KANT

This is the first full-length biography in more than fifty years of Immanuel Kant, one of the giants among the pantheon of Western philosophers as well as the one with the most powerful and broad influence on contemporary philosophy.

It is well known that Kant spent his entire life in an isolated part of Prussia, living the life of a typical university professor. This has given rise to the view that Kant was a pure thinker with no life of his own, or at least none worth considering seriously. Manfred Kuehn debunks that myth once and for all.

Kant's life (1724–1804) spanned almost the entire eighteenth century, and the period of his adulthood coincided with some of the most significant changes in the Western world, many of which still reverberate in our lives today. This was the period in which the modern view of the world originated, and this biography reveals how Kant's philosophy was an expression of and response to this new conception of modernity. His intellectual life reflects the most significant intellectual, political, and scientific developments of the period, from the literary movement of *Sturm und Drang* to such distant events as the French and American Revolutions.

Taking account of the most recent scholarship, Professor Kuehn allows the reader (whether interested in philosophy, history, politics, German culture, or religion) to follow the same journey that Kant himself took: from being a scholar narrowly focusing on the metaphysical foundations of Newtonian science to emerging as a great thinker expounding the defense of the morality of an enlightened citizen of the world.

Manfred Kuehn was a professor of philosophy at Purdue University from 1983 to 1999. He is now teaching at the Philipps-Universität Marburg.

Kant
A Biography

Manfred Kuehn
Philipps-Universität Marburg

CAMBRIDGE
UNIVERSITY PRESS

PUBLISHED BY THE PRESS SYNDICATE OF THE UNIVERSITY OF CAMBRIDGE
The Pitt Building, Trumpington Street, Cambridge, United Kindgom

CAMBRIDGE UNIVERSITY PRESS
The Edinburgh Building, Cambridge CB2 2RU, UK
40 West 20th Street, New York, NY 10011-4211, USA
10 Stamford Road, Oakleigh, VIC 3166, Australia
Ruiz de Alarcón 13, 28014 Madrid, Spain
Dock House, The Waterfront, Cape Town 8001, South Africa

http://www.cambridge.org

First published 2001

Printed in the United States of America

Typeface Ehrhardt 10.5/13 pt.   *System* QuarkXPress 4.0 [AG]

A catalog record for this book is available from the British Library.

Library of Congress Cataloging in Publication data
Kuehn, Manfred.
Kant : a biography / Manfred Kuehn
p. cm.
Includes bibliographical references.
ISBN 0-521-49704-3
1. Kant, Immanuel, 1724–1804.   2. Philosophers – Germany – Biography   I. Title.
B2797.K86 2001
193 – dc21
[B]   00-033671

ISBN 0 521 49704 3 hardback

To
Margret

Contents

Acknowledgments

THE FOUNDING of the North American Kant Society in 1986 was a significant event not only for Kant scholarship in the United States but also for me personally. I have been lucky to be able to serve as the society's bibliographer since its inception, and I am glad to observe that Kant scholarship has become a more cooperative enterprise since that time. Indeed, I have benefited greatly from the help of many friends and colleagues whom I might never have known without this institution. I cannot thank all of those who have had an influence on my work over the years, but I would like to give a special thanks to the late Lewis White Beck, who was the founding father of the society. Like many, I owe him a great debt. I am sure this book would have been greatly improved if it could have benefited from his advice, but unfortunately that was not to be.

I have, however, been fortunate to benefit from the help and advice of many others. I am very grateful to Terry Moore, who first encouraged me to think about the necessity for a new biography of Kant, and then suggested that I write it. Without him, this book would never have been written. It would have remained a dream. In writing the book, I have incurred many other debts. First among those are the ones to my friends in Marburg, who helped me greatly not only in the research, but also in the preparation of the first draft. Heiner Klemme's encouragement, help, and friendship were decisive from beginning to end. I cannot thank him enough. Werner Stark's expert advice improved the work a great deal and saved me from a number of serious errors. Werner Euler generously shared some of his unpublished work with me. Reinhard Brandt, who rightfully pointed out to me early on that any biography of Kant could be written only in Marburg, was also helpful in a number of ways. His comments on the penultimate version were especially important.

I am also grateful to the staffs of the University Library and the Library of the Institute of Philosophy at the Philipps-Universität Marburg, and of the Herder Institute in Marburg. I spent many enjoyable hours there in the summers of 1995 and 1997, as well as a few days in 1996 and 1998. Some of the preparatory work was done with the support of a summer grant from the National Endowment for the Humanities in the summer of 1988 and a fellowship at the Center for Humanistic Studies at Purdue University during the fall of 1990. This support was originally for a study of Kant's philosophical development, parts of which have been incorporated into this book. Much of the first draft was written with the support of another fellowship at the Center for Humanistic Studies during the fall of 1995. I am also thankful to Rod Bertolet, the chair of the department of philosophy at Purdue University, who made various arrangements that made it possible for me to return to Marburg in 1997.

Some of my other colleagues at Purdue, namely Cal Schrag, William McBride, and Jacqueline Mariña, graciously commented on an early draft of the first three chapters, and the comments and suggestions of Mary Norton and Rolf George significantly improved the final version of those chapters. Martin Curd read various parts and left his mark on them (I have indicated some in the text).

Karl Ameriks, Michael Gill, Steve Naragon, Konstantin Pollok, and Frederick Rauscher read the entire manuscript and made many helpful comments for which I am most grateful. Karl Ameriks and Michael Gill, especially, took such an active interest in the project that their influence is everywhere. I wish that the final product could more adequately express what I have learned from them.

Finally, I would like to thank Margret Kuehn for her support during the writing of this book and my other quixotic travails.

Cast of Characters

Borowski, Ludwig Ernst (1740–1832), one of Kant's first students; he remained friendly with Kant throughout his life. During his later years, Borowski was a high official in the Lutheran Church of Prussia. He was a frequent dinner guest during Kant's last years. He wrote one of the three "official" biographies of Kant, but did not attend his funeral.

Baczko, Adolph Franz Joseph von (1756–1823), a student of Kant's during the seventies (and a friend of Kraus). Although he lost his eyesight, he was a capable historian. A professorship at the University of Königsberg was denied him because he was a Catholic.

Beck, Jacob Sigismund (1761–1840), one of Kant's most famous early followers. He studied in Königsberg, where he was as much influenced by Kraus as by Kant. He published between 1793 and 1796 a volume of explanations of Kant's critical philosophy. Early on, he was an orthodox follower of Kant's; in his last book, *The Only Possible Point of View from which Critical Philosophy Must Be Judged*, Beck went his own way, much to Kant's chagrin.

Fichte, Johann Gottlieb (1762–1814), famous idealist philosopher. He came to Königsberg, where he wrote the *Critique of All Revelation* (1792). Kant used his influence to see that it was published. This work, which appeared anonymously, was first viewed as Kant's own. Kant's revelation of Fichte's authorship made him famous. Later, Fichte went "beyond" Kant. He severely criticized Kantian philosophy and thus drew Kant's ire.

Funk, Johann Daniel (1721–1764), a very popular professor of law in Königsberg and a close friend of the young Kant. He led a loose life, and he had a decisive influence on Hippel.

Goeschen, Johann Julius (1736–1798), came to Königsberg in 1760, where he soon became a friend of Kant and the Jacobis. He was first the master and then the director of the mint in Königsberg. He and Maria Charlotta Jacobi became lovers and married after she got a divorce. After the marriage Kant remained friendly with Goeschen, even though he never entered their house.

Green, Joseph (1727–1786), British merchant in Königsberg and the closest friend of Kant. Hippel is said to have used Green as a model for his Man of the Clock, a character who lives by inviolable maxims and strictly by the clock. Later writers transferred these characteristics to Kant.

Hamann, Johann Georg (1730–1788), one of Kant's (and Green's) close friends. Born and educated in Königsberg, Hamann was also known as the Magus of the North. He was one the most important Christian thinkers in Germany during the second half of the eighteenth century. Advocating an irrationalistic theory of faith, he opposed the prevailing Enlightenment philosophy. He was the mentor of the literary movement of *Sturm und Drang.* Herder popularized these ideas after leaving Königsberg in 1764.

Herder, Johann Gottfried (1744–1803), one of Kant's students during the early sixties. Influenced as much by Hamann as by Kant, he became one of the most important writers of the *Sturm und Drang* movement and had an enormous influence on pre-Romantic thinkers in Germany. After Kant reviewed his *Ideas* anonymously and very critically, Herder turned against his teacher.

Herz, Markus (1747–1803), one of Kant's most important students, a respondent at the defense of Kant's Inaugural Dissertation and an important correspondent for Kant after moving to Berlin in 1770. Herz became a medical doctor in Berlin, where he gave lectures on Kant's philosophy that influenced important government officials in favor of Kant.

Hippel, Theodor Gottlieb (von) (1741–1796), friend of Hamann and Kant who became the mayor of Königsberg. He wrote many humorous plays and novels. Like Kant and Schulz, he went to the *Collegium Fridericianum,* and he studied at the university during Kant's earliest years as a lecturer there. Hippel and Kant were friends but always kept a "polite" distance.

Jachmann, Reinhold Bernhard (1767–1843), closely associated with Kant between 1783 and 1794. As his amanuensis or academic helper, Jachmann knew Kant well during the years in which he published his most famous works. Jachmann and his older brother (Johann Benjamin, 1765–1832) were closely associated with Joseph Green and Robert Motherby. Johann Benjamin, also one of Kant's amanuenses, practiced medicine in Königsberg after studying in Edinburgh. Reinhold Bernhard Jachmann was one of the three "official" biographers of Kant.

Jacobi, Johann Conrad (1718–1774), banker in Königsberg and friend of Hamann and Kant. He was the husband of Maria Charlotta until their divorce in 1768. One of Kant's close friends, he took care of some of Kant's private business, such as the regular payments to his poor relatives.

Jacobi, Maria Charlotta (1739–1795), called "the Princess," who divorced Johann Conrad Jacobi and married Johann Julius Goeschen. Kant, who was a friend of both Johann Conrad Jacobi and Johann Julius Goeschen, never went to the house of the Göschens after gossiping too much about the events leading up to the divorce.

Kanter, Johann Jakob (1738–1786), book dealer and publisher who was close to Kant, Hamann, and Hippel. Kant lived for a while in a building that housed his bookshop. Kanter was the publisher of many of Kant's works.

Keyserlingk, Caroline Charlotte Amalie, Countess (1729–1791), Kant's "ideal" of a woman, the wife of Count Heinrich Christian Keyserlingk. Kant was a close friend of the family with a standing invitation to their table, where he almost always sat at the place of honor beside the countess.

Keyserlingk, Heinrich Christian, Count (1727–1787), the husband of Caroline Charlotte Amalie. Kant and the count seem to have shared many political views.

Kraus, Christian Jacob (1753–1807), perhaps Kant's most talented student during the seventies. Kraus became his colleague in 1780 and taught moral philosophy. Today he is best known as one of the people who introduced Adam Smith's ideas into Germany. Even though Kraus and Kant were good friends, even sharing a common household at one time, they had a falling out sometime before the third *Critique* was published. In some ways, Kraus was closer to Hamann than to Kant.

Lambert, Johann Heinrich (1728–1777), mathematician and philosopher. Lambert's philosophical correspondence with Kant was an important source of inspiration for the latter.

Lampe, Martin (1734–1806), Kant's servant throughout most of his life. He was a retired soldier. Lampe was rather limited in his intelligence, and Kant had constant problems with him. He had to let him go at the very end of his life because he drank so heavily that he neglected his duties as a servant.

Mendelssohn, Moses (1729–1786), famous Jewish philosopher who was Kant's literary friend and supporter. Mendelssohn and Herz became friends in Berlin after 1770. Kant thought highly of Mendelssohn, and their correspondence was important to him.

Motherby, Robert (1736–1801), English merchant, partner of Green, and Kant's close friend. Kant had a great deal of influence on the education of Motherby's sons. He also had much of his money invested in the firm of Green and Motherby

Reinhold, Karl Leonhard (1758–1823), one of the first popularizers of Kant's philosophy. Though he never met Kant in person, he made Kant a household name. After becoming professor in Jena, he abandoned strict Kantian philosophy for his own philosophy of representation. Later, as a follower of Fichte he became critical of Kant, but Kant always remained grateful to Reinhold.

Scheffner, Johann Georg (1736–1820), a friend of Hippel, Hamann, and Kant. He published risqué poems "á la Grecourt" in 1761. He became secretary in the ministry of war in Königsberg in 1765 and 1766 but retired the next year.

Schulz, Johann (1739–1805), a friend of Kant's who studied at the University of Königsberg during Kant's first years as a lecturer. He reviewed Kant's Inaugural Dissertation and, during the seventies, became court chaplain in Königsberg and lecturer in mathematics. After becoming the first defender of Kant's critical philosophy, he was appointed full professor.

Wasianski, Ehregott Andreas Christoph (1775–1831), studied theology at the University of Königsberg between 1772 and 1780. He took courses from Kant and was his amanuensis. He became a deacon in Königsberg in 1786 and took care of Kant during his last years. He was the executor of Kant's will and the third of the three "official" biographers of Kant.

Chronology of Kant's Life and Works

1724 April 22: Immanuel Kant is born.

1732 Fall: Kant begins to attend the *Collegium Fridericianum*.

1735 Birth of his brother Johann Heinrich (died 1800).

1737 Death of his mother (born 1697).

1740 September 24: Inscribed at the University of Königsberg.
Death of Frederick William I; Frederick II (the Great) becomes king of Prussia.

1746 Death of his father (born 1682).

1748–54 Private tutor in Judtschen, Arnsdorf, and Rautenburg.

1749 First book, *Thoughts on the True Estimation of the Living Forces* (*Gedanken von der wahren Schätzung der lebendigen Kräfte*).

1751 Knutzen dies.

1754 Wolff dies.
Two essays, "Whether the Earth Has Changed in Its Revolutions" (*Ob die Erde in ihrer Umdrehung . . . einige Veränderung erlitten habe*) and "On the Question whether the Earth is Aging from a Physical Point of View" (*Die Frage, ob die Erde veralte, physikalisch erwogen*).

1755 *General History and Theory of the Heavens* (*Allgemeine Naturgeschichte und Theorie des Himmels*).
June 12: Promotion to *Magister*, with the thesis "On Fire" (*De igne*).
September 27: Acquires permission to lecture at the university with the thesis "A New Exposition of the First Principles of Metaphysics" (*Principiorum primorum cognitionis metaphysicae nova dilucidatio*).

1756   January to April: Three essays on the earthquake in Lisbon.
       April 8: Applies unsuccessfully for Knutzen's position.
       April 10: Disputation on his *Physical Monadology* (*Metaphysica cum geometria
       iunctae usus in philosophia naturalis, cuius specimen I. continet monadologiam
       physicam*).
       April 25: "New Remarks about the Explanation of the Theory of Winds"
       (*Neue Anmerkungen zur Erläuterung der Theorie der Winde*) (announcement
       of his lectures for the summer semester).

1757   Easter (announcement of his lectures): "Sketch and Announcement of a Lec-
       ture Course on Physical Geography, with an Appendix whether the Westerly
       Winds in Our Environs Are So Humid because They Blow over a Large
       Ocean" (*Entwurf und Ankündigung eines Collegii der physischen Geographie,
       nebst Anhang . . .*).

1758   January 22: occupation of Königsberg by the Russians.
       Summer semester (announcements of his lectures): "A New Doctrine of
       Motion and Rest" (*Neuer Lehrbegriff der Bewegung und Ruhe*).
       December: Applies unsuccessfully for Kypke's position.

1759   Fall (announcement of his lectures): "Essay on Some Views about Optimism"
       (*Versuch einiger Betrachtungen über den Optimismus*).

1760   "Thoughts at the Occasion of Mr. Johann Friedrich von Funk's Untimely
       Death" (*Gedanken bei dem frühzeitigen Ableben des Herrn Johann Friedrich von
       Funk*).

1762   July: The Russian occupation of Königsberg ends.
       "The False Subtlety of the Four Syllogistic Figures" (*Die falsche Spitzfind-
       igkeit der vier syllogistischen Figuren erwiesen*).
       Herder becomes Kant's student (until 1764).
       Rousseau, *Emile* and *Contrat social*.

1763   *The Only Possible Argument in Support of a Demonstration of the Existence of
       God (Der einzig mögliche Beweisgrund zu einer Demonstration des Daseins
       Gottes).*
       *Attempt to Introduce the Concept of Negative Magnitudes into Philosophy (Ver-
       such den Begriff der negativen Größen in die Weltweisheit einzuführen).*

1764   Declines professorship of poetry.
       *Observations on the Feeling of the Beautiful and Sublime (Beobachtungen über
       das Gefühl des Schönen und Erhabenen).*
       "Essay on the Illnesses of the Head" (*Versuch über die Krankheiten des Kopfes*)
       in *Königsberger Gelehrte und Politische Zeitungen*.
       Review of Silberschlag's *Theory of the Fireball that Appeared on July 23, 1762*,
       in the same paper.

Prize essay for the Berlin Academy: *Inquiry Concerning the Distinctness of the Principles of Natural Theology and Morality* (*Untersuchungen über die Deutlichkeit der Grundsätze der natürlichen Theologie und der Moral*).
Lambert, *New Organon.*

1765   Fall (announcement of his lectures): "Announcement of the Organization of His Lectures in the Winter Semester 1765/66" (*Nachricht von der Einrichtung seiner Vorlesungen in dem Winterhalbenjahre von 1765/66*).
Begins correspondence with Lambert.
Application for the position of sublibrarian at the *Schloßbibliothek.*
Leibniz, *New Essays on the Human Understanding.*

1766   *Dreams of a Spirit-Seer Elucidated by Dreams of Metaphysics* (*Träume eines Geistersehers, erläutert durch Träume der Metaphysik*).
Begins correspondence with Mendelssohn.
(April 1766 to May 1772): Sublibrarian at the *Schloßbibliothek.*
Mendelssohn, *Phaedo.*

1768   "Concerning the Ultimate Ground of the Differentiation of Directions in Space" (*Von dem ersten Grunde des Unterschiedes der Gegenden im Raume*).

1769   October: Offer from Erlangen.
December: Rejection of the offer from Erlangen.

1770   January: Offer from Jena.
March: Application for professorship at the University of Königsberg.
March 31: Appointment to professor of logic and metaphysics.
Inaugural Dissertation, *De mundi sensibilis atque intelligibilis forma et principiis,* defended on August 21.

1770–81 "Silent years"; origin of the *Critique of Pure Reason* (*Kritik der reinen Vernunft*).

1771–88 Karl Abraham von Zedlitz serves as minister of education in Prussia.

1771   Review of Moscati, *Of the Essential Difference in the Structure of the Bodies of Humans and Animals.*
Lambert, *Architectonic.*

1775   Easter (announcement of his lectures): "Of the Different Human Races" (*Von den verschiedenen Rassen der Menschen*).
Crusius dies.

1776   An essay on the *Dessau Philanthropinum* (*Königsbergische Zeitung*).
Hume dies.
Summer semester: Kant becomes dean of the faculty of philosophy.
Declaration of Independence and Declaration of Human Rights.

1777   Another essay on the *Dessau Philanthropinum*.
        Tetens, *Essays*.
        Lambert dies.

1778   Declines an offer to become professor in Halle.
        Voltaire and Rousseau die.
        Lessing, *On the Education of the Human Race*.

1779–80 Winter semester: Kant serves as dean.

1780   Becomes permanent member of the university senate (until 1804).

1781   May: *Critique of Pure Reason* (*Kritik der reinen Vernunft*).

1782   Announcement of the publication of Lambert's *Correspondence*.
        "Information for Medical Doctors" (*Nachrichten an Ärzte*).

1782–83 Winter semester: Kant serves as dean.

1783   *Prolegomena* (*Prolegomena zu einer jeden künftigen Metaphysik, die als Wissen-
        schaft wird auftreten können*).
        Review of Schulze's *Attempt at a Guide toward a Moral Doctrine for All Man-
        kind Independent of Differences of Religion*.
        December: Kant buys his own house.
        Mendelssohn, *Jerusalem*.

1784   November: "Idea for a Universal History of Mankind" (*Idee zu einer allge-
        meinen Geschichte in weltbürgerlicher Absicht*) in *Berlinische Monatsschrift*.
        December: "Answer to the Question: "What is Enlightenment?"" (*Beantwor-
        tung der Frage: Was ist Aufklärung?*).
        Diderot dies.

1785   January and November: Review of Herder's *Ideas* in *Allgemeine Literatur-
        Zeitung* (Jena).
        March: "Concerning the Volcanoes on the Moon" (*Über die Vulkane im
        Monde*) in *Berlinische Monatsschrift*.
        April: *Groundwork of the Metaphysics of Morals* (*Grundlegung zur Metaphysik
        der Sitten*).
        May: "On the Wrongful Publication of Books" (*Von der Unrechtmäßigkeit
        des Bückernachdrucks*) in *Berlinische Monats-schrift*.
        November: "On the Definition of the Concept of a Human Race" (*Über die
        Bestinmung des Begriffs einer Menschenrasse*) in *Berlinische Monatsschrift*.
        Mendelssohn, *Morning Hours*.

1785–86 Winter semester: Kant serves as dean.
        Mendelssohn–Jacobi dispute (also knows as the pantheism dispute).

1786   January: "Conjectural Beginning of the Human Race" (*Mutmasslicher Anfang des Menschengeschichte*) in *Berlinische Monatsschrift*.
Easter: *Metaphysical Foundations of Natural Science* (*Metaphysische Anfangs-gründe der Naturwissenschaft*).
Summer semester: Kant for the first time serves as rector of the university.
August: Frederick the Great dies.
Review of Hufeland's essay on *The Principle of Natural Right* (*Grundsatz des Naturrechts*).
"Observations on Jakob's Examination of Mendelssohn's Morning Hours (*Bemerkungen zu Jakobs Prüfung der Mendelssohnschen Morgenstunden*).
October: "What Does 'Orientation in Thinking' Mean?" (*Was heißt, sich im Denken orientieren?*) in *Berlinische Monatsschrift*.
September: Inauguration of Frederick William II. Kant organizes the university's role in the festivities.
December 7: Kant becomes external member of the Berlin Academy of the Sciences.
Schmid, *Extract from Kant's Critique of Reason*.

1786–87   Reinhold's "Letters on the Kantian Philosophy" in *Der teutsche Merkur*.

1787   Second edition of the *Critique of Pure Reason*.

1788   Beginning of the year: *Critique of Practical Reason* (*Kritik der praktischen Vernunft*).
January: "On the Use of Teleological Principles in Philosophy" (*über den Gebrauch teleologischer Prinzipien in der Philosophie*) in *Der teutsche Merkur*.
Summer semester: Kant becomes rector for the second time.
Schmid, *Lexicon for the Easier Use of the Kantian Writings*.
Hamann dies.
July 9: The Edict on Religion.
December 19: New Edict on Religion.

1789   Beginning of the French Revolution.
Reinhold, *On the Destiny of the Kantian Philosophy until Now* and *Attempt of a New Theory of the Human Power of Representation*.
Johann Schulz, *Examination of the Kantian Critique of Pure Reason*.
Toward the end of the year: Kant begins to have difficulties concentrating on intellectual work for extended periods of time.

1790   *Critique of Judgment* (*Kritik der Urteilskraft*).
Against Eberhard, "On a New Discovery, which Makes All New Critique of Pure Reason Unnecessary Because of an Older One" (*Über eine Entdeckung nach der alle neue Kritik der reinen Vernunft durch eine ältere entbehrlich gemacht werden soll*).
"On Enthusiasm and the Means against It" (*Über die Schwärmerei und die Mittel dagegen*) in Borowski's *Cagliostro*.
Maimon, *Essay on Transcendental Philosophy*.

1791   September "On the Failure of All Attempts at a *Theodicee*" (*über das Miálin-gen aller philosophischen Versuche in der Theodizee*) in *Berlinische Monatsschrift*. Summer semester: Kant serves as dean.

1792   March 5: New and stricter edict concerning obedience to religious customs. April: "Concerning Radical Evil" (*Vom radikalen Bösen*) in *Berlinische Monatsschrift*. June 14: Failure to obtain permission to print "Concerning the Battle of the Good against the Evil Principle for Dominion over the Human Being" in *Berlinische Monatsschrift*. Schulze, *Aenesidemus*. Fichte, *Critique of All Revelation* (at first assumed to be Kant's work). France becomes a republic. Easter: *Religion within the Boundary of Mere Reason* (*Religion innerhalb der Grenzen der bloßen Vernunft*). September: "On the Old Saw 'That May Be Right in Theory, but It Won't Work in Practice'" (*über den Gemeinspruch: Das mag in der Theorie richtig sein, stimmt aber nicht für die Praxis*) in *Berlinische Monatsschrift*. Beck, *An Explanatory Extract from the Critical Writings of Kant*. Schiller, *On Beauty and Dignity*. Louis XVI guillotined.

1794   Second edition of *Religion within the Boundary of Mere Reason*. Spring and summer: Decisive actions against the "neologists" taken by the king. May: "Something on the Influence of the Moon on the Climate" (*Etwas vom Einfluß des Mondes auf die Witterung*) in *Berlinische Monatsschrift*. June: "The End of All Things" (*Das Ende aller Dinge*) in *Berlinische Monatsschrift*. July: Membership in the Petersburg Academy. October 1: Kant is censored by the king. October 12: Kant's response to the king. Fichte, *Grounding of the Entire Doctrine of Science* (*Wissenschaftslehre*) Maimon, *Attempt at a New Logic*. New General Law of the Country (*Allgemeines Landrecht*) promulgated in Prussia. Robespierre guillotined.

1794–95 Winter semester: Kant's turn to be dean for the seventh time (Kraus stands in for him).

1795   *On Eternal Peace* (*Zum ewigen Frieden*). Schiller, *On the Aesthetic Education of Man* and *On Naïve and Sentimental Poetry*. Schelling, *On the Ego as the Principle of Philosophy*. Correspondence with Schiller.

1796   Second edition of *On Eternal Peace*.
Appendix to Sömmerring's *On the Organ of the Soul* (*Über das Organ der Seele*).
May: "On a Newly Raised Noble Tone in Philosophy" (*Von einem neuerdings erhobenen vornehmen Ton in der Philosophie*) in *Berlinische Monatsschrift*.
July 23: Kant's last lecture.
October: "Solution of a Mathematical Dispute Based on a Misunderstanding" (*Ausgleichung eines auf Miáverstand beruhenden mathematischen Streits*) in *Berlinische Monatsschrift*.
December: "Announcement of the Soon to Be Completed Tract on Eternal Peace in Philosophy" (*Verkündigung des nahen Abschlusses eines Traktats zum ewigen Frieden in der Philosophie*) in *Berlinische Monatsschrift*.
Fichte, *Foundations of Natural Law*.
Beck, *The Only Possible Point of View*.

1797   *Metaphysical Foundations of the Doctrine of Right* (*Metaphysische Anfangsgründe der Rechtslehre*).
June 14: Königsberg students honor Kant's fiftieth anniversary as an author.
Metaphysical Foundations of the Doctrine of Virtue (*Metaphysische Anfangsgründe der Tugendlehre*).
"On a Presumed Right to Lie from Philanthropic Motives" (*Über ein vermeintes Recht, aus Menschenliebe zu lügen*) in *Berliner Blätter*.
November 10: Death of Frederick William II; Frederick William III becomes king.
Schelling, *Ideas for a Philosophy of Nature*.

1798   *The Dispute of the Faculties* (*Der Streit der Fakultäten*).
Anthropology from a Pragmatic Point of View (*Anthropologie in pragmatischer Hinsicht*).
"On Turning Out Books" (*Über die Buchmacherei, zwei Briefe an F. Nicolai*).
Declaration against Schlettwein.
Kant's turn to be dean for the eighth time (Mangelsdorf stands in for him).
Schelling, *Of the Worldsoul*.

1799   August: Open declaration against Fichte.
Fichte, *Appeal to the Public*.
Herder, *Metacritique*.

1800   Last publication by Kant himself.
September: Kant's *Logic*, edited by Jäsche.
Schelling, *System of Transcendental Idealism*.
Herder, *Kalligone*.

1801   November 14: Last official pronouncement.

1802   *Physical Geography* (*Physische Geographie*), edited by Rink.
Hegel, *The Relation of Skepticism to Philosophy, Faith and Knowledge*.
Schelling, *Giordano Bruno*.

1803   *On Pedagogy* (*Über Pädagogik*), edited by Rink.
        April: Kant's last letter.
        October: Last illness.
        Herder dies.

1804   February 12: 11:00 A.M.: Kant dies.
        February 28: Kant is buried.
        April 23: Memorial service at the university.
        May: Prize essay, *On the Progress of Metaphysics since Leibniz and Wolff* (*Über die Fortschritte der Metaphysik seit Leibniz und Wolff*), edited by Rink (written in 1790).
        Schelling, "In Memoriam: Kant."
        Napoleon becomes emperor.
        Code civil is enacted.

Prologue

I

IMMANUEL KANT died on February 12, 1804, at 11:00 A.M., less than
two months before his eightieth birthday. Though he was still famous,
German thinkers were engaged in trying to get "beyond" his critical philosophy. He had become almost irrelevant. His last important contribution
to the philosophical discussion had been made almost five years earlier.
This was the open "Declaration Regarding Fichte's *Wissenschaftslehre*" of
August 7, 1799. In it, he had stated clearly his conviction that all the more
recent philosophical developments had little to do with his own critical
philosophy, that "Fichte's *Theory of Science* was a totally indefensible system," and that he was very much "opposed to metaphysics as defined by
Fichte."[1] Urging philosophers not to go "beyond" his critical philosophy,
but to take it seriously not only as his own last word, but also as the final
word on metaphysical questions in general, he, in effect, took leave of the
philosophical scene. Nothing more, certainly nothing different was to be
expected from him. German philosophy, and with it the philosophy of
Europe as a whole, was taking a course he could not appreciate. Yet these
developments had little to do with the dying man in Königsberg. Some
said he had outlived his time, but he no longer took any interest in them.

"The great Kant died indeed just like the least important human being,
but he died so gently and quietly that those who were with him, noticed
nothing but the cessation of his breathing."[2] His death followed the gradual and prolonged deterioration of his mind and body that had begun in
1799, if not earlier. Kant himself had said in 1799 to some of his friends:
"I am old and weak. Consider me as a child."[3] Scheffner had found it necessary to point out years before Kant's death that everything that had made
him the genius that he was had disappeared. He had long been "*ent-Kanted*"

or "de-Kanted."[4] Especially during his last two years, no signs of his once-great mind could be observed.

His corpse was so completely dried out that it looked "like a skeleton that one might exhibit." Curiously enough, that is precisely what happened. Kant's corpse became a public sight during the next two weeks. People stood in line to see the corpse until it was buried sixteen days later. The weather was the main problem. It was very cold in Königsberg, and the ground was frozen so hard that it was impossible to dig a grave – as if the earth refused to take what remained of the great man. But then, there was no need to hurry, given the state of the body, as well as the great interest of the citizens of Königsberg in their dead celebrity.

The funeral itself was a solemn and grand affair. A large crowd was in attendance. Many citizens of Königsberg, most of whom had known Kant either not very well or not at all, came to see how the famous philosopher was put to rest. The cantata written at the death of Frederick II was adapted for Kant: the greatest Prussian philosopher was honored with music written for the greatest Prussian king. A large procession followed the coffin, and *all* of the churches in Königsberg rang their bells. This must have appeared fitting to most citizens of Königsberg. Scheffner, Kant's oldest surviving friend, "liked it very much," as did most citizens of Königsberg. Though Königsberg had ceased to be the political capital of Prussia in 1701, it was in the minds of many Königsbergers the intellectual capital of Prussia, if not of the world.[5] Kant had been one of its most important citizens. He was their "philosopher king," even if the philosophers outside of Königsberg were looking for another.

It was still brutally cold on the day of the funeral; but, as winter days in Königsberg often could be, it was also beautifully bright and clear. Scheffner wrote about a month later to a friend:

> You will not believe the kind of tremor that shook my entire existence when the first frozen clumps of earth were thrown on his coffin – my head and heart still tremble . . .[6]

It was not just the cold that made Scheffner shiver. Nor was it simply the fear of his own death, which might have been awakened in him by the hollow sounds of the frozen clods of earth falling on the almost-empty coffin. The tremor that would reverberate in his head for days and weeks had deeper causes. Kant, the man, was gone forever. The world was cold, and there was no hope – not for Kant, and perhaps not for any of us. Scheffner was only too much aware of Kant's belief that there was nothing to be expected after death. Though in his philosophy he had held out hope for eternal life and a future state, in his personal life he had been cold to such ideas. Scheffner had often heard Kant scoff at prayer and other religious practices. Organized religion filled him with ire. It was clear to anyone who knew Kant personally that he had no faith in a personal God. Having postulated God and immortality, he himself did not believe in either. His considered opinion was that such beliefs were just a matter of "individual needs."[7] Kant himself felt no such need.

Yet Scheffner, a citizen of Königsberg almost as famous as Kant, clearly had such a need. Scheffner, one of the most respectable and respected citizens by the time of Kant's death, professed to be a good Christian, and he probably was one. Scheffner was a pious, if not strictly orthodox, member of his congregation, and he was happily married. His piety had not always been obvious. During his earliest years he had been a poet of some note, or perhaps better characterized as of some notoriety. Indeed, he was still remembered as the (anonymous) author of a volume of erotic poetry in the French tradition, which had created quite a stir some forty years back. Many considered the poems to be among the most obscene verses ever written in German. Kant's reputation as an unbeliever might cast even more of a shadow on his own reputation. Furthermore, he had to have doubts about Kant's eternal soul. As a friend, he took Kant seriously. Is it surprising that these doubts cast a spell not only over the ceremony of Kant's burial, but also over Scheffner's very life?

Some of the more righteous Christians in Königsberg found it necessary to stay away entirely from the funeral. Thus Ludwig Ernst Borowski, a high official in the Lutheran Church of Prussia, one of Kant's earliest students and an occasional dinner guest during Kant's last years, someone whom many viewed as Kant's friend, stayed home – much to the dismay of Scheffner.[8] But Borowski was pursuing still higher career goals. Only too aware of Kant's shaky reputation among those in government who really counted, he felt it was better not to attend the funeral. He had serious reservations, if not about Kant's moral character then about his philosophical and political views, and he did what he felt to be most politic.

On the day after Kant's death, the *Königlich Preußische Staats-, Kriegs- und Friedens-Zeitungen* published a note, which among other things stated:

Kant, being eighty years old, died completely exhausted. His achievements in the revision of speculative philosophy are known and esteemed by everyone. His other virtues – loyalty, benevolence, righteousness, and politeness – can be missed only here in our city to their full extent. Here, the memory of the departed will remain more honored and more lasting than anywhere else.[9]

Relatively few would have disputed the fact that Kant really possessed the virtues of "loyalty, benevolence, righteousness, and politeness" that were especially singled out in this notice. Still, there were some who did feel differently. One of the earliest publications on Kant's life to appear in Königsberg was an attempt to put into question Kant's benevolence, righteousness, and politeness, while at the same time raising questions about his religious and political views. The *Remarks on Kant, His Character, and His Opinions by a Fair Admirer of His Merits*, which appeared anonymously and without any indication of its place of publication in 1804, was almost certainly written by Johann Daniel Metzger, a professor of medicine (pharmacy and anatomy) at the University of Königsberg. Kant and Metzger seem to have found themselves often in agreement. Since Kant took a great interest in medicine, the two frequently had occasion to discuss matters of mutual interest, but they also had had several disagreements concerning administrative matters at the university. As a result, Metzger had tried to embarrass Kant more than once during his turns as rector of the university.[10]

It is not altogether clear why the author thought the book needed writing. What is clear is that he had a certain degree of animosity toward Kant, and that he felt the record concerning Kant's private life needed to be set straight. Metzger's diagnosis was that "Kant was neither good nor evil."[11] He was not particularly hard-hearted, but then again, he did not have a particularly kind heart either. Metzger intimated that he probably had never given any money to anyone except his immediate family. He concluded from the evidence that Kant had once refused to contribute to a collection for a colleague whose house had burned down that he "was an egoist to a quite considerable degree."[12] Yet Metzger went on to explain, this was probably not his own fault. First, being a misogynist, Kant had never married.[13] Secondly, almost everyone deferred to Kant as the famous author. This was also the reason why he could not accept disagreement. Indeed, Metzger told his readers that Kant could become quite insulting when someone dared to disagree with him. As if that were not enough, Metzger revealed that Kant had the audacity to endorse the principles of the French Revolution, defending them even at dinners in the noblest houses. He was not afraid of being blacklisted (as it was done in Königsberg). Kant was impolite and insensitive. Furthermore, he mistreated his servants. Even his own uneducated sister, who took care of him during his dying days, was not allowed to eat at his table. "Wasn't Kant broad-minded enough to have his sister sit at his table at his side?"[14] Kant was reported to have said before his death that "he was leaving this world with a clean conscience, never having intentionally committed an injustice." Metzger concluded, "this is the creed of all egoists."[15]

While not wanting to say much about Kant's view of theology, Metzger could not help noting that Kant was "an indifferentist" – and probably worse. He was unfair to theologians, and he disliked religious people. Nor did he know much of jurisprudence; as a result he did not think highly of it. He was unfair to members of the faculty of law. While he appreciated medicine, he allowed himself to judge in areas where he was unqualified. For example, he did not know anything of anatomy, but he pronounced on subjects that presupposed such knowledge. He was also inconsistent: although a "misogynist," he liked Hufeland's *Macrobiotics,* which claimed that marriage increases a man's lifespan. Metzger claimed that he did not really want to dispute the importance of Kant's philosophy. While he was willing to admit that Kant's books contributed greatly to the fame of the University of Königsberg, he found the man lacking.

Metzger let it be known: Kant's works were great, but Kant himself was a far-from-admirable human being. He was as petty as human beings come, sharing in most of their faults. All in all, Kant, far from being a model of virtue, was an average person. He was neither particularly good nor particularly bad, but it would be better if students did not emulate him.

Metzger's short book was occasioned by other books on Kant that were meant to praise him.[16] There had already been a few biographies before Kant's death, all of them extremely flattering, but it appears to have been one book in particular that motivated Metzger, namely Johann Gottfried Hasse's *Notable Remarks by Kant from One of His Friends at Table,* which had appeared shortly before.[17] Hasse was a professor of oriental languages and theology. He and Kant became close after 1786, and Hasse frequently attended Kant's dinner parties, especially during the three years before his death. Hasse's short work was intended to be "neither a sketch of his life nor a biography," nor was it meant to "stand in the way of anyone who might have something more important or better to say about the great man." His *Remarks* are notable only because they provide evidence of Kant's incompetence during his final years.

Hasse claimed that he only wanted to "express his thankful heart." Yet most of Kant's friends wished he had not done so. In his "Declaration Regarding Fichte's *Wissenschaftslehre,*" Kant himself had alluded to the old Italian proverb to the effect that if God protects us from our friends, we can take care of our enemies ourselves, and that "there are friends who mean well by us but who act wrongly or clumsily in trying to promote our ends."[18]

Hasse's publication was clumsy and wrong-headed. Though he praised Kant's greatness and intended to give examples of his ingenuous mind and noble character, he succeeded chiefly in raising questions that are interesting in quite different respects. Thus Hasse tells us of a book that Kant was writing during his last days. The old philosopher had himself at times declared this to be "his chief work, . . . which represents his system as a completed whole," but Hasse goes on to observe that "any future editor would have to treat it with caution because, during his last years, Kant often deleted things that were better than those he replaced them with, and he also interjected much nonsense (like the meals which were planned for a given day)."[19] Many of the stories Hasse tells seem to be designed only to raise doubts about Kant's mental competence.[20]

This was not the worst aspect of Hasse's book. He also raised questions about Kant's character, and especially about his loyalty to members of his family. Thus, after pointing out that Kant spent a considerable amount each year supporting his relatives, Hasse went on to note that he "never mentioned" these relatives to anyone. He also told his readers that Kant never answered any questions about his relatives when asked, and that, when his sister came to assist him during his last years, he tried to conceal her identity from his friends – "even though he gave her food from his table." He showed his gratitude for his sister's able care by asking his friends "to forgive her lack of culture."[21] All in all, Hasse's *Notable Remarks by Kant* amount to a strange tribute. No wonder Scheffner found the book despicable, observing that "it would not be easy to put such a great number of trivialities, minutiae, and indelicacies on so few pages."[22] Metzger, on the other hand, seems to have found in Hasse's ambiguities useful reminders of Kant's true character. Indeed, his *Remarks on Kant* can be seen as Metzger's attempt to put Hasse's remarks in a more proper light.

Hasse's and Metzger's efforts were not the only biographical accounts that were published in Königsberg during 1804. Nor were they the most significant. Indeed, they were soon completely overshadowed by a project started by Kant's publisher, Friedrich Nicolovius, who saw to it that a collection of biographical sketches by people who knew Kant well during different stages of his life was published. Nicolovius was not alone. Others, like Scheffner, were also involved in urging this project along. The collective enterprise was designed, at least in part, to forestall and undermine further contributions like those of Hasse and Metzger. In this, it was quite successful. The resulting book, *On Immanuel Kant,* came to be viewed as the most extensive and most reliable source of information concerning

Kant's life and character, but it is neither as reliable nor as extensive as we might wish.

The three people who had known Kant well during different periods of his life, and who were to give accounts of Kant's life as they knew it, were Ludwig Ernst Borowski, Reinhold Bernhard Jachmann, and Ehregott Christian Wasianski. All three were theologians born and raised in Königsberg. Borowski had known Kant the longest, having attended his lectures in 1755 and remained friendly with him through the early sixties. He had also been his opponent in a disputation on physical monadology in 1756. Though he could not give a firsthand account of Kant's funeral, he could be counted on to tell the story of Kant's life from his earliest period as a lecturer until his final years. Jachmann had studied with Kant and had become closely associated with him between 1783 and 1794.[23] As his "amanuensis" or academic assistant, he knew Kant well during the years in which he published his most famous works. He could speak with authority on the eighties and nineties. Wasianski was a deacon who had taken care of Kant during his final years. He had studied at the University of Königsberg between 1772 and 1780. Indeed, like Jachmann, he had also been Kant's *amanuensis*. He could have said much about Kant's life during the seventies, but strangely enough he says nothing about these years, restricting himself to an account of Kant's last years. After Wasianski left the university in 1780, he had no contact with Kant for a decade, meeting him again only in 1790 at a wedding reception. Kant seems to have invited him immediately to his regular dinner parties, and gradually came to rely on him. Over the years he entrusted him with more and more of his personal business. Indeed, Wasianski ultimately earned Kant's complete trust. Having been chosen by Kant as his personal secretary and helper, as well as the executor of his will, he knew the aged Kant's circumstances very well.

These three theologians were expected to set the record straight. They were to tell the public who Kant really was, and they were to make sure that others who were dealing in mere anecdotes could not harm his reputation. The project was thus essentially an apologetic enterprise. As such, it had the blessings of Kant's closest friends in Königsberg. In a certain sense, they all closed ranks to "save" Kant's good name. It is important to understand this function of the book *On Immanuel Kant*, for it explains why certain things are emphasized in the book and others downplayed. The apologetic nature of the project explains also the somewhat monochromatic picture of Kant we get from the three biographies. Its authors clearly felt that there were a number of things that were "not appropriate for the public."[24]

Furthermore, each of them had prejudices and views that could only stand in the way of an objective account of Kant's life and work as a whole. For one thing, these three Königsberg theologians could not be expected to paint a colorful picture of the "all-crushing" philosophical libertine, whose audience was the world. Rather, they sketched, all gray on gray, the dull outlines of the life and habits of an old man, who just happened to have written books that made him famous. Telling us next to nothing about the first sixty years of Kant's life and more than enough about the last twenty years or so, they continued in some ways the tradition started by Hasse and Metzger. Yet, it is their picture that still largely determines the way we see Kant. Kant was made into a "flat character" whose only surprising feature was the complete lack of any surprises.

Some of Kant's friends thought that the only one who was really qualified to write about both the man and his ideas was Johann Christoph Kraus, Kant's former student, longtime friend, and colleague in philosophy. But Kraus refused to do so. Scheffner explained: "Kraus is the only one who could write about him; yet, it might be easier to cut off a piece of granite with a knife than to get him to prepare something for publication."[25] We do not know whether it was just Kraus's perfectionism that kept him from writing a biography of Kant. There may have been other reasons. Kant and Kraus had had a falling out. Though they did not quite avoid each other late in life, they did not talk to each other either. Some thought there was a certain rivalry between them – and there probably was. Metzger, who denigrated Kant's character, praised Kraus. We do not know whether this was a reason for Kraus's reluctance. All we know is that he never wrote anything on Kant. Scheffner might have been an even better candidate, but he showed no interest, or perhaps better, he urged on Borowski.[26] Another person who might have opened up new perspectives on Kant was Karl Ludwig Pörschke, professor of poetry at the University of Königsberg. An early admirer of Fichte in Königsberg, he wrote to him in 1798, reporting that Kant was no longer capable of "sustained thinking," and that he was withdrawing from society:

Since I often must talk to him for four hours at a stretch, I know his bodily and mental condition very well; he hides nothing from me. I know from intimate talks his life's story starting with the earliest years of his childhood; he acquainted me with the smallest circumstances of his progress. This will be of service when the buzzards are making noise around his grave. There are in Königsberg a number of people who are ready with biographies as well as with poems about the dead Kant.[27]

Unfortunately, perhaps, Pörschke did not publish a biography either.

Later, other friends in Königsberg did publish some of their impressions of Kant. They added a detail or an anecdote here and there, but they did not fundamentally change the earlier picture or make a revision necessary.[28] Relying on the same stereotypes, they were content to support the official biographers. This is especially true of Friedrich Theodor Rink, in his *Ansichten aus Immanuel Kant's Leben* (1805). Rink, who studied with Kant between 1786 and 1789, and who was a frequent dinner guest during the periods 1792 to 1793 and 1795 to 1801, also said little about Kant's early years and much about the old man. He reinforced the view of Borowski, Jachmann, and Wasianski. Just as they were, he was interested in defending the role of Pietism in Königsberg culture.[29] All the other biographies that appeared during Kant's lifetime or shortly after his death are still less reliable, and can be used only with the greatest of caution. Most of them are based on mere hearsay and not on any firsthand knowledge of Kant and Königsberg. We must therefore rely mainly on the three theologians from Königsberg.

The most interesting later publication was Rudolph Reicke's *Kantiana, Contributions to Kant's Life and Writings* of 1860.[30] It reprinted the materials that were collected for the memorial lecture that was held for Kant in April of 1804. Some of the details in this work contradict the claims in the standard biographies, although it appears that some of the official biographers had access to this information as well. One might well wonder why they neglected these details.

Borowski is the least reliable of these three biographers. He was a reluctant contributor. Only after having been urged by several friends (including Scheffner) did he agree to publish his contribution. He himself never tired of drawing attention to his reservations about publishing his biographical sketch. Had friends not pressured him, he would have suppressed it. His reasons are not difficult to understand. Many contemporaries had made Kant's doctrines responsible for the empty churches at Sunday services in Königsberg and elsewhere. To make matters worse, some of the more radical clerics were themselves Kantians. Borowski was more of a conservative. He was also more of an opportunist, who obeyed the orders of the king's ministers without much reflection. He felt that an endorsement or defense of Kant would not help his career. While it might not end his advancement, it could well impede it.[31]

On the other hand, Borowski claimed – at least implicitly – that he had the necessary qualifications for a Kant biographer. He argued that a biographer must be not only someone who can be trusted to know what he is reporting, but also someone who can be trusted to have "the *will* to relate the facts correctly." He artfully left it up to the reader to determine, on the basis of his "quite simple narrative," whether he himself "can and does give a faithful and true account."[32] A closer look at Borowski's account reveals that the narrative is far from simple. His contribution consists of a number of quite disparate parts, more a collage than a simple narrative. The first part, entitled "Sketch for a Future Reliable Biography of the Prussian Philosopher Immanuel Kant," dates back to October 1792. At that time Borowski had prepared a short biographical sketch of Kant for the German Society of Königsberg. As correspondence between Borowski and Kant, included in the introduction, shows, Borowski had submitted this sketch to Kant for review. Kant looked it over and made some corrections. Borowski notes what these changes were, but he does not always want to believe Kant. So, when Kant struck out the claim that he had first studied theology, Borowski insisted that he must have. The sketch is followed by another narrative. It goes over the same ground as the sketch but was written in 1804 for the purpose of the publication. Since Borowski was not very close to Kant during his final years, he relied on Pastor Georg Michael Sommer (1754–1826) for information.[33] The two narratives are followed by documents from Kant's life as well as by a comment by Borowski on another biography.[34] The comment and the book end with a peculiar warning: "One should indeed not *write* too much about someone who is dead."[35]

Borowski followed his own advice. We certainly do not find out much about Kant's life – and especially not much about his early life. There are a number of mistakes, both obvious and not so obvious.[36] Further, there seem to be many things Borowski did not tell because he seemed to feel they were inappropriate, even if they were true. At the same time, there are many things he did include because he felt they were appropriate, even though they were not strictly speaking true. To say that the contribution is an exercise in obfuscation is perhaps too harsh, but not altogether misleading. This should be already clear from the title, which reads "Presentation of Kant's Life and Character, by Ludwig Ernst Borowski, Royal Prussian Church Counsel, Painstakingly Revised by Kant Himself." As we have seen, if anything was painstakingly *revised* by Kant, it was less than one-third of what Borowski published, and it is questionable whether Kant revised even this portion *painstakingly*. As Kant himself said in the letter

Borowski included, he only allowed himself "to delete and change some things." What Kant did is therefore better described as a *casual* rather than a painstaking revision. Second, Kant did not see two-thirds of the biography at all. The second narrative is especially interesting in this regard. Its claims must be carefully compared to what we find in the first part, because in it Borowski more explicitly interpreted and characterized Kant's life and character, not restricting himself to the simple account of the facts and events we encounter in the part that Kant saw. In it, we get more of the moral of Kant's life story than of the life, which is not to suggest that we get much of Kant's life in the first part. This moral was informed by Borowski's own "heartfelt wishes" that Kant had chosen a different life than he actually had. Borowski wished that Kant

had not just viewed existing religion, and in particular the Christian religion as a need of the state, or as an institution that should be allowed to exist for the sake of those who are weak (something that is now even preached from the pulpit), but that he would have accepted and truly known the firm, wholesome, and happy aspect of Christianity . . . that he had not viewed the Bible merely as an acceptable instrument for leading and educating publicly the common people . . . that he had not viewed Jesus as the personified ideal of perfection but as the sufficiently proven messenger and son of god, the savior of mankind, that he had not, because of his fear of falling into mysticism, denied the significant value of true pious feelings, that he had participated in the public *cultus* and in the sacraments full of the grace of the Lord . . . that in all this he had been a shining example to the thousands of his students. How much good he would have done.[37]

Interestingly enough, Borowski's first attempt at a biography of Kant dates back to the time just before the king's *Maßregelung* or censure of Kant's religious views. Though there were already signs of trouble, Borowski appears not to have been aware of them in 1792. In 1804 he was all too aware of the problem, and this often interfered with the presumably "quite simple narrative."

Borowski's own faith stood more in the way of a "faithful and true account" than has been commonly realized. His story is more complex than that of Metzger, but it is informed by similar reservations, and it is therefore fraught with ambiguities. Indeed, there is evidence that Metzger and Borowski were friends, and that he therefore wished to avoid criticizing Metzger. This is regrettable. Borowski's account is mainly important for information about the years before 1783, and there is no other extensive account of that period. He left out much that might be interesting either because he did not think it was relevant or because he did not know the facts.

In any case, it is all too clear what bothered Borowski. He could not approve of Kant's religion. Rejecting both his religious theory and his religious practice, he had great difficulty in praising Kant. To be sure, he praised Kant as a moral person, but there was always the religious caveat. Borowski felt he had to make excuses. His biography thus at times takes the form of a defense: Kant was nothing like his followers; he really was a good man. Furthermore, he was nothing like his work; and even his work, if properly understood, was not as detrimental to the Christian religion as it may appear. Wherever possible, Borowski emphasized Kant's solid Pietistic background, making that background and that connection seem stronger than it was. His account must therefore be checked carefully against and supplemented by other sources. Fortunately, such sources do exist, even if they have not received the attention they deserve.

Jachmann, who was in 1804 the principal of a school near Königsberg, also had approached Kant earlier about a possible biography. Indeed, he had asked Kant in 1800 to answer fifty-six questions about his life.[38] Kant had never answered. Why, we do not know. It is interesting, however, that while Jachmann suggested in the biography that Kant had asked him to write it, Jachmann's letter, a more trustworthy source, makes clear that it was he who first approached Kant. He said that he wanted to write his biography because "the entire world wants your authentic biography and it will recognize your own contribution to it with the highest gratitude."[39] Jachmann, unlike Borowski, did not have an anti-Kantian ax to grind, and he is, at least to that extent, more trustworthy than the latter. His own outlook was more "liberal" or more "Kantian." This is shown by his *Examination of the Kantian Philosophy of Religion in Regard to its Alleged Similarity to Pure Mysticism* of 1800, which defended Kant against certain allegations.[40] Yet Jachmann's allegiance to Kant raises other problems. His biography has only good things to say about Kant, and he wrote his account from the perspective of a student who uncritically adores his teacher. Another problem is that he viewed Kant from a theological perspective: his emphasis on theology gave a peculiar slant to his account of Kant's life. Thus, Jachmann claimed that Kant liked to lecture to theologians, and that he hoped "the bright light of rational religious convictions would spread throughout his fatherland," adding that Kant "was not deceived because many apostles went off to teach the gospel (*Evangelium*) of the kingdom of reason."[41] Whether Kant had that kind of missionary zeal may very well be doubted. Jachmann's account, taken by itself, is also of limited value for a true understanding of Kant's life, and since we can check Jachmann's account against a wider variety of other sources than we can Borowski's, he is also less important. Kant was already famous when Jachmann became his student, drawing many visitors from outside Königsberg. His acquaintances paid greater attention to him when he was famous than they had when he was young and unknown.

Wasianski, regrettably, restricted himself to telling us about Kant's last few years. Indeed, it is peculiar how little he had to say about the Kant who taught him philosophy during the seventies. Since Kant's final years are the least interesting for an understanding of the background of his philosophy, Wasanski's account of Kant's decline and death is almost irrelevant for an understanding of Kant's life and thought. Wasianski cared much for his former teacher, and his account of Kant's last days is truly touching, but there are occasions on which he is less than discreet. His anecdotes about Kant's peculiarities are not much better than those of Hasse. Furthermore, insofar as he believed that he was not just polishing the image of an old man, but also engaged in providing material "for some anthropological and psychological reflections," he is playing to a different audience. When he is writing in this mood, Kant is for him an object of observation, an interesting "case," not a human being for whom he cared. His "case history" of an old man's death reveals nothing of significance about Kant the philosopher and his life in younger years.

Indeed, the greatest shortcoming of the picture painted by the three biographies is that it is almost exclusively based on the last decade and a half of Kant's life, that is, from about his sixty-fifth to his eightieth year. There is very little about Kant during his thirties, forties, and fifties, and almost nothing about the twenty-year-old Kant. All the claims about Kant's almost mechanical regularity in life – his dinners, his relation with his servant, his strange views on everyday matters, all the things that have become part and parcel of the ordinary picture of Kant – really record more the signs of his advanced age and the decline of his powers than they reveal the character of the person who conceived and wrote the works for which he is now known.

For better or worse – though mostly for worse – it is these three biographical sketches that form the most extensive, if not always the most reliable, sources of Kant's life. One can only regret that the authors of these biographical sketches were not the most qualified or the most reliable witnesses. At times, the intentions of the authors are clearly revealed. When Borowski finds, for instance, that "in its results, the Kantian doctrine of morality coincides entirely with the Christian one," we know what makes him say so, and we can discount it.[42] When Jachmann tries to downplay Kant's enthusiasm for the French Revolution by showing that, all in all, Kant was a good Prussian citizen, he is more worried about contemporary politics than about giving a true characterization of Kant.[43] Even when these intentions are not so obvious, they are always present.[44] The authors were more interested in defending what they took to be the good name of Kant (and Königsberg) than in giving an objective account. They give us an ideologically slanted view of Kant that owes more to the stereotypes of the age than to Kant's individual character. We get a caricature, not a portrait painting – well-meaning, but unreflective and without even a hint of irony.

It was ultimately because of this caricature that the German Romantics came to believe in a man who was all thought and no life.[45] Heinrich Heine summed up this view as follows:

> The history of Kant's life is difficult to describe. For he neither had a life nor a history. He lived a mechanically ordered, almost abstract, bachelor life in a quiet out-of-the-way lane in Königsberg, an old city at the northeast border of Germany. I do not believe that the large clock of the Cathedral there completed its task with less passion and less regularity than its fellow citizen Immanuel Kant. Getting up, drinking coffee, writing, giving lectures, eating, taking a walk, everything had its set time, and the neighbors knew precisely that the time was 3:30 P.M. when Kant stepped outside his door with his gray coat and the Spanish stick in his hand. . . . eight times he would walk up and down the little alley lined by Linden trees – every season, no matter whether the weather was cloudy or whether the clouds promised rain. One could see his servant, the old Lampe, anxious and worried, walk behind him, with an umbrella under his arm, like an image of destiny.[46]

An interesting image, but more a caricature of a caricature. Kant's friends in Königsberg preferred a Kant without history to a Kant with a questionable history. Heine, like many of the Romantics, disliked Kant's philosophy for the same reason that he disliked his life. Both were much too "ordinary" or "common" for him.[47] Simmel later spoke of the "incomparable personal trait of Kant's philosophy," which he saw in "its uniquely impersonal nature." Kant was a "conceptual cripple," his thinking was the "history of a mind (*Kopf*)" and not that of a real person.[48] Thus, when Arsenij Gulyga, like Heine and many others before him, claims today that "Kant has no other biography than the history of his doctrine," he joins a chorus of voices going back to the Romantics.[49] If Gulyga and Heine are right, then Kant constitutes an exception to Nietzsche's claim that "every great philosophy has so far been the self-confession of its originator, a kind of unintentional, unconscious *memoires*." Nietzsche should have made an exception for Kant.[50] Since he had no life, he could not have written any *memoires* either.

Kant, on this view, went one better than Descartes, who, according to a story popular in the eighteenth century, was always accompanied on his travels by a "mechanical life-sized female doll which . . . he had himself constructed 'to show that animals are only machines and have no souls. . . . Descartes and the doll were evidently inseparable, and he is said to have slept with her encased in a trunk at his side."[51] Kant, it would seem, actually succeeded in turning himself into a machine.

There is at least one recent psychoanalytic appraisal that aims to raise serious questions about Kant's philosophy based on the accounts of Borowski, Jachmann, and Wasianski. Hartmut and Gernot Böhme claim that "the false innocence of Kant's biography and its idealization are both equally symptoms of the kind of thinking, which has taken possession of his life and which has been made to appear harmless."[52] The Böhme brothers claim that neither Kant's life nor his thoughts were harmless or innocent. His thinking was characterized by violent structures, by repressed fears, anxiety, and strategies of repression. They declare these characteristics of his thought to be the consequences of a deformed, "mechanized" life. Though the Böhmes have argued this view forcefully, even if not always on the basis of the facts, they are probably wrong. The life of Kant that they are "analyzing" is not Kant's own but the life that others have made up. If their views have any value – and I am not altogether convinced that there is much of value in them – then their value consists more in the elucidation of the forces at work in Borowski's, Jachmann's, and Wasianski's lives than any description of the forces at work in Kant. I would like to show that there are differences of fundamental importance.[53] The Böhmes's attempt to make Kant more interesting appears to me to fail. Whatever else his life may have been, it does not provide a good example of the "structures of rationality" that characterize modern life.

Karl Vorländer, who has worked most extensively on Kant's life, emphasized the "complementary" character of the three biographies. One might speak of "complicity" and "compliment" instead.[54] Kant's "official" biographers did not really try to give a disinterested account. Their sketches were designed to peddle a certain picture of Kant, the good and upstanding citizen, who led the somewhat boring life of a stereotypical professor. We may be sure that many of the things these biographers took to be dangers to Kant's reputation would hardly be viewed as dangerous today. Some of the perceived shortcomings might even be considered virtues by later generations, and some of the perceived virtues do not look so good today. Still other features of Kant that we do not hear about might raise new and interesting questions about the person and his thought.

It is difficult, if not impossible, to get behind these texts to the historical Kant, but this does not mean that we should not try. The situation is somewhat analogous to our situation with regard to Socrates and Jesus, though perhaps not quite as problematic. There are, after all, texts written by Kant himself. There is also an extensive Königsberg correspondence, which gives us glimpses of how Kant was seen during his life. There are also sources provided by other famous citizens of Königsberg, which allow us to give more color to Kant's life. Finally, there is Metzger, who generally is just dismissed as "unreliable." But what can "unreliable" mean here? After all, even if he did not know the late Kant quite as intimately as did Wasianski, he did know him. He knew him as a colleague in the university setting, and he thus knew him in a role that Wasianski did not. Kant affected him negatively, but that does not mean that his judgment should simply be discounted. Borowski is not much more reliable than Metzger, or rather, Borowski has to be treated with the same caution as does Metzger, and insofar as Jachmann and Wasianski are engaged in "hagiography," they have to be treated just as carefully.

I must therefore disagree with those who believe that anyone who writes a biography of Kant must accept the traditional view of the evidence. Rudolf Malter summed it up as follows:

The rank order of the evidence that has long been recognized remains valid: besides the rare autobiographical utterances by Kant and the correspondence which is fundamental for any biography, the three biographies [by Borowski, Jachmann, and Wasianski] are the main basis for our knowledge about Kant, his life, his personality, and his interaction with the citizens of Königsberg.[55]

Borowski's biography, while important, should not be put into the same class with the biographies of Jachmann and Wasianski. The correspondence of Hamann, Herder, Hippel, Scheffner, and others should be considered a better source than the biographical sketches of Borowski, Jachmann, and Wasianski. If Borowski's account is inconsistent with sources independent of the biographical tradition, such as passages from letters from contemporaries of Kant, the independent evidence should be followed. In any case, if we treat the three official biographies with a healthy dose of skepticism, a much more colorful and interesting Kant will emerge.

II

During the two hundred years since Kant's death, not many full biographical treatments of Kant have been written. Though a recent bibliography of works on Kant's life takes up 23 pages and lists 483 titles, most of these concern minutiae that are of little interest even to those most keenly intrigued by Kant's philosophy.[56] Rolf George finds in a recent review of Kant biographies that there are really only "half a dozen early reminiscences, and four later full dress biographies"; the rest, he thinks, are, if not downright irrelevant, then at best only of marginal interest.[57] George is perhaps a little too harsh in his judgment. There are (a few) more books and articles of biographical interest than he is willing to admit. Yet it is undeniable that there is not as much written on Kant's life as one might reasonably expect.

Furthermore, there has never been a biography that would satisfy the most stringent requirements of scholarship. Karl Vorländer's two-volume *Immanuel Kant, Man and Work* of 1924 comes closest to this ideal, but even Vorländer did not really attempt to accomplish this task.[58] In a sense, his ambitions were higher. He did not want to write a book that would be valuable just for the philosopher and scholar, but instead wished to bring "to life the aged Kant as he lived and thought" for the general reader. The same is true of his short account called *The Life of Immanuel Kant*, which appeared in 1911 and preceded the two-volume biography.[59] Malter claimed in his preface to the fourth edition of this work (1977) that hardly any new sources for the externals of Kant's life had appeared since 1924, and that Vorländer's work thus represents in a sense the "completion" of research into the externals of Kant's life.[60] This is not quite correct. Vorländer's work is the touchstone by which all other biographies of Kant must be measured. It does indeed supersede all previous biographical treatments of Kant.[61] However, this must not be taken to mean that it is impossible to go beyond Vorländer or that Vorländer's work is based on the entire evidence. It is not. Vorländer's sources themselves are to a large extent still available, and they allow in many cases quite different interpretations. Kurt Stavenhagen's *Kant and Königsberg* of 1949 shows how much more important the Seven-Year War (the European part of the French and Indian Wars, 1756–63) were for Kant's development than Vorländer had suggested. He also tries to show that the young Kant was different from the old Kant, whom Vorländer had tried to bring to life. Vorländer did not conduct original research. He relied on articles that, although difficult to find today, can still be found. Finally, Vorländer himself was not as objective as is sometimes claimed. His Kant is to a large extent the reflection of his own views on culture and politics. Though he was careful, he overlooked certain aspects of the research that preceded his work. Furthermore, new material has been discovered. The recent work of Reinhard Brandt, Werner Euler, Heiner Klemme, Riccardo Pozzo, Werner Stark, Hans-Joachim Waschkies, and others has contributed to a better understanding of the externals of Kant's life. While we are still not in a position to understand completely Kant's role in the administration of the University of Königsberg, we do know more than Vorländer knew or was willing to reveal. Finally, a better understanding of the historical background of eighteenth-century Prussia makes it necessary to revise some of the claims that Vorländer and his predecessors have taken as being obviously true. Kant scholarship often relies – at least implicitly – on a certain picture of Kant, the man. A biography that takes into account the new evidence and the different concerns of readers almost a century later is long overdue.

This is especially true in the English-speaking world. Apart from J. W. H. Stuckenberg's dated *The Life of Immanuel Kant* of 1882, there exist only two recent translations of foreign titles, namely Ernst Cassirer's *Kant's Life and Thought* (from the German) and Gulyga's *Immanuel Kant and His Life and Thought* (from the Russian).[62] Stuckenberg wrote his biography long before many of the most important independent sources for a complete life of Kant were available. When he wrote, there existed no full edition of Kant's letters, of his reflections, or of his lectures. Nor was there much of the correspondence of Hamann and Herder available to him. Numerous other sources have been opened up since he wrote. While Stuckenberg's book still reads well, it does not satisfy the standards that must be applied today. Cassirer's biography, on the other hand, "does not dwell on the minutiae of Kant's life."[63] In other words, it does not say very much about Kant's life, concentrating almost entirely on his thought and his published writings. It is more a popular account of Kant's philosophical development than a thoroughgoing biography. Gulyga's biography might be the best available in English, but it is not widely available. This well-written life of Kant was intended for the Russian reader. It provides a welcome antidote to the other two biographies available in English, but because it is written from a perspective that is somewhat foreign to the English reader, it does not always further our understanding of Kant's life and work. Furthermore, it is not always reliable, and it overemphasizes the connections between Kant and Russian thought.

III

Biographies of philosophers have been relatively scarce in the recent past.[64] One of the most important reasons for this has to do with the way philosophy is being done in America, Australia, and England. To an analytically minded philosopher, the biography of a thinker is simply irrelevant, since it says nothing about the truth of his position and adds nothing to the soundness of his arguments. While this is, strictly speaking, true, the lack of context – or perhaps better, the substitution of an anachronistic context – often stands in the way of appreciating what a philosopher wanted to say.

Biographies of philosophers are difficult to write. They must strike a balance between representing the biographical details and discussing the philosophical work. They must neither turn into a mere tale of the philosopher's external life nor become a mere summary or general discussion of his books. If a biography concentrates too much on the accidents that make up its subject's life, it may turn out to be trite and unexciting (if only because philosophers usually did not – and do not – live exciting lives). If a biography concentrates too much on the work, it can easily become boring for another reason. The work of most philosophers does not lend itself to easy summary or general discussion. In any case, it is highly unlikely that such a summary treatment of the life work of any philosopher would add in any significant way to the philosophical discussion. Ideally, a biography of any philosopher would be both philosophically and historically interesting, and would integrate the story of the philosopher's life with a philosophically interesting perspective on his work.

While both life and thought need to be addressed, this cannot mean that these two different concerns should simply be given equal time. Matters are more complicated. A biography must integrate the two in some way. It must make clear how the life and thought of a philosopher are connected. Though it is a difficult and perhaps impossible task to establish why a certain philosopher held the views he held and wrote the works he wrote, any biography that does not address this question will probably be of limited interest.

Kant's biography would appear to be especially difficult to write. His life was that of a typical university professor in eighteenth-century Germany. His philosophical work is so dense, abstruse, and technical that it is difficult to make it accessible to the general reader. This would seem to be a deadly combination. Furthermore, Kant himself followed in his works the motto *"de nobis ipsis silemus"* ("about ourselves we are silent"). He was concerned with philosophical truth, and he wanted to be known for having advanced philosophical truths. This also has consequences for his biography. There is no journal; the details about his life are sparse. They have to be gleaned from what he let through by accident, and from the recollections of those who were closest to him. Most of these are recollections of older people about the older Kant.

Kant did have a life. Though he lived in an isolated part of Prussia, though he did not undertake any thrilling journeys, though there are no great adventures to be told, and though much of his life is summed up by his work, there is still a highly interesting, and perhaps even exciting, story to be told. This is the story of Kant's *intellectual* life, as it is reflected not just in his work, but also in his letters, his teaching, and his interactions with his contemporaries in Königsberg and the rest of Germany. Even if Kant's life was to some extent typical of an eighteenth-century German intellectual, it is of historical importance just because it was so typical. The differences and similarities between his life and those of his colleagues in other Protestant universities such as Marburg, Göttingen, and elsewhere in Germany may open up interesting perspectives for understanding not only the man but also the times in which he lived.

Kant's life spanned almost the entire eighteenth century. The period of his adulthood saw some of the most significant changes in the Western world – changes that still reverberate. This was the period during which the world as we know it today originated. Though Königsberg was not at the center of any of the significant movements leading to our world, these movements largely determined the intellectual milieu of Königsberg. Kant's philosophy was to a large extent an expression of and response to these changes. His intellectual life reflected most of the significant intellectual, political, and scientific developments of the period. His views are reactions to the cultural climate of the time. English and French philosophy, science, literature, politics, and manners formed the stuff of his daily conversations. Even such relatively distant events as the American and French Revolutions had a definite effect on Kant, and thus also on his work. His philosophy must be seen in this global context.

Yet it was within a definitely German, even Prussian, setting that Kant experienced the momentous developments that took place during the eighteenth century. Sometimes it is almost shocking to observe how much of his intellectual development was dictated by outside forces. Thus Kant's early philosophical work developed as a series of responses to the philosophical *Preisaufgaben* set by the Berlin academy.[65] It is just as difficult to understand the early Kant without discussing his relation to the literary movement of "*Sturm und Drang*" and the "cult of genius," as it would be to understand the late Kant without considering the controversy surrounding the so-called *Pantheismusstreit*.

Furthermore, Kant was part of Königsberg's particular intellectual milieu. He was not the only one in Königsberg who was interested in and affected by these changes. Hamann, von Hippel, Herder, Herz, and several others were able to contribute to the German cultural scene – at least in part – because of their experiences in Königsberg. It is important to investigate how the lives of these interesting people intersected, and how Kant was shaped by his interactions with them. While it might be an exaggeration to speak of a "Königsberg Enlightenment" in the way in which we speak of a "Berlin Enlightenment" and a "Scottish Enlightenment," it would not be entirely inappropriate either. Kant's critical philosophy needs to be seen in that context as well. So, in discussing Kant's life and works all three contexts – the global, the regional, and the local – must be taken into account.

In this biography of Kant such concerns will be taken more seriously than they have been in previous biographies. In other words, this will be an intellectual biography of Kant that shows how Kant's intellectual concerns were rooted in his period. In some ways, such an approach has similarities to such developmental studies as those of Schilpp, Vleeschauwer, and Ward, and such discussions of Kant's *Weltanschauung* as can be found in the works of Kroner and Beck. Yet it is different from these insofar as it pays less attention to standard philosophical texts and more attention to the events in Kant's life and their relation to events in Königsberg, Prussia, Germany, Europe, and North America. Without neglecting the representation of the biographical details of Kant's life and his work, I will concentrate on Kant's intellectual journey from narrow concerns with the metaphysical foundations of Newtonian physics to the philosophical defense of a moral outlook appropriate to an *enlightened* "citizen of the world."

Like Vorländer and Gulyga, I mean to present Kant in such a way that he is approachable for someone who is not well versed in Kant scholarship. Even a reader who is unfamiliar with the intricacies of the current philosophical discussion of Kant or philosophy in general should find the book readable. Kant's life is intrinsically interesting, and, unlike Vorländer and others, who primarily wanted to bring to life the older Kant, I shall focus more on the younger philosopher, who first conceived the project of a *Critique of Pure Reason*. I hope that a many-sided Kant will emerge, a Kant that looks more like a real person than the "Mandarin" of Königsberg, as Nietzsche saw him.[66]

We can learn from Kant's life as much as we can from the lives of other eighteenth-century figures – Benjamin Franklin, David Hume, Frederick the Great, Catherine the Great – whose lives were intertwined with that of Kant in intricate and sometimes not-so-intricate fashion. Indeed, we can learn from Kant's biography at least as much as we can learn from the biography of any well-known person. Perhaps we can learn even more from it because, as will become clear, Kant's character was quite consciously meant to be his own creation. He agreed with Montaigne and his Stoic predecessors that "to compose character is our duty, not to compose books, and to win, not battles and provinces, but order and tranquillity in our conduct. Our great and glorious masterpiece is to live appropriately." Whether Kant lived his life "appropriately" is an open question; and this makes his life fascinating for anyone who thinks philosophy has to make an important contribution to the understanding of our lives.

I do not really know what makes biographies so fascinating to so many readers. Is it simply curiosity about how the "famous" have lived? Is it voyeurism, an unsavory desire to glimpse the dirty little secrets of the "great"? Is it escapism, an attempt at vicarious living, a kind of romance for the more intellectually inclined? Or is it a way of trying to find meaning in our own lives? Many self-help books testify to a widely felt desire for a "successful" life. Successful people might be thought to have accomplished this elusive goal – and successful philosophers, that is, people who have reflected on what makes for success, might have more to offer than most.

As Virginia Woolf once observed, biographies are difficult, if not impossible, to write, because "people are all over the place." Their lives have no real narrative line. Yet such a line is precisely what biographers try to establish. A biography has a beginning, middle, and end; and it usually attempts to make sense of, or give reasons for, events that may simply have followed one another without being connected in any way. Some lives may indeed make sense, while others seem to be spent senselessly. Whether or not someone's life had meaning – whatever that may mean – is a question that is at least as difficult to answer as the question of whether or not our own lives have meaning. The two questions are ultimately one and the same. Thus we need not be reticent about looking at the lives of those who have gone before us in order to make sense of our own.

Of course, there is no guarantee that we will learn important and worthwhile lessons from the study of any particular life. It would be a mistake, I think, to fashion one's own life after the life of any historical figure, even if this has been done by many who ended up becoming historical figures in their own right. One cannot choose a life in the way one chooses a coat. Yet there are many ways of life, and biographies can give us some insight into their possible dangers and rewards. Kant's life was different from that lived by many Romantics, by self-styled Nietzscheans, or by other modern adventurers. Whether or not it was attractive, I have to leave to the reader. I am sure it was more interesting than the caricatures still current today.

This introduction is followed by nine chapters. Chapter 1, "Childhood and Early Youth (1724–1740)"; Chapter 2, "Student and Private Teacher (1740–1755)"; Chapter 3, "The Elegant *Magister* (1755–1764)"; Chapter 4, "A Palingenesis and Its Consequences (1764–1769)"; Chapter 5, "Silent Years (1770–1780)"; Chapter 6, "'All-Crushing' Critic of Metaphysics (1780–1784)"; Chapter 7, "Founder of a Metaphysics of Morals (1784–1788)"; Chapter 8, "Problems with Religion and Politics (1788–1795)"; and Chapter 9, "The Old Man (1796–1804)." I have tried to integrate the narrative of Kant's life and the development of his philosophy as much as possible. The sections that provide more extensive summaries of Kant's major works are clearly marked in the outline, and the reader more interested in Kant's life than in the details of Kant's philosophy should be able to avoid them, even though I do not think that this is a good idea.

Childhood and Early Youth (1724–1740)

Early Childhood (1724–1731):
"The Best Education from the Moral Point of View"

THE YEAR 1724 was not one of the most significant years in the history of the human race, but it was not wholly insignificant either. It saw the signing of a treaty between Moscow and Constantinople, designed to dismember Persia, whose territory the two powers had previously invaded. Persia's Shah Mahmoud went insane and ordered a wholesale massacre at Isfahan. Philip V abdicated the Spanish throne in favor of his son Louis – only to regain it when Louis died a few months later. The Sieur de Bienvilles, governor of Louisiana at New Orleans, proclaimed a *Code Noir* for regulating blacks and expelling Jews, while the Quakers and Mennonites published their first statements opposing slavery. In Philadelphia, a craft guild along the lines of European guilds was established. In Ireland, still a colony of England and largely exploited by absentee landlords, Jonathan Swift published *Drapier's Letters,* in which he tried to persuade the Irish to oppose a scheme by one William Wood, who had received a royal patent for issuing a new Irish coin but who planned to profit from debasing it. Peter I, known as Peter the Great, founded the Russian Academy of Sciences and Arts. Paul Dudley discovered the possibility of cross-fertilizing corn. Herman Boerhaave argued in his *Elementae chemiae* (Elements of Chemistry) that heat is a fluid, and Gabriel Daniel Fahrenheit described the supercooling of water. George Frederick Handel finished two of his lesser-known works, the operas *Giulio Cesare* and *Tamerlano.* Jean Philippe Rameau composed one of his three collections of harpsichord pieces. Daniel Defoe published *Roxana* and *A New Voyage around the World.* The second volume of Alain René Lesage's picaresque romance *Gil Blas* appeared. The Comtesse de Lafayette's posthumous *La Comtesse de Tende* came out, as did Bernard de Fontenelle's *De l'Origine des fables* (The Origin of Myths) intended to explore both the psychological and intellectual roots of mythology and to refute popular superstitions. Claude Buffier published his T*raité des vérités premières et de la source de nos jugements* (Treatise on First Truths and on the Source of Our Judgments), trying to uncover the basic principles of human knowledge, while David Hume was beginning his second year of study at the University of Edinburgh.

In Prussia, Frederick William I (1688–1740), who ruled from 1713, was hard at work, trying to centralize the state, and to amass an impressive army with the revenue from an impoverished country. During the previous year he had taken a decisive step to reform his administration, unifying it into a single board, which was known as the general directory. This institution was to become an efficient bureaucracy that cut royal expenditures while more than doubling annual income, allowing him to channel funds to his army. During 1723 he had also found time to expel Christian Wolff from all of Prussia at the behest of religious zealots, known as Pietists, in Halle. They had argued that Wolff's acceptance of the Leibnizian theory of preestablished harmony implied fatalism and could serve as an excuse for deserters from the army. Indeed, it might persuade them to desert. Frederick William I went so far as to prohibit Wolffian doctrines from being taught.[1] He thereby, quite against his intention, made this thinker a cause celèbre among those who favored Enlightenment. Wolff, ordered not to reenter Prussia at the pain of death, made the University of Marburg his home and published in 1724 one of his most successful works, namely the *Vernünftige Gedanken von den Absichten der natürlichen Dinge* (Reasonable Thoughts about the Purposes of Natural Things), a treatise on teleology in which he attempted to show how well-planned this world really is.

Most of these events in Prussia and elsewhere – in due time – were of consequence in Königsberg. Some of the king's actions had immediate effects: In 1724 Königsberg, which until then had consisted of three different cities, namely the *Altstadt* or the old city, the *Löbenicht,* and the *Kneiphof,* was united. This made the city easier to administer and government more effective. (Among other things, the unification reduced the number of gallows from three to one.) The same year also saw the return of a church official named Georg Friedrich Rogall, who was to look out for the king's interests in Königsberg. Having been educated and converted to Pietism in Halle by the enemies of Wolff, he also had the ear of his religious ruler. One of his first actions consisted in the removal from the

University of Königsberg of the most outspoken advocate of Wolffian philosophy. Christian Gabriel Fischer (1686–1751), professor of natural philosophy, met with the same fate as Wolff because Rogall informed on him in Berlin.[2]

On April 22 of this year Immanuel Kant was born in Königsberg. The *Old Prussian Almanac* associated the name "Emanuel" with this date. Accordingly, he was baptized "Emanuel." He would later change it to "Immanuel," thinking that this was a more faithful rendition of the original Hebrew. "Emanuel" or "Immanuel" means "God is with him." Kant thought that it was a most appropriate name, and he was uncommonly proud of it, commenting on its meaning even in his old age.[3] It is perhaps meaningful that he found it necessary critically to evaluate and correct the very name given to him, but it is noteworthy that the literal meaning of his name provided him with comfort and confidence throughout his life. Indeed, Kant's autonomous, self-reliant, and self-made character may well presuppose a certain kind of optimistic trust in the world as a teleological whole, a world in which everything, himself included, had a definite place.

Emanuel was the son of Johann Georg Kant (1683–1746), a master harness maker in Königsberg, and Anna Regina Kant (1697–1737), née Reuter, the daughter of another harness maker in Königsberg. Johann Georg Kant had come to Königsberg from Tilsit. His marriage to Anna Regina on November 13, 1715, opened the way for him to make a living as an independent tradesman.[4] Such craftsmen had to belong to a guild. Since the guilds strictly regulated the numbers of those who could open a business within a city, marriage to a master's daughter was often the only way for someone from the outside to break into the trade. One became an independent master tradesman in one of only two ways: either by being born a master's son or by marrying a master's daughter. Anna Regina herself was the daughter of Caspar Reuter and his wife Regina, née Felgenhauer (or Falkenhauer).[5] Caspar Reuter had also come from outside the city, namely from Nürnberg, which had old trade connections with Königsberg.[6]

A master had to have produced a "master piece" and to have obtained the right of citizenship within the city in which he conducted his business. This usually meant that he had to own real estate within the city (or at least belong to a family that did). More importantly, he had to be registered in a local guild whose special laws and customs applied to him and his entire family from the moment he entered it. To enter a guild, proof of legitimate birth of both the master and his wife had to be supplied. Traditionally, the guilds were largely independent of public authorities, and they tended to settle disputes among themselves.[7] The lives of members were ruled by old customs, which did not allow them much freedom in pursuing their business. How many apprentices and journeymen could be employed was strictly regulated. Unskilled workers were forbidden to work in any recognized trade. Prices were not set at the open market. The organization of the guilds was essentially a closed system whose rules and regulations usually guaranteed a decent living by suppressing competition. As a master of a trade, Kant's father could exercise (at least in principle) a kind of control over journeymen and apprentices that we would find unacceptable today. He would, for instance, be the one who granted the permission to a journeyman to move from one place to another. The guilds also had the authority to punish their members, an authority they exercised.

In Königsberg, every guild had its own representative in each district of the city, and each had a special account set aside to help their members in case of death, sickness, or impoverishment.[8] When a master died, the guild usually had to take care of the widow. Indeed, "the guild, just like the church, encompassed the entire life" of its members.[9] The *Handwerker* were proud and very conscious of their special position, taking great care to distinguish themselves from those they considered of lower standing. "Honor" or "*Ehre*" was important not just in all dealings of a member of the guild, but also in his or her background. A member of the guild belonged to the "respectable" classes.[10] An eighteenth-century account of the situation of craftsmen in Zurich may give us some idea about the situation in Königsberg:

The high-handedness of the so-called gentry was justly resented by members, both young and old, of what might be called the middle class of citizens. Expressions such as . . . "I am a gentleman and a citizen" were bold claims such as might be heard in altercations with those who deemed themselves superior, or with country folk or foreigners. . . . The baker from whom my parents bought their bread, Irminger, was a shrewd and experienced businessman; at the time when I myself became a citizen he was highly regarded as a master of his guild and was treated with great respect as a member of the Council. This was the case, too, with several others, and a good many craftsmen were entitled to an equal degree of respect as members of the Grand Council. The highly elitist manner of electing members to the Grand Council – they were chosen by existing Council members and the aldermen of the guilds – would inevitably have led to total domination by a patrician clique, had not the guild masters, the two principal officers, been elected by the guild as a whole. . . . It was mainly the butchers who upheld the guild system . . . they were followed by the bakers and millers, while the shoemakers and tailors had only one member apiece on the Grand Council.[11]

Working largely with leather, the harness makers were closely related to the shoemakers and saddle makers. The harness makers (*Riemer* or *courroiers*)

produced harnesses for horses, carriages, and sleds as well as other implements having to do with transportation. In Prussia they also were responsible for the outfitting of the carriages themselves. The main material they
worked with was leather, and the most important implements of their
trade were similar to those of the saddle makers. Kant's father, like most
tradesmen, had his workshop at home. While the harness makers were not
among the most prestigious of the guilds, they were part of the system. As
members of this class, the Kants may not have been rich, but they certainly
had a certain kind of social standing that demanded respect, and they took
pride in their honor. Kant, as the son of a master, had special rights, since
he was a member of the guild by birth.

The family first lived in a house located in the outer city, which had once
belonged to the stepfather of Regina Reuter, Kant's grandmother.[12] It
seems to have been inherited by Kant's grandparents, and it was owned by
them rather than by his parents. The house stood on a narrow but deep
lot. It was typical for Königsberg – three stories high. There was a shed,
a garden, and even a meadow. Though the living quarters were not luxurious, they were comfortable at least by eighteenth-century standards.
Emanuel's father appears to have earned a fairly good living, although
harness making was never a way to riches.[13] It was not as prosperous a
trade as that of the butchers and bakers, for instance, but it supported a
family well. Emanuel's father may have employed an apprentice or a journeyman at times, although it would not have been unusual had he worked
mostly by himself.[14] The Kants almost certainly had at least one maid-
servant, who also would have lived in the house. The young Emanuel was
constantly confronted with his father's business.

Emanuel was the fourth child of the Kants, but when he was born his only
surviving sibling was a five-year-old sister. At his baptism, Anna Regina
wrote in her prayer book: "May God sustain him in accordance with His
Covenant of Grace until his final rest, for the sake of Jesus Christ, Amen."
Given that she had already lost two children, the name of the new son
appeared most auspicious to her as well. It answered a real concern and
expressed a heartfelt sentiment. It was not just a pious wish. Indeed,
Emanuel's chances of living to a ripe old age were not very good. Of the
five siblings born after Kant, only three (two sisters and one brother) survived early childhood. In other words, four of the nine children born in
the Kant household died at an early age. While this was not unusual in the
eighteenth century, it could not have been easy for Emanuel's mother.

While the Kant family lived fairly well during Emanuel's early childhood, the situation worsened as he grew older. On March 1, 1729, his grandfather died. It appears that, as a result, Johann Georg Kant also took charge of the business of his father-in-law. He was now the only provider for his mother-in-law as well. He found this difficult to manage. Four years later (in 1733) the entire family moved out of the home they had occupied until then into the house of the grandmother – probably to be able to take better care of her. The new house, a smaller, more modest, one-story dwelling, also located in the outer city, provided cramped quarters for the growing family. An open kitchen, a large living room, and two or three small bedrooms, all sparsely furnished, made up the living space. The house stood right by the "*Sattlerstraße*," or the Saddle Makers' Street. This was of course the street in which, in accordance with customs going back to the Middle Ages, most of the saddle and harness makers of the city lived.[15]

The new business location was not as profitable as the old. Though Emanuel's father had never had a large business, his income declined steadily. The two most important reasons for this were increased competition from the nearby shops of the saddle makers and the increasing age of the father. The first was not just a consequence of the new location, but also a direct result of the serious crisis that the guild system underwent during the early years of the eighteenth century. Though the guild system remained powerful, it had deep problems. This is shown by the "Opinion of the Imperial Diet Concerning the Abuses of the Guilds" from August 14, 1731, which was meant to curb these abuses. Guilds were quarreling with one another, and journeyman and masters did not get along as well as they had before. The edict took away some of the rights of the guilds and curbed others, enjoining them to

become more sedate in their ways, showing due obedience to their appointed [civil] authorities. Nonetheless, it has proven absolutely necessary to abandon our former patience and to point out in all seriousness to masters and journeyman that, if they continue in their irresponsible, evil, and stubborn ways, the Emperor and the Diet might easily be moved, following the examples of other countries, and in the interest of the public, which is hurt by such criminal, private quarrels, to suppress and abolish guilds altogether.[16]

The Kant family was affected by such quarrels, but Johann Georg and Anna Regina proved themselves to be good people in the eyes of their son:

I still remember . . . how the Harness makers and the Saddle makers once had a dispute about the business they had in common (*Gemeinsame*) because of which my father suffered greatly. Yet in spite of this, my parents dealt with such respect and love with their enemies and with such a firm trust in their destiny (*Vorsehung*) that the memory of this will never leave me, even though I was just a boy then.[17]

It is easy to see how these two trades came into conflict. They were competing for essentially the same customers, and both could supply the same goods. The trade of the harness makers was very similar to that of the saddle makers, but the apprenticeship of harness makers lasted two years, that of the saddle makers three. While saddlers could make harnesses, harness makers were neither trained to make saddles nor were they allowed to do so. In competing for a limited business, the saddle makers encroached on the market of the harness makers, who fought this encroachment but ultimately lost. In some regions of Germany the trade of the harness makers had already disappeared by the time Kant was born.

Johann Georg Kant lived and worked during the period in which this trade declined in Königsberg. His business suffered as time went on, and it became increasingly difficult to make a living during the 1730s and 1740s. Johann Georg must have known he was facing a losing battle. He must have felt that the encroachment was unfair, even if he could not change it. Still, he did not allow these troubles to poison his family life, even though family and business were so closely intertwined.

How the Königsberg of the early twenties looked from the point of view of a simple journeyman can be seen from the account given by Samuel Klenner, a tanner (*Weissgerber*) who spent some time in the city:

Königsberg: The capital of Prussia Brandenburg . . . It is a large and very extensive place. I was here three quarters of a year with the master Heinrich Gallert in Rossgarten.

Every pastor must give one Ducate to the Lutheran Bishop here, who has a doctorate in the Holy Scripture because he must always review (*revidieren*) them, and he must preach wherever he goes. The king has also built an orphanage here, and he has allowed professor Francke in Halle to design it. There is a small church in it, and the public teachers of the institution give excellent sermons, even though they are called Pietists . . .

The food here, as in all of Prussia, is very plain. For almost half of the week, one receives one and the same kind of food, namely salted pork and fish. This is warmed up every day again. The bread is black, yet still quite tasty. The flour is roughly milled, and it is baked with the husks. Often the bread contains straw. The beer, by contrast, is excellent: the table beer in Prussia is often superior to the real beer in some parts of Silesia.

The journeymen cannot go into the public because of the soldiers. They must always sit in the hostels, playing cards for money – something very common in Königsberg. However, no one is allowed to sit in a pub and drink while church is on. If anyone does, he is arrested. Because the recruitment of soldiers intensified, and because they tried their best to recruit me, I traveled back to Danzig.[18]

The daily food of the Kant family was probably as monotonous as this account suggests, and frugal at the best of times. Nevertheless, it would not have been unusual for small tradesmen of the period, and it would be wrong to say that the Kants were poor – at least as long as the mother was alive.

Johann Georg and Anna Regina Kant were good parents. They cared for their children as well as they could. In fact, if we know one thing about Kant's youth, it is that he led a protected life. One of his closest colleagues reported later:

Kant told me that when he more closely observed the education in the household of a count not far from Königsberg . . . he often thought of the incomparably more noble education that he had received in the house of his parents. He was grateful to them, saying that he had never heard or seen anything indecent at home.[19]

This testimony is supported by Borowski, who wrote:

How often have I heard him say: "Never, not even once, was I allowed to hear anything indecent from my parents, or to see something dishonorable." He himself admitted that there are perhaps only a few children – especially in our age – who can look back to their childhood with such gratification as he always could and still does.[20]

Indeed, Kant had only good things to say about his parents. Thus he wrote in a letter late in life "my two parents (from the class of tradesmen) were perfectly honest, morally decent, and orderly. They did not leave me a fortune (but neither did they leave me any debts). Moreover, they gave me an education that could not have been better when considered from the moral point of view. Every time I think of this I am touched by feelings of the highest gratitude."[21]

When Johann Georg died in 1746, Emanuel, the oldest son – then almost twenty-two years of age – wrote in the family Bible: "On the 24th of March my dear father was taken away by a happy death. . . . May God, who did not grant him many joys in this life, permit him to share in the eternal joy."[22] We may assume that Kant respected and loved his father: much of his stern moral outlook can probably be traced back to this hard-working man who eked out a living for his family under circumstances that were not always easy. His mother may have meant even more to him. But he spoke of her in more sentimental terms. Thus he is reported to have said: "I will never forget my mother, for she implanted and nurtured in me the first germ of goodness; she opened my heart to the impressions of nature; she awakened and furthered my concepts, and her doctrines have had a continual and beneficial influence in my life."[23] She was "a woman of great and natural understanding . . . who had a noble heart, and possessed a genuine religiosity that was not in the least enthusiastic."[24] Kant believed not only that he had inherited his physical looks from his mother, but also that she had been most important for the first formation of his character, as well as for having laid the foundation for what he later became. He was very dear to her, and he felt favored. In his lectures on anthropology, we find him saying that it is usually the fathers who spoil their daughters and the mothers who spoil their sons, and that mothers will prefer sons who are lively and bold.[25] Yet he also said that sons usually love their fathers more than their mothers, because

children, if they have not yet been spoiled, really love pleasures that are connected with toils. . . . In general, mothers spoil . . . their children. Yet we find that the children – especially sons – love their fathers more than their mothers. This results from the fact that the mothers do not allow them to jump and run, etc. because they are afraid they might hurt themselves. The father, who yells at them, and perhaps also spanks them when they are unruly, also leads them at times into the fields where they can behave like boys and allows them to run around, play and be happy.[26]

While this is not necessarily an account of his own relation to mother and father, there is every reason to believe that he loved them both, if perhaps in different ways.

Emanuel's mother was better educated than most women in the eighteenth century. She wrote well. Indeed, she appears to have taken care of most writing in the family. She took him out on walks, "called his attention to objects of nature and many of its appearances, even told him what she knew of the nature of the sky, and admired his keen understanding and his advanced comprehension."[27]

His grandmother died in 1735. Sad as this event must have been, it may have made things easier. There was one less mouth to feed, less work for the mother, and more room for the children. In November of the same year, Anna Regina gave birth to another child, a son (Johann Heinrich). Two years later (on December 18, 1737), she died at the age of forty, worn out by nine pregnancies and the strain of taking care of her family.

As Emanuel was just thirteen when his mother died, her death affected him greatly. He is reported to have given in old age the following account of his mother's death:

[She] had a friend, whom she loved dearly. Her friend was engaged to a man to whom she had given her whole heart, without violating her innocence and virtue. Though the man had promised to marry her, he broke his promise and married someone else. As a consequence of the pain and suffering, the deceived woman came down with a deadly high fever. She refused to take the medicine prescribed for her. Kant's mother, who nursed her on her deathbed, tried to give her a full spoon of the medicine; but her sick friend refused it, claiming it had a disgusting taste. Kant's mother believed that the best way to convince her of the contrary would be to take a spoonful herself. She did, then realized her sick friend had already used the very spoon. As soon as she understood what she had done, she felt nauseated and was gripped by a cold shudder. Her imagination heightened both. When she noticed spots on the body of her friend, which she recognized as signs of smallpox, she declared immediately that this event would be her death. She laid herself down that very day and died soon thereafter – a sacrifice to friendship.[28]

Wasianski, who reported this story, also said that Kant had told him this "with the loving and tender sadness of a good and thankful son."

Is there more to this story? Does it show only love and gratitude, or does it reveal something more sinister? Does it allow us to draw conclusions about a secret resentment toward his own mother that Kant still felt in his seventies? Does Kant blame both the friend and his mother for leaving, and thus betraying him? Hartmut Böhme and Gernot Böhme have claimed that the boy really was convinced that the death of Anna Regina was a just punishment for her being a "bad" mother, and that he was conflicted about this for the rest of his life.[29] They also suggest that Kant's later view of morality as freedom from affection and desire has its roots here: Kant blamed his mother for dying, felt guilty about this, and therefore found it difficult to grieve. He "repressed" grief and guilt at the same time and therefore did not learn to appreciate the importance of our nonrational side.[30] Perhaps, but not likely. Whatever deep psychoanalytic reading the surface of this story allows, we must remember that it will be more appropriate as a reading of Wasianski than as a reading of Kant. These are, after all, not Kant's own words. Even if it were true that some of the confused emotions that plagued Kant at the untimely death of his mother still had an effect in his old age (or perhaps, had an effect again in his old age), this would not allow us to draw any significant conclusions about Kant's life as a whole. The death of his mother cannot have been easy for a thirteen-year-old, but it does not explain his later philosophical development.

Anna Regina was buried "silently" and "poor," meaning that she was buried without a procession and at a price that people of modest means could afford.[31] For the purposes of taxation the Kant household had been explicitly declared "poor" in 1740, and whereas Johann Georg had paid 38 Thalers in taxes earlier, he now paid only 9 Groschen.[32] Given this decline, it is not surprising that the family received assistance from other family members and friends. Thus, they got firewood from some benefactors, and Emanuel's studies were supported by an uncle (a brother of his mother, a shoemaker by trade) who was better off than Kant's father.[33] Later, by the

time Kant was a famous philosopher, some people tried to argue that the
Kant family was destitute, but that never appears to have been the case.
Wasianski found it necessary to address the topic, saying that Kant's "parents were not rich, but not at all so poor that they had to suffer any need;
much less [is it true] that they were destitute or had to worry about food.
They earned enough to take care of their household and the education of
their children." He also pointed out that, though they received help from
others, it was not very significant.[34] While there was no "social safety net"
in today's sense of the term, the extended family looked out for its members and provided what was necessary.

Kant did not have much in common with his brother and sisters. He
was not very close to any of them. When, during the very last days of his
life, his sister Katharina Barbara came to nurse him, he was embarrassed
by her "simplicity," even though he was also grateful. With his only surviving brother, Johann Heinrich, who was born while Kant was already
attending the *Collegium Fridericianum*, he did not have much of a relationship either. He hardly found time to answer his letters. This does not
mean that he did not scrupulously fulfill what he took to be his duties toward them. Indeed, it is clear that he supported them when they were in
need.[35] Even if he remained aloof, he never neglected his obligations to
his family.

Kant's parents were religious. They were deeply influenced by Pietism,
especially his mother, who followed the Pietistic beliefs and practices then
current in the circles of tradesmen and the less educated townspeople in
Königsberg. Pietism was a religious movement within the Protestant
churches of Germany. It was to a large extent a reaction to the formalism
of Protestant orthodoxy. Orthodox theologians and pastors placed great
emphasis on the so-called symbolic books, and they required strict verbal
adherence to their teaching. Anyone disagreeing with the traditional theological doctrines was harassed and persecuted. At the same time, they
were not overly interested in the spiritual or economic well-being of their
flock. Most of them had made comfortable arrangements with the local
gentry, and they were often disdainful of the simpler and less educated
people of the city. The Pietists, by contrast, emphasized the importance
of independent Bible study, personal devotion, the priesthood of the laity,
and a practical faith issuing in acts of charity. Pietism was an evangelical
movement, and it usually involved an insistence on a *personal* experience
of radical conversion or rebirth, and an abrogation of worldly success.[36]
Pietists believed that salvation could be found only after one had under-

gone a so-called *Bußkampf* or struggle of repentance that led to a conversion (*Bekehrung*) and awakening (*Erweckung*). In this struggle the "old self" was to be overcome by the "new self" through the grace of God. By it, the "child of the world" became a "child of God." To be a true Christian was to be born again, and to have had a conversion experience that usually could be precisely dated. This rebirth, however, was only the first step on a long road. The living faith of the converted had to be reconfirmed every day by "acts of obedience to God's commandments [which] included prayer, Bible reading, and renunciation of sinful diversions and service to one's neighbor through acts of charity."[37]

Pietism was a "religion of the heart," very much opposed to intellectualism and characterized by an emotionalism that bordered at times on mysticism. Wherever Pietism took hold, small circles of the "select" were formed. Indeed, one of the main tenets of Pietism is the view that every believer should gather at his location an "*ecclesiola in ecclesia*," or a small church of "true Christians" (*Kernchristen*), distinct from the formal church that may have strayed from the true meaning of Christianity. Its most important source of inspiration was Philipp Jakob Spener's *Pia desideria* of 1675, whose subtitle read "heartfelt desire for the improvement of the true evangelical Church that is approved by God, together with some Christian suggestions, designed to lead toward it." Its main center in Prussia was the new University of Halle, where August Hermann Francke (1663–1727) propagated Pietistic ideas with great success, and from which Pietism spread throughout Prussia.[38]

One of the most important reasons for the success of Pietism was Frederick William I, who found the Pietists useful for his own purposes. To create an absolutist state with a strong army, an effective administration, a rigid economy, and a uniform and effective school system, he relied on the most prominent members of the Pietistic movement to help him in pushing through his reforms.[39] Since these reforms were very much against the interests of the landed gentry of Prussia, who were closely allied with the more orthodox forces within the Lutheran Church, the political conflict between the absolutist king and the local nobility became also a conflict between theological orthodoxy and Pietism. This combination of political and theological motives made an explosive mixture. The king in Berlin took away many of the privileges of the landed gentry in order to propagate his own more central administration. His drive to educate the children of the poor also brought him into conflict with the landed gentry, as the time children spent in school kept them from working in their fields, and thus cut into their profits. The ensuing battle between the centralist forces in Berlin and the landed gentry was often fought with great bitterness, with the Pietists being the king's natural allies. Indeed, Frederick William I "incorporated Pietism increasingly in his organization, used it, and thus changed it, only to be changed by it in turn."[40] However one might be tempted to speak of an "unholy alliance" of religion and politics, it was an alliance that, on the whole, favored the interests of the common people rather than those of the nobility.

The Pietism taught at Halle was distinct from that taught elsewhere in Germany. Francke placed greater emphasis on an active Christian life than did other propagators of Pietism. Indeed, he enjoined a kind of social activism. Acts of charity were not just the private affair of every individual Christian, but also a common task of the Prussian Pietist community. Francke had founded a number of institutions for the housing and education of orphans and other destitute children in Halle, and he embarked on an ambitious educational project, significant far beyond Halle. The "*Franckeschen Anstalten*" were meant to give "an idea and an example to other countries and kingdoms so that the common good will come about."[41] The daily acts of charity that were required of a Pietist were often channeled into work for such enterprises as orphanages and schools for the poor. It was this Pietism of the Halle persuasion that had the most significant effect in Königsberg. Indeed, there was an immediate and direct connection between Halle and Königsberg during the first half of the eighteenth century, with the king actively supporting the transplantation of Halle Pietists to official positions in Königsberg. It was this kind of Pietism that influenced Kant's parents.

Though Pietism became dominant in Königsberg under Frederick William I, its influence reached further back. The most important early Pietists in Königsberg were Theodor Gehr and Johann Heinrich Lysius. Gehr, who had experienced a Pietistic conversion in Halle, founded a *collegium pietatis* in Königsberg, and later also a school for the poor. Gehr's school developed over the years into a gymnasium. Taken into royal protection in 1701, it obtained the name *Collegium Fridericianum* in 1703. At the same time, Lysius became the director of the school, and since he was also appointed as an "*extra ordinarius*" in the theological faculty of the University, the influence of Pietism on the culture of Königsberg increased. Indeed, he had greater official standing than any previous Pietist in Königsberg. This was a significant first victory for Pietism.

Indeed, the Pietists were at first persecuted as "street preachers without a calling" (*unberuffene Winckelprediger*) in Königsberg. They were accused of founding illegitimate schools at street corners (*Winckelschulen*), which constituted an unfair competition with legitimate schools, and also of preaching heresy. Only when the *Collegium Fridericianum* became an official institution and its director was appointed as a professor at the university did Pietism become a real threat to the orthodox forces in Königsberg. When part of the school was transformed into a church, where Pietistic preaching "drew huge audiences," it began to meet with official resistance.[42] The orthodox clergy of Königsberg, the faculty of theology, and the administration of the city did everything they could to curb the success of the Pietists in the city. Lysius was accused of spreading "*Chiliasm*" and an "unfounded hope for better times," perverting both his followers and the word of God. His followers were "simple-minded and common citizens and artisans," who, "like today's Quakers, Mennonites, enthusiasts, and other fantastic misled souls (*Irrgeister*), were allowed to open up the Holy Bible in their meetings. They could find a text or saying in it, and explain, gloss, or interpret it according to their concepts. He [Lysius] prostitutes the precious word of God and puts a waxen nose on it, as it were." Early on, most students and professors at the university ridiculed the Pietists, and the city administration and nobility were almost uniformly opposed to them. Even after the arrival of Franz Albert Schulz in 1731, Pietism remained in an embattled position.[43] Though Schulz became one of the most important figures in the intellectual and social life of Königsberg, he had to overcome great resistance. It would therefore be wrong to say that Königsberg's culture was ever completely characterized by Pietism, even if the new movement was very successful with ordinary citizens such as Kant's parents.[44]

It appears that Kant's parents, and especially his mother, sided with Schulz and were indebted to him. Kant's mother often took her older children to Bible study sessions held by Schulz, and Schulz often visited the family and even helped them by supplying firewood. Kant's earliest religious instruction outside the home came from this man, and Schulz's brand of Pietism formed the background of Kant's first formal religious instruction. For better or worse, through his parents – and especially his mother – Kant was part of the Pietistic movement in Königsberg. The conflicts between the Pietists and the more traditional elements of Königsberg society became to a certain extent his own. When the Pietists were vilified, his parents – and to some extent he himself, as well – must also have felt discriminated against.

Schulz was a complex character, marked by great ambition and a "*geheime*

Cholera" or a hidden choleric streak. Furthermore, though he might have
been willing to compromise in theology between Pietism and Wolffian rationalism, he was uncompromising in his pursuit of the common goals of
Halle Pietism and Berlin Absolutism. He not only had studied theology in
Halle and therefore been deeply influenced by Francke, but also had continued to study with Wolff, and his theology constituted an attempt to
synthesize Pietistic and Wolffian ideas, or perhaps better, to formulate
Pietistic ideas using Wolffian terminology and methods.[45] It was through
him that Wolffian philosophy, still officially prohibited in Prussia, gained
a wider recognition at the university.[46] Schulz was very much in tune with
the government in Berlin. There had been a development in the king's
views on Wolff. Frederick William I had begun to appreciate his philosophy. After reading some of his work, he no longer believed Wolffian philosophy and Pietism to be contradictory. Thus he tried to get Wolff to
come back to Prussia, and he even went so far as to order all students of
theology to study Wolff: "They must be thoroughly grounded in philosophy and in a sound logic after the example of professor Wolff."[47] Schulz
was thus the right man at the right time. His political instincts were just
as sound as his theological ones.

  This new development had important consequences for the Königsberg
Pietism that Kant's parents and Kant himself encountered. It was derived
from Halle Pietism, but was less "enthusiastic" than the latter, having a
Wolffian and thus a more "rationalistic" outlook.[48] Schulz was opposed to
an all-too-enthusiastic religiosity.[49] Just as Francke had significantly modified Spener's doctrine, at least in order to take advantage of the opportunities that presented themselves in Prussia, so Schulz modified Francke's
views under the influence of a different environment and a different time;
Königsberg Pietism cannot simply be identified with Halle Pietism. It was
of a strange variety and in many ways closer to the philosophy of the orthodox party than their disputes would suggest: their school philosopher was
not Aristotle, but Wolff.

  Schulz's actions were often determined just as much by the political
demands of the king in Berlin as by concern for the spiritual well-being
of the citizens of Königsberg. Indeed, it appears that he and his followers
often found it difficult to separate these two concerns, and under Schulz,
Lutheran pastors became more like schoolmasters than preachers. The
teaching of the basics of Christianity became ever more closely combined
with the teaching of reading, writing, and arithmetic. Not surprisingly,
therefore, Schulz soon made enemies – and not just among those opposed

to Pietism. In pursuing the program of Frederick William I against the wishes of the more orthodox clergy and their friends among the officials and nobility, Schulz incurred the wrath of many. Indeed, he was so closely identified with the king that he was very worried when the king suffered a severe illness in 1734, writing to a friend that he had already been threatened and predicting that "his head would be cut off within three days of the king's death." Some time later he reported: "Here the noise increases daily. Now even the rabble begins to get involved. Thus for some weeks I can hardly walk the street safely. In the evening I cannot leave the house at all."[50] His opponents smashed his windows, made noisy protests in front of his house as well as those of other Pietist professors, and carried signs through the streets vilifying them. Still, the Pietists persisted, viewing their opposition as the enemies of God himself, and continued to do what they saw as God's work. While others saw in them nothing but puppets of Frederick William I, they insisted that they were doing what was right. By the early thirties, the Pietists had gained the upper hand in their struggle with orthodoxy, and Frederick William I had scored a number of victories against the Königsberg local opposition to his centralist state.[51]

The fact that Emanuel grew up in this religious environment certainly had consequences for his intellectual development, though it is difficult to determine how far these went. Emanuel's religious background was frought with deep ambiguities, having a component that was seen elsewhere as contrary to the basic tenets of true faith. If Pietistic ideas had an influence on Kant very early on, they were those mediated by Schulz. It was the Pietism in Königsberg that confronted the young Kant, and not some other kind. His mother's outlook, which was described by Kant himself as "genuine religiosity that was *not at all* enthusiastic," has Schulzian traits. Still, it is unlikely that Pietism had any fundamental and lasting influence on Kant's philosophy.[52] It is even doubtful that the Pietism of his parents left any significant traces on Kant's intellectual outlook, even if Kant's earliest biographers suggest that it did. They were in no better position to make this claim than we would be today. Borowski claimed that Kant's "father insisted on industriousness and thorough honesty in his son, while the mother also demanded piety in him in accordance with the ideas (*Schema*) she had formed of it. The father demanded work and sincerity – the mother demanded holiness as well."[53] Borowski further observed that Kant "enjoyed the supervision of his parents long enough to be able to judge correctly about the entirety of their way of thinking (*Denkart*)," and that "the demand for holiness" found in Kant's second *Critique* was identical to his own mother's demands during his earliest years. In a similar vein, Rink quoted Kant as having said of his parents:

Even if the religious views of that time . . . and the concepts of what was called virtue and piety were anything but clear and sufficient, the people actually were virtuous and pious. One may say as many bad things about Pietism as one will. Enough already. The people who took it seriously were characterized by a certain kind of dignity. They possessed the highest qualities that a human being can possess, namely that calmness and pleasantness, that inner peace that can be disturbed by no passion. No need, no persecution, no dispute could make them angry or cause them to be enemies of anyone.[54]

The comments attributed to Kant show that he respected his parents and others who practiced Pietistic customs. They also show that Kant believed that his mother positively influenced his moral outlook. Yet this is far from showing that Kant's mature view was in any way close to Pietism. It may indeed be true that Kant "enjoyed the supervision of his parents long enough to be able to judge correctly about the entirety of their way of thinking," but this does not mean that he himself learned their way of thinking as a consciously formulated doctrine.[55] If anything, the passages make clear that the mature Kant did not think that there was much of a doctrine at all behind the conduct of these virtuous and pious people. He appreciated them for their actions, not for their theological theories. To claim on the basis of such slender evidence that a "vital key to understanding Kant's views is the fact that his parents were both members of the Pietist church" is consequently misleading.[56] Indeed, the two passages show that conceptually Kant could have learned very little, if anything at all, from this earliest encounter with Pietism. His praise of the moral dignity of those who were *serious* about their Pietism has, in fact, an underhanded quality, for one may, after all, say many bad things about Pietism. Kant differentiates between those who were serious about Pietism, who were living it without necessarily being able to formulate clearly any of its concepts or doctrines, and those who were not so serious about it, who did not live in accordance with its precepts, but who could talk quite well about it. Finally, as we have seen already, Borowski, himself a bishop in the Prussian Lutheran Church, is intent on downplaying the differences between the various factions of Lutheranism. His motives for connecting Kantian moral philosophy with Pietism were at least in part political. He not only wished to minimize the differences between Pietism and orthodoxy, but also wanted to show that Kant's religious views were ultimately quite close to those of the church.

What Kant received from his parents was not a training in a certain kind of religious discipline, but a warm, understanding, and supportive environment that built confidence in his own abilities and a sense of self-worth. Like his sisters and his brother, "Manelchen," as his mother called him, was loved by his parents. Indeed, they not only loved their children, but also treated them with respect. They taught by example, and they not only provided a harmonious and decent, if simple and frugal, home for all of their children, but also gave their oldest son every opportunity for advancement.

Kant gave us several clues about what he learned from his parents. He asserted late in his life that the education he received from them "could not have been better when considered from the moral point of view," and throughout his life he remarked about the ideal early moral education. Therefore, it is perhaps best to listen to Kant on what the best moral education of young children involves, and to take this as a clue to what he learned from his own parents. In his so-called Lectures on Pedagogy he differentiates between a physical education that is based on discipline and a moral education that is based on maxims. The former does not allow children to think, it simply trains them. Moral education is based on maxims. In it, he thinks, "everything is lost when it is founded on examples, threats, punishment, etc." It is necessary to lead the child to act well from maxims, not from mere habit, so that the child does not just do what is good but does it because it is the good thing to do. "For the entire worth of moral actions consists in their maxims."[57] More particularly, in order to provide the foundation of a moral character in children, "we must teach them the duties that they must fulfill as much as possible by means of examples and instructions. A child's duties are only the common duties towards oneself and others." At this point, they consist mainly in cleanliness and frugality, and they are based on

a certain dignity that a human being possesses in his inner nature, which gives him dignity compared with all the other creatures. His duty is not to deny this dignity of humanity in his own person.

Drunkenness, unnatural sins, and all kinds of excess (*Unmaessigkeit*) are for Kant examples of such a loss of dignity whereby we lower ourselves below animals. Most importantly, Kant thinks that "crawling" – the making of compliments and the currying of favors – is also beneath the dignity of man. For children it is mainly lying that is to be avoided, for "lying makes human beings the object of general contempt and it tends to rob the child of his self-respect," something everyone should have.

We also have duties toward others, and the child should learn early

> Reverence (*Ehrfurcht*) and respect for others . . . and it is very important to see to it
> that the child practice these. For instance, when a child avoids another child that is
> poorer, when it pushes the other away, or hits it, etc., one should not say: "Don't do
> that, it hurts the other; have some sympathy, it is a poor child."[58]

Instead, we must make the child aware that such behavior is contradictory to the right of humanity.

In general, Kant felt that one should not make children feel sorry for others so much as one should instill in them a feeling of duty, self-worth, and confidence.[59] This is what he thought his own parents did for him. Kant also emphasized a child's need of good examples, pointing out "for a still undeveloped human being, imitation is the first determination of his will to accept maxims that he afterward makes for himself."[60]

Kant's remarks about his parents show that he considered them as excellent examples. It is highly likely that Kant first learned of duties toward himself and others by imitating them. He also felt that children should be taught some of the concepts of religion – "only they must be more negative than positive. To let them pray empty formulas serves no purpose and it causes a wrong concept of piety. The true service of God consists in acting in accordance with God's will, and that is what children must be taught."[61] Put another way, religious concepts must strengthen moral values, not the other way around. In the *Metaphysics of Morals* he is still more explicit about the separation of morality and religion. He recommends that the moral catechism, not the religious one, should be the first to be presented to school children, claiming that "it is important in this education not to present the moral catechism mixed with the religious one . . . or what is worse yet: to have it follow upon the religious catechism."[62] It is doubtful that the old Kant would have called the education he received from his parents "ideal from the moral point of view," had religion and the "demand for holiness" pervaded it in the way that Borowski suggests.[63]

Yet Kant's moral philosophy might still have had deep roots in his early childhood. The Kants were not just Pietists; since Kant's father was a master artisan and his parents members of a guild, they must have imparted to their son the kind of moral disposition that was rooted in the ethos of the *Handwerk*, of the guilds and artisans.[64] This ethos was characterized more by a proud independence from king and lord, a spirit of self-determination and self-sufficiency (even under the most adverse circumstances) than it was by submissiveness and obedience to higher authority. The power of the guild in the early eighteenth century can easily be overestimated, but the social standing of its members can just as easily be underestimated. It is significant that Kant, throughout his life, was very conscious of his origins.

The central moral precept of the guild system was "honor" (*Ehre*). Indeed, without honor, the member of the guild was nothing. Kant's pronouncements about his parents and his sisters must be seen in just this context. When he says that he was never allowed to see anything dishonorable as a child, and that the blood of his parents was never sullied by anything indecent, he had in mind this moral conception of honor characteristic of the guilds. When Wasianski emphasizes that Schulz supported Kant's parents in a way that was compatible "with the feeling of honor shared by Kant and his parents," he is talking about precisely this.[65] Monetary handouts would not have been acceptable. Help with the supply of firewood was a different story.

For the mature Kant, however, honor was only a very incomplete expression of morality. Honorableness or *Ehrbarkeit* was merely external.[66] It therefore could not possibly capture the true nature of morality. Indeed, he explicitly points out not only that "moral culture must be based on maxims not on discipline" (because discipline concentrates on what is external, merely preventing bad habits, whereas maxims form a certain moral disposition) but also that

these maxims cannot be maxims of honor (*Ehre*), but only those of right. The former can very well coincide with an absence of character, while the latter cannot. Furthermore, honor is something entirely conventional that must first be learned as it were, and requires experience. In this way, the formation of character can come about only very late, or better, it is possible only very late. By contrast, the representation of right lies deep in the soul of everyone, even of the most delicate child. It would be very good if one led the child to ask: "Is this the right thing to do?" rather than telling it: "You should be ashamed of yourself."[67]

It is, accordingly, just as much a mistake to argue that the simple morality of the guilds, a morality based on honor, forms the root of Kant's moral theory as it is a mistake to claim that the simple Pietism of his parents explains his mature views.

While Emanuel's youth as the "son of a master" (*Meistersohn*) does not explain Kant's later philosophical development, it is important for understanding his background. Indeed, the one cannot be understood without the other. Pietism helped those who accepted it through the difficult times created by the crisis in the guild system. With its emphasis on lay priesthood, individual Bible study, and a community of the faithful, Pietism was in tune with the values of the members of the guild. Though the Pietists were also known as "*Mucker*" or "crawlers," their practices reinforced their sense of independence and autonomy. Indeed, one of the things that orthodox clergy could not accept about Pietism was that everyone was judged to be equally qualified in interpreting the Bible, and thus the sharp distinction between pastor and lay person was blurred. It was a large step from the guild members' insistence on independence from civil authority (and their more democratic understanding of societal organization) to Kant's notion of an ideal community of morally autonomous individuals, but this step was not as large as the step from faithful obedience to the word of God and fellowship of Christ to the complete autonomy prescribed by the categorical imperative. For better or worse, there is a continuity in the first, while there is a radical discontinuity in the second.[68] The independent tradesmen found the message of Pietism acceptable at least in part because it promised independence from some of the established hierarchies of eighteenth-century Prussia. What Emanuel's mother and father made of it was certainly not independent of the ethos they had grown up with. First and foremost, they belonged to the class of honorable tradesmen (*ehrbare Handwerker*), and this largely determined their moral code.

Put another way, what Kant acquired from his parents were the values of the petit bourgeoisie. He learned the importance of hard work, honesty, cleanliness, and independence. He also acquired an appreciation for the value of money. Indeed, in the only description of his parents that we have in his own words, he specifically points out that his parents left him neither money nor debts, yet prepared him well for this world. The values he acquired would not have been significantly different from the ones he might have picked up had he been born into a family of small independent tradespeople in Padua, Edinburgh, Amsterdam, or Boston at the beginning of the eighteenth century. Just as in the house of the Kants in Königsberg, religion played some role. Religious worship was not the only, nor perhaps even the most important, pursuit in that household. Hard work in serving customers, obtaining the essentials of life without having to compromise oneself, living decently, keeping up appearances appropriate to one's standing, looking out for one's family, and not being unduly indebted to, or dependent on, anyone else would have been the important concerns. Kant was indebted to his parents at least as much for these human qualities as for any specific religious doctrine or way of life. That his parents not only were interested in keeping up appearances, but also genuinely believed in the necessity of living a good life in the eyes of God, does not change this.[69] In any case, he would soon get to know Pietism from a different perspective.

School Years (1732–1740): "In the Servitude of the Fanatics"

If Kant was "touched by feelings of the highest gratitude" whenever he thought of the education he received in the house of his parents, he was horrified when he remembered his school years at the *Collegium Frideri-cianum*. Hippel, later one of Kant's closest friends, reported that

Herr Kant who also experienced these torments of youth in full measure, used to say that terror and fear would overcome him as soon as he thought back to the slavery of his youth, and this even though he remained in the house of his parents and only went to a public school, namely the then so-called "Pietistic hostel," or the Collegium Fridericianum.[70]

A similar sort of sentiment was also expressed by David Ruhnken, one of Kant's school friends. He begins a letter to Kant, dated March 10, 1771, saying: "Thirty years have now passed from the time we both groaned under that gloomy, yet useful and not objectionable, discipline of the fanatics."[71]

Kant was not as charitable as Ruhnken, and he did not think highly of the moral education he received in the "Pietistic hostel." In the "Lectures on Pedagogy" he felt it necessary to point out that "many people think their youth constituted their best years, but this is probably wrong. They are the hardest years because one is very much subject to discipline, seldom has a friend, and even less often has freedom."[72] This may sum up his view of his youth in a rather restrained way. He felt that the kind of discipline he experienced amounted to a particularly harsh form of slavery that was not only *not* very useful, but also positively harmful. "In school there is coercion (*Zwang*), mechanism, and the shuttle of rules (*Gängelwagen*). This often robs people of all the courage to think for themselves, and it spoils the genius."[73] Indeed, his later enthusiasm for educational reform, and especially his unparalleled efforts on behalf of the Institute of Dessau under the leadership of Basedow, goes to show how little he thought of the kind of education that children received at the *Collegium Fridericianum*.

What was this education that Emanuel received? He first went to school in the outer city, namely to the so-called *Hospitalschule*. This school was connected with St. Georg's hospice. It had one teacher, usually an unordained minister whose duties also included weekly visits to the city jail. Kant's teacher was Ludwig Boehm, a candidate in theology, who held this position for an unusually long period.[74] Kant learned from Boehm the basics of "reading, writing, and arithmetic" together with the other children of his neighborhood, but he did not attend this school for long. In the summer of 1732, at the age of eight, he began to take classes at the *Collegium Fridericianum*. The story, probably true, is that it was Schulz who first noticed Kant's great promise and persuaded his parents to send their son to the *Collegium* in preparation for a later education in theology. Though Schulz was not yet director of the school, he already had close connections to it. Furthermore, he was always interested in recruiting able students. So, if he noticed that Kant was a gifted child, he would have wanted him to enter the proper course – that is, the career of a minister in the service of the church – as soon as possible.[75]

The *Collegium* was, as we have seen already, a Pietistic institution. Conceived after the *Franckeschen Anstalten* in Halle, it had two goals. On the one hand, it wanted to save its charges from "spiritual corruption," and thus aimed at "implanting righteous Christianity in their hearts while they were young." On the other hand, it also aimed to improve the "worldly well-being" of the students by educating them in the humanities as well.[76] The school educated children of both nobility and commoners. Indeed, its students were being prepared for high office in civil life and the church. For a commoner like Emanuel, being accepted as a student meant an opportunity for social advancement.

Most of the students lived in the institution itself, but some were allowed to stay with their parents. Kant belonged to the latter group, even though he had to walk a long way to school and back.[77] His days were highly regimented and filled almost exclusively with schoolwork. School began at 7:00 A.M., and it ended at 4:00 P.M., with a period for lunch between 11:00 and 1:00. Classes were held six days a week from Monday to Saturday. Holidays were very few. There were only a few days off at Easter, Pentecost, and Christmas, as well as one day after the yearly public examination.[78] So Emanuel was gone from home for most of the day, six days a week, and his homework kept him busy long after he came home. Even on Sundays he would not have had much time for himself, as he had to attend church and afterward catechetical exercises. This closely supervised regimen lasted until he was admitted into the University of Königsberg at the age of seventeen.

Classes were organized differently than they were at most other institutions during that period in the sense that the students were placed into different grades solely in accordance with their ability and knowledge. So someone might attend the first year of the Latin course, while sitting in the second class of religion and the third class of Hebrew. This arrangement made it very difficult to make friends.

Each class was held in its own room, starting and ending at the ringing of a bell. Before the formal instruction began, the teacher delivered "an inspiring but short prayer" so that the work would be "more godly and more blessed while no time was lost for instruction." Before lunch and at the end of the afternoon, a verse from a hymn was sung. In all subjects the "main aim," even if this was not always explicit, was to lead the students "to God and his Glory." Teachers were admonished to view themselves as instructing under the supervision of "the all-present God."[79]

Subjects changed every hour. From 7:00 to 8:00 there were five classes of theology; from 8:00 to 10:00 there were six classes of Latin; from 10:00 to 11:00 the three highest classes were instructed in Greek, and the others took more Latin (exercises in conjugation). Between 11:00 and 12:00 students ate in rooms designed for that purpose, while a teacher read "something useful" to them. This was followed by an hour of supervised play in the courtyard. From 1:00 to 2:00 the students were instructed in different subjects – some took logic, others the history of philosophy, geography, church history, or calligraphy. From 2:00 to 3:00 Hebrew and mathematics were taught. On Wednesdays and Saturdays students who wished could also take mathematics (*mathesis*) and vocal music during the first two hours of the afternoon.

During the first year of religious instructions, the students had to memorize Luther's small catechism.[80] They were also told some of the biblical stories in an appropriate form. The second year was devoted to repeating the small catechism, supplemented by parts of Luther's large catechism, and more Bible stories. Instruction for the third year was described as "all the preceding is repeated, and anything necessary added here and there." The religious teaching of the fourth year was based on Christoph Starcke's *Ordnung des Heils in Tabellen* (Order of Salvation in Tabular Form).[81] In addition, two hours per week were devoted to an introduction to the New Testament.[82] In the fifth and final class the New Testament was taught still "more thoroughly." Two hours every week were concerned with an introduction to the Old Testament. Teachers were instructed to show "how everything could be a subject for *prayer* and be applied to a Christian life and approach."[83] The final two years were especially designed to prepare the student for the further study of theology at the university. The teachers of the school were well suited for this task, since most of them were advanced theology students at the University of Königsberg.

Emanuel did not find theology easy – or so it appears. At Easter 1735, the beginning of his third year at the school, he was in third-year Latin and third-year Greek, but only in his second year of arithmetic and religion.[84] Still, whether he wanted it or not, he received a solid preparation in theology before leaving the school. Since he had an extremely good memory until his last years, we may assume that he never forgot the doctrines that were drilled into him so early in his life.

The other classes were in the service of religious education as well. This holds true especially of Hebrew and Greek. In Hebrew, which was taught in three classes, students were expected to read the five books of Moses as well as the historical books and the Psalms of David. The fourth and fifth year of Greek were devoted not only to repetition in grammar, but also to the reading of the New Testament. Only after they had read the *entire* Greek New Testament were the students introduced to the classical Greek writers. The book they used was Johann Matthias Gesner's *Chrestomathia* (first published in 1731). It contained selections from Aristotle, Sextus Empiricus, Herodotus, Thucydides, Xenophon, Theophrastus, Plutarch, Lucian, and Herodian. Students would also read some Homer, Pindar, and Hesiod. While they would thus get some idea about classical antiquity, the main emphasis was still theological.

The backbone of the education at the *Collegium Fridericianum* was Latin.[85] Not only did the students spend the most time learning Latin, it was also by far the most important discipline. There were six classes, lasting up to eighteen hours per week in the lower grades, up to six in the higher. Most of these hours were taken up by drills in vocabulary, conjugation, declination, and the rules of grammar. By their third year, students were expected to read Cornelius Nepos; the fourth year consisted of a repetition of all of Nepos, some Cicero, and some poetry. In the fifth class they read Caesar and more Cicero, and in the sixth year Cicero (*De officiis*, among other selections), Muretus, Curtius, and Pliny. Great emphasis was placed on speaking and writing in Latin. Indeed, in the two highest classes students were instructed to talk to each other and their teachers in Latin only.

Emanuel did well in Latin, and those who knew him then thought that he would make classics his chosen field of studies. Ruhnken said that between Easter 1739 and September 1740, he himself was most interested in philosophy, while Emanuel was most interested in the classics.[86] Emanuel, David, and Johannes Cunde, another friend, together read classic authors outside of class, supplementing the meager reading list of their school. Ruhnken, who had more money than either of his two poor friends, bought the books. Already thinking of authorship, they planned to call themselves by Latinised names: Kantius, Ruhnkenius, and Cundeus.[87] Kant continued to think highly of the ancients, reading them throughout his life. Seneca and perhaps somewhat surprisingly Lucretius and Horace remained his favorites, but he also knew other classical Latin writers well. Borowski and others report that even in his old age Kant could recite from memory long passages of the works that he especially liked.[88] His interest in Greek literature was somewhat less intense. Only a few Greek words appear in his published writings, and he never used any Greek as a motto for his books. This does not imply that he could not read Greek. Nor does it mean that he was not interested in Greek philosophy. In fact, quite the opposite is true. As we shall see, it was his rediscovery of the Greeks and their philosophical project that helped him to clarify his own views at a crucial time in his philosophical development.

It is no surprise that Kant's favorite teacher was one who taught him Latin. His name was Heydenreich.[89] While he had nothing to say about any of his other teachers, Kant praised Heydenreich even late in his life. This "good" man not only fostered Kant's love of the classical Latin authors, but was also responsible for much of his knowledge of antiquity, and he was thankful to him for trying to teach him to think clearly.[90] When Kant later complained that it would be better if the schools taught "the spirit" and not merely "the phrases" of authors, he did not mean to direct this against Heydenreich. This teacher was someone who approached Kant's ideal and inspired him and his friends to study Latin authors even outside of class.

There were also classes in geography and history, but they were not of primary importance. Furthermore, since instruction in history was in good part concerned with the history of the Old and New Testaments, it seemed to the students to be an extension of religious instruction. Calligraphy, or the art of writing beautiful script, does not appear to have been very much to Kant's liking. It was the only subject in which he was demoted to a lower class from a higher.

French was not a required subject. Students could take it in three optional classes on Wednesdays and Saturdays. Kant did. While the classes did not aim at making the students fluent in the language, they were intended to provide them with the skills necessary for reading any French author tolerably well. We may therefore assume that Kant was able to read French and comprehend it when it was spoken, even if he probably never became very good at speaking it.[91] It is remarkable, however, that Kant did enroll in French, as it had to be paid for separately.[92] English did not form any part of the curriculum. Indeed, it was not taught as a special discipline even at the University of Königsberg until long after Kant had begun to teach there. Thus it is unlikely that Kant received any formal education in English. Though he could probably decipher what a certain passage was about, he could not really read it.

Arithmetic, too, was considered less important than Latin. There were only three classes given, and they did not go beyond the very basics. *Mathesis*, the more advanced mathematical discipline, was also optional (and thus had also to be paid for separately). It was designed to introduce the students to the basic principles of mathematics in arithmetic, geometry, and trigonometry. The textbook used in this course was Wolff's *Auszug aus den Anfangsgründen aller mathematischen Wissenschaften* (Extract from the Main Parts of All Mathematical Sciences).[93] The students could not expect to become very proficient in this discipline either, because the teachers were asked only to see to it that the students could understand, prove, and solve "the most important" parts of this subject. The teacher was to give them a "concept of the mathematical doctrine so that their understanding was prepared and trained for the study of the other sciences."[94] Yet even this level was probably far beyond anything that a student of theology could reasonably be expected to do. Emanuel as a result of these classes may have had a better education in mathematics than the average student in Prussia, but his early education in this discipline was dismal by later standards.

The same was true of philosophy. Though it was a regular class and not an option, it appears to have been taught only during one year. If the school's library for teachers is any indication of how the class was taught, then it was entirely Wolffian in outlook. Philosophy was one of the classes in which the students were allowed to "dispute" one another. In any case, Kant himself later remarked to one of his friends at the school (Cunde): "These men (*Herren*) could not blow into a fire any spark that lay in us for philosophy or mathematics," and his friend is said to have answered: "But they were very good at blowing it out."[95]

The educational spirit of the school is well summed up by director Schiffert's claim that "repetition is the soul of studying: so that what once has been learned is not forgotten again." There were weekly class hours set aside entirely for repetition; every class began with the repetition of material covered in previous sessions. Three weeks before the exam period the entire material covered during the preceding half-year period was repeated again. Schiffert believed that if something had been repeated three times then it "is firmly impressed in memory."[96] He was probably correct, but this method could hardly have made for exciting classes. Kant approved of this approach late in life, claiming that "the culture of the memory is very necessary, and that we only know as much as we remember." Nor was he opposed to rote methods in learning vocabulary and other matters.[97] He believed, however, that "the understanding must be cultivated as well," and that "knowing that" must gradually be connected to "knowing how." He believed mathematics was the discipline best suited for this. Since mathematics was not taught very well at the *Collegium Fridericianum*, we may assume that he did not think that the school excelled at educating the understanding.

Pietists were not opposed to corporal punishment, but neither did they view it as the best means of disciplining children. As Melton observes, discipline "in Francke's schools was comparatively mild for its day. Francke's theory of punishment reflected the Pietist effort to subjectify coercion, transfer its locus from outside to inside the individual." Indeed, the Pietists placed a great deal of emphasis on "introspection as a tool for developing self-discipline."[98] At the *Collegium Fridericianum*, every student who was to attend the communion had "to compose a report on the state of his soul" beforehand. This report had to be handed in to one of the supervisors, who examined it to determine whether or not the student was ready for communion. If that was not enough, every student also had to bring to his supervisor a sealed report from his teachers outlining whether there were any problems that would make it inappropriate for the student to partake in communion.[99] If there were significant differences between the student's and the teacher's report, the child was to be admonished.

The mature Kant had a definite aversion to the kind of introspection the students were required to engage in. Thus he said that such "observation of oneself" or the "methodical account of what we perceive within ourselves, which provides the materials for the diary of a self-observer, can easily lead to enthusiasm and insanity."[100] No doubt, his distaste for such introspection dated back to this very period of forced reports on "the state of the soul."

Though the ideal was to teach the students self-discipline, the practice was probably quite different. One of Kant's early biographers, Mortzfeld, speaks of the "leaden atmosphere of punishment" that pervaded the entire place.[101] Kant himself attested to this fact when he told Jachmann that all of his teachers, with the exception of one, had tried but failed to keep discipline by being very strict.[102] As Kant was industrious and diligent and almost always finished the class as the "*Primus*" (the student with the highest grades), he probably was not often punished.[103] However, if he could not produce his schoolbooks because he had left them behind when he stopped to play, he would have been chastised in some way.[104] Late in his life he told a story about how "when he was still a student there, an insolent boy came to the inspector Schiffert and asked: Is this the school of the Pietists? Hearing this, the inspector gave him a solid beating, saying: Now you know where the school of the Pietists is."[105] Even if Kant himself never experienced corporal punishment firsthand, it was a part of his daily experience.

During this period Kant also lost his mother. She died three years before he left the school. From then on, he and his sisters and brother had to rely on their father alone. The "leaden atmosphere" at school would have been complemented by a less than joyful climate at home. It is no wonder that Kant did not like to remember his school years.

At the end of his schooling, Emanuel was perfectly well qualified to pursue a course of studies in theology, law, philosophy, or the classics. While he could also have undertaken studies in medicine or the natural sciences, he was neither as well prepared for these disciplines nor would he have received much encouragement in school to pursue these studies. On the other hand, the *Collegium Fridericianum* prepared him well for the world of eighteenth-century Prussia. It provided a good foundation for a career in the Lutheran Church or in the Prussian state under Frederick William I.

It was not an education that encouraged critical or independent thinking. Though it was typical for the time, it probably had a greater emphasis on obedience and discipline than did comparable schools in the rest of the German countries. One of the most important ideals of Pietist education was to instill self-discipline. Pietists were not just interested in controlling the body, they also wanted to control the mind by implanting certain religious and moral principles. They were aiming ultimately at "converting" the students from "children of the world" to "children of God." To this end, they felt it was necessary to educate not only the intellect, but also the will. In fact, Francke, who inspired the Königsberg Pietists in their educational practices, felt that above all, it is necessary to break the natural willfulness of the child. While the school-master who seeks to make the child more learned is to be commended for cultivating the child's understanding, he has not done enough. He has forgotten his most important task, namely that of making the will obedient.[106]

While it might appear contradictory that a voluntary conversion was to be brought about by breaking the child's natural will, it was not so in the eyes of the Pietists. They viewed this break only as the first step in the so-called *Bußkampf* (struggle of contrition) towards the *Durchbruch* (breakthrough). Accordingly, the religious outlook that the school tried to instill in its pupils was somewhat unusual. While all the other schools of the period also placed a great deal of emphasis on formal religion, they did not require the kind of Pietistic conviction that was considered desirable by some of the Königsberg Pietists.

Not surprisingly, Kant understood this aspect of their view well – and rejected it in its entirety. It was a "hypothesis" that

the separation of the good from the evil (that forms an amalgam in human nature) is brought about by a supernatural operation, i.e. the contrition and crushing of the heart in a *repentance*, which borders on despair. Only the divine spirit can bring us to a sufficient state of repentance. We must pray for it – being contrite that we are not contrite enough.[107]

This was repugnant to him. He considered it hypocritical because the grieving and contrition were not ultimately the responsibility of the one to be converted. What was thought to lead to the radical conversion that differentiated the true Christian from the merely nominal one, appeared to him impossible. On this hypothesis, we could never know whether we really were converted, because this would presuppose knowledge of an unknowable supernatural influence. Furthermore, a Pietist could be distinguished from other people by his absolute reliance on God for everything, and by his complete rejection of any kind of moral autonomy. At the same time, a Pietist tended to exhibit a certain kind of false pride as belonging to the "select" few, those who are, as God's children, saved and form the elite of Christendom. The mature Kant rejected both aspects of the Pietistic way of life. The first was for him the expression of a "servile attitude" (*knechtische Gemütsart*).[108] The other justified in his eyes "the particular kind of disdain" that he saw *always* connected with the label "Pietism."[109] It is not clear whether he already felt this way about Pietism in 1740, but it is not unlikely, given that his friend Ruhnken wrote they both were "groaning" under the heavy discipline of the fanatics between 1732 and 1740. If Pietism had any influence on Kant at all, then it was a negative one. It may have been precisely because he was acquainted with Pietism that he came to reject almost completely any role of feeling in morality. If anything, Kant's moral and religious views betray a definite anti-Pietistic bias. Kant's emphasis on autonomy as a key to morality is also a rejection of the Pietistic emphasis on the necessity of a supernatural influence on the human will. Kant's mature philosophy is characterized, at least in part, by a struggle to legitimate an autonomous morality, based on freedom of the will, and it must also be seen as a struggle against those who would enslave us by breaking our wills. This struggle has its beginnings in Kant's youth, even if it took him a very long time to formulate his arguments against those bent on fostering a servile attitude and demeaning human nature as essentially base. It is absurd to claim that Pietism was a major influence on his moral philosophy.[110]

Emanuel's will was not broken by the teachers at the *Collegium Fridericianum,* but not for want of trying on their part. Emanuel resisted a pressure that was almost irresistible. We may be sure that he neither openly converted nor put on an act, as so many of his fellow students did. The "terror and fear" that would "overcome him as soon as he thought back to the slavery of his youth" has more to do with the pressure to convert than with any intellectual demands put upon him by his teachers. It is to this period in life that we must trace his aversion to prayer and singing of hymns and his resistance to any religion based on feeling and sentiment. In this regard, Emanuel's education was not very different from that of Frederick II, which was also described as "a chronicle of suffering."[111] Frederick's pious but brutal father, bent on making a man of what he perceived to be a womanish boy, used some of the same methods that the Pietists used on their charges. Though the externals of Kant's youth are far less dramatic, there is every indication that he became similarly resistant to conversion. Like the prince, twelve years his senior, Kant turned away from the soul searching and self-condemnation of the Pietists and toward other models. For Emanuel, these were to be found in the Latin classics; for the young Frederick, they were to be found in contemporary French literature. Both rejected the religious way of life of their parents.

This is one reason why Kant thought highly of Frederick and called his period not only "the age of Enlightenment" but also "the century of Frederick." Like Frederick, he felt that he had been "treated like a slave" in his youth, but like Frederick, he was not broken. To submit to the servitude of his teachers would have meant "self-incurred tutelage" for life. We do not know whether Kant explicitly formulated this thought for himself during his school years, but we do know that this was his considered opinion late in life.[112] As he acknowledged,

It is very difficult for any single individual to extricate himself from the tutelage [*Unmündigkeit*] that has become almost nature to him. . . . Statutes and formulas, those mechanical tools of the rational employment, or rather wrong employment, of his natural gifts, are the fetters of an everlasting minority. Whoever throws them off makes only an uncertain leap over the narrowest ditch because he is not accustomed to this sort of free motion. Therefore there are only few who have succeeded by their own exercise of mind both in freeing themselves from incompetence and in achieving a steady pace.[113]

Kant was in 1740 far from making the "uncertain leap over the narrowest ditch," and perhaps the ditch was not quite as narrow as it seemed to him when he wrote this passage.

It should be added that during Kant's youth men and women lived segregated lives in Königsberg, and the atmosphere was rather stuffy. Thus, even "pregnant" was not a word that could or should be used by young women, and showing much of the "neck, in the back or in front" was strictly *verboten*.[114] Education, especially among the class of tradesmen, was restricted to males. Indeed, it was unusual for girls to get much education beyond the bare basics of reading, writing, and arithmetic. "*Kinder, Küche, Kirche*" really did define the lives of women to a large extent. Accordingly, Kant, like almost all of his contemporaries, had little occasion for social interaction with the opposite sex during his youth.

Königsberg: "A Fit Place for Acquiring . . . Knowledge of the World"?

Kant's youth was thus characterized by a stark contrast between a loving home in which he was encouraged and accepted, and a stern and gloomy school life, in which natural inclinations were for the most part suppressed. Though both his family and his school were religious, though both were even Pietistic, the contrast between the two could not have been more striking. Kant was luckier than some of his friends. He did not have to live at the *Collegium Fridericianum*, but could escape to his home in the evenings; and since he had a long way to walk every day through the streets of Königsberg, he also got to know life from yet another side.

Königsberg is often described either as a desolate and isolated "backwater town" of eighteenth-century Germany, or as a "frontier city" of Prussia.

Both views are misleading. Königsberg had a somewhat "insular" character, being situated in the northeastern corner of Prussia, near to the Russian border, and closer to Poland than to western Prussia. Still, it was a very important city. Founded in 1255 by the Teutonic knights, it joined the Hanseatic League in 1340 and was the capital of all of Prussia until 1701. When Kant was born, it was just the capital of East Prussia, but it was still one of the three or four most important cities of the entire kingdom.[115] A considerable number of government institutions remained, along with a heavy contingent of the military. Located at a bay in the Baltic Sea, it was an important trading point, connecting all of eastern Europe with other seaports in Germany and Europe. Its dealings were mainly with Poland, Lithuania, England, Denmark, Sweden, and Russia. The main goods from eastern Europe were grain, hemp, flax, ash, wood, tar, wax, leather, and pelts, while the most important wares from the west were salt, fish, linen, zinc, lead, copper, spices, and southern fruits.[116] As a busy harbor town, it was comparable to Hamburg and other Hanseatic cities. Its main rival was Danzig.

Königsberg grew throughout the eighteenth century. In 1706 it had about 40,000 inhabitants, by 1770 about 50,000, and by 1786 close to 56,000.[117] It also remained one of the major urban centers of Prussia.[118] Königsberg was a more Prussian city than most others in Prussia. The Prussian state was still weak. Indeed, most of the people in Prussia did not identify themselves as "Prussians," but rather as "Berliners," "Westphalians," or as citizens of Cleves or Minden. Königsberg was an exception. Properly speaking, the only people who deserved the name "Prussian" were the inhabitants of Königsberg and its environs. Since the Prussian king lived in Berlin, Königsberg was more directly linked to Berlin than most other cities.

The arm of the king had a long reach, indeed. As the dispute between the Pietists and the orthodox clergy shows, Königsberg had close connections to both Halle and Berlin. Furthermore, it housed some of the important institutions of Prussia, and officials of the government were highly influential in the city. Frederick William I, though pious, was a stern monarch. No one, except his army officers, was safe from his stick. He brutally beat those whom he felt lacking in duty. Though Königsberg was usually too far away for him to take such personal actions, his decrees, edicts, and laws had an almost immediate effect there. He drew up rules in great detail for nearly everything, from the education of students, to exams at universities, to the "training of gardeners, millers, lamplighters," and preachers. The fines he imposed were sometimes excessive, sometimes strange. Any parson who preached for more than an hour was subject to a fine of two Thalers; anyone who exported raw wool abroad would suffer death by hanging (because only the export of treated wool was profitable to Prussia). A public official who had taken a small sum of public money was hanged in 1731 in Königsberg, even though the fiscal office had asked for clemency. The gallows was erected right before the palace in the city and all the officials had to watch. The corpse was left hanging all day, and then removed and left lying outside one of the city gates until the ravens had picked it clean.[119] Another official was severely punished because he refused to relocate to another city at the order of the king. Conscription was a constant danger to young men – especially to those who were tall.

Because soldiers in eighteenth-century Prussia did not live in barracks, but were billeted in civil quarters in various parts of the city, they were conspicuous and a source of frequent annoyance. The demand for new recruits was constant, and citizens were sometimes pressed into service. On some occasions recruiters invaded congregations during Sunday service and forcibly abducted the tallest and strongest men.[120] Although university students were exempt from service, they were far from safe. "How easily the edict against seizure could be circumvented is shown by the case of a student of law at the University of Königsberg named Korn. On April 29, 1729, this robust young man was seized on a street in Königsberg, plied with strong liquor until he became drunk and cursed in the presence of 'witnesses,' and was then enlisted as a moral delinquent."[121] Military life was abhorrent to most of the citizens of Königsberg. Army discipline was brutal. Soldiers were severely caned for the smallest violation of rules and procedure. Running the gauntlet thirty times was the normal punishment for resisting "with words or reasoning."[122] Drawing a weapon in resisting meant execution by firing squad. Drunkenness, unless it happened on duty, was not punished. While Kant himself, being neither strong nor tall, never had to fear the recruiters, he must have had many unpleasant experiences with the military.[123] Kant did not think highly of them, and it is likely that his dislike of the military has roots that go back to his youth.

It was hardly a liberal or enlightened climate that pervaded this city during the time of Kant's childhood and puberty. The government was oppressive and stifling, more like a feudal than a modern one. Though Frederick William I may have had the best of intentions as far as the welfare of his subjects was concerned, his delivery left much to be desired.

The city was, however, not just a Prussian garrison but an international trading port and the capital of Prussia. It still housed several important institutions of the Prussian state. It was a city of merchants as well as of bureaucrats, both rich and poor. Kant himself thought that a

great city, the central place of a realm, which houses the central institutions of its government, which possesses (for culture and science) a university, and which has a good location for marine trade, both through rivers, with the interior land and with countries of different languages and customs close and far away, such a city can be a fit place for the acquisition of knowledge of human nature as well as knowledge of the world even without travel. Such a city was Königsberg on the river Pregel.[124]

Contrary to many commentators, Königsberg was not a mere backwater.

Emanuel did not grow up in the city itself, but in its immediate environs, the "*vordere Vorstadt.*" Administratively, this section belonged to the part of the city called the *Kneiphof.* It was a residential area and at the same time a busy commercial center, housing many warehouses for grain and other trading goods, and containing many pubs and boarding houses. The *Sattlerstraße*, where the Kants lived after 1733, was precisely what the name indicates. It was a street lined with the shops and workplaces of the harness and saddle makers, a busy, noisy, and somewhat uneven neighborhood. There were also many swampy meadows, bordered by irrigation channels. As one might expect, parents needed to keep a close eye on children in these circumstances.

Emanuel's earliest playmates were from this neighborhood, and he played with them in these surroundings. His childhood friends were thus for the most part descendants of the skilled and independent tradesmen who lived in the area and formed a relatively uniform stratum of the city of Königsberg, but none of these playmates became a friend whom Kant would remember in old age. He does not say much about his early childhood games, but in one of the stories he tells us how he escaped falling into the water while balancing on a floating log. We may assume that he played all of the games that were typical for Königsberg children. Since there was water everywhere, they involved playing on and by the water in summer and ice skating in the winter.

The part of town in which Kant grew up was in other respects a dangerous place to live. Fires, floods, and storms often ravaged his neighborhood.[125] Königsberg, and especially the *Vordere Vorstadt* experienced many fires during Kant's lifetime. The house in which Kant was born burned down in 1769 during a fire that "destroyed 76 homes and 134 warehouses in the Vordere Vorstadt."[126] The fire started in early March; ten weeks later new fires were still breaking out.[127] Yet Königsberg itself was by all accounts beautiful, looking like a typical medieval German city. Because of its many bridges, it was called the "Venice of the North." Leonhard Euler (1707–1783) made the main bridges famous with his problem called "The Bridges of Königsberg."[128]

One might call eighteenth-century Königsberg "multicultural," at least in the sense that it was made up of many different peoples. Apart from a large contingent of Lithuanians and other inhabitants from the Baltic region, there were Mennonites who had come to Königsberg from Holland in the sixteenth century, as well as Huguenots who had found refuge in Königsberg. They continued to speak French among themselves, went to their own church, and had their own institutions and businesses. There were many Poles, some Russians, many people from other countries around the Baltic Sea; there was a significant Jewish community, and a number of Dutch and English merchants. These groups largely kept their own customs and traditions. While there may not have been much interaction among them, the fact that they lived in close proximity with one another and had to deal with one another at least on a business level is not insignificant.

Thus Kant did not have to travel far to become acquainted with the ways of different cultures. He grew up in an environment that acquainted him with ways of life other than those of eighteenth-century German tradesmen. Königsberg, in spite of its relative isolation, was in some ways a cosmopolitan city. In many ways, it was far less provincial than a town like Göttingen or Marburg. It was also much larger than most German university towns of the period.

It is doubtful whether the city and the opportunities for playing and learning it offered for a young boy outweighed the drudgery of school life. School would not have left him with much time to do anything but study. Indeed, the best relaxation for him and his friends was probably found in the few hours they could squeeze out of the week to read some of the classic authors they really wanted to read. By the time Emanuel was ready to leave school, he spoke and read Latin very well. As it did for so many Germans of this period, classical antiquity provided escape from the harsh realities of life, school, and church.

Frederick William I died on May 31, 1740, to be succeeded by Frederick II in the very year that Kant left school. Frederick II was known to be much more liberal in matters of religion, to be interested in philosophy and literature, and he was expected to make great changes. He came to Königsberg for his inauguration (*Huldigung*) on July 16, 1740. At this occasion, the only time he was ever in Königsberg, he left little doubt about his sentiments. When a student told him that he wanted to go for a year to study at Halle, the king asked: "Why?" The University of Halle was no good. "*Sein alle Mucker,*" that is, they are all Pietists! The opponents of Pietism in Königsberg immediately took the opportunity to blacken the reputation of Schulz, telling the king that he went to people's houses, confiscated their playing cards, and excluded them from confession and the eucharist until they gave up card playing.[129] Schulz noted that "the enemies of the realm of God mightily raise their heads," yet his own head – much to the chagrin of the orthodox – was not cut off. Because the new king succeeded where his father had failed, namely in bringing Wolff back to Halle as a professor of law and vice chancellor of the university, there were expectations that things would change in Königsberg as well and that there would be more freedom of religion. Yet the Pietists remained more influential than their enemies had hoped. Their power was on the decline, but they held onto their privileges much longer than anyone expected. Being more interested in the expansion of the territory of Prussia than in his intellectual pursuits, the new king left administrative matters more or less as his father had arranged them. He wanted to acquire a reputation for Prussia, and his ambition was, as he said, "to put all of Europe to the torch."[130]

Student and Private Teacher
(1740–1755)

The Albertina: "A University for the Growth of the Sciences"?

EMANUEL'S LIFE changed radically when he entered the University of Königsberg. During his previous school years, all his activities had been highly regimented. Upon entering the university, he experienced for the first time the freedom to study any subject that interested him and to spend the day as he chose. No one could tell him what he had to do and when. No one could force him to search his soul for depravities. He now was on his own. He left the house of his father, but did not enter any of the boarding houses that existed for students of lesser means.[1] Rather, he took up his own quarters. Having become a member of the university, or an "academic citizen" (*akademischer Bürger*), he was not directly subject to the rules administered by the officials of the city of Königsberg, but was first and foremost subject to the officials of the university. Much like the guilds, the university was a largely independent corporation. Emanuel's new status brought with it a number of rights and privileges. An academic citizen not only had the right to go to the lectures and to use the resources of the university, but also was free from the direct demands of the city and the state, which included protection from being drafted into the army.[2]

Emanuel's acceptance into the University of Königsberg was the beginning of a lifelong association with it. It was thus a highly significant event for him when the rector of the university added on September 24, 1740, the name "Emanuel Kandt" to the registry. It meant that he, the son of a master craftsman, had effectively moved from one guild into another. Yet the academic guild, or the guild of the learned (*literati*), formed a class or estate (*Stand*) of its own, which was in many ways closer to that of the nobility than to those who made their living by working with their hands or by selling goods.[3] The importance of the move from "town" to "gown" should not be underestimated. Academic citizenship was an important first step to higher honors for many young men in eighteenth-century Prussia and elsewhere. It was definitely a move up for young Emanuel.[4]

Normally, those who were inscribed in the register had to swear their allegiance to school and country and their love of the true Christian religion. This meant that for a long time neither a Catholic, nor a Jew, nor even a Reformed Protestant could be sworn in.[5] Only Lutherans were believed to be capable of loving the true Christian religion. While the Reformed could be sworn in after 1740, Catholics and Jews continued to be discriminated against.[6] Emanuel, being only sixteen years old, was exempted from this requirement. He had only to promise that he would obey. Most students had to take an examination by the dean of the faculty in order to obtain a "*testimonium initiationis*" before they could be registered. The requirements for admission, formulated by none other than Schulz, stated that

no one is to be admitted to the university who has not explicated with some competence a somewhat difficult author such as Curtius or the *Selected Orations* of Cicero
and has delivered a small oration without grammatical errors. He should also understand tolerably well what is said in Latin. In Logic he should understand the most
essential parts of the syllogism. He should also know what is absolutely necessary in
geography, history and epistolography. He should as well be able to explain and analyze at least two of the gospels, such as Matthew and John in Greek and the thirty-one
initial chapters of the Mosaic books in Hebrew.[7]

Kant, having graduated from the *Collegium Fridericianum*, would not have had the slightest difficulty in passing this test.[8] This was precisely what his studies had prepared him for. Nor should one be surprised that mathematics and natural philosophy were conspicuous only by their absence from the list of the necessary requirements.

One might have expected Kant to take the easy way and to follow essentially the same career as most of his predecessors and classmates. Had he done so, he would, after attending the obligatory courses in philosophy, have gone on to study theology. After the fifth semester, he would have become a teacher at the *Collegium Fridericianum*, or have obtained one of the numerous fellowships open to theologians. Finally, he would have been ordained as a pastor, and taken up a parsonage or become a professor of theology at the university (perhaps even both, insuring a relatively comfortable and secure income). Kant took neither a stipend nor a fellowship, nor did he ever teach at the *Collegium Fridericianum*. He chose an entirely different road. We cannot be certain which course of study Kant declared he would follow when he entered the university, because the rector failed to note the field of study for those he inscribed in 1740.[9] Still, it is more than likely that he attended courses in philosophy from the very beginning, if only because philosophy was the first subject for all students.[10] Even students intending to study theology, law, or medicine first had to study philosophy as a preparation for one of these "higher" faculties. That Kant studied philosophy at first therefore does not mean that he intended to study philosophy as his main subject. Since he was most interested in the classics during his last year at the *Collegium Fridericianum*, it is likely that he intended to make classics his occupation. Yet fairly early in his studies he changed his mind and concentrated on courses in philosophy.

Christoph Friedrich Heilsberg (1726–1806) began his studies one year after Kant. His first contact at the university was Johann Heinrich Wlömer (1728–1797), who happened to be such "an intimate friend of Kant" that they at times shared the same quarters. At the instigation of Wlömer, Kant took Heilsberg under his wing and gave him "books about modern philosophy and reviewed at least the most difficult parts of all the recitations I took with Ammon, Knutzen and Teske. All this he did out of friendship,"[11] in other words, he did not charge him for his tutoring. Kant also tutored several other students for money – but not just for money. Those he helped returned the favor in other ways as well. They provided him with luxuries, such as coffee and white bread. When Wlömer moved to Berlin, another student, Christoph Bernhard Kallenberg, gave Kant free quarters and considerable support.[12] Kant was also supported by his uncle, the shoemaker Richter, who had taken in Kant's little brother when their father died in 1746. As Heilsberg put it:

Kant lived very frugally; real need he never had to suffer, even though there were times when he had to go out while his clothes were with the menders for repairs. At those times one of the students would stay in his quarters and Kant went out with borrowed coat, pants, or shoes. If a piece of clothing was completely worn out, the fraternity had to collect money and buy a new piece, without this ever being put into account or being returned.

Kant was not given to drinking or fighting, both of which were common among the students at an eighteenth-century German university.[13] He does not appear to have taken part in any of the spoofs that the students engaged in. Thus he did not take part in the so-called *Pantoffelparade* in which the students, lining the exit of the churches in Königsberg, ostentatiously looked over and critically evaluated the young ladies as they were leaving services. His studies were more important to him than anything else. When he was a more senior student, Kant had something of a following among the younger ones. The younger students looked up to him. He not only tutored them in academic subjects but also influenced them in other ways. Thus Heilsberg reports that "Kant did not like any frivolities and even less 'going out on the town,' and he converted his listeners little by little to the same view." He was a moral force in the lives of others long before he graduated and began to teach at the university.

Kant had a serious appearance. He did not laugh often. Though he had a sense of humor, it did not show itself in ways to which other students were accustomed. He at least appreciated humor in philosophical writers. His wit was subtler than most of his comrades could appreciate. Furthermore, he had a deadpan character. Spontaneous laughter or uncontrolled joy did not seem to be in his nature. This may or may not have been the influence of his Pietistic education, which would have given him a tendency to suppress such outbursts. The children of God in Königsberg did not engage in uncontrolled and undisciplined behavior. Even late in his life his humor was dry, and his jokes were subtle and delivered with a serious demeanor. Already as a student Kant seemed to favor self-control as one of the highest virtues.

When he was criticized by someone for not laughing enough, "he admitted this shortcoming, and then added that no metaphysician could do the world as much good as Erasmus of Rotterdam and the famous Montaigne," recommending to his friends that they should make especially the latter "constant reading." He could cite many passages of Montaigne "by heart."[14] That Montaigne was so important to Kant as a student is not insignificant, but he was hardly alone in this. Many of his contemporaries, like Hamann and Scheffner, thought equally highly of him. Nor is it surprising that he continued to praise Montaigne later in his life, although he also found that Montaigne spoke too much of himself – a fault that Kant did not have.

Kant was not all work and no play. Again Heilsberg:

Playing billiards was his only recreation. Wlömer and I were his constant companions in this. We had trained ourselves to the highest skill in this game, and we seldom went home without having won. I paid my French teacher almost entirely from this income. When no one wanted to play with us any longer because we always won, we entirely gave up this means of income and chose the game of l'hombre, which Kant played well.

Even in recreation, Kant never lost sight of utilitarian considerations. Playing was also a way of making money. The Pietists, and especially Schulz, would hardly have approved of this practice.[15] For the strict Pietists, cards were the "prayer-book of the devil," a road that led straight to hell. Kant was unbothered by such considerations. Nor did these games interfere with his studies or his tutoring – quite the contrary. In one of his lectures on anthropology, he claims that playing cards "cultivates us, makes us even-tempered, and it teaches us to keep our emotions in check. In this way it can have an influence on our morality."[16] Kant would have made a good poker player.

What would Kant's academic studies at the University of Königsberg have been like? In 1700 there were twenty-eight German universities scattered throughout the different German states. Many of them were small. Total enrollment at all the German universities was only 9,000 students.[17] By 1760 that number had decreased to 7,000, even though five new universities had been founded (Breslau, Bützow, Fulda, Göttingen, and Erlangen). Heidelberg had only 80 students, and 20 of the other universities had fewer than 300. Halle and Leipzig were larger, with more than 500 students each. The University of Königsberg probably had between 300 and 500 students for most semesters during the eighteenth century.[18] Part of the reason for its relative success in attracting students was its location. The "Albertina" was the only university in eastern Prussia, and indeed one of the two major universities in Prussia. Students who wished to study somewhere else had to travel far. Königsberg also attracted students from the surrounding countries. It was an international university, with significant numbers of Poles, Lithuanians, and students of other Baltic nationalities in attendance.[19] Another advantage, at least after 1737, was the fact that theology students graduating from the University of Königsberg were the only ones in Prussia who were exempted from studying for two years at the University of Halle.[20] Indeed, theology, and the university as a whole, had been reformed in accordance with the principles established at the University of Halle.

The geographical isolation of Königsberg had disadvantages. Johann Georg Bock (1698–1762), professor of poetry and rhetoric, bitterly complained. He wrote in 1736 to his friend Johann Christoph Gottsched (1700–1766), the famous Wolffian philosopher and literary critic, who himself had studied at Königsberg between 1714 and 1723: "as you know I live here in a place where new foreign books and writings appear, just like comets, only after long years."[21] As late as 1781, Ludwig (Adolph Franz Joseph) von Baczko (1756–1823) wrote of East Prussia as a whole: We are "decried as almost a learned Siberia; and owing to the great geographical distance from Leipzig, the center of the German book-trade, it is natural that we should suffer, since all literary novelties come late to us, and authorship is hindered by the lack of bookstores."[22] When Frederick the Great visited Königsberg in 1739, he quipped that the city was better suited "to bring up bears than to be an arena for the sciences."[23]

Given Königsberg's remoteness, it is perhaps not very surprising that not all disciplines were taught equally well. Not many came to East Prussia with the express purpose of teaching at the university, and some of those who taught at the University of Königsberg were underqualified. In some courses "the teacher was not well acquainted with his discipline and wanted to learn it by lecturing (*docendo*)."[24] Some of the best talent was home-grown or consisted of people who, having been born in Königsberg, had studied elsewhere. The course offerings were uneven. Some disciplines were not taught at all; others, like chemistry, natural history, economics, and political science, were not well represented. Mathematics and physics were, by all accounts, taught poorly. Though experimental physics was taught, the experiments that could be performed with the equipment available at the university were by all accounts poor. In the natural sciences Königsberg was not among the leading universities of Europe or even of Germany at the time.

In 1744 the university had forty-four full professors (*Ordinarien*), all of them badly paid. The full professors received only a small salary; the other professors (*außerordentliche Professoren*) and the lecturers (*Privatdozenten*) received nothing.[25] They had to live entirely off the fees the students paid them for attending their lectures and recitations. None of them could have made a living without some other income. In fact, all faculty members, unless they were independently wealthy, had to have secondary incomes. This meant some other official position (*Nebenamt*), a business, or another occupation. Some ran dormitories for students, others took in students as boarders into their own households, still others had businesses, and at least one of them ran a pub. Even in Göttingen, where professors were much better paid, many had vegetable gardens. The theologians, who usually were also pastors or higher officials in the Lutheran Church of Prussia, were better off than those who taught law, medicine, or philosophy (though theologians taught even some of those disciplines). Philosophers were paid the least, but since every student had to take some courses in philosophy, there were many students in the public lectures on philosophy.

The Albertina had four schools or *Fakultäten*: philosophy, theology, law, and medicine.[26] Philosophy was also known as the "lower faculty," as compared to the higher faculties.[27] Theology was undoubtedly the most important of these. It had the most students, its teachers received the most secure income, and its faculty was also the most influential. The school of philosophy, more than those of law and medicine, was dominated by theology. Not only did several theologians teach philosophy, but theological concerns also motivated many of the philosophers who were not theologians themselves. During the first two-thirds of the eighteenth century, philosophy at Königsberg was not much more than the handmaiden of theology. How profoundly theological developments influenced the school of philosophy can readily be seen from the history of these two disciplines during the early part of the century. At its very beginning, the orientation of philosophy was almost entirely Aristotelian.[28] Descartes and other modern philosophers had very little influence on the way philosophy was taught. They appear to have been important mainly as figures that needed to be refuted. Indeed, most philosophy professors appear to have been engaged in defending Aristotelianism against the various attacks that had been leveled against it.[29] The reason for this was that the orthodox Protestant doctrine that was taught in the school of theology relied heavily on Aristotelian doctrine. As the influence of orthodoxy waned in subsequent years, Aristotelianism became less important. By the late thirties, most of its adherents had disappeared. Yet when Kant entered the university there were still Aristotelians teaching in the faculty, and Aristotelianism continued to play a role.

As early as 1715, there were several philosophers engaged in trying to find a middle way between traditional Protestant Aristotelianism and some of the more recent philosophical developments, arguing that not all of modern philosophy was bad. Thus Gottsched reported that during 1714 and 1715 he was taught philosophy in accordance with Cartesian principles and natural law in accordance with Christian Thomasius (1655–1728).[30] Gottsched also claimed that he was exposed to other thinkers, such as Locke and Leclerc, and that the spirit of free and open discussion pervaded the university during that period. In any case, that is how Gottsched later saw it. He emphasized that "the great freedom to philosophize that was prevalent at the University of Königsberg during my period of study there has protected me from the slavish way of thinking and teaching that was so common in the dominant philosophical schools."[31] It was during this period that Wolff's philosophy first became important at Königsberg. J. H. Kreuschner, preacher at the Kneiphof church, had studied with Wolff and was his first prominent adherent. Christoph Friedrich Baumgarten, a native of Königsberg and one of Wolff's first students, is said to have been the first to teach Wolffian philosophy at Königsberg. After receiving a master's degree from the University of Leipzig in 1720, he had returned to the city of his birth to teach there, and he spread what he took to be a better system. Others followed. Thus Theodor Reinhold That (1698–1735) published a book in 1724 in which he tried to show the superiority of the Wolffian method, and N. E. Fromm also advocated a strict Wolffian approach. Georg Heinrich Rast, who in 1719 had defended Leibniz's explanation of why the level of mercury in a barometer contracts just before a thunderstorm, was also close to Wolff.[32] It was he who converted the young Gottsched to Wolffian thinking.[33] Another younger teacher advocating Wolffian principles was Conrad Theophil Marquardt. Also born in Königsberg, he had studied theology in Königsberg and philosophy in Halle. While in Halle, he had become a strict Wolffian. In 1722 he defended in Königsberg his Inaugural Dissertation on preestablished harmony, and he was still teaching theology, philosophy, and mathematics when Kant came to the university. Leibniz and Wolff were not the only philosophers taught at Königsberg. Students were exposed to many different thinkers, and a one-sided Wolffianism does not appear to have been the rule. Thus even Gottsched, who saw in Wolff an escape from an eclecticism that "mixes up very different ideas and principles" and that left him without orientation, could remain relatively independent. His first academic treatise was called "Doubts about Leibnizian Monads"; and his Inaugural Dissertation about the "genuine notion of divine omnipresence" shows that he was preoccupied with Wolffian problems but did not uncritically accept all of Wolffian doctrine.

This freedom to pursue different philosophical ideas did not last long. Pietism, which had been influential among ordinary citizens in the city of Königsberg for some time, also gained the upper hand at the university. Because of a number of strategic appointments by the king, Lysius and his Pietistic friends were finally able to dominate the theological faculty in 1725. They immediately introduced decisive changes in what could be taught.[34] Not only did they eliminate all patristic studies but, following the lead of their colleagues in Halle, they also confronted Wolffian philosophers head on. They had already succeeded in having Fischer expelled from the university, from Königsberg, and from all of Prussia in 1724, but they continued to argue that Wolff's views ultimately amounted to atheism. This was, of course, a most powerful warning to all other Wolffians.

The Pietists also restricted freedom in other ways. Lysius had been rather liberal in his view of so-called middle things, *adiaphora*, or matters of indifference. He was not strictly opposed to dancing, for instance. Rogall, on the other hand, was uncompromising, seeing the devil's work in all such things. The tone accordingly changed, and a still more austere version of Pietism took hold in town and at the university. Soon the Königsberg establishment hated Rogall even more than they had despised the Pietists who had preceded him.

Both the orthodox and the Wolffians tried to resist, of course, and Pietism did not gain in prestige among the established clergy, faculty, and city officials. Ultimate success at the university also continued to elude them. Thus Rogall observed that there were "many artisans and often also soldiers who reveal in a simple-minded way the state of their heart. Only among the students and the officials (*Honoratioren*) the evangelical message of Jesus Christ will not take effect . . ."[35] Most of the students had laughed at them, but not for much longer. The king continued to intervene. In 1726 he decreed that theology had to be taught according to the principles of Halle. He delivered the final blow in 1728, when he ordered that every candidate for a pastorate in the East Prussian church needed a *testimonium pietatis et eruditionis*, or a "certificate of piety and education," from the Pietist Abraham Wolff in Königsberg before he could be appointed.

This gave the Pietists unprecedented power, which they wielded uncompromisingly. Even before this decree they had often threatened their opponents with "telling the king."[36] From then on, every theology student was absolutely dependent on them for a position that would afford him a living.[37] From 1730, as a direct result of the king's decrees, the Pietists possessed what amounted to a monopoly in the theological faculty. No theology student who cared about his future could afford to disagree openly with the Pietist professors or to be friendly with those who were not Pietists. So while the courses of the Pietists were exceedingly well attended, the orthodox professors lectured to almost-empty rooms. The students were no longer laughing.

These developments in theology also had consequences for philosophy. Freedom of philosophical expression disappeared.[38] In 1727, lecturing in accordance with Wolffian texts was explicitly prohibited in Königsberg, and Wolff's works were no longer allowed to be distributed.[39] Accordingly, J. G. Bock complained in 1729 that the "university is in so miserable a condition that it does not seem unlike a trivial school; philosophy is afflicted with a hectic fever, and the other sciences are also poorly enough cultivated."[40] The hectic fever of Pietism threatened to kill off philosophy altogether, or so it seemed to some. The Wolffians gave in – at least publicly. More quietly, they continued to advocate and teach Wolffian philosophy. Ultimately, in Königsberg as elsewhere, the Pietistic actions "hardly interfered with the spread of Wolffian ideas."[41] Yet many a promising career, such as that of Marquardt, was effectively over. None of the younger Wolffian or orthodox lecturers could hope for advancement of any kind, and most of those who had not given up teaching when Kant entered the university remained mere lecturers. They had not been promoted simply because they were not Pietists.

The most important of the orthodox opponents of Pietism was the theologian Johann Jakob Quandt (1686–1772), who had already opposed Lysius. He was a highly educated and, by all accounts, very talented theologian and a specialist in "Oriental" languages, who also knew English, French, and Dutch. Quandt had an extensive library of books in all of these languages. Considered as one of the best preachers in all of Prussia, he advocated a rational (*vernünftig*) orthodox faith.[42] Not a Wolffian himself, he was close to many of the younger instructors who were influenced by Wolff.[43] Though he became increasingly more isolated at the university over the years, he remained influential in the city. He had the ear of those who were in power locally, namely the nobility and the public officials in Königsberg (including much of the clergy). Still, the orthodox forces were marginalized. The conflict between the Pietists and the orthodox was a part of the political struggle between the forces of the central government in Berlin and the local government and nobility in Königsberg (and elsewhere), and the king had the upper hand in this struggle. Nevertheless, the influence of Quandt and his followers should not be underestimated. The power of the Pietists continued to increase until 1740, but they were never in absolute control, and this was to a large extent due to Quandt.

Another peculiar development in the intellectual history of the university began in 1732. In August of that year, Bock wrote to Gottsched: "You will not be little surprised when your brother tells you that the Wolffian philosophy is now imported here by those from Halle themselves, and that they praise it in front of everyone as the best kind. . . . Who would have been able to imagine such a transformation some time ago? Even a year ago it would have appeared to be incredible, if someone had prophesied this . . ."[44] What had happened? Schulz had arrived in the meantime.

As one of Schulz's students said, "This most learned man taught me to get to know theology from another side in that he brought so much philosophy into it that one was forced to believe that Christ and all his apostles had studied in Halle under Wolff."[45] Thus Wolff's philosophy became more important again when Schulz took the leadership of the Pietistic faction in Königsberg. The Wolffians in Königsberg could breathe more easily. Indeed, Schulz promoted Wolffian philosophy as long as its adherents endorsed the basic truths of Christianity as he saw them, and since most Wolffians were far from being atheists, there was a truce between the Wolffians and the Pietists.

None of this meant a return to the free philosophical discussion that Gottsched had known when he had studied in Königsberg. The apostles may have sounded like Wolff, but they were still apostles conceived in the Pietistic mode. J. G. Bock wrote in 1736 to Gottsched: "Our academy does not look at all similar to the one that my brother left, and I only would like to say that I have not been able to get a *collegium poeticum* together within a year and a half."[46] Poetry, theater, and other nonreligious diversions were still considered frivolous, worldly, "of the devil," and thus actively discouraged. All efforts had to be directed towards the well-being of the human soul in accordance with Pietistic principles. Wolffian philosophy was considered useful in this regard, and it could therefore be tolerated, but only insofar as it supported Pietistic conviction. Cölestin Christian Flottwell (1711–1759), professor of German rhetoric and another friend of Gottsched's in Königsberg, wrote on April 2, 1739: "The school of theology is in a frenzy and at this time the Spanish inquisition is milder than it is."[47]

The orthodox faction in Königsberg did not help this situation, since it did everything in its power to discredit the Pietists. In one bizarre incident, redolent more of the Middle Ages than of the Enlightenment, the orthodox faction tried to defame Salthenius, one of the most prominent Pietists, by accusing him of being in league with the devil – and not entirely without foundation. Salthenius, as an adolescent in Sweden, had indeed written a letter to the devil in his own blood, promising the devil his body and soul in return for a pouch of money that would never run out. He placed the letter under an oak tree for delivery, but it never reached the addressee. Instead, it was picked up by a farmer, who immediately notified the authorities. Salthenius was convicted and received the sentence of death, which was later commuted to a month in prison. Finding it wise to leave his native Sweden, Salthenius went to Germany. After studying and converting to Pietism in Halle, he became first the inspector of the orphanage in Königsberg, then the inspector of the *Collegium Fridericianum*, and finally associate professor of logic and metaphysics in 1732. The orthodox preachers did not find it was beneath them to report on Salthenius' youthful sin,

notifying the king in 1737 of his pact with the devil. While they were un-
successful in having him removed, it is not difficult to imagine the sensation this created in Königsberg.[48] Flottwell, as a Wolffian taking the side
of the orthodox, reported with disgust to Gottsched: "our theological faculty consists of men who either have perjured themselves more than once,
like Dr. Schulz, or who are stupid, like Dr. Kypke, or who are conceited
and envious, like Dr. Arnoldt, or who have become a friend with the devil
himself . . ."[49]

This was more or less the situation at the University of Königsberg when
Kant entered it in 1740. Though Frederick II had promised change, the
change was not quick in coming. It was still very important, especially for
those who intended to study theology, to choose the right courses and the
right teachers – and the right teachers were still Pietists or those who were
sufficiently close to them. Kant was probably aware of this from the beginning, and if he was not, he would have been made aware of it by the
following event as related by Heilsberg:

> Kant introduced Wlömer and me to teachings about ordinary life and customs. One
> should acquaint oneself with all the sciences and exclude none, not even theology. [It
> should be studied] even if one did not intend to earn one's living by it. We, that is,
> Wlömer, Kant, and I [Heilsberg] decided therefore to attend in the next semester the
> public readings of Schulz . . . who is still highly esteemed. We did it. We did not miss
> an hour and we took copious notes, and we repeated the lectures at home so well that
> we passed the exams, which this honorable man often administered, with such high
> grades that he asked all three of us to stay behind at the end of the last lecture. He asked
> us about our names, our [knowledge of] languages, our teachers, and about our inten-
> tions in studying. Kant said he wanted to become a medical doctor. . . . [He asked:] "Why
> are you studying theology?" (It was, unless I am mistaken, systematic theology.) Kant
> answered: "from thirst of knowledge," to which the great man answered: "Well, if that
> is the case, then I have no objections, but if you change your mind before you graduate,
> and if you choose the calling of the preacher, call on me with confidence. You shall have
> the choice of a position in the country or one of the cities. I can promise you this, and
> I will, if I am still alive, keep my word. Here, take my hand and leave in peace."[50]

If Kant had not already known the importance of such connections, he knew
now. His answer reveals a certain confidence in his abilities, and a sense of
how important it was to him to be free to study anything he wanted. When
he attended Schulz's lectures after his first two years at the university, he
was interested in them for philosophical reasons. Kant could easily have
entered the ministry. He had all the right qualifications, but he lacked any
inclination to pursue this course.

What was Kant's course of study? Like most students, he most likely took philosophy courses until the event Heilsberg describes. These courses included logic and metaphysics, which were given every year in alternate semesters by the professor of logic and metaphysics, and ethics and natural law, which were given in the same fashion by the professor of moral philosophy. The professor of physics lectured on theoretical and experimental physics every year, taking either one or two semesters, and the poetry professor gave lectures in rhetoric and history.[51] Apart from these lectures by the full professors, which did not have to be paid for, there were several lectures and courses that required payment and were given by the full professors, the associate professors, and the lecturers. Kant probably attended, sooner or later, all of the free public lectures, and he also must have taken a number of the courses offered for payment.

When Kant was a student, the philosophical faculty had eight full and a number of associate professors and lecturers.[52] They taught everything from Greek, Hebrew, rhetoric, poetry, and history, to logic and metaphysics, practical philosophy, mathematics, and physics. Since the philosophical course (*cursus philosophicus*) was mainly designed to prepare the students for one of the higher faculties, relatively few of the students sought a degree in that discipline. Yet visitors to Königsberg marveled at how many metaphysicians there were at this university compared to most others in Germany.

Given the history of the schools of theology and philosophy between 1710 and 1740, it should not be surprising that the members of the faculty had varied philosophical backgrounds and outlooks. First of all, there was Johann Adam Gregorovius (1681–1749), an Aristotelian, who was primarily interested in defending the moral philosophy of Aristotle against more modern attempts at ethics. In the *Wöchentliche Nachrichten* of 1741, he said, among other things:

I cannot make a secret of the fact that the philosophy of Aristotle has been so maligned and ridiculed since so many new systems have appeared after the beginning of this century . . . that no dog would take a piece of bread from an Aristotelian, even if it had not been fed for five days. . . . This public disregard of antiquity led me entirely to abandon Aristotle from honest conviction. Subsequently, I had to learn every new system as soon as it appeared in order to teach it to the youthful students who were only interested in the newest (*splitterneue*) philosophers. . . . I had . . . as great an attendance and applause as any. Yet after I got tired of the constant change . . . I began to compare all the new doctrines with the ancient one. Yet I had to learn that the hate and disregard which those inexperienced in these matters have against Aristotle also met me.[53]

Gregorovius was not ignorant of modern philosophy. He just did not think it was superior to the Aristotelian philosophy and was prepared to argue this, even if to relatively empty classes. While we do not know whether Kant attended his lectures, his "thirst of knowledge" would not have stood in the way of doing so. It is more than likely that he, who after all wanted to study the classics, did not miss the opportunity to listen to Gregorovius in 1740.[54]

Gregorovius's approach differed markedly from the one Kant had experienced at the *Collegium Fridericianum*. Kant observed in his *Metaphysics of Morals* that with some justification "it is thought improper not to defend the ancients, who can be regarded as our teachers, from all attacks, accusations, and disdain, insofar as this is possible." Then he pointed out that it is "a foolish mistake to attribute preeminence in talents and good will to the ancients in preference to the moderns just because of their antiquity."[55] It is likely that when he wrote this he also had some of his own former teachers in mind. He could have known orthodox Protestant Aristotelianism firsthand. Whether Kant took courses with Quandt, the most famous member of the orthodox party, is not known, but it is unlikely because Quandt hardly ever felt it necessary to teach. Gregorovius was soon succeeded by Carl Andreas Christiani (1707–1780), who had come from Halle to Königsberg to teach practical philosophy. He was a Pietist and a protégé of Schulz.[56] Kant may have gone to his lectures as well.

The second full professor was Johann David Kypke (1692–1758), who belonged to both the theological and the philosophical faculty. He taught from 1725 to 1758. Being one of the older Pietists, he was less inclined to appreciate Wolff. Rather, he was an eclectic, wavering between Aristotelianism and Pietism. In an advertisement of his lectures from 1731 he stated that, depending on what the students wished to hear, he could lecture either in accordance with the "proven peripatetic (Aristotelian) method or in accordance with that of Budde or Walch." Budde and Walch were two of the foremost followers of Thomasius, the other founder of the German Enlightenment besides Wolff. Thomasius himself came under the influence of Pietism while he was in Halle, but he later developed a more independent position again.[57] Budde and Walch were radical Pietists and opponents of Wolff.[58] Accordingly, they would have been more or less "safe" choices in Königsberg before the arrival of Schulz, but there were times when Kypke lectured on logic in accordance with Rabe's Aristotelian textbook *Philosophical Course or First Compendium of the Philosophical Sciences Dialectics, Analytics, Politics, Comprehending also Ethics, Physics and Meta-*

physics. Deduced from the Most Evident Principle of Right Reason Following the Scientific Method.[59] In any case, Rogall ordained in 1738 that everyone who went on to theology had to read this work.[60] Again, it is likely that Kant attended his lectures as well. In them, he not only would have become more closely acquainted with Aristotelian philosophy, but also would have heard about some of the more recent critics of Wolffian philosophy, the Thomasians. Kypke's *Brevissima deliniatio scientarum dialecticae et analyticae ad mentem philosophi* of 1729 was certainly one of the works that impressed on Kant the distinction between analytic and dialectic that was later to become so important in the *Critique of Pure Reason.*[61] Kant lived in Kypke's house during his first years of teaching at the university, so he had at least some acquaintance with him.[62]

Then there was the professor of poetry and eloquence J. G. Bock, the good friend of Gottsched and a bitter enemy of the Pietists. He had philosophical interests, but they were not his most pressing concerns. He opposed the Pietists for many reasons, but the fact that they stood in the way of students taking courses in poetry was one of the most important ones. Again, it is more than likely that Kant attended his public lectures, though we may doubt that he found them very important.

Perhaps more interesting than either of these three was Marquardt, who beginning in 1730 was an associate professor of mathematics. Until his death in 1749 he gave lectures in logic and metaphysics that were said to be very popular. In his dissertation of 1722 he had given his unqualified support to preestablished harmony in the question of the mind–body relation. This is highly significant, for during the period under consideration it was more or less universally assumed that only three systems were possible that could explain how substances could be related to each other, a question that was of course especially important for understanding the relation of mind and body. The first of these was the system of physical influx, which held that the change in a substance B is sufficiently and immediately founded in another substance A. This position was usually associated with Aristotelianism, and sometimes also with Locke. The second was occasionalism, which involved the belief that the change in substance B and the change in substance A are both directly caused by God. This was ascribed to the Cartesians and especially to Malebranche. The third position, the Leibnizian view of preestablished harmony, claimed that both A and B are indirectly caused by God via two harmonized series of changes. This was called the system of universal (or preestablished) harmony. Wolff himself had come into conflict with the Pietists over just this problem. The main reason for this was his guarded and limited endorsement of Leibniz's theory of preestablished harmony in the *Reasonable Thoughts of God, the World and the Soul of Human Beings as well as of All Things in General* of 1720. The sections concerned with the human soul led him "against his expectations to the Leibnizian theory," although he did not endorse preestablished harmony as the absolute truth but only as the most reasonable hypothesis. He was soon attacked by the Pietists. They argued that universal harmony contradicted the freedom of the will required by the true Christian faith.

Marquardt was much less timid than Wolff himself, arguing that all bodily phenomena could be completely explained at the level of bodies. At the same time, these phenomena could also be explained at the more fundamental level of the substances, because the soul could create all representations on its own. Since God had to create the best of all possible worlds, he had to have established a correspondence between body and soul, or phenomena and substances.[63] Marquardt supplemented his a priori argument by a posteriori arguments that were meant both to prove preestablished harmony and to disprove occasionalism and physical influx. As a strict Wolffian, he remained opposed to the Pietism expressed in Wolffian terms that became common in Königsberg under Schulz. Kant may or may not have taken courses in philosophy and mathematics from him.

Still more important, perhaps, were Carl Heinrich Rappolt (1702–1753), Johann Gottfried Teske (1704–1772), Christian Friedrich Ammon (1696–1742), and Martin Knutzen (1713–1751). Rappolt was an associate professor of physics. He was more or less Wolffian in orientation, but was also deeply influenced by British sources. Rappolt was also a declared enemy of Pietism. His views had been influenced mainly by Kreuschner, the first Wolffian in Königsberg, and by Fischer, the Wolffian who was most hated by the Pietists. It was Fischer who caused Rappolt to abandon his studies in theology and to turn towards physics. Annoyed by the Pietist intrigues, he wrote in 1728 to Gottsched: "Here all science seems to be without use, and one does not so much consider whether someone has learned something solid as whether one knows to adapt to the manners of Halle."[64] He had good reason to be angry. Teske, favored by the Pietists, was appointed a full professor of physics in 1729, even though he had studied physics for only two years.[65] In 1729–30 Rappolt went to England to study physics and mathematics, and in 1731 he obtained the degree of *Magister* in Frankfurt (Oder). In 1731 and 1732 he lectured repeatedly on the English language,

English culture, and English philosophy (*Scholae Anglicana linguae hujus culturam cum philosophia copulabit*).[66] He also taught philosophy and gave lectures on Pope (mainly for money).[67] Lindner, one of Kant's friends, is known to have learned English from him. Hamann liked him and was close to him. Kant's love of Pope seems to date back to this period, and it appears that it was Rappolt who first acquainted him with Pope. It is also possible that Kant got to know other British authors through him.[68] While we do not know definitely that Kant took Rappolt's courses, we must assume that he took at least those of Ammon, Teske, and Knutzen. Since Kant in 1741 was already tutoring Heilsberg and others on the material of the courses given by Ammon, Knutzen, and Teske, we may assume not only that he had attended their lectures, but also that he attended them very early in his studies.[69]

Ammon was a lecturer (*Privatdozent*) in mathematics. He began as an Aristotelian, but had moved closer to Wolff long before Kant entered the university.[70] His *Lineae primae eruditionis humanae in usum auditorii ductae,* which appeared in 1737, was a short summary of the subjects that students had to master in the philosophical curriculum. Being more eclectic than narrowly Aristotelian or Wolffian, it was adopted as a textbook in a number of lecture courses. Because Ammon died in 1742, Kant could not have tutored many times for Ammon's courses. Nevertheless, through Ammon he would have been exposed to the approach of the Aristotelians, even if he never went to the lectures of any other Aristotelian. Kraus did not have a high opinion of Ammon, saying that having seen a mathematical tract of his, he could only call him a dilettante (*Stümper*).[71] Whether that distinguished him from Kant's other teachers is difficult to say.

Teske, who had received his position at least partially as a result of efforts by Lysius and Rogall, taught both theoretical and experimental physics.[72] While he did not have as rigorous a training in science as Rappolt did, he was close to Pietism. Borowski spoke highly of him, describing him as a good teacher and person. At Kant's promotion to *Magister,* Teske said that he had learned a great deal from Kant's dissertation.[73] While Borowski claimed that Kant considered the memory of this man "holy," Kraus, who should have known better, maintained that Kant had "a low opinion of Teske and rightfully so."[74]

Teske worked mainly on problems concerning electricity. He was said to have been one of the first scientists to claim that "electrical fire" was identical to the "material of lightning." He was proud to say that some of his experiments had shown "how useful it [electricity] was also in the medical sciences."[75] His pride was his collection of 243 "physical and mathematical instruments," acquired throughout his life.[76]

Teske not only introduced Kant to experimental physics, but he also formed his early views on the matter of electricity. This is significant, for Kant never gave up his basic view of the nature of electricity and fire, and in this way Teske's influence continued throughout Kant's life. His thesis for the degree of *Magister* was entitled "Succinct Exposition of Some Meditations on Fire," and dealt with just those subject matters that a student of Teske might be expected to work on. Accordingly, it is Teske who must be considered Kant's *Doktorvater,* and his praise of the dissertation must have meant much to Kant at the time.

Teske's courses in experimental physics were quite impressive. Johann Friedrich Lauson, in a feeble attempt at poetry, described how Teske used equipment to memorable effect, producing electric charges to create heat, sparks, and flashes, electrifying his students, lighting alcohol, and producing a glow in a wire even under water. Lauson's poem does not make clear precisely what conclusions Teske drew from his experiments, but we know he thought that electricity and lightning were of the same nature. He knew how to entertain his students with effects of electricity, but he did not lead any of them to become a great scientist.[77] Kant was enough attracted by Teske's investigations of electricity and fire to write his dissertation on this topic. Though Teske claimed that he had learned from Kant's dissertation, we may safely assume that it was informed not just by the literature to which he refers, but also by Teske's speculations and calculations. Regrettably, Teske has received little attention from Kant scholars.

One of the best known and most influential philosophers at Königsberg was Knutzen. Many former students were proud to have studied with him. Thus Hamann said in his autobiography:

I was a student of the famous Knutzen in all parts of philosophy, mathematics, and in private lectures on algebra, and I was a member of the physico-theological society that was founded by him, but did not succeed.[78]

Although Kant never mentioned him in any of his writings, Knutzen is usually thought to have had the greatest influence on Kant. Borowski claimed that "Knutzen meant most to him among all his teachers, and he delineated the course of . . . [Kant] and others that would allow them to become original thinkers and not mere followers."[79] Kraus observed that Knutzen was the only one "who could have had an influence on his [Kant's] genius," surmising that "what unlocked Kant's genius under Knutzen and led him to the original ideas that he put down in his natural history of the heavens was the comet of 1744, on which Knutzen published a book."[80]

When Kant entered the university, Knutzen was a relatively young associate professor who taught logic and metaphysics. He had been a student of both Ammon and Teske.[81] Most importantly, he was a Pietist in the Schulzian fashion, that is, he followed the Wolffian method while engaging and criticizing many of the tenets of Wolffian philosophy in a serious way. In 1734, at the age of twenty-one, he had defended his dissertation, "Philosophical Comment on the *Commercium* of the Mind with the Body, Explained by Physical Influx." In this work he criticized Wolffian philosophy, but also expressed his appreciation for the Wolffian approach. Accordingly, he had some difficulties. Wolffian philosophy was still officially prohibited, and so the public speech on this work (*Redeaktus*) was held up for a year because of protests by the orthodox.[82] The orthodox faction was delighted to be able to pay back the Pietists in this particular way.

Knutzen was not really a Wolffian. While his philosophical concerns were to a large extent dictated by Wolff, his position was fundamentalist Christian. Thus his dissertation dealt with the issue that was most contentious between the Pietists and the Wolffians, namely, the question concerning the relation of mind and body. Taking what was essentially an anti-Leibnizian, and thus to a lesser extent an anti-Wolffian, position, he argued that the theory of preestablished harmony was just as wrong as occasionalism, and that the only reasonable theory was that of physical influx. At the same time he accepted the view that bodies consisted of absolutely simple parts. This meant that the interaction of mind and body was not the interaction of radically different substances (a problematic idea) but the interaction of simple elements with one another. Since the idea of physical influx was in the minds of many scholars connected with Locke (and corpuscularianism), it would not be entirely inaccurate to say that Knutzen defended the Lockean position. In any case, he had developed a new theory, meant to be an alternative to the Leibniz–Wolffian one. In his earlier dissertation for the *Magister* degree, he had attacked another doctrine bound up with Wolffian philosophy, namely, the view that the world may have existed from eternity.[83] For Knutzen, as for any Lutheran, the world was created and designed by God with a definite end in mind. It could not possibly be eternal.[84] To say that Knutzen was a "Wolffian" is therefore misleading. "His pietism belongs in its basic outlook to the great Spener-Francke line."[85] His thinking was at least as much influenced by British as by German sources.

All his works show that he knew and appreciated British philosophers more than the traditional picture suggests. Even Erdmann, who does his best to characterize Knutzen as a Wolffian, has to admit that his philosophical views are closer to the British than to the German philosophers. They do indeed "point in the direction of the empiricist skepticism and idealism of English [*sic*] philosophy."[86] As far as epistemology was concerned, Locke and his followers informed Knutzen's thought more than Wolff and his school. Gottsched saw this clearly. He accused Knutzen of being too close to Locke in his discussion of sensibility.[87] For Knutzen, just as for Locke, internal and external sensation forms the basis of all knowledge. Without the materials given us in sensation, the principle of contradiction does not allow us to know anything.[88] There can be no doubt that Knutzen read Locke's *Essay* and that he considered it important. Indeed, he constantly referred to Locke in his lectures and advised his students to read him, and at the time of his death he was still working on a translation of Locke's *Of the Conduct of the Human Understanding.*[89]

In 1740, the year that Kant entered the university, Knutzen published in German his *Philosophical Proof of the Truth of Christianity*, which would become his most successful work, and the one for which he was best known in the eighteenth century.[90] In it, he defended Christianity against British Deism, and especially against Toland, Chubb, and Tindal.[91] Since Deism constituted as much a threat to Christianity as Wolffianism did, the Deists were an important object of criticism not just for the Pietists but also for the orthodox. In writing this book, Knutzen not only showed how firmly his views were rooted in the theological discussion of Königsberg, but also revealed his intimate knowledge of a then relatively unknown aspect of British philosophy. The book also provides a good insight into Knutzen's theological outlook.

The *Philosophical Proof* contains such "theorems" as "We have the duty to obey God" (§ 12) and "God *must* punish the perpetrators" (§ 17), as well as such "propositions of experience" as "We are all guilty of not obeying God" (§ 13). From these theorems and propositions Knutzen derives other theorems, such as: "Everyone must expect severe punishment after death" (§ 19). We need, accordingly, to be saved – and we can be saved only if we are told that, and told how we can be saved. "In short, the necessity of divine revelation is founded on the necessity of the means of salvation (*Begnadigungsmittel*), and revelation presupposes the latter" (p. 42). This proves that Tindal, who had argued that we need only natural religion, was wrong. This is not all; Knutzen goes on to prove that either there is no revelation at all, or the Christian revelation is the only one. Since the first disjunct is false, the second one must be true. In similar fashion he proves the doctrine of the trinity and other dogmas, proving in the end not just the truth of Christianity, but the Lutheran version of it as the only true one. The methodology of the book is Wolffian, but its spirit could hardly be further removed from Wolffian philosophy.[92]

Yet being popular and engaging, Knutzen became almost immediately one of Kant's favorite teachers, the one who had the most important early influence upon the young student. Borowski claimed that Kant "attended his classes in philosophy and mathematics without a break."[93] If this is true, then his weekly schedule during the first semester would have included the following courses from Knutzen: four hours of mathematics, four hours of philosophy, one hour of logic "in outline," as well as exercises in disputation. In the second semester he would have taken a more advanced course in logic, another course in mathematics, in which Knutzen introduced "select minds" to higher mathematics, and again exercises in disputation; and in the fourth semester he would have taken practical philosophy. Later, he probably attended lectures in rational psychology, natural philosophy, natural law, rhetoric, mnemonics, algebra, and the analysis of the infinite.[94] During his first few semesters he must also have attended Teske's classes in physics and Ammon's classes in mathematics.[95] In his third year he went to Schulz's lectures in systematic theology. The lectures he and Wlömer appear to have attended covered theology insofar as it is based on revelation, but there may have been others.[96] Some of Borowski's remarks suggest that he also attended Schulz's other lectures.[97] They would have included a course on "theology: thetic–antithetic," in which he taught Christian dogmatic in a dialectical arrangement that reminds one very much of Kant's own later dialectic. To these classes, we may safely add a number taught by such people as Rappolt, Marquardt, and Gregorovius. Even if Knutzen was Kant's favorite teacher, he was not his only one. He sought, after all, the most well-rounded education that might be obtained in a place like Königsberg.

In 1743 appeared a book by an anonymous author with the title *Reasonable Thoughts on Nature by a Christian Friend of God. Who [sic] is Nature? That It Is Powerless without His Omniscient Limitation. And How through the One, Divisible Power Everything in This World Is Possible Only in and through the Mediate Causes in Accordance with the Efficacy or Action, which Has Been Given to It.* The author was the notorious Christian Gabriel Fischer, who had returned in 1737 to Königsberg after having promised to adhere to doctrines of the true faith.[98] Starting from Wolff and Leibniz, he advocated a point of view that can only be called Spinozistic, thus challenging not only the Pietists, but also the orthodox. The theologians had major problems with its open Spinozism, but even greater ones with Fischer's specific views on the holy trinity, the denial of the doctrine that Christ was both all human and all divine, and his denial of other theological dogmas. After a pastor preached openly against Fischer and his book on New Year's Day, the book became something of a best-seller. Fischer himself was excluded from the Eucharist. He was not allowed to remain the godparent of his grandchild, and he was advised to go to the Reformed church from then on.[99]

The book was, of course, forbidden – but only after it had created a great sensation. Curiously, it was the orthodox faction (and not the Pietists) who moved against Fischer. Receiving in this case no opposition and even quiet support from the Pietists, they succeeded in having the book banned, but they did not succeed in harming Fischer beyond that. Frederick William II, the great benefactor and protector of the Pietists, who had also at times listened to the orthodox in religious matters, was no longer there; and Frederick II not only advocated religious tolerance but also was an atheist. In his youth he had praised to Voltaire Christian Wolff's *Reasonable Ideas of God, the World, the Soul of Man, and of All Things in General* "as the key to every mystery in the universe," only to be rebuffed by Voltaire. Frederick II had long outgrown such speculations, being much more skeptical and cynical than any of the Wolffians could ever be, with a preference for all things French in intellectual matters. He had little use for religious squabbles in general and for those in Königsberg in particular.[100]

If the Pietists and the orthodox needed any sign that the situation had changed again, Frederick II's inaction was that sign. Defamation on purely religious grounds would no longer succeed. As long as someone was obedient and a good citizen, the king would not interfere. On the other hand, the events of 1744 show again and only too well that religious controversy, persecution, and censorship continued to play a role in Königsberg, and that the dispute between the orthodox, the Pietists, and those advocating modern philosophy continued. These disputes were always simmering below the surface, and it did not take much for them to erupt in heated public debate. We may assume that Kant took an active interest in the controversy over Fischer's book, which was very close to his own concerns. Kant might have disagreed with Fischer's claim that his book was the proper antidote to "atheists, naturalists, Epicureans, Stoics, and many other Free-thinkers, who have no proper concept of God and his actions through his creation," but he could have wholeheartedly agreed with Fischer's rejection of the claims made by the theological faculty that they were the proper judges of this work. A "philosophical system . . . founded merely on reasons known by the intellect from experience" had to be judged by philosophers and scientists, not by theologians.[101] Not much later, Kant himself offered such a system.

The year 1744 was important for another commotion and controversy. In 1738, Knutzen had predicted that a comet that had been observed in 1698 would reappear in the winter of 1744.[102] When a comet appeared, Knutzen became an instant celebrity in Königsberg, and gained a reputation as a great astronomer well beyond the confines of Königsberg. Knutzen's *Rational Thoughts on the Comets, in which is Examined and Represented Their Nature and Their Character as well as the Causes of Their Motion, and at the Same Time Given a Short Description of the Noteworthy Comet of This Year,* published in 1744, was, according to Kraus, responsible for awakening Kant's interest in science, and it was this book that led Kant to write his own *Universal Natural History and Theory of the Heavens,* which appeared eleven years later.[103] Like Knutzen's other students, Kant may have viewed him as a hero.

Doubts soon arose. Euler showed both in letters to Knutzen and in an article that appeared later in 1744 that Knutzen's prediction had *not* come "true," that the comet of 1744 was *not* identical to the comet of 1698, and, at least by implication, that Knutzen did not know enough physics.[104] He argued that it would be "at least four to five hundred years" before the comet could be seen again.[105] Yet this refutation did not seem to matter to most of the people in Königsberg, and most certainly it did not matter to Knutzen and his students. They never acknowledged that Knutzen's prediction had been wrong. In a poem written for the occasion of his burial, he is compared with Newton, Leibniz, Locke, Descartes, and Bayle.

Knutzen's work on the comets was in any case largely motivated by theological concerns. It was written in part as a response to a tract entitled "Attempt of a Consideration of the Comet, the Deluge, and the Prelude of the Final Judgment; in Accordance with Astronomical Reasons and the Bible . . ."[106] Its author was Johann Heyn, who had become notorious as a follower of William Whiston. Among other things, Heyn argued in this tract that the ancient fear of comets as a bad omen was well founded. Knutzen objected to this view. For him, just as for Newton and Wolff, comets were just small planets circling the sun. They took a regular course that could be computed. Though of great interest to the physicist, they did not have to be feared as bad omens. Knutzen concluded, therefore, that Heyn was an alarmist and an obscurantist. Intending to defeat the fear of comets "in its last stronghold," he vehemently attacked Heyn.[107] Heyn responded in kind, accusing Knutzen not only of plagiarism – the prediction had already been made a year earlier in the *Leipziger gelehrte Anzeigen* – but also suggesting that he had not sufficiently proven the identity of the comet of 1698 and the comet of 1744. Knutzen and his students seem to have dismissed Heyn's reference to Euler, just as they rejected Euler's criticism itself.

Knutzen's understanding of scientific and mathematical matters was inadequate to the task of advancing the discussion of the more technical aspects of physics. He did not belong to that "small elite" of scientists on the continent who understood the details of Newtonian physics.[108] His knowledge of calculus was especially deficient. Relying more on mechanical models than on calculations, he had some general understanding of Newton's *Principia* but could not make any original contribution to science. Nor was he willing to draw a sharp line between science and metaphysics. Theological and apologetic concerns dictated what could and could not be accepted at least as much as did scientific views. As a scientist, he was rather limited even by eighteenth-century standards.

Kant followed the comet controversy with at least as much interest as he had the dispute centering on Fischer's book earlier in the year. He became very interested in the subject of cosmogony, and this was one of the reasons why his earliest works deal with such matters. On the other hand, the controversy about Knutzen's comet may also have led to disenchantment with his teachers. Euler's criticisms may have made Kant realize Knutzen's shortcomings as a scientist. In any case, one of the people to whom Kant sent his first work was Euler; and in one of his first essays he dismissed the study of comets as irrelevant to understanding planets such as the Earth.[109]

During his years of study at the University of Königsberg, Kant became acquainted with many different approaches to philosophy, theology, and the natural sciences. While many scholars have viewed the university as more or less outside of the main stream of the intellectual developments of the eighteenth century, or as completely dominated by Pietism, this was not the case. First, any student at the University of Königsberg during the relevant period was exposed not only to Pietistic and Thomasian doctrine, but also to the philosophy of Wolff and his followers. The presentation of

Wolff would have been critical and largely negative, but he was openly discussed. Pietism in Königsberg contained a heavy dose of Wolff, and it was for that reason different from Pietism elsewhere. Furthermore, there were also convinced Wolffians in Königsberg. Few Wolffians were in official positions at the university, but Marquardt was, and there were others among the educated clergy. This had an influence on the discussion. People like Fischer, who held views even more radical than those of the stricter Wolffians, stoked additional fires as well. Secondly, Aristotelianism, while waning, still formed part of Königsberg's intellectual climate at the time. Yet it was not just that the Aristotelian terminology was still pervasive; the substance of Aristotelian logic and metaphysics was not entirely absent either.[110] There may have been few convinced Aristotelians, but the eclectic spirit of some of the earlier Pietists kept this view alive. Finally, and perhaps most importantly, Königsberg scholars were already looking to Britain for the decisive philosophical developments, while the other German universities – with the exception of the new University of Göttingen – remained absorbed in the minutiae of the Wolffian and Thomasian dispute.[111]

Professors like Quandt, Salthenius, and Knutzen, however different they may have been on almost every other matter, saw the real danger to religion coming from the British Isles, not from German philosophers; and some of them – most notably Knutzen – saw the real solution there as well. Furthermore, many of these religious conservatives were epistemologically radical. Bayle and Montaigne were seen not so much as endangering faith, but as refuting a way of thinking the faithful need not adopt. All the ferment of the period and all the recent philosophical ideas were present in Königsberg: it was not an intellectual backwater. The practitioners of philosophy at the university were neither the brightest nor the boldest, but they were competent, and some of them, (Knutzen, for instance) were sound in philosophy. An intelligent young man, such as Kant undoubtedly was, could have picked up all that was necessary for a solid grounding in the discipline, and he would have been provided with all the materials necessary for contributing to what he might have conceived of as the "Growth of the Sciences."[112]

On the other hand, in the physical sciences and especially in astronomy, Königsberg did not have the best the eighteenth century had to offer. Its scientific mediocrity was typical of most other universities in Europe, but it meant that Kant was not well prepared to make original contributions to either theoretical or experimental physics. Apart from the fact that Kant himself was not very mechanically inclined – he later often asked his students to construct physically impossible mechanical models – he also did not find the proper support in the University of Königsberg. Teske's electrical experiments were perhaps the closest he got to real experiments in the sciences. Anything of interest in Kant's early writings on physics attests therefore at least as much to his ingenuity as to his education.

Estimation of the Living Forces: "What Unlocked Kant's Genius?"

Borowski agreed with Kraus that Kant came into his own around 1744, but, more sensibly, he picked out Kant's first work as revealing his independent genius, claiming that Kant "began to work on the *Thoughts on the True Estimation of Living Forces* . . . four years after entering the university."[113] Borowski also claimed that it was "Knutzen *and* Teske" who converted Kant from a study of the classics to philosophy, and who led him in "an unexpected direction," namely, into "the barren fields of philosophy." Their "philosophical, physical, and mathematical lectures, which were indeed excellent for awakening genius and were very entertaining (many of Teske's students still gratefully remember him), powerfully attracted Kant." Borowski says nothing about the comet. Instead, he refers the reader to the Preface to Kant's first work as evidence.[114]

Kant's Preface does not tell us what brought him to write this work. It is an apology of sorts. Kant admits that it might be considered presumptuous of him – a completely unknown author – to criticize such famous thinkers as Newton and Leibniz. He argues that such an undertaking, while it would have been dangerous in earlier times, is now appropriate: "We may now boldly dare to regard the fame of Newton and Leibniz as nothing whenever it would stand in the way of the discovery of the truth," and we should "obey no other authority than that of the understanding."[115] Later in the text he says of metaphysics: "Our science, like many others, has indeed reached only the threshold of a genuinely thorough science. It is not difficult to recognize the weakness in many of the things it attempts. One finds often that prejudice is the greatest strength of its proofs."[116] Neither Teske nor Knutzen are mentioned here (or indeed in any other of his published works).[117] Instead, we find Kant affirming his belief that "at times it is not without benefit to have a certain noble trust in one's ability" and that it might not be the best approach to continue on "the broad highway."[118] He goes out of his way to "declare publicly" that he honors and respects "*the great masters of our knowledge*" whom he is going to attack in this work.[119] In an uncharacteristically immodest way, he proclaims: "I have already prescribed the route I want to take. I will begin my course and nothing shall prevent me from continuing it."[120]

These passages show that Kant has become an independent thinker, and also that he is confident he can make an original contribution to natural philosophy. They do not tell us what led to this – at least not directly. Yet perhaps they do so indirectly. In this work Kant is addressing not just his colleagues in Königsberg, not just the members of the academy, but the German public as a whole. Still a student, he dares to become a participant in what he takes to be a central dispute between some of the most famous thinkers of his age. In a sense, he is going over the heads of his professors, bypassing the discussion within the university, as it were, and asserting his right to be an equal participant in the philosophical discussion of the period.

It is just as interesting to note again what Kant does not do. If he had followed the common career of a talented philosophy student at the University of Königsberg, he would have written a dissertation in Latin, submitted it, become a *Magister* of philosophy, and then begun teaching at the university or at one of the high schools in Königsberg.[121] One of the questions that must therefore be asked – but to my knowledge never has been – is: "Why did Kant not present this early work as a dissertation to the university?"[122] Instead of expending his energy on fulfilling an academic requirement that would have allowed him to pursue his interests by teaching the very things he was interested in, why did he choose to write this work in German? He could have written it in Latin, and he must have been sufficiently confident of its merit. Instead, he wrote a work that could not possibly have advanced him institutionally. At the very least, this act could make him seem presumptuous and make enemies for him in Königsberg.

We do not know for certain why Kant chose this course of action, but the tone of defiance that comes through in his introduction suggests that it was connected to the situation that existed in the institution he attended. In the dedication he talks of his "low" status or "*Niedrigkeit*," and in the book itself he repeatedly speaks of himself as "common" or "*schlecht*." His attack on "the great masters of knowledge" was not directed just at Leibniz and Newton, and his insistence that nothing would hinder him in achieving his goals suggests that he was talking not only to the German public in general but also to the Königsberg academic community in particular. He wanted to be noticed. He felt insufficiently appreciated by the members of the philosophical faculty – and perhaps especially by Knutzen. Or was there perhaps – at least in his eyes – positive disregard and discrimination against him? Was he treated in the way he thought he deserved? His planned dissertation may in fact have been dismissed by those who would have had to approve it, or he may never have planned to submit the work as a dissertation because he felt it would be rejected.

There is evidence that Kant was not as well appreciated as Borowski would have us believe. Borowski claimed that "Knutzen, a wise judge of heads, found in Kant excellent talents, encouraged him in private conversations and later lent him Newton, and, since Kant liked it, anything else he wanted from his rich library."[123] It is of significance that he made these claims in passages that Kant himself did not see, and that in the passages that Kant did see, he said only that Kant attended Knutzen's classes, and that he was the teacher whom Kant liked most.[124] This may well be true. It may also be true that Knutzen lent him Newton – something that was not unusual at a time when there was no university library.

It is obvious from the record that Knutzen did *not* regard Kant as one of his best students. Kant was not even mentioned by Knutzen's early biographers as one of his students. On the other hand, there is evidence that one of his favorite students was Friedrich Johann Buck (1722–1786). Not much older than Kant, Buck held at least on one occasion *repetitoria* (review sessions) for Knutzen. Buck was also the one who continued Knutzen's lectures after his death in 1751, and he continued Knutzen's scientific correspondence. Clearly, Knutzen considered Buck to be much more important than Kant. Another student Knutzen valued more than Kant was Johann Friedrich Weitenkampf (1726–1758). He had entered the university two years after Kant, but Knutzen, the "wise judge of heads," regarded him so highly that he had him read at the bicentenniary of the University of Königsberg – significantly also in 1744 – a speech on how useful academies are for the welfare of nations. Knutzen also saw to it that this speech was published. Kant, perhaps understandably, did not like Weitenkampf. In his *General Natural History,* he attacked Weitenkampf in a pointed fashion, claiming that Weitenkampf's arguments against the infinity of the world – which also expressed one of Knutzen's main concerns – prove only that he is one of those who do not know enough about metaphysics.[125] Indirectly, Kant dismissed Knutzen as well.

How little Knutzen thought of Kant is shown also by the fact that Kant's name is not to be found among the many students mentioned as outstanding in his correspondence with Euler.[126] Thus Borowski's report may well be misleading: Kant was not necessarily a protégé of Knutzen. The great Knutzen, predictor of the course of comets, was not his mentor, and he did not support his further career. If Kant did not become a theologian "because he was opposed to Pietism," then Knutzen – had he found this out – would have had grounds for disliking Kant. At the very least, he would have had grounds for predicting a dim future for Kant in Königsberg.[127] Kant, on the other hand, must have disliked some of Knutzen's propositions of "experience." The work he began in 1744 may have been more of a reaction against Knutzen than one that was positively inspired by Knutzen.

To be sure, the work shows every sign of coming out of the intellectual milieu fostered by Knutzen. It is more speculative than mathematical, even if it deals with a question that was still important.[128] Euler's *Mechanica sive motus scientia* of 1736 had already moved the question to a different plane.[129] He had tried – with great success – to formulate and solve the problems of mechanics-dynamics in a mathematical way. It is not clear whether Kant, as a student of Knutzen, whose mathematical skills were hardly up to the task of understanding Euler's *Mechanica*, knew this work then. In any case, Kant framed the problem in metaphysical terms, just as one would expect from anyone who went through this school.

In other ways, the *True Estimation of the Living Forces* shows – at least indirectly – that Kant was on his own. Nothing would prevent him from "taking his course." In old age Kant made clear to one of his biographers that he had tried from his "youth" to be autonomous and independent of everyone, so that he "could live for himself and his duty, and not for others. This independence he declared . . . to be the foundation of all happiness."[130]

In his first public expression of independence, Kant wrestled with one of the central disputes in German natural philosophy during the early part of the eighteenth century, namely the problem of the measurement of force. Late in the previous century, Leibniz had opposed the Cartesian theory that matter was completely inert. Leibniz saw Cartesian physics as an attempt to explain all of nature by what he called "dead force." He differentiated between this "dead force" (*vis mortua* or *conatus*) and "living force" (*vis viva*). Living force was for him also the force of motion. Dead force, he thought, did not arise from motion itself but initiated new motion and explained changes in motion. This distinction was connected to the difference between the Cartesian and the Leibnizian account of the world. Whereas the Cartesians believed that "the nature of body consisted of inert mass (*massa*) alone," Leibniz argued that something else needed to be postulated to account for the phenomena.[131] Saying that he did not care whether this principle was called "form," "entelechy," or "force," he claimed that it was central for understanding motion. The Cartesians were wrong in equating a body's moving force with the (scalar) momentum, the product that results from multiplying the quantity of motion (speed) with the weight of the body. He argued that there was an important difference between speed and force, and that more than twice the force must be present to give something twice the speed, and that living force actually equals mv^2 (where m = mass and v = velocity). This theory of how force is measured thus has deep roots within Leibnizian metaphysics, and some of the arguments Leibniz adduces are more metaphysical than empirical in nature. The Newtonians, who were not interested in such hypotheses, also opted for an account of moving force in terms of "momentum" rather than "living force." The dispute between the Leibnizians and the Cartesians was fierce. What was the true measure of force? Was it Descartes's momentum or Leibniz's "living force?" Newton, whose position about the activity of matter was intermediate between the positions of Descartes and Leibniz, made the problem more difficult.[132] Like Leibniz, he criticized the Cartesian concept of inert matter and included forces in his conception of matter, but Newton emphasized what he called the *vis impressa*, which corresponded to Leibniz's *vis mortua*, and he tried to exclude *vis viva* entirely from physics. On the other hand, both Leibniz and Newton thought that there was a "force of resistance" proportional to the quantity of matter, resident in every body, and this fitted "neatly into Leibniz' general account of matter as dynamic."[133]

Kant began his discussion explicitly with some "metaphysical concepts."[134] He wanted to mediate between the parties, arguing that both parties were wrong and that neither of them could describe all of nature. He thought the Leibnizians had perhaps the most severe problems. Mathematics proved them wrong, because it "allows no other measure of force than the old *Cartesian* one."[135] The mathematical definition of "body" allows only external relations between bodies as far as mechanics is concerned. Most of the book is concerned with showing that the Leibnizian arguments against this position are insufficient.

In a somewhat surprising turn of argument, Kant goes on to argue in the third part of his book that the mathematical definition of "body" is not necessarily the only or the correct definition of physical bodies. He now "presents a new estimation of the living forces as the true measure of force in nature."[136] Arguing that the axioms of mathematics may exclude certain characteristics that physical or natural bodies may nevertheless really possess, he tries to show that they may therefore contain an internal principle that causes them to exert force. Such a body may "increase within itself the force which has been awakened in it by the cause of an external motion."[137] Kant calls the motion caused by such an internal principle a "free motion," that is, a motion whose speed always remains the same. The measure of the speed of bodies in free or infinite motion, as he also calls it, is living force. While the measure of all other motions is momentum, free motion must be understood along Leibnizian lines. What is important to Kant is that living force is possible only if there are free motions.[138] Yet we cannot prove that there are free motions. We can only assume them as a hypothesis. The theory of living forces is also only a hypothesis, and this is, as Kant points out, all that Leibniz meant to say in the *Theodicee*.[139] Kant's new theory turns out to be a defense and modification of Leibniz's theory of living forces.

It also seems to be related to Newton's ideas about "active force." *Vis inertia* was not sufficient for Newton to explain the variety (or perhaps better, the quantity) of motion, which is constantly decreasing and always "upon the decay." We must therefore, he argued, postulate active principles, which explain why the world does not come to a standstill. Newton could never decide "what that principle is, and by means of [what] laws it acts on matter." It was "a mystery," and he did not know how it was related to matter.[140] Kant thought that he could connect this thought with Leibnizian ideas about living forces.

The doctrine of living forces was connected to the theory of monads. Leibniz believed that a completely materialistic or mechanistic explanation of the phenomena was impossible and therefore posited form, entelechy, and force as an internal principle of substances. Kant accepted this view. When he differentiates between mathematical bodies and natural bodies, and when he assigns an internal force to natural bodies that enables them to have free motion, he seems simply to be following Leibniz, but he is not. Rather, he is following, or perhaps better, developing, Baumgarten, a Wolffian who moved closer to Leibniz than did any of his other Wolffian contemporaries. Baumgarten tried to defend preestablished harmony against physical influx by giving up the claim that monads do not act on each other. Like Kant, he claimed *"monades in se mutuo influunt"* ("monads influence each other").[141] This is – or it seems to be – different from what Leibniz proposed. Leibniz did not believe that monads interact, or that they stand in real external relations with each other.

Though some of Kant's (and Baumgarten's) observations were meant to modify Leibniz's view, these modifications were not meant to be of a fundamental nature. In fact, Kant claims that if he had more time, he would show that his theory could do justice to Leibniz's "theory of universal order and harmony," which has been made so "praiseworthy" by Leibniz's view of living forces. Indeed, he goes so far as to claim that he has completed "some sketches" in which he is doing precisely that.[142] Kant seems to say that he accepts the Leibnizian theory of preestablished harmony. Indeed, his "new system" may be understood as giving a new foundation for this Leibnizian doctrine.[143] Yet Kant's preestablished harmony is different from that of Leibniz in the sense that what is preestablished is not just the internal states of substances, but both the internal states of substances *and* their interactions. Furthermore, their interactions are of primary importance for establishing a world. Still, Kant remains a Leibnizian in one crucial respect: the order of the world is preestablished, and the internal principles of the substances are in harmony with their external relations.[144] This means that he accepts a modified theory of preestablished harmony as the correct systematic account of the world as a whole.

While Kant accepts physical influx as the correct account of certain kinds of motions, he thinks that it cannot explain all of reality. It can only account for external causality. The internal principles of substances obey different laws. God (and his preestablished harmony) is required to keep the internal and external forces in harmony. What consequences does this have for our understanding of a passage that occurs very early in the book, and that is often used to argue that Kant was an influxionist? In this passage, Kant claims that "an acute author was kept from perfecting the triumph of physical influx over preestablished harmony by nothing more than by this slight confusion of concepts, from which one can easily extract oneself as soon as one pays attention to it."[145] This confusion concerns the soul. In particular, it concerns the question of whether the soul, being an immaterial being, can cause motion in matter. Kant argues that this question loses its paradoxical appearance as soon as we understand that the soul can and must be said to have a "place" or "*Ort.*" Claiming that the word "place" means just the "mutual interaction of substances," he can argue that any substance that interacts with other substances has a place. If the soul has a place – and it does – then it can interact with other substances. This means that the problem of how a soul can cause motion can be solved. Kant also claims that it would be better to speak of force "in terms of effects in other substances, which, however would not be further determined," and not in terms of motion.[146]

It has often been suggested that Kant had Knutzen in mind here. Knutzen did indeed maintain that the soul had a place or was "*in loco.*" He had also tried to prove that the theory of physical influx was *probable* on the basis of the "locality" of the soul. His argument went something like this: (1) The soul is "*in loco*" (in a place) because it is embodied. (2) That the soul possesses movement of its own is proved by the fact that its body moves often. Therefore, (3) the soul possesses a movement of its own. Therefore, (4) it can move other things. The problematic character of premises (1) and (2) is too obvious to need discussion. Neither Descartes nor Leibniz would have seen anything more in them than a confusion of what was at issue in the mind–body problem. Kant simply claims that to have "a place" or to be "*in loco*" means to stand in "mutual interaction" with other substances. This claim – regardless of whether it has any other merits – is preferable to Knutzen's. His work seeks then to improve his teacher's account. Not only does he intend to replace probability with certainty, he also wishes to correct Knutzen.

More needs to be said. First, Kant is sarcastic: a slight confusion prevents perfect triumph – and is the confusion really that slight? If the "acute author" is indeed Knutzen, then this is a put-down. Second, there is no reason to suppose that Kant really believed that physical influx would ever triumph over preestablished harmony in the way Knutzen believed it could, that is, by replacing it. What Kant says is quite compatible with the view that physical influx was a perfect triumph in one area, namely, as far as dead force and external causality is concerned, but not as far as the systematic account of the whole is concerned.

The theory of preestablished harmony in its strictest form was unacceptable to Knutzen and the other Pietists in Königsberg for theological reasons. It seemed to them to conflict with a belief in the freedom of the will and to lead to a thorough determinism and fatalism. Thus, while Knutzen uses the word "monad," his monads are different from Leibniz's. They are characterized by "intellect and free will" ("*intellectu et libera voluntate*"), and they are entirely immaterial. Knutzen explicitly rejects Leibniz's theory that monads mirror the universe and that they are the substantial unities that make up all things. "*Substantia simplex sive monas*" (simple substance or monad) is identical to "*spiritus,*" or mind, for him. Kant, in adopting Leibniz's "theory of universal order and harmony," was thus arguing for a position unacceptable to Knutzen and the Pietists. In some ways, his position in the *Living Forces* is as close to those of Marquardt and Rappolt (and even Fischer) as it is to the Pietistic position. Neither Knutzen nor

anyone else in the Pietistic faction would have been open-minded enough
to overlook this departure from the party line, even if they could have forgiven the quip about the slight confusion of a certain "acute author." To
use Wolffian principles was one thing, but to endorse the theory of preestablished harmony was quite another.

The book may thus be viewed as an act of defiance. Kant rejected one
of the major tenets of his teacher. It is an expression of his "opposition to
Pietism," and it could not pass the scrutiny of the Pietists. This probably
explains in part why it could not become a doctoral thesis and why he felt
he had to leave Königsberg.

The process that led to this break had started as early as 1744. One of
the reasons it took so long for him to leave can be found in an important
event in Kant's personal life. The year 1744 was significant not just for the
Fischer controversy and for Knutzen's comet. Late that year Kant's father
fell seriously ill, suffering a stroke which led to his death "of complete exhaustion" a year and a half later, on the 24th of March 1746.[147] This radically changed Kant's life. His older sister was twenty-five, his two younger
sisters were seventeen and fourteen, and his little brother was only nine
years old. It is likely that two of the sisters were already out of the house,
working in someone else's household, and that only his youngest sister and
his brother were at home. Kant, as the oldest son, was all at once responsible for the entire family. The sister probably could have taken care of the
father and brother tolerably well, and the older sisters as well as their relatives helped. Nevertheless, some of the work fell to Kant, and his freedom
of study was severely hampered. Kant must have taken his duties seriously.
In the *Metaphysics of Morals* he gives the example of a man who gave up
his plan to pursue some pleasurable activity "immediately, though reluctantly, at the thought that by carrying it out he would omit one of his duties
as an official *or neglect a sick father*," and who in doing so proves his freedom in the highest degree.[148] This example was not fictional.[149] He must
have spent a significant amount of time at home with his family during
1745, and it is likely that he wrote most of his *Estimation* during this very
period, when he was unable regularly to attend lectures and recitations. In
any case, he did not submit the book to the censor until the summer semester of 1746, that is, not until after his father had died.[150]

Kant left Königsberg shortly after August 1748.[151] A significant part of
the two years between his father's death and his departure must have been
spent taking care of the estate. As Kant himself says in a late letter: not much
was left after everything was settled. Still, it would have taken time to sell

the house, the tools, and the equipment of his father, and to see to it that his brothers and sisters were taken care of. No matter what motive Kant might have had for leaving Königsberg, he could not have departed before those matters were settled. During this period (in 1747) Kant also added a number of emendations to the book and wrote the dedication to Johann Christoph Bohlius, a professor of medicine at the University of Königsberg. He lived at least part of the time with a fellow student who helped him – as did his uncle. After his family affairs had been settled, however, there was little to keep him in Königsberg – especially since he saw no possibility of advancing at the university.

His book was noticed. There were some reviews.[152] Gotthold Ephraim Lessing wrote a derisive epigram about it, saying:

> Kant, commencing the hardest of courses,
> is daring the world to educate,
> and investigates the living forces.
> But his own he fails to estimate.[153]

In his anthropology, Kant observes the following:

The age at which we obtain the complete use of reason may be determined as follows: [i] as far as the facility (to use it competently to achieve any goal) is concerned it is approximately the twentieth year, [ii] as far as calculation (to use other human beings for one's own purposes) is concerned, it is the fortieth year, and [iii] the age of wisdom begins around sixty. The latter age is entirely negative. We are finally able to recognize all the foolish mistakes we made in the first two.[154]

This suggests that he felt he had the necessary maturity to deal with technical questions of philosophy at age twenty-two or twenty-four, but that he had no clear idea of what this would bring him. Lessing's epigram was certainly false, if it is taken as a prediction of what Kant would do. Properly, Lessing suppressed this epigram in later editions of his work.

Private Teacher: "There May Never Have Been a Worse Hofmeister"

While Kant's student years were not easy – and not just for financial reasons – they must, on the whole, have been rewarding. They were years of freedom and intellectual growth. In 1748, having concluded his formal studies at the university and having lost his father, he was facing an uncertain future. He was entirely on his own at the age of twenty-four, and his life changed fundamentally. Borowski claimed that "because of a lack

of means he became a private teacher (*Hofmeister*), and took up employment
first with the reformed preacher Andersch in Judtschen, then at the estate
von Hülsen close to Arensdorf, and finally with the Count Keyserlingk."[155]
This decision to become a private teacher was not directly caused by the
death of his father.[156] Nor could it have been simply "lack of funds," because that had always been a problem. It is doubtful that it was his first
choice to leave Königsberg to teach young children in the country. Why
did he not try to find a place as a teacher at one of the schools in Königsberg? To be a *Hofmeister*, or a "lackey companion and teacher," who usually was not much better than a servant, could not have been a desirable
prospect.[157] It may have seemed to him to be the only way to support himself. Indeed, it was usually the only way for young and poor academics, who
had neither a future at the university nor the right kind of letter of recommendation, to bridge the gap between the years of study and a position
as a pastor, teacher, or official of the government. It was meant to be an
"interim position."[158] Yet, this wait was usually long, and success was far
from assured.

Kant was uncommonly lucky in his choice of employers, Pastor Andersch,
Bernhard Friedrich von Hülsen, and the Keyserlingks. He was probably
in Judtschen between fall 1748 and fall 1751.[159] Judtschen was close to
Königsberg, and Pastor Andersch belonged to the Reformed Church, that
is, to the Calvinist denomination, not the Lutheran one. He ministered to
the French Huguenots, who had come to Prussia under Frederick William
I.[160] Judtschen was a fairly prosperous town, settled by these Huguenot
immigrants. Both the pastor and judge were usually French-speaking, and
so the German-speaking pastor was an oddity. He had been given his position over the protests of his French-speaking congregation in 1728. Over
the years he had become more and more acceptable to them, and was eventually well liked by many of the farmers. On the other hand, Andersch had
problems with his Lutheran colleagues.

Having a good income, Andersch could afford to educate his five sons
well. Kant was hired to teach three of them. One of Kant's charges was
Timotheus (1736–1818), who later became a wine merchant in Königsberg.
He also became Kant's friend. His older brother, Ernst Daniel (1730–
1802), had already left the house to go to high school in Berlin. He later
studied theology and became a pastor of the Reformed Church in Königsberg. Not much is known about Kant's stay in Judtschen, but he had some
social relations with the members of the congregation, being asked twice

to be godfather during this period. Though the pastor's family spoke German, Kant also had to speak French to at least some of the members of the congregation. If so inclined, he could have practiced his French quite easily.[161] He also had to attend some of the services at the Reformed Church, and while Andersch was probably no great theologian, his sermons were different from those of the Königsberg Pietists. Given the differences between strict Lutheran and Reformed Protestants – differences that for a long time prevented anyone belonging to the Reformed Church from taking an oath of allegiance to the University of Königsberg – it is significant that Kant allowed himself to become a godfather to someone from the Reformed Church.

After three years in this community, Kant left to enter the services of von Hülsen, a Prussian knight who owned a large estate near Arnsberg. The town was located approximately sixty miles southwest of Königsberg.[162] There, Kant instructed the three older sons of the family, probably for several years. This family liked him, for after he left, they continued to write to him and to "make him a participant in any interesting occasion in the family."[163] When he was back in Königsberg (August 10, 1754) Kant sent them two textbooks in history and Latin as well as pictures for the youngest two boys, asking that everyone be "a good example" to this "little fine man," who was born in 1750.[164] Two of the sons later lodged with Kant when they studied at the University of Königsberg, and Kant later recommended teachers for the children of one of his former charges.

Kant himself thought that he was probably the worst private teacher, or *Hofmeister*, who ever lived. "One of his most unpleasant" dreams was that he was again such a teacher. He also admitted that the profession of a teacher "always appeared [to him] as the most bothersome." But he was very likely a better teacher than he thought.[165] The way in which the families of his pupils stayed in contact with him suggests that they thought him to be a good teacher and a good person. Their friendly overtures also suggest that he probably did not have to suffer the ignominies that many poor private teachers had to endure in noble families.

During his time as a *Hofmeister*, Kant not only polished his manners and his skills in polite society, but also pursued independent studies. We do not know how much time Kant had for private study, but Borowski claims that he drew up the basic outline of some of his later works during this period and even produced drafts of parts of them: "he collected in his miscellanies from all the parts of human knowledge all that seemed somehow useful to him – and he still thinks with great satisfaction back to this period."[166] Kant never gave up his academic citizenship and continued to be a "student." He probably always planned to return to the University of Königsberg.

By August 1754, after about six years of absence, Kant was back in Königsberg, preparing his dissertation, working on his second major German work, and preparing essays that would appear in short order. The university had changed during his absence. Knutzen was dead, and some of Kant's fellow students had already obtained positions. Many others had left and taken positions outside the university or outside of Königsberg. Kant himself was single-minded in his pursuit of a position at his alma mater. At the same time, he probably was also the supervisor of a member of the Keyserlingk family who was studying at the University of Königsberg.[167] In any case, during that year he published two essays in the weekly *Königsbergische Frag- und Anzeigungs-Nachrichten*. The first, entitled "Investigation of the Question whether the Earth Has Experienced a Change in Its Rotation . . . ," appeared in the issues of June 8 and 15. It was meant to answer a question formulated for a public competition by the Berlin Academy. Though the deadline was at first 1754, the Academy extended it on June 6, 1754, for another two years. When Kant decided to publish this essay, he did not know of the extension. Kant claimed that he could not have achieved the kind of perfection required for winning the prize because he restricted himself to the "physical aspect" of the question.[168] More importantly, he used the essay to call attention to a book that would soon appear with the title, "Cosmogony or Attempt to Derive the Origin of the Cosmos, the Formation of the Heavenly Bodies and the Causes of Their Motions from the General Laws of the Motion of Matter According to Newton's Theory."[169] The second essay was on "The Question whether the Earth is Aging, Considered from the Point of View of Physics." It appeared in six parts in August and September of 1754. In it, he tried to clarify what the question means "*without* considering the comets, which some have, for some time now, found easy explanations for any extraordinary event."[170] Comets are just as irrelevant to the question of the aging of the earth "as earthquakes and fires are to the question of how buildings age."[171]

At the same time, Kant was also working on the book he had already called attention to in his essay. Its final title was *General Natural History and Theory of the Heavens, or an Essay on the Constitution and Mechanical Origin of the Whole Universe, Treated in Accordance with Newtonian Principles*.[172] Kant knew that it would appear dangerous to those of "true faith," if only because it would immediately be recognized as belonging to the tradition of "Lucretius or his predecessors Epicurus, Leucippus, and Democritus." Not denying its heritage, he argued that he "did not begin to plan this enterprise until he was certain that he was safe with regard to the duties of religion."[173] He claimed he knew that he was again (or still?) treading on dangerous ground, but that he had to continue on his course: "I see all these difficulties, yet I do not despair. I feel the whole strength of these hindrances, which stand in the way, but I do not give up."[174] Kant also must have known that the despair and the difficulties were not necessarily as great as all that, if only because the king – and he was the one who ultimately was going to make or break his career – would not be overly worried by "the duties of religion." It was hardly an accident that the book was dedicated to him. What was an accident was that the publisher of the book went bankrupt, and that the court impounded his entire stock. The *General Natural History* did not cause so much as a murmur among the zealots – only a review. The book was even less successful than his first, but by this time he had also planned his academic advancement at the university.

The Elegant *Magister*
(1755–1764)

First Years (1755–1758): "An Excellent Brain"

O N APRIL 17, 1755, Kant handed in his dissertation for the *Magister* degree in philosophy. It was entitled "Succinct Meditations on Fire," and was not much more than an uncontroversial exposition of views derived from those of Teske.[1] His uncle Richter paid the necessary fees for Kant's promotion.[2] Four weeks later there was a public examination, and on June 12 he received the doctorate. Hahn, who was the professor who had first inscribed Kant's name into the register of the citizens of the university, gave a lecture "On the Honorable Titles of the Old Jews at Their Academic Promotions: Rabh, Rabbi, and Rabbon." Kant's topic was "On Easy and Thorough Instruction in Philosophy."[3] Borowski noted that there was "a rare congregation of learned men," and that "the entire auditorium showed through its quietness and attention the proper honor to the *Magister* to be."[4] Kant had achieved a reputation, or at least some notoriety. The scholars and intellectuals connected with the University of Königsberg were expecting much from him. That this is true can also be seen from one of Hamann's letters to his brother, in which he asks that Kant's dissertation be sent to him, for Kant is "an excellent brain" ("*fürtrefflicher Kopf*").[5] In 1755, Kant was no longer an unknown quantity – at least not in Königsberg.

In order to be able to teach, or to receive the "*venia legendi,*" Kant, like every other scholar, had to defend another dissertation. In fulfillment of his requirement, Kant submitted his "New Exposition of the First Principles of Metaphysical Knowledge," which he defended on September 27, 1755. In this work he attempted to answer the question, "What are the ultimate grounds of the possibility of truth?" or "What must be granted for anything else to be true?" Kant discussed and rejected as truly basic the two basic principles of Leibniz and Wolff, namely the principle of contradiction and the principle of sufficient reason. The first, which amounts to the claim that it is impossible for the same thing to be and not to be at the same time, is really just the definition of the impossible, and is subordinate to the principle of identity. Indeed, the principle of identity would be the basic principle, if it were one principle, but Kant argued that it really consists of two: the principle "whatever is, is," which holds for positive truths, and the principle "whatever is not, is not," which holds for negative truths. Nevertheless, the principle of contradiction is a basic principle in the sense that it is irreducible and necessary, even if it is not the very first principle.

In the same way, Kant modified and defined the principle of sufficient reason. Calling it, with Christian August Crusius, the principle of determining reason, he rejected Wolff's definition of it as circular, raised a number of difficulties with regard to it, but ultimately defended it. In particular, he addressed Crusius's claim that this principle leads to the "Stoic fate," thus "impairing all freedom and morality." This argument was not new, but Crusius had put it forward "in greater detail and more forcefully."[6] Therefore, the principle of sufficient reason had to be defended anew. Kant did so at length, thus endorsing again one of the basic tenets of Leibnizian philosophy. Rejecting two other principles that were usually thought to follow from the principle of sufficient reason, he offered two principles of his own: (1) the principle of succession, that is, substances can change only insofar as they are connected to other substances; their reciprocal dependence determines how much they change; and (2) the principle of coextension: "finite substances by their mere existence are unrelated," and they are related only insofar as they are maintained by the will of God as the common principle of their existence. The divine intellect maintains them "in a systematic pattern of mutual relations."

Kant meant to offer a new system. He called it "the system of the universal connection of substances." It can do justice to what is correct in the theory of physical influx as well as to what is correct in the theory of preestablished harmony, but it should not be identified with either. This dissertation thus represented in an important sense the promised sequel to the *Living Forces*. Kant tried to show how efficient causality with regard to the external relations of substances is compatible with changes "that happen internally" and are based on internal principles. Efficient causality represents dead forces, the internal changes represent living forces, but God ultimately is the source of both, and God keeps them in harmony.

This work outlined the metaphysical underpinnings of the kind of middle system that the *Living Forces* had proposed. It was intended to overcome the defects of the "crude theory of physical influence" and the defects of Leibniz.[7] The harmony that Kant spoke of was not *pre*-established, but was established by "the mutual connection of things." At the same time, Kant believed that this system was compatible with true faith. Characteristically, he closed the dissertation by noting that there are certainly

those who are consumed with a passion to hunt down distorted conclusions from published works, and are clever at extracting a kind of venom from the way others think. As a matter of fact, it is perhaps possible that even in these views of ours, they may twist something into a bad meaning . . . I believe it is my part to let them luxuriate in their opinion and not to worry that anyone perhaps may be disposed to judge my work incorrectly. My business is to continue vigorously along the straight path of investigation in a way appropriate to science. Accordingly, I ask, with proper respect, that those who desire to see the liberal arts prosper may favor my efforts.[8]

Echoing the Preface to the *Living Forces*, he promises to continue on the course he started there without worrying about those who might continue to persecute him for religious reasons.

Closely connected to the dissertation or the "New Exposition" was the dissertation of 1756, entitled "The Use in Natural Philosophy of Metaphysics Combined with Geometry, Part I: Physical Monadology." Frederick II had ruled that one could obtain the position of full professor only after holding at least three public defenses. The "Physical Monadology" was submitted to fulfill this requirement.[9] Kant defended it on April 10, 1756. This work represents a further explication of the systematic background of his physical theories. We can see that his fundamental position had not changed between 1746 and 1756. He was still opting for the system that mediates between Newton or Descartes and Leibniz. A full account of reality must involve monads, or "active beings," whose nature cannot be explained by mathematical space with its arbitrary definitions. "Space . . . is divisible *in infinitum*, and does not consist of simple parts."[10] Bodies, on the other hand, consist of simple elements, which cannot be divided any further. One of Kant's most central points of the "Physical Monadology" was to show that the indivisibility or simplicity of monads is not contradictory to the infinite divisibility of space. Kant offered as a reason that space, as Leibniz had pointed out, is not substantial but "a phenomenon of certain external relations of substances."[11] The monad "occupies" space by its activity. It hinders other things from entering into its sphere of activity. Indeed, the "force by which the simple element of a body fills its space is the same as that which others call impenetrability. If the former force is denied, there cannot be a place for the latter."[12] While Kant's middle system shares certain features with Boscovich's doctrine, it is perhaps more indebted to Baumgarten, for whom impenetrability was also the basic character of physical monads. Kant probably was encouraged in this view by Euler, who in his *Recherches sur l'origin des forces* of 1752 had also argued that impenetrability was one of the basic characteristics of matter.[13] Characteristically, however, he did not accept – at least at this time – Euler's arguments for absolute space, but continued to hold onto the Leibnizian view.

While Kant wanted his system to be identified neither with physical influx nor with universal harmony, it generally seems to have been viewed as either the one or the other. The Pietists would have been very worried about its similarities to preestablished harmony, but it was not just the Pietists with whom Kant had to contend. The traditional Wolffians were opposed to his attempt to mediate between the theory of physical influx and the more Leibnizian theory of Baumgarten. Flottwell wrote on April 20, 1756:

The young men are hopping like woodpeckers around us older ones. They are pursuing us with envy, with derision, and with new thoughts; and God knows that, just as it goes with jurisprudence in Prussia, so especially philosophy is made into a waxen nose. A young *Magister* has already proven that there is a *simplex compositum* (a simple complex), which has no parts, however. Therefore *simplex* and *spiritus* must be *in spatio* and *loco*. Mr. Crusius' philosophical new births make just as much noise as Klopstock does in poetry and rhetoric. Anyone who has neither time nor year for investigating such dallying (*Tändeley*) is called an *ignoramus*, and it still is true: this is the best world.[14]

So much for Kant's efforts at showing that infinite divisibility of space was not opposed to simple physical monads: it represented mere dallying for the older Wolffians.

The feelings of Hamann and other younger intellectuals in Königsberg were more ambivalent. Thus Hamann, in responding to Lindner, said that he had not found the dissertation as enjoyable as he had expected, and he also tried to convince Lindner that Kant's view, according to which monads have elastic, repulsive and attractive forces, was "more natural" than the view that they are individuated by representations. He reported: "I, for my part, have often asked myself when confronted with Kant's bright ideas (*Einfälle*): why hasn't anyone thought about the matter in this way before? It seems so easy to accept his view. Perhaps the continuation will bring better materials, and I am curious to read them." Hamann was more interested in the promise of what was to come than in what Kant had delivered. He expected Kant "to abstract more purely about the concept of space than others," after having refuted "different deceptions of the power of imagination."[15] Hamann did not find everything he was looking for, but Kant's "bright ideas" did fascinate him. What we see in Hamann's letter may well be a glimpse of the earliest reputation of Kant. He had many "bright ideas," which looked promising, even if they were not always well thought out.

Kant's academic disputations form the background of the more popular work on cosmogony that appeared in 1755, namely the so-called *General History*. The plan for writing this work dated back to 1751, when Kant read in the *Hamburgischen freien Urtheile* a review of Thomas Wright of Durham's theory of the universe.[16] Parts of the work were probably written during his absence from Königsberg, but it was most likely completed there.[17] In any case, it was published "at the advice of his friends" so that his system would be noticed by the king and therefore might be further investigated and perhaps be given mathematical precision by others.

Some philosophical scholars believe that the *General History* contradicts the claims that Kant advanced in his formal Latin writings or that, at the very least, the work is so different in style and doctrine from them that it almost seems as if it had been written by a different man. But this is not really so. To be sure, the academic writings are very formal. They had to be. Kant had to obey the language and the form of the academy. The *General History* addresses a wider audience. It deals, moreover, with a strictly physical problem, namely the material origin of the world. The other writings deal either with exclusively metaphysical problems or with problems concerning the application of metaphysics to physics. In the *General History*, metaphysics has receded into the background. In it, Kant wanted to show how we could explain, by mechanical principles alone, how the world arose. The mechanical principles were of course those of Newton.[18]

Kant postulated, "as an immediate consequence of God's being," a kind of basic matter that fills the entire universe. Though this basic matter had from the start a basic striving for perfection, implanted in it by God, it was at first without motion. The first motion cannot come from God; it must be derived from the forces of nature itself. Kant tried to derive it by using the force of attraction, which causes the matter, which is unevenly distributed in the universe, to contract into a central body. On the other hand, there is also the force of repulsion, which causes the parts of matter that are moving toward the central body to collide and form other bodies, which move in different directions. Through the interactions of the forces of attraction and repulsion, rotation resulted, and numerous planetary systems slowly formed. The process took millions of years. It did not happen at an instance, as many of the creationists held. Perhaps more importantly, Kant held that it would continue forever. The universe is infinite in space and time. If this was not enough to raise eyebrows in Königsberg, Kant went on to speculate that we are not the only inhabitants of this universe but that there is intelligent life on other planets. Though Kant did not raise the question whether Christ died for extraterrestrials as well, or whether perhaps he had to die on other planets again, it would have been a question uppermost in the minds of most of his readers in Königsberg. When Kant imagined that it might be possible that our soul continued to live on one of these other planets, he stepped over the line of theological propriety. There was also a long section called "On Creation in the Entire Extent of Its Infinity in Both Space and Time," in which Kant argued that though the world had a beginning, it did not have an end. In this context he also fiercely contested some of the theories of another student of Knutzen – Weitenkampf – who, like his teacher, had argued against the infinity of the world.

More important than these theological musings is the fact that Kant did not use any theological principles to explain nature. Teleological considerations based on God's plans or on the principle of sufficient reason had no place in physics for him. Kant's mechanistic explanation of the world dispensed with them. All that he needed was matter and force. "Give me matter, and I will show how the world arose."

The doctrine Kant developed in the *General History* was very similar to a theory put forward in 1796 by Laplace. Accordingly, it was known and highly esteemed during the nineteenth century as the "Kant-Laplace Theory."[19] However, it does not seem to have had much of an impact during Kant's own life. Partly as a result of the bankruptcy of his publisher, most of the copies of Kant's book were destroyed (*eingestampft*), and the rest was distributed only during the sixties, without causing much of a stir. So, Kant's second attempt at becoming a popular writer known beyond the confines of Königsberg had also failed. It is even doubtful whether Frederick II, to whom the volume was dedicated, ever saw the work.

As a *Magister* and *Privatdozent* or lecturer, Kant was now allowed to teach university courses.[20] He received no salary from the university, having to make a living from the fees he could collect from the students who attended his lectures. How much money he had and how well he lived, would depend upon the number of students he attracted. It was a difficult way of making a living, and many other lecturers had to rely on other income.

The lectures and disputations of the *Magisters* were held not in official lecture halls of the university, but in private lecture halls that the *Magisters* either owned or rented. Borowski reports:

> I attended his first lecture in 1755. He lived then in professor Kypke's house in the *Neustadt,* and he had there a fairly large lecture hall. It, as well as the stairway and the entrance hall, were filled with an almost incredible number of students. This seemed to make Kant quite embarrassed. Unused to this situation, he almost lost his composure, spoke even more softly than usual, often correcting himself. This just gave us a more lively and wonderful impression of the man whom we presumed to be the most learned and who seemed to us just modest and not fearful. In the next lecture matters were already quite different. His delivery was, just as in the following lectures, not only thorough, but also liberal-minded and pleasant.[21]

All professors and lecturers had to base their lectures on a textbook or "compendium." Some of them followed them slavishly and pedantically. Borowski tells us that Kant did not follow his compendia strictly.[22] Rather, he only followed the order in which the authors had arranged the materials and gave his own observations and theories under their headings. Often he digressed and added observations, which, according to Borowski, were "always interesting." Apparently, he developed early the habit of cutting off these digressions when they began to lead too far from the subject at hand, saying "and so on" or "and so forth." Kant exhibited his dry humor in the lectures, apparently never giving a cue as to when it was proper to laugh. He himself "almost never laughed," and "even when he caused his listeners to laugh by telling some funny anecdote," he was stone-faced.[23] Unusual attire of students he found disconcerting.

Kant's delivery was not characterized by great attention to didactic methods. He did not repeat his points, and he failed to clarify everything so that even the slowest of his students could follow. To "force them to understand" was, according to this early student, not Kant's approach. Everyone had to pay attention, or he was left behind. Kant did not appreciate extensive note-taking, believing that many of the note-takers copied what was unimportant, and neglected what was truly important. Questions asking for clarification he accepted gladly – at least in his younger years. According to Borowski, Kant's

> lectures were freely delivered, spiced with wit and good humor, often with quotations of books he had just read, and at times with anecdotes, which, however, were always relevant. I never heard him utter (sexual) ambiguities with which many other teachers

wish to enliven their talks and with which they drive good and well-raised youths from their lecture halls.

Kant eschewed "followers," saying: "You will not learn from me philosophy, but philosophizing, not thoughts merely for repetition but thinking."[24] He suggested that his students order their accumulated information under different headings in thought and always ask themselves when they read or heard something new, "Under which heading or in which order does this belong – where do you put it?" He also advised his students to prepare a commonplace book (*Miszellaneen*), ordered in accordance with the different sciences, to aid their perhaps deceptive memories.[25]

Kant was a popular lecturer from the beginning; his lecture halls were always full. In February 1757, Gottlieb Immanuel Lindner inquired in a letter, "is *Magister* Kant still safe from the court of inquisition that investigates wit?"[26] Hamann's brother writes to Lindner: "*Magister* Kant lives happy and content. Quietly, he recruits those who attend the lectures of the clamorous (*marktschreierische*) Watson, and he weakens with industry and true learning the apparent applause of this youth."[27] The competition and jealousy among the different young lecturers was intense. Even modest financial success, which was necessary for survival, was hard to come by, and it had to be fought for vigilantly and steadily.

Not everyone liked Kant. Scheffner, who was boarding with L'Estoq, explicitly points out that he attended the lectures by Watson on Horace and aesthetics, "but none by Kant, against whom the director of my studies had an antipathy, and whom he never invited into his house."[28] Instead, he attended most of the courses given by L'Estoq himself. These included "among other things *jus naturae*, Hobbes' *De cive*, which he, as I learned to see in later years, really did not understand quite correctly. Against Hobbes's *Leviathan* he warned us most seriously, so that I dared to read him only later."[29] In Kant's lectures he would not have heard such serious warnings. What he would have heard instead could be gathered from Borowski, who reported:

During the years in which I was one of his students Hutcheson and Hume were especially estimated by him, the former in the discipline of ethics, the latter in deep philosophical enquiries. His power of thinking received a special new impetus especially through Hume. He recommended these two thinkers to us for careful study. As always, he was interested in travel books. . . . Why should I be more extensive here? In short, Kant left nothing untried and unexamined that is contributed by good writers to the store of human knowledge.

Only theological works, of whatever kind they may have been, but especially exegesis and dogmatic theology, he never touched. . . . he had read Stapfer's foundations of theology many years ago. His knowledge in this discipline really did not go beyond what he had learned in Schulz's lectures on dogmatic theology in 1742, 1743, which was also the year in which Stapfer's book appeared.[30]

Kant's special interest in Hutcheson and Hume is quite in keeping with the spirit of the time. Hume's first *Enquiry* appeared in German in 1755, and Lessing's translation of Hutcheson's *A System of Moral Philosophy* appeared in 1756 under the title *Sittenlehre der Vernunft*. Mendelssohn and others in Berlin were at the time just as interested in Hume and Hutcheson as were Kant and others in Königsberg. That these interests found their expression in Kant's lectures almost immediately shows among other things how carefully he paid attention to developments in Berlin.

As in today's universities, lectures were given during certain circumscribed periods of the year. During the summer semester, courses were taught from the end of April or beginning of May until the middle of September. In the winter semester, they were taught from the middle of October until the end of March or the beginning of April. Kant thus had two breaks of about a month in April and in September-October.[31] There were also breaks in the middle of the semester, that is, four weeks in July-August (a "dog-days break" or *Hundstagsferien*) and another four weeks around Christmas and New Year's.[32] Professors lectured for a total of eight months of the year. During the other four months they had time for other work and relaxation.

During the semester the pace was grueling. A lecture course usually took four hours a week, with either two or four meetings a week. On the "main days," Monday, Tuesday, Thursday, and Friday, the full professors gave the public lectures for which the students did not have to pay. The lecturers and associate professors had to arrange their hours around these events. On Wednesdays and Saturdays some teachers at the university gave private tutorials and colloquia. Kant also sometimes conducted disputation exercises on these days, which lasted an hour each day.[33]

To earn a living, Kant had to give many lectures. In the first semester (winter 1755–56) he lectured on logic, metaphysics, mathematics, and physics. In the summer semester of 1756 he added geography, and in the next, ethics, never lecturing less than sixteen hours and at times up to twenty-four.[34] Kant's textbook in metaphysics was usually Baumgarten's *Metaphysica*, which had first appeared in 1739, and in logic it was Georg Friedrich Meier's *Auszug aus der Vernunftlehre* of 1752.[35] Baumgarten was the most Leibnizian among all the Wolffians, and Meier was Baumgarten's student and follower. This meant that Kant's core lectures were essentially based on the most radical brand of Leibnizian–Wolffian philosophy. During the first semester he followed Baumeister, "even though he would have preferred to follow Baumgarten." When he circulated a piece of paper to ask his students which text they would prefer, and someone made a very strong appeal for Baumgarten, he offered that person private instruction.[36] Kant's copies of these books were interleaved with empty pages on which Kant wrote his own notes. Over time, these pages filled up completely, and he had to use the margins. Some of these books have survived, and they are extremely useful for understanding Kant's philosophical development. Borowski reports that "at times he also carried a separate notebook . . . into which he transcribed marginalia."[37] In the ethics lectures he always used Baumgarten's *Ethica* as a textbook. It appears that he usually lectured on mathematics over two semesters, covering arithmetic, geometry, trigonometry in the summer, and mechanics, hydrostatics, aerometry, and hydraulics in the winter. He used sometimes Wolff's *Anfangsgründe aller mathematischen Wissenschaften* (1710), and sometimes the shorter *Auszug aus den Anfangsgründen aller mathematischen Wissenschaften* (1713).[38] His lectures on physics and natural science were, at least during the fifties and early sixties, based on Johann Peter Eberhard's *Erste Gründe der Naturlehre* (Leipzig, 1753).[39]

This was a difficult schedule, but it shows that Kant attracted students. Nevertheless, "during the first years as lecturer, his income through his lectures was very small." While he had an "iron reserve" of twenty gold coins (*Friedrichsd'or*), he never touched it. Instead, he sold some of his books. He had to wear the same coat until it was worn out, and his friends offered to buy him a new one, but he refused.[40] The first two or three years were difficult. After that, it got better. He had earned a reputation as a good teacher. Borowski spoke of "a truly rich remuneration for his private lectures (which, as I know for certain, he received already in the years 1757 and 1758)."[41] As a successful lecturer, Kant earned an income that allowed him to live the life appropriate to his status. As he later told one of his publishers, he "always had a more than sufficient income," could afford two rooms, a "very good table," that is, good meals, and could even employ a servant.[42] He also assured him that those were "the most pleasant years of his life." On the other hand, he warned Sigismund Beck later in life that "the subsistence which is based merely on giving lectures is *always* very deficient (*mißlich*)."[43] It is therefore likely that Kant was not in a position to accumulate much money during this period, and that he was very dependent on a steady income made by lecturing.[44]

In 1756, Knutzen's professorship of logic and metaphysics was to be filled again. Kant applied with a letter to the king, saying that philosophy was "the most important field of his efforts," and that he never had lost any opportunity to teach logic and metaphysics.[45] He did not obtain the position. Indeed, it appears that his letter never reached Berlin, but was simply filed.[46] Kant continued to try to better his situation by obtaining a position at a local school, the *Kneiphöfische,* but "he did not pass."[47] The committee appointed instead one Wilhelm Benjamin Kahnert. This appears to have been in 1757, after Kant had already taught for four semesters at the university.[48] The position for which Kant applied had become vacant (on October 11, 1757) as a result of the death of Andreas Wasianski, the father of one of Kant's biographers. It was not unusual for a private lecturer at the university to teach also at a local high school until he obtained a professorship at the university. Kahnert had already taught two years at the *Löbenicht* school before applying for the new position. He also was much better at obeying the rules of Pietistic discourse than Kant ever was. It is difficult to imagine that Kant could ever have written the following, which is characteristic of Kahnert (and other Pietists):

> I will recognize with David my misdeeds, for His grace is great, and I will be ashamed with David, and will consider myself unworthy, and with the poor sinner (*Zöllner*), I will direct my eyes towards heaven, and I will beat my sinful breast in sorry (*wehmütigen*) motions of remorse and say: Oh God, forgive this poor sinner during this holy time of advent! and I will return with the lost son and say: "Father, I have sinned . . ."[49]

Perhaps it was very predictable that Kant would "fail," given his lack of previous experience and proper devotion. Indeed, it may have been precisely because he "was opposed to Pietism" that he did not get the position he had applied for.

His life was not all work or bad luck, of course. Kant had also good friends. Among these was Johann Gotthelf Lindner (1729–1776), who during this period was not in Königsberg. Michael Freytag (1725–1790), Georg David Kypke (1723–1779), and Johann Daniel Funk (1721–1764), who were also friends of Lindner, played perhaps a greater role in his daily life then.[50] Hamann, who himself was a close friend of Lindner, and who knew the others well, was not as close to Kant, but he belonged to the same circle of acquaintances. Kant and Freytag had known each other from the days of the *Collegium Fridericianum*. Freytag had studied in Königsberg, and he taught at a high school (the *Domgymnasium*) in Königsberg from 1747 until 1767, when he left to become pastor in a neighboring village. He died in 1790. During the fifties, he and Kant were very close.

Kypke, half a year younger than Kant, had studied with Kant both at the *Collegium Fridericianum* and at the University of Königsberg, but, unlike Kant, he had become a member of the faculty relatively early.[51] In 1746 he was appointed as associate professor in Oriental languages, and in 1755 he was promoted to full professor. In addition to his specialization in Oriental languages, Kypke also held lectures on the "English language," which awakened a great deal of interest in all things English among his students.[52] He translated Locke's *Of the Conduct of the Human Understanding* in 1755, which some believe was a very important work for Kant early on.[53] In any case, Kypke and Kant were close not only in their philosophical concerns during this period, but also in other ways.[54] Hamann wrote to Lindner in 1756:

> Wolson seems to live very merrily. I was once with him in Schulz's garden where I found *Magister* Kant . . . Mr. Freytag, and professor Kypke. The latter now lodges in their house and has his own household because of which he has gained much weight. They talk here of a recommendation which he gave for a maid, and in which he otherwise praised her, but then noted that she was *obstinata* and *voluptuosa*. Yet one must imagine his accent and his facial expressions in order to find what is funny in the things we laugh about when they are told.[55]

At least early on, Kypke, "an acute and often satiric judge of the arts," placed great emphasis on elegance.[56] From 1755 until 1777 Kypke was the governmental inspector of the synagogue in Königsberg. It was the task of this inspector to make sure that the phrase "for they bow down and prostrate themselves before what is vain and futile and pray to a god who cannot help" in a prayer said at the end of each service was *not* used. The allegation was that it referred to the Christians. Kypke had his own reserved seat in the synagogue and he received a salary of one hundred Thalers for the service.[57]

Funk, who was a doctor of jurisprudence and junior barrister at the court, was an even closer friend than Kypke. "With him he was really friendly."[58] "He interacted most with him."[59] Borowski tells the following interesting story, which probably took place during the break between the winter semester of 1755–56 and the summer semester of 1756:

> Once, during his first years of teaching, I went early in the morning with Dr. Funk to him [Kant]. A student had promised to come this morning and pay his honorarium for

a lecture he had attended . . . Kant claimed that he really did not need the money. Still, every fifteen minutes he came back to the point that the young man would not appear. A few days later he came. Kant was so disappointed that, when the student asked whether he could be one of his opponents at the upcoming defense, he did not accept him, saying: "You might not keep your word, not come to the defense, and thus spoil everything!"[60]

The defense was that of Kant's *Physical Monadology* on April 21, 1756, where Borowski was one of the opponents.[61]

Funk was an extremely interesting character, leading what might be called a loose life. He also gave lectures in jurisprudence. Hippel, who studied with him during the relevant period, observed that he learned more from him than from those with greater titles:

> Just because he had to live off his lecturing, he was by far the best among the teachers (*Magister*). Even at that time it appeared to me that the gentlemen in having other positions (*Nebenstellen*) had one or more concubines besides their betrothed wife. My good old Funk, who had married the widow of professor Knutzen, someone very famous in his own time, was not without a resting bench besides his conjugal bed, but his lectures were as chaste as the bed of a cleric.[62]

Apparently, Funk was popular not only with his students, but also "with the ladies." In this he contrasted sharply with his wife's first husband, who lived, as someone put it, the life of a "complete pedant."[63]

Kant and his friends had varied interests, and the circles they moved in were neither those of the Pietists nor even those of the more conservative Wolffians. Not only their views, but also their lives were less constrained than theirs. During these years, "Kant was not bound by firm dietetic rules, and he did many things just for pleasure."[64] The next few years accentuated this trend.

The Russian Occupation (1758–1762): "A Man who Loves Truth as Much as the Tactfulness of Good Society"

While Königsberg was relatively quiet, there had been war. Frederick had marched into Saxony with 61,000 men on August 29, 1756. The ensuing Seven-Year War, proved costly for Prussia. When the Prussian army lost a battle at Groß Jägersdorf against the Russians, they had to give up Königsberg. Luckily, there was no fighting in Königsberg itself. On January 22, 1758, with all church bells ringing, the Russian general William of Fermor marched into Königsberg and occupied the castle, which the Prussian field marshal had left not long before. The Prussian administration together with representatives of both nobility and commoners handed over the keys to the city to the general, and a five-year-long Russian occupation of the city began.[65] Soon after, all officials had to swear an oath of allegiance to the empress Elizabeth. Russian money and Russian holidays were introduced, and a Russian governor of the city was appointed.

There was some resistance to the Russians. Most of it came from the clerics. They were opposed not only to the frequent marriages of Russians to Königsberg women (which usually involved becoming a member of the Orthodox Church), but also to the lifestyle of the Russians in general. Any Russian victory called for a service commemorating and celebrating the occasion. One of the more upstanding clerics, the preacher of the *Schloßkirche*, Arnoldt, once gave a sermon on Mica 7:8, "Rejoice not against me, O mine enemy (*Feindin*): when I fall, I shall arise." He was accused of having slandered her majesty and threatened with expulsion. Though he promised to retract, he never had to do so because at the assigned service a number of students created a panic by yelling "Fire!" at an appropriate moment. There were other incidents. The director of the Royal German Society, Pisanski, had forgotten to remove the word "Royal" from the door of their conference room. The society was outlawed, and even its library had to be removed from the public building; but on the whole not much changed.[66] Prussian officials continued to do the work they had done before, and everyone continued to draw the same salary. The Russians especially favored the university and its members. The army officers attended many lectures, and the professors were invited to official receptions and balls, which they had not been allowed to attend before. All in all, the Russian occupation was good for Königsberg.[67] While some professors kept their distance from the Russians, others became familiar with them. Kant belonged to the latter group. While he never stooped to the fawning that one of the instructors of poetry, Watson, engaged in, he did get along.

The Russians contributed to a change in the cultural climate of Königsberg. There was more money, and there was more consumption. This is well acknowledged by one of Kant's closest acquaintances, Scheffner, who said: "I date the genuine beginning of luxury in Prussia to the Russian occupation." All at once, there was more social activity in Königsberg. Many merchants, who were accumulating wealth as suppliers of the Russian army, gave large parties, and Königsberg "became a lively (*zeitvertreibender*) place."[68]

For some, the Russian occupation meant liberation from old prejudices and customs. The Russians liked everything that was "beautiful and well-mannered." The sharp distinctions between nobility and commoners were softened. French cuisine replaced the more traditional fare in the houses of those who were better off. Russian cavaliers changed the social intercourse, and gallantry became the order of the day. Drinking of punch was the rage. Dinners, masked balls, and other diversions almost unknown in Königsberg, and frowned on by its religious leaders, became more and more common. Society was "humanized."[69] Some undoubtedly saw this "humanization" as leading to a significant decline in morality, but others viewed it as a liberation. Hippel spoke of a *"Seelenmanumission,"* or the freeing of his soul from slavery, which forever changed his attitude to life. He ended his studies of theology and began his career in administration.[70] Many other intellectuals were equally affected by the new freer, worldlier way of life prevailing in Königsberg.

Kant gained from this new situation. First, his finances improved during these years. He not only taught many officers in his lectures, especially in mathematics, but also gave them private instructions (or *privatissima*), which were, as he himself points out, very well paid.[71] As an added bonus, he was often invited to dinners. Second, he also enjoyed at many parties the company of Russian officers, successful bankers, well-off merchants, noblemen and women, and especially the circle of friends of the family of Count Keyserlingk. The latter, having anticipated trouble with the Russians, had moved out of Königsberg to their estate some distance from the city. However, as it turned out, the Russians were more interested in paying compliments to the beautiful countess, Kant's "ideal of a women," and in attending their parties than in creating problems for them.

Kant developed a special relation with the Keyserlingks. He was asked to come to their estate to educate one of their sons.[72] He was picked up in a horse-drawn carriage, and Kraus reports that on the way back he had time to reflect on the difference between his own early education and that of a nobleman. He also knew other officers. As late as 1789 he received a letter from one Franz, duke of Dillon, a captured Austrian officer, who stayed in Königsberg as a prisoner of war until at least 1762. He wrote:

It was a happy accident that I just saw your name in our newspaper and saw that you are still alive and that you also enjoy the favors of your king . . . I just took a few happy glances at what has passed. The memory of many very pleasant hours, which I passed in your company, brought true pleasure to my mind. At the gentlemen's G. and C. and even in our clubs a thousand of witticisms were witnessed, which, without touching on learned matters, were very useful to a young man (as I then was). In short, the benevolence and the friendliness with which I was treated makes Königsberg inestimable for me.[73]

Kant then moved freely in what was high society for Königsberg: noble officers, rich merchants, and the court of the count.

The Keyserlingks had definite cultural interests, especially in music, and their palace was appointed with the most beautiful furniture, china, and paintings. The countess was also interested in philosophy and had earlier in her life translated Wolff into French, which goes a long way toward explaining why Kant was appreciated early on and made a regular dinner guest. Kant occupied almost always the place of honor to the right of the countess.[74] Kant's association with this family was to last more than thirty years. He felt great respect for the countess, who was three years younger than he was. After her death in 1791, he called her "an adornment of her sex" in a footnote to his *Anthropology*. There was, of course, never any romantic involvement. The social distance between Kant and the countess was just too great for that thought even to arise. The countess presented to Kant, however, the type of woman he might have wanted to marry, if that had been at all possible.

Kant became a person of elegance during this period, someone who shone at social events with his intelligence and wit. He became an elegant *Magister* ("*ein eleganter Magister*"), someone who took great care of his outer appearance, whose maxim was that it was "better to be a fool in style than a fool out of style." It is our "duty not to make a distasteful or even unusual impression on others."[75] As late as 1791 a Danish poet found it "pleasing that Kant prefers a somewhat exaggerated elegance (*Galanterie*) over carelessness in dressing."[76] He always followed also the "maxim" that the colors of one's dress should follow the flowers. "Nature does not create anything that does not please the eye; the colors it puts together always fit precisely with each other." Accordingly, a brown coat required a yellow vest. Late in his life Kant preferred mottled (*meliert*) colors. During the period under consideration, he was more inclined to extravagance, wearing coats with golden borders, and a ceremonial sword.[77] He cut a figure quite different from his more clerically and Pietistically inclined Königsberg colleagues, who wore more modest black or, at most, gray.[78]

Kant was a very attractive man: "His hair was blond, the color of his face fresh, and his cheeks showed even in old age a healthy blush." His eyes were particularly arresting. As one contemporary exclaimed: "From where do I take the words to describe to you his eye! Kant's eye was as if it had been formed of heavenly ether from which the deep look of the mind, whose fiery beam was occluded by a light cloud, visibly shone forth. It is impossible to describe the bewitching effect of his look on my feeling when I sat across him and when he suddenly raised his lowered eyes to look at me. I always felt as if I looked through this blue ether-like fire into the most holy of Minerva."[79]

Yet at 5 feet, 2 inches (1.57 meters) tall, and of slender build, he was neither athletic nor an imposing figure. His chest was somewhat sunken, which made breathing difficult, and he could not endure heavy physical exertion. At times he complained of a lack of air. Delicate and sensitive, he was also subject to allergic reactions. Freshly printed newspapers would make him sneeze. Accordingly, if he dominated a conversation or social function, it was not by his physical presence but by his charm and wit. In many ways he embodied the ideal of an intellectual and man of letters fostered during the period of the Rococo in Germany and France.[80] Accordingly, it is not at all unlikely that Kant did indeed advise the young Herder that he should "not brood so much over his books, but rather follow his own example."[81]

How important elegance was in Königsberg during the period, and to Kant especially, can also be seen from Borowski, who reports that in one of Kant's disputation sessions a student had proposed the thesis "that interaction in general, and especially among students must be connected with grace (*Grazie*)." Kant did not reject this thesis, but he explained that the common German concept of "*Höflichkeit*" or "politeness" really meant "courtly" or "noble" manners, and was thus connected to a certain estate. Instead, he argued that one should aim at a certain kind of "urbanity."[82] In other words, though Kant "mixed with people in all the estates, and gained true trust and friendship," he never forgot where he came from.[83] The republican ideals he later formulated in his political writings were thus rooted in his personal life.

The topic of elegance in the eighteenth century was inevitably bound up with relations between the sexes. Kant, who never married, and who – as far as we know – never had sex, is often thought to have had little to do with women, but this is false. In addition to being the darling of the Countess Keyserlingk, Kant also socialized with a number of other women, who remembered him long after they had separated. The earliest was perhaps Charlotte Amalie of Klingspor. She wrote to Kant in 1772 that she felt certain he was still her friend "just as you were then," that is, after the middle of the fifties, and she assured him that she had benefited from his "benevolent instruction" that "in philosophy truth is everything and that a philosopher has a pure faith." She thanked him as well for having sent her long before Christoph Martin Wieland's "Reminders to a Girlfriend" (*"Erin-*

nerungen an eine Freundin") and for having tried to educate her as a young woman through pleasant conversation. That Kant sent her this poem by Wieland gives us at least some idea of how he felt about her.[84] Nor is it insignificant that the poem is by Wieland, whose poems are uncharacteristically witty, lucid, and light for a German of any century. This poem belongs to those that are characterized by an enthusiastic and sentimental Platonizing morality that emphasized abstinence rather than fulfillment. Wieland himself later felt that this high-strung abstinence had hurt him more than a cruder form of debauchery would have. How Kant felt about this we can only surmise. His elegant conduct suggests sentiments similar to those expressed by the early Wieland. The poem's most important reminder to the girlfriend is to remember and contemplate the "holy thought" that she is carrying "the Godhead's image: reason" and the "supreme power to know the truth."

When Heilsberg says that Kant was "no great devotee (*Verehrer*) of the female sex," he did not mean that Kant looked down on women or that he was a misogynist, but rather that he was not someone for whom sexual exploits were important as a means of proving himself. "He felt marriage to be a desire and to be a necessity," but he never took the final step. Once there was "a well brought up and beautiful widow from somewhere else, who visited relatives." Kant did not deny that she was a woman with whom he would have loved to share his life; but "he calculated income and expenses and delayed the decision from one day to the next."[85] The beautiful widow visited other relatives, and she married there. Another time he "was touched by a young Westphalian girl," who had accompanied a noble woman to Königsberg. He was "pleased to be with her in society, and he let this be known often," but again he waited too long. He was still thinking of making an offer of marriage when she reached the Westphalian border.[86]

After that, he never thought of marriage again. Neither did he appreciate suggestions from friends in that regard, preferring not to go to a party if there were likely to be exhortations in this direction. During his early years, marriage would indeed have been difficult for financial reasons. He himself is said to have quipped that when he could have benefited from being married, he could not afford it, and when he could afford it, he could no longer have benefited from it. He was not alone in this. Many a scholar in eighteenth-century Germany had to endure the same fate and live the life of a celibate simply because he could not support a wife and children. Some found rich widows, who could support them, but they were exceptions.

Whether Kant ever really understood women is an open question. That

he understood them less and less as he grew older is very likely. That his
view of the social and political role of women was largely traditional is without a doubt also true, but it is not entirely so. Kant was influenced by more
progressive views, and he in turn influenced such views.[87] Given that in
Kant's time there were no female students, and that he encountered women
only in clearly circumscribed and mostly very formal social contexts, not
much more could be expected.

University business went on as usual during the years of the Russian
occupation. When Kypke died in 1758, and his position of full professor
of logic and metaphysics became open, Kant applied for it – again without
success. It was instead given to Buck, one of Knutzen's favorite students,
who had taught longer and was perhaps more deserving. Buck, Flottwell,
Hahn, Kant, Thiesen, and Watson had applied, but only the names of
Buck and Kant were forwarded to Petersburg. Buck was initially endorsed
as the most suitable candidate, but as a result of objections by Schulz, who
was the rector of the university during that year, Kant and Buck were both
recommended as competent.[88] Schulz supported Kant only after a meeting during which Schulz asked Kant "solemnly: Do you really fear God
with all your heart?"[89] The answer must have been satisfactory, though it
seems that Schulz did not so much favor Kant as he disapproved of most
of the other candidates. Indeed, one may wonder whether he really wanted
Kant, who looked to him much weaker than Buck, or whether he wanted to
make Buck look stronger by putting forward both names rather than Buck's
alone. In any case, some of the others, like Flottwell and Hahn, were unacceptable to Schulz under any circumstances. Academic success continued
to elude Kant.

Kant and Hamann: "Either a Very Close
or a Very Distant Relation"

While Kant was not a revolutionary in matters of gender or sex, he was a
nonconformist in matters of religion. This is shown again by some of the
events of 1759. Hamann, who had belonged to Kant's circle of acquaintances at least since 1748, and who was close to several of Kant's friends,
had left Königsberg in 1752. After a number of years as *Hofmeister,* during
which he acquired a substantial debt, he entered the services of the merchant house of Berens in Riga. He had already become one of the closest
friends of Johann Christoph Berens (1729–1792) during his years of study
at the University of Königsberg. In 1757 the company sent him to London,

where he experienced nothing but failure, squandering even more money and living a most undisciplined life. He also came into close contact with members of the London homosexual community. Finally, overcome with guilt, he lost all his previous moral and religious convictions. He had been deeply influenced by Enlightenment ideals, but now Hamann slowly fought his way back to the belief that Christ and the church were the only salvation not just for himself, but for everyone. This "conversion" has often been described as a Pietistic *Durchbruch*, and it does share certain features with it. In many ways, however, it was more a return to an orthodox Lutheran faith, in which scripture is accepted as the sole authority and in which hope for salvation comes from faith alone (*sola scriptura* and *sola fide*). When Hamann returned to Königsberg in March of 1759, after having been received "surprisingly well" by the Berenses in Riga (and after a failed proposition of marriage to their daughter), he was a changed man. Having given up the Enlightenment ideals he had shared with Berens, Lindner, and others – including Kant – and having embraced a fundamentalism of the most uncompromising sort, he was almost unrecognizable to his old friends. When Berens came for a visit to Königsberg in the summer of 1759, he enlisted Kant in trying to convince Hamann that he should give up what could only appear to the world as foolishness. On July 12, 1759, Hamann wrote to his brother: "At the beginning of the week I was in the company of Mr. B. and *Magister* Kant at the Windmill where we ate a country dinner together in the tavern there. . . . Confidentially, our association does not have the former intimacy, and we impose on ourselves the greatest restraint to avoid any appearance of it."[90] Later that month Berens and Kant visited Hamann and tried to persuade him to translate some articles from the French *Encyclopédie*, but to no avail. Instead, Hamann fired off a letter to Kant, which began:

Most honored *Magister:* I do not blame you for being my *rival* (*Nebenbuhler*) and that you have enjoyed your new friend for whole weeks, while I only see him for a few scattered hours, like a phantom or a clever informant . . . I shall, however, bear a grudge because your friend insulted me in introducing you into my solitude. . . . If you are Socrates, and your friend wants to be Alcibiades, then you need for your own education a genius. . . . Allow me therefore to be called your genius as long as it takes me to write this letter.[91]

Hamann went on to try to convince Berens and Kant that a Christian faith should be the result of consistent philosophizing, appealing to Hume for support. Philosophy can only lead to skepticism, and skepticism leads to belief. Reason was not given to us to make us "wise," but to make us aware of our "folly and ignorance" in all matters. Hume argued that we cannot "eat an egg and drink a glass of water without" believing. Philosophy therefore leads to a fideistic position.

Hamann used the German word "*Glaube*" here, and "*Glaube*" means both "belief" and "faith." Ingeniously (or perversely) exploiting the ambiguity, Hamann asked: If Hume needs such *Glaube* "for food and drink, why does he deny *Glaube* when he judges of matters that are higher than sensuous eating and drinking?"[92] Indeed, he later said that he was "full of Hume" when he wrote this, and that it was Hume who had shown this to him. This invocation of Hume for his fideistic conclusion was also a direct attack on Kant, whose lectures had been given a new impetus by Hume just then, but in a quite different direction.

In the aftermath of this episode Hamann published in 1759 an essay entitled *Socratic Memorabilia*.[93] In it, he tried to show, among other things, that Berens and Kant, together with all of their contemporaries, were wrong in trying to supply a rational justification of experience. Renewing the argument of the letter, he claimed that experience involves belief at its most fundamental level. "Our own existence and the existence of all things outside us must be believed, and cannot be determined in any other way," he claimed, and he argued that if "there are proofs of truth which are of as little value as the application which can be made of the truths themselves, indeed, one can believe the proof of a proposition without giving approval to the proposition itself."[94]

Hamann believed that any consistent reading of Hume leads to viewing his philosophy as a defense of fideism.[95] This was not entirely unreasonable. Hume found, for instance, that "upon the whole . . . the *Christian Religion* not only was at first attended with miracles, but even at this day cannot be believed by any reasonable person without one. Mere reason is insufficient to convince us of its veracity: And whoever is moved by *Faith* to assent to it is conscious of a continued miracle in his own person . . ."[96] This seems to sum up what has sometimes been discussed under the title of "Hume's fideism." Hume can be – and has been – taken to endorse the view that religious beliefs are unjustifiable, and that they *therefore* require something like a "leap of faith." Hume's critique of rationalist theology can thus be taken as purely orthodox Protestant teaching. Hume himself invited such a reaction when he observed: "I am the better pleased with the method of reasoning here delivered, as I think it may serve to confound those dangerous friends or disguised enemies to the *Christian Religion*, who have undertaken to defend it by the principles of human reason. Our most holy religion is founded on *Faith*, not on reason; and it is a sure method of exposing it to put it to such a trial as it is, by no means, fitted to endure."[97] Hamann believed that Hume had undermined the very foundations of all intellectualism and Enlightenment philosophy, and that he was for that very reason important. He saw in Hume a skeptic in the tradition of Bayle. Others in Königsberg, who were friends of Hamann and Kant, namely Hippel and Scheffner, appreciated Montaigne, Bayle, and Hume precisely for such religious reasons. None of them saw any contradiction between skepticism and religious beliefs. On the contrary, they viewed skepticism as a necessary prelude to a genuine religious faith. It was for that reason that they thought Hume was entirely compatible with traditional religious beliefs.

The *Socratic Memorabilia,* which made Hamann famous throughout Germany, was not the only consequence of this episode. Hamann did not give up communicating directly with Kant. Later in the year he sent Kant a series of letters in which he criticized Kant's plan to write a physics textbook for children and at the same time offered his help in writing it.[98] Apparently Kant had proposed to write such a book. If it had ever been written, it would – at least in part – have been based on his *General History,* though he might also have offered some of the ideas put forward in the physical monadology. It would most certainly have offered a completely mechanistic explanation of the world in accordance with Newtonian principles, and would not have presented the biblical account of creation. Kant would have presented an alternative to the biblical account, and, whatever else the physics for children might have become, it would have been a work in the service of the Enlightenment. Hamann saw this and accordingly rejected the very idea. Kant should not try to "pervert" children in this way:

To preach to the learned is just as easy as to deceive honest people. Nor is there danger or responsibility in writing for the learned because most of them have already been so corrupted. That even the most fantastic author can no longer confuse them . . . a baptized philosopher will know that more is required in writing for children than a wit a la Fontanelle and a wooing style.[99]

He also pointed out that Kant was wrong to think that he could easily change his perspective from that of an academic philosopher to that of a child.

Or do you expect children to be more capable than your adult students who have difficulty in following you in the patience and the speed of your thinking? And, since your proposal also requires a thorough knowledge of the world of children, which can be acquired neither in the elegant nor in the academic world, all this seems so fantastic to me that I would be in danger of getting a black eye on a fantastic ride just because I am inclined to what is fantastic.[100]

Hamann insisted that a physics textbook for children must be based on the biblical account of creation, and his help was predicated on Kant's conversion to Hamann's Christianity. His offer of assistance was thus not genuine but a kind of payback to Kant for trying to reconvert him. Hamann was also teasing him with the notion of having to become "childlike," that is, Christian. He himself assumed in several passages the role of the child, asking Kant to have a "heart for children."[101]

It is unsurprising, therefore, that Kant did not respond. Hamann, however, found Kant's silence disconcerting. One of the reasons for this has to do with another interesting development in Königsberg during 1759. Daniel Weymann (1732–1795), a fervent admirer of Crusius, had defended on October 6, 1759, a dissertation on "*de mundo non optimo*" in order to receive permission to lecture at the university. Kant published an advertisement of his lectures on October 7, entitled "An Essay on Certain Considerations Concerning Optimism." Kant's concern with such considerations can be traced back to his drafts for a response to a question formulated for an essay competition by the Berlin Academy in 1753.[102] The immediate occasion for it was Weymann's dissertation. Outlining, "in some haste," a number of remarks that he claimed would make it easier to understand the dispute over the question whether or not this world is the best of all possible worlds, he basically attacked Crusius's position against Leibniz, taking the side of Mendelssohn and Lessing. Leibniz's doctrine that God created the best of all possible worlds was neither new nor unorthodox. What was new was the use to which he put it in his proposed solution to the problem of evil. Leibniz's use of the idea may be questionable, but the idea itself made sense. Indeed, "not every extravagance of opinion deserves the trouble of a careful refutation. If anybody were so bold as to assert that the Supreme Wisdom could find the worse better than the best . . . I should not waste my time in attempting a refutation. Philosophy is put to poor use if it is employed in overturning the principles of sound reason, and it is little honoured if it is found necessary to mobilise her forces in order to refute such attempts."[103] Instead, Kant tried to prove that there is indeed a possible world beyond which no better world can be thought. He did not once mention Weymann, but it was clear enough to anyone in Königsberg whom he had in mind. In any case, Weymann took the bait and published a rejoinder, which appeared just a week later.[104] This led to some commotion. Kant chose to remain silent. In a letter to Lindner of October 28 he stated his reasons:

A meteor has recently made its appearance above the academic horizon here. *Magister* Weymann has sought in a rather disorderly and unintelligibly written dissertation against optimism to make a solemn debut on this stage which has just as many clowns as Helferding's theater. His well-known immodesty made me decline his invitation to act as a respondent. But in the program of my lectures which I distributed the day after his dissertation appeared and that Mr. Berens will bring to you together with the one or other little piece, I briefly defended optimism against Crusius without thinking of Weymann. Nevertheless, his gall was raised. The following Sunday he published a pamphlet against the presumed attack – full of immodesty, distortions, etc.

The judgment of the public and the obvious impropriety to get involved in exchanging blows by fist with a Cyclops, not to mention the rescue of a pamphlet that may already be forgotten when its defense appears, obliged me to answer in the most proper manner: by silence.[105]

Perhaps Weymann deserved the silent treatment, but he was hardly wrong in thinking that Kant, in attacking Crusius, was also dismissing his dissertation as unworthy of even a thought or a mention. One thing is certain – since Weymann's dissertation represented for the most part a summary of Crusius, and since it was clear to anyone that he was a follower of Crusius, everyone in Königsberg would have understood Kant's pamphlet to be an attack on the new *Magister*.

There was not much love lost between Weymann and Kant. They were competing for the same students, and Weymann was more successful than Kant. Andrej Bolotov (1738–1833), who attended Weymann's lectures during this period, reported that Weymann secretly tried to enlist students of other professors and that the others, "all" Wolffians, according to Bolotov, were opposed to him and made his life difficult. The Pietist Weymann had great influence on the students, with the result that

many of his students distanced themselves from their former teachers and, following the *Magister* Weymann, now already equipped with better rules, thoughts and proofs, became genuine opponents of those professors and were no longer to be defeated in ordinary dispute.[106]

Moreover, the philosophy that Weymann preached, namely that of Crusius, had the added benefit of "transforming any person who came close to it, even if he did not wish to, almost automatically into a Christian."[107] Bolotov also "personally laid eyes on the great, or more bluntly put, the muddle-headed Kant," dismissing his "Wolffism" just as he had that of all the other professors in Königsberg.[108] When Bolotov left Königsberg, he gave Weymann a sheep's pelt to keep him warm.[109]

What was Kant up to in attacking Weymann's position? One might perhaps say that battle lines were being drawn. Weymann's dissertation was stating his convictions and defining an agenda. Kant raised doubts about the consistency and philosophical value of such an agenda. The students, who at that time were choosing the lectures for the coming semester, also knew what was at stake in this dispute. On the one side there was a new lecturer, intent on bringing renewed vigor to the Pietist camp by defending Crusius's ideas; on the other side there was another fairly young teacher, trying to revise philosophy by modifying Baumgarten's theories in the direction of British philosophy. It was another skirmish in the long battle at the university between those who saw philosophy as the handmaid of a certain kind of theology and those who saw it as an autonomous discipline.

Like Kant, Hamann had little respect for Weymann. He gave the following report:

I only looked into his dissertation, and I lost all desire to read it; I went to the auditorium and I lost all desire even to hear. Stay at home, I said, so that you do not get angry or make others angry with you. I actually went to the defense of the dissertation. *Magister* Kant was asked to oppose, but he declined; and he printed *instead* an invitation for his lectures, which I will keep for you. He also sent me a copy. I do not understand his *reasons*, but his bright ideas are blind puppies, which were brought prematurely into the world by a bitch. If it was worth while to refute him, I would have tried to understand them. He appeals to the *whole* in judging the world. For this we need knowledge that is no longer *made of pieces*. To argue from the whole to a fragment is like arguing from the unknown to the known.[110]

When Kant did not answer Hamann's letter on the physics textbook for children, Hamann felt he had been treated just like Weymann. He claimed that this was "an insult to [him]."[111] He attacked Kant, saying: "You are proud, to tell you the truth . . . You may treat Weymann in any way you wish, as a friend I demand a different treatment. Your silence in regard to him is more cowardly and despicable than was his stupid critique of your essay. You treat me the same. I will not let you go unpunished."[112] Earlier Hamann had predicted that his relation to Kant would in future be either very distant or very close.[113] It would be the former for some time to come, and it was never *very* close. This is not surprising. What is perhaps surprising is that Kant and Hamann continued to have any relation at all. Between Weymann and Kant, on the other hand, there could not be any relationship whatsoever. Kant had made an enemy, who would from then on indict his work with great vigor but little understanding.

Kant found teaching exciting – at least at first. By October 1759 it had become burdensome. Thus he wrote to his friend Lindner:

> I, for my part sit daily in front of the anvil of my lectern and strike it in the same rhythm with the heavy hammer of lectures that resemble each other. At times an inclination of a more noble kind leads me to extend myself beyond this narrow sphere, yet need, present immediately, with an impetuous voice calls me back to the hard labor without delay and with a truthful voice . . .
>
> Yet given the place where I am and the small expectation of abundance, I am satisfied with the applause with which I am honored and with the advantages I draw from it, and I dream my life away.[114]

Kant seems tired and unhappy. Still, the letter may have been written in a moment of despair, and such moments are not necessarily characteristic of how someone sees life.

Hippel, who was his student during the summer of 1758 and the winter of 1758–59 – after having first "attended the entire philosophical course of Buck," the lectures of Teske in physics, Langhansen and Buck in mathematics, Kypke in logic, Greek with J. G. Bock, Flottwell in German stylistics as well as Hebrew and some courses in theology – had little to say about Kant as a lecturer.[115] Though he attended lectures in "philosophy and physical geography," as well as in metaphysics, he did not find them especially remarkable. He was much more impressed with old Schulz's lectures in dogmatic theology.[116] Being more influenced by Pietism than Kant was, he probably found Kant not only too difficult, but also unwholesome. This does not mean that Kant took less care in preparing and delivering his lectures; he simply could not afford to neglect them, because his livelihood depended on them. It does show, however, that his style did not appeal equally to all students.[117] Johann Schulz (1739–1805), who became Kant's friend late in life, was also a student then. Like Kant, Schulz had been prepared for university studies at the *Collegium Fridericianum*. Whether he attended Kant's lectures is not entirely clear. He did not identify himself as Kant's student when asked to do so later, but Borowski, who should have known, said he was indeed one of the best of Kant's students.[118] In any case, Kant's thought appears to have begun to influence Schulz only in 1770. Kant, in his earliest years of teaching, was perhaps a good lecturer, but he was one of many, and his ideas were not radically new.

A student who was close to Kant during this time was one Johann

Friedrich von Funk (1738–1760), who later died from exhaustion in Königsberg. One of Kant's most peculiar publications deals with his untimely death. It was written in the form of a letter to Funk's mother, in which Kant praised the character of her son and used the occasion to reflect on the meaning of life.

Every human being makes his own plan of his destiny in the world. There are skills he wants to learn, there are honor and peace, which he hopes to get from them, and lasting happiness in conjugal life and a long list of pleasures or projects make up the pictures of the magic lantern, which he paints for himself and which he allows to play continuously in his imaginations. Death, which ends this play of shadows, shows itself only in the great distance and is obscured and estranged by the light, which envelops the more pleasant places. While we are dreaming, our true destiny leads us on an entirely different way. The part we really get seldom looks like the one we expected, and we find our hope dashed with every step we take . . . until death, which always seemed far away, suddenly ends the entire game.[119]

Under these conditions, the wise man concentrates "on his great destination beyond the grave," and he will be "rational in his plans, but without being stubborn, hopeful that his hopes will be fulfilled, but without being impatient, modest in his wishes, but without being censorious, trusting without insisting, and active in fulfilling his duties, but ready, with Christian resignation, to obey the command of the Highest, when it pleases Him to call us from this stage amidst all our striving."[120] We should always remember this, and we should get used to thinking of such things in the bustle of our daily business tasks and recreations. Tedium, as well as excitement, controversy, and pleasure, could soon come to an end.

Herder, Student of Kant (1762–1764): "Initiated, as It Were, into the Roussiana and Humiana"

The Russians left Königsberg in 1762. The empress Elizabeth had died on December 25, 1761, and Peter III, a simpleton and Prussiaphile, who was more at home in Holstein than in Russia, had taken her place. As an ardent admirer of Frederick, Peter III not only ceased all hostile activities, but also entered into an alliance with Prussia to declare war on Denmark (a traditional enemy of Holstein). Not surprisingly, he managed in short order to alienate almost everyone who counted in Russia. In Königsberg, the Russian commander officially ceased to be in charge, but the troops remained there. On June 28, Catherine took over power in a coup d'etat led by her lover. Almost immediately, the Russian commander issued a declaration that the Russians were again an occupying force. The new empress, however, was not interested in keeping the occupied territories, and she ordered the Russian soldiers, who had not been paid for a number of months, back to Russian soil, thus in effect canceling the alliance with Prussia and withdrawing from the war. As the Russians left, the Prussian high administration returned. Hamann could write to Lindner on July 10: "On Monday peace was declared here. . . . Yesterday evening, the administration met here. Lauson's wish has been fulfilled. He always prayed that the professor of poetry would not die until the Prussian administration was here." J. G. Bock had died two days earlier, and the chair of professor of poetry was vacant. The king of Prussia would fill it, not the empress of Russia.

Again, there do not appear to have been any great problems connected with the change of administration. Kant, in any case, made the change without difficulty. As he had been giving *privatissima* to Russian officers before, so he was now teaching the Prussian officers. His connections with these officers were facilitated by the small military school (*école militaire*) in Königsberg, which gained in importance after the Seven-Year War. Since Frederick the Great wanted his officers to be better educated, he required them to take classes in mathematics and other useful subjects.[121] Hamann wrote in February of 1764 that Kant "now holds a class (*Collegium*) for General Meyer and his officers, which brings him much honor and advantage, because he dines [with the General] almost every day and is fetched in a carriage to give his lectures in *mathesis* (mathematics) and physical geography."[122]

The General Meyer, the commander of a regiment of dragoons in Königsberg, was a man of rare education. Kant gave a lecture course on mathematics and physical geography for several officers in his house. . . . He often dined there because the General was a bachelor like Kant. Besides the officers many of the most honorable scholars were invited. Meyer was very concerned with elegance, and he would give his officers a stern look, if they did not behave properly at the table. When Kant, who sat opposite to the General on one occasion, spilled red wine on the most exquisite table setting, everyone was shocked. The General, in order to avoid an awkward situation, spilled himself an entire glass, and, since the conversation was dealing with the Dardanelles, he drew with his fingers their outlines in the spilled wine . . .[123]

Kant became a good friend of this General Meyer. At the same time, Kant also continued his visits to the Keyserlingks and his other social obligations.

During these years, the life of the elegant *Magister* became more and more hectic and more and more worldly. Daniel Friedrich von Lossow, who was the general of the hussar regiment in Königsberg, became an important figure in Kant's life. He not only invited Kant often to his estate in Gold-app, at the eastern border of East Prussia (approximately seventy-five miles from Königsberg), but also asked him to obtain for him binoculars and glasses. Furthermore, he appreciated Kant's advice concerning the filling of the positions of field pastors. Kant thought little of common soldiers. Someone who could endure the life of a soldier, with its lack of autonomy, had to have a mean (*niederträchtiger*) character, from his point of view. On the other hand, he did enjoy the company of the more educated officers.

Things other than social occasions diverted Kant as well. Thus he re-ported to Borowski how he had witnessed an operation on a Lieutenant Duncker and on that occasion had spoken to the doctor about operating on someone who was born blind, so that he might make him see. The doctor

was willing to do the operation, provided he found the patient suitable for it after ex-amining him. A society of good friends has already been engaged to take up the cost for his nursing as long as the cure will last here. Accordingly, I cannot lose any time. I ask you humbly to tell me the name of the boy from Lichtenhagen or whatever the name is of the place we talked about earlier. [Please tell me also] the name of the parish to which the father belongs and if possible the name and the whereabouts of the noble-man or administrator who is in charge of the village.[124]

Kant's interests were not merely or perhaps even primarily philanthropic. He was more interested in observing firsthand the operation and its con-sequences. It is likely that he wanted to find out more about what and how a person born blind can see at first. The famous Molyneux problem also concerned Kant in Königsberg.[125]

Herder came to Königsberg in August of 1762.[126] Recommended by Hamann, he first worked at Kanter's bookshop, reading almost all day, and was soon noticed by Kanter as a talented young man, one deserving of en-couragement and help. Apparently, Kanter asked Kant to allow Herder to visit his lectures without a fee. After an exam, in which Kant found Herder to be well enough prepared for university studies, he was allowed to attend lectures. As Herder said himself, he studied "especially the different parts of philosophy with *Magister* Kant, philology with professor Kypke, theol-ogy in its different fields with Dr. Lilienthal and Arnold."[127] He also attended Teske's physics lectures. Indeed, they were at the time probably the most important to him.[128]

At that time Kypke had his quarters no longer with Kant but far out-side of the city (*Vorstadt*), where he grew carrots and onions and sold them from his garden.[129] Kant lived and taught in the so-called *Magister*'s alley (*Magistergasse* or *Magisterstraße*), much closer to the university.[130] This was traditionally a street on which many among the faculty at the university lived. We may assume that Kant grew neither carrots nor onions; as a citizen of both the academic and the elegant world he would have had neither the time nor the inclination to do so. Instead, he enjoyed life as the elegant *Magister*. There were times when, having enjoyed conversation and wine a little too much, he had difficulty "finding the entrance (*Loch*) into the *Magister*'s alley."[131]

When not invited to dinner, Kant ate at Gerlach's, a "billiard house in Kneiphof," close to where he lived. Borowski points out that during his "earlier years he went from lunch, after finishing his lectures, to a coffee house, had conversations about the events of the day there or played a game of billiards. At that time he also loved to play a game of l'hombre at parties in the evening because he believed it activated his mind."[132] This was followed by a long walk, often in the company of friends or students, whom he asked to join him after he had finished lecturing for the day. Again, the topics of conversation were not necessarily scholarly but ranged far and wide.[133] After coming home, he continued to work, doing mostly his reading. Often, of course, he was invited to friends and acquaintances in the evening, hence his occasional difficulties in finding his way home.

Herder, on the whole agreeing with Borowski's earlier account of Kant's teaching, reported that his

lectures were the most entertaining talks. His mind, which examined Leibniz, Wolff, Baumgarten, Crusius, and Hume, and investigated the laws of nature of Newton, Kepler, and the physicists, comprehended equally the newest works of Rousseau . . . and the latest discovery in science. He weighed them all, and always came back to the unbiased knowledge of nature and to the moral worth of man.[134]

Kant was thirty-eight when Herder studied with him, and Herder always thought that these were Kant's best years. Long after the two had a falling out, Herder raved: "more than thirty years ago I knew a youth, the originator of the critical philosophy himself, and I attended all his lectures, some repeatedly, during the years of his greatest flourishing."[135] He

had the most cheerful sprightliness of a youth . . . his open brow, made for thinking was the seat of clarity; and the most profound and pleasant speech came from his eloquent mouth. Jest, wit, and caprice were in his command – but always at the right time so that everyone laughed. His public lecture was like an entertaining conversation. He spoke about his author, thought on his own, and often beyond the author. During the three years I listened daily to his lectures I never noticed the smallest trace of arrogance. He had an enemy, who wanted to refute him . . .[136]

Herder emphasized that Kant's only concern was the truth, that he wanted no part of sects and parties, and that he did not seek mere followers. Apart from Weymann, he seemed to have no enemies. Kant's "philosophy awakened one's own thinking."[137] He was a man of the world. "Human beings, nations, natural history, physics, mathematics, and experience were the sources from which he enlivened his presentation."[138]

Herder exaggerated. He was writing more a hagiography than a biography. Nevertheless, Herder's account of this period is not entirely misleading. Others felt the same way. Thus another student, Christian Friedrich Jensch, supported Herder, saying

how interesting Kant was in his lectures. As if in an enthusiastic state, he appeared and said: "this is where we stopped last time." He had learned his main ideas so deeply and so vividly that he now lived in them and in accordance with them for the entire period; and often he paid little attention to his textbook.

He lectured on Baumgarten. His copy was covered with notes all over. Hume, Leibniz, Montaigne and the English novels of Fielding and Richardson, Baumgarten and Wolff are mentioned by Kant as the works from which he learned the most. He thought very highly of *Tom Jones*.[139]

Herder also spoke of the effect that Kant had on him. He felt "captured by the grace of the Kantian presentation, and caught up in (*umschlungen*) a dialectical web of words in which he no longer thought of himself."[140]

A number of Herder's notes, taken in Kant's lectures, have survived.[141] In the very short and incomplete notes on logic, we learn that the Stoics "exaggerated virtue" and that "no philosopher can be a Wolffian, etc. because he must think for himself. Wolff and Crusius had to define and prove everything. Though they had examples of such errors before their eyes, they still asserted their own errors." Kant advocated eclecticism, saying "we will take what is good wherever it comes from," and he talked of the "noble pride to think for oneself and to discover our own mistakes first." Though we must look for truth before we look for beauty, he told his students "we demand in all knowledge also beautiful things . . . otherwise they are disgusting."[142] The notes from the mathematics lectures tell us little about Kant's views, but just follow the textbook, and the notes on physics show that Kant was still concerned with the problem of the divisibility of mathematical and material space, accusing the textbook of confusing the two kinds of space. Both subjects seem to have been of little interest to Herder, and his notes on them contain nothing of great interest.[143] In this respect they contrast sharply with the notes from the lectures on moral philosophy and metaphysics, which are very extensive and highly interesting.[144]

The notes on moral philosophy show that Kant did indeed take the moral sense to be the basis of morality. He talked of Hutcheson and claimed that "one should investigate the feeling of the *natural man*, and this is better than our artificial one: Rousseau has visited (*aufgesucht*) it."[145] The "supreme law of morality is: act according to nature. My reason can err; my moral feeling only when I uphold custom before natural feeling."[146] He asked: "Does that mean we can establish moral law without God?" He answered: "Of course it does." In fact it is easier to found it on our nature: "the culture of moral feelings should precede the culture of obedience."[147] "Can an atheist be tolerated in society?" It depends: if they base their atheism on moral grounds, they are dangerous and cannot be tolerated; if their atheism is based on logical reasons, then they are "not so dangerous for society."[148] Therefore, Spinoza should not have been damned. "Does a Christian ethics have to precede philosophical ethics?" No, on the contrary! When "Pietists make the idea of religion dominant in all conversation and discourse, while it can be concluded from their common behavior that this idea has lost the sense of novelty, they are nothing but gossips."[149] The Spartans let their females walk naked "until they were nine – the males until thirteen . . . our artificial virtues are chimerical and so vice originates when what is hidden is regarded as vice."[150] "Society is the true spice of life, and it makes the *dignified* (*würdige*) person useful; and when the learned cannot converse, this is the result of their assiduity, or of the scorn of society. The latter is founded on the lack of knowledge of the world and the value of scholarship. The scholar must be able to converse with all classes because he is outside of all classes . . ."[151]

Rousseau plays an important role in these lectures, and this is not just due to Herder's literary preferences. Kant himself had come under the influence of Rousseau. In a famous autobiographical reflection from this period, found in the "Remarks on the Observations of the Beautiful and Sublime" ("*Bemerkungen zu den Beobachtungen über das Gefühl des Schönen und Erhabenen*"), he mused:

I am myself by inclination a seeker after truth. I feel a consuming thirst for knowledge and a restless passion to advance in it, as well as a satisfaction in every forward step. There was a time when I thought that this alone could constitute the honor of mankind, and I despised the rabble who knows nothing. Rousseau set me right. This blind prejudice vanishes; I learn to respect human nature, and I should consider myself far more useless than the common laborer if I did not believe that this view could give worth to all others to establish the rights of man.[152]

These "Remarks" were written almost immediately after the publication of the *Observations*. They show that Kant was impressed by Rousseau – so much so that he felt he had to "read Rousseau so long until the beauty of expression no longer interferes; and only then can I rationally examine him."[153] Rousseau exhibited such an "uncommon acuity of mind, such a noble turn of genius, and such a sensitive soul" that there was perhaps never a writer comparable to him. This positive impression is, however, almost immediately followed by "alienation about peculiar and contradictory opinions, opposed to what is generally viable."[154]

Accordingly, Kant soon became critical of Rousseau. Though he followed for a time Rousseau's method, and though Rousseau's *Emile* influenced him in the choice of philosophical topics during the second half of the sixties, he was never a slavish follower of Rousseau. Kant's "Remarks" show how Kant thought that Rousseau's method was important for the doctrine of virtue and how he thought Rousseau could help to improve the ancients.

Still, Rousseau was important to Kant during the early sixties for philosophical and personal reasons. Green and Kant must have talked about Rousseau quite frequently. Rousseau had an effect on the character Kant was beginning to form. Rousseau "set him right." Perhaps it is not an exaggeration to speak of a "Socratic turn" in Kant that took place during this period. Yet his advertisement of his lectures on ethics in 1765 does not even mention Rousseau.[155] Rousseau may have been the first who "discovered" under the variety of human appearances "the deeply hidden nature of humanity and the hidden law whose observance may justify destiny," but Kant did not think that Rousseau described this hidden nature correctly.[156] Hutcheson, Shaftesbury, and Hume were better guides in this regard – or so Kant thought in 1765.

Herder's most extensive and most careful notes were taken in Kant's metaphysics lectures. They give a very good indication of what Kant thought during the period: "Crusius's principle" – whatever is must be somewhere and at some time – is wretched and unproven.[157] Metaphysics should be not only thorough, but also beautiful.[158] Parts of the lecture notes are very direct. Thus "Wolff errs" and "Crusius errs," and "Baumeister [is] the wretched *interpreter* of Wolff":[159] perhaps "Malebranche's philosophy is better than that of Leibniz";[160] but it is space which "must be the first *actus* of the divine all-presence of God, through which the things come into connection (*nexus*)."[161] On the other hand, "the status *post mortem* is very probable, the entire world would equal nothing without rational beings," and so on.[162]

Kant's presentation of the concepts, arguments, explanations, and hypotheses, and of his own theory, was very condensed. Different points followed each other in rapid succession, and it must have been difficult for the young students to follow him. Part of the effect he had on his students had thus more to do with feeling. They became persuaded "that things of the highest importance were being said about matters of the utmost urgency: things which at all costs [they] must understand," but to their chagrin they could not understand, and so they made it their business to try to understand.[163] Herder himself found another way out. He told Caroline Herder:

My soul could not be well in this realm of death, of lifeless concepts without basis and ground. After each lecture in metaphysics I ran into the open with a poet – or I read Rousseau or a similar writer, in order to waken and lose these impressions . . . for they hurt me.[164]

He wrote the draft of an "An Essay on Being," which, though often thought to be pure Herder, is probably closer to Kant's ideas at that time than traditionally thought.[165] Herder: "Being cannot be proven – the existence of God cannot be proven – no idealist can be refuted – all existential propositions, the largest part of human cognition *cannot* be proven – *rather,* everything uncertain; no! *not* uncertain [even though] *not* at all provable . . ."[166] A number of poems have survived in which Herder put Kant's and Rousseau's ideas into verse. Indeed, Kant had at least one of these read during his lectures.[167]

There can be little doubt that Kant was an inspiring lecturer during this period. Nor can there be much doubt that he was interested not only in teaching philosophical theories to his students, but also in teaching them how to live, by recommending a certain way of life. He then thought that philosophical reflection had to have an important place in life, but that it was neither all nor perhaps even the most important thing. Elegance and appreciation of the beautiful in nature and literature were more important to him than dry book knowledge. Herder also drew attention to this, calling Kant the "observer of society," who looked "for the great and beautiful in man and in human characters, and the temperaments and motivations of the sexes, and virtues and finally of national characters." He praised Kant's nuanced views and observations in psychological matters, calling him the "German Shaftesbury."[168] Again, Herder exaggerated, but his exaggeration nevertheless adds a facet to our understanding of Kant's intellectual temperament. He was not the dry physicist and metaphysician that one might expect from reading his Latin dissertations. Kant was definitely European in outlook. He not only read and appreciated the current German, French, and English authors, but he tried to put their theories into praxis. Furthermore, there was a definite literary flavor to his life. He strove to be a man of letters, not just a scholar, and that set him apart from most of his colleagues at the university.

Herder, on the other hand, was shy, withdrawn, and without social graces. He did not have many friends, though he was close to Hamann and learned from him literature, theology, and English. Hippel, who had been on an extended journey to Russia, returned to Königsberg at about the time that Herder first arrived there. The journey had convinced Hippel that he was not cut out for theology, and he had become much worldlier. He disliked Herder – or at least he could not take him seriously. He made constant fun of this student of Kant's and friend of Hamann's, and he disparaged Herder's first literary efforts.[169] Like Kant, Hamann, and Herder, Hippel also had literary ambitions, and, very much like them, he inclined toward sentimentalism. But Herder's gushy, emotional, and exaggerated style was not to his taste. Kant was more forgiving, hoping that Herder's enthusiasm would diminish with age.

Kant also had reservations about Herder's approach to life. When Herder left Königsberg, Kant told him not to "brood so much over his books, but follow his own example. He [said that he himself] was very social, and only in the world can one educate oneself. (And really, *Magister* Kant was then the '*most elegant*' (*galanteste*) man of the world, wore bordered clothes, a *postillion d'amour*, and visited all the coteries)."[170] Hamann reported about the same period:

> . . . swept along by a whirlpool of societal diversions, he [Kant] has many works in his head: *Morality*, an Essay on a new metaphysics, an excerpt of his physical geography, and a great number of small ideas, from which I also hope to profit. Whether the least of it will come to pass is still in doubt.[171]

Kant spent "perhaps most afternoons and evenings in society . . . not infrequently participating in a suite of playing cards, and often returning home only past midnight. If he was not invited to a meal, he would eat in a restaurant, together with several educated persons. It was there that he met . . . von Hippel and that the two got to know each other better, and this was the period during which they met often."[172] Kant was, in other words, a central figure in Königsberg social circles. He had great promise, but there were questions about whether he would fulfill it. Hamann himself found it necessary to assure Mendelssohn in Berlin that "Kant is a man who loves the truth as much as the tactfulness of good society."[173] He was far from sure, however. Some of Kant's friends had a loose lifestyle, and this seemed to influence Kant. Hamann felt Kant could go one way just as well as the other: he could lose himself completely in social diversions; or he could make something more solid of his "bright ideas." The "wild" philosopher might turn out something worthy, and he might not.

Kant's Philosophical Works of the Period: "Traces of His Spirit"

When Kant first began teaching at the university, he had already published a number of books, dissertations, and articles. During the years between 1756 and 1762 he published only three pamphlets, advertising his lectures, and one essay of a personal nature. These were the "Announcement of a Lecture in Physical Geography" (Easter 1757), the "New Doctrine of Motion and Rest" (Easter 1758), "Considerations on Optimism" (fall 1759), and the "Thoughts at the Occasion of the Premature Death of Sir Johann Friedrich von Funk" (1760). All of these were occasional pieces. They give us some insight into Kant's concerns during this period, but they hardly constitute a substantial contribution to philosophy – nor were they meant to. They were for local consumption, not meant to further his stature as an author. Indeed, part of the reason for the later increase in Kant's productivity may also have had to do with Johann Jakob Kanter (1738–1786), the enterprising book dealer, who began publishing his own books at this time and had need for new publications.[174]

At the end of this period of Kant's life, by contrast, he published five much more significant works, not only meant for a wider audience, but also intended to be original contributions to the philosophical discussion of the time. These are *The False Subtlety of the Four Syllogistic Figures* (1762), the *Attempt to Introduce the Concept of Negative Magnitudes into Philosophy* (1763), *The Only Possible Argument in Support of a Demonstration of God's Existence* (1763), the *Observations on the Feeling of the Beautiful and Sublime* (1764), and the *Inquiry Concerning the Distinctness of the Principles of Natural Theology and Morality* (1764), the so-called "Prize Essay." Apart from these more substantive works, Kant also published a short "Essay on the Illnesses of the Head" in the *Königsberger Gelehrte und Politische Zeit-ungen* in February of 1764; and a review of a book that offered a theory of the "fireball" that had appeared in the sky on July 23, 1762, was published in March of 1764 in the same journal.[175] So, the period ended as it started: with a flurry of literary activity.

Most of this was written after October 1762, that is, after the Russians had left Königsberg. It almost seems as if Kant now took up where he left off when the Russians marched into Königsberg, now again pursuing wider philosophical recognition in Germany. The first of these post-Russian publications was not very different from his pamphlets advertising his lectures. Indeed, it most likely started out as such a pamphlet. Kant described *The False Subtlety* as the "product of a few hours," and he said that his main purpose was to introduce some materials that he could not extensively treat in his lectures on logic.[176] The work was probably concluded by early fall 1762. In any case, Hamann could already quote from it in a passage written on November 17.[177] It is not a highly original work. Its thesis that the Aristotelian theory of syllogism is too elaborate was already well known. Most of what Kant says in the work can already be found in Wolff, Thomasius, Meier, and Crusius.[178] No more should be expected from an expanded pamphlet advertising his lectures.

The "Prize Essay" was written for a competition sponsored by the Berlin Academy. The question was whether "the metaphysical truths in general, and the first principles of *theologiae naturalis* and morality in particular, admit of distinct proofs to the same degree as geometrical truths; and if they are not capable of such proofs, one wishes to know what the genuine nature of their certainty is, in what degree the said certainty can be brought, and whether this degree is sufficient for complete conviction."[179] The question was published in June of 1761, but Kant began to work on it only late, and he sent his essay off at the very latest possible date (December 31, 1762). Furthermore, he himself remarked that it was far from being a finished product.[180] This makes sense. Since the Russian occupation lasted until early July 1762, and since the Russians, in spite of their great friendliness, would not have looked with great favor on a member of the university who was dealing with the enemy, he probably started it only after Königsberg was again in Prussian hands.[181] Mendelssohn received the first prize, but Kant's *Inquiry* was judged to be of almost equal merit. As a matter of fact, Kant's essay does not even come close to Mendelssohn's much more polished effort. Perhaps there was also a bit of politicking at work in the academy to reward someone from Königsberg.

Kant's essay represented a more radical departure from traditional German philosophy, and that may have played a role as well. Mendelssohn had answered the question affirmatively in a traditional Wolffian (or rather Baumgartian) fashion. Kant followed Newton. Indeed, he explicitly claimed that his method was that of Newton, and he argued that mathematical certainty was different from philosophical certainty. Though the one was not greater than the other, the methods were quite dissimilar. While mathematics could follow the synthetic method, metaphysics had to follow the analytical method. Stipulative definitions, which form the basis of mathematical construction, have no place in philosophy. Philosophy must proceed analytically. Construction and intuition are unavailable here. The metaphysician must take the concepts as they are given in experience, and analyze them. Nevertheless, there are examples of certain knowledge in metaphysics. Not surprisingly, they turn out to be his own arguments as given in the *New Elucidation*. More surprisingly, perhaps, Kant is at the same time convinced that much less has been achieved in the metaphysics of morals than in the rest of metaphysics. Indeed, the title of the last section of this work expresses his belief that "The Primary Grounds of Morals Are, in Their Present State, Not Yet Capable of All Requisite Evidence." This formulation stands in stark contrast to the penultimate section, which was meant to establish that "The Primary Grounds of Natural Theology Are Capable of the Greatest Philosophical Evidence." Kant concludes in the final section of this essay

that, although it must be possible to attain the highest degree of philosophical evidence in the fundamental principles of morality, nonetheless the ultimate fundamental concepts of obligation must first be defined with more certainty. In this respect the task is greater in practical than in speculative philosophy, since it is still to be settled whether it is simply the cognitive faculty or whether it is feeling (the primary inner ground of the appetitive faculty) which decides the basic principles of practical philosophy.[182]

The reason for this claim seems to be the lack of clarity about the *formal* principles of morality. Kant argued that while we know that the principles of natural theology are principles of reason, we do not know this of the moral principles. He claimed that philosophers had only realized recently that the faculty of truth is cognition, whereas the moral faculty is "feeling" or "sensing." What is good is disclosed by "feeling." He claimed that it was important not to mix up the two. His view tended toward the thesis that in morality, feelings are basic, and that the understanding can only have the task of clarifying moral concepts by showing how they arise from "simple sensations of the good." He argued that "if the sensations of the good are simple, the judgment, 'This is good,' is completely indemonstrable and a direct effect of the consciousness of the feeling of pleasure associated with the conception of the object." He also claimed that we do in fact possess many simple sensations of the good, and that we must therefore admit many unanalyzable conceptions of the good. They give rise, according to Kant, to certain material principles of morality that are necessary conditions for any particular obligation. It is in "this respect Hutcheson and others have provided a start toward some excellent observations."[183] Kant must also have had in mind Hume's "pleasing sentiment of approbation," which is experienced by a disinterested spectator who has reasoned much and made many nice distinctions. Kant's discussion of the *material* principles of morality derived thus largely from British sources.

These material, sense-based principles were insufficient for Kant, however. He thought they stood in need of primary formal principles that are the necessary condition for acting morally *in general*.[184] Kant said that he was sure "after long consideration of this subject" what these primary formal principles are. They are the basic principles of the Wolffian ethics of perfection: "Do the most perfect thing that can be done by you," and "Refrain from that whereby the greatest perfection possible through you is hindered." Kant was unsure where these formal principles came from, whether from sensation or from cognition. That is the fundamental problem that he needed to solve before he could achieve "the highest degree of philosophical evidence in the primary bases of morality."[185]

At this point Kant seemed to think that while we know very little about moral obligation, we can know a great deal about God. The principles of natural theology have the highest philosophical evidence. Those of the metaphysics of morals have not – or so Kant says. This is quite in keeping with his *Only Possible Argument*, written around the same time. Kant closes this book by saying that it "is absolutely necessary that one should convince oneself that God exists; that His existence should be demonstrated, however, is not so necessary."[186] There is no reason to believe that Kant was disingenuous in saying this. Though he was very much opposed to a certain kind of theology, he did believe that there was a God. Furthermore, he was convinced that he had offered the best – indeed, the only – proof. Later he apparently lost faith in both his proof and God. As his friend in old age, Pörschke, witnessed: "He often assured me that even when he had been *Magister* for a long time, he did not doubt any dogma (*Satz*) of Christianity. Little by little, one after the other, they broke off."[187]

The *Concept of Negative Magnitudes* is another important product of these years. Kant probably completed it by June 1763, and it was published in the same year. In it, Kant opposed using the mathematical method in philosophy, while at the same time arguing that mathematics may be usefully employed in philosophy. He differentiated between logical opposition, or contradiction, and real opposition, or a conflict of forces. Nothing that contains a logical contradiction can exist. Accordingly, whatever is contradictory in the logical sense is nothing. However, an object that involves real opposition is possible. Impenetrability is an example of this. It is "negative attraction," or a force by means of which a body hinders another body from occupying the place it occupies. Kant also adduces other examples taken from psychology and morality to show that it makes sense to speak of negative magnitudes. There are many objects that contain forces that are opposed to each other, even though, because they cancel each other out, nothing seems to be happening. Yet only a spark may be required to set something in motion that is based on these opposing forces.

All of this seems to be quite compatible with his earlier system, according to which an external influence may awaken an internal change. Indeed, it may be seen as a further explication of that view. The explication of real reasons (*Realgründe*) seems to be based again on Baumgarten, and the estimation of the function of living forces seems to be the same as before.[188] Real reasons are internal, not external. There is something "great and . . . important" in Leibniz's claim that "the soul with its power of representation comprises the entire universe."[189] Still, Kant's distinction between real and ideal reasons is meant to be different from that of Crusius and Wolff. Real reasons are those reasons that do not simply follow the law of contradiction. They are not known by judgments but by concepts. These concepts may be analyzed into "simple and un-analyzable concepts, whose relation to what follows cannot be made distinct."[190] This represents the limit of the knowledge of all causality.

Kant poses clearly for the first time the question of the validity of the causal relation: "How am I to understand *that something exists because something else exists.*"[191] The relation cannot be logical or merely epistemological (like Crusius's ideal reason). There must be a real reason, but the question is what it is. Perhaps we will never know. Only analysis will tell. Kant promises such an analysis. He will not be content with such words as "cause," "effect," "force," and "action." He will try to see whether he can "by analysis reach more simple concepts of real reasons so that ultimately all our cognitions of these relations end in concepts of simple and unanalysable real reasons."[192]

This is a view with which a Leibnizian could live quite well. In any case,

the anti-Leibnizianism that many scholars have perceived in this piece just
does not seem to be there. The real reasons for all concepts are contained
in the "activity of our mind. External objects may contain the conditions
why they originate in one way or the other, but not the power to create
them."[193] On the other hand, there is clearly foreshadowed Kant's later
acceptance of Hume's critique of causality. There need be no contradiction here. Mendelssohn, a little earlier, had argued that Hume's analysis
of causality is compatible with Leibniz's view, and Kant may have held the
same view.[194]

Though *The Only Possible Argument*, perhaps his most important book
of this period, also has a publication date of 1763, it goes back to a much
earlier period. Indeed, its origin can be traced back at least to the fifties,
when Kant was working on cosmogony, and a rudimentary version of the
argument is already present in the *Nova Dilucidatio*. As Kant himself points
out: "The observations, which I present here, are the fruits of lengthy reflection. Because many other commitments have prevented me from
devoting the necessary time to it, these observations show characteristic
signs of haste and are incomplete."[195] It is not hard to guess at the "commitments" to which Kant is alluding. Though there may have been other
philosophical projects, they were mostly social obligations.[196] Kant certainly finished the essay before the middle of December of 1762. He had
probably been working on this book for quite some time. Borowski reported
that before he published it, he lectured for an entire semester on a "Critique
of the Proofs for the Existence of God."[197]

In *The Only Possible Argument* Kant tried to show that the argument
from design or the physico-theological proof of the existence of God is
insufficient. It can at best prove God as a craftsman, but not God as the
creator of matter itself. He also rejects the arguments of Descartes and
Wolff, who try to prove God's existence by concepts alone. The ontological argument, as Descartes devised it, cannot work because "existence is
not a predicate at all."[198] Wolff's argument, based on the empirical concept of existence and the notion of an independent thing, also fails. Kant
argued that "what is under investigation here is whether the fact that something is possible does not presuppose something existent, and whether
that existence, without which not even the internal possibility can occur,
does not contain such properties as we combine together in the concept of
God."[199] His answer is that it does. "The internal possibility of all things
presupposes some existence or other."[200] Accordingly, there must be something whose nonexistence would cancel all internal possibility whatsoever.
This is a necessary thing. Kant then tried to show that this necessary thing

must have all the characteristics commonly ascribed to God. Therefore, God necessarily exists. This a priori step in Kant's argument is followed by a step a posteriori, which was intended to establish the necessity of an absolutely necessary being. He argued that matter itself contains the principles that give rise to an ordered universe, and this, he thought, leads us to the concept of God as a Supreme Being, which "embraces within itself everything which can be thought by man."[201] God includes all that is possible or real. In other words, Kant offered an ingenious argument that combined a sort of ontological argument with a "purified" physico-theological argument.

This work showed Kant at the height of speculative power, but in many ways it was a throwback to the fifties as well. It was influenced by the *Essai de Cosmologie* and the *Examen philosophique* (1758) of Maupertuis. It also shows effects of Euler. In the main, it consisted of criticisms of Wolff and Crusius, and it presented important modifications of Baumgarten's metaphysics. Kant also spoke highly of Hermann Samuel Reimarus's *Abhandlungen von den vornehmsten Wahrheiten der christlichen Religion* (1754) and of Derham, who had already played a role in his *General History*. Vorländer is not altogether wrong to view *The Only Possible Argument* as the last work of Kant's "*naturphilosophische*" period. Even if one may doubt whether there was such a "period" in Kant's life, it surely enough represents the continued pursuit of old concerns more than the beginning of something new.

Given this explicit critique of Crusius, *Magister* Weymann could not fail to respond to *The Only Possible Argument,* and he did so – quickly. On January 14, 1764 he published "Reservations Concerning The Only Possible Argument of *Magister* Kant in Support of a Demonstration of the Existence of God." He accuses Kant of not having understood Crusius, and of not being able to provide arguments against atheism. As an example of Weymann's immodesty, the following two passages will perhaps suffice:

You talk somewhat disparagingly of the logical smelter in which concepts are purified. Every philosopher must experience this heat in his youth. This is why so few thorough thinkers can be found within the world of philosophy. For most of them are kept away by the fear of this smelter, and to be able to call themselves philosophers still, they cover philosophy with the mask of elegance (*Galanterie*).[202]

Furthermore,

At the same time you defend the case of the Idealists, for they also place the world in a "somewhere" (*Irgendwo*), but only in a thought somewhere, just as we ascribe to the garden the same shape that we see in an optical box.[203]

So Kant had already been accused of being an idealist in 1763, almost twenty years earlier than is generally known.

The reaction outside Königsberg was more favorable. Resewitz reviewed the book positively in the influential *Briefe die neueste Literatur betreffend.*[204] This review made Kant well known throughout Germany. Most importantly for Kant, however, it made his name in Berlin. Krickende, who had studied in Königsberg and then gone to Berlin, wrote to Scheffner in November 1764:

> *Magister* Kant has here [in Berlin] uncommon credit. Sack and Spalding have sung him a true panegyric song, and called him the subtlest philosophical brain, who had the gift to present the most abstract truths in the simplest way and to make them distinct for everyone. *Magister* Weymann is an oxymoron in the judgment of the examiners, and the scribbling of two lifetimes will not get him out of that. . . . There will soon be signs and miracles at the University of Königsberg, . . . and meteors to be seen.[205]

As a matter of fact, Krickende's prediction was premature.

If *The Only Possible Argument* represented a reworking of old ideas, the *Observations* dealt with new concerns. In it, Kant's aesthetic and literary preoccupations come to the fore. The work was written more from the point of view of an "observer" than from that of a "philosopher." It has four sections. The first introduces the concepts of the beautiful and the sublime, the second shows how these concepts are exhibited by human beings in general, the third shows how they are represented in men and women, and the last how they are found in nations. Much of the *Observations* must strike us as dated, as the expression of sentiments long since become passé. A woman is to have a "beautiful understanding" and a man a "deep understanding"; and a learned woman might as well grow a beard. "The Spaniard is earnest, taciturn, and truthful." The "Italian appears to have a feeling mixed from that of a Spaniard and that of a Frenchman," and so on. Some of his observations seem silly today, others are annoying, and still others touching. To be sure, there is irony in some of these passages. Kant's writing is playful at times, but this does not mean that he did not endorse most of what he said.

I am not sure whether the little book "richly discloses the personality of the author."[206] In fact, it is somewhat doubtful that it does. If any of Kant's books wears "the mask of elegance" or *Galanterie*, it is this one. What we get is not so much heartfelt sentiments as the prejudices of an era. Though Kant shared these prejudices, of course, they are not what defines his personality. That some of these prejudices survive in his lectures on anthropology as long as he lectured on this subject does not make them any less dated. They must be understood as signs of the time, not as Kant's own achievements. More importantly, perhaps, Kant later abandoned many of the views he presented in this book. He found:

> Among men there are but few who behave according to *principles* – which is extremely good, as it can so easily happen that one errs in principles, and then the resulting disadvantage extends all the further, the more universal the principle and the more resolute the person who has set it before himself.[207]

Principles are bad because they may exaggerate mistakes. "Indeed!" one might be tempted to say in light of later developments. Kant's mature moral philosophy depends on exactly the opposite point of view. How different the gallant *Magister* was from his later self. Bright ideas might be dangerous, but not as dangerous as bright ideas made into solid principles.

4

A Palingenesis and Its Consequences (1764–1769)

Kant at Forty: "When Does One Acquire One's Character?"

O N APRIL 22, 1764, Kant turned forty. This was a significant event, at least in Kant's own view of his life. According to his psychological or anthropological theory, the fortieth year is of the greatest importance. We may be able to use reason satisfactorily when we are twenty, but "as far as calculation (to use other human beings for one's own purposes)" is concerned, "it is the fortieth year" in which we reach maturity.[1] Even more significantly, Kant believed that it is in our fortieth year that we finally acquire a character.

No one who in his way of thinking is conscious of having character can have such character by nature. Rather, it must always be acquired. We may also assume that the foundation of this character and its beginning will be unforgettable. It is like a kind of rebirth, like a certain solemn kind of promise to oneself. Education, examples, and teaching cannot gradually bring about this firmness and constancy in principles, but it comes about only through an explosion, as it were, which follows all at once upon the dissatisfaction with the state of vacillation of instinct. There will perhaps only be few who have tried to accomplish this revolution before their thirtieth year and even fewer who have firmly founded it before they are forty. The attempt at becoming a better human being in fragments is a futile undertaking, for one impression disappears as we work on another. The foundation of a character is indeed the absolute unity of the internal principle of how to live in general.[2]

Character is thus not something we are born with or something that might happen to us. It is our own creation. We make or adopt our character, and to have a good character is the ultimate moral achievement.

Only insofar as we have a character do we have moral worth. It is our duty to form a character in the moral sense. Kant's moral psychology is

144

also a psychology of character. Indeed, it is this character that is the focus of Kant's concern. Whatever happens at forty, it has deep moral implications:

> That someone has a character can only be proved by his having adopted as his highest maxim the principle to be truthful in his inner confession to himself as well as in his dealings with anyone else.[3]

Accordingly, the maxim relevant first and foremost for judging character is that of truthfulness.

Kant offered many variations on this theme in his lectures on anthropology, claiming that only at forty can we begin to form a correct conception of things because then we have lived through varied situations of life. Before forty, hardly anyone is capable of correct judgments concerning the true value of things.[4] He also emphasized that character is possible only if our inclinations are still sufficiently strong to cause us to take interest in things, but not so strong as to become passions. All this will probably happen at the age of forty. Character requires a ripened understanding. Curiously, Kant also believed that forty marks the year in which the power of memory begins to weaken. Accordingly, we must have collected all the materials for thinking before that year. After forty, "we cannot learn anything new, though we can expand our knowledge."[5] Whatever we will accomplish after forty in intellectual matters is thus a function of the materials we have collected before that time and of the characteristic judgment that develops around forty. It will be the result of our knowledge and our character.

Character is built on maxims. Yet what are maxims? Kantian maxims are for the most part really ordinary sorts of things – at least in the way he described them in the context of anthropology. They are precepts or general policies that we have learned from others or from books, and that we choose to adopt as principles to live by. They show us to be rational creatures, or creatures who are capable of guiding their actions by general principles and not just by impulse. Yet and this is important, Kant did not think that they originate simply from our own reasoning. They are not primarily private principles but subjects of public discourse. Indeed, Kant insisted that conversations with friends about moral matters provide a very good way of clarifying our moral ideas. Maxims, in a sense, are all around us; the question is which we should adopt.

Maxims are not, moreover, restricted to moral contexts. Kant seems to believe that it is good to have maxims in every situation. To live by maxims, that is, to live in a principled way, is to live rationally. Maxims prevent us

from acting impulsively, from being swept away by emotions and thus acting foolishly. Though we know this well from Kant's writings, some of us
may be annoyed by his insistence that we really can act only in one of two
mutually exclusive ways – either by instinct or by reason – and that "as
human beings we live according to reason, and should therefore limit the
incentives (*Triebfedern*) of animality by maxims of reason and not allow any
inclination to become too strong."[6] That's pure Kant. Insistence on rationality is one of the essential aspects of Kant, and it should not be expected
that Kant would contradict in his anthropology lectures what he endorsed
in his published works. So, nothing surprising here.

What might be surprising, at least to those who have read recent secondary literature on Kant's ethics, is that maxims are meant to be relatively
and perhaps even absolutely constant. It does not seem to make sense for
Kant to speak of maxims that are temporarily adopted. Maxims that would
serve us at a certain moment or on one occasion, but that might be abandoned again at other times, are not really maxims in Kant's sense of the
word. This does not mean that once a maxim has been universalized it does
indeed hold universally, even if I never have to act on it again. Rather, it
means that maxims are the kind of things that we must act on all the time.
They are real principles by which we live. Once we have adopted something
as a maxim, we need to follow it. So, a maxim must be the kind of rule that
can be followed, that is, one that has relevance in our daily lives, not some
artificial principle. Thus "Always be first through the door" and "Never
eat fish on Friday" are indeed maxims, but a principle such as, "Whenever
it is Friday, and the sun is shining, and there is a white piece of paper lying
at this intersection, and there are exactly five leaves on the tree to the right,
I will not obey the red light" is not a maxim. Such a "principle" is not the
kind of rule we can live by. Even "Never eat fish on Friday" is a maxim, in
Kant's sense, only if the person who formulated it is willing to live by it
for the rest of his life. Constancy and firmness are required characteristics
of maxims. Once accepted, they must not be revoked – ever. Or so Kant
suggests.

Given this irrevocable character of maxims, it should not be surprising
that there must be relatively few, in Kant's view. Maxims are really the most
basic rules of conduct and thinking. We should not, therefore, attribute to
Kant the view that it is necessary to formulate maxims for every particular
act we can imagine. This is another reason why it would be a mistake to
think of our moral life as one of constant evaluation of maxims of action.
The adoption of a maxim should be viewed as a rare and very important

event in a human life. Maxims, at least "maxims" in the sense of the anthropology lectures, are *Lebensregeln,* or rules to live by. Maxims are therefore not to be understood as "free-floating, isolated decisions ... that stand in no connection with an enduring moral agent with a determinate nature and interest," as Henry Allison suggests as a possibility.[7] Maxims always refer to enduring moral agents. Indeed, they make sense only if we assume an agent. They are expressions of rational agency. If we truly knew the maxims of a rational agent, we would also know a great deal about the moral agent. Since the maxims are the very rules she lives by, the maxims would tell us what kind of person she is. Nor would we have to observe every action of the agent in order to determine her maxims. The patterns of her behavior would be enough to tell us something about the rules she has chosen to live by.

Maxims do not merely express what kind of a person one is; they constitute that person, in some sense. They constitute the person as character. In other words, to have a certain set of maxims and to have character (or to be a person) is one and the same thing. This is perhaps the most important point of Kant's anthropological discussion of maxims. Maxims are character-constituting principles. They make us who we are, and without them we are, at least according to Kant, nobody. As he puts it, character "is based on the rule of maxims"; to have a certain character means to have certain maxims, and to follow these maxims. Indeed, it is only when our "maxims are constant" that "we call them character." Perhaps it is still too weak to say that maxims are character-building principles, for character seems to be constituted by maxims. As free and rational beings, we can and must adopt principles according to which we live, and it is for that reason that character may "be defined also as the determination of the freedom (*Willkür*) of human beings by lasting and firmly established maxims." Insofar as character is indeed the characteristic mark of human beings as free and rational beings, living by maxims makes us what we should be. It is for this reason that Kant believes that the "mark of human beings considered as freely acting beings is, strictly speaking, his character." It is for this reason that he identifies character with our "way of thinking" (*Denkungsart*), which is opposed to the "way of sensing" (*Sinnesart*). Putting it differently, he says, "character is a certain subjective rule of the higher faculty of desire [i.e., will], ethics contains the objective rules of this faculty. Accordingly, character makes up what is characteristic of the highest faculty of desire. Each will . . . has its subjective laws, which constitute, however, its character."

To have character is not necessarily to have a morally good character. There are good characters and there are bad characters, and while Kant believes that it is better to have character in either sense than to have no character at all, good or moral character is better. How do we judge whether character is good or bad? By the maxims, of course! Maxims are decisive for judging the goodness of our character because the goodness of character depends upon the goodness of the maxims. If someone has a good character, then she also has good maxims, and if someone has good maxims, then she has a good character, and this is all that counts. (Someone without maxims is neither good nor bad. He is not moral at all but simply an instrument or a thing, ruled by his animal instincts.) Furthermore, the actions are not very important – at least not directly. In the anthropology, Kant goes so far as to say that actions really do not matter at all, and that it is really just the maxims that count in moral evaluations: "what is decisive in practical matters is not whether one has done a good action at one time (or other), but rather it is the maxim."[8]

"Someone who does not have character does not have maxims either."[9] Indeed, "character depends on the rule of maxims." It is the distinguishing mark of human beings as freely acting beings, and "it is called the *Denkungsart* or the way of thinking."[10] In other words, character limits freedom by maxims and consists in the firmness of maxims. Only a man with a constant character can be called good. To be good, he must have good maxims, and they must be constant. We are worth only as much as our maxims are worth. This means that we must legislate for ourselves, and that we must not rely on our feelings and inclinations. Indeed, character cannot be based on feelings, but must always be founded on maxims of reason. They have a definite purpose and are not free-floating rules. All this has relevance for a better understanding of Kant's mature philosophy, but it is also extremely important for understanding Kant's own development as a person. Since discovery, formulation, and adoption of maxims make for character, the moral rebirth of a person amounts to the beginning of a life according to maxims.

It is safe to assume that Kant underwent such a rebirth at about forty, and that as a result of it he consciously withdrew from the "whirlpool of societal diversions," which had swept him along before. Here is the source of what Borowski called "Kant's true nature according to all who knew him, namely his constant striving to live in accordance with reasoned principles, which were at least in his *own* view well founded." He strove to "formulate certain maxims in all large and small, important and unimportant matters, which always formed the basis [of his actions] and to which one always had to return. These maxims gradually became intertwined so much with his self that his actions always proceeded from them, even when he was not aware of them at the time."[11] This also had great consequences for the many "bright ideas" that characterized his mental life. They were to be put into the service of a universal theory, but first the theory itself had to be formulated.

The advice he gave to Herder on leaving Königsberg might have been withdrawn not long after it was offered. Perhaps it is not altogether wrong to characterize the revolution and rebirth that Kant underwent as the result of a "life crisis."[12] If Kant's foundation of his own character coincided with his fortieth year, then it coincided with a number of other significant developments in his life.

First of all, around 1764 his circle of friends changed dramatically. Kypke, who had moved to the outskirts of the city to raise carrots and onions, was no longer as close to Kant as he had been during earlier years. Indeed, as early as April 1761, Hamann reported that Kypke was building a "house at the garden, and lets his profession lay fallow for a time."[13] This included his professional friendships as well. It also appears that he never really returned to cultivating the arts. His garden seemed to provide more than enough fulfillment. Kypke never made any further contribution to the intellectual discussion of the time. His interests and those of Kant began to diverge so much that they no longer had much to talk about.

More importantly, however, in April, just days before Kant's fortieth birthday, Funk, Kant's closest friend, died suddenly. His entire circle of friends was in an uproar. Hamann reported on April 21 (the evening before Easter Sunday) that there had nearly been a brawl about who was to bury his corpse. The Prussians and the *Kurländers* both insisted that they had the right to put him to rest. Kant, a Prussian, was charged with organizing a memorial event (*Ehrengepränge*), but the officials prohibited it. Neither party was allowed to have a public event. Instead, Funk was buried at night. Hippel, a *Kurländer*, composed an elegy to Funk. Hamann expected that the "other party," that is, the Prussians, which most prominently included Kant, would do the same. It is not known whether the Prussians did follow suit, but we may be sure that none of these developments made it easier for Kant to deal with the loss.

We do not know how he grieved, but since he was a sensitive human being, Kant surely could not have been without a great deal of sorrow. His fortieth birthday could not have been a happy one. His grieving would not

have been very different from the way in which we all experience it. There
was denial, there were feelings of guilt, and, most importantly, there were
sustained attempts at coming to terms with the loss and his own life. The
loss of his friend meant more to him than the deaths of most people before and after. In any case, Funk's death provided him with ample occasion
for reflection on life, death, and "the true value of things," and such an
experience of human mortality could have been one of the reasons for the
"palingenesis," or "rebirth," or the "explosion . . . which follows all at
once upon the dissatisfaction with the state of vacillation of instinct." If
only because of the death of Funk, the period 1764–65 was very important for Kant, indeed.

The religious – even Pietistic – overtones in Kant's account of the origin of character cannot be overlooked. In another account of the necessity
of our rebirth he draws a definite parallel to the religious conversion described by the Pietists. Unsurprisingly, this account reveals an intimate
understanding not only of the Pietistic doctrine of rebirth, but also of orthodox Christianity. Differentiating between the Spener–Francke and the
Moravian–Zinzendorf *Bekehrungslehren,* both of which were mystical for
him, he claimed that both declare that what is supersensible is also supernatural. They maintain that a miracle is necessary either for becoming a
Christian or for achieving a Christian way of life.[14]

It would be a mistake, however, to view Kant's conversion as a religious
one. For he advocated what was essentially a moral solution to the problem.
In fact, he claims that morality is "the genuine solution of that problem
(of the new man)."[15] He claims: "There is something in us that we can never
cease to wonder at once it has entered our sight, and this is what also elevates the idea of *humanity* to a dignity which one might not expect in *man*
as the object of experience."[16] The specific description of moral rebirth
and character that Kant offered later, in *The Dispute of the Faculties,* is perhaps couched in a language that was not available to Kant in 1764–65, but
its substance and its general characterization are quite compatible with his
earlier view. By acquiring a character one becomes a new person (*neuer
Mensch*). We recreate ourselves in accordance with maxims. Kant is thus
in this sense further away from Rousseau, who believed that virtue was a
gift of nature, and closer to Hume, who believed that we needed to "cul-
tivate" our natural interest in morality.[17] For Kant, virtue is artificial, not
natural. We must create ourselves anew from the materials of our previous
lives – or so he suggests. Though Kant's theory of the "new man" may sound
Christian, it also has definite Stoic elements. Indeed, the triumph of the

man of character over the oscillations of feelings and passions, his realization that the moral law gives human beings dignity far beyond any other animal, and his self-mastery by maxims – all these aspects of Kant's view of character align him more closely with these pre-Christian philosophers than with the Pietists.[18] Indeed, even the Platonic ideal of the "wise and serene character, always consistent with itself" is closer to Kant's view than is that of the latter-day Christians.[19]

The new Immanuel Kant that emerged after 1764 was different in other respects as well. Again, this was the result of maxims. In a rare autobiographical note Kant tells us:

Because of my narrow and flat chest, which leaves little room for the movements of heart and lung, I have a natural inclination to hypochondria, which *in my earlier years bordered on despair of living.* But the consideration that the cause of this congestion of the heart was merely mechanical and could not be changed soon made me completely disregard it so that there was calmness and joy in my head even though I felt constricted in my chest . . .[20]

This sounds very much like a description of a mild form of angina pectoris (chest pains caused by insufficient oxygenation of the heart muscle). Since this condition was first accurately described by London physician William Heberdeen in 1768, we may assume that at least the description of his ailment goes back to the time around 1768, though Kant may have viewed it in a similar way even earlier.

Kant felt that to escape hypochondriacal states we should go about our "daily business" (*Tagesordnung*) and concentrate on the things we must do. Our maxim should be to focus on other matters and especially on philosophical problems, and this, Kant is sure, will enable us to overcome the states of anxiety to which we might otherwise fall victim. Orderliness is a source of mental health. A life in accordance with maxims not only makes us virtuous, but has other "advantages" as well.[21]

Though the history of hypochondria goes back to antiquity, it was an especially fashionable disease in the eighteenth century. It was all the rage among intellectuals.[22] Throughout "most of its history it was linked to melancholia, which, being one of the four directions a personality could tend toward, was a common temperamental type."[23] Richard Burton in his successful book on *The Anatomy of Melancholy* of 1621 differentiated among many kinds of melancholy, of which "hypochondriacal melancholy" was only one. It arose for him "from the bowels, liver, spleen, or membrane called *mesenterium*" and was also called "windy melancholy, which Laurentius subdivides into three parts from those three members, *Hepatick, splenetick, meseraick.*"[24] Burton's book was apparently a favorite of Hamann's, and Kant probably knew it as well. The "hypochondriacal winds" of his *Dreams of a Spirit-Seer,* and the essay on the "Illnesses of the Head" suggest at the very least that he knew of the concept. By the end of the eighteenth century hypochondria had turned into one of the commonest disorders, afflicting persons from every social stratum.[25] It is not surprising that Kant believed he suffered from it. Nor was he alone, since Hamann and Kraus were also professed hypochondriacs.

James Boswell and Samuel Johnson were also afflicted by it. Indeed, Samuel Johnson's advice to Boswell was quite compatible with Kant's advice to himself: "constant occupation of the mind, to take a great deal of exercise, and to live moderately, especially to shun drinking at night." Hypochondria could be a merely imagined sickness, but often it was not. Nor would it be correct to think that it was merely a disease of the mind. This is also what Kant believed. Though hypochondria has to do with fantasy and is largely based on the whims of the afflicted, "it is an evil, which probably intermittently migrates through the entire nervous system, regardless which part of the body is its main location. It attracts primarily a melancholic vapor around the seat of the soul," and this is why the patient feels almost every sickness of which he hears, why he likes to talk of his afflictions and likes to read medical books. Yet, "in society he sometimes is overcome by good cheer, and then he laughs very much, eats well, and is commonly viewed as a healthy person."[26] If he is overcome by some strange idea that might cause him to laugh inappropriately in the presence of others, or "if some dark representations awaken in him a violent inclination (*Trieb*) towards something evil, and if he is anxious and afraid that it might erupt (though this might never happen), then his state has similarity to insanity, even if there is no danger. The evil is not deeply rooted; it disappears either by itself or through medication, at least insofar as the mind (*Gemüt*) is concerned."[27] Kant knew what he was talking about. Indeed, in claiming that hypochondria has both a physiological and a psychological component he seems to be talking about himself.

Kant did not have just a vague feeling of discomfort, amplified by brooding concern. It was not just that he had a tendency to believe that he had sicknesses, which he might not have had; there was also an underlying physiological cause of these feelings. The emotions or feelings that *"bordered on despair of living"* were at least in his own mind and probably also in reality connected with his narrow chest, which made breathing difficult and made it more difficult for his heart to work. He suffered from a mild form of scoliosis or curvature of the spine. His muscles were always weak and undeveloped, and his bone structure was unusually delicate. He easily could overexert himself. Later in his life (1778) he said that he was never sick, but that he was never really healthy either. He was "healthy in a weak way." The only way he felt he could maintain this precarious state, he claimed, was by "a certain uniformity in the way of living and in the matters about which I employ my mind."[28]

Connected with his delicate body was a great sensitivity. He spoke himself of his "sensitive nerves." Thus he was affected greatly by even small changes in his environment. Therefore, he was very attentive to his bodily needs from very early on. Worries about his bodily well-being naturally led to worries about other matters. Kant was a worrier, but anxiety or worry that causes distress was – and is – no harmless affliction. Kant's attempt to overcome it by concentrating on matters at hand seems to be as relevant today as it was then. Reflecting on such anxieties and worries seems only to amplify them and is therefore self-defeating. Kant's own regimen was perhaps just a simple and simple-minded form of mental hygiene, but it is not uninteresting to observe that Kant found it necessary to engage in it. It was an approach born of need, not of idleness. To try to engage in activities that are incompatible with the worries seems to be much more productive in the long run. In any case, it turned out to be more productive in Kant's case. Nor does it seem to be entirely unattractive. George Bernard Shaw once said that the "true joy of life" was "the being used for a purpose recognized by yourself as a mighty one, the being thoroughly worn out before you are thrown on the scrap heap; the being a force of Nature instead of a feverish, selfish little clod of ailments and grievances complaining that the world will not devote itself to making you happy." Kant's new character was born of similar considerations.

It was this revolution that made possible Kant's later achievements. It was also the core of his mature philosophy. This does not mean that Kant "mechanically ordered" his life so that he could create the body of his work. Later, that is, after 1775, when he was over fifty, he began to worry about whether he would have enough time to finish what he then believed he had to say, but he did not have these worries in 1764, when he was not yet sure what he really had to say. Did Kant deceive himself when he claimed that he *created* his character, and that he consciously *formulated* his new maxims? Were his views only rationalizations of processes that had nothing to do with choice? Were these developments the beginning of the end of Kant's life? Some have argued that, but it seems to beg the question.[29] Perhaps it is not altogether false to say that at forty there began a process in which Kant's external life became more and more predictable, and that this ultimately led to a dramatic increase in his literary productivity. Yet to say that this was "a peculiar process of mechanization in Kant's external life which favored his inner life . . . [and that] the dying of the periphery led to the intensification of activity at the center of the psyche" is both too fanciful and too simple-minded.[30] To say that Kant's conception of character was "the only possible solution" to his life's problem appears to be just as naïve as to claim that the "life at the limit (*Grenze*), as the philosopher must lead it, is always a life in crisis . . . a life whose 'possibility' cannot be described and a life which does not conform to any plan."[31] Of course, we as human beings – Kant included – can plan our lives. These plans do not always turn out the way we want them to turn out, but that is a different story.

Kant's newfound appreciation of maxims not only was rooted in the desire to escape the unpleasant experiences of death, hypochondria, and despair, but also was connected to other developments in his daily life. During the time around 1764–5, Kant made new friends. Most important among these new friends was Joseph Green, an English merchant who had come to Königsberg when he was very young. Green was a bachelor like Kant, but he lived a different life from the one Kant had lived until then. Rather than being driven by the whirlpool of events, Green lived by the strictest rules or maxims. Indeed, he followed the clock and calendar pedantically. Hippel, who wrote a play called *The Man of the Clock* in 1765, is thought to have modeled this man after Green.[32] "Green was distinguished by his character as a rare man of strict righteousness and true nobility, but he was full of the most peculiar characteristics – a true *whimsical man* [English in the original], whose days followed an invariable and strange (*launenhaft*) rule."[33] Green traded in grain and herrings and also in coal and manufactured goods.[34] He was the "greatest and most highly esteemed among the merchants in the English colony of Königsberg."[35] Yet he was less interested in pursuing his business than in reading books "about new inventions and travels of discovery," living "the life of a hermit."[36] According to one observer, he was "more a scholar than a merchant," and his education was much superior to that of the other merchants of his day.[37] It is perhaps not surprising that Kant found his friendship so valuable.

We cannot be entirely sure when Kant came to know Green, but it was sometime before 1766, and perhaps as early as 1765. In 1766, when Green was on business in England, Scheffner wrote to Herder: "The *Magister*

[Kant] is now constantly in England, because Rousseau and Hume are there, of whom his friend Mr. Green sometimes writes to him."[38] Two weeks later he related a number of anecdotes concerning Hume and Rousseau to Herder, which obviously come from the letters of Green to Kant. It has been said that Green and Kant first met each other at the time of the American Revolution, and that their relationship started with a heated dispute about it. Kant took up the side of the Americans and Green that of the English.[39] This cannot be true, of course, though it may well be that their dispute was about an earlier episode that ultimately led to the American Revolution, namely the Stamp Act of 1765. It led to riots in Boston and elsewhere in August of that year, which forced the British Parliament to revoke the act later that very same year.[40] This would mean that Kant's friendship with Green dates back to the summer of 1765. This much is sure, that by 1766 they were close friends; and at least from that time on Kant was a constant and very regular visitor at Green's house. Kant's regularity was probably – at least at first – due more to Green's punctuality than to that of Kant, for it was said that the neighbors could set their clocks in accordance with the time at which Kant left Green's house in the evening: at seven o'clock the visit was over.

A number of anecdotes illustrate how strictly Green adhered to his rules and promises. Kant and Green were said to have once agreed to take a leisurely trip in a horse-drawn carriage to the country at 8:00 A.M. the next day. Green, who was already waiting for Kant at 7:45, left precisely at 8:00 even though Kant was nowhere to be seen, and when he passed Kant a little later on the road, he just drove past him, with Kant vigorously signaling for him to stop. It was against Green's maxim to do so. The character of Hippel's comedy who corresponds to Green mocks his future son-in-law because he "gets up whenever it occurs to him – at 7:00, at 8:00, at 9:00 – for he does not have, like other honest people, his coffee and tea days. No! He hardly knows half an hour beforehand whether he will drink tea or coffee. His lunch is dictated by his hunger . . ." He praised himself: "I do not get up because I have slept enough, but because it is 6:00 A.M. I go to eat not because I am hungry, but because the clock has struck 12:00. I go to bed, not because I am tired, but because it is 10:00 P.M."[41]

A *Magister*, who plays a role in the play, objects that it is a mistake to think "that learned works follow the same rules as the letters of merchants, which must be written because it is the day for the mail. A dissertation – by the hangman! – is not a bank draft. With such works one cannot keep hours."[42] Kant probably still would have agreed with the *Magister* at this time, but little by little he learned to write philosophy like a bank draft, and he kept hours for writing as well.

The two became very close, and Green's effect on Kant cannot be overestimated. Like Kant, Green loved Hume and Rousseau. "The association with the highly original and most righteous Englishman Green assuredly had not just a small influence on Kant's way of thinking and especially on his study of English authors."[43] When he was around Funk, Kant loved to play cards, went to the theater, listened to concerts, and pursued other diversions. He was a man of the town. Soon he gave up playing cards to please Green.[44] His visits to the theater became rarer, and late in life they ceased almost altogether. Green was completely tone deaf. Thus he could distinguish poetry from prose only by the way it was printed on the page, and he found the way poems were printed on the page disorienting. Kant, "at least in his early years, listened to good music with pleasure." He gave up that custom as well.[45] Borowski frequently contrasts in his biography what Kant did "earlier" and what he did (or better: did *not* do) "later," bearing witness to the profound changes that took place after 1764. The elegant *Magister* with a somewhat irregular and unpredictable lifestyle changed into a man of principle with an exceedingly predictable way of life. He became more and more like Green. Kant slowly adopted Green's way of life – or so it would seem. The days of the whirlpool of social diversions were coming to an end – not suddenly, but slowly: maxim by maxim.

They completely trusted each other, and they shared most of their thoughts and feelings with each other. Yet their friendship did not, at least if we are to believe Kant himself, rely on "mere feeling," but on "principles." It was a "moral" friendship, not a merely "aesthetic" one.[46] Kant's view of maxims, as necessary for building character, was, at least in part, indebted to Green's way of life. It was not an accident that in the lectures on anthropology in which Kant spoke of maxims, he often claimed that the English had the most solid understanding. He himself relied on the judgment of his English friend.

A close friend of both Kant and Green was Robert Motherby (1736–1801) of Hull. He had come to Königsberg at the age of eighteen as the result of an inquiry by Green, who was looking for a reliable assistant. Motherby could not speak any German when he first arrived, but he soon became indispensable to Green in all his business dealings. Green later made him his partner in the firm, and when Green died, Motherby inherited the firm. Kant continued to visit Motherby after Green's death and was a close friend of the family. Through these English merchants Kant got to know others within their circle of acquaintance, such as the Englishman Barcklay, the Scottish merchant Hay, and the French merchants Toussaint and Laval. Motherby married one of the ten daughters of Toussaint (Charlotte).[47] Still, it was Green who became the most intimate friend Kant ever had.

In 1768, Hamann wrote: "I was day-dreaming several days ago when I was at my friend Green's. Then, I heard Kant claim that we cannot expect any new and important discoveries in astronomy because of its perfection. I remembered, as if in a sleep, that I hated the new hypotheses of astronomy so much that I could have annihilated them . . ."[48] In practicing the art of conversation, Green and Kant discussed most things. Such conversations probably followed more often than not the schema Kant describes in his lectures on anthropology. A conversation, according to this view, has three parts; a narrative or story, a discussion, and jest. The conversation begins with someone telling a story, which is then discussed. This discussion may get heated. "If the discussion or *raisonnement* becomes too serious and threatens to become an argument, then it would be lucky if there is someone with wit at the table who might give the dispute a different direction."[49] The story might take an inordinately long time, but Kant was confident that the conversation would sooner or later be directed to discussion, and that therefore wit would have to be introduced sooner or later. However, "a conversation that consists only of jest and joking is unbearable and tasteless." Indeed, it is almost "like a dream" because it does not have any coherence.[50] We may only hope that Kant's assurance that "we cannot expect any new and important discoveries in astronomy because of its perfection" was an expression of his wit, rather than a part of his contribution to the discussion. Other topics of conversation in 1768 would have been the London bread riots, during which government grain stores were looted by the mob, and the fact that the price of bread in Paris had reached the high price of four sous per pound. Green was a merchant after all.

The firm of Green, Motherby & Co. also took care of most of Kant's money. Indeed, Borowski claimed that Kant "invested his savings in the most advantageous way – something in which his friend Green took one hundred times greater care than he did himself."[51] While it is not known when Kant began his investments in the firm, we do know that in 1798 he had accumulated 43,000 guilders in it, which was a very significant amount of money.[52] Given the size of his savings, the meagerness of his income throughout his life, and the power of compound interest, it is more than likely that he started to invest small amounts of money early. Kant understood that the maxim of putting aside regularly smaller amounts of money has more significant rewards than trying to save large amounts late in life. In any case, these developments must be seen against a stark economic background. Prussia was affected in 1763 by a severe financial crisis, which had started in Holland. Even before there had been inflation in Prussia, caused by Prussia's debasement of its currency to pay for the Seven-Year War. The economy basically was stagnant, and it did not get better until the seventies. In 1763, food was so scarce in Berlin that people stood in long lines at the entrances of the bakeries "and fought terribly about the half-baked bread, which was of inferior quality.[53]

Those who had to live on fixed incomes were especially severely affected by these developments. Though Kant did not live on a fixed income, he did have to live on the fees paid by students, and there were fewer students in the sixties and seventies than there had been in the fifties. Nonetheless, the financial situation in Königsberg was not as bad as it was in Berlin, because Königsberg was much more closely tied to Poland and the other eastern European countries. Still, the citizens of Königsberg were not helped by the developments in Berlin. There can be little doubt that Kant had to live much more frugally during most of the sixties than during the time of the Russian occupation, or after he became a full professor in 1770. Money, as we have seen, was never unimportant to Kant, but it was particularly important between 1762 and 1764.

On November 11, 1764, a large fire broke out in Königsberg, which lasted a week and destroyed 369 houses, 49 warehouses, and the Löbenicht church. It also took many lives. The fire may have been a case of arson. Its devastation reminded all of the citizens of Königsberg, including Kant, how precarious life really is.[54]

Kant's Method of Teaching:
"The Genuine Method in Philosophy is Zetetic"

During 1764 there were several indications that Kant's name had begun to be noticed. Not only had his works received good reviews, but they were also discussed seriously at other universities. One sign of this was a disputation by a *Magister* Cleß at Tübingen, which was sent to Kant late in 1764. Ploucquet had presided at the defense. One half of the book was simply the Kantian text. In the other half, Kant was "interpreted, supplemented, and sometimes refuted with great respect."[55] More importantly, there was official recognition from Berlin. In August of 1764 the university received a letter authorizing it to fill the post of full professor of poetry, which had been vacant since J. G. Bock's death. In the letter Kant's name was specifically mentioned: "We know through some of his writings a certain *Magister* there, whose name is Immanuel Kant. His writings reveal a very thorough learning." The letter went on to ask, was he suitable for the position, and would he be inclined to accept?[56] Kant's answer was: "No, but he would be very interested in the position of logic and metaphysics, which might soon open up." He was confident that a more appropriate position was in reach, and he did not opt for what appeared to him second best. He would soon reach what was one of his most important goals – at least as far as his official career at the university was concerned. This was another reason for reflecting on what he had accomplished so far, and what he wanted to do with the rest of his life. As one reason for anxiety, other reasons may have surfaced.

Kant declined to take a position that would have meant a steady income, certain that he would get a more suitable position sooner or later.[57] The next opportunity of official support did not amount to much, though it was better than nothing. It came when the sublibrarian of the *Schloßbibliothek* retired. The *Schloßbibliothek* basically amounted to the university library, though it was not heavily used. Kant applied for this position in November 1765 and received it in February of 1766. He was paid the salary of 62 Thalers per year.[58] The library was open twice a week, on Wednesday and Saturday between 1:00 and 4:00 P.M. The old sublibrarian had left the library in disarray. Kant and his superior (Friedrich Samuel Bock) had to reorder the books and compare the holdings with the catalogues. If this was arduous and mind-numbing work, it was not made much better by the fact that the rooms of the library were not heated during the winter. Sublibrarian Kant therefore sat much of the year – six hours a week – with "stiff hands" and "frozen ink" in dark rooms, which did not allow him to read or write at all. He had to be there, even if there were hardly any patrons during the long Königsberg winters. On the other hand, the new regular salary improved his "very deficient subsistence."[59]

This salary allowed Kant to change his residence in 1766. He had never liked the noise that came from the commercial vessels that used the river Pregel, which was close to his quarters, and from the many carriages that brought Polish wares into the city. Accordingly, he moved into the house of his publisher Kanter.[60] His large house – sometimes described as the old City Hall – contained apartments, lecture rooms for Kant and other professors, as well as some rooms for students. It also was the location of Kanter's bookstore, which had the atmosphere of a coffeehouse. Kanter not only sold books, which could be inspected by the professors, but also published the *Königsbergische Gelehrten und Politischen Zeitungen,* which the professors and even the students – at least on certain days – could read without payment. The intellectuals of Königsberg made this bookstore into a central cultural institution and meeting place. Visitors often made it their first stop. Beginning in the summer of 1768, the bookstore was adorned with the portraits of some of the most important cultural representatives of Königsberg and the rest of Prussia, including Mendelssohn, Hippel, Scheffner, Lindner, and of course Kant, who had published some of his works with Kanter.[61] Kant also benefited in other ways from living in Kanter's house. He could, for instance, borrow all the books he wanted and take them up to his apartment. Furthermore, at times he saw a manuscript even before it was printed, and he was kept up-to-date on the literary and social gossip, whether he wished to be or not.

The position of professor of poetry was given on October 24 to Lindner, one of Kant's closest friends from his student years. Indeed, it appears that Kant himself used his influence in Königsberg to obtain this position for Lindner.[62] Lindner's return to Königsberg was significant for Kant. After the loss of Funk, Lindner could have become the most important of his academic friends. Funk had not been a faithful husband – like Kant, he was interested at least as much in gallantry as in scholarship. Lindner was less interested in matters of gallantry and more in literature. Though one might suppose that his interests were more compatible with the new character Kant began forming at the time, there is no evidence that the two continued their friendship. One of the reasons for this might have been Lindner's theological views. He later became court preacher in Königsberg and Hamann's confessor.[63] By all accounts, he was closer to Hamann than to Kant.

Kant continued to teach a heavy load. He tried to teach students how to philosophize, but he did not see himself as teaching his students the truth in a systematic fashion. In his "Announcement" of his lectures for the winter semester of 1765–66 he argued that a skeptical method is best in philosophy.[64] He told his prospective students that he was not going to teach philosophy ("which is impossible"), but rather how to philosophize:

The true method of instruction in philosophy is *zetetic,* as it was called by some of the ancients (derived from *zetein*). It is searching, and it can become *dogmatic,* that is, *decided* through a more developed reason only in some parts.[65]

Using the old Pyrrhonic characterization of the Skeptics as inquirers who "persist in their investigations," he also explicitly pointed out in his lec-

tures that this was the very name that was used by Sextus Empiricus to refer to the "skeptic discipline."[66] Though Kant did not seem to want to deny
that philosophy can become dogmatic, he did not suggest that it had become so to any large extent. He was already fairly certain as to why metaphysics was "still so imperfect and insecure." Philosophers misunderstood
its characteristic method. It is not synthetic, as commonly supposed, but
analytic.[67] This is as true of metaphysics as it is of ethics. Indeed, Kant
argued that though ethics has a better reputation than metaphysics, it was
just as imperfect. It may appear more thorough because the human heart,
or sentiment, tells us what is right and wrong before we have thought about
it. However, these distinctions have not been drawn very clearly. Therefore,
we should be just as skeptical about ethics as we are about metaphysics.

His lectures in metaphysics began with a short introduction into "empirical psychology," followed by a discussion of material nature. He then
went on to present ontology as the "science of the universal attributes of
objects," and the difference between immaterial and material being, paying special attention to rational psychology. Finally, he considered the cause
of all things or the "science of God and the world." The order was dictated by Kant's pedagogic concerns. The young students were to be introduced first into particular matters of interest to anyone, and only afterwards
into the more difficult abstract metaphysical theories. Kant thought that
this had the added benefit that a student who lost interest after empirical
psychology would at least have learned something that would be useful in
life.[68] Logic, according to the "Announcement," can be treated in two ways –
either as a critique and law of common sense, or as a critique and law of
science. Kant claimed he would treat it in the first way, so that it would be
useful in the daily life of his students. Moral philosophy deals not only
with what should be done, but also with what actually takes place. It has an
anthropological basis, which deals with the nature of man "that always
remains." Physical geography is meant to give the students knowledge of
geography in the widest sense of the word, and thus to help them understand their place in the world. All the lectures had a clear practical peda-
gogical objective. Kant claimed that he wanted to make a difference in the
lives of his students, to teach them something useful. For this reason, he
wanted to make himself understood.

One of the most important of his students during the period between
1764 and 1769 was Marcus Herz (1747–1803). He was born in Berlin as the
son of a synagogue scribe. After studying the Talmud, he went to Königsberg in 1762 to become an apprentice at the house of Joachim Moses
Friedländer, a banker and merchant of some standing. Königsberg had one

of the "largest, most significant, and most enlightened Jewish communities in Northern Europe."[69] Supported by Friedländer and others, he matriculated at the university. He was inscribed in the register of the university on April 4, 1766. This was not a matter of course. Rules that allowed Jews to study at the university without special permission were instituted only by the end of the sixties. No Jew ever obtained a professorship during Kant's lifetime. Catholics had the same problem. Interestingly, though, Kant later supported another Jewish student of his in trying to obtain a position in the faculty of medicine, but ultimately had to give up.[70] Herz attended the lectures Kant gave in the semester immediately following his "Announcement."[71] What he heard in 1766 would not have been very different from what Kant had taught during the previous semester. Herz is said to have made "many a good poem between Kant's lectures."[72] He himself claimed that his studies "of languages and philosophy" in Königsberg were accompanied by "constant and uninterrupted pain, which I might call torture." He succeeded only by "the greatest effort."[73] He became a good friend of Kant's, probably serving as one of his most intimate partners in philosophical discussions during this period. Thanking Kant, he later wrote:

> It is you alone whom I have to thank for the happy change in my circumstances, to whom I am indebted for my entire self. Had it not been for you I would even now, like so many of my brethren drag a burden of prejudice, lead a life inferior to that of a beast . . . I would be nothing.[74]

We get many hints about how well acquainted Herz was with Kant's views from the later correspondence between the two.

Herz also had an effect on the Jewish community in Königsberg, since he encouraged others to learn modern languages and acquaint themselves with non-Jewish literature. He appears even to have been able to convince "Jewish beauties" that it was elegant to have a copy of Baumgarten's *Metaphysics* on their make-up tables.[75] After moving to Berlin, he actively popularized Kant's philosophy there in the late seventies. He thus became one of the most important early followers of Kant.[76] Nonetheless, like Herder and several other early students of Kant, he never could appreciate Kant's mature philosophical position.

By the end of 1769, Kant received "a call" from the University of Erlangen, a small Prussian institution far away from Königsberg. He was offered the first chair of theoretical philosophy (logic and metaphysics). The position was well funded. Kant provisionally said yes. On December 13,

1769, Kant received the official offer. He had to make his final decision, which was negative. As he explained:

Renewed and many powerful assurances, the appearance of a perhaps close vacancy here, the attachment to my home town (*Vaterstadt*) and a very wide circle of acquaintances and friends, but first and foremost my weak bodily constitution, suddenly rise up in my mind so powerfully against the undertaking so that I can find peace of mind only where I have so far always found it, even if under burdensome circumstances.[77]

This reads like not just a decision not to go to Erlangen, but a maxim to stay in Königsberg. He feigned "defects of character," which he hoped would excuse him in Erlangen (and, of course, in Berlin), but it is clear that he himself had come to terms with his lack of the spirit of adventure, and that he was more than content to stay and to be who he was, a citizen of the University of Königsberg.

A Literary Circle: "A Comedy of Five Acts"

Perhaps as a result of living in the house of the bookseller Kanter, Kant became part of "a literary circle which formed itself and to which the world must perhaps be thankful for a number of reflections."[78] It was also called "a *learned society*" or a "learned circle." Hippel said that its regular members were General (*Oberstleutnant*) von Lossow, who was the chairman, the baroness of Thile, the president, *Magister* Kant, *Herr* and *Frau* Jacobi, and the master of the mint, Goeschen. "Among the extra-ordinary members there were – very many."[79] Hippel also claimed that he was at only one of the meetings of the society. Some of the members of the society also met less formally outside of the regular meetings, and with other friends. He would have met most if not all of them on a number of occasions. Hippel's ironic distance from this public society can be explained, at least to some extent, by his own involvement with the more clandestine, but more politically motivated, club of the Freemasons. While Kant never joined their ranks, many of his friends were members.

"Literary societies" were all the rage in Germany during the last third of the eighteenth century. Most of them were similar to the larger and more formal reading societies, which also existed throughout Germany. In the absence of public libraries, reading societies were formed because books and magazines were relatively expensive. Members of the reading societies could read many more books, magazines, and newspapers than they otherwise could have afforded. Joint subscriptions were their main benefit, but

literary debate also proved to be important. Not all reading was literary, of
course. Acquisition of practical knowledge by its members also formed an
important part of a reading society's mission. Reading societies "adopted
a democratic organizational structure . . . the highest authority was the
general meeting, usually held on a monthly basis. . . . As a rule, in addition to the general assembly, there was also an elected committee consisting of a chairman, a treasurer and a secretary."[80] Egalitarianism
formed the basis of these societies. Class and rank were at the very least
supposed to be irrelevant, even if they were not always without their effect. They were Enlightenment in practice – serious business, in other
words. Henriette Herz (1764–1847), the wife of Markus Herz, wrote late
in her life that "one read then differently from now." Reading was done in
"community." One bought fewer literary works, and one read them together, talking about them with each other. "One had the goal of educating
oneself (*sich zu bilden*), a word which now has become almost one of
ridicule."[81] Because that is what people wanted, learned men and even famous scholars did not think it violated their standing if they taught those
who wanted to learn. "Often they presented in a social and very mixed circle what our scholars of today would think worthy only for their students
and other scholars."[82] That Kant felt it necessary to participate in such an
enterprise shows how seriously he took the concerns of the Enlightenment. It is probably no accident that his student and friend, Henriette's
husband, became active in very much the same way, but it is perhaps just
an accident that the literary societies in Berlin, and especially those connected with Henriette and Marcus, have received so much more attention
than the one in which Kant was involved.

The formal literary society was loosely connected to Kant's circle of
friends. This was not uncommon either. Literary friendship circles, in contrast to literary societies, "often assumed the character of private literary,
or learned and philosophical, circles revolving completely around convivial
conversation or philosophical debate."[83] They were more pleasure than
business. That this was true of the Königsberg circle cannot be doubted.
We know what some of its meetings were like from Hippel's correspondence of the period. Sometime in 1767 he wrote to Scheffner:

professor Lindner has also acted *magnifice*, and has given a dinner one evening for the
professor Will, Amon, Kant, Hamann, my own insignificant self and Mr. Kanter. In
Friedrichstein W* was in his own element. As happy as a prince and witty as a poet of
dithyrambs [or wild Bacchanalian songs]. We extemporized a burlesque in which he
played his part so well that I became curious to see his pieces for the theater. As much

as K* has told me about it, I cannot find anything new in them. In other respects W* was very reserved, according to Kant and Goeschen. But I thought it was a small town attitude. Kanter's wife, who undoubtedly does not like it that every day they eat and drink at their house, made a terrible scene.[84]

Nothing staid and reserved about this meeting! Even if Kant would have found at least some of the goings-on tasteless and might have felt uncomfortable at times, there he was. He knew what he was talking about when he later condemned such diversions. Still, he probably enjoyed himself. The influence of Green and his own maxims was still clearly circumscribed and limited, and the social pleasures still held a great deal of attraction for him.

The most important members of the society, at least as far as Kant was concerned, were Johann Julius Goeschen (1736–1798), Johann Konrad Jacobi (1717–1774), and his wife Maria Charlotta Jacobi (1739–1795). Goeschen had come to Königsberg after the Russian occupation as the new master of the mint. His friends therefore usually simply called him the "master of the mint" or "*Münzmeister.*" Kant and Goeschen were close during these years. The two undertook many things together, especially between 1764 and 1768. Thus they were often seen together.[85] Jacobi, a dealer in metals, had come to Königsberg in 1751, and Kant's friendship with him went back to his earliest years as a *Magister;* he was obviously quite intimate with him.[86] He could ask for favors and did receive them. In 1767 he influenced Jacobi to arrange for Hamann the position of secretary and translator at the customs office.[87] He also was close enough to him to reject other favors. When Jacobi offered to buy him a new coat because the one he was always wearing was threadbare, Kant did not accept.[88] He also was somewhat close to Jacobi's younger wife. In any case, there is a note by Jacobi's wife to Kant on June 12, 1762:

Dear friend: Aren't you surprised that I am undertaking to write to you as a great philosopher? I believed to find you yesterday in my garden, but since my girlfriend and I sneaked through all the avenues and could not find you in this circle of the sky, I busied myself with making you a band for a sword, which is dedicated to you. I lay claim to your society tomorrow afternoon. "Yes, yes, I will be there," I hear you say. Good, then, I will expect you, and then my clock will be wound as well. Please forgive this reminder. My girlfriend and I send to you a kiss by sympathy. The air in Kneiphoff is hopefully the same as here so that the kiss does not lose its sympathetic force. Live happy and well, Mrs. Jacobi (*Jacobin*).[89]

Kant visited the house of the Jacobis frequently. Therefore, not too much should be made of the playful tone of the letter. It has been suggested that especially the "winding of the clock" has reference to the opening scene of *Tristram Shandy*, which deals with Tristram's conception. Yet even if the winding of the clock may have sexual overtones, the allusion was probably more an expression of literary playfulness than it was an invitation to deceive her husband. In fact, Kant was probably closer to Johann Konrad Jacobi than he was to her. Jacobi was a very educated person in his own way, being able to correspond with businesses abroad in five languages.[90] They would have shared many more interests with one another than with the young Maria Charlotta. She was twenty-two years younger than her husband, and fifteen years younger than Kant.

Kant and Maria Charlotta were friendly with each other, but she appears to have been more interested in him than he was interested in her. At the beginning of 1766, when Maria Charlotta, known to everyone simply as "the Princess," was in Berlin to cure a problem with her eyes, she responded to a letter by Kant. In it, she alluded to many evenings that Kant, Goeschen, and Jacobi had shared during her absence, and she assured Kant that her husband's well-being was the only thing that gave her satisfaction, mockingly scolding Kant for not being willing to accompany her on the voyage home.[91]

Königsberg at that time had a lively theater culture, and Kant and his friends took part in it. Though there was no standing ensemble, it did have a theater building with three hundred seats. Goeschen, Jacobi, Hippel, and Kant often went together to the theater, where Jacobi and Goeschen had rented a booth. Some of the plays they would have attended were: Voltaire's *Zaire, Coffeehouse,* and *Alzire,* Weiße's *Haushälterin, Candidates,* and *Crispus,* Goldoni's *Pamela, or the Rewarded Virtue* and *The Cavalier and the Dame,* Molière's *Miser,* and Lessing's *Miss Sarah Sampson.* They must have seen Hippel's *Man of the Clock* and *Servant and Master,* and they attended many others that were popular at the time. The *Königsbergische gelehrte und politische Anzeigen* published reviews of most of them, and many appear to have been written by Hippel. These performances helped shape Kant's intellectual outlook in general and perhaps some of his particular philosophical views as well.

Voltaire's *Coffeehouse,* for instance, was, as the reviewer notes, baptized "a translation of Hume," and it represented for him the greatest compliment to the English that anyone could pay them. Both the titles of the plays and the reviews show that Königsberg was by no means a cultural backwater but actively participated in the developments of the time. The reviewers were not always complimentary to the actors, and Lauson, the poet who could versify everything from electrical experiments to burials, is said to have "barely escaped a drubbing by one of the insulted actors."[92]

The literary circle was short-lived, broken up by an affair between Goeschen and Maria Charlotta. The two got entangled in a relationship, which ultimately led to the divorce of the Jacobis. On September 17, 1768, Hippel wrote to Scheffner:

Next Monday Jacobi will be divorced from his wife. The cause of the divorce is adultery. She not only admits to it, but she proclaims that she committed it because she wanted to get a divorce and be rid of such a "worthless fellow," as she says. Her hope is, without doubt, that Goeschen will marry her. If Goeschen has given her hopes, he is culpable, but if he really fulfills them, then I am at a lack for any word. His reputation is suffering terribly, and everyone – the Jacobi woman the most – says he will marry her. . . . He, Jacobi, not only wanted to assume all the guilt, but he also, on his knees, offered her the contract. . . . The Princess Jacobi has fallen. The entire world despises her . . .[93]

Not quite a year later, Goeschen and the divorced Maria Charlotta, the fallen Princess, were making plans to get married. Hippel wrote: "The entire city is talking: Goeschen will marry the Jacobi, only Kant and I do not speak about it because he has not said a word to *us*."[94] On the other hand, there was quite a bit of talk about the roles of Kant and Hippel in this affair. Some of the people in Königsberg seem to have found it difficult to believe that these two men were entirely innocent. This gossip was not just spoken but also committed to writing by members of the literary circle. Enough talk, in any case, that Hippel could find:

Even this has to be tried: to be in the mouths of the entire public. The feeling of righteousness must be enough for us here, but then it is enjoyable to see how people have to stifle themselves when one meets them, and when they talk of such things. The one makes excuses, avoids one, another eats more than usual, and then must take medicine the next day – Let us, my dear friend, overcome such things and endure a world which, in one word, is not for us.[95]

Kant's experience was like that of Hippel – and perhaps worse. When Goeschen and Maria Charlotta got married on October 23 1769, Hippel attended the wedding, but Kant did not. In fact, he never visited the Goeschens as long as Jacobi was alive. As Hippel said:

You just wanted to have some news about *Magister* Kant? This is a comedy in five acts, which I cannot possibly perform today . . . Kant is a really good boy, and he is and will remain my very good friend, but he said so many peculiar things about the present wife of the master of the mint and the former *Geheime Rätin* to her husband, and he has been so indignant about this marriage that he is careful not to show his face at her house.[96]

Kant was upset by the developments. He took the side of the former husband, said bad things about his Princess, and then found it difficult to visit her after the divorce and the new marriage. He was emotionally involved. In the end, he found it easiest to break off all contact, probably forming the maxim never to enter their house.[97] In the "Remarks," in which women play a large role, he had already noted: "A women narrows a man's heart. The marriage of a friend usually means the loss of a friend."[98]

It is not difficult to understand what happened. Maria Charlotta, who in 1768 was just twenty-eight years old, was married to a fifty-one-year-old man. Her husband could easily have been her father. Furthermore, Jacobi, at least by some accounts, was not among the most faithful of husbands himself. She gradually tired of the marriage. At the same time, Goeschen, just three years older than she was, attracted her interest. They fell in love and committed adultery. Instead of trying to hide her unfaithfulness, Maria Charlotta took matters into her own hands, got a divorce, and then married the man she really loved – not paying much attention to the scandal that ensued. The resolve with which she acted and the willingness with which she took risks were remarkable, if not admirable.

Kant, by contrast, who was forty-four and closer in age to her former husband than to either Goeschen or Maria Charlotta, found the matter neither remarkable nor admirable. Before her involvement with Goeschen, Maria Charlotta may have been interested in Kant, but after the affair she probably held a grudge against him for things he had said about her. Though he was invited to the Goeschen household many times, he did not go. If we can believe Jachmann, his reason was loyalty to her divorced husband.[99]

Kant found it very difficult to sort out his various emotional attachments, loyalties, duties of fidelity, gratitude, and non-maleficence than did the old and new partners in marriage and their other friends. He ultimately acted in what Hippel considered an indelicate and clumsy manner, deciding to cut off contact with Maria Charlotta and his closest friends. We can only imagine what he said and did, and how this affected his friends, since Hippel never relates to us the comedy in five acts. Still, it is clear that Hippel, who had a great gift of observation, found it worthy of a comedy. One might regret that he never wrote it, or one might be glad he never did – but at least one thing is certain: Kant would have been one of the characters at whose expense we would laugh today. Kant himself recognized that he did not play an admirable role in the affair. If the good citizens of Königsberg had been asked to serve as judges of Kant's character during this period, many would have judged it to be ambiguous.

If the Goeschen affair did not provide enough material about the literary elite in Königsberg to exercise the wagging tongues, they soon had more: Kanter's wife was unfaithful to her husband not long after. Kanter became the laughing stock of Königsberg. As usual in such cases, advice was not lacking. Krickende, who saw Kanter on one of his trips to Berlin, wrote to Scheffner that "he should not take so many trips" because peculiar things happened to "beautiful young women when their husbands were not at home."[100] Hippel was less charitable: "This woman has shown the truth to me: a stupid wife is still easier to seduce than an intelligent one, and there is also more honor and more tranquillity with the latter."[101]

If Kant had some interest in marriage before these scandals, he probably lost all of it as a result of them. Maria Charlotta appears to have irreversibly colored his view of women and marriage. This is certainly true of Hippel. Thus he wrote in his *Essay on Marriage* of 1769: "In truth, only a fool, a knave, or a priest are capable of marriage. The last one is used to be bound by duties, the knave hopes that his wife is unfaithful, and the fool believes that she is faithful."[102] He himself had decided a year earlier that he would never get married. Indeed, his decision was so firm that he thought, "this knot would hardly ever be untied."[103] Nor did Hippel ever change his mind. Kant's reservations about marriage probably date back to some time after this period. In March of 1770, he still appears to have been willing. In any case, during that year Hippel wrote to Scheffner that he had seen Kant, and that he was "not sure whether" Kant, having received assurance that he would become the professor of mathematics, "might not present himself as a bridegroom at any minute, for one says that he is not entirely disinclined to dare to take this unphilosophical step."[104] But Kant never did. Having reached the age of forty-six, having seen what happened to some of his friends, he had ambiguous feelings about marriage. In any case, we know from his lectures on anthropology that he believed "a younger wife dominates an older husband and a younger husband an older wife."[105] Given the customs of the period, the prospects could hardly have seemed propitious to him.

Kant formulated the maxim: "One mustn't get married." In fact, whenever Kant wanted to indicate that a certain, very rare, exception to a maxim might be acceptable, he would say: "The rule stands: One shouldn't marry! But let's make an exception for this worthy pair." Rules and maxims could have exceptions, and not just as far as marriage was concerned; but just as only the exceptional marriage was for him an acceptable exception, so maxims could be violated only rarely. Kant's phrase was borrowed from a man named Richey, who in 1741 wrote a poem in which he tried to prove by means of the principle of sufficient reason that one should not marry, or perhaps, that one "does not have to" (*muß nicht*) marry. Whether consciously or unconsciously, Kant changed the "*muß nicht*" to "*soll nicht.*"[106]

During these years he became still more firmly rooted in the literary world of Königsberg. He came to know most of the aspiring younger writers of Königsberg as well as the more established authors in one way or another. Hamann, one of the central figures, was well known to Kant, even if the two did not always see eye to eye. Hippel, who had been a friend and student of Funk and a pet enemy of Herder's, was a good friend of Hamann's during this period, but he also became close to Kant. Lindner, Kant's friend from their student years, had returned to Königsberg in 1765. Whether the professor of poetry shared Kant's enthusiasm for Richey's poem on marriage may be doubted, but they shared many views on German literature. Scheffner, having published risky poems "á la Grecourt" in 1761, held the position of secretary in Königsberg between 1765 and 1766. He became the best friend of Hippel during this period.[107] After he left Königsberg, he still kept in close contact. Thus he says:

> Since I visited Hippel every Christmas and Easter, and so my former acquaintance with Kant was also renewed, who, as the entire world now can read, could combine wit and earnestness in society. We often found very happy conversation at Kant's between 7:00 and 8:00 in the evening. Here I also came into closer contact with J. G. Hamann, who was a man of iron firm character with a heart full of love for humanity, an unlimited fantasy, and a truly remarkable mixture of childishness and the vehemence of a passionate human being. Without wishing to teach others, he had a great influence on the spirit of his young friends, which was very advantageous for them. His house was a chaotic magazine.[108]

Scheffner tried to enlist Kant for his own interests, but without success. Thus he wrote to Herder that Kant was "too lazy" to read Huartes carefully or to collaborate with him on a review of Herder's *Fragmente.*[109] Kant himself had other plans. He was no longer interested in a critique of books and systems, but was becoming increasingly interested in a critque of philosophical reasoning itself.

Dreams of a Spirit-Seer (1766): "Character, Ambiguously Expressed"

The *Dreams of a Spirit-Seer* is perhaps Kant's most curious book. The plan to write it, or at least to write something on spirit-seeing and Swedenborg, goes back to at least the summer of 1762, but probably not to a time much earlier than that.[110] In a letter to Charlotte von Knobloch, Kant explained how his interest in Emanuel Swedenborg (1688–1772) was piqued. Kant pointed out that it was unlikely "that anyone ever noticed in him any trace of a way of thinking inclined to the miraculous or a weakness that could led to credulity." He also claimed that he had never believed in spirits or been afraid in cemeteries, following the rule of healthy reason, which, he found, in general speaks against such apparitions. Yet Swedenborg's predictions, or better, miraculous visions, seemed to be at least prima facie reliable. They pointed in the direction of a proof of the reality of another world. Thus Swedenborg was said to have reported the precise events that were taking place in Stockholm when he was fifty miles away.[111] The witnesses of these "sightings" were for Kant absolutely reliable. So something had to give; either the natural laws governing sight were incomplete, or Swedenborg and his witnesses were mistaken. Kant had difficulty in finding anything that undermined the credibility of these events. Thus he was "longingly" waiting for a book Swedenborg was to publish soon in London. When he read the book, he was disappointed and amused by parallels between the speculations of Swedenborg and those of academic metaphysicians.

By November 6, 1764, Hamann reported to Mendelssohn that Kant, "to whose society I now restrict myself," will "review the *Opera omnia* of a certain Schwedenberg [*sic*]," and expressed his hope to be able to send soon a "small treatise by *Magister* Kant *in lieu* of an antidote" to Mendelssohn. Kant had thus written a part or a preliminary version of the *Dreams* before this time. Hamann was well informed; perhaps he even had in hand some part in the project. The history of its publication was also peculiar. It was not sent to the censor in manuscript form, as it should have been. Kanter submitted a printed copy and was fined 10 Thalers, or the equivalent of one-sixth of Kant's yearly salary as a sublibrarian. Kanter's excuse was that the manuscript was "very illegible." It had been sent to the printers page by page for that reason. Kant himself confirms this, trying to find an excuse for the bad organization of the book in this procedure. He "was not always able to see in advance what ought to be introduced early on to facilitate the better understanding of what was to follow . . . and certain elucidations had subsequently to be omitted because they would have otherwise appeared at an inappropriate place."[112] On the other hand, Kant seems to have trusted his former student Herder to understand the parts of the work without having seen the whole, since he sent him the book piece by piece as it was printed.[113] Since Borowski tells us that Kant usually sent only the entire work at once, the *Dreams* appear to be exceptional even in that regard. There was a rush to judgment in this matter. Why, we do not know.

The *Dreams* is the only book for which Kant ever came close to apologizing. Though it was published anonymously, he accepted responsibility for it. Thus on April 6, 1766, he wrote to Mendelssohn:

> The estrangement you express about the tone of my little work proves to me that you have formed a good opinion of the sincerity of my character, and your very reluctance to see that character ambiguously expressed is both precious and pleasing to me. In fact, you will never have to change this opinion. For, though there may be flaws that even the most steadfast determination cannot eradicate completely, I shall certainly never become a fickle or fraudulent person, having, during what must have been the largest part of my life, learned to do without as well as to scorn most of the things that tend to corrupt one's character. The loss of self-respect, which originates from the consciousness of an undisguised way of thinking, would thus be the greatest evil that could befall me, but which most certainly never will befall me. Although I am personally convinced with the greatest clarity and satisfaction of many things which I will never have the courage to say, I will never say anything that I do not mean (*dencke*).[114]

Kant thus tried to downplay the tone, which Mendelssohn had found troublesome. The book was not serious enough. Metaphysics was important and should not be made light of. Kant tried to reassure Mendelssohn. Still, in affirming his steadfast character as a philosophical author, he indirectly apologizes for the ambiguous style or tone of the work. This tone is perhaps best characterized by a passage from the end of the third chapter. A Victorian translator of the work rendered it as follows:

> Therefore, I do not at all blame the reader, if, instead of regarding the spirit-seers as half-dwellers in another world, he, without further ceremony, despatches them as candidates for the hospital, and thereby spares himself further investigation. But, if anything then is to be treated on such basis, the manner of such adepts of the spirit-world must be very different from that based upon the ideas given above; and if, formerly, it was found necessary at times to burn some of them, it will now suffice to give them a purgative. Indeed, from this point of view, there was no need of going back as to metaphysics, – for hunting up secrets in the deluded brain of dreamers. The keen Hudibras could alone have solved for us the riddle, for he thinks that visions and holy inspirations are simply caused by a disordered stomach.[115]

The last sentence, whose scatological German outspokenness the bowdlerizing translator thought "hardly bearable in English," should read: "The keen Hudibras would have been able to solve the riddle on his own, for his opinion was: if a hypochondriacal wind should rage in the guts, what matters is the direction it takes: if downwards, then the result is a f − ; if upwards, an apparition or an heavenly inspiration."[116]

The same kind of sentiment can also be found in the "Essay on the Illnesses of the Head" of 1764, in which Kant is for the most part content
simply to classify the appearances of these illnesses, without trying to find
their roots. Yet, at the very end of the paper he does find it necessary to say
that their roots are probably to be found "in the body, and for the most part
in the digestive parts rather than in the brain." They are not caused by
thinking but have an origin in nonmental excesses. Thus Kant finds it
might be better for a doctor to prescribe a higher dose of a purgative to a
"learned loudmouth" than for a philosopher to refute him. Because, if

> according to Swift's observation, a bad poem represents only a cleansing of the brain,
> and if by means of it many harmful humors are expelled to make the sick poet more
> comfortable, then why cannot an inferior and brooding book represent the same? And
> in such a case it would be advisable to prescribe to nature another route of purification
> so that the evil can be aborted thoroughly and in a quiet place, without troubling the
> public with it.[117]

Mendelssohn did not appreciate this kind of humor. It appears that he was
a Victorian before his time, but he was correct about one thing, the passage
of the *Dreams* is uncharacteristic of Kant's writing as a whole – though
perhaps not of the sense of humor he would have had to suppress in mixed
company, or at least in some of the mixed company he was part of. The literary circle of which he was part – for better or worse – was less prudish
than many of the other circles in Königsberg.

The *Dreams* seem to belong to the genre of satire. In the book Kant makes
fun of Swedenborg's visions of a spirit world as the effects of "hypochondriacal winds" that have taken a wrong direction. Yet to characterize the
book as a satire is not to do it justice. Its satirical elements are put into the
service of a theory or – at the very least – a certain view of how the world is.
In this way, it is not without similarity to Hamann's *Socratic Memorabilia*.
Hamann also used satirical elements to support a theory, which was held
in all seriousness. Yet whereas Hamann used philosophy to illustrate and
support his theory of faith, Kant used a certain kind of faith to illustrate
the shortcomings of philosophy. Though the full title reads "*Dreams of a
Spirit-Seer, Illustrated by the Dreams of Metaphysics*," he seemed to think
that the spirit-seer's dreams illustrate, or put into relief, the dreams of metaphysics. It was a book for everyone and for no one. It "will fully satisfy the
reader; for the main part he will not understand, another part he will not
believe, and the rest he will laugh at."[118]

In the "practical conclusion" of the *Dreams*, Kant asserts that it is one
of the achievements of a wise man that he can "select from among the

innumerable tasks before us the one that humanity must solve."[119] The task
that humanity must solve is one that lies not in a world beyond this one, but
in the here and now. The book concludes "with the words with which
Voltaire, after so many sophistries, lets his honest Candide conclude: 'Let
us look after our own happiness, go into the garden, and work.'" This happiness and the work that must be done are closely bound up with morality.
Indeed, the entire book may be read as an argument for a naturalistic foundation of morality and against founding morality on the hope of a better
state in another life. In this way, it follows Hume's sentiments. Though Kant
believes that there probably never was a righteous man who could admit to
himself that with death everything comes to an end and that life has no
meaning beyond what we can find in this life, he nevertheless claims that
"it seems to be more in accordance with human nature and the purity of
morals to base the expectation of a future world upon the sentiments of a
good soul, than, conversely, to base the soul's good conduct upon the hope
of another world."[120] What we need is a simple moral faith. We need to realize that knowledge of that other world is neither possible nor necessary. It
is "dispensable and unnecessary."[121] In fact, the difference between someone who is wise and someone who is not is the realization of just this. A
sophist, in an unreasonable "craving for knowledge," may set no other limits to what is knowable than "impossibility." Science, however, teaches us
that there are many things we cannot know. Reason will convince us that
there are many things we do not need to know. In fact, to "be able to chose
rationally, one must know first even the unnecessary, yea the impossible;
then, at last, science arrives at the definition of the limits set to human reason by nature."[122]

The theoretical conclusion of the first part of the book seems to be exactly parallel to the practical conclusion of the second part. Kant claims
to have discovered a pneumatology, which "may be called a doctrinal conception of man's necessary ignorance in regard to a supposed kind of beings," namely spirits. The theoretical conclusion may be formulated as a
maxim, which is entirely negative. Kant declares:

And now I lay aside this whole matter of spirits, a remote part of metaphysics, since I
have finished and am done with it. In future it does not concern me any more. . . . It is
. . . a matter of policy, in this as in other cases, to fit the pattern of one's plans to one's
powers, and if one cannot obtain the great, to restrict oneself to the mediocre.[123]

It would be tempting to see in these conclusions the first, even if incom-
pletely expressed, theoretical consequences of Kant's revolution and re-

birth, and perhaps that is precisely what they are. However, it would be easy to exaggerate the importance of the work. It does not represent a revolutionary break with the past. His theory remains essentially the same as before. Just as in his earlier works, he holds that "spiritual essence is mostly present in matter, and that it does not act upon those forces which determine the mutual relations of elements, but upon the inner principle of their state."[124] He defends the Leibnizian view that there must be an internal reason for external efficiency. As for those "half-dwellers in another world," that is, those who believe in a separate spirit world, they belong in the hospital.

Kant's Philosophical Development between 1755 and 1769: "Seeking the Honor of Fabius Cunctator"

There are many different accounts of the various positions Kant is supposed to have held during his precritical period. I believe most of these to be mistaken. Kant did not so much have an all-inclusive metaphysical position as he was searching for one. The reminder Kant wrote for himself in his copy of the *Observations* is characteristic of the whole period:

Everything goes past like a river and the changing taste and the various shapes of men make the whole game uncertain and delusive. Where do I find fixed points in nature, which cannot be moved by man, and where I can indicate the markers by the shore to which I ought to adhere?[125]

Kant was searching more than he was expounding fixed positions during most of the sixties, and the nature of this search was more important than the sequence of different positions he held during that period.

The word "nature" presents the fundamental outlook of Kant's position at that particular time. It was in nature that he tried to find fixed points and criteria for judging human action, not in reason; and Rousseau loomed large in the background of this view. Indeed, Kant was a naturalist in the way in which most of his contemporaries were naturalists. This problem still occupied Kant during 1765–66, as his "Announcement of the Character of His Lectures during the Winter Semester of 1765–1766" shows. Kant points out that ethics might seem to be more secure than metaphysics but in fact is not. It seems scientific and thorough, but is neither.

The cause of this is that the distinction between good and bad in actions and the judgment concerning moral justice can easily and correctly be recognized immediately by the human heart and what is called *sentiment* [*Sentiment*] and without the detour through proofs. Therefore – because the question has often been decided before we have rational principles – it is not surprising that one has no difficulty in accepting as acceptable reasons which have only an appearance of being sound.

Rather than following that route, Kant would try to supplement and make more precise "the attempts of Shaftesbury, Hutcheson and Hume, which, though imperfect and defective, have nevertheless come farthest in the discovery of the first principles of all morality."[126] This text also gives us some indication as to where Kant hoped to find these principles. In the "Announcement" of 1765 he tells us that he will "always consider philosophically and historically what actually *happens* before I indicate what *ought to happen*," and that he will clarify the method according to which human beings should be studied. We should not concentrate only on their changing shapes that are the result of the environment they are found in, but rather should concentrate on "the *nature* of man that remains always the same, and upon his peculiar place in creation." This will tell us what we should do while we seek the highest physical and moral perfection, while we fall short of both in various degrees. Kant seems confident that what nature tells us and what reason tells us will turn out to be the same.

It has become customary to divide Kant's so-called precritical period, that is, the time before 1769–70, into at least two different phases. The first is often called his "rationalist period," and the second his "empiricist period." According to this view, the first of these distinct phases lasted roughly from 1755 to 1762, while the second began about 1762–3 and ended in 1769. Its clearest formulation goes back to Erich Adickes, the editor of Kant's "*Handschriftlicher Nachlass*" for the Academy edition of Kant's works. Adickes called the first period Kant's "original epistemological standpoint," and he argued that at that time the "tendency of *Kantian epistemology* was, in accordance with its *aim* and *method, rationalist*."[127] Indeed, he went so far as to claim that Kant belonged during the first period to "the Leibniz-Wolffian school." Though he admitted that Kant was also influenced by Christian August Crusius, he still believed that Kant was so close to Leibniz and Wolff in his aims, his method, and his fundamental principles that "he can be called their disciple."[128] While not wanting to deny the existence of "empiricist elements" in Kant's thought and acknowledging that Kant was influenced by Newton even then, Adickes still held that Kant was basically and most characteristically a rationalist during the fifties. Kant not only was a methodological rationalist, that is, somebody who believed that we should favor logical or mathematical procedures in our search for scientific truth, but he also accepted the rationalist view of the world that is sometimes called necessitarianism. Kant was at least at first convinced that "nature" was constituted by an ordered whole of necessary connections, and that it was the philosopher's task to determine those things that could not possibly be otherwise.

Adickes detected a shift toward a more empiricist position in the writings of the early sixties, and he believed that this shift is visible in three of Kant's claims. Contrary to his earlier position, Kant now held that: (1) being is not a predicate or determination of any thing; it can, therefore, not be proved by argument, but can only be experienced; (2) logical contradiction is entirely different from real opposition; and (3) the logical ground (*ratio* or reason) of something is quite different from its real cause (*ratio* or reason).[129] He believed that Kant's tendency towards empiricism became stronger over time. While during the early sixties he was well on the way toward empiricism, his writings of 1766 show that he had become a full-fledged empiricist.[130] Nevertheless, it would be wrong, according to Adickes, to call the Kant of this period a skeptic in the Humean fashion. In fact, he argued that it would even be wrong to think that Kant was very much influenced by Hume's way of philosophizing. The influence of Hume came only later, that is, in 1769. Furthermore,

even during the time in which Kant came closest to empiricism, his ethical and religious *Weltanschauung* did not change. Then as always, it formed the background and, perhaps better, the basis for his thinking. The speculations of rational psychology and theology were still as attractive to him as they were before. There was only one difference: what earlier were scientific claims and demonstrations, are now private opinions and subjective proofs. However, they are for this reason no less secure than the earlier assertions.[131]

This then is the picture that forms the background to most of the interpretations of the critical philosophy: Kant started out as a more or less orthodox Wolffian; he then came under the influence of empiricism, but the empiricist influence never went to the deepest core of his philosophical convictions. This deepest core remained always essentially *rationalistic*.

Many scholars have attempted to refine Adicke's rough outline and have introduced more periods and subdivisions into Kant's development, speaking of many different more or less radical "*Umkippungen,*" "*Kehren,*" or conversions on Kant's part.[132] While most scholars appear to have followed Adickes's view of the period from 1755 to 1769 as a development away from a fairly orthodox rationalism and toward some form of empiricism, they have varied widely in their emphasis on who influenced Kant when,

and to what extent. Not all have accepted Adickes' emphasis on "rationalism," and some have argued that empiricism was of greater importance for
the early Kant.[133] Furthermore, depending on whether they took as the
guiding thread of their discussions the problem of the method of metaphysics, the problem of space, the nature of the self, the problem of causality, the concept of existence, the problem of God, or that of moral (and
aesthetic) judgment, different scholars conceived of different periods
and considered different influences as important. Whereas those more interested in metaphysical topics have tended to emphasize the importance
of Leibniz and Wolff on the one hand, and that of Crusius and Hume on
the other, those more concerned with morals have stressed the supposedly
Pietistic background of the early Kant, or the influence of the "moral
sense" school on Kant during the early sixties, and the lasting effects of
Rousseau on Kant that began around 1764. Accordingly, there are almost
as many different conceptions of the specifics of Kant's early development
as there are philosophical scholars discussing it. The changes ascribed to
Kant are often more the expression of the wishes of the scholar in question
than a conclusion determined by the evidence. Herman-J. de Vleeschauwer
was certainly correct when he observed:

Praise for the superhuman genius of Kant conjoined with the claim that he changed his
mind every decade like a dizzy fool who cannot master the direction of his own thought
is surely evidence of a fundamental contradiction. The majority of biographies devoted
to him, however, appear content to accept a contradiction of this nature.[134]

The lack of agreement on the specifics of Kant's "development" before 1769
and the contradictory character of the many accounts suggest that none of
the accounts offered so far is entirely correct.

   One of the reasons for the lack of agreement is an uncritical and unreflective use of the terms "rationalism" and "empiricism." Though these
labels make some historical sense when used to refer to the broad outlines
of the philosophical discussion in the seventeenth century, they are not
precise enough to provide a useful characterization of most of the important thinkers even of that period.[135] Was Berkeley a "British empiricist" or,
as has been argued, an "Irish Cartesian?" In what sense was Locke an "empiricist"? Recent discussions have shown that, if he was an empiricist, he
was not one in the sense in which it is usually assumed – and Wolff was
hardly the model of a "rationalist" either. It is probably not quite fair to
say that "Wolff's philosophy is . . . a confused mixture of rationalistic and
empiricistic elements," but it is certainly true that "it is impossible to clas-

sify it as consistently one or the other."[136] The same point must be made a fortiori about Kant's contemporaries.

Kant, from the very beginning of his philosophical training, knew of the limits of Wolffian philosophizing, and he never accepted it without reservation. Most importantly, however, it would have contradicted not only the spirit of the age, but also the way Kant understood himself. Diderot had praised the "eclectics" in the *Encyclopédie* as independent thinkers who were subject to no master, who critically investigated all doctrines, and who accepted only those things that are witnessed by their own *"expérience"* and their *"raison."* Most significant German thinkers of Kant's generation wanted to be "eclectics" in this sense. They aimed to be *"Selbstdenker,"* independent thinkers in the service of science and humanity, not members of some sect. Though most of them were educated in a more or less Wolffian spirit, they were by no means orthodox Wolffians. Kant was no exception in this regard. He, like many of his contemporaries, dared to think for himself. Therefore, discussions of the early Kant's "empiricism" versus his "rationalism" need to be taken *cum grano salis.*

This is only part of the problem, however. The very conception of Kant's "precritical development" poses another, perhaps even more fundamental, problem. In order to be able to give a coherent account of any kind of development, we must have at least some idea about the end product of that process. We must be able to specify what counts as development "toward" that goal, and what is an "aberration." Only if we know what it is that counts as the goal or final achievement can we trace the stages of such a process. However, there is no such final goal toward which the early Kant developed. His critical philosophy represents – as he himself tells us – the beginning of something new. It was the result of a sudden, decisive, and radical change in his philosophical outlook, not the fruit of a long, focused search.[137] Therefore, it is misleading to speak of the "development" of the early Kant in any but a very rough or approximate sense. Toward the end of the so-called precritical period, namely on May 7, 1768, Kant confessed to Herder that he was "not attached to anything," and he went on to say:

with a deep indifference towards my own opinions as well as those of others I often subvert the entire structure and consider it from several points of view in order to hit finally perhaps on the position from which I can hope to draw the system truthfully.

Kant was deeply skeptical not only about the philosophical theories advanced by others, but also about his own attempts, admitting himself that he had not been able to arrive at a position that he could accept as the truth. He goes on to say in the same letter that

since we have been separated, I have allowed in many parts room for other views. While my attention has been directed at recognizing the true end and the limits of human abilities and inclinations, I believe that insofar as morals are concerned, I have finally succeeded to a large extent. I now work on a metaphysics of morals. And I imagine that I can indicate the obvious and fruitful principles as well as the method which viable attempts must follow in this kind of knowledge, even if they are often useless.[138]

So while he believed that he had reached more secure ground in ethics, he was far from being certain even in this field. His approach was characterized by a great deal of skeptical reserve.

Kant never was a convinced skeptic, but he was in some ways skeptical about his very enterprise. It may therefore prove useful to make clearer what kind of skepticism Kant had assimilated. If we define skepticism as a "thesis or claim concerning some group of statements, namely, that each of the members is doubtful in some way and to some degree," and if we take different disciplines to consist of such groups or sets of statements, then we can differentiate between epistemological, ethical, religious, and metaphysical skepticism.[139] Each one of these skepticisms is "local" to some discipline, and does not necessarily involve the kind of "global" doubt that is usually attributed to the skeptic. Indeed, some forms of skepticism might not even cover an entire discipline, but could be restricted to a subset of claims within a discipline. Different forms of skepticism may also vary in accordance with the strength of their doubt. Thus an epistemological skeptic may doubt whether we, in fact, know whether certain kinds of claims are true, or he may doubt whether it is possible in principle to know the truth of a certain kind of claim. Kant's musings of 1768 show he was a skeptic about philosophical and especially metaphysical claims. He may even have come close to being a global skeptic about metaphysics, not being "attached" to anything. However, his skepticism does not appear to have been one of great strength, for he was not convinced that metaphysics is impossible in principle, but rather that, as a matter of fact, the true metaphysical system had not yet been discovered. His skepticism regarding the theoretical parts of metaphysics was stronger than that regarding the metaphysics of morals. While not doubting the possibility of scientific knowledge and the validity of moral claims, he was uneasy about the metaphysical accounts given of these matters. This uneasiness can be described as a form of *metaphysical* skepticism, or as a skepticism concerning the method followed in metaphysics.[140]

Kant excused himself in a letter to Lambert, dated September 2, 1770, for having failed to answer the latter for four years, by saying that he could not have brought himself to send "anything less than a clear outline of this science [metaphysics] and a determinate idea of its method."[141] He claimed that he had found this outline and the corresponding idea of the method only a year earlier, namely in 1769. It was thus a kind of methodological skepticism that preceded Kant's first attempts at critical philosophy.

That some form of moderate metaphysical and methodological skepticism characterized for Kant the stage for his own critical philosophy can also be seen from some of his frequent descriptions of the development of metaphysics – which, in some ways, are really semi-autobiographical accounts of his own development. Thus he claimed that the "first step in matters of pure reason, marking its infancy, is *dogmatic.* The second step is *sceptical;* and indicates that experience has rendered our judgment wiser and more circumspect" (A761=B789), while the third step is constituted by his *critical* philosophy. In the Preface to the first *Critique* he argued that the rule of metaphysics was at first "dogmatic" and "despotic," that internal disputes as well as "*sceptics,* a species of nomads" often challenged this rule, and that "in more recent times" Locke had attempted to put an end to the controversies between different forms of dogmatism and skepticism, but that he had failed:

And now, after all methods, so it is believed, have been tried and found wanting, the prevailing mood is that of weariness and complete *indifferentism* – the mother, in all sciences, of chaos and night, but happily in this case the source, or at least the prelude, of their approaching reform and restoration. For it at least puts an end to that ill-applied industry which has rendered them thus dark, confused, and unserviceable.[142]

This indifferentism was for Kant not the effect of "levity but of the matured judgment of the age, which refuses to be any longer put off with illusory knowledge" (Axi).[143] It was, he thought, the harbinger of change for the better, a necessary prelude to the "tribunal" of the "critique of pure reason" (Axii). Kant had reached the stage of indifference at least by 1768.

It would, however, be wrong to restrict this "indifferentism" or "methodical skepticism" only to the final stage of a development that Kant underwent between 1755 and 1768. Skeptical reserve and respect for the skeptical tradition (both ancient and modern) appear to have played a considerable role in Kant's thought from the very beginning. Thus he observed in one of his earliest reflections (roughly dated around 1752-56) that differences in opinion give rise to skepticism; and he talked with apparent approval of "a reasonable Pyrrhonism," whose basic principle says that we must postpone a decisive judgment whenever the rules of prudence do not require us to act in accordance with certain rules, whenever there are distinct reasons to the contrary, and whenever it is not necessary to decide."[144] Metaphysics and ethics fulfill all three requirements of this basic principle, and we may assume that Kant was well aware of this.

This Pyrrhonic maxim of the advisability of postponing judgment remained important for Kant, as is shown by notes that Herder took as a student. There we find the following observations:

> *Pyrrho*, really a man of great merit, founded a sect in order to go down another road, to take down everything. *Pyrrho:* the universal *dogmata* (except those of mathematics) are uncertain. His successors went farther. *Socrates* seems to have been somewhat of a Pyrrhonist. The certain [principle] that makes happiness should be assumed. He was a practical philosopher.[145]

He also wrote down: "The Pyrrhonian *'non liquet!'* is, as a wise oracular saying, supposed to make difficult and hateful our *empty* brooding."[146] These passages show not only that Kant was acquainted with Pyrrhonism, but also that he did not reject it outright. In fact, Pyrrho is explicitly called "a man of merit." Comparing Pyrrho to Socrates, he considered Pyrrho's principle of nonevidence as useful in keeping us from engaging in certain kinds of useless intellectual activity. Furthermore, Kant identified the end of the skeptic as a moral one. It is also significant that Hume played a large role in these lecture notes, and that Kant's view of the role of philosophy was entirely negative. Thus he argued, apparently thinking himself to be in agreement with Hume, that philosophy "now has only the use of preventing us from doing anything that would be worse; and if it makes us moral, then only indirectly."[147] Kant then valued Hume for the same reasons he valued Pyrrho. Both were for him important as examples of how to employ the skeptical maxim that judgment in metaphysical matters should be postponed.

How much Kant appreciated the skeptical method can also be seen from his *Dreams of a Spirit-Seer*, which is perhaps his most skeptical writing. In it he observes that even though he might not have insight into the secrets of nature, he is confident enough "not to fear any enemy, however terribly equipped . . . to make in this case the attempt of opposite reasons in *refutation*, which, among scholars really is the skill to prove to each other one's ignorance."[148] Furthermore, he goes on to attempt to show that we cannot possibly know anything of spirits or minds. The *"mundus intelligibilis"* or "immaterial world" is unknowable. He therefore believed that he was justified in taking a strong skeptical position regarding this particular part of metaphysics, and he claimed that he would from then on put aside the entire matter concerning spirits as finished and completed. A wide field of metaphysics would no longer concern him – or so he thought in 1765.

In the letter to Mendelssohn of April 6, 1766, he confessed that, though he valued metaphysics and considered it neither trivial nor dispensable, he still thought that with regard to "the stock of knowledge currently available, which is publicly for sale . . . it [is] best to pull off its dogmatic dress and treat its pretended insights *skeptically.*"[149] Beck has aptly called this phase in Kant's thought "quasi-Humean."[150] Kant, in the fashion of a true skeptic, attempts to provide what he describes as a "propaedeutic" or, using more skeptical terminology, a "*catarcticon.*" He was well aware that the "*catarcticon*" usually is purged together with the impurities it is administered to purge.

Not only was Kant not an orthodox Wolffian early on, he never became a convinced empiricist either. Indeed, both his early students go out of their way to make clear that Kant was not a "follower" in any sense, but somebody who wanted to find his own way. As Herder put it: "He was indifferent to nothing worth knowing," looking to find the truth wherever it could be found, and not subscribing to any particular system. Kant was an "eclectic" and "*Selbstdenker*" in very much the same way as most of his contemporaries. Dieter Henrich has claimed that "Kant became aware of the general situation of ethics at the middle of the eighteenth century through the opposition between Wolff's *philosophia practica universalis* and Hutcheson's moral philosophy, and his first independent formulation of an ethical theory resulted from a critique of these two philosophers."[151] While this is not altogether false, it is not the whole truth either. There was no thoroughgoing *opposition* of Wolffian and Hutchesonian ethics in Germany. The Germans were not willing to abandon completely metaphysics of the Wolffian type, but they were willing to admit that the traditional Wolffian account was seriously incomplete *because* it had neglected the phenomena of sensation. They discovered that British philosophers also had something to offer; and since the relevant works were not only extensively reviewed in many German journals, but for the most part also translated quickly, many Germans were led to formulate a new problem or task for themselves. The works of Locke, Shaftesbury, Hutcheson, Hume, Smith, Ferguson, and almost every other British philosopher of note were full of problems that needed solutions and observations that needed to be explained, if

German philosophy of the traditional sort was to succeed. Most of these problems seemed to have to do with the analysis of sensation in theoretical, moral, and aesthetic contexts. Central among all of these was the problem of a "moral sense." Many Germans thought that the British observations could be built into a more rational account without substantial loss, and their fundamental task became one of explaining how Wolffian *theory* could account for the (apparently recalcitrant) *facts* discovered by the British. Thus many philosophers conceived of their task – at least at first – as one of (more or less simply) incorporating British "observations" into a comprehensive "theory."

As Moses Mendelssohn noted at the occasion of a review of Edmund Burke's *A Philosophical Enquiry into the Origin of Our Ideas of the Sublime and Beautiful:*

> The theory of human sensations and passions has in more recent times made the greatest progress, since the other parts of philosophy no longer seem to advance very much. Our neighbors, and especially the English, precede us with philosophical observations of nature, and we follow them with our rational inferences; and if it were to go on like this, namely that our neighbors observe and we explain, we may hope that we will achieve in time a complete theory of sensation.[152]

What was needed, he thought, was a *Universal Theory of Thinking and Sensation;* such a theory would cover sensation and thinking in theoretical, moral, and aesthetic contexts.[153] It would be comprised of British "observations" and German (read: Wolffian) "explanations." He admitted that such a reduction to reason might appear difficult in the case of moral judgments, since our moral judgments "as they present themselves in the soul are completely different from the effects of distinct rational principles," but that does not mean that they cannot be analyzed into rational and distinct principles.[154] He suggested that our moral sentiments are "phenomena, which are related to rational principles in the same way as the colors are related to the angles of refraction of light. Apparently they are of completely different nature, yet they are basically one and the same."[155] The problem concerning a "moral sense" was for the Germans thus not an isolated issue. It was one important part of the broader problem concerning the relation of sensibility and reason in general. The question was: how could one unified theory be given of sensation and reason? The different attempts at answering this question reveal that almost everybody thought that an answer could only be found by showing or presupposing that these two apparently different faculties are really expressions of one and the same faculty, that sensations and thoughts were part of one continuum. Some emphasized the sensitive part of this continuum as basic, though most opted for the intellectual one; but, and this is most important to remember, all accepted what may be called the "continuity thesis" concerning sensation and cognition.[156]

It was for this reason that Hutcheson's observations on the "moral sense" could also form the starting point for Kant; and it was for precisely this reason that he thought that "the attempts of Shaftesbury, Hutcheson and Hume, . . . though imperfect and deficient, have nevertheless come furthest in the collection of the first principles of all morality"; and finally it is for this reason that he himself engaged in such observations. Because the principles of morality can be gleaned from empirical observation of what seems to be a special sense, but might not turn out not to be so, we can start our analysis with it. Given the danger inherent in the rationalist procedure of definition, we should start with such evidence. Still, this was more a procedural point than a foundational one. Kant's position was compatible with the kind of rationalism that Mendelssohn subscribed to. In this account of human nature, reason played as important a part as the moral sense. Kant could not make up his mind which was more important. This does not mean that Kant was confused about his own position. He was wavering between reason and moral sense as between two radically different approaches to the foundation of morals. For Kant, like his contemporaries, subscribed to the "continuity thesis." Indeed, there is nothing in Kant's pronouncements about moral sense in his published works between 1760 and 1770 that radically distinguished him from his German contemporaries. He considered observations in the British style very important, and sometimes he emphasized them. When he said, "under the name of the 'moral feeling,' Hutcheson and others have provided a start toward some excellent observations," he did not mean that Hutcheson and the others got it essentially right.[157] Like Mendelssohn, he thought that they had made a good start, but that their principles need to be reduced to "the highest degree of philosophical evidence." Accordingly, he could argue in the *Observations on the Feeling of the Beautiful and the Sublime* of the same year that

true virtue can be grafted only upon principles such that the more general they are, the more sublime and nobler it becomes. These principles are not speculative rules, but the consciousness of a feeling that lives in every human breast and extends itself much further than over particular grounds of compassion and complaisance. I believe that I sum it all up when I say that it is *the feeling of the beauty and the dignity of human nature.* The first is a ground of universal affection, the second of universal esteem.[158]

This passage does not imply that all of morality is based upon a moral sense or feeling. At best, it shows that virtue presupposes feelings, leaving open the question on what are the principles upon which moral judgments ultimately are based. Yet even this cannot be the whole story, for when Kant speaks about the necessity of subordinating one's own inclination to one that has been so generalized that it covers all of humanity, he had in mind certain intellectual operations that generalize initially particular feelings. This means that true virtue presupposed for Kant understanding or thinking as well. Thus a person led by sympathy to help a needy person rather than to repay a debt incurred earlier would violate his duty of justice, and would thus clearly not be virtuous. Kant went so far as to claim that sympathy is "weak and always blind." General rules are needed for true virtue, and these cannot come from any feeling.[159] This suggests that Kant could not have believed even in 1763 that moral judgments are simply based on feeling. It is really the business of reason to analyze and clarify the complex and confused concept of the good by showing how it emerges from simple sensations of good.[160]

Kant's thought underwent a radical change when he came to believe that reason and sensation cannot be understood as continuous. In the Inaugural Dissertation of 1770 there was no longer any continuity or bridge between sensation and reason. He then saw the two faculties as radically discontinuous, and *therefore* he argued that the earlier approach could not possibly work. It was this break that defined the difference between Kant's precritical view on ethics and his critical view. The rejection of the continuity thesis marked the end of Kant's search for fixed points in *human nature*, and the beginning of his search for them in pure reason. This change was connected to moral considerations and to a new theory of space and time.

In the essay "Concerning the Ultimate Foundation of the Differentiation of Directions in Space" of 1768, Kant argued that space is not an object of external sensation but "a fundamental concept, which makes all these sensations possible in the first place." He also assures us that it is not "a mere entity of reason." It is more than that. Yet he is far from certain that he has shown the latter, and he ends on a skeptical note, saying that

there is no lack of difficulties surrounding this concept when one, through ideas of reason, tries to grasp its reality, which is evident enough to the inner sense. But this is a constant difficulty in philosophical investigations concerned with the first data of our cognition. But this difficulty is never so decisive as the one which emerges when the consequences of an accepted concept contradict the clearest experience.[161]

Here Kant still accepted the continuity thesis, and in this essay space was not only not a form of sensible intuition, but also was conceived in Newtonian terms: it was an independent reality for him. But soon after he published this essay, Kant changed his view on both the continuity thesis and the nature of space. This happened in 1769. This did not mean, of course, that he would present his new theory without further delay. It only meant that he now believed that he knew what theory he intended to defend. This theory was ultimately to provide his newfound character with a philosophical justification and defense.

5

Silent Years (1770–1780)

The Inaugural Dissertation: "Genuine Metaphysics without Any Admixture of the Sensible"

IN JANUARY OF 1770 Kant was offered a position at the University of Jena. Given his response to the University of Erlangen, it would have been very surprising if he had accepted. In any case, later that year the long-awaited opportunity for advancement in Königsberg came closer. On March 15, 1770, Langhansen, professor of mathematics, the man who had administered his entrance exam to the university, passed away. Kant lost no time. In a letter dated March 16, Kant submitted a request to Berlin for consideration in the matter. He did not want Langhansen's position. Instead, he suggested an exchange. Christiani, who had taught moral philosophy as well as mathematics until then, and who was the son-in-law of Langhansen, should take over the free position. Kant adduced as a further reason for this the fact that the professor of mathematics was traditionally also the inspector of the *Collegium Fridericianum,* and that Christiani had the greatest claim to this position. Since this position came with good benefits, as well as with a free apartment at the school, Christiani would likely be interested. Kant was not. Should a switch between himself and Christiani not be possible, he suggested a switch between himself and professor Buck, who held the position of professor of logic and metaphysics, and who was also associate professor of mathematics. Pointing out that Buck had obtained this position "only at the occasion of the Russian *gouvernement,*" and that he himself had "all the recommendation of the academy," he thought that such a switch would be harmful neither to justice nor to public utility.[1] It seems clear that he would have rejected the professorship in mathematics, just as he had earlier rejected the professorship in poetry, and that the only thing that would do for him was either the chair of moral philosophy or the chair of metaphysics and logic.

On March 31, just fifteen days after submitting his request, Kant was declared *Professore Ordinario der Logic und Metaphysic*. Kant had finally obtained the position he had wanted at least since 1755. Buck was less happy. Neither Kant nor the Prussian authorities appear to have consulted him. Buck complained about this, saying that "he had never even thought of asking for the professorship in mathematics," and that "Kant himself brought him unexpectedly the High Royal Patent without talking with him or making friendly inquiries about this beforehand."[2] Obviously, there was not much love lost between Kant and Buck, Knutzen's favorite student and successor. Kant could not care less about Buck. He got what he wanted. Well regarded in Berlin, he directly pursued his own interests, completely disregarding what one might consider good manners or even moral sense. Kant's disregard for Buck's fate may have been occasioned by his feeling that he, and not Buck, had deserved the position in 1759, and that Buck only got what was coming to him anyway. Kant never thought very highly of Buck as a philosopher.

Kant's new salary was 160 Thalers and 60 Groschen, or about 100 Thalers more than he received as a sublibrarian, and about 40 Thalers less than he would have received in Jena.[3] His income (now about 220 Thalers) was still modest, but it allowed him to live in relative comfort. In fact, his salary as a professor alone was comfortable enough for Kant; he resigned his position as sublibrarian in May of 1772.

Before Kant could assume his position, he had to defend publicly a so-called Inaugural Dissertation in Latin. He did so on August 21, 1770. Three students (one from the faculty of theology, another from the faculty of law, and a third from the liberal arts) and two colleagues were the opponents. Kant had chosen Herz, now a student of medicine, to take up the office of the "respondent," or the defender of Kant's thesis. This was a great honor for Herz. Still, it was almost denied to him, for Kant had to overcome "strong objections of the university senate" to having Herz perform this role.[4] The dissertation was entitled "*De mundi sensibilis atque intelligibilis forma et principiis*," or "On the Form and Principles of the Sensible and Intelligible World." Though it was really not much more than a hastily composed thesis, written to satisfy the academic requirements for the professorship, it presented for the first time important aspects of the critical philosophy. Kant himself considered this occasional piece as the true end of his "precritical period" and as the beginning of his "critical philosophy." Thus when he was approached by Johann Heinrich Tieftrunk about the publication of a collection of his minor writings in 1797, he answered: "I accept your proposal of putting together a collection of my minor writings. However, I would not like to have included anything before 1770, so that it would begin with my dissertation *de mundi sensibilis et intelligibilis forma* . . ."[5]

One of the most important new doctrines of Kant's Inaugural Dissertation was his radical distinction between "intellect" and "sensation." In this work Kant for the first time explicitly argued that these two faculties are independent and irreducible sources of two entirely different kinds of knowledge. He defined sensibility as "the receptivity of the subject through which it is possible that its representative state be *affected* in a certain manner by the presence of an object," and intelligence as the "*faculty* of the subject through which it is able to represent things which cannot by their own nature come before the senses of their subject."[6] Intellectual knowledge has nothing in common with sensitive knowledge. Indeed, he argued that we must assume two worlds, a *mundus intelligibilis* and a *mundus sensibilis*. Each of these worlds obeys its own principles and exhibits forms peculiar to it, and each of them has its own objects: "The object of sensibility is the sensible, that which contains nothing but what is to be cognised through the intelligence is intelligible. In the schools of the ancients the former was called *phenomenon* and the latter a *noumenon*."[7] Phenomena are "representations of things *as they appear*," noumena are "representations of things *as they are*."[8] It would therefore be a serious mistake to regard sensibility as nothing but confused thinking, or thinking as nothing but distinct sensation. To use Kant's own words, "The sensitive is poorly defined as that which is *more confusedly* cognised, and that which belongs to the understanding as that of which there is a *distinct* cognition. For these are only logical distinctions which *do not touch* at all the things *given*, which underlie every logical distinction."[9] Kant singled out for special criticism "the illustrious Wolff," who "has, by this distinction between what is sensitive and what belongs to the understanding, a distinction which for him is only logical, completely abolished, to the great detriment of philosophy, the noblest of the enterprises of antiquity, the determining of the *character of phenomena and noumena* . . ."[10] Yet Kant believed that not just Wolff but every modern philosopher, more or less uncritically, had accepted this thesis. By contrast, he wanted to return to the enterprise of antiquity, proclaiming the necessity of a "genuine metaphysics without any admixture of the sensible."[11] To be sure, sensitive knowledge presupposes the use of certain concepts of the understanding; but this use of the understanding is merely logical, or perhaps better, merely formal. It is of secondary importance compared to the real use of the understanding by means of which "the concepts themselves, whether of things, or relations, *are given*."[12]

This new thesis of the radical discontinuity of sensibility and intellect is closely connected with two other doctrines that make their first appearance in this work – namely, that of the subjectivity of space and time, and that of the essentially rational nature of morality. Space and time are no longer intellectual concepts. They are subjective forms of our sensibility. Spatio-temporal objects, or phenomena, are precisely not things in themselves. All of science deals with mere phenomena. Whereas he had tried to explain space in his earliest writings as an effect of the internal principles of physical monads and had differentiated between mathematical and physical space, in 1770 Kant accepted only one kind of space. It was then only a formal characteristic of the sensible world, which could therefore be a criterion for distinguishing phenomena from noumena. One of the rules important for keeping metaphysics pure from any admixture of the sensible reads: "If of any concept of the understanding whatsoever there is predicated generally anything which belongs to the relations of space and time, it must not be asserted objectively; it only denotes the condition, in the absence of which a given concept would not be sensitively cognizable."[13] Spatiality and temporality are negative criteria that allow us to exclude concepts from pure metaphysics.

Kant still believed in 1770 that there were concepts independent of space and time in the required sense and that a genuine metaphysics, freed of anything that is merely sensible, was possible. In other words, he still believed that he could make interesting and significant claims about "things which in themselves cannot be the objects of the outer senses (such as man possesses)."[14] He thought it was important that we can make claims about immaterial things that are "altogether exempt from the universal condition of *externally, namely spatially, sensible things*."[15] He argued for a dogmatic end of the understanding that was different from its merely negative elenctic purpose that would keep the sensitive distinct from the noumenal. This dogmatic end was so important to him because "in accordance with it the general principles of the pure understanding, such as are displayed in ontology or in rational psychology, lead to some paradigm, which can only be conceived by the pure understanding and which is a common measure for all other things insofar as they are realities."[16] The pure principles of the understanding were thus for Kant of the utmost importance for evaluating the reality of things.

He thought that by means of the pure principles we could think a primordial being that would allow us to evaluate all derivative beings. It would be a model, form, or paradigm of which all other things were just imperfect copies.[17] This paradigm was "noumenal perfection," which came in two senses, namely, "perfection either in the theoretical sense or in the practical sense. In the former sense it is the Supreme Being, GOD; in the latter sense it is MORAL PERFECTION. *Moral philosophy*, therefore, insofar as it furnishes the first *principles of judgment*, is cognised by the pure understanding and belongs only to pure philosophy."[18] Accordingly, moral principles were intellectual. This meant that they concerned things in themselves or noumena and that they belonged among the formal principles of the *mundus intelligibilis*. Moral concepts could therefore not be reduced to sensibility. It would be impossible for us to obtain these concepts by analyzing sensations. Wolff's mistaken acceptance of the continuity thesis had led him away from realizing this origin of moral concepts in the pure intellect. He thus undermined the "noblest enterprise of antiquity." Kant, by contrast, hoped to show that moral philosophy insofar as it "is cognised by the pure understanding and belongs only to pure philosophy" is objective. It does not in any way depend upon the subjective conditions of sensibility, and it is firmly grounded in certain knowledge claims that are "altogether exempt from the universal condition of *externally, namely spatially, sensible things.*" It was for this reason that he thought we must pursue "a pure metaphysics without any admixture of the sensible." These ideas were the origins of Kant's idealism, and they were essentially *Platonic.*[19]

The purely rational or intellectual concepts were "connate" to the pure intellect. They were "abstracted by attention to its actions at the occasion of experience from laws inborn in the mind." They "never enter into sensual representations as parts of it." Therefore, they could not possibly be abstracted from these sensual representations, but had to come from the intellect alone. Kant mentioned as examples of such concepts not just "possibility, existence, necessity, substance, cause . . . with their opposites and correlates," but also "moral concepts" in general, and the "*perfectio noumenon*" in particular.

The "*perfectio noumenon*" in its theoretical sense "is the Supreme Being, God" and in its moral sense, "moral perfection." While he concentrated in the Inaugural Dissertation on the theoretical sense of the *perfectio noumenon*, he did point out that "moral philosophy, so far as it supplies first principles of moral judgment, is known only through the pure intellect and itself belongs to pure philosophy."[20] In 1764 Kant could not decide whether it was reason or the senses that supplies us with the first principle of moral judgment; by 1770 he had decided in favor of reason. However, Kant's concept of reason of 1770 is very different from that of 1764. While the earlier concept consisted of generalized perceptions, the view of 1770 was characterized by a certain "ideal" that is independent of sensation. This "ideal" represented for Kant the "maximum of perfection which is called by Plato an Idea." It provided him with "the common measure and principle whereby we have knowledge," and it was identical with the "*perfectio noumenon.*"

Indeed, this ideal was the highest expression of our intellect. Therefore, the most important concerns of pure reason had to be the determination of the characteristics of this ideal. It was not only "the principle of knowledge" but also "the common measure of all other things so far as real." Kant thought not only that we know things through God, but also that those things have reality only insofar as God has brought them into existence. Our answers to the epistemological, ontological, and moral questions turned for him on the same principle, namely "God . . . as the ideal of perfection," or the *perfectio noumenon*. So intellectual concepts have a twofold use. First, they had what Kant called the "elenctic use," or the "negative service of keeping sensitive concepts from being applied to noumena," and second, they had a dogmatic use in establishing true knowledge of reality.

Kant intended the Inaugural Dissertation to be a mere sketch of a new method that would "occupy the place of a propaedeutic science, to the immense benefit of all who would explore the innermost recesses of metaphysics."[21] The most important aspect of this method was for Kant a clear distinction between principles of sensitive cognition and principles of intellectual cognition, and the "all-important rule" for which he argued was that we must "*carefully prevent the principles proper to sensitive cognition from passing their boundaries and affecting the intellectual.*"[22] Kant was never again to abandon this position on thought and sensation. However, he was forced to change his mind on the way in which he defended it. In 1770 he believed that reason could secure the foundation of a universal moral theory only in knowledge of things "as they are," and he believed that we could have this kind of knowledge through reason.

Kant concluded the Inaugural Dissertation with a promissory note for a "more extended treatment" of these matters. Though he did not want to present in his sketch the positive ideas for reform, he thought he had provided a foundation for such a reform. The *Critique of Pure Reason,* which appeared eleven years later, was the fulfillment of this promise. In it, Kant presented to the public for the first time the results of deliberations that had preoccupied him during the intervening years. Its publication ended more than a decade of "silence" – and hard work.

First Reactions: "We Are . . . Not Yet Sufficiently Convinced"

The Inaugural Dissertation was reviewed in the *Königsberger gelehrte und politische Anzeigen* on Friday, November 22, and Monday, November 25, 1771. The reviewer was Johann Schulz, who was at that time pastor in a town named Löwenhagen. Schulz first duly noted the importance of the dissertation, saying that it was different from most academic exercises and that it promised the purification of metaphysics from any admixture of the sensible. Then he offered a detailed summary of the work. In the second part of the review, he was more critical. Thus he rejected Kant's claim that intellectual intuition was impossible. Though this claim "is basic to the entire dissertation," it is "unprovable" because the soul can see "*itself*" and everything that happens at present in it by internal sensation. It does not matter whether these sensations are of external or internal things. Since time was not just the form of sensation for Kant, but also of thinking, he could not deny that intellectual intuition was impossible on the basis of the claim that it was in time. Indeed, Kant wanted to show that space and time were just principles of the sensible world, but they might well be principles of both the sensible and the intelligible world, and Kant should prove why this was impossible. Kant might be right about this, but he certainly did not prove it. Schulz also objected to Kant's principle of the form of the intellectual world. Kant thought that it consisted in the dependence of everything on one. The reviewer "had no hesitation in simply declaring this to be incorrect." Kant proved that all substances in this world must depend on a single necessary cause, but he did not prove the converse, that all substances that depend on the one cause must make up one world. Kant had made an important beginning in investigating the difference between the sensible and the intellectual, but much work still remained to be done. Schulz said that though "we are not yet sufficiently convinced, the vistas, which this work opens up are nevertheless so estimable that we know of no work, which could provide better materials for the improvement of metaphysics."[23] Kant called the "honest pastor Schulz" the "best philosophical head he knew in the region."[24] He said that his objection about time as the form of inner sense was "the most essential" that could be made to his system, and that it "occasioned considerable reflection on his part."[25]

At this time, there had already been other responses. Sulzer, in a letter of December 8, 1770, found Kant's theory "not just thorough but important." He had one small problem: until now he had been convinced that Leibniz's view of space and time was correct, that the concepts of "space" and "time" differed from those of "duration" and "extension." The latter pair consisted of simple concepts, the former of complex concepts that could not be thought without the concept of order. He agreed with Kant on the "natural influx of substances," and had thought of it as Kant did for a long time. He also had ideas about the difference between the sensible and the intelligible, and he was looking forward to hearing more.[26] There were also criticisms. Mendelssohn had written to Kant on December 25, 1770:

Your dissertation has now reached my eager hands, and I have read it with much pleasure. Unfortunately my nervous infirmities make it impossible for me of late to give as much effort of thought to a speculative work of this stature as it deserves. One can see that this little book is the fruit of long meditation, and that it must be viewed as part of a whole system. . . . The ostensible obscurity of certain passages is a clue . . . that this work must be part of a larger whole . . . since you possess a great talent for writing in such a way as to reach many readers, one hopes that you will not always restrict yourself to the few adepts who are up on the latest things, and who are able to guess what lies undisclosed behind the published hints.

Since I do not count myself as one of these adepts, I dare not tell you all the thoughts that your dissertation aroused in me. Allow me only to set forward a few, which do not concern your major theses but only some peripheral matters.[27]

A nice put-down; Mendelssohn criticized Kant, who had just received a professorship because he was such a popular teacher and writer, for being obscure. After pointing out that he himself had said something on infinite extension that was very close to what Kant put forward in the dissertation (and that he would send him the second edition of his *Philosophical Writings*), he criticized him for identifying Shaftesbury's moral instinct with the Epicurean feeling of pleasure. His most important criticism concerned Kant's conception of time. Kant had claimed in the dissertation that we know what the word "after" means only because of an antecedently formed concept of time.[28] Mendelssohn found that the word "after" may indeed have at first only chronological meaning, but that it is possible to use it for any order in general "where A is possible only when or in case B does not exist. In short, it can mean the order in which two absolutely (or even hypothetical) things can exist."[29] It's just a matter of language that it seems to be temporal. For similar reasons, the principle of contradiction needed the condition "at the same time"; but more important than this, Mendelssohn revealed that he could not convince himself that "time is something merely subjective." His argument ran like this: Succession is a necessary condition of the representations of finite minds. Finite minds are not just subjects, they are also objects of representation in the minds of God and other human beings. Consequently, succession is also necessarily objective. If succession is a reality in representing creatures, then why can it not be a reality in sensible objects? The objections to this way of conceiving time are far from obvious. Time, which according to Leibniz is a phenomenon, has, like all appearances, both subjective and objective aspects. "The subjective is the *continuity*" we attribute to it; the objective is the succession of alterations that are equidistant consequences [*rationata*] of a common ground."[30]

About two months earlier Lambert had criticized Kant's "excellent dissertation" in a letter to him. Lambert recognized that Kant's speculations had their source in his own work. Kant wanted to make a sharp distinction between sensible and intellectual things, and he claimed that things that involved space and location differed in kind from things that must be eternal. He himself had said as much in the *New Organon* of 1764, but, and this was important, he had spoken only of existing things, whereas Kant wanted this to apply to all things. Are the truths of geometry and chronometry sensible or also intelligible, that is, eternal and immutable? Perhaps they are both. In any case,

Till now I have not been able to deny all reality to time and space, or to consider them mere images and appearance. I think that every change would then have to be mere appearance too. And this would contradict one of my principles (No. 54 *Phenomenology*). If changes have reality, then I must grant it to time as well.[31]

There must be something in existing objects that corresponds to time and space.[32]

Kant knew already in June 1771 that Herz, his student and respondent, would publish in 1771 his *Reflections from Speculative Philosophy* (*Betrachtungen aus der spekulativen Weltweisheit*), a commentary on his Inaugural Dissertation.[33] He expected much from it. Though he later, following a review by Lambert, did not think so highly of it, he did consider it important, at least at first.[34]

The book is written as a series of letters to a friend about Kant's philosophy. Though much of the book is just a summary of Kant's position, Herz also offered a number of criticisms. Kant had been content just to discuss the differences between what is subjective and what is objective, and to show that sensible cognition is concerned only with something subjective, while rational cognition aims at "the objective in things" and to delineate the principles at work in each.[35] Herz declares,

> I believe, however, that I can maintain with great persuasiveness that there exists a much too great difference even between the relations of things as we determine them in accordance with the laws of pure reason and what is true of these things independently from our cognition. I base this on nothing less than the nature of our cognition in general. Locke shows that it extends never further than to the qualities which these things have. . . . But what makes the substrate, which has all these qualities, can itself not be a quality again. . . . It thus ceases to be an object of our cognition . . .[36]

We cannot know things in themselves in any sense. Whatever the principles of the intelligible world amount to, they do not amount to knowledge of things in themselves. Kant must be wrong about the latter point.

In the context of the discussion of Crusius's "principle of accidentality," which amounts to the claim that "whatever exists contingently has at some time not existed," he pushes this argument further. If he had used Locke with regard to the concept of substance, he now argues essentially along Humean lines:

> *Magister* Kant believes that we fall into this error because we erroneously transform into a condition for the object what is in our subjective knowledge the most certain sign of the accidental character of the thing (namely our knowledge that it did not exist at one time). Perhaps it will not be entirely disagreeable, if you follow me farther back . . . I have already said something about the difference between absolute and hypothetical necessity earlier. If it has been established that nothing can exist without a reason, then the latter must apply to everything apart from the absolutely necessary being. . . . Since accidental things necessarily presuppose a reason and can therefore exist only as a consequence, we must, I believe, investigate the concepts of cause and effect further. . . . So much seems certain: the repeated observations of two successive events are the only thing that provided us the occasion to expect them in accordance with the rules of probability as constantly conjoined with each other, and to call that which was prior in time *cause,* and that which was later in time *effect.* The concept of time, which has entered into both concepts, and which thus belongs to them just as it belongs to all experiential knowledge, is so conjoined with them in our representation that we cannot think cause and effect without space and time even in pure rational cognitions where space and time are not present.[37]

Herz claims, in other words, that causality is just as infected by sensibility as any other concept. It cannot be legitimately used in a purely rational metaphysics. Causality presupposes temporality. In other words, Kant had not been radical enough.

If this was not sufficient to call Kant's attention to Hume's relevance for the new purely rational metaphysics, then the following must have helped. The *Königsberger gelehrte Zeitung* published on July 5 and 12, 1771, a text entitled "Nachtgedanken eines Skeptikers" (Night Thoughts of a Skeptic), which presented a dramatic monologue in the fashion of Edward Young's *Night Thoughts on Life, Death, and Immortality* (1742–45), a book that was very popular in Germany at the time. As was quite common, the author of the text was not identified. Since its prose sounded very much like that of Johann Georg Hamann, who was not only known to be deeply influenced by Young, but who was also the managing editor of the paper and frequently published his own writings in this paper, many readers in Königsberg and elsewhere would have identified Hamann as the author of the piece.[38] Yet Hamann was not the author of these "Night Thoughts." He was only the translator, and the real author was David Hume.[39] Kant would have known that.

The "Night Thoughts of a Skeptic" represented a translation into German of the Conclusion of Book I of Hume's *Treatise*. In the *Treatise* itself, the translated section is simply called "Conclusion of this book."[40] Hamann gave it a more dramatic, yet quite fitting title. He also obviously tried to obscure the origin of the text in other ways. Where Hume said in his text "in England," Hamann put *"in unserm Land"* or "in our country," and he completely left out the last paragraph of Hume's Conclusion, because it would have made clear to every reader that it was part of a much larger work.[41]

In the Conclusion of Book I of the *Treatise*, Hume discussed the causal principle, but the thrust of his discussion here was entirely different from that in the first *Enquiry*. In the *Enquiry*, Hume simply argued that our knowledge of any particular causal connection cannot be based upon reasoning a priori, but "arises entirely from experience, when we find that particular objects are constantly conjoined with each other." In the Conclusion of Book I of the *Treatise*, he emphasized that the connection between cause and effect "lies merely in ourselves" and that is "nothing but" a "determination of the mind." In the *Enquiry*, it could appear that the causal connection, though itself not objective, was somehow based upon the objects themselves. In this passage, Hume claims that the causal relation is entirely subjective. We may want to "push our enquiries, till we arrive at the original and ultimate principle" of any phenomena, but we cannot.

The discovery of the subjective character of the causal relation "not only cuts off all hope of ever attaining satisfaction, but even prevents our very wishes; since it appears that when we desire to know the ultimate and operating principle, as something, which resides in the external object, we either contradict ourselves, or talk without meaning." Here the question of the very possibility of metaphysics is asked in the context of a discussion of the causal principle, and this must have become immediately clear to Kant – whether before or after reading Herz does not matter. Kant agreed with Hume that the connection or tie between cause and effect was a "determination of the mind." Though he found this determination in pure reason and not in the imagination, his problem was the same as Hume's: how can we go from "that in us which we call 'representation' to the object?"

This did not exhaust Hume's problem, for in the Conclusion of Book I, the problem of causality is placed in a wider context. It is not just that the understanding forces us to "either contradict ourselves, or talk without a meaning." Hume also found fault with his fundamental principle of imagination. It also leads "us into error when implicitly follow'd (as it must be)." For this principle "makes us reason from causes and effects and convinces us of the continu'd existence of external objects, when absent from the senses. But tho' these two operations be equally natural and necessary in the human mind, yet in some circumstance they are directly contrary, nor is it possible for us to reason justly and regularly from causes and effects, and at the same time believe the continu'd existence of matter. How then shall we adjust these principles together?"[42] It leads to fundamental and, if Hume is correct, inevitable contradictions. Clearly more work was needed.

From Hamann's point of view there was, of course, more at stake. It was his attempt at criticizing pure philosophy. The title of his translation captured very well the existential despair of the Humean text that is so uncharacteristic of Hume. To give just a few examples:

But before I launch out into those immense depths of philosophy which lie before me, I find myself inclined to stop a moment in my present station, and to ponder that voyage which I have undertaken, and which undoubtedly requires the utmost art and industry to be brought to a happy conclusion. Methinks I am like a man, who, having struck on many shoals, and having narrowly escaped shipwreck in passing a small frith, has yet the temerity to put out to sea in the same leaky weather-beaten vessel, and even carries his ambition so far as to think of compassing the globe under these disadvantageous circumstances. My memory of past errors and perplexities makes me diffident for the future. The wretched condition, weakness, and disorder of the faculties, I must employ in my enquiries, encrease my apprehensions. And the impossibility of amending or correcting these faculties, reduces me almost to despair, and makes me resolve to perish on the barren rock, on which I am at present, rather than venture myself upon that boundless ocean which runs out into immensity. This sudden view of my danger strikes me with melancholy; and, as it is usual for that passion, above all others, to indulge itself, I cannot forbear feeding my despair with all those desponding reflections which the present subject furnishes me with in such abundance.

Here is the passage with which the first installment of the "Night Thoughts" ends:

The intense view of these manifold contradictions and imperfections in human reason has so wrought upon me, and heated my brain, that I am ready to reject all belief and reasoning, and can look upon no opinion even as more probable or likely than another. Where am I, or what? From what causes do I derive my existence, and to what condition shall I return? Whose favour shall I court, and whose anger must I dread? What beings surround me? and on whom have I any influence, or who have any influence on me? I am confounded with all these questions, and begin to fancy myself in the most deplorable condition imaginable, environed with the deepest darkness, and utterly deprived of the use of every member and faculty.

Verfremded in this way, the Humean text makes a powerful statement. It emphasizes the uselessness and danger of a certain way of philosophizing, and it expresses a despair that is claimed to be the inevitable result of relying *too much* on reason. Philosophical reason necessarily leads us astray. It cannot solve our problems, be they philosophical or otherwise. Hume's Conclusion might in this way serve as a warning against too much and too serious philosophizing and abstract thinking.

I have little doubt that Hamann intended precisely this message to come across, that he translated the piece as a warning to those who relied too much on philosophical reasoning and on pure reason, urging them to come back to the fold of ordinary life and to a faith that needs no other justification than itself. This was one of Hamann's most important views. Philosophy understood as a foundational and rational enterprise that could solve all our problems, is itself a problem for him. Hamann had found Hume useful in precisely this context before. In 1759 he had used Hume's *Treatise* in his *Socratic Memorabilia* to remind rationalist thinkers, and especially Kant, that Hume's skepticism pointed beyond their very project. Arguing against Plato's misinterpretation of Socrates and invoking Shaftesbury's Platonism as a veil of "unbelief," Hamann had emphasized Socratic ignorance, and he had suggested that Hume's philosophy demonstrated, perhaps against its own intentions, that any fundamental reliance on reason was a mistake. What we must rely on is sensibility and faith.

By publishing in 1771 the translation of the Conclusion of Book I of the *Treatise*, Hamann wanted to accomplish the same thing, namely to remind those who relied all-too-confidently on reason that this is always a serious mistake. Furthermore, the text also holds out reliance on natural beliefs or *Glaube* as a solution to the inevitable despair that follows from philosophizing. Human nature is not only stronger than human reason, it also provides the solution to all the problems that philosophy creates. Be a philosopher, but above all be a man. Don't take philosophy too seriously. Be skeptical even of skepticism. Rely on faith rather than reason. The main addressee was Kant, but he meant to remind his public of this as well. The translation of Hume should be seen as Hamann's veiled response to Kant's dissertation. Hamann reminded Kant that his new dogmatism about pure reason, a dogmatism very much at odds with his earlier "pseudo-Humean" phase, is a dead end, promising only the kind of despair that Hume evokes in the "Night Thoughts." He also reminded Kant that Hume had already overcome this despair with his concept of "belief" or "faith." Yet Kant, who was listening to Hume, Lambert, Mendelssohn, and Herz in revising his speculative philosophy, did not have ears to hear Hamann's more radical criticism.

Kant's Moral Philosophy Around 1770:
"All Morality Is Based on Ideas"

That the first data of *moral* experience greatly concerned Kant in 1769 can be seen from his notes for the lectures of that period. In them, Kant contrasts sharply those systems that found morality on feeling with those that found it on reason. Indeed, he claims that all moral systems must be divided in that way: they derive morality either from feeling, or from reason.[43] Accordingly, he is also concerned with reevaluating the role of the moral sense. In 1764 he had emphasized the importance of the moral sense for *both* the first formal and the first material principles of morals. Around 1770 he made claims like the following: "The doctrine of moral feeling is more a hypothesis to explain the phenomenon of approval that we give to some kinds of actions than one which could determine maxims and first principles that hold objectively and tell us how we should approve or reject something, or act or refrain from acting."[44]

Kant now begins to emphasize the *dependence* of moral feeling on a logically prior and independent rational principle. Thus he claims:

The moral feeling is not an original feeling. It is based on a necessary internal law that makes us view and feel ourselves from an external point of view. We feel ourselves in general, or in the personality of reason, as it were, and we view our individuality as an accidental subject, or as the accidents of the universal.[45]

The conditions without which the approval of an action cannot be universal (cannot stand under a universal principle of reason) are *moral.* . . . The approval of an action cannot be universal, if it does not contain grounds for approval that are without any relation to the sensible motives of the actor.

Accordingly,

The first investigation is: What are the *principia prima diiudicationis moralis* . . ., i.e. which are the highest maxims of morality and which is their highest law?

2. What is their rule of application . . . to an objection of *diiudication* (sympathy of others and an impartial spectator)? 3. What transforms moral conditions into *motiva*, i.e. on what is their *vis movens* and thus their application to the subject based? The latter are first the *motivum* that is essentially connected with morality, namely the worthiness to be happy.[46]

These passages reveal Kant's continuing debt to Hume's account of moral approval in terms of "the particular structure and fabric of the mind" of a judicious spectator, and they contain also the beginnings of Kant's account of morality in terms of generalized maxims and pure reason. Indeed, the feeling of "ourselves in general," or the feeling "the personality of reason," has definite similarities to his later account of the "divine man within us." It is as if the external and essentially "Humean" spectator has become internalized and idealized. Hume thought he could account for moral judgment in terms of a "pleasing *sentiment* of approbation" by an unbiased and disinterested spectator. Kant develops the idea of a completely rational observer of himself, or perhaps better, of an agent split in two, namely, a nonrational actor and a rational observer of these actions.[47] Hutcheson and Hume believed (and the early Kant suggested) that morality was based in the final analysis on a moral sense. Kant sharply differentiates between moral judgments that are purely rational and theoretical, that is, without application, and the application of such principles, which presupposes feeling. He explicitly says, "one must consider morality purely without any *motiva sensualis.*"[48] He also pointed out that "our system is the doctrine of freedom subordinated to the essential laws of the pure will" and claims that this is the agreement of all actions with one's personal worth.[49] It is only these rational grounds that are objective; the sensitive ones are merely subjective. "The categorical necessity of free actions is the necessity in accordance with laws of the pure will, the (hypothetical) or conditional necessity is that in accordance with the affected will."[50]

In these notes Kant rejects Hutcheson's account of morality outright, arguing that the "principle of Hutcheson is non-philosophical because it introduces a new feeling as a basis for explanation. Secondly, while Hutcheson suggests that the laws of sensibility are objective reasons," a moral feeling – being sensible – cannot provide the foundation for objective moral laws.[51] Such a foundation can only come from reason – or so Kant argues in some of these reflections. He now claims:

The concept a priori alone has true universality and is the principium of rules. Virtue can only be judged in accordance with concepts and therefore a priori. Empirical judgment in accordance with intuition in pictures or experience gives no laws, but only examples, which demand a concept a priori for judging.

Therefore "all morality is based on ideas."[52] Furthermore, Kant claims that "the practical sciences determine the value of the theoretical ones. . . . They are the first in intention. The goal is prior to the means. However, in execution the theoretical ones are first."[53]

Kant later made a number of cryptic remarks about the "primacy of pure practical reason." They may have historical significance, for the beginnings of his critical philosophy are to a large extent moral. The development of Kant's moral view is important for understanding any part of his mature theory. Only reason shows that we are autonomous and possess dignity. This is why it is necessary to develop a "genuine metaphysics without any admixture of the sensible." Such a metaphysics would constitute the only true knowledge we have of ourselves and would give foundation or justification to our character.

Almost everything that Kant says about character in anthropology can be translated to what he says about will in his moral philosophy. "Character" is the appearance of the will; a good character corresponds to the good will, and an evil character to an evil will. Indeed, "will" is "character," but character "completely freed from everything which may be only empirical and thus belong to anthropology." When Kant parenthetically defined character in the second *Critique* as the "practically consistent way of thinking (*Denkungsart*) in accordance with unchangeable maxims," he hinted at just that.[54]

Kant's philosophical theories seem to have caught up with his life. At forty-six, Kant had formulated the beginnings of his philosophical justification of the character he had begun to develop six years earlier. Yet it was only a beginning. It would take another fifteen years of hard work before he published his final views on these matters, and when he did so, he talked so much of pure reason, the categorical imperative, and duty that character did not seem to be as important to him as it really is.

Herr Professor: "They Went to Kant's Lectures to Gain a Reputation"

As a *Magister*, Kant had to give many lectures just to support himself. Though his position as sublibrarian gave him added income during the latter half of the sixties, he still lectured twenty-two hours on five different subjects in 1770. He found this difficult. His health was poor.[55] To Herz, who had left Königsberg for Berlin at the beginning of August, he complained about "being overburdened with courses."[56] As soon as he became "professor Kant," he could relax a little. From then on he could lecture less. Still, he did not drastically reduce his teaching load. He still taught sixteen hours most semesters, and sometimes more. Furthermore, he had to teach more students than before.[57] The professorship brought with it new duties. He had to give the public lectures that were required of any full professor. It was not just the content of these lectures that was prescribed, but also the time. Kant had to start lecturing at 7:00 A.M. Waking up early was not easy for Kant – at least at first. Kant wrote later: "In the year 1770, when I took up the professorship in logic and metaphysics that made it necessary for me to begin lecturing at 7:00 A.M., I hired a servant who had to wake me."[58] Until that time Kant had never lectured before 8:00 A.M. So one of the regularities in Kant's life was imposed on him by the government. It was not his choice to get up so early; it was his public duty.

Kant had already been lecturing on new topics beginning in the late sixties. One of these was natural law, on which he lectured beginning in 1767, but not on a regular basis. Another subject he began to treat was "philosophical encyclopedia, with a short history of philosophy," which he taught six times between the winter semester of 1767–68 and the winter semester of 1771–72.[59] After his promotion he began to teach subjects he really liked, like anthropology in 1772–73, and rational theology in 1774.[60] Especially the lectures on anthropology, which he would hold in every winter semester from 1772–73 on, were important. They were to become the most accessible of all his lectures.[61] While students dreaded his lectures on logic and metaphysics, they seem genuinely to have enjoyed his lectures on anthropology.

Toward the end of 1773, Kant had written Herz – someone who justifiably could be assumed to have the greatest interest in the subject – that he was offering a *colloquium privatum* on anthropology, and that he was planning to transform this subject into a proper academic discipline. His main purpose in doing so was:

> To introduce by means of it the sources of all the sciences that are concerned with morals, with the ability of commerce, and the method of educating and ruling human beings, or all that is practical. In this discipline I will, then, be more concerned to seek out the phenomena and their laws than the first principles of the possibility of modifying human nature itself.[62]

Kant also assured Herz that this wouldn't be dry academic stuff, but an entertaining occupation, and that his empirical observations were meant to teach his students the rudiments of prudence and even wisdom. He also felt it necessary to point out explicitly that he would not address questions concerning the mind-body relation. If we take this seriously, then we may say that Kant's lectures on anthropology were first conceived as a kind of empirical psychology in the service of practical concerns. Empirical psychology was traditionally treated in metaphysics. Kant broke with this tradition. Indeed, from the time he began lecturing on anthropology, he no longer treated that subject very extensively in his lectures on metaphysics.[63] The lectures were "popular" both in the sense that he treated his subject matter "popularly" and in the sense that his lectures were well attended. He also lectured on mineralogy in the winter of 1770–71, responding to a demand from the minister in Berlin that mineralogy and the laws concerning it (*Bergrechte*) should be taught in Königsberg. Kant, who was charged with the supervision of a collection of rocks and minerals, was probably better qualified than anyone else in Königsberg to teach it, and so he did; but only for a semester.[64]

Kant still lectured every day. During the summer semester he usually taught logic, and during the winter, metaphysics. Thus in the summer of 1770 he taught (on Monday, Tuesday, Thursday, and Friday) logic from 7:00 until 8:00, and then again from 8:00 until 9:00 (privately), and "universal practical philosophy as well as ethics" from 9:00 until 10:00. On Wednesdays and Saturdays he lectured on physical geography from 8:00

until 10:00. He also gave a course on encyclopedia every day from 10:00 until 11:00. In other words, he taught twenty-two hours a week.[65] In the summer of 1776, he taught logic, theoretical physics, and physical geography, and held a *"repetitorium"* in logic. This meant he taught six fewer hours than he had six years earlier. There were also other duties.

In the summer semester of 1776 Kant became dean of the faculty of philosophy the first time. The deanship of the faculty of philosophy at the University of Königsberg had to be taken up by the full professors in turn. Kant served six times as dean. As a dean, he was also a member of the senate, which was the body that supervised all academic and administrative matters. It also was the court in which all university disputes were decided, including those of academic citizens and their families.[66] Kant found membership in this body to be a burden. Another duty of the dean was the examination of the incoming students. There would have been some seventy or eighty of them.[67] Some of his colleagues accused Kant of not examining the young people with the required strictness. He seems to have been satisfied if the students did not betray "complete neglect." Nor did he restrict their freedom as much as others would have liked, feeling that "trees grow better when they stand and grow outside, and they bring more fruit in this way than if they were grown by artifice in a hothouse . . ."[68] Kraus believed that Kant was not strict because he disliked the entire business and because it interfered with his other work, but there is also evidence that not everyone thought he was "easy" in his role as examiner. Thus Jachmann told of an incident that supports a different view. When Jachmann was graduating from his high school in Königsberg, the director saw to it that all the students were quickly taught another logical system. *Magister* Weymann, "a follower of Crusius and a declared enemy of Kant" had taught them philosophy.[69] The director feared that this might not be sufficient, and that Kant would fail his students.[70]

In the next semester (the winter of 1776–77) Kant had to teach for the first time a course on "practical pedagogic," which each of the professors of the faculty in philosophy had to teach in turn. Not surprisingly, Kant used Basedow's *Methodenbuch* of 1770, which applied his philosophy of common sense in opposition to idealism as well as to "harmonism," that is, to Leibniz.[71] The touchstone of common sense for Basedow was utility. Only what is useful should be taught. We have already seen that Kant was influenced by such ideas in his "Announcement." While he would not have liked everything in this textbook, Kant did appreciate the spirit in which it was written. When it was again Kant's turn to teach "practical pedagogic" in 1780, he used another text, namely his colleague F. S. Bock's *Textbook of the Art of Education for Christian Parents and Future Teachers of the Youth.*[72] The register of academic courses had a note beside the title of the course: "by Royal Decree."[73] In his lectures on anthropology Kant continued to praise Basedow.[74]

Some of the most important students who went to Kant's lectures during the seventies were Jakob Michael Reinhold Lenz (1751–1792), Christian Jakob Kraus (1753–1807), and Baczko. Lenz, who later became one of the famous writers within the *Sturm und Drang* movement, studied with Kant between 1769 and 1771. He wrote one of the poems celebrating Kant's promotion. Entitled "When His High and Noble Herr Professor Kant Disputed for the Honor of professor on August 21, 1770," it is well designed to reveal the poetic genius of Lenz. It is interesting as a document of what he and his contemporaries thought a professor should be, and what they saw in Kant. Thus we find him emphasizing Kant as someone in whom both virtue and wisdom can be found, one who lived and honored what he taught. Lenz probably slept during the lectures on moral philosophy, because he did not seem to realize that wisdom, at least according to the classical theory of the virtues, is a virtue itself. On the other hand, it may simply have been a compromise necessary to make the poem rhyme. In any case, what Lenz lacked in philosophical sophistication he made up for with enthusiasm. He praised Kant because as somenoe

> Whose clear eye never was bedazzled by the ostentatious
> Who, never crawling, never called the fool sagacious
> Who many a time reduced to shred
> The folly's mask, which we must dread.

We may wonder whether "the fool" was Buck, and whether the folly to be dreaded was a certain kind of religiosity. As if what he had said was not enough, he ended the poem by saying:

> You sons of France! Despise our Northern region
> Ask if ever a genius has here arisen:
> If Kant still lives, you will not hazard again
>   to ask this question.[75]

Lenz's intellectual outlook showed traces of Kantian influence. He knew and appreciated Shaftesbury and Hume, and he believed that the source of morality was the moral sense. Like Kant, Lenz thought the moral sense should not to be understood as a simple faculty, but as "a felt necessitating (*Nötigung*) to agree with a universal will." Though the feelings of sympathy and aesthetic harmony were important to him, it was ultimately the *summum bonum* that was important. In his "Essay on the First Principle of Morals," Lenz argued, very much like Kant, that morals "must be based on firm and inviolable principles," and that there are no actions that are more in conflict with human nature than those without a goal.[76] He also affirmed the centrality of the *summum bonum,* and the idea that the *summum bonum* should be sought within us. He agreed that there was not just one principle of morality but two. He developed the view that these two principles of morality could be found in the inclination to become perfect and the inclination to become happy, that there is a moral faith, and that this faith is the *complementum moralitatis.* All of these ideas were compatible with Kant's. To some extent, they were just extensions of the views Kant held during the period in which Lenz was his student.

Perhaps one might go further and say that Kant influenced the very way in which this essay is written.[77] Lenz alluded to his "usual way to spread out some easy and apparently unconnected remarks about the first principles of morals," and said "opinions . . . will count for me as genuine coin until I can exchange them for better ones." In this he was closer to the Kant of the *Observations* than to the Kant of the Inaugural Dissertation, but he was close to Kant. There is a certain family resemblance between the writings of Lenz and Herder, and the early Kant may have been responsible for this, at least in part. He may have had a more important and, as it were, subterranean influence on thinkers who developed very differently from the way in which he developed. This influence was not so much on the rationalistic elements of the eighteenth century, but on those who were opposed to a one-sided reliance of reason.

Kraus, who came to study at the University of Königsberg in October 1770, was similar to Lenz in his intellectual outlook.[78] He officially entered the University of Königsberg on April 13, 1771, and that is where he stayed until his death.[79] Apart from some trips to other parts of Germany, he remained for the rest of his life in Königsberg. In time, he became one of Kant's closest friends and colleagues. Kraus was the nephew of Pastor Buchholz, who was his mother's brother. When he first came to Königsberg his uncle supervised him. Since Buchholz was also Hamann's confessor, Kraus was almost immediately introduced into the intellectual circles of Königsberg. Like all beginning students, he started out with courses in the faculty of philosophy. He attended Kant's lectures during his very first semester, became interested, and soon had heard all them, and Kant, in spite of the great number of students in his lectures, had not failed to notice Kraus's exemplary attentiveness and lively interest. Because Kraus never went to lectures simply in order to have been there, but because he wanted to obtain new materials for thinking and research, he formulated many questions, reservations, doubts, obscurities and other thoughts, which disturbed him and almost made him insane. Yet in part because of his bashful and shy nature and in part because of the stark distance between the academic teacher and the students that still existed then and which made a friendly exchange between them very rare, he did not dare to visit Kant. But he obtained his wish in another way. He became a member of Kant's disputation class and once he offered such deep objections to the great philosopher and betrayed such an ability for philosophical thought (*Speculation*) that Kant began to wonder about the young man and asked him to stay after the lecture so that he could get to know him better. It almost appears as if Kant sought out his student. For the student this was an event of the greatest importance . . . without Kant, who became his one and only, Kraus would perhaps never become what he became.[80]

Kraus liked Kant and Kant liked Kraus – and the professor of philosophy looked out for his student. When Kraus's uncle died in 1773, he was without any support. His parents had died before he came to Königsberg. Kant began to support Kraus. In 1774 he recommended him to supervise a young baron in his studies at the university. Kraus obtained the position and received a substantial salary. He lived with the young baron at Kanter's house, close to Kant.

After having attended all of Kant's lectures, Kraus turned toward other studies in 1774. He learned English and mathematics on his own. He read widely, appreciating especially Butler's *Hudibras,* all of Shakespeare, Laurence Sterne's *Tristram Shandy,* "to form his mood (*Laune*) and wit," Rousseau and Spinoza, "to educate his understanding," and "Tindal, Morgans, Hobbes, and all the anti-religious wits, which teach me to doubt and to accept the true claim that the Bible is not meant for speculation." He also read Voltaire and, as a teacher in "speculation," that is, metaphysics, Hume. Kraus may have been influenced as much by these readings as he was by Kant's lectures. Though Kant looked at Kraus as his student, Kraus was not willing to follow Kant's new critical philosophy.

Indeed, after 1775, Kraus, like Herder before him, came more and more under the influence of Hamann, who on August 14 of that year told Herder that Kraus "is a great genius, both in philosophy and mathematics. He broods over problems . . . He is the teacher of my son and his father."[81] But a year later (August 10, 1776) he wrote: "Kraus has become a complete stranger to me and is translating, on Green's recommendation, Young's

Political Arithmetic for Kanter." But he then confided that Kraus "worked on something – what it was perhaps neither one of us knew. He became sick over it because he over-exerted his faculties."[82] This was not the last reference to Kraus's inability to finish his own work. Later that year Hamann complains that Kraus, in spite of his great talent, has a "secret, sneaky, inexplicable something" about him that, "like a dead fly, spoils the best ointment."[83] He also complained about Kraus's inclination to disorderliness. Given that Hamann was not a paragon of orderliness either, this was significant.

The context of these remarks is provided by Kraus's wish to participate in the Prussian Academy's prize essay competition on the sources of the two original faculties of the soul. Since he "believed that he had the entire work ready in his head, he thought he could put his thoughts easily to paper. My credulousness and curiosity caused me to encourage him, since it was entirely impossible for me to reveal his ideas. . . . He always pretended to work on it, and expressed his hope that it would soon be finished. He became sick over it in body, spirit, and mind."[84] When Hamann looked at his papers he found nothing, or at least, nothing worthwhile. Herder, whose work *On Knowing and Feeling in the Human Soul* was submitted to the competition, had, of course, a great deal of interest in this subject matter.

Kant, who was working on his *Critique of Pure Reason*, which dealt with the same problem, would have been just as interested. He thought highly of Kraus, even making excuses for him. Thus he wrote to Herz:

> A certain misology, which you regret to have noticed in Kraus . . . originates, like many an expression of misanthropy, from the fact that in the former one loves philosophy and in the latter people, but finds both ungrateful, partly because one expected too much of them, partly because one is too impatient in awaiting the expected reward for one's efforts from the two. I also know this sullen mood; but a kind glance from either of them soon reconciles us with them again and serves to make our attachment stronger . . .[85]

This is telling not only about Kraus, but also about Kant. By the time he wrote this, he had been working for at least nine years on the *Critique*, and he was impatient himself. Furthermore, he was gradually finding out that he could expect very little from metaphysics, and in any case much less than he had hoped for in 1770. Whether the same thing held for people is not so clear, but it is not unlikely that it did. Kraus must have disappointed Kant at times, just as he had disappointed Hamann.

Whatever Kraus's problems may have been, Kant continued to take care of him. He obtained another position for him in the house of the Keyser-

lingks, which paid him 200 Thalers just for supervising one of their relatives. During the years 1779 and 1780, Kraus took a trip to Berlin and Göttingen, becoming a Freemason on the way and making many important
friends and acquaintances. "One evening in Göttingen he was invited to a
garden party at which many professors, including Johann Georg Heinrich
Feder, were present. The conversation was steered to the philosophy of the
day. Kraus mentioned that Kant had a work in his desk (the *Critique of
Pure Reason*), which would most certainly cost philosophers anxiety and
sweat. The gentlemen laughed and said that from a dilettante in philosophy
something like this was hardly to be expected."[86] If only they could have
spoken to some of Kant's students.

Baczko, who later became a historian of Königsberg, studied at the Albertina between 1772 and 1776. He also went to Kant's lectures. In his
autobiography he gives the following account:

> Kant had then begun his brightest period. He lectured metaphysics without payment,
> when I entered the university. I attended his lectures right away and I did not under-
> stand them. Given the estimation of Kant's name and the suspicions that I have always
> entertained about my abilities, I came to believe that I had to put more time into my
> studies. Therefore I asked everyone of my acquaintances whether they did not own
> books on metaphysics or other philosophical disciplines. Soon I got the works of Wolff,
> Meier and Baumgarten, but also some very poor books, which I read with great exer-
> tion. I worked through entire nights, labored uninterrupted for twenty hours and more
> over a book and learned nothing.
>
> As well as lacking the occasion, I was too proud and stubborn to confess my igno-
> rance to others and to ask them for help. . . . I began to believe that some of Kant's stu-
> dents knew even less than I did. I began to believe that they went to Kant's lectures in
> order to gain a reputation. I began to tease some of them, declaring all of philosophy
> useless.[87]

Still, Baczko goes on to declare that Helvetius's *On the Spirit of Man*,
d'Argens's *Philosophy of Bon Sens*, Brucker's *History of Philosophy*, as well
as some things by Grotius, Hobbes, Gassendi, and philosophers like them,
did turn out to be useful after all.

Baczko's experience, which probably was not untypical, shows that Kant's
lecture style had changed. He no longer aimed at elegance and popularity,
but cultivated a certain kind of obscurity that made it very difficult for
students to understand him. He gained the reputation of being a difficult
philosopher. There were a number of students – not altogether untypical
at a German university – who were impressed by the depth or obscurity of
Kant. They went to his lectures just because they did not understand them.
Kant was not unaware of this. When he was asked in 1778 whether he could

not provide a set of lecture notes as a source of information for his new philosophy, he wrote back that it would be difficult for a variety of reasons. His main reason was that "metaphysics is a course that I have worked up in the last few years in such a way that I fear it must be difficult even for a discerning head to get *precisely* the right idea from somebody's lecture notes. Even though the idea seemed intelligible to me in the lecture, still, since it was taken down by a beginner and deviates greatly both from my formal statements and from ordinary concepts, it will call for someone with a head as good as your own to present it systematically and understandably." Two months later he again complained that "those of my students who are most capable of grasping everything are just the ones who bother least to take explicit and verbatim notes; or rather they write down only the main points, which they can think over afterwards. Those who are most thorough in note taking are seldom capable of distinguishing the important from the unimportant. They pile a mass of misunderstood stuff under that which they may possibly have grasped correctly."[88] Kant knew that there were many students who had problems with his lectures, and it is clear that he did not much care about it. He talked to those who "are capable" and not to those who are incapable. Indeed, he might well have catered to the taste of those students who liked obscurity.

Kant made one other telling remark in this context. He said: "Besides, I have almost no private acquaintance with my listeners, and it is difficult for me even to find out which ones might have accomplished something useful."[89] By 1778 Kant seems to have isolated himself almost completely from his students. For the most part, he did not know them, and they seem not to have known him. Kant no longer seemed to care much whether his students got something "useful" out of his lectures on logic and metaphysics. He seemed more interested in developing his own theory. Though his lectures on anthropology and physical geography were easier and more accessible, emphasizing the useful, much like his earlier lectures in metaphysics, this does not seem to have implied closer contact with most of his students. In any case, he wrote to Herz in 1778 that he "shortened the section on empirical psychology when he began to lecture on anthropology."[90] This alone would have made the lectures on metaphysics harder.

Baczko was an exception: he did get to know Kant "because [he was] his frequent listener." Furthermore, while he might not have had success with books on metaphysics, he did have success with anthropology. Kant noticed Baczko because the student could help him with many examples. Indeed, Kant encouraged Baczko to make anthropology his main field of study.

Baczko said he would have followed Kant's advice if the University of Königsberg had allowed him to become a *Magister*. Alas, as a Catholic, he was not allowed to do so.[91] Another reason why Baczko came closer to Kant than most students was his friendship with Kraus:

There were then also living a number of students at Kanter's house. One of them was . . . professor Kraus. I soon felt a heartfelt attachment for him, and we were inseparable friends throughout our academic years. Our first meeting was, however, somewhat peculiar. I found myself in a position of pressing need, so that I could not heat my room. For this reason I took off my boots as soon as I came home, put on an old overcoat, and went to bed. When I wanted to write, I put a board, which I kept for just that purpose, on the blanket. Now, since Kant always had his lecture room heated very well, and since I was taking a recitation from him from 8:00 to 9:00, and another recitation by Jester from 10:00 to 11:00, I often remained in Kant's lecture room from 9:00 to 10:00. He did not lecture during that period, and I remained unnoticed by anyone. To pass the time I always brought some book. Kraus, who exhibited a quite remarkable impulsiveness, saw a book at my desk even before Kant had started his lecture. He took it right away into his hand, and since he . . . probably viewed me as an unimportant and ignorant person, he was surprised to see that I had brought Segner's *Cursus mathematici*. So he asked me in his special tone: "My dear soul, what are you doing with this book?" The question annoyed me, and I answered in almost the same tone: I sing from it when I do business (*commercire*). He looked at me and laughed; I laughed with him.[92]

Kraus had a great deal of influence on Baczko's philosophical outlook. Indeed, the philosophical books he appreciated were just the ones that Kraus also would have appreciated. Through Kraus, Baczko came to know Hamann better as well, and thus was introduced to the literary world of Königsberg.

As a result of the pox, Baczko lost his sight in one eye at the age of twenty in 1776. In 1780, his other eye had to be operated on to remove a cyst. The operation was not successful. As a result, he also lost his sight in that eye and became completely blind.[93] Yet this did not prevent him from becoming a successful historian. He first employed a boy to read to him several hours a day, and then hired a student to do so. Others in Königsberg admired Baczko for his skill and persistence. Baczko explains that even

Kant, who – I do not know for what reason – had an aversion to blind people, was so good to visit me. He confessed this aversion to me, adding that I was not blind because I possessed sufficient concepts from intuition and instruments, which overcame the lack of sight.[94]

Whatever the cause of Kant's aversion, he visited his former student, fulfilling what he must have seen as his duty. Baczko appreciated this. Not everyone today would appreciate Kant's behavior or feelings.

More important for the spread of Kant's philosophy was perhaps Anton Willich, who studied medicine at Königsberg beginning in March of
1778. He also attended Kant's lectures between 1778 and 1781. In 1792,
after graduating as a medical doctor, he went to Edinburgh, where he soon
became part of a friendship circle around Walter Scott.[95] His *Elements of
Critical Philosophy* of 1798 was one of the first books on Kant in Britain.
Though Willich was not an important philosophical mind in his own right,
he testified to the powerful influence Kant had on his students during this
period.[96]

One student, who did not – or perhaps better, could not – attend Kant's
lectures was Salomon Maimon (1754–1800). He came to Königsberg during 1779. His account makes clear why:

> When I arrived there, I went to the Jewish doctor, explained to him my proposal to
> study medicine, and begged for advice and support . . . he referred me to some stu-
> dents who lodged in his house. As soon as I showed myself to these young gentlemen,
> and told them what I wanted, they burst out into loud laughter. Certainly, they were not
> to be blamed for this. Imagine a man from Polish Lithuania, of about twenty-five, with
> a stiff beard, tattered dirty clothes, whose language is a mixture of Hebrew, Yiddish,
> Polish and Russian, with grammatical inaccuracies, who claims that he understands
> the German language, and that he has attained some knowledge of the sciences. What
> were the young gentlemen to think?
>
> They began to poke fun at me, and gave me to read Mendelssohn's *Phaedo*, which by
> chance lay on the table. I read in the most pitiful style, both on account of the peculiar
> manner in which I had learned the German language, and on account of my bad pro-
> nunciation. Again, they burst into laughter; but they said I must explain to them what I
> read. This I did in my own fashion; but as they did not understand me, they demanded
> that I should translate what I read into Hebrew. This I did on the spot. The students,
> who understood Hebrew well, fell into no slight astonishment, when they saw that I
> had not only grasped correctly the meaning of this celebrated author, but also ex-
> pressed it felicitously into Hebrew.[97]

The students advised Maimon to go to Berlin. He followed their advice,
met Herz and Mendelssohn there, came under their influence, and became
a philosopher of sorts. Much later, he read Kant's first *Critique* and became
one of the most important early followers of Kant.[98] We can only speculate
about what might have become of him had he been able to attend Kant's
lectures in 1779.

Kant not only lectured to many students and attracted at least one
promising follower during the seventies, he succeeded on another front as
well. In December 1775 the ministry in Berlin sent a warning to the University of Königsberg, in which it requested that the lectures be made more

effective. Kant and his colleague Reusch were praised. Weymann and Wlochatius were censured. The ministry did not want the heads of the students "obscured by useless speculation" but wanted to see them learn "truly useful concepts," and the letter explicitly said: "we do not like to see that Crusius's philosophy is taught in Königsberg, since the most learned scholars are long convinced of its uselessness. From now on, this shall cease."[99] The teaching of Crusius was thus effectively forbidden in 1775. Weymann was eliminated as Kant's rival. It was only in 1789 that he was allowed to teach again, in spite of a negative recommendation by the university senate, which "was co-signed by Kant," of course.[100] But he did not teach for long. This time the students heckled him until he gave up. Though 1789 was a time in which Weymann's religious views were welcome in Berlin, Crusius was by then a real anachronism.[101]

Karl Abraham Freiherr von Zedlitz (1731–1793), minister for matters of church and education, was responsible for the warning. One of Frederick II's progressive ministers, he founded a chair of pedagogy at Halle (1779), generally planned for the better education of teachers, supported the founding of new schools, and continued to push for the centralization of school administration. Later, in 1787, he instituted an *Oberschulkollegium* (a national board of education). He had taken a liking to Kant. Thus he asked in February of 1778 whether he might nominate Kant as a professor of philosophy at Halle, with a beginning salary of 600 Thalers. Halle was much larger and much more prestigious, and Kant would have effectively become the successor of Wolff, a great honor. He declined, only to have the offer raised by 200 Thalers, with the title of *Hofrat* thrown in. Still, Kant decided to stay in Königsberg, where he drew a salary of only 236 Thalers and had no opportunity to become *Hofrat*. Neither the opportunity to teach many more students, nor the more central location of Halle, nor even the good name of the university there, were sufficient to make him move. The reason was his belief that he had been given only a "comparatively small dose of the force of life."[102]

In August of the same year, von Zedlitz asked Kant in a letter to use his influence so that students would not concentrate their studies so much in the higher faculties. Though studies in the higher faculties promised a career in theology, law, or medicine, philosophy and the liberal arts might be more useful for them in the long run.[103] Von Zedlitz was well acquainted with Kant's philosophy through Herz, who was spreading the word about Kant's philosophy by lecturing and writing about it. In 1778, von Zedlitz attended lectures by Herz on "Kant's rational anthropology."[104] Herz wrote that he was "always the first in my room and the last to leave."[105] In 1779, von Zedlitz took a course on psychology with Herz, and again he did not miss any session. When Kraus was in Berlin in 1779, he also got to know von Zedlitz well. The secretary of the high minister wrote to Kant: "in the reflection of these two we get to know your light."[106] Kant was now famous in Berlin. Everyone, it appears, expected great things from him. He clearly had some weight. But the reflection of Kant's light was somewhat distorted. Kant's views had changed, and what von Zedlitz saw was an earlier Kant, not the Kant of the *Critique of Pure Reason*.

Kant always had close friends among his colleagues.[107] Funk and Kypke were important to him during his earlier years as a *Magister* but not later. While Funk died long before Kant became professor, Kypke drifted into the life more characteristic of a small farmer than of a scholar. He became a stranger. Kant had occasion more than once to disapprove of Kypke's conduct. Thus in 1777 Kypke, governmental inspector of the synagogue beginning in 1755, caused a controversy that quickly led to the elimination of that office. Early in that year the Jewish community moved the place of Kypke's reserved seat in the synagogue. Considering the new location less dignified, he was not amused, and he therefore submitted on April 5, 1777, a letter of complaint to the Royal Ministry of State in which he also aired other misgivings. The most important complaint centered on the *Alenu* prayer, which was offensive to some Christians. This prayer included the phrase "for they bow down and prostrate themselves before what is vain and futile and pray to a god who cannot help," which some took to mean Christians. To remove the possibility of insult, the use of the phrase was forbidden by a royal edict dating back to 1703, and one of the duties of the governmental inspector of the synagague was to see to it that the phrase was not spoken. Kypke claimed that the prayer was not spoken loudly enough but merely "muttered," implying that the Jews actually *were* saying the offensive phrase. He also complained that they did not inform him in a timely manner of the psalms that would be read in upcoming services, making it impossible for him to object to them. Reprimands and perhaps more serious punishment were in order – or so Kypke felt. The Jewish community defended itself and submitted a testimonial by Mendelssohn, namely, the "Thoughts on Jewish Prayers, Especially on the '*Alenu* Prayer.'" Mendelssohn argued convincingly that the prayer was much older than Christianity and therefore could not have been directed at Christians. The testimonial caused more dispute and some intemperate rejoinders by Kypke, but it ultimately resulted in the elimination of his position in 1778.[108]

Though he received a raise in salary to compensate him for the loss of the 100 Thalers income from his supervisory activity, this was not the outcome he wanted. Kant, who had selected the Jew Herz as his respondent in the defense of his *Magister* thesis, had little sympathy for Kypke. Count Keyserlingk, Kant's friend and protector, played a decisive role in bringing this affair to its proper end.

During the seventies two of his younger colleagues seem to have been especially important to Kant, namely, Johann Gottlieb Kreutzfeld (1745–1784) and Karl Daniel Reusch (1735–1806). Lindner, professor of poetry, died in March of 1776. The person chosen to replace him was Kreutzfeld, also a good friend of Kraus and Hamann. In fact, the three had already studied English together for a long time, and Hamann claimed that he had taught Kreutzfeld the rudiments of that language.[109] Kreutzfeld also was a student of Kant. In his defense of his Inaugural Dissertation, "Concerning Sensory Illusion and Poetic Function," Kraus was the respondent, while Kant gave a commentary on the thesis.[110] Kant maintained a somewhat close relationship with this student of his as well. Whether this relationship with Kreutzfeld was closer than that with Reusch, professor of physics from 1772, singled out by von Zedlitz, together with Kant, as a teacher to be emulated, is not clear. In any case, Reusch and Kant discussed not just Fahrenheit's thermometer and lightning rods, but also many other questions. When Reusch met Kant on one of his regular walks, he often accompanied him.

After 1780, it was Kraus who was his most important colleague. For in June of 1780 Christiani, who was a full professor of moral philosophy already during Kant's years as a student, died unexpectedly. Kant wrote almost immediately to von Zedlitz to recommend Kraus for the position. At the same time, he asked Hamann to write to Kraus in Göttingen in order to prepare him.[111] Just two months later, Hamann was writing to Herder, fully convinced that Kraus would get the position.[112] Kraus "left Göttingen as a designated (*berufener*) professor. On the way home to Königsberg that fall, he obtained the title of *Magister* at the University of Halle. On January 4, 1781 he arrived in Königsberg "as professor of moral and political philosophy."[113] This was highly significant not just for Kraus, who could thank Kant for his professorship, but also for Kant, who had succeeded in having the second most important position in philosophy occupied by his friend and one of his best students.[114] We may be sure that his support for Kraus was not just dictated by personal but also by political considerations. Just as the Pietists had earlier dominated the way philosophy was taught at the university by seeing to it that the right appointments were made, so Kant was trying to make sure his views were propounded not just by him. By the end of 1780, ten years after his own appointment, he had succeeded in what had been one of his goals from the beginning.

Another person who became an important friend and ally of Kant during these years was Schulz, the reviewer of his Inaugural Dissertation. In 1775, he was appointed as a deacon at one of the churches (*Altroßgarten*) in Königsberg. During the same year, he became a *Magister* and doctor of philosophy and then defended his Inaugural Dissertation, entitled *"De geometria acustica seu solius auditus ope exercenda. Dissertatio I."* Kraus was one of the opponents. Schulz from then on held lectures on mathematics and astronomy. In 1776, he was appointed as court chaplain at the *Schloß-kirche.* Although he was very close to Kant in his intellectual outlook, the two did not seem to have close personal relations. Indeed, they seem to have communicated mostly by way of letters, which was somewhat unusual.

Social Life: "I Got All That I Ever Wished For"

One of the reasons why Kant wanted to remain in Königsberg was his circle of friends and acquaintances. Kant felt comfortable in the city of his birth. He continued to be invited often to attend dinners and parties by most of the major families in town. He mixed with nobility at the Keyserlingks' court and with the important merchant families in Königsberg just as much as with the officers of the Prussian army. His visits at the Keyserlingks' lasted for "many years and without interruption." The countess liked Kant especially, but the count also seems to have respected him. Kant got to know the "noble way of life" there, which, according to Kraus, he understood so well. His "elegance" (*Gewandtheit*) and his "delicate" behavior were quite rare among scholars. "Kant always sat at Keyserlingk's table at the place of honor, immediately beside the Countess, unless some foreigner was there, who according to protocol had to sit at that place."[115] The astronomer and geographer Johann Bernoulli (1744–1807), who visited Königsberg during 1778, wrote:

I ate at lunch at the count of Keyserlingk with a scholar, whom the University of Königsberg honors as one of its greatest members, professor Kant. This famous philosopher is in his social intercourse such a lively and polite man, and he has such an elegant (*fein*) way of life that one would not easily expect such a deeply searching mind in him. But his eyes and his face betray a great wit, and their similarities with d'Alembert was really noticeable. This scholar has in Königsberg many adherents. This may well be explainable by the fact that there are more metaphysicians here than at other universities. He offered now a course, which was greatly appreciated, and which had as its goal to provide his students with correct concepts of men, their actions, and from the manifold events and acts that happen in human life. Various stories and anecdotes gave spice to these lectures and made them still more instructive and popular. Herr Kant had not published philosophical writings for a long time, but he promised that he would soon bring out a little volume (*Bändchen*).[116]

The "little volume" of which Bernoulli speaks would of course be the *Critique*. Kant himself in the summer of 1778 had no idea how long the book would become. Perhaps he did believe that the many sketches he had collected could be condensed into a rather short version.

Kant's friendship with Green was also an important factor in his decision to stay in Königsberg. He frequently went to visit Green's house in the afternoon. By the seventies, Green relied almost entirely on his associate Motherby for his business. Since Motherby paid more attention to it than Green had, the business increased more and more in importance. Kant and Green were very close at this time. He is reported to have discussed every sentence in the *Critique* with Green.[117] If these discussions were important to Kant – and by all accounts they were – he could not have left Königsberg during the seventies for that very reason alone.

The conversations with Green and his guests formed an important part of Kant's life then. For it was through Green that Kant got to know a number of other people. First among those was Motherby. In fact, every Sunday, Kant and Green went together to Motherby's for dinner. Another, less likely friend of Kant, who also regularly visited Green, Motherby, and Hay, was the Pastor Sommer, who knew English very well. Sommer was also a good friend of Hamann, Hippel, and Kraus. Indeed, Hamann called Sommer Kraus's "shadow."[118] During the "earlier years, Sommer also participated in journeys to the country, which were attended by Kant as well."[119] Reinhold Bernard Jachmann, Kant's biographer, and his brother Johann Benjamin Jachmann, both students of Kant, also belonged to the circle of acquaintances that met at the houses of these British merchants.[120]

These social bonds were not all that held Kant in Königsberg. He also felt that the city was perfect for him in other ways. Writing to Herz, he explained:

I got all that I wished for, namely a peaceful situation that is exactly fitted to my needs: in turn occupied with work, speculation, and society, where my easily affected, but otherwise carefree, mind and my even more capricious body, which however is never sick, will be occupied without strain. All change makes me anxious, even if it seems to contribute greatly to the improvement of my situation. I believe I must pay attention to this instinct of my nature, if I still want to lengthen somewhat the thread, which fate spins very thinly and delicately for me.[121]

It would be easy to dismiss Kant's fears today, but we should realize the hardships that any extended trip would have presented in the eighteenth century. A move from one city to another was not an easy matter, and if Kant's health was as delicate as he believed it to be – and there really is no reason to doubt this – then his cautiousness was not altogether unreasonable.

Around the end of 1777 Kant did move out of Kanter's house into quarters "at the Ochsenmarkt." Borowski detailed the reason as follows: "he was driven out of his [Kanter's] house by a neighbor, who held a cock on his property, whose crowing often interrupted Kant in his meditations. He offered to buy the animal from the neighbor at any price to obtain peace from the loud animal. Yet he did not succeed to persuade the stubborn neighbor who could not at all comprehend how the cock could bother Kant."[122] Again, it was noise that made Kant move.

The new quarters could not have been very comfortable. Kraus, who moved into the very same rooms (after Kant vacated them to move into a house of his own), complained about them in the very cold winter of 1786. Thus he spoke of "my broken rooms, in which my fingers get stiff and my thoughts stop."[123] Kant, who placed the greatest emphasis on well-heated rooms, would not have appreciated the new drafty abode either. But Kraus, just like Kant, seemed to like the peacefulness of the surroundings. He took up Kant's quarters at the Ochsenmarkt because he wanted to escape from his own noisy neighborhood. Thus he wrote in April of 1783 that the lack of progress in his work "must be the fault of the most horrible street noise because I am not entirely thoughtless. But I cannot keep my thoughts together at all. As soon as it is no longer necessary to heat, I will move to the back [of the house] where at least no carriages go by."[124] The drafts seem to have been so bad and the situation so irreparable that the owner later bricked in the windows altogether. It was thus not so easy for a young professor at the University of Königsberg to find acceptable rooms. After all, they not only had to house him, but also had to provide him with large enough lecture rooms. Price certainly was a consideration as well.

Kant only rented rooms and did not really maintain a household. He thus had to eat out every day. Indeed, this was a constant in Kant's life. From the time of his earliest years as a *Magister* until about Easter of 1787, when he finally set up his own "economy" or household, he had to eat at a restaurant. Thus he wrote to an early biographer, who had claimed that he was not well off financially during his early years as a *Magister,* that he was even then capable of "paying for a very good table." Like many bachelors in the eighteenth century, he ate his main meal in a restaurant or pub (*öffentliches Speishaus*). The main meal was, as customary in Germany until fairly recently, at lunchtime. Borowski pointed out that "he always had an agreement with the owner that he would find good and decent society there." Once he left a house of this kind because a man, who otherwise was quite reasonable, had gotten into the habit of speaking very slowly and with some pathos about even the most insignificant matters. Kant disliked ostentatiousness. Especially at lunch, he preferred conversational tone without any artifice. Indeed, he himself never made a great effort at avoiding "common expressions" and was even given to a certain "provincialism" in his language.[125] In other words, he spoke like an East Prussian; and the East Prussian dialect was deft. It struck people who spoke only High German as rather direct – and how direct Kant could be can be seen from his *Dreams.*

Kant stopped going to another place when certain people "tried to join in without being invited, expecting that he would lecture them at lunch and answer their objections. He wanted . . . to free himself from anything that exerted the mind and, as he used to say, 'give honor to the body.' But apart from those, anyone from any social class was welcome."[126] Those who wanted to be special he disliked. He felt that "a philosopher might be more at home in a farmer's pub than among distorted heads and hearts." For years Kant took his lunch at Zornig in the Junker Street, with completely uneducated and ignorant majors and colonels. When a judicial official came to this party, Kant declared that this man was "hammering his head full," and he therefore left.[127] Later he went to Gerlach's, which was "a billiard house in the Kneiphoff." It appears that Kant ate at Gerlach's for most of the time between 1755 and 1770.[128] Zornig or Zornicht was a "coffee and guest house," which was close to the *Prinzessinenplatz,* where Kant later built his house; and it was also close to where Hippel lived. If the descriptions are reliable, then Zornig was a somewhat more exclusive place than Gerlach's. Still, for more than thirty years Kant ate lunch at a pub, and during that time he mixed with a great variety of different people. Kant thus did not always live the withdrawn life that many people associate with a philosopher of his standing. Far from it: when he was not invited to a dinner party, he ate in the company of men with very different backgrounds from his own, and he enjoyed it.

The choice of entrees was also important to Kant. Nothing too fancy, the meat well-done, good bread, and good wine. During his early years he preferred red wine, late in life he liked white wine better. He loved to eat at a leisurely pace, and, if he liked a particular dish, he inquired about the recipe and how it was prepared. But he was also free with his criticism. Hippel later joked that "sooner or later he would be writing a *Critique of the Art of Cooking.*"[129]

His daily schedule then looked something like this. He got up at 5:00 A.M. His servant Martin Lampe, who worked for him from at least 1762 until 1802, would wake him. The old soldier was under orders to be persistent, so that Kant would not sleep longer. Kant was proud that he never got up even half an hour late, even though he found it hard to get up early. It appears that during his earlier years, he did sleep in at times. After getting up, Kant would drink one or two cups of tea – weak tea. With that, he smoked a pipe of tobacco. The time he needed for smoking it "was devoted to meditation." Apparently, Kant had formulated the maxim for himself that he would smoke only one pipe, but it is reported that the bowls of his pipes increased considerably in size as the years went on. He then prepared his lectures and worked on his books until 7:00. His lectures began at 7:00, and they would last until 11:00. With the lectures finished, he worked again on his writings until lunch. Go out to lunch, take a walk, and spend the rest of the afternoon with his friend Green. After going home, he would do some more light work and read.

This was the "peaceful situation that is exactly fitted to my needs: in turn occupied with work, speculation, and society." It was a regular or even regulated way of life, but it was hardly mechanical. Lecturing, writing, and reading were interrupted by conversation, relaxation, and even play. No doubt, Green's influence had had its effect. Kant's "character" had begun to form. It was characterized by his "constant striving to act in accordance with thought-out maxims, which – at least in *his* opinion – were well founded principles, and by his eagerness to formulate maxims in all the greater and smaller, more and less important matters, from which he always began and to which he always returned."[130] His "maximized" life was not – at least not at this point – disadvantageous to his work or life. Indeed, his life according to maxims seems to have made both his work and his life more pleasant. They contributed to the smooth and regular flow of his life that he valued over everything.

It was very much like the "life of the skilled artisan" or craftsman that Dohm idealized as "the most happy one possible in our civil society." Like the ideal member of the guild, Kant was "troubled by neither nagging fears nor delusive hopes about the future; he enjoy[ed] the present with a pure and perfect joy, and expect[ed] tomorrow to be exactly like today. . . . He [was] happy with his own lot in life, and suspect[ed] . . . that the upper classes [were] less so with theirs."[131] His father had never achieved this goal, but Kant had done so. That this state also had similarities to the ideal life as described by the Stoics and the Epicureans is, of course, no accident either.

Kant did not have to worry about money. Though the merchants in Königsberg went during the seventies through a severe crisis during which forty-seven firms went bankrupt because of the partition of Poland (just when the economy was improving in the rest of Prussia), Kant was financially secure.[132] The firm of Green, Motherby & Co., with whom Kant had invested most of his money, was not among the firms that had to fear bankruptcy. Having more dealings with England and Holland, they were not as much affected by these national developments.

Nor did Kant have to deal with the unexpected vagaries of business or family life. He was engaged in precisely the kind of activities that he enjoyed most. His servant Lampe took care of all practical matters. He saw to it that Kant had clean clothes, that he woke up on time, that he had the needed supplies. He took care of Kant's rooms, and did all the errands, but he did not live with Kant. Having his own quarters, he was less satisfied with his bachelor life. Indeed, at some time during his employment he took a wife – against Kant's wishes. Kant had indeed a legal say in such matters. He could have prohibited it, and probably would have done so if Lampe had given him a chance, but he married secretly and thus created an additional expense for Kant, if only because Lampe now "needed more" by way of support.[133]

If Kant was conservative in the particulars of his relation to his servant, he was more liberal in his broader social concerns. Clearly, his religious views were less than orthodox. This is shown by an incident that had to do with one of his former students, namely Herder, who had already become famous in his own right by the middle of the seventies. He had published in 1768 and 1769 works on literature and aesthetics, which got him noticed.[134] In 1774 he published a work *On the Oldest Document of the Human Race*. Kant was obviously interested in this work of a former student and close friend of Hamann's, for on April 6, 1774, he wrote to Hamann for help in understanding the work, which concerned the book of Genesis and its precedents in Egypt. He was not sure he understood what Herder was up to and asked Hamann to react to his interpretation, but "if possible in the language of human beings. For I, poor son of this earth, am not organized to understand the divine language of *intuitive reason*. What one spells out in common concepts and in accordance with logical rules I can indeed grasp. Also, I just want to understand what the main point (*Thema*) of the author is, making no claim to understand it in its entire dignity and evidence."[135] Irony aside, Kant really was interested. Hamann obliged, answering the very next day. The book had four points: (1) The history of the beginning of the world, that is, "the oldest document," is not one that was originally written by Moses. It originates from the very fathers of humanity. (2) It is not to be understood as a mere poem. Indeed, it is more reliable and more genuine than the most common physical experiment. (3) It is the key to all mysteries of civilization and the sufficient reason of the difference between civilization and barbarism. (4) To understand it, we only need to rid ourselves of modern philosophy. Not surprisingly perhaps, Kant still did not understand. In his next letter he found Herder's main point in the claim that God gave language to human beings, and, together with it, all the rudiments of science. The first book of Moses reveals these. It is therefore the most reliable and purest document. But: "What is the sense of this document?," and how do we know that it is genuine and pure? Hamann answered one more time, but he hardly fulfilled Kant's wishes. Interpretation or understanding is God's business. To understand nature, we must accept God's word. The exchange seems to end where their earlier exchange also ended. Neither a physics for children nor a physics for adults can do without faith. Hippel wrote to Scheffner somewhat later that "Kant does not like the *Document* at all, and my only consolation is that he does not understand it completely."[136] Kant had nothing to say in response to Hamann.

Kant's answer to Johann Kaspar Lavater (1741–1801) – one of the new friends of Herder, who also wanted to become a friend of Kant's – can give us a clue to what Kant thought. Lavater had asked Kant for his judgment on a treatise on *Faith and Prayer*. Kant wrote on April 28, 1775: We must differentiate between the true doctrine of Christianity and its expression (*Nachricht*). The true doctrine coincides with a purely moral faith that God will support all our genuine efforts at doing good, even if their success might appear not to be in our power. The adulation of the teacher of this religion (Jesus) as well as the asking for favors in prayer and devotion is inessential.[137]

The entire exchange between Kant and Hamann had a subtext that is usually completely neglected, for Hamann was at that time beginning his campaign against Johann August Starck (1741–1816), who had arrived in Königsberg on September 28, 1769, moving into Kanter's house and living "door to door" with Kant.[138] He was a Freemason, and there were rumors that he had converted to Catholicism. Starck claimed that he had been initiated into the secrets of Freemasonry of Medieval Templarism, and he succeeded in converting the Königsberg lodge into one of "strict observance." At the same time, he was successful in obtaining a professorship at Königsberg. In October of 1773 Starck defended a dissertation, "On the Use of the Old Translations of Holy Scriptures," and in March of 1774 another dissertation on the highly controversial topic of "Heathen Importations into Christendom." In the latter he argued that Christians had taken over many of their rites from heathens, and that many Christian customs could be traced back to the mystery cults of the ancient world. The Christian rites should be understood in this light. While they should perhaps not be completely removed, as the Mennonites demanded, they should be carefully evaluated, since many of the differences between the confessions depended just on them. Still, religion should not be held hostage to such externalities. "The goal and purpose of all religions is that they direct the gaze of human beings from this earth to heaven, that true virtue, love of God and fear of God grow in men's breasts. If even the external rites take on the substance of the doctrine in order to achieve this, then religion has reached its goal."[139]

Hamann felt himself challenged. Enlisting Kypke's help, he was preparing a refutation.[140] When Hamann answered Kant's letter about Herder's *Oldest Document* on April 7, he complained that the theological faculty had given to a "Roman-Apostolic-Catholic Heretic" and "Crypto-Jesuit" the title of doctor, and he wondered whether he would be able to do two things at the same time, that is, both defend Herder and attack Starck.[141] Kant answered:

There is nothing strange in the new academic appearance for me. Once a religion is put in such a position that critical knowledge of ancient languages, philological and antiquarian scholarship make up its basic foundation, on which it is built at all times in all nations, then someone, who knows Greek-Hebrew-Syrian-Arabic-etc. and who is also acquainted with the archives of the ancient world, will be able to lead all the orthodox wherever he wants to lead them. They may look as unhappy as they wish, they are like children. . . . Considering this, I fear very much for the long duration of the triumph without victory, accomplished by the re-installer of the Document. For he is opposed by a closed phalanx of masters of Oriental language, which will not let such a prize be taken from their territory by someone who is uninitiated.[142]

With this, Kant, who lived "door to door" with Starck, dismissed Herder's work out of hand. He also seemed to be taking the side of Starck. This was certainly how Hamann saw it.

Kant, while not a Freemason himself, took the side of the Freemason against the fundamentalist Christian, Hamann. While he disliked the secrets of Freemasonry as much as the rites of Christianity, he appreciated their fundamental goals. It was certainly no accident that many of his friends were Freemasons, but some of them seem to have been even more conflicted than Kant was. Thus Hippel, one of the leading Freemasons in Königsberg, was also a believing Christian. He found the two difficult to reconcile, especially since he was also a friend of both Hamann and Kant. We can only imagine the conversations that Hippel, Kant, and others had about these matters, but it is important to remember that they were concerned about these issues and that discussion of them played an important part in their lives. When Hamann attacked "highly praised reason, with its universality, incapability of error, its enthusiasm, certainty and evidence" as a "false idol (*Ölgötze*), who has been given divine attributes by a crass and superstitious unreason," he attacked Starck together with Kant and Hippel.[143] When Hippel satirized in his *Kreuz- und Querzüge* certain abuses in the society of Freemasons, he was not only trying to draw a line between himself and people like Starck, but also seemed to be criticizing Kant.[144]

Starck advanced quickly at the university. This was clearly due – at least in part – to his good connections in Berlin. He held the right views, as far as the officials of Frederick II were concerned, and his connections with Freemasonry did not hurt him either. Kant, who could thank very much the same people for obtaining his own professorship, would have felt at least some affinity with Starck. They talked with each other, and it is clear that they found points of mutual interest. In any case, the similarity of Kant's views with those of Starck can hardly be overlooked. Kant may even have written to Hamann at Starck's request.

If Kant felt some affinity with Starck, he had little or no appreciation for another newcomer to Königsberg, who also came to live in Kanter's house, namely Abraham Johann Jakob Penzel (1749–1819). He had arrived in Königsberg after fleeing from Würzburg, where he had been involved in a duel. In Königsberg he was tricked into enlisting in the Prussian army, ending up in a regiment stationed in Königsberg. There Penzel became a good friend of Kraus and Hamann. A geographer and a classicist by training, he had translated Strabo; and before the unfortunate incident in Würzburg he had been well on his way to pursuing a literary career. Many people in Königsberg felt sorry for him, and some worked toward having him excused from military service, but after some initial success, this attempt failed. Frederick II himself decreed that Penzel was to remain a soldier because of his "immoral life style."[145] Kant disliked Penzel, apparently for the same reason, and Hamann reported to Herder on October 14, 1776, that Kant "had always been against him [Penzel], and considered him to have a base character because he was able to endure his status as a soldier so well . . ."[146]

Kant was always interested in education. This was not just because of his reading of Rousseau's *Emile* during the early sixties; it was something that he had worried about at least from his time as a *Hofmeister*. His lecture given at the occasion of becoming *Magister* was, after all, "Of the Easier and More Thorough Presentation of Philosophy." In 1774, this interest in education received a new impulse through Johann Bernhard Basedow's (1723–90) founding of a progressive school, the *Philanthropinum* in Dessau. The *Philanthropinum* was conceived in a very "progressive" spirit. It almost immediately provoked extensive discussions in the German journals. Basedow aimed at educating his students to become "philanthropists," who would lead a "patriotic and happy life of contributing to the common good." Basedow aimed at the education of the human being as a whole. He emphasized practical knowledge over mere intellectual training. His school week included not just drill, but "*Wandertage*" or day-long "outings" into nature. He emphasized athletics, and he attacked the rigid distinction between "work" and "play," insisting on frequent breaks and on teaching languages not by rote memorization but as a kind of game. Students were to be taught physics and other subjects by experimenting themselves and by looking at objects (*Realien*) that they might never have seen. They were to be educated to become independent citizens who could take care of themselves in their future lives. Religious education was to recede into the background. Indeed, Basedow felt that no prayers should be taught to children until they were ten years old.[147] In other words, Basedow's approach was radically different from the Pietistic education Kant himself had suffered through.

Many of the practices advocated by Basedow are now part of the mainstream of pedagogic thinking, but when he first proposed and practiced them, they were controversial. Thus J. G. Schlosser (1739–99), who was later to be severely criticized by Kant for his obscurantism, argued in 1776:

> The vocations of men are in most cases so incompatible with the all-around development of their faculties [advocated by Basedow] that I would almost say that one cannot start early enough to encourage the atrophy of two-thirds of those faculties; for most men are destined for vocations where they cannot use them in later life. Why do you castrate oxen and colts when you prepare them for the yoke and the cart, yet wish to develop the totality of human powers in men similarly condemned to the yoke and the cart? They will jump the furrow if you give them the wrong preparation, or kick against the traces until they die.[148]

The cynicism of Schlosser's position is unpalatable, but it was not uncommon. Many believed that

> it suffices for the ordinary rustic of the countryside and the ordinary artisan of the cities – the two groups of people who compose the majority of Prussian subjects – that their education give them correct conceptions of religion and of their duties as subjects . . . and that it remove prejudices which might prove disadvantageous to the effective performance of their traditional occupation. Knowledge of 'higher things' can only prove harmful to them.[149]

Knowledge of more than what religion and the government required might make ordinary people discontented and rebellious. Consequently, they would be better off not knowing.

Kant was opposed to such thinking. Indeed, he endorsed the method of the *Philanthropinum*. In 1776, he wrote at the request of Motherby, "a local English merchant and my dear friend," to Wolke, then the director of the school, asking that Motherby's son be admitted to that school. He also volunteered that "Mr. Motherby's principles agree completely with those upon which your institution is founded, even in those respects in which it is furthest removed from ordinary assumptions about education." After describing in great detail what the boy could and could not do, he pointed out that in "matters of religion, the spirit of the *Philanthropinum* agrees perfectly with that of the boy's father." He did not want the boy to be taught "devotional exercises directly," but only indirectly, "so that he might eventually do his duties *as if* they were divinely inspired." No wooing of favor or flattery in prayer should be encouraged. Righteousness should be the only concern. It is for this reason that "our pupil has been kept ignorant of religious service."[150] Kant, who together with Green was invited every Sunday to the house of Motherby, probably had a hand in teaching this pupil, and the expression "our pupil" was not a slip of the pen.

The *Philanthropinum* needed students. It was in constant need of money.

Accordingly, there was many an appeal to its supporters to enlist students and to donate money. Kant rose to the occasion. He not only saw to it that Motherby's son went to the school, but also wrote an article for the *Königsberger gelehrten und politischen Zeitungen,* recommending the school's principles with great ardor.[151] He wanted not only students to be sent to the *Philanthropinum,* but also future teachers, so that they could spread the good message. His student Kraus was to be the "Prussian apostle." If this was not enough, Kant also collected money for the *Philanthropinum,* and then wrote another article advertising both the school and its magazine. Since "governments these days do not seem to have money for the improvement of the school," he appealed again to private citizens of means to support the new school, saying at the end of the article that those who wanted to subscribe to the magazine of the *Philanthropinum* could do so between 10:00 A.M. and 1:00 P.M.[152] Though the school continued to suffer financial problems, Kant did not give up. He continued to support it in a variety of ways, getting a former student of his to collect subscriptions and to become a teacher there, writing encouraging letters to the leaders of the school, and even offering one of its former directors, Campe, the highest position in the Prussian Church that goes with a full professorship in theology (altogether, a salary 1200 Thalers). Just a hint from Campe's (and Kant's) friends in Berlin would be sufficient to get him the position. Campe declined.[153] Kant, on the other hand, continued to follow the developments at Dessau with great sympathy and interest. It was just the kind of thing that could lead to a quick "revolution" in the schools. Only a revolution could succeed where slow reforms had failed.[154]

Vorländer thought it was "touching" (*"rührend"*) how Kant supported the *Philanthropinum* in even the smallest details. Yet "touching" is hardly the right word. Apart from belittling Kant's engagement in this cause, it suggested that ultimately small details are not for "great thinkers." In fact, there was little that was small or unimportant about Kant's campaign for the reform of practical education. Kant was committed to this great democratic ideal of the Enlightenment. Like his membership in the short-lived "learned society" during the sixties, Kant's engagement in the cause of education shows that he cared about his fellow citizens who were deprived of the knowledge of "higher things." He was not just a theoretician as far as Enlightenment was concerned, he was actively engaged in spreading it in Königsberg. What the Pietists and his colleagues close to his old school, the *Collegium Fridericianum,* thought about this is not difficult to imagine. His active support of the *Philanthropinum* must have seemed like a slap in the face.

In July of 1777 Moses Mendelssohn, one of the most important German philosophers of the late Enlightenment, came for a visit to Königsberg.[155] He was perhaps the dominant force on the German philosophical scene between 1755 and 1785. His work in aesthetic theory and on the nature and role of sensibility was especially influential, and it would be difficult to understand the development of German thought from Wolffian rationalism to Kantian idealism without paying close attention to Mendelssohn. If he was received like royalty by the Jewish community, he was treated with almost equal respect by the philosophical community. Kant and Hamann were especially happy to see him. After a trip to Memel, Mendelssohn stayed another ten days in Königsberg (August 10–20). Kant wrote to Herz in Berlin:

Today Mr. Mendelssohn, your worthy friend and mine (for so I flatter myself), is departing. To have a man like him in Königsberg on a permanent basis, as an intimate acquaintance, a man of such gentle temperament, good spirits, and Enlightenment – how that would give my soul the nourishment it has lacked so completely here, a nourishment I miss more and more as I grow older! I could not arrange, however, to take full advantage of this unique opportunity to enjoy so rare a man, partly from fear lest I might disturb him . . . in the business he had to attend to locally. Yesterday he did me the honor of being present at two of my lectures, *à la fortune du pot*, as one might say, since the table was not prepared for such a distinguished guest . . . I beg you to keep for me the friendship of this worthy man in the future . . .[156]

One may well wonder what difference such a Mendelssohnian influence might have made to Kant's critical enterprise. Would the *Critique of Pure Reason* – which Kant was busily writing at that time – have looked any different? We will, of course, never know the answer to such questions.

The Developing Conception of a Merely Propaedeutic Discipline: "Obstacles"

In his *Prolegomena to Any Future Metaphysics* of 1783, Kant "*openly confess[ed]*" that

the reminder of David Hume was the very thing which many years ago first interrupted my dogmatic slumber and gave my investigations in the field of speculative philosophy a quite new direction. I was far from following him in the conclusions at which he arrived by regarding, not the whole of his problem, but a part, which by itself can give us no information. If we start from a well-founded, but undeveloped thought which another has bequeathed to us, we may well hope by continued reflection to advance farther than the acute man to whom we owe the first spark of light.

He further claimed that the *Critique of Pure Reason* was "the execution of Hume's problem in its widest extent."[157] Indeed, I take this to mean that Hume did not just strike the first "spark" by which "light might have been kindled," did not merely provide the suggestion that first interrupted Kant's dogmatic slumber and that gave his investigations in speculative philosophy a quite new direction, but that Hume determined the final outlook of the theoretical part of critical philosophy. It should be clear in any case that the *Critique* was not the effect of a flash of brilliant insight, conceived all in one piece during a few months of uninterrupted work. Rather, it was the result of a long development, the outcome of many meditations and much work over a period of more than eleven years. Some of the delay can be blamed on interruptions by official duties and on ill health. The most important cause for the *Critique*'s delay, however, was the formulation of the very problem and its solution, and the problem's formulation and solution were not separate events, but different aspects of the same process.

This process had begun with the Inaugural Dissertation. Yet in 1770 Kant had no inkling that it would take him such a long time to deliver the "more extended treatment" of the discussion of the Inaugural Dissertation. Indeed, the treatment he envisaged then could not have gone far beyond the dissertation itself. When he sent the work to Johann Heinrich Lambert, Moses Mendelssohn, and Johann Georg Sulzer in Berlin, hoping for a reaction before he published the final version, he indicated very clearly that he thought that not much more work was necessary. Writing to Lambert about the dissertation in September of 1770, he claimed that the summary of the new science he proposed could be made in "a rather small space," requiring only a "few letters." It would be easy, because Kant knew precisely what was required. He told Lambert:

For perhaps a year now, I believe that I have arrived at a position that, I flatter myself, I shall never have to change, even though extensions will be needed, a position from which all sorts of metaphysical questions can be examined according to wholly certain and easy criteria. The extent to which these questions can or cannot be resolved will be decidable with certainty.

Indeed, Kant was confident that he could make this *"propaedeutic discipline . . . usefully explicit and evident without great strain."*[158] Though he would not be able to work on it during the summer, he would use the winter to finish the practical part, or the "metaphysics of morals."

The objections and criticisms made by Herz, Lambert, Mendelssohn, and Schulz caused Kant to rethink the project. Thus in June 1771 he wrote to Herz regarding the letters of Lambert and Mendelssohn that these two men had "entangled [him] in a long series of investigations."[159] He was now working on his book

under the title *The Limits of Sensibility and Reason*. It would contain and treat somewhat extensively the relation of the basic concepts and laws that are meant for the world of sense together with the sketch of the nature of aesthetics, metaphysics and morals. I spent the winter going through all the materials for this, surveyed, weighed and calibrated everything. However, I finished the outline for this only recently.[160]

Almost a year later, in February 1772, he reported to Herz that "so far as my essential aim is concerned, I have succeeded and . . . now I am in a position to bring out a 'Critique of Pure Reason'."[161] But it turned out that he was not ready, after all. At the end of 1773 he wrote to Herz that he could perhaps have published something, and that he had spent "great effort . . . on the not inconsiderable work that I have almost completed." Because he did not want to present something incomplete, he had held off publication until the following Easter.[162]

  Yet three years later – by the end of 1776 – he realized that he would not be finished with the *Critique* "before Easter," and that he needed "part of next summer" as well.[163] In the summer of 1777 he spoke of "an obstacle" that kept him from publishing it. This obstacle was "nothing but the problem of presenting these ideas with complete clarity." His "investigations which earlier were devoted piecemeal to varied topics in philosophy have gained a systematic form, and have guided me gradually to the idea of the whole which first makes possible the judgment about the value and the interdependence of the parts."[164] At the beginning of April 1778, Kant had to deny rumors that parts of the *Critique* were already in print. He blamed distractions that hindered him from publishing a book that would "not take up many sheets of paper."[165] Thus the summer of 1778 saw him working "indefatigably" at the *Critique*, still hoping to finish it "soon."[166] He had at this time "little sketches" ("*kleine Entwürfe*").[167] Work on these sketches took Kant again much longer than he had anticipated, for it was *three* years later, namely on May 1, 1781, that Kant could write to Herz that in "the current Easter book fair there will appear a book of mine, entitled *Critique of Pure Reason*." This book, he said, contained "the result of all the varied investigations, which start from the concepts we discussed under the heading sensible world and the intellectual world."[168]

Soon after its publication, Kant had to defend himself against charges that he had introduced in his book an esoteric new language that made it all but impossible to understand his philosophy. He blamed this difficulty on the way in which the published version was written. In a letter to Garve in 1783, he admitted that, although he had taken a long time to think through the different problems, he put together the text that was finally published rather quickly. Therefore,

the expression of my ideas – ideas that I had been working out painstakingly for more than twelve years in succession – was not worked out sufficiently to be generally understandable. To achieve that I would have needed a few more years instead of the four or five months I took to complete the book.

Kant was thus one of the first to admit that his writing was more difficult than it might have had to be, but he excused himself by pointing to his relatively advanced age (he was by then nearly sixty) and his fear that he might not be able to finish the system as a whole if he spent too much time polishing his writing. But he also hoped that people would "get over the initial numbness caused unavoidably by a mass of unfamiliar concepts and an even more unfamiliar language (which new language is nevertheless indispensable)." The "main question," the question "on which everything depends" was formulated clearly enough, or so he thought.[169]

There were thus at least *two* different decisive events in Kant's philosophical development toward critical philosophy, one occuring around 1769 (the rejection of the continuity thesis), the other taking place around 1771 (the discovery of Hume's problem). If these events were the first two "steps" toward the *Critique,* then they were followed by a third step that was perhaps less decisive, but was nevertheless very important, namely, Kant's formulation of the systematic whole around 1778. First, the criticisms by others and his reading of the last section of Hume's *Treatise* forced him to reconsider his strong claims for the ability of reason. The culmination of this development can be seen in his letter to Herz of February 21, 1772. Significant parts of Kant's philosophical position of 1775 can thus be found in the so-called *Duisburg Nachlass* and in some of the transcriptions of his lectures. It was only during the period between 1777 and 1780 that he "discovered," or better, began to formulate, the principle governing the whole, and thus also began composing the main sections of the *Critique.*[170]

What had first been conceived as a short book that would present an elaboration of the doctrines advanced in the Inaugural Dissertation, had become a very long book indeed. It was 856 pages long, and most of its parts were entirely new. The final result of the investigations he had first undertaken with Herz was very different from the outcome first anticipated. The book had not only become longer, but its tone and subject matter had also changed significantly. In fact, less than thirty pages of the *Critique* correspond closely to the earlier treatment. The so-called Transcendental Aesthetic, or the discussion of space and time, was still recognizable as part of the doctrine of the dissertation, but that was about it. The Transcendental Analytic with its discussion of the categories and the principles of the understanding, and the Transcendental Dialectic with its discussion of the Antinomies, meant to reveal an essential contradiction of rational principles and to establish a merely regulative use of the ideas of reason, were not only not foreshadowed by anything in the earlier work, but were incompatible with certain parts of the dissertation.

When Kant wrote to Lambert in September 1770 that he had arrived a year earlier at a position that he would "never have to change, even though extensions will be needed," he could not possibly have predicted the doctrine he advanced in the *Critique*. His position, though perhaps fundamentally the same, did change in parts. Thus, unlike the Inaugural Dissertation, the *Critique* was not so much concerned with keeping intellectual cognitions pure, as it was an attempt to show that intellectual cognition was possible only insofar as it had a relation to sensitive cognition, and that sensitive cognition was possible only on the assumption of intellectual cognition. Whereas he emphasized in 1770 the *distinctness* of these two faculties, he insisted in 1781 on their *interdependence:* "Without sensibility no object would be given to us, without understanding no object would be thought. Thoughts without content are empty, intuitions without concepts are blind" (A51=B750).[171] This was an important shift. He still accepted the discontinuity thesis, of course, but it now had only a negative function as far as pure knowledge of noumenal entities was concerned. The path from the Inaugural Dissertation to the *Critique* was thus not as straight as Kant had first believed it would be. In a reflection written around 1776–68, he found:

Even if I can only convince people that they must wait with the development of this science until this point has been determined, then this work has achieved its goal.
In the beginning I saw this doctrine in a twilight, as it were. I attempted quite seriously to prove propositions and their contradictions, not in order to erect a skeptical doctrine, but because I suspected an illusion of the understanding, [and attempted] to discover what it consisted in. The year 1769 gave me a great light.[172]

The *Collegium Fridericianum* in the eighteenth century

Immanuel Kant, 1791 (miniature by Gottlieb Doppler, 1791, Bildarchiv
preussischer Kulturbesitz)

Frederick II or Frederick the Great (Bildarchiv preussischer Kulturbesitz)

Karl Freiherr von Zed-
litz, Prussian minister of
education and supporter
of Kant (Ullstein Bilder-
dienst)

Johann Georg Hamann
(Museum für Hambur-
gische Geschichte)

Johann Gottfried Herder
(Schiller Nationalmuseum,
Marbach)

Johann Gottlieb Fichte
(Bildarchiv preussischer
Kulturbesitz)

Friedrich Heinrich Jacobi
(Schiller Nationalmuseum,
Marbach)

Karl Leonhard Reinhold
(Ullstein Bilderdienst)

Kant's house (Bildarchiv preussischer Kulturbesitz)

The castle and Kant's house

At the beginning of the seventies, Kant was far from being clear on the significance and implications of the doctrine that he put forward in the Inaugural Dissertation. Even if the beginnings of the critical doctrine go back to about 1769, this does not mean that the problem of the *Critique* in its entirety was discovered all at once. Most of the contents of that work were conceived and written later, in the late seventies.

In a logic tutorial he gave in 1792, Kant confessed to his students that he had at first no clear idea about what should be the *goal* of his first *Critique,* and that he had to think hard about it. Indeed, he used his initial confusion about the goal of the first *Critique* as an example to show his students the importance of proper meditation. Thus he told them that anybody who writes or thinks methodically must know (1) what precisely it is that he wants to establish, and (2) what is decisive for establishing it. One student noted:

> Now he mentioned as an example how much effort it had cost him to know what it was that he really wanted [to establish] when he first had the idea to write the *Critique of Pure Reason,* and that he finally found that it could be formulated in the question: are synthetic a priori propositions possible? – Yes; but what is decisive here is that we can give them corresponding intuitions. If this cannot be done, then they are not possible. From this we can see how meditation is facilitated by this method.[173]

So it was not only that the different parts of the *Critique* were conceived, one by one, over a period of approximately eleven years, but also that the "essential point" underwent some development and change during that time. It took some time for Kant to realize what the point of his critical philosophy really was. Kant may have been in possession of some of the elements of the later critical philosophy already, but he had no clear idea of what they meant, or of how they fitted into the larger picture that he would draw in 1781. Indeed, he probably had a very different conception of the larger context then. The development of the final critical view took at the very least until late 1771. For, if we can believe his letter to Herz of February 1772, he had achieved clarity about his "essential goal" only then. However, it is likely that he was still much more confused than he knew then. It is more likely that all the pieces fell into place only in 1777, when his "piecemeal" investigations into "varied" topics finally led him to "the idea of the whole" of a merely propaedeutic discipline.[174]

This view of the origin of Kant's *Critique* is indirectly supported by Kant's public "Declaration Concerning the Authorship of von Hippel" of December 1796. In it, he claimed that some fragments of his doctrines "concerning a system, which I had in my head, but which *I could only accomplish during the period from 1770 to 1780* gradually found their way into my lectures," where they were picked up by Hippel.[175] Kant's critical philosophy was thus first introduced to the German public not by Kant himself, but by Hippel, who had published *Lebensläufe nach aufsteigender Linie, nebst Beilagen A, B, C* (Descriptions of Life in an Ascending Line, with Additions A, B, C). This novel appeared in three volumes in 1778, 1779, and 1781.

In these volumes Hippel used some passages from Kant's encyclopedia and anthropology lectures almost verbatim, and was therefore (later) accused of having plagiarized Kant. Kant defended Hippel in his "Declaration" against the charge of plagiarism, and he also confirmed that Hippel had used notes from his lectures. Hippel's book also contained a fictionalized account of Kant in the role of examiner, and many other allusions to the Königsberg professor. Indeed, Kant played a large part in the work as the "Grandfather professor" and "His Spectability."[176] Hippel allowed himself some spoofs of Kant's character. In the examination scene, His Spectability, "as the dean of the faculty is usually called," suggests that "it is customary to examine foreigners either not at all or only very little." Hippel knew of the accusations that Kant was too easy in his examinations.

His Spectability is happy because he had just become a grandfather the night before. Kant's servant Lampe appears as the grandmother:

Just as we were about to blind ourselves with a great deal of metaphysics (*uns . . . ins Ague zu sträuen*), when, lo and behold, the nightcap (*Hausmütze*) of His Spectability jerked open the door and looked through a small crack. But one could see that the old woman still had a light in her eye. She directed a beam into the room. This reminder was to make her loving husband realize that they had an appointment with their grandson this evening. It was evident from the face of His Spectability that He knew what was owed to a look through a small crack. It went over and over. – I do not know whether I will be able to imitate this over and over in writing.

The moral maxims, His Spectability started after this look through the small crack (I do not know why?), show how we may become worthy of happiness, the pragmatic ones show how we can obtain it.

This scene may have to do with the fact that Lampe had taken a wife (and become a father) without informing Kant. It is known that Kant was unhappy about this.

Kant had said in his encyclopedia lectures: "As far as we are concerned, we understand a joke, and we are not upset if the philosopher does not live as he teaches." Hippel, who in his novel contrasted natural and artificial

philosophy, finding natural philosophy to be the genuine article and artificial philosophy a "waste of time," found: "Could there be a more fitting
motto for artificial philosophy than 'gentlemen, you will understand a joke?'
Its emblem would be the *camera obscura*."[177] Kant's critical philosophy
seemed as artificial to Hippel as it did to Hamann.

"All-Crushing" Critic
of Metaphysics (1780–1784)

T HE EIGHTIES and early nineties were the years during which Kant
wrote most of the books for which he is now famous. During these
years he lived mostly for this work. The resulting body of work is awe-
inspiring. While much of it has its roots in his thinking and lecturing during the preceding twenty or so years, the dedication to his work during this
period was truly noble. Most of what people think when they hear the name
"Kant" was created during this period. Most of the stories about Kant can
also be traced back to this period. Still, the author of the three *Critiques* was
not simply the old man who wrote them. Kant had already lived a longer
life than most people in the eighteenth century could hope for, and his mature work was just that: mature. It would have been unthinkable without the
preceding years; and that means both the earlier years, during which he
was a something of a dandy, a foppish man of society, and the silent years
of quiet resolution that resulted from his mental rebirth. William James
differentiated between those who are "once-born" and those who search for
a "second birth" that will "convert" them, will change their "habitual center of . . . personal energy."[1] Kant belonged to the "twice-born." Though
his conversion was not a conversion to religion but rather an areligious
moral conversion, it was important, for it was what ultimately determined
or informed his critical philosophy. Born of crisis, its effects are everywhere
in Kant's mature philosophy. Even if there remains little to be told about
this crisis, it shows that Kant's rationalism or intellectualism was not easily achieved but the result of a struggle that continued during the years in
which he was creating his critical corpus.

Hypochondria remained a problem for Kant until his death. But whereas
he had to worry about heart palpitations during his earlier years, he now
was more anxious about the state of his bowels, as can be seen from one of
Hamann's letters to Herder in April 1783. He had visited Kant, who, he said,

is the most careful observer of his *evacuations*, and he ruminates often at the most inappropriate places, turning over this material so indelicately that one is often tempted to laugh in his face. The same thing almost happened today, but I assured him that the smallest oral or written evacuation gave me just as much trouble as his evacuations a posteriori created for him.[2]

As early as 1777 Kant had written to Herz about "insufficient exoneration," about "accumulating feces" or constipation, resulting in "bloatedness" and the need to take purgatives, which left his constitution in a state of turmoil. He took an entire page to discuss his symptoms, his approach to obtaining relief, and a theory that might explain both.[3] Nor were the complaints restricted to the lower part of his body. Kant felt that it was ultimately the obstructions of the bowels that caused distractedness and periods of confused thinking (*benebelter Kopf*) from which he was beginning to suffer. These complaints, though comical-sounding, made his life quite miserable. Nor were they merely mental phenomena. His digestive system was in some kind of disorder, and the medical knowledge of the time did not admit of a real cure. Accordingly, Kant's attempts at managing the symptoms by dietetic means were really the only course open to him. His overanxious concern with the state of his body was the result of a real need. Kant was getting close to sixty years old. Many of his younger friends would die at a much younger age. Hamann died when he was fifty-eight, Hippel died at age fifty-five. Both lived much harder than Kant; and Kraus, who was almost as careful as Kant, failed to reach fifty-five. Furthermore, the last years of his three friends were punctuated by serious illnesses, while Kant never got seriously ill. When he published his *Critique*, he was fifty-seven, and he would live almost another twenty-three years. He himself attributed his long life to the hypochondriacal care with which he watched his body.

Since we can no longer hope to discover the physiological cause (or causes) of these symptoms – Kant himself thought it was a problem with his stomach (*Magenmund*) – we should be careful in speculating about them. To claim that the affliction was psychosomatic, or that it was caused by his philosophy, is just as much a mistake as it is to claim that his philosophical achievement was in some sense caused by his hypochondria.[4]

Kant's critical philosophy may well be viewed as a "dietetic" response to metaphysical excesses, but this is only one way of viewing it – and not the most important one. As he himself pointed out, dietetic regimen as "the art of prolonging human life leads to this: that in the end one is tolerated among the living only because of the animal functions one performs – not a particularly amusing situation."[5] Philosophy, on the other hand, deals – at least according to Kant – with what transcends the mere animal functions we perform. Whether we like it or not, this is what Kant's "second birth" or palingenesis signified. It turned him away from the worries that characterized his daily life, and made him the philosopher we know. His philosophy was meant to help transform us into autonomous moral agents. To speak with Alexander Pope, this autonomy makes man "the glory, jest, and riddle of the world."

The *Critique of Pure Reason:*
"Nothing More than Two Articles of Belief?"

Kant claimed, as we have already seen, that he wrote the *Critique* within a period of four to five months, "as if in flight." Other evidence supports this. As late as June 11, 1780, Hamann wrote to Herder: "Kant is still working on his Morals of Healthy Reason and Metaphysics, and he is proud of his being late because it will contribute to the perfection of the work."[6] On August 15, he reported that Kant expected he would be finished with the *Critique* by Michaelmas, then about six weeks away, and on September 7 he wrote to Hartknoch that "professor Kant will keep his word and finish at Michaelmas. He is on the fence as to whether to publish with you or with Hartung. He really would like to have it printed here [in Königsberg]."[7] We may therefore assume that Kant began writing the final version in May or June of 1780. It was probably written in the same way that most of his other works were written. Borowski, who claimed that there was not much to say about the way Kant wrote his works, described it as follows:

He first conceived a general outline in his head; then he worked it out more explicitly; added some passages here and there, writing on little pieces of paper, which he inserted into the hastily written first draft. After some time, he revised the entire manuscript again, and then copied it for the printer in its entirety in his clean and clear writing.[8]

Jachmann reported that "Kant himself assured [him] that he did not write down a single sentence in the *Critique of Pure Reason* unless he had presented it to Green and had his unprejudiced judgment which was not bound to any system."[9] If this is true, and there is no reason to doubt it, then Kant's *Critique* is not so much the work of a solitary and isolated thinker as the product of a collaborative effort. Granted, all the ideas were Kant's, and he was presenting his own system. Yet we may wonder how Green's judgment changed the first draft of the *Critique*. Jachmann claimed that Green had "undoubtedly a decisive influence on his [Kant's] heart and character."[10] He probably also directly influenced the first *Critique* as well as some of the later works. In any case, there are many phrases and idioms in Kant's work that can be traced back to the language of merchants, such as "borrowing," "capital," and so forth.[11] Furthermore, the works written after Green's death are more difficult to read than the ones Kant wrote while his friend was alive.

When Kant said he wrote the *Critique* in "four to five months" he was referring, of course, only to the last stage of writing and copying the manuscript for the printer. The final general outline went back at least a year earlier, and some of the first drafts dated from the early seventies. Some of these early drafts have survived – for instance, parts of the discussion of the Principles of Pure Reason, the so-called *Duisburg Nachlass*, as well as an early dedication of the *Critique* to Lambert from about October 1777. It reads:

You have given me the honor of writing to me. At your request I attempted to develop the concept of a method of pure philosophy, and this occasioned some observations designed to refine that still obscure concept. As I progressed, the outlook widened, my answer to you was delayed without end. This work may serve as an answer as far as the speculative part is concerned. Since it is the result of your demand and suggestion (*Wink*), I'd wish that you make it entirely your own by trying to develop it further . . .[12]

Kant's work appeared too late for Lambert, however. He died in 1779. Whether he would have understood (or liked) it better than his other contemporaries is far from clear. In any case, there are many who would argue that for the others it did not appear too late, but too early. The *Critique of Pure Reason* would change, if not the world, then at least philosophy.

The first proofs arrived in Königsberg on April 6, 1781. Hamann read them as they arrived in Königsberg and as Kant gave them to him. On May 5, he was complaining about the length of the work. "Such a fat book is neither fitting for the author's stature nor for the concept of pure reason, which he opposes to the lazy and *arse-like* (*ärschlich*) reason, that is, my very own reason, which loves the force of inertia and the *hysteron proteron* from taste and purpose."[13] Finally, he received a bound copy of the entire *Critique* on July 22, 1781, "for breakfast."[14]

Kant's critical philosophy can be viewed as an attempt to answer three fundamental questions of enduring philosophical significance: "What can I know?" "What ought I to do?" and "What may I hope for?" He may be said to address the first of these questions in the *Critique of Pure Reason*, but he does not answer the question directly. He seems to be primarily interested not in the general question of what we can know, but in the narrower question of what can be known with absolute certainty and without any qualification. In his terminology, this question is "What can we know a priori and in complete isolation from experience?"[15] Put differently, what Kant tries to answer is the question of whether the kind of knowledge sought by metaphysicians – including himself – is possible. The bulk of his work is meant to show that traditional metaphysics rests on a fundamental mistake, since it presupposes that we can make substantive knowledge claims about the world independent of experience, and Kant argues that we cannot validly make such claims.

Kant calls the claims of traditional metaphysics "synthetic a priori judgments," and he argues that it is impossible to know anything a priori about the world as it is independent of experience. But he does not simply follow the route of previous empiricist philosophers, who considered all knowledge to be derived from experience alone and thus tried to trace all knowledge back to sensation and reflection. Kant thought, rather, that all knowledge has an a priori component. As he had already argued in the Inaugural Dissertation, we supply the form to the knowable world. Indeed, the formal aspects of the knowable world are constituted by the cognitive apparatus that we, and every other finite being like us, must have; and it is this cognitive apparatus that allows us to make synthetic a priori judgments about the world. These synthetic a priori claims are not about reality per se. They are about reality only as it is experienced by beings such as we are. Only because we possess certain cognitive principles that enable us to experience the world can we make synthetic a priori claims about the world as it appears to us. For that very reason, these claims cannot be claims about the world as it is independent of our conceptual apparatus. Thus metaphysics can tell us only about the presuppositions of experience, or the conditions that must be fulfilled for any experience whatsoever. Kant now calls all investigations about the possibility of a priori knowledge "transcendental," and thus refers to his inquiries as "transcendental philosophy."

Kant describes these a priori epistemic conditions as "forms" to which knowledge is necessarily subject. He now distinguishes three such forms, namely, (1) the forms of sensibility, (2) the forms of the understanding, and (3) the forms of reason.

The first of these, the forms of sensibility, are space and time. They are not characteristics of "things in themselves," but are merely subjective conditions for our knowledge of the world. However, because we cannot but view the world as spatial and temporal, things in space and time, or "the appearances," are objective for us. Kant says that they are "empirically real" but "transcendentally ideal." If we were constituted differently, we might be able to "see" (or intuit) things as they are in themselves and not just as they appear to us. As finite beings, we cannot experience anything without our senses. Space and time are necessary conditions of any experience for us. As such, they provide us with a priori knowledge of the world of our experience. We can know that the world of experience must have certain spatial and temporal characteristics. Geometry and arithmetic are the sciences dealing with synthetic a priori judgments that are based on space and time. Most of what Kant has to say in the Transcendental Aesthetic, that is, the section dealing with the a priori forms of sensibility, can already be found in the Inaugural Dissertation.

Second, our knowledge is dependent on the forms of the understanding, or on a number of basic a priori concepts. Kant discusses these a priori concepts in the first part of the Transcendental Logic, also called the Analytic of Concepts. Borrowing a term from Aristotle, he calls these basic concepts categories. Though similar to his view in the dissertation of 1770, his view here differs in some respects. For one thing, in the earlier work he had given an open-ended list. In the *Critique*, he claims that there must be exactly twelve such categories, and he is sure that he has derived them with a strict proof from a single principle. The categories now consist of the basic concepts of quantity (unity, plurality, and totality), quality (reality, negation, and limitation), relation (inherence, causality, and community), and modality (possibility/impossibility, existence/nonexistence, and necessity/contingency). They can accordingly be arranged in a table consisting of four groups, each containing three categories. Kant tries to derive them in a chapter entitled "The Transcendental Clue to the Discovery of All Pure Concepts of the Understanding," usually called the Metaphysical Deduction.

The categories appear to have a wider application than the concepts of space and time because we seem to be able to make claims about things that are not part of our spatio-temporal world. Many philosophers use the concept of causality, for instance, in talking about God and in devising proofs for his existence, but they also claim that God is neither in space nor in time. Kant, like Hume before him, is convinced that this is a mistake. Yet he rejects Hume's contention that the concept of cause must be restricted to experience because it has been derived from experience; the categories are a priori concepts and therefore independent of experience.

Though they make experiential knowledge possible, they might also make other kinds of knowledge possible. Indeed, that they make purely metaphysical knowledge (of nonspatial and nontemporal objects) possible had been a fundamental thesis of his Inaugural Dissertation. It is the task of the Transcendental Deduction to show that the categories are necessary for experiential knowledge and insufficient for knowledge of objects independent of space and time.

Kant tries to show that while the categories per se are independent of experience, their use is necessarily restricted to spatio-temporal experience. They are designed for us to think about objects of experience, or appearances. His Transcendental Deduction, one of the most difficult passages in the first *Critique,* is essentially an attempt to establish this restriction on our use of the categories. The details of Kant's arguments are admittedly messy. It is not always clear what Kant means or how he takes himself to have proved particular points. Nonetheless, the general strategy is clear. Kant intends to show that the categories are possible concepts only insofar as they make experience possible; when applied to anything that goes beyond experience, they become merely empty words:

The Transcendental Deduction of a priori concepts has thus a principle according to which the whole inquiry must be directed, namely, that they must be recognized as a priori conditions of the possibility of experience, whether of the intuitions which are to be met with in it or of the thought. Concepts which yield the objective ground of the possibility of experience are for this reason necessary (A94=B126).

The Deduction shows that the categories, which, he claims, may be assumed as given because of the Metaphysical Deduction, are necessarily presupposed in any possible experience (which is also presupposed as given). Kant intends to show that the use of the categories is justified insofar as it is related to this experience.

This is one of the most important differences between the categories or concepts of the understanding, and the ideas or concepts of reason, which constitute Kant's third "form," or the forms of reason. The latter are discussed in the second part of the Transcendental Logic, namely the Transcendental Dialectic. Ideas cannot form "the basis of any objectively valid synthetic judgment," while "through concepts of understanding reason does, indeed, establish secure principles, not however directly from concepts alone, but always only indirectly through relation of these concepts to something altogether contingent, namely possible experience" (A737= B705). Thus he can say that any principle of the understanding has "the peculiar character that it [the principle] makes possible the very experience which is its own ground of proof" (A737=B705), and this implies not only that experience would not be possible without these categories, but also that we cannot establish the objective validity of the categories without relating them to possible experience, which, per se, is "something entirely contingent."

Before moving on to the ideas, Kant discusses the universal principles of knowledge, which are based on the categories (Analytic of Principles). The so-called Schematism of the Pure Concepts of the Understanding, which introduces this part of the *Critique*, is easily its second-most-difficult chapter (after the Transcendental Deduction). In the Schematism chapter, Kant argues that a merely logical discussion of the categories is insufficient. Such a discussion abstracts from the fact that we always employ the categories in thinking and thus in time. We must therefore explain how these pure concepts enter into our thinking. "We must be able to show how pure concepts can be applicable to appearances" (A138=B177). Kant thinks that "obviously there must be some third thing, which is homogeneous on the one hand with the category, and on the other hand with the appearance . . ." (A133=B177). These are what he calls "the transcendental schema" or the schemata of the categories. These schemata are rules that relate the pure to what is given through the senses. There are accordingly schemata for quantity, quality, relation, and modality. What all these rules have in common is that they are given in time. Indeed, the "schemata are . . . nothing but a priori determinations of time in accordance with rules" (A145=B184). These rules concern the time-series (quantity), the time-content (quality), the time-order (relation), and the scope of time (modality).

The Principles of the Understanding are the judgments that the understanding actually achieves, given these general schemata. Again, Kant thinks that the table of the categories "is the natural and the safe guide" (A148=B187). There are accordingly Axioms of Intuition (quantity), Anticipations of Perception (quality), Analogies of Experience (relation), and Postulates of Empirical Thought (modality). It is under these headings that Kant tries to solve some of the most important problems of traditional metaphysics and gives them a place in his system, along with the problems of substance, causality, and reality in general.

Yet one of the most important consequences of this part of Kant's view is drawn only later in the Dialectic, where he tries to show that the traditional proofs about the nature of the soul, about the world as a whole, and about God must be unsound. They cannot establish knowledge in any sense. If they are taken as establishing knowledge, they inevitably lead us to contradict ourselves. Kant tries to show that rational psychology, philosophical cosmology, and rational theology are doomed to failure, at least if understood as purely theoretical enterprises. These are the chapters of the *Critique* that earned him the name of "*Alleszermalmer*" (all-crushing). Indeed, Kant appears to leave little of traditional metaphysics and ontology standing. The end result of his critical labors may seem to resemble Hume's skepticism.

Kant puts this result in a different way – and in a way that eventually caused great problems for him. He argues – perhaps better, asserts – that this result is equivalent to saying that we cannot know noumena, but only phenomena, or that we cannot know things as they are in themselves but only as they appear to us. Thus we can never know what holds the world together in its innermost being, or what things are apart from our conceptual apparatus. We cannot even know who or what we ourselves ultimately are. We can have a negative conception of what a noumenon is, that is, we can say what it cannot be. Thus it cannot have spatial or temporal characteristics. Since space and time are forms of intuition, that is, part of the epistemic conditions necessary for knowledge of appearances, things in themselves – that is, things apart from how we must perceive them – cannot have perceptual characteristics. But we cannot have a positive concept of a noumenon. It is merely a limiting concept, a placeholder for a position that no human concept will ever reach.

In the Paralogisms of Pure Reason, Kant tries to show that the traditional claims about the human soul – that it is substance, that it is simple, that it is a unity, and that it is possibly related to things in space (the four classes of the categories are again at work here) – are based on fallacious reasoning (i.e., on a paralogism). Kant claims that there is a transcendental ground that tempts us to draw conclusions that do not follow from any evidence that could possibly be given to us. To be sure, whenever we think, we experience ourselves as subjects. But whenever we do so experience ourselves, we can be sure that we are only "appearing" to ourselves, and that these experiences do not provide insight into who we "really" are, independent of experience. Empirical psychology deals with this phenomenon. We know just as little about who we "really" are as we know about things in themselves. Kant readily acknowledges that there seems to be a "second" self, that is, the self that "has" the appearance or is "doing" the experiencing. In his language, this is the "I think," which is a part of every thought or concept. It is the "vehicle" of all concepts (A 342=B399). Kant also acknowledges that the "I" of this "I think" seems independent of experience and is indeed the presumed object of rational psychology, but, he argues, it is impossible to know anything about this "I" as an object of pure thought. For it can never be such an object. Whenever we try to focus on it, it recedes. We can investigate it as a logical presupposition of all thinking, the "vehicle" of all concepts, but then we are engaging in transcendental logic, which does not allow us to go beyond the categories, and therefore cannot take us beyond experience. We can treat the "I" as an empirical object of inner intuition, but this is by definition different from rational psychology. In other words, we have no access to our self as a thing in itself.

Kant's critique of rational psychology is followed by the explicitly dialectical parts of Kant's first *Critique,* namely the four antinomies in the Antinomy of Pure Reason. They concern traditional problems of cosmology. The results of this section are equally negative. Kant attempts to expose the necessarily fallacious character of all the arguments developed by traditional metaphysicians about a number of fundamental problems, namely whether or not (1) the world has a beginning, (2) there is something simple, (3) there is freedom, and (4) there is an absolutely necessary being. Kant ingeniously argues that the arguments for asserting these claims are just as good as the arguments for denying them. Both the thesis and its denial follow logically from basic principles of reason; and this is what he calls the antinomy of reason. Reason seems ultimately flawed. It is not reliable, and it cannot possibly answer the very questions that it inevitably raises.

A closer look at the third antinomy, concerning the problem of freedom, reveals his strategy. Kant argues in the thesis that "causality in accordance with the laws of nature is not the only causality from which the appearances of the world can one and all be derived" (A445=B473). We also need another kind of causality, namely that of freedom. To prove this thesis, Kant offers an indirect proof. Assuming that this thesis is false, he thinks he can derive a contradiction: the series of causes in accordance with the laws of nature leads to an infinite regress, but an infinite series has no beginning, and thus has no first cause. Therefore the assumption that "causality in accordance with the laws of nature is the only causality" there can be, must be false. Similarly, if we assume that there is another kind of causality than natural causality, we are led to a contradiction. A causality of freedom is either lawful, but then it is just nature; or it is lawless, and thus "abrogates those rules through which alone a completely coherent experience is possible" (A447=B475). We can prove both the thesis and the antithesis, and therefore ultimately neither. Reason cannot demonstrate what it claims to know. Traditional metaphysics must therefore be considered a failure.

Kant follows a similar strategy in the three other antinomies, believing he can prove in this way that rational cosmology in its entirety amounts to nothing but "dialectical play." Strangely enough, however, he does not think that this proves that this kind of cosmology is useless. There may be no ultimate answer to such metaphysical problems, yet these problems arise inevitably from the principles of knowledge. Just as there are certain perceptual illusions that are unavoidable, so there are these rational illusions. As the very first sentence of the *Critique* states: "Human reason has the peculiar fate in one species of its cognitions that it is burdened with questions which it cannot dismiss, since they are given to it as problems by the nature of reason itself, but which it also cannot answer, since they transcend every capacity of reason" (Avii). These questions are bound up with the very essence of finite rationality and therefore also with our own nature. We cannot help asking these questions, and we need to search for their answers. Reason has an inevitable interest in them. Furthermore, the totality of the theses constitutes a coherent position, and the totality of the antitheses constitutes another coherent position. Kant calls the former "the dogmatism of pure reason" and the latter "the principle of pure empiricism." His sympathies ultimately seem to lie with the dogmatic position. Empiricism is an unsatisfying position, therefore it can never be popular. It is in reason's interest and our own that the theses be true. For each thesis, we are better off if we believe that the position presented by the thesis is true, and that the position expressed by the antithesis is false. That is, according to Kant, the reason why we should believe in the dogmatic position. No more, no less.

The same may be said about the results of his discussion of God in the Ideal of Pure Reason. We must assume that God exists, but we cannot possibly prove it. Kant's arguments are original and convincing. His critique of the traditional proofs of the existence of God are perhaps the most persuasive part of the first *Critique*. Looking first at the ontological proof of the existence of God, Kant argues that existence is not a real predicate, and that therefore any attempt to prove God's existence from the idea that he possesses the perfection of existence is bound to fail. Conceptually, there is no difference between an imagined hundred dollar bill and a real one. It is just that the imagined one will not purchase anything. An imagined perfect being has no purchasing power either.

The other two kinds of proofs, namely, the cosmological proof and the physico-theological proof (otherwise known as the argument from design), fare no better. They make more sense – up to a point. Still, they do not prove the existence of God, as God is understood by theists. The cosmological proof, according to Kant, runs thus:

If anything exists, an absolutely necessary being must also exist. Now I, at least, exist. Therefore an absolutely necessary being exists. The minor premise contains an experience, the major premiss the inference from there being any existence at all to the existence of the necessary. The proof therefore really begins with experience, and is not wholly a priori or ontological. For this reason, and because the object of all possible experience is called the world, it is entitled the cosmological proof. (A604f=B632f)

For Kant, this proof, which he himself endorsed in his *Only Possible Argument*, hides many pseudo-rational principles and a "whole nest of dialectical assumptions, which the transcendental critique can easily detect and destroy" (A 609=B637). Indeed, given what he thinks he has proven in the section on the antinomies, it cannot possibly work.

Kant also believes that the physico-theological proof fails, although he has more respect for it. Indeed, he claims that this

proof always deserves to be mentioned with respect. It is the oldest, the clearest, and the most accordant with the common reason of mankind. It enlivens the study of nature, just as it itself derives its existence and gains ever new vigour from that source. It suggests ends and purposes, where our observation would not have detected them by itself, and extends our knowledge of nature by means of the guiding-concept of a special unity, the principle of which is outside nature. This knowledge again reacts on its cause, namely, upon the idea which has led to it, and so strengthens the belief in a supreme Author [of nature] that the belief acquires the force of an irresistible conviction. (A624f=B652f)

It is not a proof. In particular, it cannot prove that there is a perfect being, such as the theistic God. Indeed, neither the cosmological nor the physico-theological argument can do that, for both presuppose that the ontological argument is valid, and both therefore fail.[16] The last argument has persuasive force. It does not prove what it is intended to prove, but it helps us to understand nature as an ordered or created whole.

The subject matters of the dialectic are, accordingly, far from being entirely useless. They have to do with fundamental questions that are unavoidable for us. Kant believed that they are expressions of deep "interests" of reason that cannot simply be dismissed. Metaphysical speculation is as inevitable for us as breathing. These questions concern the forms of reason – what Kant calls the "transcendental ideas." The ideas, which are for Kant restricted to God, freedom, and immortality, do not afford any kind of knowledge beyond that which is possible through space and time and the categories. They can give rise only to a kind of rational faith.

The belief that these concepts are satisfied (i.e., that God, freedom, and immortality are real) is central to Kant's so-called "moral faith." Though Kant himself was not religious and was opposed to any form of external religious worship, he did believe that morality inevitably leads us to the acceptance of certain tenets of traditional theism. In his later essays on religious matters and especially in his *Religion within the Limits of Mere Reason* of 1793, Kant will attempt to develop the parallels between revealed religion and philosophical theology. We will also see that, in true Enlightenment fashion, he will claim that all that is essential in religion can be reduced to morality, but he does not reject the main tenets of traditional religion. They are valuable, if only we realize that they are not knowledge, but "nothing more than two articles of belief" (A831=B839), namely the belief in God and the belief in immortality.

Thus even after reason has failed in all its ambitious attempts to pass beyond the limits of all experience, there is still enough left to satisfy us, so far as our practical standpoint is concerned. No one, indeed, will be able to boast that he *knows* that there is a God, and a future life; if he knows this, he is the very man for whom I have long [and vainly] sought. All knowledge, if it concerns an object of mere reason, can be communicated; and I might therefore hope that under his instruction my own knowledge would be extended in this wonderful fashion. No, my conviction is not *logical,* but *moral* certainty; and since it rests on subjective grounds (of the moral sentiment), I must not even say, '*It is* morally certain that there is a God, etc.', but '*I am* morally certain, etc.' In other words, belief in a God and in another world is so interwoven with my moral sentiment that as there is little danger of my losing the latter, there is equally little cause for fear that the former can ever be taken from me. (A828f=B856f)

Some might scoff at the idea that this is all that philosophy can achieve, but Kant believed that it is not only more than enough, but also a good thing, that in matters that concern us all, no one is privileged. The "highest philosophy cannot advance further than is possible under the guidance which nature has bestowed even upon the most ordinary understanding" (A830=B858).

First Reactions to the *Critique:* "Too Much like Berkeley and Hume"

When the *Critique* first appeared, Kant expected not only that he would be understood, but also that other scholars would rally to support his project.

He was eager to hear Mendelssohn's judgment about it. When he heard from Herz that Mendelssohn had put the book away and was not going to get back to it, he was "very uncomfortable," hoping it would "not be forever." Mendelssohn was, he thought, "the most important of all the people who could explain this theory to the world; it was on him, on Mr. Tetens and you [Herz], dearest man, that I counted most."[17] He also hoped to enlist Garve "to use [his] position and influence to encourage . . . the enemies of [his] book . . . to consider the work in its proper order" and to make his problem understood. "Garve, Mendelssohn, and Tetens, are the only men I know through whose co-operation this subject could have been brought to a successful conclusion before too long, even though centuries before this one have not seen it done."[18] In the same vein he wrote to Mendelssohn "to encourage an examination of [his] theses," because in this way "the critical philosophy would gain acceptability and become a promenade through a labyrinth, but with a reliable guide book to help us find our way out as often as we get lost."[19] At the same time, Kant was beginning to suspect that it would not happen, and that "Mendelssohn, Garve and Tetens have apparently declined to occupy themselves with work of this sort, and where else can anyone of sufficient talent and good will be found?"[20] Mendelssohn himself claimed that a nervous disability had made it impossible for him to analyze and think through the works of "Lambert, Tetens, Platner, and even those of the all-crushing Kant." He claimed to know them only through reviews and from reports of his friends, and he said that philosophy for him "still stands at the point at which it stood in approximately 1775."[21]

One of the first reviews of the *Critique* appeared on January 19, 1782, in the *Göttingische gelehrte Anzeigen*. It characterized Kant's work as belonging to the British tradition of idealism and skepticism. Indeed, the only philosophers the reviewer explicitly mentioned were Berkeley and Hume. He found it most interesting that Kant wanted to offer a "system of higher, or . . . transcendental idealism," and he suggested that it was "based upon our concepts of sensations as mere modifications of ourselves (upon which Berkeley also primarily built his idealism) and upon those of space and time." He also called attention to the fact that Kant's objection to a substantial self had already been used by Hume and others before him. Kant did not seem to have chosen the middle way between exaggerated skepticism and dogmatism, and he did not lead his readers back to the most natural way of thinking. Rather, Kant's arguments are those of a "*Raisonneur*" who wants to leave common sense behind by opposing to each other two genera of sense: the inner and outer one, or by wanting to merge or transform these two into each other. When the form of internal sensation is changed into that of external sensation, or when it is mixed up with the latter, materialism, anthropomorphism, etc. result. Idealism is the product of contesting the rightful title of outer sense besides inner sense. Skepticism at times does the one and at other times the other in order to mix and shake everything into confusion. In some ways, our author does so as well. He does not recognize the rights of inner sensation . . . But his idealism still more contests the laws of external sensation and the resulting form and language natural to us.

In short, Kant was too much like Berkeley and Hume.

The review was by Garve, but Feder had heavily edited it. The passages comparing Kant to Berkeley and Hume had been added by Feder, who later wrote a great deal against Kant's idealism, offering what he called "Anti-idealism in Accordance with the Simple and Solid Principles of Common Sense." Thinking that Kant was obviously as indebted to Berkeley as he was to Hume, he could not understand why Kant wanted to put so much distance between his own thought and that of Berkeley.[22] For better or worse, this review set the tone and the agenda for the next decade or so. It became usual to view Kant as a skeptic in the Humean fashion, and to oppose him with appeals to language and common sense.

Hamann, Kant's friend and critic in Königsberg, essentially agreed with the Garve–Feder assessment. Kant was a skeptic in a Humean sense, and therefore indebted to Berkeley. In a manuscript that remained unpublished during his lifetime, Hamann observed that

a great philosopher has maintained that general and abstract ideas are nothing but particular ones, annexed to a certain term which gives them a more extensive signification at the occasion of individual things. Hume declares this assertion of the Eleatic, mystic and enthusiastic Bishop of Cloyne, George Berkeley, to be one of the greatest and most valuable discoveries which has been made in the republic of letters in our time.

First of all, it appears to me that the new skepticism is infinitely more indebted to the older idealism than this accidental, individual and occasional remark shows to us. Without Berkeley, Hume would hardly have become the great philosopher the *Kritik* declares him . . . to be. But concerning the important discovery itself: it lies open and revealed in the mere usage of language of the most common perception and observation of the *sensus communis*, and it does not need special insight.[23]

Hamann had just been reading Malebranche and Beattie's *Essay on Truth* in order to find out about the sources of Berkeley's idealism, and thus had a special reason to see these connections, but pointing them out was appropriate. Like Feder, Hamann accused Kant of being an idealist in Berkeley's sense, and he also accused Kant of being inconsistent in praising Hume so much while rejecting Berkeley so thoroughly. Without Berkeley, there would be no Hume; without Hume, there would be no Kant. Therefore without Berkeley, there would be no Kant. Furthermore, Kant's antinomies are for Hamann antinomies not of reason but of language. When Hamann ironically called himself a "misologist," he was calling attention to this. Philosophers have been misled by language for the longest time, and Kant was no exception; indeed, in his disregard for language, he was even more misled by it than others before him. Accordingly, Hamann argued that a critique of language and its functions was more necessary than overly subtle philosophical inquiries into the nature of pure reason. It is on this that he tried to base his own *Metakritik*.[24]

In 1782, Hamann also planned another work that was to be called *Schiblimi, or Epistolary Findings of a Metacritic*. He meant to include the following parts:

The first epistle deals with the printed version of Hume's *Dialogues;* the second with the hand-written one [i.e., his own translation of Hume that was never published and appears to be lost] and Mendelssohn's judgment; the third compares Jews and philosophers; the fourth is a warmed over translation of the last chapter of Hume's first part of human nature which in 1771 appeared in a couple of Supplements under the title "Night Thoughts or Confessions of a Skeptic." The fifth will certainly deal with Kant . . .[25]

So Hamann still thought in 1782 that the "Night Thoughts" were relevant to his dialogue with Kant. What bothered Hamann most in Kant's *Critique* was Kant's emphasis on pure reason and purely formal characteristics, and Kant's tendency to downplay sensation and faith. In other words, what Hamann found most bothersome was Kant's Platonism. While he admired Kant's critique of rational theology, he rejected entirely Kant's rationalism as a mysticism of the Platonic sort. Again, Hamann defends his fideism and attacks Kant's (even more) radical intellectualism by relying on Hume's arguments.

Kant's contemporaries viewed the *Critique* as the work of a skeptic. To them, he was a Humean. There was not only no fundamental incompatibility between the critical enterprise and Hume's skepticism, there was continuity; and this was a continuity they did not like. They accused Kant of being a negative skeptic like Hume. As the review of the *Critique* in the *Göttingische Anzeigen* pointed out, it could serve as a good corrective to exaggerated dogmatism. It could sharpen the mind of those who read it, but it relied too heavily on skeptical arguments and thus was too radical. For this reason Kant was led toward the sort of idealism that Berkeley had defended.

Later in 1782, there was a review in the *Gothaische gelehrte Anzeigen*. It was more positive, if only because it restricted itself to a summary of the work, calling attention to Kant's theory of space and time in particular. The book contributed to the "honor for the German nation." It was "a monument to the nobility and subtlety of the human understanding," but its contents would also be "incomprehensible to the greatest majority of the reading public." It was mainly for "the teachers of metaphysics."[26]

Prolegomena: Not for "Mere Learners, but . . . Future Teachers"

On February 4, 1782, the *Königsbergische gelehrten und politischen Zeitungen* published a short announcement of the first volume of Lambert's *Correspondence* as the first installment of an edition of Lambert's posthumous works. Its purpose was to invite subscriptions, and its author was Kant. He argued that the project was important and that the publication of Lambert's works might help stem the tide of products by "the deviant (*verunartet*) taste of the times." People had come to like the "insipid plays of wit or mere copies of products, which are either outmoded or just foreign." He expressed his hope that Lambert's works would also help to "enliven the zeal of the learned men for the spread of useful and thorough science, which has almost expired, and to make them complete the project that Lambert started, namely to found a confederation, which would put up a united front against the ever-increasing power of barbarism, and which would re-introduce thoroughness into science by improving certain methods, which are still defective."[27] In other words, Kant was hoping that others would endorse his own project of a critique of pure reason, which he viewed as a continuation of Lambert's suggestions. This was also a first response to those who either ignored his work or received it negatively.[28] One of the reasons Kant praised Lambert's correspondence was because it contained his own letters to Lambert. Indeed, the letters show how close his project was to that of Lambert and that Lambert took his work seriously. His *Critique* should be seen as the continuation of the work started by Lambert.

Kant felt himself ignored by those on whom he had counted and treated like an imbecile by those whom he did not respect. The review in the *Göttingische gelehrte Anzeigen* was especially to blame. Its author had, he felt, completely misunderstood the work. So, soon after the appearance of this review, he began to think of a more popular and shorter treatment of the subject matter of the *Critique*.

The result of his thinking was the so-called *Prolegomena to Any Future Metaphysics, which May Be Called a Science,* which appeared in 1783. While it would be wrong to regard the book simply as a reaction to the review in the *Göttingische Anzeigen,* it is clear that this review had angered Kant very much, and that he felt he had to answer the critic in Göttingen. Accordingly, the *Prolegomena* contained many overt and some not-so-overt references to the review. Though it ended up as a sustained polemic against the Göttingen review, it did not start out that way. In a letter to Herz, written shortly after the appearance of the *Critique,* Kant spoke of its subject matter as "the metaphysics of metaphysics," and hinted that he had some idea how it could be made "popular." If he had started with the subject matter of the Antinomies and talked about it in a "flowery" style (*sehr blühenden Vortrag*), he could have made his readers curious about the sources of the contradictions.[29] In another letter, written about a month later, he expressed his dissatisfaction with how he had expressed his views. Advancing age and "worrisome illnesses" had made him publish the book sooner than would perhaps have been advisable.[30] These second thoughts seem to have been the cause of his willingness to write a "popular extract suitable for the general reader," or "in popular style."[31] By September 15, 1781, he seems to have promised to Hamann and Hartknoch that he would indeed write such a work.[32] But Hamann did not know late in October what the work would be like, having heard rumors that it might be either a short extract or a textbook (*Lesebuch*) on metaphysical subjects.[33] When the Göttingen review appeared in January of 1782, the plan changed. Kant now began to write a "prolegomena of a still to be written metaphysics," and a response to the Göttingen reviewer.[34] In late August the book had been written and was being copied by Kant's amanuensis. By September it was finished, but its publication was delayed until April of 1783.

Berkeley, Hume, and their critics play a much larger role in the new book than they had in the *Critique.* Kant's reaction to being compared to Berkeley was very different from his reaction to being compared to Hume. While he was incensed at being called a Berkeleyan idealist, and vehemently protested that there were no similarities whatsoever between him and the Irish bishop, he was not opposed to being called a Humean, provided only that it was understood what it meant to be a "Humean." He tried to put as much distance as possible between himself and "all genuine idealists, from the Eleatic school to Berkeley."[35] Their position is contained in the "formula: 'All knowledge through the senses and experience is nothing but sheer illusion, and only in the ideas of the pure understanding and reason is there truth'."[36] His position amounts to a reversal of this idealism: we can speak of truth only in knowledge through the senses and experience. The ideas of pure reason are mere fictions. (Whether Berkeley would have accepted this characterization of his thought is, of course, a different story.)

On the other hand, Kant openly confessed that Hume had interrupted his dogmatic slumber and that in the *Critique* he was pursuing "a well-founded, but undeveloped, thought" of Hume. Indeed, he referred to his first *Critique* as "the working out of Hume's problem in its greatest possible extension."[37] No wonder he was known among his friends as the "German Hume." If Kant's account of "Hume's problem" is considered against this background, a number of things become immediately obvious. First, the references to Reid and his followers are no accident. Kant tries to downplay their importance, and by attacking them, he is also attacking Feder and the philosophers close to him. Second, Kant tries to explain his relation to Hume. Thus he tells us that

Hume started in the main from a single but important concept in metaphysics, namely that of the connection of cause and effect. . . . He challenged Reason, who pretends to have conceived this concept in her womb, to give an account of herself and say with what right she thinks that anything can be of such a nature, that if it is posited, something else must thereby also be posited necessarily; for that is what the concept of cause says. He proved irrefutably: that it is wholly impossible for reason to think such a conjunction a priori and out of concepts. For this conjunction contains necessity; but it is quite impossible to see how, because something is, something else must also necessarily be, and how therefore the concept of such an a priori connection can be introduced. From this he inferred that Reason completely deceives herself with this concept, in falsely taking it for her own child.

The question was not whether the concept of cause is correct, useful, and in respect of all knowledge of nature indispensable, for this Hume had never held in doubt; but whether it is thought a priori by reason, and in this way has an inner truth independent of all experience, and hence also has a more widely extended usefulness, not limited merely to objects of experience; this was the question on which Hume expected Enlightenment. He was only talking about the origin of this concept, not about its indispensability in use; once the former were determined, the conditions of its use and the extent of its validity would have been settled automatically.[38]

Kant is also aware of Hume's skepticism, but he believes this skepticism is a consequence of Hume's inability to understand how the concept of causality can be thought purely a priori. Indeed, he tells us, Hume's skeptical conclusion was "hasty" and "incorrect." If only for this reason, Kant never thought of "listening to him [Hume] in respect of his conclusions."

This alone should be enough to show that he did not consider this particular skepticism as deserving of an answer.

Kant did not object to being regarded as close to Hume. From his own point of view, Hume was more an ally or predecessor than an adversary. Though Kant did not follow Hume in all details and rejected Hume's skeptical conclusions, the differences were not very significant to him. There are surprisingly few remarks that are critical of Hume in his theoretical works, and there are none that are hostile. Instead, Kant constantly emphasized the importance of Hume in his published works. In his lectures he advised his students to read Hume's works "many times." To sum up, Kant thought that Hume offers the following argument:

(1) Assume the causal relation to be rational.
(2) If a relation is rational, it can be thought a priori and on the basis of concepts.
(3) For objects to be causally related, they must stand in a necessary relation, such that if one object is posited, the other one must also be posited.
(4) It is impossible to see by reason alone how the existence of one object necessitates the existence of another.
(5) Therefore, "it is wholly impossible to think such a conjunction a priori and out of concepts."
(6) Therefore, the causal relation is not rational.
(7) Therefore, it is impossible to understand "how the concept of such an a priori connection can be introduced."
(8) Therefore, it must have some other source or sources, and the most reasonable ones are imagination and custom.
(9) But imagination and custom can produce only "subjective" necessity.
(10) Metaphysics requires necessity based on intersubjectively valid concepts.
(11) Therefore, metaphysics is impossible.

Kant thinks that the argument ending with (6) as a conclusion is sound. Hume "proved," he says, "irrefutably: that it is wholly impossible for reason to think such a conjunction a priori and out of concepts."

What Kant does not accept is (7) and the conclusions founded upon it. He cannot, if only because this would show that the science of metaphysics is impossible. In order to save the science of metaphysics, or to show how it is possible, he must show how it is possible to introduce the concept of such a connection a priori. There is no reason for Kant to accept (7), in any case. From the fact that the causal relation cannot be shown by reason to be a priori, it does not follow that it cannot be shown to be a priori in some other way, just as it does not follow from the fact that I cannot determine the smell of an open sewer by sight that I cannot determine its smell in any other way. Thus Kant thinks he can make a plausible case that the causal connections have "their origin in pure understanding." Thus he argues that

(12) It is possible to introduce the concept of a priori connections by deducing them from the pure understanding.

One can make a distinction between "local skepticism," or a skepticism that relates only to a certain class of propositions, and "universal skepticism," or a skepticism that involves the doubting of the justifiability of any knowledge claim. Kant believes that Hume essentially establishes a form of "local skepticism," with "universal skepticism" being a hasty conclusion founded upon the former. Moreover, Kant does not see Hume as denying the existence of necessary synthetic judgments, but only as denying a certain way of justifying them. So Kant thought that he needed to give only a limited answer to Hume. All he had to do was justify synthetic a priori judgments, whose existence was admitted by Hume.

Kant's *Prolegomena* approaches the problem of the *Critique* from this perspective. First, there is the relatively short Introduction, in which Hume gets so much attention. Assuring his readers that to do metaphysics is as natural as breathing, that it "can never cease to be in demand – since the interests of common sense are so intimately interwoven with it," he argues that it needs reform precisely because of Hume's successful critique of causality.[39] Secondly, he characterizes the peculiarities of all metaphysical knowledge, which, of course have to do with the synthetic a priori nature of its subject matter. Finally, he summarizes the contents of the first *Critique*, using a new organizing principle. He asks four questions: (1) "How Is Pure Mathematics Possible?", (2) "How Is a Pure Science of Nature Possible?", (3) "How Is Metaphysics in General Possible?", and (4) "How Is Metaphysics Possible as a Science?"

Kant finds the answer to the first question in the subject matter of the Transcendental Aesthetic. Pure mathematics and its synthetic a priori cognitions are possible because space and time are a priori forms of intuition. The answer to the second question can be found in the first part of the Transcendental Logic. Science and its a priori cognitions are possible because we have the categories and the principles. "The understanding does not derive its laws (a priori) from, but prescribes them to, nature."[40]

The third question deals with the subject matter of the Transcendental Dialectic or with the ideas of pure reason as they concern psychology, cosmology, and theology. These ideas arise naturally when we employ the categories "as mere logical functions," which "can represent a thing in general . . . [or] *noumena,* or pure beings of the understanding (better, beings of thought)."[41] Just because these ideas are products of thinking, they cannot be incomprehensible. They are principles that allow us to achieve completeness and synthetic unity in experience. The first *Critique* had proved just this (at least according to Kant).

In the Conclusion, Kant argues that "Hume's principle," that is, the admonition " 'not to carry the use of reason dogmatically beyond the field of all possible experience,' should be combined with another "principle, which he [Hume] quite overlooked, 'not to consider the field of experience as one which bounds itself in the eyes of our reason.' " He further claims that, since his first *Critique* effects just such a combination, it "here points out the true mean between dogmatism, which Hume combats, and skepticism, which he would substitute for it."[42] Kant endorses here what may be taken to be the outcome of Hume's "mitigated" or "consequent" skepticism. Although Hume's principle needs to be complemented in ways that bring him into conflict with Hume, Kant nonetheless accepts Hume's principle.

The formulation "not to carry the use of reason dogmatically beyond the field of all possible experience" is very Kantian and very un-Humean, and this is not just a matter of style. Where Kant speaks of "possible experience," Hume would have spoken of "the usual course of experience" or "what actually has been experienced." So it might be said that Kant's interpretation of "Hume's principle" distorts Hume. It is clear, though, that Kant believes that this principle sums up an important aspect of Hume. Furthermore, it is a fair rendition of Hume's systematic intention as expressed in a great number of passages that are meant to criticize that "considerable part of metaphysics" that is "not properly a science, but . . . which would penetrate into subjects utterly inaccessible to the understanding . . ." and that present arguments for the cultivation of "true metaphysics . . . in order to destroy the false and adulterate."[43] It is more than clear that Hume believes that he has shown that we cannot go beyond experience. Because "we can go beyond the evidence of our memory and senses" only by means of the relation of cause and effect, and because this relation itself "arises entirely from experience," all arguments in moral, political, and physical subjects that are "supposed to be the mere effects of reasoning and reflection . . . will be found to terminate, at last, in some general principle or conclusion, for which we can assign no reason but observation and experience."[44] For Hume, the principle that "all the philosophy will never be able to carry us beyond the usual course of experience" is most important for undermining "the foundations of abstruse philosophy, which seems to have hitherto served only as a shelter to superstition, and a cover to obscurity and error." It essentially fulfills thus the negative task of limiting the sphere of metaphysics. In addition, according to Hume, the principle also has the positive effect of liberating us from "religious fears and prejudices" and supporting in this way a more humane moral outlook on life, strengthening the "easy and obvious philosophy."[45] The negative theoretical strictures are meant to contribute to a more positive moral outlook. For Hume, the principle may even have positive religious consequences, because it shows that if there is a "true" religion, then it must be based on faith. By limiting "the principles of human reason," this principle may make room for faith.

What Kant calls "Hume's principle" sums up the most fundamental tenet of Hume's mitigated skepticism, but it also sums up the most important outcome of Kant's first *Critique*. For what Kant in the *Prolegomena* calls "Hume's principle" is nothing but a different formulation of what Kant identifies in the very same context as the

proposition, which is the resumé [*Resultat*] of the whole *Critique:* Reason by all a priori principles never teaches us anything more than objects of possible experience, and even of these nothing more than can be known in experience.[46]

Kant admits here that "the resumé of the whole *Critique*" is essentially a negative principle. It limits our use of reason and thus also the scope of metaphysics. When one disregards the phrases characterizing reason as having a priori principles, as one may do here without distorting the intent of the sentence, Kant simply says that "reason never teaches us anything more . . . than can be known in experience."

Like Hume, Kant believes that this negative theoretical principle has a positive moral point, for it has "the inestimable benefit, that all objections to morality and religion will be for ever silenced, and this in Socratic fashion, namely, by the clearest proof of the ignorance of the objectors" (Bxxxi).[47] Contrary to Hume, Kant believes that this principle is not the last word on the issues addressed in speculative philosophy. Hume's principle needs a friendly amendment. Taking his point of departure from Hume's criticisms of deism and theism, Kant finds that

Hume's objections to deism are weak, and affect only the proofs and not the deistic assertion itself. But as regards theism, which depends on a stricter determination of the concept of the Supreme Being, which in deism is merely transcendent, they are very strong and, as this concept is formed, in certain (in fact in all common) cases irrefutable.[48]

Because the deistic concept of God is vague, representing "only a thing containing all reality, without being able to determine any one reality in it," Kant's objection to Hume's arguments against deism does not amount to much. Kant's opposition to Hume's critique of theism is, by comparison, much stronger. He believes that the common thread of all of Hume's arguments against theism is the charge of anthropomorphism, and thus claims that for Hume anthropomorphism is "inseparable from theism" and that this is what makes theism "contradictory in itself." Kant agrees that "if this anthropomorphism were really unavoidable, no proofs whatever of the existence of a Supreme Being, even were they all granted, could determine for us the concept of this Being without involving us in contradictions." Kant also believes that he can offer an argument that does not depend upon anthropomorphism, and that he can therefore "make the difficulties which seem to oppose theism disappear."[49]

According to Kant, Hume has overlooked a principle that may be called the "boundary principle." It tells us that there may be things that are beyond experience. We should therefore not expect too much from experience. Kant claims that experience has boundaries, and that these boundaries cannot be found within experience itself. His talk of boundaries is not easily understood, yet it goes to the very heart of his philosophy: the distinction between appearances and things in themselves. So much is clear for Kant: boundaries (*Grenzen*) are different from limits (*Schranken*), for "bounds (in extended beings) always presuppose a space existing outside a certain definite place and enclosing it; limits do not require this, but are mere negations which affect a quantity insofar as it is not absolutely complete." Kant believed that mathematics and natural philosophy allow of limits, but not of boundaries. While we can admit that there may be things that are inaccessible to scientific study, this has no consequence for scientific inquiry per se, since we can never arrive at them as barriers to further enquiry, or as something beyond which we cannot go. If a scientific question can be properly formulated, then it can, in principle, be answered. We can never say that scientific knowledge is completed, or that nothing new can be learned about nature. Science allows of continuous progress. This is not so for metaphysics. It has both limits and boundaries. In fact, Kant believes that metaphysics leads us necessarily toward boundaries. If we push our inquiries in metaphysics far enough, we will arrive at

questions that can – indeed must – be asked, but that cannot be answered
in metaphysics itself. Hume's "empiricism" may be a good strategy for
science (at least up to a point), but it is a bad one for metaphysics. In any
case, not all metaphysical questions can be answered. The boundary principle is meant to restrict Hume's principle so as to prevent us from going
too far along the road Hume wanted to travel.

Put differently, Hume's principle simply tells us to refrain from doing
something, while the boundary principle also tells us to do something. Indeed, the boundary principle seems to tell us to do something that Hume's
principle, taken by itself, might prohibit. It suggests that we should look
beyond possible experience, so as to modify or restrict Hume's principle
in particular cases, namely in those cases that have to do with the boundaries of experience, whatever they may be. We must admit that appearances
do not exhaust all of reality. Appearances presuppose something that appears, which is "distinct from them (and totally heterogeneous)," namely,
a thing in itself. While we cannot *know* what is beyond experience, we can
still *think* it. In fact, Kant claims that we *must* think about such things, and
that reason itself forces us to do so. We must, Kant argues, at least *assume*
things external to reason. One of these is the existence of God as a de-
signer, for "without assuming an intelligent author, no comprehensible
ground for design and order can be stated without falling into patent ab-
surdities. Although we cannot prove the impossibility of such design
without an original intelligent author . . . there yet remains . . . a sufficient
subjective ground for assuming such an author."[50] This "subjective ground"
is the "need of reason" that we encountered earlier. It is the reason why Kant
had to "deny knowledge to make room for faith."

The answer to the fourth question – "How Is Metaphysics Possible as
a Science" – should now also be clear. Metaphysics, which exists as a human
need and a "natural disposition of reason," is possible as a science of our
necessary conceptual framework.

In order that a science of metaphysics may be entitled to claim . . . insight and conviction, a critique of pure reason must exhibit the whole stock of a priori concepts, their
divisions – according to the various sources (sensibility, understanding, reason), together with a clear table of them, the analysis of these concepts, with all their consequences, and especially the possibility of synthetical knowledge a priori by means of a
deduction of these concepts, the principles and the bounds of their application, all in
a complete system.[51]

Kant's *Critique* and *Prolegomena* are today usually read as works by an
antiskeptical philosopher. Accordingly, the question of whether or not Kant

refuted skepticism in general and Hume in particular is a central concern in most discussions of Kant's critical philosophy. There is a consensus, that is, at least in large parts of the English-speaking world, that Kant was essentially an antiskeptical philosopher, even if there is less agreement about the success or failure of Kant's arguments against skepticism. As Ralph C. S. Walker puts it:

> Any list of the great philosophers has to include Kant. His influence on philosophical thinking . . . has been immense, and his work remains of the most immediate contemporary relevance. For he faces up to the most fundamental problem that confronts philosophers, and tackles it in a more illuminating way than anyone has done before or after. This is the problem which scepticism raises.

According to this view, Kant is the great philosopher he is *because* of his thoroughgoing antiskepticism, and those who are seriously trying to answer the skeptic today "have nearly always done so by developing, or amending Kant."[52]

Many others would agree. Barry Stroud, for example, argues that although Kant's "comfortable anti-skepticism" ultimately fails, it does contribute "to our understanding of the complex relation between the philosophical theory of knowledge, on the one hand, and the inquiries and claims to knowledge that we make in everyday and scientific life that are presumably its subject matter, on the other."[53] For Stroud, these positive contributions are a function of Kant's thorough antiskepticism. Yet they may be the result of Kant's genuine appreciation of the skeptical position. Though Stroud admits that "Kant's rejection of all forms of skepticism nevertheless comes out of a full acknowledgment of its powerful appeal," he never asks why skepticism has such a powerful appeal for Kant.[54] While still others find Kant's antiskepticism less "comfortable" than does Stroud, they do agree that Kant was an antiskeptic. Thus Richard Rorty contends that we should set Kant aside as part of the larger task of moving beyond "the notions of 'foundations of knowledge' and of philosophy as revolving around the Cartesian attempt to answer the epistemological skeptic."[55] Since, for him, Kant is also the very ideal of an antiskeptical philosopher, Rorty takes his own view to be necessarily "anti-Kantian." Rorty is trying to persuade us that a "post-Kantian" culture is possible and desirable, and he would like us to "see philosophy neither as achieving success by 'answering the skeptic,' nor as rendered nugatory by realizing that there is no skeptical case to be answered."[56] For Rorty the story is more complicated. We do not have to go down the road of either Hume *or* Kant.[57]

This antiskeptical interpretation of Kant has – at least initially – a certain amount of philosophical and exegetical appeal. Kant describes the general outlines of his critical project in different ways. For example, he says that it is a "tribunal which will assure to reason its lawful claims, and dismiss all groundless pretensions . . . in accordance with its own eternal and unalterable laws" (Axi), or the solution of "the general problem: How is knowledge from pure reason possible?"[58] As such, it also is for him an attempt to "decide as to the possibility or impossibility of metaphysics in general" (Axii), and is meant to enable reason "to follow the secure path of a science, instead of, as hitherto, groping at random, without circumspection or self-criticism" (Bxxx). On the other hand, the *Critique* is also intended to be "a happier solution" to "Hume's problem," or "the execution of Hume's problem in its widest extent."[59] As Kant tells us, it was occasioned by Hume's "suggestion" or "reminder" or "objection" concerning causality, which "first interrupted [his] dogmatic slumber and gave [his] investigations in the field of speculative philosophy a quite new direction."[60] But we are also told by Kant that he "was far from following" Hume in his "conclusions," for Hume "ran his ship ashore for safety's sake, landing on scepticism," whereas he himself succeed in establishing a new "formal science."[61] Indeed, Kant thought that his work finally "points out the true mean between the dogmatism which Hume combats and the skepticism which he would substitute for it."[62] Given these pronouncements, it may seem reasonable to say with W. H. Walsh that Kant had two projects, or that he was preoccupied with "two major issues, that of the nature and possibility of metaphysics, and that of the countering of scepticism." Kant wanted to accomplish two different things. On the one hand, he intended to show that there could be a descriptive sort of metaphysics, having to do with the "necessary framework of experience," and, on the other hand, he also "hoped to counter Hume."[63]

Nonetheless, Kant's project was different from the one that Walker, Walsh, Stroud, and Rorty attribute to him. Kant did not mean to refute a global skepticism about all claims to objective knowledge. Rather, he saw himself as responding to a local skepticism. This local skepticism concerned the possibility of claims to knowledge made in metaphysics, and not the possibility of knowledge claims in general. He was concerned to show that some of the particular claims metaphysicians are wont to make are indeed possible or justifiable. Refuting a local skepticism concerning the possibility of certain metaphysical claims is different from refuting a global skepticism concerning "objective truth." Universal skepticism for Kant is – at best – a hasty conclusion founded upon metaphysical skepticism. Therefore, it needs no response. All he had to do was to justify a priori synthetic judgments in a different way, not by reason, but by some other cognitive faculty.

Furthermore, Kant did not see Hume as denying the truth of necessary synthetic judgments, but only as denying a certain way of justifying them. If Hume had not admitted the presence of any kind of necessity in the causal relation, Kant would have begged Hume's question, and those who claim that Kant misunderstood Hume's intentions and that he thus misconstrued his task would be correct. Again, Kant is correct. Hume admitted that our complex idea of causality does indeed contain the idea of necessity. In fact, the account given in the *Prolegomena* so closely follows Hume's analysis of causality in the *Treatise*, Book I, Part III, section III, "Why a Cause Is Always Necessary," one might be tempted to assume that Kant had access to a "defective copy" of Hume's *Treatise* (and he might well have had such access, as Hamann owned the entire book and sometimes lent it to Green).[64] It is thus clear that Kant thought he needed to give only a limited answer to Hume.

Kant's ultimate concerns were moral, and perhaps even religious. Accepting the validity of the empiricist approach to science and to the growth of knowledge, Kant wanted to save morality from becoming too naturalistic and too relativistic. He wanted to show that even in the absence of knowledge of absolute reality, morality has a claim on us that is itself absolute and incontrovertible. It is this moral claim on us that elevates us above the beasts. It shows us to be rational in the way that Plato had insisted that we are rational. The *Critique* and the *Prolegomena* showed not only why Plato's own approach was wrong, but also why the Humean approach, if properly understood, was not as inimical to a more rationalistic outlook as many had supposed until then. A healthy dose of skepticism injected into idealism was just what was needed to show that while we have a higher purpose, we cannot know what Plato thought we could know. In a footnote reminiscent of his sarcasm in the *Dreams*, Kant finds that

High towers and metaphysically great men resembling them, round both of which there is commonly much wind, are not for me. My place is the fruitful bathos of experience; and the word transcendental . . . does not signify something passing beyond all experience but something that indeed precedes it *a priori*, but that is intended simply to make knowledge of experience possible.[65]

Kant's *Prolegomena* was meant to offer a sketch of this system according to the "analytic method." It presupposes that science (as mathematics and physics) is actual and works backward to first principles. The *Critique* starts from more general first principles and follows the "synthetic method."[66] Neither of them contains the whole system. Kant continued to work on it for the rest of his life. Indeed, while he was working on the *Prolegomena* and settling into his new house, he was also working on the further development of his system, and in particular on its moral part. Finally, after almost twenty-five years, he could concentrate on the Metaphysics of Morals that had first motivated him to engage in the critical project.

One of the first public occasions for a closer investigation of moral matters was a book by one Johann Heinrich Schulz (1739–1824), of which Kant wrote a review. The book was entitled *Attempt at a Guide toward a Moral Doctrine for All Mankind Independent of Differences of Religion, together with an Appendix on the Death Penalty.*[67] Its first part had appeared in 1783, and its author was a preacher in Gielsdorf who had become notorious as an atheist or "preacher of atheism."[68] He was also called the *"Zopfprediger"* or *"ZopfSchulz"* (Ponytail Schulz), because he refused to wear the traditional wig that preachers had to wear and donned a ponytail instead. Schulz argued in this book that there was no such thing as free will, and that human behavior, just like the behavior of any other living being, was completely determined. "As far as the will is concerned, all inclinations and instincts are contained in just one [principle], namely *love of self.* Though every human being has a particular *mood* (*Stimmung*) in this respect, this mood can never depart from a general mood. Self-love is always determined by all the sensations in their entirety, but in such a way that either the more obscure or the more distinct sensations have a greater part in this determination."[69] When only obscure sensations determine self-love, we call the resulting action "unfree." Actions are called free when they are the result of conscious representations, but this does not mean that we are really free. It's all due to our mood, or the totality of our sensations at any one time. Therefore, the distinction between virtue and vice is illusory, moral praise betrays a lack of sophistication, and punishment is unjust.

Against this view, Kant pointed out that Schulz's theory had similarities to that of Priestley; that Martin Ehlers, a professor in Kiel, had recently argued for a similar position; and that it had become common among British preachers. He could also have mentioned Frederick the Great, who had said,

I shall never be dissuaded from my conviction that regardless of how much noise he makes in the world man is only an infinitely tiny creature, an unnoticeable atom in relation to the universe. . . . Instruments of an invisible hand, we move without knowing what we do; statesmen and warriors are no more than puppets in the hands of providence, which guides the world at will.[70]

Kant objects to the fatalism inherent in Schulz's position, taking up Frederick's analogy and claiming that it "turns human conduct into a mere puppet show" and completely obliterates the concept of moral obligation (*Verbindlichkeit*). But

the "ought" or the imperative that distinguishes the practical law from the law of nature also puts us in idea altogether beyond the chain of nature, since unless we think of our will as free this imperative is impossible and absurd and what is left us is only to await and observe what sort of decision God will effect in us by means of natural causes, but not what we can and ought to do *of ourselves* as authors.[71]

Even the greatest skeptic or the convinced fatalist must act "*as if he were free.*" This is because anyone who wants to pursue "righteous conduct in conformity with the eternal laws of duty," and not be "a plaything of his instincts and inclinations," must presuppose it.[72] This would include Frederick.

At the very end of the *Prolegomena*, Kant had dared the reviewer of the *Göttingische Anzeigen* to reveal his identity. Garve took the bait and wrote to Kant on July 13, 1783, saying that he could not call the review his because it had been changed. Only some of his phrases had been retained, and some things had been interpolated. Indeed, he claimed that he was at least as angry at the review as Kant was. He also asked Kant not to make public use of the letter. It would be wrong to make difficulties for the editor. Garve had forgiven the editor, and he had also given him permission to revise and shorten the review. Kant was satisfied. On August 7, 1783, he answered Garve, saying that he had never believed that "a Garve" could have written the review. He also expressed his hope that Garve would help him in making clearer his goals to the enemies of the *Critique.* Just a little later, on August 21, when he received the original review as reprinted in the *Allgemeine deutsche Bibliothek*, he was disappointed. Garve's original review was really no better than the one that had appeared in the *Göttingische Anzeigen.* It was just longer, and it did not mention Berkeley by name. Kant complained, and he felt he was being treated "like an imbecile."[73]

Literary success seemed to be denied to him. Still, Kant was more successful in Königsberg. Hamann wrote on October 26, 1783, that Kant was lecturing on "philosophical theology" with an "amazing" number of students in attendance, while at the same time working on the "publication of the rest of his works" and "conferring with *Magister* and Court Chaplain Schulz, who also is writing about the *Critique*."[74]

Kant had sent Schulz a copy of the *Critique* on August 3, 1781, saying that he had proved his acuity in his review of the Inaugural Dissertation, and in fact had "penetrated the dry material best among all those who judged the book." Since Schulz had spurred him on to continue his thoughts, he was sending him the result, that is, the *Critique*, hoping that he would have the time to examine and judge it. Schulz appears to have had little time – or his study of the *Critique* took a very long time – for he only answered on August 21, 1783, that he had read the book and was willing to publish a review. In fact, he sent Kant a manuscript that summarized the work, and added a number of questions that he wanted clarified.[75] Kant answered on August 22, sending him the Garve review for examination, saying it was better thought through than the one published in the *Göttingische Anzeigen*. He also said that he had heard through Jenisch, their common student, that he had a draft of his evaluation, and he asked Schulz to hold back the review, and to think about how others might be instructed to approach the work. It would be a good thing if Schulz thought of his project as a book, rather than as a review. Four days later, Kant wrote another letter, saying that Schulz had "penetrated deeply and correctly into the spirit of the project," and that he had "almost nothing to change" in the manuscript. If he transformed the review into a book, then a few passages on the Dialectic should be inserted. Kant promised that he would send Schulz some materials soon, but he never got around to doing it.[76] Part of the reason for this was perhaps that Schulz himself had noticed some omissions and remedied the shortcomings. Kant finally wrote to him on the eve of publication, answering some of the questions Schulz had raised earlier, expressing his hope that Schulz could still use his answers to change the manuscript: "For nothing can be more desirable for the enemies than to find lack of uniformity in the principles."[77]

Kant was happy, for on March 4, 1784, he sent to Schulz a coin that had been occasioned by the very book on which he was commenting. "A number of my students had kept secret the plan to surprise me with such a sign of sympathy. They were so effective that I only found out about it when I received last Sunday an exemplar in the mail from Berlin. . . . I have heard that Mendelssohn thought out the symbol and motto, and it honors his acuity."[78] He also said that he really did not like such ostentatious expression of approval, "but what can one do, if one's friends like to think different." Hamann wrote on March 25 that "the golden coin, which was given to Kant last Wednesday, has 1723 instead of 1724 as the year of his birth, and there are a number of other little things that diminished his joy about the honor given to him."[79] One may hope that the joy in Schulz's book was less adulterated. In any case, the book was published late in 1784 under the title *Exposition of Kant's Critique of Pure Reason,* with the author's name spelled "Schultz" rather than "Schulz." Kant had a defender – at least in Königsberg.

His Own House (1783):
"Quite Romantic," but "Close to a Prison"

On December 30, 1783, after having lived in rented quarters for all of his adult life, Kant bought a house of his own. He felt that he could now afford it, but he must also have felt that he needed it more than ever. Renting meant occasional moves. When and why would not always be up to him, and this meant a certain lack of security. It meant that Kant was not master of his own affairs in some fundamental respects. At fifty-nine, Kant was finally ready to change this. Having achieved autonomy in matters intellectual, Kant was also intent upon becoming autonomous in more concrete ways – and it was high time, as old age was not far off. Kant's purchase was also a way of preparing for his declining years.

The house Kant bought had belonged to a portrait painter named Becker, who had recently died. Hippel, whose own property bordered on Becker's, was instrumental in the deal. He told Kant that the property was for sale, and he wrote to Kant on December 24, the day before Christmas, that he had found out that the house was not yet sold, and that if Kant were to make an offer, he would probably be successful.[80] Kant acted right away. Indeed, he wrote down notes and questions about what had to be done on Hippel's very letter. Thus he asked whether there was only one stove in the house, where precisely the borderlines of the property lay, whether he should take out a wall between two smaller rooms and the room that was to become the lecture room, and when the house would be free. The answer to the last question was: "in March." Kant made notes about the costs of the necessary renovation on the back of a short letter, dated February 21, 1784. Work appears to have begun at that time. By the end of April, somewhat worried about the details and delays, he wrote to Johann Heinrich Fetter, a contractor whom he had hired to supervise the renovations for him:

> ... you have accepted the supervision of my building, and you have thus taken a great worry from me because I am entirely ignorant in such things. I have no doubt that the master craftsmen, whom I have told to follow your instructions, will follow them without objections.

Apparently, the builders had given him bad advice. They had told him that certain parts of the house could be renovated, which was impossible. They had brought too many bricks. The date on which the renovations were to be finished had to be pushed back. Kant asked Fetter to make sure that he could move into his house on May 22, because he had to move out of his old quarters by that time. Ordinary worries interfered with his work, and it is perhaps no accident that he published only two short essays in 1784.

He was able to move in on May 22; and by July 7, 1784, he had paid off all the mortgages and encumbrances on the house. The house was now truly his.[81] He asked that the insurance on the house be increased from 4,000 to 7,500 Guilders, which was what it had cost him. Still, not everything was in order. On July 9, 1784, Kant found it necessary to write to Hippel about noise. This time it was not the crowing of a cock, but the singing of prisoners.

> You were so good to promise to act on the complaint of the residents of the street at Schloßgarten in regard to the loud (*stentorische*) prayers of the hypocrites in the prison. I do not believe that they have reason to complain about the presumed danger to the salvation of their souls, if their voices are lowered so that they could hear themselves even by closed windows ... and without screaming with all their might then. They could still receive the favorable judgment of the warden that they are god-fearing people. This seems to be their real concern anyway. He will hear them, and they are really asked only to discipline their voices to a degree that is sufficient for the pious citizens of our city to feel saved in their houses. One word to the warden ... will be enough to curb this abuse and will help the person whose quiet state you have many times tried to help so graciously ... [82]

Nothing more is heard from Kant about unruly singing of hymns after this, but it appears that Kant never really obtained the peace and quiet he had always sought for his work. Religious devotion would continue to noisily intrude into his daily business. Borowski reports that all he achieved was that the windows were closed. The "nonsense" continued.[83]

Nor was this the only problem. Kant also found it necessary to complain about some of the boys who played in his street and threw stones over his fence. Complaints to the police did not help. The officers refused to act until someone in his household was hurt. Kant was bitter: "There will only be a right to punish [them] when I am sick or dead!"[84]

There were also other distractions. During the winter semester of 1783–84, Kant was dean again.[85] During his tenure, Metzger complained about who was to teach which lectures in the faculty of medicine. First he sent this complaint to Berlin; later, he talked in secret to someone who used the information in an anonymous attack on the faculty of medicine in Königsberg, which appeared in a journal published in Jena. Some of the senators of the university, including Kant, who, as dean of the faculty of philosophy, was a member of the senate that semester, wrote to Berlin to support the faculty of medicine against Metzger. In fact, they called Metzger a "suspicious witness," and they formulated this suspicion further by pointing out that Metzger was not always "motivated by disinterested eagerness in his official dealings." This was not all. In this same context, a professor of medicine in Jena named Gruner insulted the faculty of medicine at Königsberg. The professors at Königsberg wanted to extract an apology from him. Kant, as dean and advisor to the rector, counseled against such a course of action, not because he wanted to avoid disputes, but because he was convinced that there was little hope of success.[86] Metzger, of course, knew about all of this. Nor was this the last time that the two clashed over administrative issues. Kant had gained another enemy in the university.

At least the location of Kant's new home was idyllic. Hasse described it as follows:

On coming closer to his house, everything announced a philosopher. The house was something of an antique. It stood in a street that could be walked but was not much used by carriages. Its back bordered on gardens and moats of the castle, as well as on the back buildings of the many hundred years old palace with its towers, its prisons and its owls. But spring and summer the surroundings were quite romantic. The only trouble was that he did not really enjoy them . . . but only saw them. Stepping into the house, one would notice the peaceful quiet. Had one not been convinced otherwise by the open kitchen, with the odors of food, a barking dog, or the meowing of a cat, the darlings of his female cook – she performed, as he put it, *entire sermons* for them – one might have thought the house was uninhabited. If one went up the stairs, one would have encountered the servant who was working on preparing the table. But if one went through the very simple, unadorned and somewhat smoky outbuilding into a greater room which represented the best room, but which was not luxurious. (What Nepos said of Atticus: *elegant, non magnifies*, was quite true of Kant.) There was a sofa, some chairs, upholstered with linen, a glass cabinet with some porcelain, a secretary, which held his silver ware and his cash, and a thermometer. These were all the furnishings, which covered a part of the white walls. In this way, one reached through a very simple, even poor-looking, door a just as destitute sans-souci, into which one was invited by a glad "come in" as soon as one knocked. (How fast my heart beat, when this happened for the first time!) The entire room exuded simplicity and quiet isolation from the noises of the city and the world. Two common tables, a simple sofa, some chairs, including his study-seat, and a dresser, which left enough space in the middle of the room to get to the barometer and thermometer, which Kant consulted frequently. Here sat the thinker in his wooden half-circular chair, as if on a tripod . . .[87]

Kant's furnishings were by all accounts simple and inexpensive. He was opposed to opulence in principle. In this, he was quite different from some of his friends, and most notably from Hippel, who lived in a veritable palace, with select and valuable furnishings and artwork. Kant found such ostentation distasteful. Kraus once defended himself for not having adequate furnishings in his quarters by appealing to Kant, who "had just said rather unflattering things about people who buy too many things for their household."[88] The only picture in Kant's house was a portrait of Rousseau that was hanging over his writing desk.[89] At times, the walls of his study were blackened by the smoke from his pipe, the stove, and the lights, "so that one could write with the finger on the wall."[90] Indeed, Scheffner once did just that while he was listening to a conversation between Hippel and Kant, whereupon the latter asked him why he wanted to destroy the ancient patina, and whether such natural wallpaper wasn't better than one that was bought.[91]

In the afternoons Kant visited his old friend Green, who found it increasingly more difficult to go out of his house because of his gout.[92] Hamann had already reported to Herder in October 1781 that two of his acquaintances were suffering terribly from gout, that Green was suffering from it in his abdomen and his intestines, and that he had "chased" it into his feet with heated wine. He mentioned that he had met Kant at Green's house and talked to him about the *Critique,* which he had earlier accused – much to Kant's consternation – of perpetrating mysticism. In June of 1782, Hamann wrote again to Herder of another visit to Green's house, where Kant was present.[93] Indeed, Hamann frequently met Kant at Green's house.[94] They talked of literary events – for instance, the publication of Hume's *Dialogues Concerning Natural Religion,* which Hamann thought was full of poetical beauty. While Green could hardly have appreciated this, he agreed with Hamann that the book was "not at all dangerous."[95] In June 1782, Hamann fulfilled his promise to give to Green "the three parts of Hume's *On Human Nature*" – another hot topic of conversation among Green, Hamann, and Kant.[96]

Jachmann tells the following story:

> Kant . . . would find Green sleeping in his easy chair, sat down beside him, reflected on his own ideas, and also fell asleep; the bank director Ruffmann, who usually came after Kant, did the same, until Motherby came into the room at a certain time and woke them. They then spent the time until 7:00 P.M. engaging in the most interesting conversations. The fellowship broke up so punctually at 7:00 P.M. that I often heard neighbors say that it could not be yet 7:00 because professor Kant had not yet passed by.[97]

On Saturdays they would stay until 9:00 P.M., and were usually joined by the Scottish merchant Hay. Before leaving they would have an evening meal that consisted of cold sandwiches.

This is how Kant would spend most of his days: He still got up at 5:00, drank his tea and smoked his pipe. He then prepared his lectures. In particular, he lectured on Mondays, Tuesdays, Thursdays, and Fridays from 7:00 to 8:00 A.M. on metaphysics (during the winter semester) or logic (during the summer semester), and from 8:00 to 9:00 on natural theology or ethics; on Wednesdays and Saturdays he taught physical geography and anthropology from 7:00 or 8:00 to 10:00 A.M.[98] He also sometimes held exercises in logic or metaphysics on Saturday. After his teaching, Kant worked some more on his books until 12:00. He then got formally dressed, went out to eat, and spent the afternoon in the company of his friends, talking about everything worth talking about (and probably some things not worth talking about), did some more reading and working in the evening, and then went to bed.[99]

This was, for the most part, a life that was not untypical of professors in Königsberg and elsewhere in Germany. The only thing that was perhaps not typical about Kant's life was the great role that socializing with his friends assumed in it. Kant was a very gregarious and social being – not so much the solitary, isolated, and somewhat comical figure that many have come to see in him. Dialogue was more important to him than many people now want to admit. His critical philosophy is an expression of this form of life, and it makes sense first and foremost in the context of this form of life. What Kant "crushed," or meant to crush, in his *Critique* were the monsters that impeded this life. It was born of dialogue, something that the large role of "dialectic" in it should already have made more than clear. As such, it can also be seen as an attempt to show why different positions within the conversation should not be assumed dogmatically to present the only truth, and why everyone engaged in the conversation of mankind should be assured an equal say.

Though now in new quarters, Kant still usually lectured twelve hours a week (four hours of public lectures, that is, either logic or metaphysics, and eight hours of private lectures).[100] His lecturing became more and more of a chore. One of his students described his lecture style during the eighties as follows:

His oral presentation was simple and without affection. In Physical geography and in anthropology he was lively. The former had a more general appeal, and it was well suited to his talent as a story-teller. The latter gained from his incidental observations of minute details either drawn from his own experience or from his readings – especially from that of the best English novelists. One never left his lectures without having learned something, or without having been pleasantly entertained. The same was true for those who were able to follow his logic and his metaphysics. But Kant probably wished that the greater part of his students, no matter how industrious they were, should have exhibited greater interest in this subject. It cannot be denied that his presentation lost already during the early eighties . . . much of its liveliness, so that one could believe at times that he would fall asleep. One was re-enforced in this view by observing how at times he suddenly caught himself and gathered his apparently exhausted faculties. . . . Yet he never missed even an hour.[101]

Kant, contrary to other professors, not only was very strict in collecting his fees, but also had those students who attended his lectures free, or who were repeating them, sign up, and "did not allow those who wanted to re-peat them for the second time."[102] His main reason for this was that there was limited space, and that those who repeated took away chairs from those who came for the first time. This does not mean that monetary consider-ations did not play a role. He was making every effort to deliver a good product, and he deserved to be paid. His product might be different from that of his father, but just as a tradesman would, he insisted on being paid for his work.

In 1783, Kant was no longer a young man, and it showed in his lectures. At sixty, he had taught the same courses for almost thirty years – year af-ter year. He had complained during his earliest years (when he had to teach many more courses) about the mind-numbing difficulty of this enterprise. It reminded him at times of the punishment of Sisyphus. How much harder it must have been when he was sixty – and there was no end in sight, as re-tirement in the sense in which it is known today did not exist. A professor taught as long as he could. In Kant's case, that would be another fifteen years; and then there were all his concerns about the success of his criti-cal project, which was not doing as well as he had hoped it would. He had to put greater effort into making it better understood, while at the same time pushing it forward into moral philosophy.

Kant still had an effect on some of his students. In 1782, one of Kant's "best students," a young Jew named Elkana, went insane, and people blamed Kant for having "fed the undisciplined industriousness, or rather conceitedness, of this unhappy young man."[103] Hamann thought that Kant's "mathematico-metaphysical" worries were probably not the only thing that was to blame, but he did not seem to find Kant entirely blameless either.[104] Elkana ran away from Königsberg, eventually made it to England, and returned to Königsberg after having been introduced to Priestley. Upon his return, he was more interested in how to desalinate saltwater than in philosophy, but he did not improve otherwise. The court chaplain Schulz, "Kant's first apostle" and "exegete," together with his wife, took him into their care. Whether this caused his wish to convert to Christianity is not clear, but he did become a proselyte.[105] Kant's difficult philosophical theories were not the healthiest fare for young students.

Another important student was Daniel Jenisch (1762–1804), who began his studies in the summer semester of 1780. He was close not only to Kant, but also to Schulz and Hamann. Hamann considered him "one of our best heads."[106] Jenisch left Königsberg in 1786 with a letter of recommendation from Kant, addressed to Biester, and he later translated George Campbell's *Philosophy of Rhetoric* into German. In the Preface he tried to show that Kant's philosophy was close to that of the Scottish commonsense philosophers, and he praised Kant so much that one of the reviewers found it necessary to criticize him for his uncritical adoration of the Königsberg philosopher.[107]

Kant's most important student during this period was Jacob Sigismund Beck (1761–1840). He began his studies at the University of Königsberg in August of 1783, and he continued them first in Halle in 1789, and then in Leipzig. Since he disliked Leipzig – and especially Platner, one of Kant's more famous opponents – he returned to Halle again, to study with such Kantians as Ludwig Heinrich Jakob (1759–1827).

While studying in Königsberg, he was, like many of Kant's students, more of a friend to Kraus than to Kant – and he was always independent.[108] He wrote later to Kant: "I have had a great deal of trust in you, but I also confess that, in the difficulties, which pre-occupied me a long time, I often wavered between trusting you and trusting myself."[109] In other words, Beck did not succumb in Königsberg to the force of Kant's philosophy. Rather, this happened when he was away from Königsberg. It took him "several years" to think himself "into the spirit of the critical philosophy," which, "along with mathematics," became the best companion of his life.[110] Beck's correspondence with Kant between 1789 and 1797 is very important for understanding Kant's mature philosophy, if only because Kant wants Beck to understand his theory correctly. Although he became one of the most important first expositors of Kant's critical philosophy, he also became the first Kantian who significantly departed from the orthodox way of doing things. In so doing, he prepared the way for Fichte, Schelling, and Hegel.

Founder of a Metaphysics of Morals (1784–1787)

K ANT SENT the *Groundwork of the Metaphysics of Morals* to the publisher at the beginning of September 1784.[1] The book appeared only
eight months later, in April of 1785. But it was actually longer in coming
than that, being rooted in concerns that Kant had first formulated twenty
years earlier, and that had been on his mind ever since.[2] He began to tackle
those concerns directly toward the end of 1781 or the beginning of 1782. As
early as May 7, 1781, Hamann asked Hartknoch, the publisher of the first
Critique, to prod Kant to publish his metaphysics of nature and morals.
Hartknoch suggested this to Kant in November of the same year, and
Hamann could tell Hartknoch at the beginning of 1782 that Kant was indeed working on the *Metaphysics of Morals*, though he could not tell him
whether Kant would publish it with Hartknoch.[3] Yet it took Kant another
three years to finish a work on the metaphysics of morals, and what he published was not the *Metaphysics of Morals* itself, but a preliminary investigation toward such a *Metaphysics*.

There were many reasons for the delay. First, the task of producing a
popular short version of the *Critique*, the *Prolegomena*, got in the way. Secondly, Kant's personal life intruded. Buying and renovating his house was
particularly distracting. Though he was confident in the summer of 1783
that he would finish something on moral philosophy during the winter, it
still took almost another year for him to finish the *Groundwork*.[4] In any
case, it is far from clear that what Kant was working on during this time
was the *Groundwork*. His letter to Mendelssohn of August 1783 suggests
that it was something else, namely "a textbook of metaphysics in accordance
with the . . . critical principles, compressed for the purpose of academic

lectures."[5] What he hoped to finish was the first moral part of this text-book, but, as so often happened, this work developed along different lines.

One of the reasons for this was the publication of Garve's *Philosophical Remarks and Essays on Cicero's Books on Duties* in 1783.[6] This book brought home to Kant not only the importance of Cicero, but also his continuing effect on Kant's German contemporaries. Kant knew Cicero well, of course. During his last two years of high school at the *Collegium Fridericianum*, he had read most of his *Epistolae ad familiares*, many of his speeches, and also *De officiis*.[7] He had always appreciated Cicero's style, arguing that "true popularity" in philosophy could only be achieved by reading and imitating Cicero.[8] Even if he had not come close to this ideal in the first *Critique*, Kant still hoped to accomplish it in his moral writings. Garve was important. He had dared to criticize Kant's first *Critique* in a review, and Kant had been moved to criticize Garve in turn. Thus Hamann reported early in 1784 that Kant was working on a "counter-critique" of Garve. Though the title of the work was not determined yet, it was intended to be an attack not on Garve's review but on Garve's *Cicero* – and it was an attack that would constitute a kind of revenge.[9]

Hamann, who took great interest in literary feuds, was initially excited. But he was soon disappointed. For six weeks later he had to report that "the counter-critique of Garve's *Cicero* had changed into a preliminary treatise on morals," and that what he had wanted to call first "counter-critique" had become a predecessor (prodrome) to morals, although it was to have (still, perhaps?) "a relation to Garve."[10] The final version did not explicitly deal with Garve. Only much later, in his 1793 essay "On the Old Saw 'That May Be Right in Theory, but It Won't Work in Practice'," did Kant publicly respond to Garve. It is significant, however, that he read Cicero in Garve's translation, and that he carefully looked at Garve's commentary while writing the *Groundwork*. Though he may have been more interested in Garve than in Cicero, the latter had a definite effect on his views concerning the foundations of moral philosophy.[11] What was to be a mere text-book treatment of well-rehearsed issues became a much more programmatic treatise. It is therefore no accident that the terminology of the *Groundwork* is so similar to that of Cicero – "will," "dignity," "autonomy," "duty," "virtue," "freedom," and several other central concepts play similar foundational roles in Cicero and in Kant.[12]

There are large areas of agreement between Kant and Cicero. They both thought that ethics is based on reason and is opposed to impulse, and they both rejected hedonism. Cicero used such phrases as "conquered by pleasure" and "broken by desires" to describe actions that fall short of virtue and moral character, while Kant argued that only actions done from duty alone were moral, while any action motivated by pleasure was nonmoral. Both Cicero and Kant offer a duty-based theory of morality.

Though Cicero, like Kant, considered duty and virtue to be the fundamental concepts of morality, Cicero opted for a form of eudaimonism, which held that whatever is in accordance with duty will also turn out to be ultimately more pleasant than what is in contradiction to virtue. Ultimately, duty, like all things, derives from nature:

From the beginning nature has assigned to every type of creature the tendency to preserve itself, life and body, and to reject anything that seems likely to harm them, seeking and procuring everything necessary for life, such as nourishment, shelter and so on. Common also to all animals is the impulse to unite for the purpose of procreation, and a certain care for those that are born.[13]

Duties are based ultimately on these tendencies. Dutiful actions may therefore be characterized as "following nature." What is our duty is also what is natural, and Cicero's claim that we should follow nature is perhaps the most famous precept of his moral philosophy.

Cicero did not derive his duties from nature in any straightforward way. First of all, nature has given reason to human beings, and reason is their essential character. Therefore, duties are based on reason as well. So, for Cicero there could be no conflict between following nature and following reason. What is truly rational is also natural. Second, nature, "by the power of reason, unites one man to another for the fellowship both of common speech and life."[14] We are social animals, who need others not just for the necessities of life, but also for company and for flourishing. We need the approval of others, and the moral life is fundamentally concerned with such approval. We do not want just to be seen as good or honorable, we also want to be good or honorable. Accordingly, the duties must be derived from the fundamental "sources of honorableness." There were four such sources for Cicero: (1) perception of truth (ingenuity), (2) preserving fellowship among men, (3) greatness and strength of a lofty and unconquered spirit, (4) order and limit in everything that is said or done (modesty, restraint). These four sources seem to him "bound together and interwoven."[15] Most duties have their origin in all of them, though some may be traced to just one of these sources. Much of Book I of *On Duties* is taken up with the attempt to show "how duties have their roots in the different elements of what is honorable."[16] Duties dealing with the "communal life" influence all the others.[17] The "duties that have their roots in sociability conform more to nature than those drawn from learning." Therefore, he examines more thoroughly "what are the natural principles of human fellowship and community."[18] Duties having to do with our sociability take precedence over some of the other duties, such as devotion to learning, for instance. As Cicero puts it in Book I, "Let the following, then, be regarded as settled: when choosing between duties, the chief place is accorded to the class of duties grounded in human fellowship."[19] The other sources of honorableness are really closely related to the second. Thus loftiness of spirit reveals itself only in a fight for "common safety." It cannot be exhibited in a fight for one's own advantage. Modesty, restraint, or what is "seemly" is at least in part bound up with one's social role. We are social animals, and ethics is the study of ourselves within society. Cicero differentiates between things that are proper for us to do because of our universal nature or because of the characteristics we share with everyone, and those that we must do because we are the individuals we are.

Each person should hold on to what is his as far as it is not vicious, but is peculiar to him, so that the seemliness that we are seeking might more easily be maintained. For we must act in such a way that we attempt nothing contrary to universal nature; but while conserving that, let us follow our own nature, so that even if other pursuits may be weightier and better, we should measure our own by the rule of our own nature. For it is appropriate neither to fight against nature nor to pursue anything that you cannot attain.[20]

What our own nature is depends to a large extent on our social role. Sociability or communicability is accordingly the most important principle from which duty derives. This is clear from the very terms Cicero uses. "Honorableness" and "the honorable" are translations of "*honestas*" and "*honestum*." Both have to do with the holding of an office or an honor. Duties are thus essentially related to one's social standing. They are bound up with something that is public, part of the sphere of the *res publica* or the community. Duties make little sense outside of society. They are not internal or subjective principles, but public demands on us. Insofar as some of these duties are based on sociability as such, some duties will be universal, but they remain duties we have as "citizens of the world."

Garve did not have any fundamental objection to any of these aspects of duty in Cicero. He endorsed the view that duty was ultimately based in human nature, that it could be traced back to the principles of self-preservation and human fellowship, and that happiness (*Glückseligkeit*) is not only at the root of duty, but is also always a motivating factor in moral decisions. Less clearly, he also viewed honor as one of the most fundamental concepts of morality. Indeed, when he summarizes the true content of human duties in a book that offers his own views on the most general principles of ethics, his first rule reads:

Act in such a way that you will appear in your conduct as a reasonable and noble man, and that you express the character of an enlightened and forceful mind . . .[21]

We must act with a view to how we will appear to others. To be sure, these "others" are perhaps best understood in terms of a disinterested spectator conceived after Adam Smith and David Hume, but it is society that is expressed in these others.

Honor was still important in eighteenth-century Germany. Indeed, it may be characterized as one of the central moral precepts of the Prussian *Ständestaat.* The estates and the guild system were pervaded by it just as much as was the nobility. Honor may even have been more important to the citizens of the larger towns and cities in Prussia than it was to many members of the nobility. Without honor, a member of a guild was nothing. To be dishonored was to be excluded from the guild. *Ehrbarkeit* or honorableness was almost everything.[22] So when Garve argued that each profession had its own moral code, that it should have its own code, and that philosophers should make distinct the "obscure maxims which people of different professions follow," he seems to be endorsing a most important aspect of Prussian society. Kant's political and historical essays of the previous year show that he had far surpassed this view. He was not worried so much about the particularities of Prussian or even European society as he was concerned with the destiny of humanity as a whole. Prussia was just one episode in the narrative of a universal history from a cosmopolitan point of view.

As the son of a master artisan who was an important member of a guild, Kant had directly experienced the kind of moral disposition or ethos that Cicero and Garve were talking about. Indeed, it always remained an important notion for him.[23] Yet it was not fundamental to morality. Honorableness or *Ehrbarkeit* was for Kant a *merely* external form of morality, or an *honestas externa.*[24] He realized clearly that it depended on the social order, and for this very reason he rejected it as the basis for our maxims. The ground of moral obligation, he says, must not be found "in the nature of man nor in the circumstances in which man is placed, but must be sought a priori solely in the concepts of pure reason."[25] "Honor" and "honorable" could therefore not possibly capture the true nature of morality. A

Ciceronian ethics that remains founded on common life, expressed by
such concepts of honor (*honestas*), faithfulness (*fides*), fellowship (*societas*),
and seemliness (*decorum*), is too superficial and unphilosophical for Kant.
For this reason, Kant rejected not just Cicero but all those who were trying to develop a Ciceronian ethics. Moral duties cannot be derived from
honor or honorableness in any way. They are based on something we find
in ourselves and in ourselves only, namely, the concept of duty that we find
in our heart and in our reason. Morality is about who we genuinely are or
who we should be, and this has, according to Kant, nothing to do with our
social status.[26]

In rejecting "honor," Kant also implicitly rejects one of the fundamental principles of the society he lives in. The distinction of different estates
has no moral relevance. As moral agents we are all equal. Any attempt to
defend or justify social differences by appealing to morals must be rejected
as well. The conservative status quo must be challenged. In the context of
Prussia of 1785, these views must be called revolutionary. On the other
hand, they can also be characterized as an adaptation and further clarification of Frederick's own moral code to every moral agent and thus also
to every citizen of Prussia. Frederick had claimed that a

> true prince exists only to work and not to enjoy himself. He must be dominated by the
> feeling of patriotism, and the only goal to which he aspires must be: to achieve great
> and benevolent measures of the welfare of his state. To this goal he must subordinate
> all personal considerations, his self-love as well as his passions. . . . Justice must always
> be the primary concern of the prince; while the welfare of his people must have prece-
> dence over every other interest. The ruler is far from being the arbitrary master of his
> people; he is indeed, nothing other than its first servant.[27]

Kant seems to be saying that we also must subordinate all personal considerations, self-love, and passions to the only goal to which it is worth aspiring, namely, to be moral. This has nothing to do with feeling and everything
to do with reason and the "idea of another and far worthier purpose of one's
existence."[28] We are in this way no different from the king – something
Frederick himself would not have disputed.

One of the more important reasons that led Kant to reject honor as a
genuine moral principle was his belief that anyone who relied on maxims of
honor rather than on maxims of pure morality also relied on self-interest
as a significant part of moral deliberations; and he was clearly right about
this. It is not so clear whether he was right when he later claimed against
Garve and Cicero that

the concept of duty in its total purity is not only incomparably simpler, clearer, and more comprehensible and natural for everyone's practical use than any motive drawn from happiness, or mixed with happiness and with considerations of happiness (which always require a great deal of skill and thought). In the view of even the most common human reason, the concept of duty is far stronger, more penetrating, and more promising than any motives borrowed from the self-interested principle of happiness . . .[29]

On May 2, Hamann told Herder that Kant was "working hard on perfecting his system." The counter-critique of Garve had become a "forerunner" of moral philosophy.[30] At the beginning of August he reported that Kant was still indefatigably working on it, and that now his academic helper (amanuensis) Jachmann was also busy with it.[31] So by that time, the final version of the text was already being prepared and the *Groundwork* was more or less finished.

The *Groundwork* is a most impressive work. It is forcefully written, and it shows Kant at his best. Curiously enough, it was Kant's first extended work exclusively concerned with moral philosophy or ethics. No matter how much his previous works are characterized by moral concerns, Kant always places them in a larger metaphysical context. The book consists of a short Preface, three main sections, and short concluding remarks. Though it takes up only about sixty pages, it may well be Kant's most influential work.[32] The Preface starts from an observation on the common division of philosophical disciplines among the ancients into physics, ethics, and logic. Kant argues that this division is "perfectly suitable" for some purposes, but claims that it obscures a more important distinction between material and formal sciences. Indeed, every science has both a formal and a material part. While the formal part deals with the logical or mathematical principles underlying the science, the material part concerns its particular subject matter.

Kant's entire critical philosophy was meant to contribute to the formal aspect of science. His moral philosophy is no exception. It concentrates upon the merely formal aspects of morality, leaving aside the empirical content, which belongs to anthropology, for Kant. He thinks that it is "clear of itself from the common idea of duty and of moral law" that moral philosophy ultimately cannot deal with empirical concerns.[33] Because its claims are universal, the form of moral philosophy must be just as much a priori as that of theoretical philosophy. Still, the *Groundwork* was not designed to deliver all of the metaphysics of morals. Kant claims that he sought only to describe and establish "the *supreme principle of morality*."[34]

Kant's procedure involves two steps, first an analytic part and then a synthetic one. In the analytic part he develops an analysis of the common idea of this supreme moral principle and determines its nature and its sources. The central concept of the first section, which is entitled "Transition from Common Rational to Philosophic Cognition," is that of a good will (corresponding to the idea of a good character in anthropology).[35] Kant claims that a good will is not good because of its effects or because it produces some preconceived end, but only because of its own volition. Indeed, a good will is the only thing that is good without any qualification. In order to explain what he means by a good will, Kant introduces a distinction between acting from duty and acting in accordance with duty. He apparently thought that duty is what a good will would will. Still, many of our actions, which are in agreement with what a good will would will, do not really deserve moral praise because they are done from an ulterior motive. They are not done simply because they are our duty but because they happen to be in our interest. They thus accord with duty, but they were not done from duty. Indeed, we may assume that most of our actions are done in accordance with duty and not from duty. We always may have – and usually do have – self-serving interests in what we do. We may be honest, for instance, not simply because honesty is always the right course of action, but rather because honesty is the best policy, or because we simply "like" to be honest. So, a shopkeeper who treats all his customers with equal fairness and does not take advantage of strangers or children, may do so not because he is convinced that this is the moral thing to do, but because he realizes that it will be good for business in the long run. When we help a needy person, we may do so because it makes us feel good, or because we hope that other will follow the same policy. None of these are truly moral motives for Kant. Since self-interest seems to be inextricably interwoven with our actions, it is quite possible that a moral act has never been committed, but this does not mean that we should not strive to perform such acts.

Thus, actions have moral worth only when done from duty. But this moral worth is not to be found in the purpose or the goal that they are meant to attain. They have their moral worth only in the subjective principle of volition that they express. Kant calls this practical principle of volition "the maxim." As we have seen, maxims are general principles of action. They define not so much particular acts as certain courses of action. In the context of anthropology or psychology, they can be described as character-building devices. In the context of pure moral philosophy concerned with the formal aspect of morality, they are decisive in determining whether a will is morally good or not.

It is the "good will" that is the "concept that always takes first place in estimating the total worth of all our actions and constitutes the condition of all the rest."[36] But insofar as maxims are subjective principles of volition, that is, volitions "under certain conditions and hindrances," willed by a will that is either good or not good, maxims are what need to be evaluated. Good maxims, or maxims that have moral worth, are those maxims that a good will would will, while bad maxims, or maxims without moral worth, are maxims that a good will could not will. Kant goes on to argue that this means that any maxim that involves motivations that are not motivated by duty itself, but are merely in accordance with duty, are maxims that a good will could not will. Indeed, he identifies an *absolutely* good will or "a will good without any qualification" with a will whose principle is "the universal conformity of its actions to law." That is, an absolutely good will is a will whose volitions proceed from the principle that "*I ought never to act except in such a way that I could also will that my maxim should become a universal law.*"[37] As we have seen, Kant believed that this principle, which he later identifies as the categorical imperative, is contained in common human reason and is thus both accessible and accepted by every moral agent. Not every philosopher would agree with that claim.

In the second section of the *Groundwork* – called "Transition from Popular Moral Philosophy to Metaphysics of Morals" – Kant goes on to argue that, even if "it is always doubtful" whether any given act is done from duty, it is still the case that only acts done from duty have moral worth. Only a pure moral philosophy that recognizes this can make sense of morality.[38] Moral concepts cannot be derived from experience, but they have their origin a priori in pure reason. They are, he claims, not derived from human reason, but from "the universal concept of a rational being as such."[39] A pure moral philosophy deals with a pure will, that is, a will which has motives "that are represented completely a priori by reason alone," and *not* with human volition, which is characterized by empirically based motives.[40]

This ideal of a pure will differentiates Kant's metaphysics of morals from the Wolffian conception of a universal practical philosophy. Wolff's thought dealt with volition in general, Kant's philosophy deals with pure will. Wolff's approach can be compared to that of logic in general, which deals with all kinds of thinking, while Kant's is close to transcendental logic, which investigates "the special actions and rules of *pure* thinking, that is, of thinking by which objects are cognised completely a priori."[41] Kant, in other words, does not intend to deal with the everyday situations of ordinary moral agents. He deals, rather, with an ideal of pure reason that is entirely a priori.[42] This ideal, which he calls the categorical imperative, is not "given in experience." It is "an a priori synthetic practical proposition," whose very possibility is difficult to "see."[43] Indeed, Kant ends his book by emphasizing that "we do not . . . comprehend the practical unconditional necessity of the moral imperative." We only "comprehend its incomprehensibility," and this "is all that can fairly be required of a philosophy that strives in its principles to the very boundary of human reason."[44]

So morality for Kant is an enigma. The ultimate condition of the possibility of morality cannot be understood. One might be tempted to say that it is a brute fact, even if it is the brute fact that one is rational and thus has the "idea of another and far worthier purpose of one's existence." That the "mere dignity of humanity as rational nature, without any other end or advantage to be attained by it – hence respect for a mere idea – is yet to serve as an inflexible precept of the will" is, Kant openly acknowledges, a paradox. True morality is an ideal yet to be instantiated in the world, but it is the only ideal worth striving for. This is in the end what his idealism amounts to. Kant knew, moreover, that this notion of the "dignity of humanity" would have explosive consequences if adopted by the citizens of Prussia and the rest of Europe, even if he himself was careful to downplay the revolutionary implications of his work.

Kant formulates the categorical imperative, that is, the unconditional command of morality, in three different ways, all of which are supposed to be equivalent. In its first formulation it reads: "*act only in accordance with that maxim through which you can at the same time will that it become a universal law.*"[45] The second formulation says: "*So act that you use humanity, whether in your own person or in the person of any other, always at the same time as an end, never merely as a means.*" The third version amounts to the claim that "every rational being" must be understood "as one who must regard himself as giving universal law through all the maxims of his will."[46] Kant most clearly identifies it as the "formal principle" of the maxims in which an agent views himself as a lawgiver in the kingdom of ends, with the command: "Act as if your maxims were to serve at the same time as a universal law (for all rational beings)."[47] Though Kant – followed by most of his commentators – seems to favor the first version of the categorical imperative, it is really the last one that is most fruitful for Kant's further argument, for it is what allows him to introduce the idea of a kingdom of ends as opposed to a kingdom of nature, and to distinguish autonomy from heteronomy.

Kant's idea of autonomy, which he also calls the "supreme principle of morality" and which is therefore the principle that the *Groundwork* sets out to establish, amounts to the claim that we, as rational beings, are a law unto ourselves, or that we are free to give ourselves our own laws.[48] To be sure, the laws we give ourselves must be such that they can be valid for any rational being. This does not take anything away from Kant's radical position that no one – no priest, no king, no God – can give us moral laws or dictate morality to us. We are not just to be responsible for ourselves, we are also to be masters of ourselves. Morality thus presupposes freedom.

It is for this reason that the concept of freedom becomes "the key of the explanation of the autonomy of the will."[49] But freedom is just as enigmatic as the categorical imperative. It "cannot be proved as something real in ourselves and in human nature."[50] "We must presuppose it if we want to think of a being as rational and endowed with consciousness of his causality with respect to actions, that is, with a will, and so we find that . . . we must assign to every being endowed with reason and will this property of determining himself to action under the idea of freedom."[51]

Kant's reasoning is circular, and he knows it. He needs to presuppose freedom to make the claim that the categorical imperative captures the essence of morality. He also needs to presuppose that the categorical imperative is the essence of morality in order to trace "the determinate concept of morality back to the idea of freedom."[52] Kant thinks he can solve the problem, or at least mitigate it, by claiming that we take "a different standpoint when by means of freedom we think ourselves as causes efficient a priori than when we represent ourselves in terms of our actions as effects that we see before our eyes." From the first point of view, we belong to an "intellectual world" of which we have "no further cognizance," that is, to the world of things in themselves.[53] From the second point of view we belong to a world of appearances that Kant had delineated so well in the *Critique of Pure Reason* to make room for faith. The *Groundwork* is therefore in an important sense nothing more than a further spelling out of one of the articles of belief of the first *Critique*. It shows that freedom as autonomy is "the supreme principle of morality." It also offers the first exact statement of the categorical imperative. The *Groundwork* does no more – but that in itself constitutes one of the greatest achievements in the history of philosophy. Yet, by so doing, Kant placed philosophy in a rather more "precarious position" than the one in which Garve (and Cicero) had left it – arguing that "there is nothing in heaven or on earth upon which it depends or is based."[54]

Other Ideas: Against "Laziness and Cowardice"
and for "Careful Adherence to Principle"

As soon as Kant had sent his *Groundwork* to the publisher, he began to work
on some contributions to the *Berlinische Monatsschrift*.[55] The first of these
was his essay entitled "Ideas for a Universal History from a Cosmopolitan
Point of View," which appeared in the November issue of the *Berlinische
Monatsschrift* of 1784.[56] The essay was a response to a remark published in
the *Gothaische gelehrte Zeitungen* on February 11, in which it was claimed:

> It is a favorite idea of Herr professor Kant that the ultimate goal of the human race is
> the establishment of a perfect constitution. He desires that a philosophical historiog-
> rapher would undertake it to write a history of mankind from this perspective in order
> to show whether mankind has come closer to this final goal at some time, has strayed
> from it at other times, and what still remains to be done to achieve it.

In the essay Kant argues that such a historiography is possible only if we
assume that nature (or perhaps better, Nature) has certain characteristics.
Put in another way, he claims that a certain Idea of Nature is a necessary
condition of "universal history from a cosmopolitan point of view." Therefore, we may say that if a "universal history from a cosmopolitan point of
view" is legitimate, then a certain idea of Nature is also legitimate. Therefore we can also say that the "universal history" forms a *"justification* of
Nature – or rather perhaps of *providence.*" Indeed, Kant claims that such
a project "is no mean motive for adopting a particular point of view in
considering the world." For, he says,

> what is the use of lauding and holding up for contemplation the glory and wisdom of
> creation in the non-rational sphere of nature, if the history of mankind, the very part
> of this great display of supreme wisdom which contains the purpose of all the rest, is
> to remain a constant reproach to everything else? Such a spectacle would force us to
> turn away in revulsion, and, by making us despair of ever finding any completed ra-
> tional aim behind it, would reduce us to hoping for it only in some other world.[57]

So Kant argues for a teleological view of Nature by arguing that such a view
is required for a history of the progress of humanity. This strategy of argument is, of course, reminiscent of that of the "transcendental arguments"
Kant puts forward in other contexts. Nevertheless, it must be observed that
his "justification of Nature" is weak. Only if we think that such a history
(or "grand narrative") is possible or necessary, do we have to accept his conclusion. The presupposition of the Idea of Progress is not a presupposition
necessary for action, as is the presupposition of the Idea of Freedom.

"Freedom" clearly takes center stage here as well. The essay starts with the same contrast between freedom of the will and the natural world of phenomena that is already familiar from the first *Critique* and the review of Schulz. Indeed, Kant characterizes history (or better, historiography) as concerned with the temporal sequence of phenomena. He just hopes that "if it examines the free exercise of the human will *on a large scale,* it will be able to discover regular progression among freely willed actions."[58] Such a regular progression would not be due to any rational purpose of humanity, but would have to be ascribed to nature itself. He seeks "a guiding principle" for a history of "the free exercise of the human will *on a large scale.*"

To this end, Kant formulates in somewhat dogmatic fashion and with little defense nine propositions. The first maintains that all natural capacities of a creature are "destined" to be fully developed sooner or later. If nature has a plan, then the plan must be fulfilled. In the second proposition, he claims that our reason is such that it can be developed fully only in the species, not in an individual. Our lives are too short to allow the latter. Third, "nature has willed that man should produce entirely by his own initiative everything which goes beyond the mechanical ordering of his animal existence, and that he should not partake of any other happiness or perfection than that which he has procured for himself without instinct and by his own reason."[59] Fourth, nature brings about the full development of our natural faculties by an antagonism within society. In the long run, this antagonism leads to a law-governed social order. Kant calls this the "unsocial sociability." Though people may not be able to bear one another many a time, they still seek the approval and respect of others. Fifth, the greatest problem for the human species posed by nature is the development of "a civil society which can administer justice universally."[60] This is, according to the sixth proposition, both the most difficult and the last problem to be solved by humanity. This is because man is an animal who needs a master, at least when he lives together with other human beings, because he has a tendency to abuse the others. This master can ultimately be found only in man himself, and that makes the task difficult, indeed impossible: "for from such crooked wood as man is made of, nothing perfectly straight can be built."[61] Another part of the reason this is so difficult becomes clear from the seventh proposition, which states that a perfect civil constitution presupposes a "law-governed external relationship with other states, and cannot be solved unless the latter is also solved."[62] Thus, eighth, the history of the human race as a whole can be regarded as "a hidden plan of nature" to bring about both a perfect civil constitution and law-governed external relationships between the states that will allow full development of all our natural capacities. This is the reason why a universal history from a cosmopolitan point of view not only must be possible, but may even further the purpose of nature itself.

While this might seem to be a mere academic exercise, it has for Kant the most practical consequences, for it shows, among other things, that we should

observe the ambitions of rulers and their servants, in order to indicate to them the only means by which they can be honorably remembered in the most distant ages. And this may provide us with another *small* motive for attempting a philosophical history of this kind.[63]

The philosopher may not be able to do much to further the ends of nature, or to contribute to the development of a perfect constitution, but there is something he can do as the judge and critic of those who rule. Kant took this role seriously from at least 1784. What he says about the law-governed external relationship with other states can be read as an implicit criticism of Frederick's warlike and militaristic policies.

In December of that same year he published his essay "What Is Enlightenment?" – again in the *Berlinische Monatsschrift*. Kant dated it September 30, 1784. The essay represents a response to a question by Johann Friedrich Zöllner (1748–1805), who was a member of a group of Enlightenment thinkers centered in Berlin. In response to an article in the *Monatsschrift*, whose author had advocated that priests and ministers should no longer play a role in marriage, and that the religious ceremony of marriage contradicted the spirit of the Enlightenment, Zöllner argued that the principles of morality were already in decline (*wankend*) and that the disparagement of religion could only accelerate this process. One should not, "in the name of *Enlightenment* confuse the heads and hearts of the people." In a note in the text, he asked: "What is Enlightenment? This question, which is almost as important as 'What is truth?' should really be answered before one starts to enlighten! And yet, I have not found an answer to it anywhere."[64]

This was the question that Kant meant to answer. He was by no means the only one who addressed this question. A dispute ensued. Kant's answer was the most philosophical, or perhaps better, the most principled one, but it was far from being the only one. He maintained that Enlightenment is humanity's destiny, whereas most of the other papers were concerned with more practical issues.

The essay ends by noting the paradox that Frederick's Prussia presents.

It allows freedom of thought in religious matters that a free state does not dare to allow. Its "well-disciplined and numerous army" is "ready to guarantee public peace," and it is because of this threat to the individual freedom of the citizen (civil freedom) that greater freedom of the spirit is possible, at least according to Kant:

> When nature has unwrapped . . . the seed for which she cares most tenderly, namely the propensity and calling to *think* freely, the latter gradually works back upon the mentality of the people (which thereby gradually becomes capable of *freedom* in acting) and eventually even upon the principles of *government*, which finds it profitable to itself to treat the human being, *who is now more than a machine,* in keeping with his dignity.[65]

Again, philosophy is assigned the role in state of bringing about what nature's plan has been all along. Freedom of thought will lead to greater civil freedom, or so Kant seems to believe. "The hindrances to universal Enlightenment . . . are gradually becoming fewer." Whatever else one may say of Frederick, he is "a shining example" of a monarch who shows that it is not necessary to play the guardian of the people in the arts and sciences. "No monarch has yet surpassed the one whom we honor."[66] Freedom in Frederick's Prussia was freedom of thought "chiefly in *matters of religion.*" It did not extend to political freedom, for instance. Kant acknowledges this, but thinks that this is a significant sign of things to come.[67]

What is Enlightenment for Kant? It is, he says, in the first sentence of the essay, "the human being's emergence from his self-incurred minority." Put positively, it is the stage of mankind's maturity. Minority is for Kant the "inability to make use of one's own understanding without direction from another. It is self-incurred when its cause lies not in a lack of understanding but in a lack of resolution and courage to use it without direction from another." We should have the courage to think for ourselves. This is expressed by the motto of the Enlightenment "*Sapere aude!*" or "Dare to be wise!"[68]

It is just "laziness and cowardice" that stand in the way of the Enlightenment now. While it may be difficult for any individual to extricate himself from tutelage, a public has a greater chance. The only thing that is required is freedom, and indeed only the "least harmful" freedom one can imagine, namely "the freedom to make *public* use of one's reason in all matters."[69] By public use of reason, he means the use of reason by a scholar or writer "before the entire public of the world of readers." It is ultimately nothing but the freedom of the press. Kant, somewhat curiously from today's perspective, is ready to concede that private use of reason, that is, the use of reason within a civil post or office (which would include that of a university professor) may and indeed should not be free. Here one must obey. We must pay our taxes, and a minister or priest must teach what the church decrees.[70] To restrict public enlightenment would be "a crime against human nature."[71] While Kant does not want to say that he lives in an "enlightened age," he is willing to say that he is living in an "age of Enlightenment," that is to say, in an age in which small steps toward an enlightened age are possible.

Not everyone agreed that this kind of enlightenment was possible or even a good thing. In 1784, Kant's former student Herder published his *Ideas on a Philosophy of the History of Mankind* with the publisher of the first *Critique*. It represented the first volume of a very ambitious enterprise. In that same year a new journal was established that was to become most important in the further discussion of Kant's own philosophy, namely the *Neue allgemeine Literaturzeitung* of Jena. Kant was asked in July whether he would not be willing to make "at least a few contributions" and whether he would be interested in reviewing Herder's *Ideas* in particular.[72] He agreed, probably after looking at Hamann's copy of the *Ideas*.[73] The review of Herder's book was to be "a trial." It was due on November 1, and it appeared in one of the first issues of the journal, namely on January 6, 1785.[74] As was customary, the review appeared anonymously.

Kant's judgment of this work of his former student was negative, and he did not hold back. Perhaps he even went out of his way to insult Herder. Thus in the introduction of the review, he did not talk so much about the book as about the author, saying that he was "ingenious and eloquent," demonstrating again his "renowned individuality," and going on to note that

his is not logical precision in definition of concepts or careful adherence to principles, but rather a fleeting, sweeping view, an adroitness in unearthing analogies, in the wielding of which he shows a bold imagination . . . combined with a cleverness in soliciting sympathy for his subject – kept in increasingly hazy remoteness – by means of sentiment and sensations.[75]

He does not expect much from the book, but he will try to seek out its main theses insofar as they might be profitable.

After a detailed summary of the stages of Herder's argument in the *Ideas*, Kant summed up "the idea and final purpose of Part I" as follows:

The spiritual nature of the human soul, its permanence and progress toward perfection, is to be proved by analogy with the natural forms of nature, particularly their structure, with no recourse to metaphysics. For this purpose, spiritual forces, a certain invisible domain of creation, are assumed for which matter constitutes only the framework. This realm contains the animating principle which organizes everything in such a way that the schema of the perfection of this organic system is to be man. All earthly creatures, from the lowest level on, approximate him until finally, through nothing else than this perfected organic system, of which the essential condition is the upright gait of the animal, man emerged. His death can never more terminate the progress and enhancement of the structure already shown before copiously in other creatures. Rather a transcendence of nature is expected to still more refined operations in order to further him thereby to yet higher grades of life, and so continuously to promote and elevate him into infinitude.[76]

As Herder had claimed, "the current condition of man is probably the intermediate stage between two worlds . . . the middle link between two interlinking systems of creation. . . . He represents two worlds in one to us and that accounts for the apparent duality of his essence. . . . Life is a battle, the flower of pure, immortal humanity a painfully acquired crown."[77]

Kant did not understand. He did not understand the argument by analogy, because what Herder stated as an analogy is a disanalogy. How can the similarity between man and all other creatures prove that man is immortal, or the middle link between mortality and immortality, when all other creatures decompose? Individuals are completely destroyed – or so it would seem. Herder's idea of a self-constituting organic system is an idea that lies entirely outside of the sphere of empirical investigation. It is mere speculation. The author may be praised for having thought for himself, and for a preacher, this took courage, but his "execution is only partially successful."[78] Kant closed by expressing his hope that philosophy would help Herder in "pruning . . . superfluous growth." Flighty imagination, "whether metaphysical or sentimental," will not get us anywhere.

Hartknoch had told Herder on a visit in 1783 that Kant believed the lack of attention to his first *Critique* was the result of Herder's influence.[79] Was the review therefore a personal reaction? Probably not – at least not entirely. For Kant, the champion of the Enlightenment as the destiny of mankind, had deep philosophical reasons to oppose what seemed to him only unprincipled flights of imagination that obfuscated what was really important. Herder's book was not just a "superfluous growth," but a weed that needed to be rooted out. Furthermore, Kant himself did not seem to think the review was a devastating one. Nor did Hamann. He wrote to Herder just before the issue of the journal containing Kant's review appeared, and he revealed that Kant was the author: "It will perhaps not be uncomfortable for you to know that our Kant reviewed you. In any case, keep it to yourself and do not reveal me."[80] He also told Herder that he had obtained a copy of the review, and that it is waiting to be sent to Herder.

In December 1784, Kant sent to Biester two other essays, "Of the Volcanoes on the Moon" and "On the Injustice of Counterfeiting Books." The first appeared in the March issue of the *Berlinische Monatsschrift* of 1785. In it, Kant took up an observation by Aepinus in the *Gentlemen's Magazine* of 1784 that was meant to show that Herschel's discovery of a volcano on the moon (in 1783) confirmed his own theory that the roughness of the surface of the moon had to be explained by volcanic activity. Kant argued that Herschel's discovery did not confirm Aepinus's conjecture, because some of the features of the moon could also be explained by nonvolcanic activity. After a discussion of the details of such an alternative, he turned toward a more general point that was of greater interest to him, namely, that the features of all the objects in space (*Weltkörper*) "originated in very much the same way. They all were first in a fluid state."[81] Kant thought that their globular shape proved this. Given that they were fluid, and that their fluidity presupposes heat, he asked where the heat might have come from originally. Buffon's explanation, which derived it from the heat of the sun, from which they all originated, was not satisfactory. Kant proposed instead that when bodies formed by the aggregation and densification of gassy matter, the warmth of the gasses also increased. This would explain also the heat of the sun, in accordance with physical laws that still hold. One thing we should do under no circumstances, however, is to appeal to God's will and plan whenever we have difficulty explaining a phenomenon.

The essay "On the Injustice of Counterfeiting Books" appeared in the May issue of the *Berlinische Monatsschrift* of 1785. It presented an argument against the illegitimate republication of books, based not on the claim that property rights attach to copies of books, but rather on the idea that a publisher is the agent of someone else, namely the author. He is thus not so much selling books on his own account, but rather doing it for the author. If someone reprints a book without permission of the author, he is acting on behalf of the author without being authorized to do so. He must therefore reimburse the author or his agent for any damage he might have caused by this transaction. Kant's essay is a tightly argued defense of this claim and some supplementary principles. Since he was by this time the author of many books, he had an obvious interest in establishing that illegitimate reprinting was unjust and should be punished by law. It might also show that his books were beginning to sell better, and that they were therefore candidates for counterfeit reprinting.

It may have been a purely theoretical interest as well. As Kant wrote to Biester at the end of 1784, he was "constantly brooding over ideas, and so I do not lack material, but only a particular reason to choose from it. There is also a lack of time, since I am occupied with a pretty extensive project (*Entwurf*), which I would really like to finish before the approaching incapacity of old age." He also observed that in the popular essays

I always completely think through my subject but I also must always fight with a certain disposition to being prolix. But I am, if you will, so bothered by the multitude of things, which offer themselves for a complete treatment, that, though capable of it, I fall short of perfecting the idea because I have to leave out some matters that seem necessary for it. In this case, I understand myself quite well, but cannot make it clear and satisfactory for others. The suggestion of an understanding and honest friend can be useful in this. I also would like to know sometimes which questions the public would most like to see solved.[82]

Kant had, of course, an "understanding and honest friend" in Königsberg, namely the merchant Green. Some friends outside of Königsberg did not understand.

The Controversy with Herder: Against Denying "Reason That Prerogative which Makes It the Greatest Good on Earth"

Herder reacted just as one would have expected. In a letter to Hamann on February 14, 1785, apparently written before receiving the letter from Hamann that revealed Kant as the author, he said:

In Jena they announced last year with great pomp a new literary magazine, and Kant was mentioned as one of the first contributors. And behold, in the 4th and 5th issue, one finds a review of my *Ideas*, which is so malicious, distorting, metaphysical, and entirely removed from the spirit of the book from beginning to end, that I was surprised. But I would never have expected that Kant, my teacher, whom I never knowingly insulted in any way, was capable of such a mean-spirited act. The reviewer teases me with my profession, sets three or four fires, so that if there is no conflagration it won't be his fault. I thought back and forth, who in Germany could write so completely outside of the horizon of Germany and the book until finally it was first rumored and then openly said: it was the great *metaphysicus* Kant in Königsberg, Prussia. At the same time I read the "Idea for a Universal History of Mankind, but [which] is supposed to be from a cosmopolitan understanding;" and as I read the essay I learn also about the reviewer, but not about the character of the man. For how malicious and infantile it is to read the plan of an incomplete, nay even barely started, book from its Preface, to take an idea from it and use it in the fashion of the book, while acting as if there was no book of this kind in the world. . . . Good that I now know what I can expect from the *Magistro VII. Artium;* happy that I do not need his childish plan that man was created for the species and the most perfect governmental machine (*Staatsmaschine*) at the end of time. What I ask of you, dearest friend, is that you will not in future continue to communicate to him my writings *prima manu* (first hand) and no longer give him my regards. I leave the metaphysical-critical throne of judgment to Mr. Apollo on which he puffs himself up, because for me it is full of haze and prattling (*gacklichen*) clouds. You may not tell him that I know of the review or the reviewer . . . I will be happy, if I startle his idol of reason or entirely lay waste to it. His professorial instructions to me are thoroughly indecent. I am forty years old and no longer sit on his metaphysical school bench. The fistula is caused by my failure to follow the Herr professor not in his beaten track of conceptual fancies (*Wortgaukeleien*). . . . [The metaphysician's] pride and his unbearable self-importance, which is also demonstrated by Kant's letters to Lambert, is nothing if not laughable.[83]

Herder could not understand; and unable to forget, he could not forgive either. What is most interesting, perhaps, is that he not only objected to the review, but also seems to accuse Kant of plagiarizing the basic conception of his own *Ideas for a Philosophy of the History of Mankind* in his "Ideas for a Universal History from a Cosmopolitan Point of View." It cannot be denied that there is a similarity between the two enterprises, and that Kant used Herder's *Ideas* as a foil, but he formulated a radical alternative to Herder's view. Kant used none of Herder's ideas. Perhaps Kant's review was not a sign of good judgment, but it was hardly as mean-spirited as Herder wanted Hamann to believe.

Hamann did not believe. At first, he did not say anything about Herder's reaction to Herder himself. Yet he still talked to him about Kant. Thus he wrote on April 14, 1785, that he had borrowed an exemplar of the just released *Groundwork* from Hippel, had read through it in a few hours, and had found that "in place of pure reason he talks in this work of another figment of the imagination and idol: the *good will.*" He added: "that Kant is one of our *sharpest* minds even his enemy must admit, but regrettably, this acuity is his evil demon, almost like that of Lessing . . ."[84] Only on May 8 did Hamann broach the subject of Kant's presumed mean-spiritedness. Implicitly criticizing Herder's followers as "*bona fide* admirers of what they do not understand," Hamann pointed out that he himself owed much to Kant, and that, just like Herder, he had every reason to avoid an open conflict with Kant. He went on to excuse Kant: "If one disregards the *old Adam* of his authorship, he truly is an obliging, unselfish, and basically noble and well-intentioned man of talents and merits." Further-more, "in your *Ideas* there are some passages which seem to be directed against his system like *arrows*, though you may not have thought of him – and I also very much suspect that much in the review was not meant as you misunderstood or interpreted it to be." There are always two sides to every story, and "all our knowledge is fragmentary."[85]

By the "*bona fide* admirers of what they do not understand," Hamann meant primarily a reviewer of Herder's *Ideas* in the February issue of the *Teutscher Merkur*, who had attacked Kant. The reviewer was Karl Leon-hard Reinhold, and the review was entitled "Letter of the Pastor of *** to the E. of the T. M. Concerning a Review of Herder's *Ideas* . . ." Kant re-ceived the issue and decided to answer. By the end of March, he had al-ready sent off his response to Jena, and it appeared in the journal's ap-pendix to the month of March. Kant defended himself by saying that he had followed "the maxims of conscientiousness, impartiality, and moder-ation, which this gazette has taken as its guide."[86] The clergyman, Kant went on to say, was wrong to accuse the reviewer of being a metaphysician who tried to reduce everything to abstract scholastic distinctions. The reviewer knew the anthropological observations quite well and respected them as empirical evidence, but "the reasonable use of experience also has its limits."[87] Analogies cannot be used to bridge the "immense void between the contingent and the necessary," and to the clergyman's assertion that "healthy reason, acting freely, recoils from no idea whatever," Kant an-swered that what he had in mind was simply the *horror vacui* with which ordinary reason recoils from ideas by means of which "absolutely nothing can be thought." He also pointed out that his judgment of the book was motivated by a proper regard for Herder's present fame "and still more for his future renown."[88]

Kant reviewed the second part of the *Ideas* in the *Allgemeine Literatur-zeitung* of November 15, 1785. He wrote the review very quickly, having received a copy of the work only on November 8.[89] In the first few pages, Kant simply summarizes Books 6 through 10 and points out that the tenth book is nothing but a recapitulation of Herder's *The Most Ancient Document of the Human Race*. He then goes on to note that the extracts of existing ethnic accounts that make up Books 7 and 8 are "ably edited," "master-fully managed," "accompanied by penetrating personal judgment," and contain "beautiful passages rich in poetic eloquence."[90] This is only a prelude to the question of whether the poetic spirit that enlivens the book does not get in the way of the author's philosophy – "whether frequently the tissue of daring metaphors, poetic images and mythological allusions does not serve to conceal the corpus of thought as under a farthingale instead of letting it glimmer forth agreeably as under a translucent veil."[91] Of course, Kant thought they did; and he gave a number of examples to show this. He thought that the work would have benefited from a greater critical reserve in the marshaling of presumed evidence. He also disliked Herder's rejection of the concept of race and "especially . . . the classification based on hereditary coloration."[92] Excusing himself as unqualified to judge what Herder had to say about the education of the human race on the basis of ancient texts – not being a philologist and not being at home "outside" of nature – he went on to defend some propositions that Herder chose to attack. The first of these is the claim that "man is an animal that needs a master." Herder had called this an "easy" and "vicious" principle in the book. It was, of course, a principle Kant had espoused in his own "Ideas." After defending it as a principle that was not vicious but salutary, he ironically added that it might nonetheless have been put forward by a vicious man.[93]

Herder did not like this installment of the review much better than the first.[94] He prayed: "God deliver us from this evil." But Kant was not yet finished with Herder. In November 1785, he published in the *Berlinische Monatsschrift* an essay on "The Definition of the Concept of the Human Race," which was, at least in part, an answer to Herder.[95] In it, he tried to show that race must be based on inherited traces, such as skin color, and he claimed that therefore there are just four races – namely, the white, yellow, black, and red. Furthermore, he argued that there are no characteristics other than color that are inevitably inherited. This also meant for him that children of mixed marriages necessarily inherit characteristics of both races, and that they inevitably pass these characteristics on to their children. He rejected the idea that the different races originated from different kinds (*Stämme*) of people. Rather, he thought that there had been *one* original kind of humanity, which possessed the four different possibilities within itself, and that the differentiation into races had proceeded in accordance with adaptations made necessary in different regions of the world. There are no different species of humanity, only different races. The whites cannot be differentiated as a separate species of human being from the blacks; and there are no *different species of human beings at all;* such an assumption would deny the unity of the kind from which they all must have originated."[96]

Herder had argued that the concept of race did not make any sense. The differences between human beings are "as varying as they are unnoticeable . . . colors fade into each other; the formations serve the genetic character, and in the end they are all just shades of one and the same great painting that has covered the earth over all space and time."[97] Slavery cannot be justified. It is not only cruel, but also criminal. Whatever differences there are, they are the result of climate. Kant disagreed with Herder, and he claimed the concept of race was justified and useful. (This did not mean, of course that he disagreed with the conclusions Herder had drawn from his rejection.) Kant argued again that there were real differences between human beings, even if they were only differences of pigmentation.[98] As he had pointed out in his review of Herder's second volume of the *Ideas*, this small difference was the only difference between his and Herder's view.[99]

While Kant declined to write reviews of the subsequent volumes of Herder's *Ideas*, he did publish another essay on a problem from Herder, namely, his "Conjectural Beginning of the Human Race." Its roots go back to the early seventies and Kant's correspondence with Hamann about *The Most Ancient Document of the Human Race*, but its immediate occasion was Book 10 of Herder's *Ideas*. Kant sent the essay to Berlin on November 8, 1785, and it was published in the January issue of the *Berlinische Monatsschrift*.[100] In it, he argued that conjecture about the beginning of the human race might be justifiable as "a history of the first development of freedom from its origins as a predisposition in human nature."[101] Starting from Genesis, Chapters 2–7, he argues that the first human being must have been able to "*stand* and *walk;* he could *speak* . . . and indeed *talk* – i.e. speak with the help of coherent concepts . . . – and consequently *think*."[102] Though Kant thought that these abilities must have been acquired, he also thought he could assume them, because he was only interested in the development of human behavior from the ethical point of view. At first, man only followed instinct, and he was happy. But "reason soon made its presence felt." With the help of the imagination, it invented desires without any natural basis. First, luxurious tastes developed; second, sexual fantasies made the fig leaf necessary, and "the first incentive for man's development as a moral being came from his *sense of decency*."[103] Next came the ability to anticipate future needs, and finally the realization that we are the "end of nature," that we are different from all other animals. This realization raises "man completely above animal society" and gives him a "position of *equality with all rational beings* . . . [as] *an end in himself*."[104] In a most characteristic passage, Kant claims that

Before reason awoke, there were no commandments or prohibition, so that violations of these were also impossible. But when reason began to function and, in all its weakness, came into conflict with animality in all its strength, evils necessarily ensued. . . . From the moral point of view, therefore, the first step . . . was a fall, and from the physical point of view, this fall was a punishment that led to hitherto unknown evils. Thus, the history of *nature* begins with goodness, for it is the *work of God;* but the history of *freedom* begins with evil, for it is the *work of man.*[105]

Kant argued that while this story shows that reason and freedom must look like a loss to the individual who must blame himself, they also are a cause for admiration and praise if we take the point of view of the species. For man's destiny is the "progressive cultivation of its capacity for goodness."[106]

In the concluding note Kant addresses a malaise to which thinking people are subject and of which the unthinking are completely ignorant, namely "discontent with that providence by which the course of the world as a whole is governed."[107] Kant thinks that contentedness with destiny is absolutely necessary for progress in the cultivation of goodness. Blaming fate interferes with working on oneself to get better. The malaise is expressed in fear of war, dissatisfaction with the shortness of life, and the yearning for a golden age in which all of our needs are met. Kant tried to show that wars are necessary, that the shortness of life is beneficial, and that a golden age is not really desirable. What appear to be undesirable features of the world are in fact conditions of the possibility of progressive cultivation of our capacity for goodness. Every individual therefore should realize that he has "every justification for acknowledging the action of his first ancestors as his own, and that he should hold himself responsible for all the evils which spring from the misuse of reason."[108] We would have done precisely the same as our ancestors did. Therefore we should be content. Things are not going from good to evil, but from worse to better.

Herder disagreed, of course. For him, the "savage who loves himself, his wife and his child . . . and works for the good of his tribe as for his own . . . is . . . more genuine than the human ghost, the citizen of the world, who, burning with love for all his fellow ghosts, loves a chimera. The savage in his hut has room for a stranger . . . the saturated heart of the idle cosmopolitan is a home for no one."[109] Herder might have started out as a student of Kant, but he had become an enemy. What one of them considered progress, the other considered to be harmful and an impoverishment of humanity. Further, Herder continued to view their conflict as merely personal. Kant, however, believed he was fulfilling his duty. In the very last sentence of his "Conjectures," he said, "Each individual is for his own part called upon by nature itself to contribute toward this progress to the best of his ability."[110] Perhaps there was a personal component to Kant's critique of Herder, but if there was, it was much less significant than Herder believed. Kant had begun to view himself as a political force, contributing to the progress of mankind.

Hamann disliked Kant's essay "What is Enlightenment?" for reasons very similar to Herder's, and he continued to write against Kant, even though he published none of these attempts. Thus he asked in a letter to Kraus, written on the fourth Sunday of Advent in 1785, "what kind of conscience does it take for a thinker (*Raisonneur*) and a speculator (*Spekulant*), who sits with his night cap behind his stove, to accuse those of minority of *cowardice*, when their guardian has a well-disciplined army to vouchsafe his infallibility and orthodoxy. How can one make fun of their laziness, if their enlightened and self-thinking guardian . . . does not even consider them to be machines but mere shadows of his own greatness . . .?"[111] What bothered Hamann had also bothered Lessing long before, when he wrote to Nicolai: "please do not talk to me about your Berlin freedom; it is really confined to the single freedom of bringing to market scurrilous anti-religious pamphlets. . . . Just wait until someone should appear in Berlin to raise his voice for the rights of subjects and against exploitation and despotism . . . you will then see what country in Europe is in fact characterized by the worst slavery at the present day."[112] The Prussia of Frederick the Great might be a great place for "examined" intellectuals like Kant, but – or so Hamann thought – it was hardly a great place to live. Kant's essay added insult to injury.

Though he tried to excuse Kant's behavior to Herder, and though he never completely approved of Herder's *Ideas*, Hamann was intellectually closer to Herder than to Kant. While it is perhaps no accident that beginning in about 1785 the letters between Hamann and Herder decreased in number, this did not mean that Hamann disapproved of Herder's project. Just as Herder's importance in Hamann's correspondence decreased, the importance of Friedrich Heinrich Jacobi increased greatly.

Metaphysical Foundations of Natural Science: "All Natural Science Proper Requires a Pure Part"

On March 28, 1785, Hamann had written to Herder that Kant was working on "new contributions to the *Berlinische Monatsschrift*, on his Metaphysics of Nature and on Physics. The principium of his morality will also appear at this Easter book exhibition. His appendix against Garve did not materialize; rather, he is said to have shortened the work. He seems to suffer from diarrhea, and I am worried that he will lose his reputation as an author by writing too much."[113] Indeed, it is amazing how much Kant wrote between the spring of 1784 and the fall of 1786. He produced not only the *Groundwork*, five major essays, and three installments of his review of Herder's *Ideas*, but also two other essays, a Preface to Jakob's *Examination of Mendelssohn's Morning Hours* (1786), and another major work, the *Metaphysical Foundations of Natural Science*. Even if he was drawing on partial drafts from years of teaching and had an amanuensis who helped him to prepare the final copy, the quantity and quality of his output is still astounding.

On September 13, 1785, Kant could write that he had finished a book during the summer but that, since he had injured his hand, the manuscript would have to stay on his desk until Easter.[114] The book indeed appeared at the following Easter convention of book dealers in Leipzig. In the September 13 letter he explained the purpose of the book as follows:

> Before I go on to the promised Metaphysics of Nature I first had to deal with something that is really only a mere application of it, but which still presupposes an *empirical* concept, namely the basic metaphysical grounds of the doctrine of bodies and, in an appendix, the doctrine of the soul.[115]

The doctrine of the soul was dropped. As Kant explained in his Preface, empirical knowledge of the soul can never become scientific. "Mathematics is inapplicable to the phenomena of the internal sense and their laws."[116] There is only as much science in a subject as there is mathematics. Therefore, the doctrine of the soul, which must be based on inner sense, cannot form part of the *Metaphysical Foundations of Natural Science*.

Kant had to write this book because he believed that science required apodictic certainty. Merely empirical certainty is not enough, but apodictic certainty can only be a priori. Therefore, we have natural science "only when the natural laws are cognized a priori," and this means that "all natural science proper requires a pure part upon which the apodictic certainty sought by reason can be based."[117] This pure part can come only from the universal laws of thought, which are ultimately based on the categories. Kant's approach was to consider what he took to be the central concept of the book, that is, matter, under "all the four headings of the understanding," namely quantity, quality, relation, and modality.[118] Therefore, the book has four chapters, concerning the metaphysical foundations of phoronomy, of dynamics, of mechanics, and of phenomenology. In his explication, Kant followed the mathematical method, "if not with all strictness . . . at least imitatively."[119] For this reason, the chapters are somewhat tediously subdivided into explications (or perhaps better translated, "definitions"), observations about them, propositions, principle(s), and proofs. This structure makes it difficult to summarize the argument of the book.

In his first chapter, Kant offers explications or definitions of matter, motion, rest, and composite motion, and he formulates the following principle: "Every motion as object of a possible experience can be viewed at will either as a motion of a body in space that is at rest, or as rest of the body and motion of the space in the opposite direction with equal velocity."[120] Kant deals with "phoronomy," that is, with matter conceived purely kinematically without regard to the causes of motion. Defining matter as "the movable in space," he uses the occasion to differentiate between a "space which is itself movable" that "is called material, or . . . relative space," and space "in which all motion must ultimately be thought . . . which . . . is called pure, or also absolute, space."[121]

In the second chapter, which is concerned with the metaphysical foundations of dynamics, that is, with forces as the cause of motion, Kant deals with the concept of matter being guided by the categories of reality, negation, and limitation. He first defines matter as "the movable in space insofar as it fills space," explicating the notion of "filling a space" as resistance to "everything movable that strives by its motion to press into a certain space."[122] This gives rise to Proposition 1: "Matter fills a space, not by its mere existence, but by a special moving force."[123] The six definitions and seven propositions that follow spell out the consequences of this "metaphysical-dynamical" conception of matter. Thus he defines attractive and repulsive forces, and finds that matter fills space by the repulsive force (Proposition 2). He then argues that matter can be compressed to infinity, but is impenetrable (Proposition 3). He is attacking Descartes, among others, in Proposition 3. Descartes had argued that extension entails what Kant calls "absolute impenetrability."[124] He then tries to show that matter is infinitely divisible (Proposition 4), that the force of attraction is necessary for the possibility of matter as well (Propositions 5 and 6), that attraction is an immediate action of one material body upon another through empty space (Proposition 7), and that there is an original attractive force that is infinitely extended throughout the universe (Proposition 8).

Kant believed that he had succeeded in showing that everything real in objects of the external senses that is not simply a spatial characteristic "must be regarded as force." Therefore he also believed that he had "banished from natural science as an empty concept" the idea of solid or absolute impenetrability.[125] Because the "mechanical mode of explanation . . . under the name of atomistic or corpuscular philosophy" depends on the concept of absolute impenetrability, that is, absolute hardness, he also believed that he had disproved it. This theory might be "very convenient for mathematics," and it might have been very influential from Democritus to Descartes, but it does not make sense.[126] This of course also has consequences for Kant's understanding of the theory of Newton and his followers. Since this theory involves atomism, Kant must reject this aspect of Newtonianism. But Kant's idea of force captures another aspect of Newton's thought, namely, his insistence on universal gravitation. Kant may be seen as trying to save the Newtonians from their own misunderstandings.[127]

In the third chapter, on the metaphysical foundations of mechanics, Kant defines matter as movable just insofar as it has "a moving force."[128] That is, he supplements the definition of the second chapter, which would hold even if matter were at rest. It is here that Kant introduces and attempts to prove the laws of motion. Though Kant's laws of motion are related to Newton's three laws of motion, Propositions 2, 3, and 4 do not correspond exactly to Newton's First, Second, and Third Laws of Motion. Although Kant calls his Proposition 2 the "first law of mechanics," it is not Newton's First Law – nor his second or third – but the principle of the conservation of "quantity of matter (i.e., mass). Kant's Proposition 3 (what he calls the "second law of mechanics") is almost the same as Newton's First Law (the principle of rectilinear inertia). One of the differences between Newton and Kant is that Newton talks about force, whereas Kant says "cause." Kant's Proposition 4 is almost the same as Newton's Third Law. There is no explicit Kantian demonstration of Newton's Second Law.

Kant formulates his laws within a metaphysical rather than a scientific context. This metaphysical context relies heavily on his own epistemological views as developed in the first *Critique.*[129] In Chapter 4, "The Metaphysical Foundations of Phenomenology," Kant defines matter as the movable "insofar as such can be an object of experience."[130] Relying on the distinction between empirical and absolute space, he argues that absolute space is "nothing at all." All motion must have reference to some other empirically given matter. Therefore, absolute motion is absolutely impossible. On the other hand, if all motion must have reference to some other empirically given matter, then this also means that we cannot have a "concept of motion or rest in relative space and valid for every appearance."[131] Yet we need such a concept to make sense of the notion of *relative* space.

Therefore, we must think of absolute space as a regulative idea of reason, or so Kant claims.

Though Kant is a Newtonian as far as science is concerned, his project of providing Newtonian physics with a metaphysical foundation indicates a more Leibnizian bent of mind. Kant's contemporaries did not know what to make of the book. Thus a review of the book that came out three years after its first publication and two years after its second edition remarked with some surprise that until then only one review of the work had appeared.[132] Johann Gottfried Karl Kiesewetter, one of Kant's students, noted as late as 1795 that "hardly anyone" had bothered to work on the *Metaphysical Foundations of Natural Science.*[133] The same might be said of Kant. As soon as he finished writing the manuscript, he turned to other matters.[134]

Kant's Intervention in the Pantheism Dispute: For "Pure Rational Faith"

In July 1780, Lessing admitted to Jacobi – at least according to Jacobi (and only after Lessing's death in February of 1781) – that he was a Spinozist.[135] Such an admission would have been risky, given that Spinoza was thought to be a "satanic atheist," and his pantheistic theory was considered a "monstrous hypothesis." If such an admission had become public, Lessing would most certainly have been embroiled in the greatest controversy of his life. It would have proved that he was not a theist, and that his rationalism had led him to deny the reality of a transcendent God. Jacobi tried to use this and other information from his conversations with Lessing to prove that he had understood the man better than some of his best friends (who included Mendelssohn). Thus he began a correspondence with Mendelssohn about Lessing's alleged Spinozism. Mendelssohn was incredulous and, wanting to save his friend's good name, tried to convince Jacobi that whatever Lessing had said, he could not have meant what Jacobi took him to mean. This correspondence remained private until 1785, when Jacobi heard that Mendelssohn was about to publish a book called *Morgenstunden* (Morning Hours), in which he would also discuss the problem of pantheism and thus respond to Jacobi's claims at least in an indirect way. Afraid that Mendelssohn would reveal their private controversy, Jacobi decided to preempt him by publishing a book, *On the Doctrine of Spinoza in Letters to Mr. Mendelssohn,* which also appeared in 1785 and made public Lessing's alleged confession and Mendelssohn's private letters to Jacobi.

His justification was that this revelation served a greater cause. Lessing was simply more consistent than all the other rationalist thinkers, and his intellectual honesty deserved to be acknowledged for what it was. Indeed, Jacobi argued that Spinozism was no different from any other speculative system; it was just more consistent. Thus "Leibniz–Wolffian philosophy is no less fatalistic than the Spinozistic, and leads the persistent inquirer to the foundations of the latter. Every path of demonstration issues in fatalism" or Spinozism.[136] He also argued that the only alternative was faith.

Jacobi soon found himself severely criticized not just for his indiscretions but also for his views. In particular, he was attacked as an obscurantist who unphilosophically appealed to faith. In 1786, Thomas Wizenmann, a friend of Jacobi's, tried to defend Jacobi, maintaining in his *Die Resultate der Jacobischen und Mendelssohnischen Philosophie von einem Freywilligen* that Mendelssohn's conception of "common sense" and Jacobi's principle of *"Glaube"* were in the final analysis identical.

Kant, who followed the dispute with great interest, was encouraged by the editor of the *Berlinische Monatsschrift* to intervene on Mendelssohn's behalf – especially since Jacobi was claiming that his position was close to Kant's.[137] Kant was willing. He had already written to Herz that he had long planned to write something about Jacobi's oddity (*Grille*).[138] In August 1786 he submitted his essay "What is Orientation in Thinking?" Far from simply defending Mendelssohn against Jacobi, he used the occasion to give another introduction to his own practical philosophy.

Kant took as his point of departure Mendelssohn's heuristic principle (or maxim) that "it is necessary to orientate oneself in speculative reason . . . by means of a certain guideline which he sometimes described as common sense . . . sometimes as healthy reason, and sometimes as plain understanding,"[139] This maxim, Kant argued, undermines not only Mendelssohn's own speculative metaphysics but leads to zealotry and the complete subversion of reason. Kant agreed with Wizenmann: Jacobi's faith and Mendelssohn's common sense amount to one and the same thing. Kant's project was thus to save Mendelssohn from himself, as it were, and to show against Jacobi that reason has the resources necessary for belief. We can orient ourselves by a subjective means, namely by "the feeling of a need which is inherent in reason itself."[140] This need of reason is twofold: it is a theoretical need and a practical need. The first, already explored in the *Critique of Pure Reason,* is expressed by the conditional that says, "if *we wish to pass judgement* on the first causes of things, especially in the ordering of those purposes which are actually present in the world," then we must assume that God exists.[141] But we have a choice in this matter, that is, it is not absolutely necessary to pass judgment on first causes. The practical need of reason, by contrast, is absolutely necessary and not conditional. In this case, Kant claimed, we must pass judgment. "For the purely practical use of reason consists in the formulation of moral laws," which lead "to the idea of the highest good that is possible in the world."[142] This highest good consists of a moral state in the world in which the greatest happiness coincides with the strictest observation of moral rules. It has thus two components for Kant. The first is morality in accordance with the categorical imperative (as already discussed in the *Groundwork*); the second is happiness in proportion to moral worth. But there is no necessary relation between morality and happiness. Indeed, often it seems the case that bad things happen primarily to good people. Nevertheless, we must believe that eventually good deeds will make a difference in the world. Thus reason needs to assume that happiness in proportion to moral worth is possible, even though nature itself cannot be expected to bring it about. Only an intelligent and all-powerful moral agent can be expected to do this. Therefore, the highest good makes it necessary for a moral agent to assume that there is another cause that makes the highest good possible. This can only be a supreme intelligence that has moral concerns, that is, God. Therefore, we must assume the existence of God. The final point is new, and it anticipates a central argument of the *Critique of Practical Reason*.

Kant then went on to point out that this need of reason does not enable us to know that God exists. It only justifies a belief. Still – and this seems to be Kant's most important concern in the essay – this is a rational belief. "Every belief, even of a historical kind must be . . . rational (for reason is always the ultimate touchstone of truth); but a rational belief is one which is based on no other data than those inherent in pure reason."[143] Rational belief is what should take the place of Mendelssohn's "healthy reason." It is what gives us orientation in speculation. This rational belief is not just a belief in certain articles of faith, recommended by reason; it is also a belief in reason itself. Both Jacobi and Mendelssohn seem to have lost this belief, and both have therefore opened the door to zealotry.

Zealotry is inimical to freedom of thought, which is only possible if we submit to reason and its laws. Trying to "emancipate" oneself from reason amounts to throwing away freedom of thought. The "maxim of the independence of reason from its *own need* (i.e., the renunciation of rational belief) is called *unbelief*." This rational unbelief is undesirable and will lead to libertinism or "the principle of no longer acknowledging any duty."[144]

Only if we continue to accept that prerogative of reason that "makes it the greatest good on earth, namely its right to be the ultimate touchstone of truth," only then are we worthy of freedom, and only then can we hope to further the enlightenment not just of individuals but of an era. Mendelssohn ultimately did not trust enough in reason. Jacobi denied reason altogether and opted for faith. In this, he was, as Kant clearly understood, close to his friend Hamann and his former student Herder. Kant pleads with them as "friends of the human race" not to give in to the temptation of irrational fears and hopes and to continue to work against superstition and zealotry, or for Enlightenment. His pleas fell on deaf ears – at least with those who really counted. Mendelssohn, who might have listened, had died before Kant even wrote the essay. Hamann, Herder, Jacobi, and those who were close to them had not just given up hope in the promise of Enlightenment, but had long since embarked on a quest to seek new goals. "Objectivity," a notion so important to Kant, was for them something to be overcome. They were intent on substituting a poetic vision of nature for mere scientific and moralistic reasoning. For Kant, this represented a loss of nerve that could only have bad consequences.[145]

The essay "What Is Orientation?" is closely related to Kant's "Some Remarks on L. H. Jakob's *Examination of the Mendelssohnian Morning Hours*," which appeared as a Preface to Jakob's book in 1786. Jakob approached Kant in March of 1786, asking whether the rumor that Kant was going to write something against Mendelssohn was correct. If it was not, then he, Jakob, would like to undertake that task. Kant answered that the rumor was false, and he encouraged Jakob to proceed, even promising him to contribute to the project.[146] The Preface is the fulfillment of this promise. Kant appears to have sent it to Jakob at about the same time that he sent "What Is Orientation?" to Biester.[147] So he worked on both pieces at the same time.

The Preface takes up the same concerns that Kant expressed in his "What is Orientation." Mendelssohn's appeal to common sense throws into doubt the very enterprise of a critique of pure reason. Kant criticizes two of Mendelssohn's "maxims" in particular, namely his claim that all the disputes between philosophical sects are ultimately nothing but semantic quibbles, and his repeated attempts to silence questions long before they have been properly considered. Using the problem of freedom versus determinism as an example, Kant tries to show that Mendelssohn was wrong in calling it merely a verbal dispute. It is an important issue, even if dogmatic metaphysicians cannot resolve it. To show how Mendelssohn closed the debate on important questions too early, Kant uses a passage of the *Morning Hours* in which Mendelssohn said: "When I tell you what a thing causes or suffers, then do not ask the further question 'What is the thing?' When I tell you what concept you must form of a thing, then the other question 'What is the thing in itself?' does not make any sense." Referring to his own theory as developed in the *Metaphysical Foundations of Nature*, Kant points out that we can only know space, things in space, the spatiality of these things, and motions, that is, external relations. Could someone like Mendelssohn really say that this is the same as knowing the thing in itself? The answer, Kant claims, can only be no. Therefore the question makes sense. We can ask "what this thing in itself is, which in all these relations is the subject."

To be sure,

If we *knew* the effects of a thing which really could be qualities (*Eigenschaften*) of a thing in itself, then we would no longer be permitted to ask what the thing in itself is apart from these qualities, for it is then just what is given by these qualities.[148]

Kant then goes on to say that he will probably now be asked (by Mendelssohnians) to give examples of such qualities that "would permit one to differentiate them and by means of them things in themselves." He answers:

this has long been done – and it was you who did it. Just look at how you obtain the concept of God as the highest intelligence. You think in it only *true* reality, that is, something that is not just the opposite of negations . . . but also and primarily opposed to the realities in the *appearance* (*realitas phaenomenon*), like all the realities which are given to us by the senses and which are therefore called *realitas apparens*. . . . Now, if you diminish all these realities (understanding, will, godliness, power, etc.) by degrees, they still remain always the same as far as their quality is concerned. Thus you get the qualities of the things in themselves, which you can also apply to other things, different from God.[149]

Noting that it is "peculiar" that we can determine our concepts of things in themselves only by first reducing all reality to God, and only then applying it to things themselves, he claims that this is the only way to separate (*Scheidungsmittel*) what is sensible appearance from what can be considered by the understanding as a thing in itself. It pays to pursue questions as far as possible – or so Kant thought.

During this time Kant also worked on his review of Gottlieb Hufeland's *Essay on the Basic Principle of Natural Law* (Leipzig, 1785).[150] It appeared in the *Allgemeine Literatur-Zeitung* of April 1786. Kant had been sent the book by the author in October 1785, and then been asked by the editor of the journal to review it.[151] He liked the book. After a short and complimentary summary, he focused on what he took to be one of the author's principal points, namely, his view that "principles which concern only the form of the free will without regard for any object" are insufficient for "practical law and thus also for the derivation of obligatoriness."[152] Hufeland argued that this deficiency could be supplied by the principle that enjoins human beings to seek the perfection of all rational beings. Kant then went on to report that the main characteristic of the author's system was the claim that all natural rights are founded in a prior natural obligation. Yet Hufeland also claimed that the doctrine of obligation does not really belong to that of natural right, something with which Kant disagreed. It should be clear that Kant could not agree to most of what Hufeland had to say. Nevertheless, he was content simply to summarize his views, saying it would be "inappropriate" for him to object on the basis of his own views – something that, curiously enough, did not hold him back in most of his other reviews and essays from this period.[153]

Another project that occupied Kant during this time was the second edition of the *Critique of Pure Reason,* which appeared in 1787. As early as April 7, 1786, Kant had written that the book, "against all expectations," was entirely sold out and that a new edition might appear within half a year. It would be "new and much revised," in order to clear up some of the misunderstandings that had arisen. "Much will be shortened, some new materials, which will serve a better explanation will be added." But "changes in the essential I will not have to make because I thought about these matter long enough before I put them on paper. Furthermore, I also repeatedly reviewed and examined all the claims that belong to the system, and I always found them to be confirmed in their relation to the whole."[154] He also told the correspondent that he would have to wait to work out his system of metaphysics in order to win time for the system of moral philosophy, a sister project, and one far easier to complete than the first.

The work on the revisions of the first *Critique* was more difficult than Kant had imagined. In any case, he complained to Hamann about how difficult (*schwer*) they were in early January of 1787, only to send them off to the publisher two weeks later.[155] The new Preface, dated April 1787, was written later – probably after the proofs had arrived. But, despite the difficulties (or perhaps because of them), the revisions of the first *Critique* turned out to be less extensive than Kant himself had envisioned eight months earlier. There was a new motto, a new Preface, a partially revised Introduction, a new version of the Transcendental Deduction, a Refutation of Idealism, a new version of the chapter on the paralogisms, a partial revision of the chapter on phenomena and noumena, and a number of minor changes and additions. All of these changes were designed to make the book easier and to play down the "idealistic" component of the work. There was also a slightly greater emphasis on moral and religious problems, which can be explained by Kant's more clearly formulated concerns about these matters during the years between the first publication of the *Critique of Pure Reason* and the second edition. However, on the whole, the work remained the same.

Kant's philosophical theories were being discussed in Königsberg. Especially his moral philosophy seems to have been the focus of attention of some. Thus Hamann went on April 17, 1787, to a church service where Karl Gottlieb Fischer (1745–1801), one of Kant's earliest students in Königsberg, was preaching on the Sermon of the Mount and arguing that the command "Do not judge!" really meant "Be gentle in judging!" This also meant for Fischer that we must realize that we can judge only actions and not dispositions or *Gesinnungen*. "*Gesinnungen* cannot be judged."[156] With this, Fischer might seem to have taken a position opposite to that of Kant. Yet insofar as Kant also claimed that we could not really know our dispositons, they were not as far apart as they might seem. Whether Kant would have appreciated this sermon as much as Hamann is doubtful, although he generally did like to read Fischer's "carefully crafted" sermons.[157]

Critique of Practical Reason: "The Starry Heavens above Me and the Moral Law within Me"

The *Critique of Practical Reason* carries a publication date of 1788. However, copies of the work were already available in Königsberg at Christmas of 1787, and Kant had finished the manuscript almost six months earlier. On June 25, 1787, Kant wrote to Schütz: "I have finished my *Critique of Practical Reason* so far that I think I will send it next week to the printer in Halle."[158] He went on to say that this work was better suited than any other to deal with his critics. He mentioned Feder and Abel, but he had in mind others who had criticized him as well.[159] Feder's *On Space and Causality*, which had appeared earlier that year in Göttingen, was an attempt to prove against Kant that there could be no a priori knowledge.[160] J. F. Abel's *Plan of a Systematic Metaphysics* (Stuttgart, 1787) was an unsystematic and eclectic theory that was, according to Kant, designed to establish a kind of knowledge that was supposed to be somewhere in the middle, between a priori and empirical knowledge.[161] He also informed Schütz that he would not review the third part of Herder's *Ideas* because he had to "work on the *Foundation of the Critique of Taste*."[162]

The second *Critique* follows the main outlines of the first. It has a long first part, entitled "Doctrine of the Elements of Pure Practical Reason," and a short "Doctrine of the Method of Pure Practical Reason." The first part is divided into an Analytic and a Dialectic. It also has a Deduction, a Typic (corresponding to the schematism in the first *Critique*), as well as an Antinomy. But the second *Critique*, and especially the Analytic, also shares some characteristics with the mathematical method of the *Metaphysical Foundations of Natural Science*. There are definitions, theorems and problems, and observations, though deduction seems to be substituted for proof. It is not always clear whether the subject matter demands the divisions and the methodical treatment Kant provides for it, or whether this is due to Kant's forced attempts to make the second *Critique* conform to the first. But the work does succeed in clarifying the concerns of the *Foundations* and of the more popular essays and reviews that preceded it.

According to the *Groundwork*, moral philosophy has three tasks: (1) to identify and establish "the supreme principle of morality," (2) to examine pure practical reason critically, and (3) to establish a metaphysics of morals.[163] Kant believed he had accomplished the first task in the *Groundwork*, and he thought in 1785 that the other two tasks could be accomplished easily in another work to be entitled the *Critique of Practical Reason*. Since the metaphysics of morals was "capable of a high degree of popularity and adaptation to the common human understanding," the third task would be easy enough. But the second task turned out to be much more complicated than he had thought, and so the second *Critique* accomplished no more than the second task. The *Metaphysics of Morals* had to wait for another day.

Whereas much of his theoretical work was concerned with showing that reason has much less power than had been assumed by his rationalistic predecessors, Kant's moral philosophy may be seen as an attempt to show that morality is the exclusive domain of reason. Since "freedom" is also one of the basic ideas to which theoretical reason leads us, it forms the point at which the two *Critiques* come together. Kant believes that the second *Critique* shows that "freedom" is a genuine concept, that is, not a mere thought, but something that has a genuine foundation in morality. Nevertheless, Kant insists that we cannot know ourselves to be free in any strict sense. It is our moral experience, or perhaps better, the experience of our morality, that gives us the right to believe in the reality of freedom. Furthermore, morality and freedom also give us the right to believe in the reality of two other ideas of reason, namely those of "God" and "Immortality." He argues that we must "postulate" the reality of these ideas in order to be able to act as moral beings in this world. Without immortality and God, we would be condemned to moral despair. Moral action should lead to greater good in this world, but it usually does not. Happiness and worthiness to be happy do not usually go together in this world. If we want to establish a connection between the two, we must assume that they will be made to coincide by God in the long run. In this way, the notions of "God" and "immortality," as prerequisites for the realization of the *summum bonum* or the highest good, make possible the moral enterprise for Kant, and therefore we must believe in their reality.

All these ideas are anticipated in prior works. Here they are just revised, expanded, and put into what Kant takes to be their systematic context. Thus the Analytic explicates first the central issues of the *Groundwork*, that is, the notions of a categorical imperative, freedom, and autonomy. It then goes on to deduce the principles of pure practical reason, that is, the moral law as "a law of causality through freedom and hence a law of the possibility of supersensible nature."[164] Kant then shows that we have a right in the practical context to extend our concepts beyond the sphere that is delimited in the theoretical and speculative context. While this is not an extension of knowledge, it is not blind belief either. In the Dialectic he develops this idea, which he had already introduced in "What Is Orientation?" and in his remarks on Jakob's *Examination*. We are allowed to postulate the immortality of the soul and God's existence, because they are required by morality and in particular by the possibility of the highest good. This means that belief in God is based in the nature of morality, and so we cannot justify morality with reference to God. In a famous passage Kant says:

> Two things fill the mind with ever new and increasing admiration and reverence the more often and more steadily one reflects on them: *the starry heavens above me and the moral law within me.* I do not need to search for them and merely conjecture them as though they were veiled in obscurity or in the transcendent region beyond my horizon; I see them before me and connect them immediately with the consciousness of my existence.[165]

It is our autonomy that is the basis of the moral law, not God's commands or demands on us. The "upright man may well say: I *will* that there is a God, that my existence in this world be also the existence in a pure world of the understanding beyond natural connections, and finally that my duration is endless."[166] From the point of view of traditional theology, Kant turned things upside down.

Kant and His Colleagues and Friends:
"Fired Up by Prejudices?"

In the winter semester of 1785–86 Kant was dean again. One of the more significant events was the application of Isaac Abraham Euchel (1756–1804), one of Kant's students, to be allowed to teach oriental languages at the university, that is, to obtain the degree of *Magister*. Kant supported the application on the basis of Euchel's excellent knowledge of the languages, knowing full well that the theological faculty would not like to see a Jew teach a subject central for them.[167] The application failed simply because Euchel was Jewish. A similar attempt by Baczko, a former student of Kant, also found Kant's support. It also failed. As a Catholic, Baczko could not become *Magister* either. Hamann wrote:

> A certain Mr. Von Baczko, who is blind and lame but has an active and restless head, has written a history of Prussia and wants to become *Magister*. But he is a Roman Catholic, and they cannot be accepted in accordance with the statutes. This man gets loud and is insistent; he even threatened the Minister von Zedlitz with public insults because he did not answer his letters . . .[168]

All in all, this was not a pleasant situation.

Again he came into conflict with Metzger, who was doing his best to become rector during that year. Metzger was confident, but Kant resisted his attempts, and in the end Metzger did not succeed.[169] In the following semester, the summer of 1786, it was Kant's turn to become the rector of the university for the first time.[170] To obtain this position, one had to be a member of the senate. The position of rector changed every semester, with the ten senior members of the senate taking regular turns. Kant had become one of the ten "seniors," which included the four most senior members of the philosophical faculty, only in 1780.[171] It appears that Kant did not object when it was argued by some in 1786 that he should not become rector because the complicated system regulating the turns did not favor him.[172] Kant himself seems to have believed that it was not his turn, and it took some effort by Kraus to prove to everyone's satisfaction that Kant should be rector.[173] Hamann reported to Jacobi in this connection that Kant "acted in this matter in a very noble philosophical way, which did honor to his good character, which no one can deny him."[174] At the ceremony during which Kant assumed the office and gave a speech, a former student, who suffered from mental illness, interrupted him. Just as the student had gotten up on the podium beside Kant and was beginning to read his announcement, he was forcibly removed by "a superior number of hands."[175]

Kant found the position of rector burdensome. One of the things he had to do during this time was to prepare and lead the ceremonies of the university at the occasion of the inauguration of Frederick William II on September 19, 1786.[176] This involved a great deal of pomp and circumstance. On September 18, he and some other members of the university senate had an audience with the king, but he did not go to the actual ceremony at the university. Why he did not go is unknown.

Kant also had to see to the distribution of free passes and coins made for the occasion of the inauguration. Kant let the senate decide by vote, and he only offered the advice not to allow any rabble to attend the festivities. Metzger, with whom Kant had had a run-in during the previous semester, found it necessary to note in his protocol of the activities to the senate that Kant failed to do a number of things in regard to the festivities. He had not invited all the professors and emeritus professors to a church service in honor of Frederick the Great; he had not asked the senate to ratify which senators were to attend the king's audience; and the members of the senate who went to the inauguration festivities had not been properly elected. Kant's procedure had been chaotic (*tumultarisch*), and he had not followed due course and proper procedures.[177] This was not the only dispute. As rector, he also came into conflict with the Jewish community in Königsberg about having held up the collection of money for a memorial picture that was to be put up in memory of Mendelssohn. Hamann said that Kant was upset about these allegations and let the Jewish community know that, by law, it was the Jews alone who should bear the cost for a memorial of one of their own.[178]

Kant was not the most effective administrator. Hippel observed that, while the philosopher could recite long passages from mathematical and philosophical books "almost verbatim or verbatim" and memorize name registers with lightning speed, he could not even keep track of three different things in administration.[179] One of the earliest biographers observed:

His other academic business as dean of the faculty of philosophy and as a member of the senate, remained of secondary importance compared with that of teaching and writing. Kant did not especially distinguish himself in this regard. Not that he considered these matters as unimportant. No! But they required a kind of statutory knowledge that he never had the desire to acquire in its full extent. They also required a kind of business-like life that he was incapable of living. This was the reason why in such cases he dealt with these matters routinely when he had to act on his own. But when it was a matter of the academic community, he went along with the plurality vote."[180]

Kant, according to this view, did not assume a leading role in the university. Hippel, who said that Kant and Kraus might be great scholars but that they were incapable of "ruling a land, a village, or even a chicken coop – not even a chicken coop," clearly believed that this was the case.[181]

This is an exaggeration. To be sure, measured by Hippel's own organizational talents, Kant fell short. Yet even if Kant did not know how to rule, he knew how to influence people within the university context; and if he never "contradicted the plurality vote," it was perhaps because he was at least to some extent responsible for the way the vote went. It was no accident that most of the major appointments to the faculty of philosophy at the University of Königsberg after Kant's promotion to full professor were such that he either did or could have endorsed them. It was no accident that his students Kraus and Pörschke were later his colleagues. It was not an accident that the court preacher Schulz, his staunchest defender, received a professorship in mathematics, and that the entire philosophical faculty thus acquired a more and more Kantian outlook. Kant took an active interest in this outcome. He pulled strings to get the results he desired, and he knew what he was doing.

He also took an interest in other matters, such as the status of the poor, the relation of the university to the military offices, and in the role of the faculty of medicine in the university.[182] Administrative matters, without doubt, were of secondary concern to him. Yet this does not mean that they were unimportant as far as he was concerned. As we will see, they were a significant part of his life, not only because they took up much of his time, but also because some issues were important from his enlightened point of view.[183]

Hamann, Kraus, Hippel, and others called him "the theoretician." Frederick William II thought highly of the "theoretician" at this point. He not only arranged through the count of Herzberg to meet Kant, but he also gave him a yearly bonus of 220 Thalers from his own account.[184] At the end of 1786, Kant became a member of the Academy of Sciences in Berlin.[185] Some of Metzger's frustration had to do with just this.

Rink, who was a student of Kant from the summer semester of 1786 on, described Kant's relation to his colleagues as follows:

Kant never needed those mean-spirited devices to get students that are regrettably still common at the university today. Never did he belittle his colleagues, never did he want to impress by rodomontades, never did he seek approval by making questionable jokes and sexual innuendo. . . . I still feel insulted when I remember how an otherwise honorable man, who was once present as a witness, and who saw and heard all this himself, could allow himself to be carried away by passion and put the character of this noble sage into a different and less positive light. . . . Peace be with the ashes of both. Both were searching for the truth, though each in a very different way; here they did not meet as sister stars; there they will.

His colleagues were never and especially in earlier times (*durchweg und in älteren Zeiten*) as peaceable toward him as Kant was toward them. Yet there were only a few who felt they were over-shadowed by him. . . . Since his unquestionable good character did not offer any target . . . they aimed at his religious principles. . . . But all his younger colleagues, most of whom had been his students, loved and honored him.[186]

Kant still taught almost every day, but after 1787 he gave only four hours of public lectures and four hours of private lectures a week.[187] Even if his lectures were no longer exciting, his fame and his role in the university assured that he had many students. His lectures were packed. Students had to come an hour early in order to reserve a place in his lecture room.[188] Some of his most important students during this time were Hamann's son, Johann Michael (1769–1813), and Jachmann, his amanuensis and later biographer. Once, Kant planned to use Schulz's *Exposition* as his textbook in metaphysics, but he never did so.[189] He liked to lecture on rational theology – and especially if there were many theologians among his listeners. He "hoped that especially from this course, in which he spoke so clearly and convincingly, the bright light of rational religious convictions would spread though his entire fatherland, and he was not deceived, for many apostles went from there and taught the gospel of the realm of reason."[190]

By this time, age had already taken its toll. Kant, now in his early sixties, suffered from a number of ailments. None of them were serious. Still, taken together, they made life bothersome and teaching more difficult. Thus Rink observed that at this time Kant could no longer see well with one of his eyes (thinking it was probably the left), and that he constantly complained about the fad of using gray paper in books rather than white and said that the print was often much too faint.[191] Kant also had serious problems with digestion. Indeed, Hamann found that this problem "was one of the most important anecdotes with which the critic entertains his morning guests, which he even must retell the count Keyserlingk before dinner, much to the hearty laughter of my satirical friend . . ."[192]

Despite such problems, Kant's public demeanor was nothing if not proper. Reusch, the son of one of Kant's colleagues, reported that students watched when

> Kant walked across the square of the *Albertinum* to go to a senate meeting, or some academic festivity. . . . He was always very cleanly dressed. His serious face, somewhat tilted to the side, and his regular gait not too slow, drew respectfully admiring looks. . . . The light sand-colored coat, which later was replaced by one of a deeper brown, should not be thought remarkable. Light colors of all kinds were in vogue then, and black coats were reserved for funerals and mourning. In warm days he went, according to the fashion of the day, with his hat on the golden knob of his wooden staff. His head was adorned with a finely powdered wig. Silk stockings and shoes also belonged to the usual outfit of a well-dressed gentleman. . . . But when, after the act of inaugurating the rector, the new rector and the professors, all in the order of the different faculties, walked to the cathedral, Kant would walk past the entrance of the church, unless he had just become rector himself.[193]

Religious observances played no part of his life. In conversations Kant would say: "I do not understand the catechism, but I once did understand it."[194]

Kant was gaining a reputation, not just in Königsberg, as an atheist.[195] He himself was reported to have feared that he could lose his position.[196] Indeed, his *Critique of Pure Reason* was becoming notorious. By this time, there had already been books written for and against Kant. There had been Schulz's *Exposition* (1784), K. Chr. Schmid's *Lexicon for the Easier Use of Kant's Critique* (1786), and his *Extract from Kant's Critique of Reason* (1786).[197] Johann Bering taught Kant's philosophy in Marburg, though this was almost immediately prohibited by a government order.[198] In Halle, it was Jakob who taught Kant's works. In Göttingen, Feder and Christoph Meiners were arguing against Kant. In many other places, Kant's philosophy was hotly debated. Mendelssohn had referred in his influential *Morning Hours* of 1785 to the "all-crushing" Kant. The volume of literature for and against Kant was increasing exponentially. By 1786, Kant was famous, if not infamous. His philosophy, difficult as it is, was in vogue.

Some of his contemporaries were very upset. They accused Kant of spreading a dangerous philosophy. Just as there were people in Königsberg who thought that Kant's philosophy had made a young student insane, there were philosophers at other universities who drew similar conclusions. Meiners wrote in the Preface to his *Outline of Psychology* of 1786:

> Anyone who has had occasion to notice the impression which the Kantian writings have made upon young people will really feel the truth of the remarks which Beattie made on the occasion of similar experiences: nothing is more injurious to taste and good judgment that the subtleties of the older and newer metaphysicians, which favor verbal disputes and lead to nothing but doubt and obscurity. These musings exhaust the power

of the spirit without reason, deaden the love of true learning, draw the attention away from the concerns of human life as well as from the works of art and nature which warm the heart and heighten the imagination. Finally, they unsettle the powers of the understanding, spoil good principles, and poison the source of human happiness.[199]

It could not be denied that there were signs this was true. Thus in Jena two students fought a duel because one had accused the other of not understanding the *Critique,* claiming that he needed to study it for thirty years before he could hope to understand it and then for another thirty years before being allowed to comment on it.[200]

Kant himself was almost as passionate. He still was not the picture of predictability and regularity that his surviving friends would later present. In April 1786, just after Mendelssohn died, Kant was present at a dinner party at which Mendelssohn's philosophical talents were impugned. Kant had always thought highly of Mendelssohn, and he rose to his defense. He spoke of his "original genius (*Originalgenie*) and his *Jerusalem* almost to the point of enthusiasm. The first he is reported to have seen in the skill with which Mendelssohn was able to make every circumstance useful to himself, and to put every hypothesis into the best possible light." Things seem to have gotten out of hand, and the verbal exchange became so heated "that Kant left full of ill will, and behaved almost rudely and uncivilly against the bank director Ruffman." Even Hippel, Kant's good friend, "was amazed and not very satisfied."[201] Hippel had a right to be unhappy, as he was the host of the party. Hamann took this occasion to characterize Kant, saying:

Kant is a man whose talents are just as great as his intentions (*Gesinnungen*) are good and honorable. So he gets very much fired up by prejudices, but he is not ashamed to deny them, to abolish them, and to swear them off. He only has to be given some time to reflect for himself. He likes talking better than listening. *In puncto* of his system and the fame he has acquired through it, he is at the moment rather sensitive and more presumptuous, as you can imagine yourself. But that is not entirely his fault, but for the most part the fault of the dear public.[202]

The incident reveals Kant's loyalty to a dead friend's memory. It also shows Kant was not the cold fish, the well-regulated machine that he would later gain the reputation of having been. He did not live his life mechanically. Hamann, who should know, reports that by nature he was passionate and impulsive – both in the way in which he lived his life and in the way in which he philosophized. The regularity with which he lived his life did not come easy to him. It was a difficult achievement. The same may be said of his philosophy.

To say that "the trouble with Kant" was that he was "a wild and intellectually irresponsible arguer," whose "innate leaning that way must have been enhanced by the intellectual isolation of Königsberg, which must have preserved him from serious criticism," is clearly an exaggeration.[203] For one thing, Königsberg was not intellectually isolated, and for another, his arguments are not all that bad. The mature Kant was not any more a wild thinker than any other philosopher. But he started out as a wild thinker. His critical philosophy was just as much the result of self-discipline as was his moral character. It was also more than that, raising, at the very least, "a lot of fascinating questions."[204] Hamann said that he had "fought many a hard fight with Kant," and that at times had been "obviously wrong" and perhaps had even wronged Kant. Yet "Kant still remained my friend in spite of this."[205] He could abstract from differences in philosophical argument in his friendships, and he was a loyal friend. That the dispute with Herder ended in bitter enmity was probably not of his choosing. Kant was proud of his achievement, and he was affected by his hard-earned fame as a writer. If we can believe Hamann, then "his pride [was] of the most innocent kind in the world."[206] Herder's pride was not quite so innocent, as some of his nasty comments about Kant show.

It was during this time that Herz, another one of Kant's former students, sent him a book, *Über den Schwindel* (On Dizziness). Kant seems to have been indifferent. He did not read it and had the book put onto the shelves as soon as it arrived, saying that he was not suffering from dizziness.[207] Borowski suggested that Kant was no longer Herz's friend and surmised that "Kant certainly never read the dedication, even though he knew from Herz's letter that there was one."[208] Borowski's suggestion that Kant was no longer Herz's friend, based on a sarcastic quip by Kant, need not necessarily be taken seriously.[209] The exemplar Herz had sent did not have a dedication. Kant's indifference was the result of his lack of interest in purely psychological questions.

He also offered financial support to some of his former students who had become friends. Jachmann, for instance, said that when his brother went to study medicine in Edinburgh, Kant offered 500 Thalers to him, which he, however, never took advantage of. Kant apparently was disappointed.[210]

On the other hand, Kant also expected things from his friends. Thus he enlisted the help of Kraus in an attempt to defend his philosophy against Meiners's allegations that his philosophy led to immorality. Kraus wrote in December of 1786 that he was working on "a defense of his friend Kant, who was bitterly insulted by Meiners in Göttingen, and who asked me to write an apologia."[211] This was to take the form of a review of Meiners's *Outline of the History of Philosophy*. Kraus tried several times to say no. But Kant did not let up, and so finally Kraus accepted the task.[212] Apparently, like all attempts at writing something original, "it cost him frightful strain and so much time that someone else might have been able to write an important book in it."[213] He began his review in the middle of December 1786, but he finished it only some time in early March of 1787. While he was proud of the review as a "true piece of bravura" (*Kunststück*), he also said that Kant had really "forced him" to write it.[214] Meiners had tried to explain away Kant's (still fairly recent) success as an aberration, claiming that if the public knew the history of philosophy better, they would not fall for his critical philosophy. Kraus criticized Meiners's history as unreliable and explained Kant's "unexpected" success by saying that it showed the philosophical public agreed with Kant. The review appeared in the first week of April. Kraus told Hamann later that month that Kant had not been satisfied with the review, that he had changed it, and he offered to provide him with a reconstruction of the review "as he had intended or written it."[215] So Kant was not above putting a great deal of pressure on a friend to further the cause of his critical philosophy. Such pressure could only strain the friendship.

Nor was Kraus the only one on whom Kant put pressure. The court chaplain Schulz, who had published an *Exposition of Kant's Critique of Pure Reason* in 1784, was also pressed into service in the fight for the *Critique*. Schulz was more willing. In any case, Schulz published at least seven reviews on Kant and works relevant to Kant in the *Allgemeine Literatur-Zeitung* during the years following the publication of his *Exposition*.[216] But Kant's relationship with Schulz was not without strains either. Thus Kant was upset when Schulz published on December 13, 1785, a review of J. A. H. Ulrich's *Institutiones logicae et metaphysicae* in the *Allgemeine Literatur-Zeitung*. The work was important, for it contained criticisms of the Transcendental Deduction. The reviewer had added his own doubts, and Kant did not like it. In a long footnote to his *Metaphysical Foundations of Natural Science*, he answered:

I find doubts expressed in the review of professor Ulrich's *Institutiones* . . . not against [the] table of the pure concepts of the understanding, but to the conclusions drawn therefrom as to the limitations of the whole faculty of pure reason and therefore all metaphysics. In these doubts the deeply probing reviewer declares himself to be in agreement with his no less examining author. Since these doubts are supposed to touch the main foundation of my system . . . they should be reasons for thinking that my system . . . far from carried with it that apodictic conviction requisite for compelling an unqualified acceptance.[217]

Hamann wrote to Herder on April 4, 1786, that Kant had been "in an extraordinarily bad mood" about the review, but that Schulz had defused the situation by visiting Kant first. They had a long conversation, and they parted on friendly terms. "The clergyman had looked into the philosopher's cards and Kant . . . was more bitter in the heat of the moment than he himself would have liked. This weakness was betrayed by his amanuensis and was afterwards covered up. In any case, Kant is in spite of his impetuousness (*Lebhaftigkeit*) a naïve (*treuherzig*) and innocent man. But he is just as little able to keep silent as Jachmann, who is of the same sort and also a very young and sanguine person."[218] Schulz, who had been a lecturer at the university for the longest time, became professor of mathematics in 1786.

The Death of His Best Friend and the Consequences: A "Changed . . . Way of Life"

It is often assumed that Kant's life changed when he bought his own house, and that he no longer went out in the evening but sought society only in the afternoon.[219] Part of the reason for this was not his change of residence (in 1783) but the death of his best friend Green on June 27, 1786.[220] During the final months Kant was "very worried about his old friend Green, with whom he is every day punctually until 7:00 P.M. and on Saturdays until 9:00 P.M. He is as much as accounted for; and he is incapable of leaving his bed, where alone he finds life bearable."[221] Green's death "changed Kant's way of life to such an extent that he never attended another societal event in the evening (*Abendgesellschaft*), and that he entirely gave up evening meals. It appeared as if he wished to spend the time of day that was previously devoted (*geheiligt*) to the most intimate friendship as a sacrifice to his close friend (*Busenfreund*) quietly alone until the end of his life."[222] Just as the death of Funk had led to a fundamental change in Kant's life, so now the death of Green led to new changes. Though he still went to Motherby's house every Sunday, and though he had many other friends, he lived a much more withdrawn life from now on. It is almost as if a part of himself died with his friend; he seemed to withdraw from the kinds of activities that they had enjoyed together. This is also the time at which Kant began set up "his own economy." He no longer took his meals outside the house, but hired a cook and began to give dinner parties at his home. There can be little doubt that he did this to continue the tradition started by Green. Kant did not embark on this new venture alone. He asked Kraus, his former student and closest colleague, to participate.[223] The practice began on Easter 1787. At first, they would be alone, but gradually the invited circle of friends grew larger. The first guests were Hamann and his children. They had wanted to visit Kraus, but were told by Lampe, whom they met on the way, that Kraus was with Kant. Accordingly, they went to Kant's house: "We found the two bachelors in a cold room, completely frozen, and Kant ordered right away a *bouteille* of good wine. . . . When I have to drink one glass, I cannot easily stop. Kraus was sitting there like a poor sinner, he had hardly eaten half of his small portion . . ."[224]

Hamann invited himself more than once during 1787.[225] But he left Königsberg at the beginning of 1788 to go to Münster and Düsseldorf, where he had great admirers. The main reason was his desire to get personally acquainted with Jacobi. Hamann died soon after he left, in Münster. Kraus was devastated.[226] Kant, who never had become a close friend of Hamann and who usually met him because they were part of the same circle of friends, was less affected.

Others who were regularly invited were Hippel, Jensch, Scheffner, Vigilantius, Karl Gottfried Hagen, Dr. Rink, professor Pörschke, professor Gensichen, bank director Ruffmann, city inspector Brahl, Pastor Sommer, candidate Ehrenboth, Motherby, and the brothers Jachmann.[227] They were all leading citizens of Königsberg, and they included high government officials, preachers, and merchants. The complexion of this little society or club changed as some of his friends died and others were invited. When Kant died, there were still about twenty-four of his *Tischfreunde*, who followed his coffin.[228] These were the people with whom he spent most of his time during his last years. They knew him better then anyone else alive at that time, though they did not know him very well, as the dinners were in the end rather formal occasions.

Kant was always elegantly dressed and took great care of his external appearance, but Kraus did not pay much attention to such matters. He let himself go and was often seen in old and worn-out clothes, which were frequently soiled by tobacco stains from Kraus's snuff.

When he shared his table with Kant and also went more frequently to other social occasions without thinking of replacing his badly worn clothes with better ones, Kant once took the occasion to steer the conversation to clothes and said to Kraus: 'Listen,

Herr Professor, you should now really have a new coat made for yourself.' Kraus took
the philosopher's suggestion very well, and with fun and wit the conversation continued by discussing as an important matter the color, the material, and the cut of his new
clothes; and within a few days Kant received his newly clad Kraus with praise and
laughter.[229]

Apparently, it was not only Kant who reminded Kraus to take care of his
clothes. Even his own students made a point of telling him that he could
not go to official occasions dressed as he was.

When these two philosophers went together on their walks through
Königsberg, which they frequently did, they were "the object of amaze-
ment." Kraus and Kant looked very much the same. Both were short and
very lean. They looked like brothers, but their manners were different.
Kant was deliberate and hardly ever showed his emotion. Kraus was lively
and animated, a fast speaker, who was quick to laugh even at his own jokes.
Kraus also liked to walk quickly, but when he went with Kant they proceeded at a slow pace. Kant had his head almost always turned toward the
ground and tilted to one side. His wig was almost always out of order and
lying on his shoulder. This complemented Kraus's usually disheveled appearance. The pair must have been the very picture of two absent-minded
professors.

Kant and Kraus had quite different ideas about philosophy, but it appears that they thought – Kant especially – that their theories were complementary rather than opposed. Kant was the theoretician, whose philosophy Kraus thought was "pure speculation, which floats, as it were, above
life, and considers life only in a speculative concern." Kraus thought that
Kant was "the greatest master of his time." But he also felt that philosophy
needed to be applied to real life. He was the practical philosopher, interested in economics and law. So in his courses on moral philosophy he taught
in accordance with David Hume and Adam Smith. He also taught many
other courses on practical matters, such as economics and applied mathematics. Many felt that Kant and Kraus formed the two poles for study at
the university of Königsberg. Each contributed something important, and
together they gave to the students salutary philosophical balance.

Kant liked Kraus very much.[230] Jachmann, who should have known because he was Kant's amanuensis during this period, describes it as follows:

Kant was an especially honorable friend of Kraus. He spoke almost daily of him with
expressions of true devotion, and he assured me that he admired the learnedness
and the zeal of the great man for the common good just as much as his character. That

the friendship of the two men was intimate and close can already be seen from the fact that professor Kraus was Kant's companion at table until Kraus set up his own household.[231]

Yet this is somewhat misleading. Kraus was "not a guest at Kant's table; he ate there every day and he paid his part." Furthermore, it "did not last very long," and the reason was not so much that Kraus set up his own household, but rather that the two had a falling out.[232]

Kant's social dinners were also a way of combating loneliness. They were the high points of his day, and he always anxiously awaited his guests. Usually three or four of his friends were invited, and sometimes – especially in later years – Kant invited those who had come to see the famous philosopher in Königsberg. Hasse described how he waited for his guests at 1:00 P.M., often still sitting at his work desk, but sometimes already turned toward the door:

Wherever or however he was sitting, his face was clear, his eyes lively and his demeanor friendly, even if he did not quite fulfill the anxious expectation of those who saw him for the first time. And when he talked, he uttered oracles indeed and was bewitching. Now he reminded his servant to serve, handed out himself the silver spoons from his secretary, and was hurrying with everything he had to say to the table. His guests preceded him to the dining room, which was just as unadorned and simple as the other rooms. One sat down without ceremony, and when someone was getting ready to say grace or to pray, he interrupted them by telling them to sit down. Everything was neat and clean. Only three dishes, but excellently prepared and very tasty, two bottles of wine, and when in season there was fruit and dessert. Everything had its determinate order. After the soup was served and almost eaten, the meat – usually beef that was especially tender – was carved. He took it, like most dishes, with English mustard, which he prepared himself. The second dish had to be one of his favorite foods (almost every day the same thing). He ate so long and so much of this until his last days that he filled up his belly with it, as he said. Of the roast beef and the third dish, he ate little. When he was taking his soup, and he found the meat in it nice and tender, he was extremely happy (and if not, he complained and was somewhat upset); and then he said: Now, my gentlemen and friends! Let us also talk a little. What's new?

He preferred that the mealtime was devoted to relaxation and liked to disregard learned matters. At times he even cut off such associations. He most loved to talk about political things. Indeed, he almost luxuriated in them. He also wanted to converse about city news and matters of common life.[233]

This could take a long time. Someone who visited him during the nineties observed that "Kant could sit till seven or eight in the evening, if only someone stayed with him."[234] Kraus, on whom Kant relied most for company during this period, was often the one who stayed.

Idealism or Realism: No Object "External to Us in a Transcendental Sense"?

Kant's star continued to rise outside of Königsberg. Reinhold's "Letters on the Kantian Philosophy" in the *Teutscher Merkur* in 1786–87 did a great deal to popularize his critical philosophy. The after-pains of the pantheism dispute moved his philosophy into the very center of the philosophical discussion. Jacobi had published in 1787 a book entitled *David Hume on Belief, or Idealism and Realism* to respond to criticisms that he was an obscurantist faith mongerer. In the book, he tried to show that he had used the word "*Glaube*," which can mean both faith and belief, not in the sense of "faith" but in the same sense in which Hume had used the word "belief" (which was indeed translated into German as "*Glaube*").

More importantly, the book had an Appendix entitled "On the Transcendental Idealism." In it, Jacobi criticized Kant severely. In some sense, the critique constituted nothing but the further development of Hamann's ruminations and observations on Kant's "critical idealism." In another sense, it was a further development of Reid's critique of Hume. Like Reid, Jacobi concentrated on the issue of the reality of external objects.[235] For, Jacobi noted,

what we realists call real objects, or objects independent from our representations, the transcendental idealism regards only as internal beings. These internal beings *do not represent anything at all of an object that could be external to us, or to which the appearance could be related. They are completely devoid of all real objectivity and are merely subjective determinations of the soul.*

Moreover, according to Kant,

we even introduce ourselves the order and regularity in the appearances, which we call *nature,* and we could not have found it, if we had not, or if the nature of our mind had not originally introduced it.

Therefore,

the Kantian philosopher leaves the spirit of his system completely behind, when he says that the objects make *impressions* upon the senses, occasion sensations in this way, and *give rise to* representations. For according to the Kantian doctrine, the empirical object, which can only be an appearance, cannot be external to us and thus be at the same time something other than a representation . . . The understanding *adds* the object to the appearance.[236]

Yet however much it is contrary to the Kantian view to say that objects make impressions upon our senses, it is impossible to understand how the Kantian view could even get started without this presupposition.[237]

In other words, Kant's categories of the understanding are really qualities of sensation. Jacobi asked why the "laws of reason" are more necessary than "laws of sensation." Why are laws of thought "objective," while laws of sensation are only "subjective"? These questions can be put, according to Jacobi, not only to Kant, but to all rationalists. For, as Jacobi saw it, the rationalists' affirmation of reason and denigration of the senses was nothing but a prejudice. He argued that the Kantian system itself presupposed laws of sensation, and that the categories are faint copies or shadows of basic principles of sensation. Without presupposing such principles of sensation, the Kantian system would be impossible.

Jacobi went on to argue that a transcendental idealist could not even attain the conception of an object that is "external to us in a transcendental sense."[238] The conception of such an object is based upon the "truly wonderful revelation of sensation." Only the realist can attain the conception of such an object, since for him sensation is the passive state of being acted upon. But this feeling is only "one half of the entire state, a state which *cannot be thought merely in accordance with this one half.*"[239] It necessarily involves an object that has caused this state. External sensation necessarily suggests a really existent external object, and the laws that lead common sense toward such objects are not laws of thought but laws of sensation. We must assume that things in themselves affect us. Jacobi claimed that "*without* this presupposition I cannot enter into the system, but *with* this presupposition I cannot remain within the system."[240] Kant's philosophy had removed itself too far from sensation and ordinary language. By trying to "purify" thought of the influence of the suggestions of sensation and the concepts of thought from the influence of ordinary language, critical philosophy becomes nihilism. There is, thus, no such thing as "pure reason." Reason is always "contaminated" by sensation and ordinary language (just as Hamann had argued in his *Metacritique*). Thus, any critique of reason must necessarily involve a critique of the preconditions of reason, namely a critique of sensation and ordinary language.

Jacobi's rejection of the Kantian "thing in itself" was only a part of this project, but it was the criticism that ultimately proved most influential. Herder also weighed in with a book called *God, Some Conversations*, which appeared in 1787. In it, Herder tried to rehabilitate Spinoza, and thus to lift the pantheism dispute to a higher level.[241] He also aimed a number of thinly disguised cheap shots at Kant. These developments did more to spread Kant's ideas than did the efforts that his friends undertook at his behest, but Kant was not happy about them. Nor should he have been. For they contained the seeds that would lead his younger contemporaries to reject his system even before his death.

8

Problems with Religion and Politics (1788–1795)

Strained Friendship: "Writing for Kant"

KANT had said in his Preface to the second edition of the *Critique of Pure Reason* (April 1787) that he would no longer engage in disputes with his critics because he would be spending all his time working out "the system behind this propedeutic" (Bxliii). Jachmann observed that during this time, which was that

of the greatest maturity and power of his mind, when he was working on the critical philosophy, he had no greater difficulty than to think himself into the system of someone else. Even the writings of his enemies he could understand only with the greatest effort because he could leave his own original conceptual system only for short periods. He usually admitted this himself and usually gave to his friends the task to read for him, and to report to him the content, i.e. the main results, of foreign systems in comparison to his own, and it was perhaps for this reason that he left the defense of his system against his enemies to his students and friends.[1]

This statement of Jachmann is a little misleading, because Kant did not just "leave" this task to his students and friends; he actively encouraged and sometimes even *forced* them (if only by his powers of persuasion) to defend his system. One of the friends enlisted to this task was Schulz, who produced four reviews of books on and by Kant in 1787, one in 1788, and some pieces on Kant for Eberhard's *Philosophisches Magazin* in 1790.[2] Another one was Kraus. Schulz had little difficulty with his task. Kraus, on the other hand, found it very difficult to write, either for Kant or for himself. His review of Meiner's *History of Philosophy* in 1787 had cost him "frightful strain" and three months of his time. Kant asked for more.

Kraus's next project was a review of a book by Ulrich, namely his *Eleutherology, or On Freedom and Necessity*. It appeared on April 25, 1788, in the *Allgemeine Literatur-Zeitung,* and it was finished soon after the review of the *History*. Kraus received even more "help" from Kant with this book review than he did with the first. On March 28, Kraus wrote to the editor that he was sending him two reviews, one by him (which concerned a book in comparative linguistics) and one that was *"not entirely his,"* namely that of the *Eleutherology*. Kant had sent him some materials, and Kraus had used them.

Ulrich advocated a kind of compatibilism. Kraus criticized him for failing to show that determinism (or "natural necessity," as he called it) and morality are indeed compatible. He examined especially one claim by Ulrich, namely, that a human being "ought to become other or better, and he can become so; *however no human being as of now can be other or better than he is.*"[3] For Kraus, this did not make sense. We could not say "now, after the end of a year, the citizens of Jena's conduct during the preceding year absolutely had to be just as it was, whereas before the beginning of the year it did not have to be as it turned out to be."[4] In general, if all actions were necessary or completely determined in the past, then they must also be determined in the present. Ulrich, Kraus maintained, should not have tried to make freedom comprehensible. Rather, he should have admitted that freedom is incomprehensible – as Kant had done. Indeed, Kantian philosophy is "worthy of a genuine philosopher, who insists upon scientific evidence where it is to be had . . . but also frankly acknowledges ignorance where it cannot be remedied."[5] Ulrich's objections to Kant – at least according to Kraus – were based on the erroneous assumption that we know not only that freedom is real but also "how it is constituted."[6] We do not know the latter, because we do not have nonsensible intuitions.

The next project for which Kant enlisted Kraus was a review of the third part of Herder's *Ideas*. Kant himself was busy with other things, for during the summer semester of 1788 he was again rector. The review never came to fruition. Though Kraus had committed himself to it in 1787, he only began to work on it early in 1788. Kraus was still working on the review in July, reporting he had pushed off this "ugly labor" and then taken it up again "only from duty" at least ten times; and then,

All that I am writing now I could have written two months ago, if Kant had not always kept me from doing it. He even gave me some of his thoughts on pantheism in order to clarify the main point of my review. But this made things more difficult; for I have lost my own way, and I cannot see myself following Kant's ways.[7]

This is one of the reasons why Kraus never finished the review, but there was another reason as well. Hamann died on June 21, and Kraus, devastated, found it impossible to continue to write. In a letter of February 1, 1789, he spelled out the reason as follows: "I told him [Hamann] of my enterprise in a letter . . . [the review] was a contest of love: who would win the approval of our teacher? Would it be Herder or me? This is what made my work attractive and important. I admit that I never worked on anything with such effort as I worked on this review."[8]

This is peculiar. The review that had begun as a defense of Kant had turned into a "contest of love" for Hamann's favor. Kraus was conflicted from the beginning. He had to criticize Herder in order to please Kant and was thereby taking the risk of upsetting Hamann. At the same time, Kraus's report also indicated a shift that had occurred during his work on the review. At about the time of Hamann's death, Kraus realized that he could not follow Kant's approach, and that he had either to follow his own approach or to give up the project. Indeed, Kraus formulated to himself perhaps for the first time how different his approach was from Kant's:

In general . . . everything metaphysical is foreign to my nature, and it is useless to force me to do metaphysics. I can accomplish the goal of my review only . . . if I view pantheism as a product of nature.[9]

In other words, he would follow either the approach of Hume's *Natural Religion* or none at all. Kant's metaphysical way of looking at religion was really foreign to him. In fact, in later self-characterizations Kraus never failed to point out his tendency toward naturalism and aversion to metaphysics. He often also included a quip about how absurd it is to speak of a philosophy that is characterized by the proper name of a person. Thus "Kantian philosophy" seemed to him a monstrosity.

Perhaps this break between Kraus and Kant was inevitable, but Kant did not help matters. In pushing Kraus to do work that he did not want to do, and in trying to persuade Kraus to promote the critical position with arguments that were not really his, Kant crossed the line. One of Kraus's friends wrote:

When Kraus was writing for Kant – for that is what really happened with his aforementioned metaphysical reviews – Kant first gave him a diamond ring, as a *pretium affectionis*. Kraus was very moved, and showed it to me then. Yet it was not long until the two men had to give up the union (*Verbindung*) into which they had entered with this ring, namely to live only for each other.[10]

Whatever one makes of Kant's gift and the union of the two men reported by this friend of Kraus's, it is clear that they soon became very distant.[11]

While working on these reviews, Kant and Kraus were also continuing their common economy, and they seemed to get along quite well. Like Kant, Kraus suffered greatly from difficulties with digestion and other hypochondriacal complaints. So the two had much to talk about, and Kraus took Kant's medical advice willingly. In August of 1787 he wrote, for instance:

My Kantian diet is, if its benefits continue, a gift of new life. I take only water from between the lunches at noon. This helps me greatly. It is also good that I gain time by not having an evening meal, and even better that I am cheerful because of it.[12]

As their philosophical disagreement became more and more obvious and troubling to Kraus, the dinners became less and less pleasant. Kraus found it increasingly difficult to accept his teacher's disagreement. Their common economy "did not last very long" as a result.[13] As one witness to the crucial occasion said, "Kraus, upset with Kant, who had contradicted him, interjected: 'soon I won't be able to distinguish muddy from clear water.' Next Tuesday (the day I usually went to Kant), I no longer found Kraus there."[14] This was sometime in 1789.[15]

This witness did not recall what precisely the argument was about. He thought that it was just that two such strong-minded people could not possibly coexist peacefully, that they were like two trees that had been planted too close together and whose branches had to come into conflict. In any case, as we know from someone else, one day Kraus told Lampe that he

should never ask him again to come to Kant's dinners. Kant was very upset. With a certain degree of anxiety, he said to his friends, that he would be able to find some peace, if he could know the reason why Kraus had withdrawn in such a way. But he did not know at all how he was to have insulted Kraus.[16]

Kraus's behavior was certainly peculiar. It may be characterized as rude and could perhaps even be characterized as a sign of ingratitude. Why did he not speak to Kant himself? Wouldn't common decency have required him to explain to Kant why he felt he could no longer see him? Even if Kant had imposed on him in the writing of the reviews, and even if Kraus found it difficult to speak to him, he could have written a letter. If Kant had openly and clearly insulted him, there would have been no need. But he had not done that. Perhaps he felt so bad about the entire affair and found it so difficult to talk to Kant that a clean break was the easiest for him. In any case, in a letter to Jacobi, written in the fall of 1789, he declared that he never had felt bad about having forgiven someone who had insulted him, "but the memory of anger, impatience, and insulting disputatiousness to which I succumbed myself does bother me terribly, and in the best of moods I cannot help but find such emotions at least foolish."[17] Perhaps this referred to his altercations with Kant, and perhaps it was just that Kant brought out the worst in him and that the retreat was a way of saving himself from such troubles.

Neither Kant nor their common friends really knew what irked Kraus. They made up stories. Someone believed that Kant had refused to take Kraus's money when he offered to pay his share.[18] Most found the reason in some disagreement during conversations they had had – and apparently there had been many. One of their last disputes was on the question of whether there had ever been a great man who was also a Jew. Kraus is supposed to have defended the Jews as "a smart (*geistreich*) and talented nation," whereas Kant was supposed to have argued that there had never been a truly great Jewish man. But, as Kraus's biographer has noted, Kraus never said anything positive about Jews anywhere else and was, in fact, convinced that Jews could never be good citizens. It is even said that he had a certain kind of personal antipathy toward Jews he knew. As a good friend of Hamann, whose anti-Jewish rhetoric certainly comes close to what some would call anti-Semitism, one would also not expect him to be too much concerned with defending Jewish honor. Kant, on the other hand, thought highly of Mendelssohn and had defended him against insults, and had many Jewish students whom he considered to be talented and capable. Herz was only the most important of these.[19] If there was such a dispute, it is more likely that the positions were reversed. In any case, any such disagreement would not have been the cause of their falling out, but merely the occasion. The real problem went deeper.

Kant never talked about possible reasons for Kraus's dissatisfaction. He continued to think highly of him and never said a bad word about him. Kraus never stated his reasons openly and clearly either, but it appears that he made a number of veiled comments. Thus he said that he disliked the long hours of sitting and talking after dinner that were common with Kant. They took too much time away from his work. It is also clear that Kraus was increasingly critical of Kant's philosophy. He called it useless and impractical, and found it absurd that there should be a "Kantian" philosophy.

Kraus had every reason to feel used by Kant, but Kant probably had no idea why he might have felt that way. Writing came easily to Kant, and he believed that Kraus was his friend and ally. Kraus seems never to have had the courage to face Kant and tell him that he felt used, that he was pressured into writing things that he did not want to write, and that the long dinners took away too much time. Instead, they had disputes about other things that were of less importance to Kraus. Finally, he simply and – at least from Kant's point of view – suddenly broke off their relationship altogether. If this does not reflect well on Kraus, it does not reflect well on Kant either. He was insensitive, wrapped up in his own concerns, and unable to understand the person who was to be his friend. This is why Metzger called Kant an egoist.

Still, the two never quarreled in public, and Kraus visited Kant again during Kant's last year of life. The two also arranged it so that they had adjacent places at dinner parties to which both were invited. Otherwise, they kept their distance. Kraus never became the kind of friend that Green had been. While Kant had many acquaintances with whom he was on friendly terms, there was no longer anyone with whom he could share his thoughts and whom he could ask for completely disinterested advice. Kant now was alone in a way in which he had never been before.

In Society (Tuesday, December 16, 1788): "Even Natural Religion Has Its Dogmatism"

Though Kant now had his own household, and though he regularly invited his friends for dinner, this did not mean that he no longer went out. As we have seen, on Sundays he usually ate at the house of Motherby. As Borowski reports, "he was sought at the table of the upper class as well as at the happy meals of his friends, and he never declined an invitation by anyone at noon time – invitations for the evening he always rejected . . ."[20] This must have been difficult for him at times, as he loved to go out – and apparently not only for pure enjoyment but also for moral reasons:

Although a banquet is a formal invitation to excess in both food and drink, there is still something in it that aims at a moral end, beyond mere physical well-being; it brings a number of people together for a long time to converse with one another.

Yet a banquet remains a "temptation to something immoral," and the question is: "How far does one's moral authorization to accept these invitations to intemperance extend?"[21]

Kant had a standing invitation at the palace of the Keyserlingks, and that is where he usually could be found on Tuesday afternoon.[22] Kant was one of twelve scholars and "other interesting people" who could always attend dinner there.[23] He impressed other guests not only by "his extra-ordinary knowledge . . . which extended to the most disparate matters," but also by his "beautiful and witty conversation."[24]

Kant was a friend of this house for thirty years. It was characterized by the loveliest society (*Geselligkeit*) and men of the most excellent minds were at home as soon as their moral character was estimated as highly as their brain. Kant loved the society of the deceased Countess, who was a very witty and educated woman. I often saw him there, so polite and entertaining that you would never have expected the deep thinker in him, who brought about such a revolution in philosophy. In societal conversation he could at times clothe even the most abstract ideas in a lovely dress, and he analyzed clearly every view that he put forward. Beautiful wit was at his command, and sometimes his speech was spiced by light satire, which he always expressed with the driest demeanor.[25]

Kant, who could be funny in a direct and obvious way when he was in the company of his equals, could also be subtle and witty in noble society.[26] He spoke both languages, so to speak, and he knew how to act in both worlds, for they were still two quite different worlds in the Königsberg of the late eighteenth century, no matter how much progress had been made in advancing equality.

The world of the nobility could appear strange to an outside observer. Thus one visitor related that he found some of the behavior of the old Keyserlingk disconcerting:

The old man appeared, when we sat down at the table, in a very warm overcoat made from linen and decorated with the order of the black eagle. After soup, two servants took off the overcoat, and he now revealed a formal coat also of linen and with the order of the black eagle. When the roast was served, he handed that coat over as well and now the Count was sitting there in a light silk dress that did not lack the order of the black eagle either. Had there been another transformation, I could not possibly have suppressed an admiring outcry; but as it was, for dessert there appeared only the two grandchildren of our well-meaning host, children from about five to seven years, in gala dress, powdered locks (*Flügellocken*) and with a sword on their sides, which perfected the comical view.[27]

We do not know whether Kant, who was quite used to this scene, found it equally funny. The attitude of detached critique and amusement that this commoner expressed would have been more familiar to him than the metamorphoses of his host.

Even after the count was dead, the dinner parties continued. This is clear from a scene Hippel recorded on the evening of Tuesday, December 16, 1788.[28] Hippel, who by this time had transformed himself from a commoner into a member of nobility, was in the habit of recording conversations and other events that he might use later in *verfremdeter* form in his novels. This sketch shows what was on the minds of Kant and other intellectuals in Königsberg at the time. As always, it had to do with developments in

Berlin in which Kant had a special interest. Kant said remarkably little in this particular conversation. As we shall see, there were reasons for this.

> Before dinner, the usual questions and answers about how one feels and doesn't feel, which, because the heroine of this piece just came home from taking the baths, have more parts and more emphasis than usual.
>
> *Countess of Keyserlingk* to me: You have to separate us, however inseparable we were until now.
>
> I: The more advantage for me.
>
> *Lady von Recke:* It was extraordinarily pleasant to me to see you before I depart.
>
> I: I could not count on this extra-ordinary pleasure, since My Lady wanted to depart earlier.
>
> *Lady von Recke:* The first letter of the alphabet that I mentioned to you shall now come to word.
>
> I: I have often asked myself what it could be that interested My Lady; yet, here as elsewhere, I discovered that I do not belong among either the minor or the major prophets and interpreters (*Deuter*).
>
> *Lady von Recke:* After dinner you will be so good as to give me the honor of visiting me in my room.
>
> I: When and where My Lady commands.
>
> *Lady von Recke:* You were the first who told me about the promotion of Herr von Wöllner to minister. – You have heard the story of the sword of faith, haven't you?
>
> I: Yes, and one can see from it that the crown prince is not entirely satisfied with the edict on religion.
>
> *Lady von Recke:* In no way, and the prince as well as every thinking person will be just as unhappy about the edict on censorship.
>
> I: Young Carmer assured me of the correctness of this – only, I knew nothing of its contents.
>
> *Lady von Recke:* Its main content is that nothing against the Augsburg Confession, nothing against the State –
>
> I, falling in: And indeed *nothing* at all be written, or be written about nothing.
>
> *Lady von Recke:* They want the Protestants to have a dead Pope, just as the Catholics have a living Pope.
>
> I: And yet, Luther was so little satisfied with His Popishness that he explicitly demanded that one go on beyond him.
>
> *Lady von Recke:* I assure you that I did not find a line against the edict on religion in the bookstores of Berlin.
>
> I: This means that My Lady does not know the Remarks by Würzer either?
>
> *Lady von Recke:* No. You know his fate, don't you? He really was brought to Spandau.
>
> I: I heard that, but I do not know who passed that judgment on him.
>
> *Lady von Recke:* The Great Chancellor
>
> I: But he did not pursue this investigation of him any further, as someone wrote to me.
>
> *Lady von Recke:* Quite right. The king reserved his right to judge Würzer himself. But you know what the best part is: he dedicated the book to the king, the king answered him quite favorably, and a few days letter he is thrown in jail.
>
> I: That's entirely new to me.

Countess of K.: Without doubt, it was at the instigation of the Principal Minister that he was put before the inquisition. Do you know this Principal Minister?

Lady von Recke: No, but I have heard a great deal about him.

Countess of K.: I happened to be in Berlin when he married his wife, and as Minister von Finckelstein got really worked up over this. All Berlin said that he loved the mother and married the daughter.

Lady von Recke: I can show the letter of the empress to the Geheime Rat in any case.

Countess of K.: Certainly, but the letter must remain secret, for the empress alludes to a ruler (*Fürst*) who should not be far from here. Did you read Würzer then?

I: Preface and Dedication to the king. And there I found a very mediocre author and otherwise nothing further.

Lady von Recke: They inquired with whom he was acquainted, and his answer was: with the hangman, with two Jews, and two weeks ago I was at Dr. Biester's. Biester was indicted and interrogated. And he said, if it was a mistake that I heard from *Magister* Würzer that he wanted to write his book, if it was a crime to be a mediocre writer, then Herr Würzer and I are culpable. – They let Biester go right away. – God!

There was a political discourse in which the officers were very active. Kant, as did I, declared that the Russians were our main enemies.

Lady von Recke and the Countess were of a different opinion and *for* the Russians. Lady von Recke assured us that the Emperor was hated and not respected in his own country, . . . and that there would probably be no war.

I wished for war and I got war, which, however, was soon over, because I only wished for war so that there would be a longer and more solid peace. The Mamsell Reichardt, a companion of Lady von Recke, always interrupted *interveniendo* when the poor Elisa wanted to in accordance with her appetite. I took care of the appetite, for one has to give it at least one vote, even though Mamsell Reichardt remained the president of this tribunal.

Of Enlightenment, Air Ships, etc.

Prof. Holzhauer, as a friend of the friend Göcking: It cannot yet be determined what damage the religious edict could do. No one can always vote with his church, even if there were a thousand edicts.

Lady von Recke: All right, but hypocrisy will be extra-ordinarily furthered, fed and cultivated in this way. To me: You will read the letter of the empress, won't you?

To Kant: I am an enemy of all dogmatism, and I think religion must be in the heart.

Kant: Yes, but even natural religion has its dogmatism.

Lady von Recke: But then it must be very comprehensible.

A little dispute about natural science, which, I maintained, was the most important enemy of superstition; against which professor Kant objected that it depended on entirely different principles. All true, I said. Yet it teaches nevertheless how the miraculous can be explained, and thus dispels the fear and the false idols of superstition, since superstition is based on miracles. Much about Blomhard who had permission to go to Breslau and Königsberg.

Countess Keyserlingk: What in the world does he want to do in Königsberg?

Exactly, I thought to myself, since Your Excellency is so exact, while having an income of 5000 Thalers a year, that there exists not a single house, etc.

Of the idea to make the Churfürst of Saxony the King of Poland.

The injuriousness of this plan to our state, etc.

The Countess Keyserlingk.: If my husband was still alive, he would certainly have made clear to the king by means of a concrete deduction that his best ally is Russia, that the house of Austria is his real enemy, and that it will always remain such an enemy.

Lady von Recke: Those Saxons who surround the king. – Something about Saxony, while the Mrs. Colonel Heykings started something with Kant.

The Countess Keyserlingk: Russia really has no interest in taking anything from us. Kurland is a real wall of separation.

I: I still do not believe that they do not have any interests in East Prussia and the properties in former Poland, given the trade in the Baltic sea, etc.

The Countess did not change her mind, and the Lady von Recke supported her in this as a courageous Russian women.

After dinner
Lady von Recke and Kant

Lady von Recke: What do you think of my dispute with Starck?

Kant: I am sorry that My Lady has to contend with a man who is so energetic, smart and proud. My Lady should stop and not read another word of his writings.

Lady von Recke: But that would really be too timid; I have once made a sacrifice for the truth, I will finish it.

Kant: But could one not get evidence from France?

Lady von Recke: But how?

Kant: There must be people who still live by the Library, and who know about everything; and since so many citizens of Kurland travel there – letters should work.

Lady von Recke: You know how our young people are traveling today. Libraries are the last coffeehouse they visit –

The society dispersed and left, or rather, left the stage. Lady von Recke had it arranged that I would be asked not to leave before I saw her alone.[29]

This conversation is symptomatic of a fairly recent change in the political atmosphere. Frederick William II and his advisors had decided soon after the inauguration that religion needed to be defended. The king had liked Kant, giving him special honors at the very beginning of his reign. Yet, given Kant's religious views and his ever-increasing reputation as "the all-crushing Kant," the new king soon regretted his support of Kant. Much like the unfortunate Würzer, who was at first accepted by the king but later thrown into prison, Kant had a right to be concerned.

Frederick William II was no Frederick the Great. Without a firm character, he followed his advisors more than his own will. It has been said that he "was over-dependent on these advisors, and as his advisors advocated divergent views his policies necessarily lacked consistency."[30] His private life was characterized by several sexual scandals of the most sordid kind, while his public policy was marked by a campaign for religious righteousness. Thus, after becoming king, he was no longer satisfied with having both a wife and a concubine, but had to get married again and commit bigamy. Yet, at the same time, he was preaching to his subjects about the importance of following the church. Frederick William II thought that religion and morality went hand in hand, and therefore did everything to strengthen religion. The hypocrisy he exhibited in his crusade for religious rectitude, while living a most unedifying life, was of course not lost on his subjects. He had neither the moral nor the political authority of his father.

This lack of leadership also showed itself in the religious policies of Frederick William II. Influenced by the obscurantist Rosicrucian Order, he surrounded himself with zealots intent on bringing an end to the evils of rationalism. One of the most important of these Rosicrucians was Johann Christoph Wöllner (1732–1800), who had inducted the king into the secret order himself.[31] Frederick Wilhelm II more or less succeeded in making Rosicrucianism the semi-official ideology of Prussia, thus doing his best to overturn the reforms of Frederick II and his rationalist ministers. Wöllner was his right-hand man in this attempt, and Wöllner's main ambition was to replace von Zedlitz, one of Kant's greatest supporters in Berlin – and the very model of an "enlightened" minister, and therefore almost evil incarnate to Wöllner. On July 3, 1788, Wöllner finally saw success. He obtained a number of posts, but most importantly, he became minister of ecclesiastical affairs. On July 9, 1788, the Edict Concerning Religion was issued, followed on December 19, 1788, by the Edict of Censorship. The first required strict orthodoxy of all preachers. It stated, among other things,

We have noted with regret . . . that many Protestant pastors allow themselves unbridled liberty in the treatment of the dogma of their confession. . . . They are not ashamed to warm up the miserable, long refuted errors of the Socinians, deists, naturalists, and other sectarians, and to spread them among the people with impertinent impudence under the much abused banner of *Aufklärung* [Enlightenment]. They denigrate the respect in which the Bible has been held. . . . They throw suspicion upon – or even make appear superfluous – the mysteries of revealed religion . . .[32]

The purpose of the second edict was to provide the tool for suppressing all writings that were not strictly orthodox. Rationalist preachers were faced with preaching either righteous doctrine or resigning. It was no surprise, therefore, that the Edict Concerning Religion was extremely unpopular among Prussian intellectuals. Hippel's sketch shows that this was also a concern in Königsberg. Kant must have been worried about losing his position. The conversation took place just three days before the Edict was announced. Biester, with whom he had the closest connection, had been

interrogated, and a writer had been thrown into the Spandau jail simply because of what he had written. This may well be why he did not have much
to say about this topic.

The conversation about Starck was perhaps more interesting to Hippel,
the Freemason, than it was to Kant. Still, Kant knew Starck well from his
time in Königsberg. The two had had close connections more than twenty-
five years earlier, and Starck still had family in Königsberg, having married someone from Königsberg in addition to being related to Kraus.[33] In
any case, Starck had broken with Freemasonry in 1785, and he had tried to
expose what he now took to be the follies of Masons in a novel called *St.
Nicaise.* Hamann had already accused him of being a crypto-Catholic and
Jesuit during the early seventies. Since the *Berlinische Monatsschrift* had
close ties with Freemasonry, Starck was soon attacked in its pages, and his
enemies repeated the accusation of crypto-Catholicism. But they did not
appear to know that he had, as a matter of fact, converted to Catholicism
on a stay in Paris. In Königsberg, this was known.[34] The only question was
how to prove it. In any case, because Starck soon became one of the enemies of the French Revolution, which Kant enthusiastically endorsed, this
conversation is of interest as well. Hippel's sketch introduces some of the
most important problems with which Kant had to wrestle during the next
decade. But there is one characteristic contrast between Kant's role in this
conversation and his role in public discussion. He said little in this conversation, but he had a great deal to say about the taking away of "the single freedom" (Lessing), namely, the freedom of speech that Frederick the
Great had granted. Frederick William II was about to return Prussia to the
state of affairs prevalent during Kant's youth. Given how important he
thought freedom of thought and speech was for the development of
mankind, Kant could not be quiet – and he was not. From now on, religion would play a much more important role in his publications than it had
before. This was due not only to the development of his own critical project but also to external political circumstances.

The Revolution: "I Have Seen the Glory of the World"

On July 12, 1789, in Paris, far away from Königsberg, developments that had
long been in the making and that had formed the subject of many a conversation among Kant and his friends, finally came to a head. France was
bankrupt as a result of the Seven-Year War, intervention in the American
Revolution, and wasteful spending. Jacques Necker was appointed minister

of finance and secretary general. But the financial crisis did not significantly improve. People were starving. As a last resort, Louis XVI called the Estates-General, in the hope it would pass the badly needed fiscal reforms. It convened at Versailles in May of 1789. From the beginning, the deputies of the Third Estate, supported by many members of the lower clergy and by a few nobles, were pushing for thoroughgoing political and social reforms. Resisting the king, they proclaimed themselves the National Assembly on June 17. They also took an oath not to separate until a constitution had been drawn up. On July 11, the king dismissed Necker. This led to a rebellion of the citizenry of Paris. The soldiers of the *Garde Française* joined the mob, and on July 14 they stormed the Bastille. The regime of Louis XVI was overturned, though he nominally remained king. On July 16, he reappointed Necker and dismissed the troops. Two days after that, he "acknowledged the new authorities born of the insurrection."[35] The results of the Revolution were soon felt in all of France. On August 4, 1789, the Assembly abolished all feudal privileges. In a swift current of events, the old order had vanished more quickly than anyone had thought possible. The spirit of the new order was expressed in a preamble to a constitution still to be written. As one historian puts it,

It was a noble and well written text, often close to the American model. The essence was expressed in a very few sentences. . . . Firstly, what had been done on 4 August: "Men are born free and live free and with equal rights." What rights? Liberty, property, safety and resistance to oppression, with all that derives therefrom: civil and fiscal equality, individual liberty, the admissibility of everyone for all employment, *habeas corpus*, non-retroactive laws, guarantee of property.[36]

All of intellectual Germany watched the events with great interest. There were some outbreaks of violence in the Rhineland. But there was no mass movement toward revolution.

Some major intellectual figures in Germany, such as Goethe and Möser, were opposed to the Revolution from the beginning. Still, most – at least at the beginning – supported it enthusiastically. Older writers such as Klopstock and Wieland endorsed its goals. Younger authors such as Herder, Schiller, and Fichte (all three of whom were influenced by Kant) wrote enthusiastically for the cause of the Revolution. Kant himself was just as inspired by it as were his students. As one of his acquaintances said, trying to correct Fichte's mistaken view that Kant took no notice of the French Revolution, "He lived and moved in it; and, in spite of all the terror, he held on to his hopes so much that when he heard of the declaration of the republic he called out with excitement: 'Now let your servant go in peace to his grave, for I have seen the glory of the world.'"[37]

Friedrich Gentz, who had studied with Kant in 1783, felt the same way. He wrote to Garve in December of 1790:

The revolution constitutes the first practical triumph of philosophy, the first example in the history of the world of the construction of government upon the principles of an orderly, rationally-constructed system. It constitutes the hope of mankind and provides consolation to men elsewhere who continue to groan under the weight of age-old evils.[38]

Gentz, together with many others, soon changed his mind. The Revolution was soon declared as the work of wicked men, Freemasons and Illuminati. Those who criticized the existing order were called "Jacobin," and "a rain of oppressive edicts fell on Germany."[39] Starck, the "crypto-Catholic" with roots in Königsberg, was one of the chief proponents of this view. Kant, on the other hand, remained a steadfast adherent of the Revolution, as his subsequent publications show.

Kant did not defend the Revolution only in public. It also was an important topic in his private dealings. Metzger took it as a mere "peculiarity of Kant's character," and not as a "vice," that Kant

for many years defended with great frankness and fearlessness his principles, which were favorable to the French Revolution, against anyone (including men of the highest offices in the state) – whether he did so during his last years I do not know. There was a time in Königsberg when everyone who judged mildly, and not even with approval, was called a *Jacobin* and was blacklisted. Kant was not deterred by this to speak at noble tables for the goals of the revolution, and they had so much respect for the man that they did not hold his views against him.[40]

On the other hand, at least if we can trust Borowski, Kant himself could not take disagreement on this matter. "Open contradiction insulted him, if it was persistent, it made him bitter. Certainly, he did not push his view on anyone, but he heartily disliked disputatiousness. When he observed it more than once [in someone], he preferred to avoid occasions that would lead to it. Thus he said right away to a man whom everyone knew thought entirely different about the French Revolution than he did: "I think it would be best, if we did not talk about it at all."[41] In matters concerning this momentous event, he was very dogmatic.[42] He thought the Revolution a good thing and worried only that it would take a "fruitless" direction. Terror or scandal did not seem to trouble him greatly. Indeed, it was "very difficult, if not impossible to change his view, even if it contradicted the facts."[43]

The politics of the Revolution was his favorite topic of conversation, and he was so curious about the new developments that "he would have walked for miles to get the mail." Reliable private information gave him the greatest joy.[44] As late as 1798, he "loved the task of the French with all his soul, and all the outbreaks of immorality did not make him doubt that the 'representative system was the best.'"[45] He was "openly a republican." The court chaplain, a professor of mathematics and defender of Kant, was apparently one of the few who held the same view.[46] So was Kraus, who also took great interest in the events in France and "changed entirely into a republican."[47]

The *Critique of Judgment* (1790): "Functionality without a Purpose"

Almost immediately after finishing the second *Critique* in the summer of 1787, Kant went on to "work on the *Foundation of the Critique of Taste.*"[48] When it finally appeared in 1790, it had turned into the *Critique* itself.

Two years before he published this "final part of the Critique," he wrote an essay, "On the Use of Teleological Principles in Philosophy," which appeared in *Der Teutsche Merkur* of January and February 1788. The essay was occasioned by criticisms of two of his papers, "Concept of a Human Race" and "Conjectures on the Beginning of Human History," which had appeared late in 1786 in *Der Teutsche Merkur.* The author was Johann Georg Adam Forster, the younger son of the famous geographer Johann Reinhold Forster. Kant wanted to respond, and Reinhold asked in October of 1787 whether Kant could not give his public approval of the "Letters on Kantian Philosophy." The essay represented for Kant an opportunity to do both, even though the two matters had little to do with each other.[49]

Kant attended to his second concern at the very end of the paper, saying that the author of the anonymous "Letters" had his full approval and that he and the anonymous author were working toward a "common cause," namely, the cultivation of a "speculative and practical reason in accordance with firm principles."[50] He also thanked the author, and in the very last paragraph, in what appears to have been a postscript, he identified Reinhold as the author of the letters, expressing his satisfaction that he had recently been appointed professor of philosophy at Jena. Indeed, Kant really must have been pleased that another one of his adherents had obtained a position: his philosophy was gaining in influence at the academy.

In the essay itself, Kant first tries to clarify his concept of "race" and to answer Forster's criticisms. In particular, he rejects Forster's idea that there are only two races, Negroes and whites, and that there were two basic origins (*Stämme*) of the human race. Kant insists that there are four races, all of whom have one origin. Forster's position is not only needlessly complex, but also does not account well for the differences among humans. Furthermore, if Forster is right in claiming that human beings originated separately in two different parts of the world, and if the differences among humans justify speaking of four races, then Forster should admit that there were four different kinds of human beings at first. Much of the discussion must strike the contemporary reader as tedious at best, and offensive at worst – an example of the latter being Kant's considered opinion that Negroes (like gypsies) have an inherited aversion to hard labor and will never make good farmers.[51]

Kant's second concern is more philosophical. He wants to answer Forster's criticism that his insistence on teleological principles is unscientific, and that he allowed theology to intrude into science in the "Conjectural Beginning." Kant points out that he does not mean to question the idea that nature needs to be explained empirically, using merely causal principles. Unlike those who speak of "basic forces" of matter, which are supposed to be responsible for the creation of nature and natural kinds, he does not introduce empty or unscientific concepts. His view of ends is very different. Teleology does not proceed along hylozoistic lines, and it is not an attempt to override the causality of nature. Indeed, the "teleological principle in nature must always be empirically determined." The same would be true of the ends of freedom, if nature had first provided us with the objects of volition, that is, with needs and inclinations, and then allowed us to choose. "But the *Critique of Practical Reason* proves that there are pure practical principles that determine reason a priori and which therefore give ends to reason a priori." While teleology cannot explain nature completely, because it is restricted by empirical conditions, we must expect completeness from "a pure doctrine of freedom." Because morality must be viewed as something that is realizable in nature, moral teleology must also be applied to nature. It is justified to that extent.[52]

Kant takes up these same concerns again at the end of the third *Critique*. They were important to him from the beginning of his thought about aesthetic matters. It has been argued that Kant's work on the book proceeded in three distinct steps. Thus, John H. Zammito, basing himself on prior work by Michel Souriau, Gerhard Lehmann, and Giorgio Tonelli, distinguishes three phases – an aesthetic phase (summer 1787–88), a cognitive turn (early 1789) characterized by "reflective judgment," and an ethical turn (late summer or fall 1789), in which the concept of the "supersensible" was central.[53] This last phase is thought to have "resulted directly from Kant's struggle with pantheism."[54] If this is right, then Kant worked specifically on the third *Critique* for over three years, influenced largely by outside forces. Zammito believes it was mainly Herder who was important. Indeed, he views Kant's third *Critique* primarily as an attempt to answer Herder, claiming that the third *Critique* "was almost a continuous attack on Herder" and that especially most of the Critique of Teleological Judgment must be read as an argument in which Herder functions as the "unnamed antagonist." Indeed, the "origins of the Third Critique lie in Kant's bitter rivalry with Herder."[55] This is what forms the most important contextual background of this work. Herder's new dogmatism, hylozoism, and artistic understanding of science needed to be refuted before Kant's criticism could succeed.

It is true that Kant thought Herder needed to be refuted, but – and this is important – he himself did not want to do this. He tried to delegate this job to Kraus, declining to refute Herder because of his desire to work on the third *Critique*. It is unlikely, therefore, that this work turned into a mere polemic against Herder. The conflict between Kraus and Kant also shows that Kant did not suddenly, in the fall of 1789, begin to think about pantheism. Indeed, he had already written notes for Kraus before June of 1787. Zammito's key question, "Why did teleology intrude?" or "Why did teleology 'insinuate itself into' a work on aesthetics?," is anachronistic. Kant's contemporaries would not have seen this as an intrusion. They would have viewed it as an issue that was closely connected to the problems Kant was addressing. Physico-theology, or the consideration of the "structure of the world with all its order and beauty," was closely connected to considerations that today belong to aesthetics.[56] Aesthetics was still not a very well-defined discipline, and it was a different enterprise from what we understand it to be today. Finally, Kant's letter to Reinhold in December of 1787 makes it quite clear that teleology was an important part of his project from the beginning.[57] This is just what might be expected, given that teleology had played an important part in Kant's thinking beginning in high school. The interconnections between teleology and theology had already interested Kant in the *General Natural History*.[58] There was no need for Herder to bring this problem to Kant's attention.

Kant's third *Critique* is often read simply as a treatise in aesthetics, and its first part does indeed deal essentially with aesthetic problems. In it, Kant argues that although aesthetic judgments are based on feeling, their claims to objective validity are not based on these feelings themselves but upon a priori principles of judgment that are preconditions for such feelings. Kant also deals in this work with the problem of the unity of his own system, the general problem of the apparent purposiveness of nature, the problems arising from a presumed necessity of applying teleological concepts in biology, and some theological concerns.

The *Critique of Judgement* is divided into two parts, the Critique of Aesthetic Judgment and the Critique of Teleological Judgment. Both parts have an Analytic and a Dialectic, but the Dialectic of Teleological Judgment is followed by a long Appendix on the method of applying teleological judgment and a general remark on teleology.[59] Kant's divisions are largely expressions of his desire for architectonic neatness. However, especially in the second part, these architectonic concerns seem to get in the way rather than help. The Appendix and Note are as long as the Analytic and Dialectic together. It is far from clear whether the division, which may have served Kant well in the first *Critique*, serves any essential function here.

The Critique of Aesthetic Judgment deals with the problem of the validity of aesthetic judgments. This problem arises from a peculiarity of the claims we make about aesthetic matters. When we claim, for instance, that "this painting by Rembrandt is beautiful" or that "the Grand Canyon is sublime," we express our feelings and do not make claims to objective knowledge. At the same time, such claims, which may be called judgments of taste, are meant to be more than mere reports of what we feel. We are convinced that there is more to such judgments, that they state something of universal significance. What justifies such convictions?

In the Analytic of the Beautiful, Kant first outlines four characteristics of judgments of taste, or rather, of one of their subjects, namely beauty. He tries to show that we may impute universality because judgments of taste are estimations of objects in which we find delight or aversion apart from any interest we may have in them. So what is beautiful delights us without any interest. Second, the beautiful is something that pleases universally, apart from any concept we have of it. Kant argues that judgments about pleasure cannot possibly approach the intersubjective validity of judgments about objects. But that would be required if such judgments were to involve concepts. Third, beauty is "the form of functionality of an object, so far as it is perceived apart from the representation of a purpose."[60] Differentiating between two kinds of beauty, namely, free and dependent beauty, where free beauty presupposes no concept of what the object should be and dependent beauty does presuppose such a concept, Kant argues that judgments of taste concern, strictly speaking, only the first kind. Judgments that involve perfection really always have an intellectual component. Finally, the "beautiful is that, which, without a concept, is cognized as an object of *necessary* delight."[61] Judgments of taste mean to exact agreement from everyone; they impute that we have a common sense. This means that they "presuppose the existence of a common sense . . . which is not to be understood as an external sense, but as the effect from the free play of our faculties of cognition."[62]

Kant defines the sublime as that which "is great *per se*."[63] It is similar to the beautiful for him insofar as it pleases on its own and does not presuppose any concepts. Whereas the beautiful always involves a question about the form of the object, the sublime can be encountered even in objects without form. It involves a representation of limitlessness. Whereas delight is connected with quality in beauty, it is connected with quantity in the sublime. Accordingly, Kant tries to show that judgments about the sublime, which must of course involve the categories, are in their quantity "universally valid," in their quality "independent of interest," in their relation "subjectively final," and in their modality "necessary."[64] This is the same approach that he followed in discussing the beautiful. However, while there is only one kind of beauty, there are, Kant claims, two kinds of the sublime, the mathematical and the dynamical. The mathematical sublime is related to the faculty of cognition, the dynamical sublime to the faculty of desire. The one leaves the mind at rest; the other moves it.

The results of Kant's discussion of the beautiful and the sublime are the following definitions: (1) The "*beautiful* is what pleases in the mere estimate formed of it (consequently not by the intervention of any feeling of sense in accordance with a concept of the understanding). From this it follows immediately that it must please apart from all interest." (2) The "*sublime* is what pleases immediately because of its opposition to sense."[65] It is "an object (of nature) whose representation determines the mind to regard the elevation of nature beyond our reach as equivalent to a presentation of ideas."[66] While ideas cannot be presented because their objects are nonnatural or supersensible, the feeling of the sublime enlivens these otherwise abstract concepts. It "expands the soul." The sublime must always have reference to our way of thinking or to maxims "directed to giving supremacy over sensibility to the intellectual side of our nature and the ideas of reason." Kant argues:

Perhaps there is no more sublime passage in the Jewish Law than the commandment: Thou shalt not make unto thee any graven image, or any likeness of any thing that is in heaven or on earth, or under the earth. . . . This commandment can alone explain the enthusiasm which the Jewish people, in their moral period, felt for their religion. . . . The same holds good of our representation of the moral law and our native capacity for morality.[67]

Whatever the feeling of the sublime contributes to the ideas, it does not provide them with graven images.

Kant compares his "transcendental exposition" of aesthetic judgment to Burke's "physiological" account of it, just as he had compared his Metaphysical Deduction in the first *Critique* to the physiological account given by Locke; and he is quick to point out that such an empirical deduction may be a first step toward a critique of taste, but that is not sufficient. Only if we assume that there is an a priori component to judgments of taste, can we really pass judgment on the judgment of others about what is beautiful or sublime.

If there is such an a priori component, then, in the Kantian scheme of things, we also need a deduction of some sort. But he makes short shrift of this demand, claiming that the exposition already given of the judgments of the sublime in nature "was at the same time their Deduction."[68] Only the judgments of taste need a deduction. Since an objective principle of taste is impossible, given the peculiarities of judgments of taste, this deduction cannot be objective either. "Although critics, as Hume says, are able to reason more plausibly than cooks, they must still share the same fate."[69] What can be proved is subjective necessity, no more but also no less. We must show how a judgment is possible which, on the one hand, is based exclusively on an individual's own feeling of pleasure in some object but which is, on the other hand, imputed to every possible observer of the object as a necessary attendant to it. This necessity can only be based on "that subjective factor which we must presuppose in all men (as requisite for a possible experience in general)."[70] This is to be found in the communicability of all sensations, and thus in the *sensus communis*.

Kant elucidates what the fundamental propositions of this *sensus communis* are by referring his readers to three maxims of the common human understanding (or common sense), namely (1) to think for oneself, (2) to think from the standpoint of everyone else, and (3) always to think consistently. While it is not clear whether the remarks on nature and art that follow and round out Kant's discussion in the Analytic are helpful to critics, the critics certainly would be better off today, if they followed these principles.

The Dialectic of Aesthetic Judgment is very short (just five paragraphs).

In it, Kant states and claims to solve the antinomy between the thesis that the judgment of taste is nonconceptual, for if it were, it would be open to dispute, and the antithesis that the judgment of taste is conceptual, because there is a diversity of judgment and consequently dispute.[71] Kant assures us that "all contradiction disappears . . . if I say: The judgment of taste does depend on a concept (of a general ground of the subjective functionality of nature for the power of judgment), but this concept does not allow us to cognize or prove anything about the object because it is indeterminable in itself and unfit to be a cognition."[72] This shows again how closely taste and morality are connected. Beauty is a symbol of morality.

Taste makes, as it were, the transition from the charm of sense to habitual moral interest possible without too violent a leap. It does so by representing the imagination even in its freedom as functional for determination of the understanding and by teaching that we can also find free delight even in objects of sense without sensual charm.[73]

In the Critique of Teleological Judgment, Kant argues that mechanical accounts of nature cannot make sense of organic form. They cannot explain the origin even of a blade of grass. Nature seems to be designed. Everything seems to have a function. To account for this, Kant formulates a principle of reason to the effect that "Everything in nature is good for something; nothing in it is in vain." While this is a subjective principle, that is, a maxim, and merely regulative and not constitutive, it is nevertheless "a clue to guide us in the study of natural things."[74] Therefore, it is indeed a principle "inherent in science." Since it is just a maxim, it does not need a deduction.

On the other hand, it does give rise to an antinomy, namely the conflict between the claim that "All production in nature is possible on mere mechanical law" and its contradiction, "Some production of such things is not possible on mere mechanical laws."[75] Strictly speaking, however, we cannot make either claim. We should restrict ourselves to the subjective maxims that say: "All production in nature *must be judged as being* possible on mere mechanical law" and "Some production of such things *cannot be judged as* possible on mere mechanical laws." There is no contradiction between these two maxims. In fact, each may have its place in science, and, as long as we are careful to apply the second maxim sparingly, it does not stand in the way of rigorous science.

The problem of teleology gives rise to the problem of design, and design seems to lead almost naturally to theology. The emphasis must be on "almost." Picking up on concerns that had surfaced in his dispute with

Herder and Forster, and that had played a large role in Kraus's break with him, Kant discusses pantheism and theism as solutions to the problem of teleology. His claim is that both fail. The Spinozistic idea of a unified substrate that underlies both thought and nature (extension) "can never produce the idea of finality," and the concept of a "living matter is quite inconceivable" in any case.[76] While theism also fails, it has an advantage over all other systems because in "attributing an intelligence to the original being it adopts the best mode of rescuing the finality of nature" from being a merely empty ideal, and it also introduces "an intentional causality for its production."[77]

Teleology is neither a branch of natural science nor a branch of theology. It belongs to the science of the critique, namely to

> the critique of a particular cognitive faculty, namely judgment. But it does contain a priori principles, and to that extent it may, and in fact, must specify the method by which nature has to be judged. . . . In this way the science of its methodical application exerts at least a negative influence . . . in the theoretical science of nature. It also in the same way affects the metaphysical bearing which this science may have on theology, when the former is treated as a propaedeutic to the latter.[78]

The ultimate end of nature as a teleological system is, as Kant had already pointed out years earlier, a particular kind of human culture, that is, "a constitution so regulating the mutual relations of men that the abuse of freedom by individuals striving one against another is opposed by a lawful authority centered in a whole, called a *civil community*."[79] This community should be embedded in a cosmopolitan whole.

What justifies the view that man is the end of nature? Morality. Only human beings are autonomous. Only they are capable of unconditional legislation, which is an end "to which all of nature is teleologically subordinated."[80]

Physico-theology is "physical teleology misunderstood."[81] Just as the teleological system of nature must be understood from the point of view of moral development, so theology must take its clue from morality. Giving a new gloss of the argument for postulating God as a condition for the possibility of the highest good, Kant argues that "it is as necessary to assume the existence of God as it is to recognize the validity of the moral law."[82] A theological ethics is almost as much of a "monstrosity" as a theological physics. What is possible is an ethical theology. Its cornerstone is not the existence of God but that of human freedom.

Kant was worried that his third *Critique* would meet with the same fate as the *Groundwork* and the second *Critique*, that is, that it would take many months before it appeared. For this reason, he changed publishers. The third *Critique* appeared with de la Garde in Berlin. He recommended Kiesewetter as the copy editor to the publisher.[83] He sent the first part of the manuscript to Berlin on January 21, 1790, and the second part on February 9, and a final small part on March 3. The Preface and the Introduction were sent on March 22.[84] By April 20 he was correcting the proofs, albeit with great reluctance. He found the work tedious.

Appreciation from a "Genuinely Philosophical Public" and Enmity from "Popular Philosophers"

At the same time, Kant's philosophy continually increased in importance and influence in Germany. Especially Reinhold's *Attempt of a Theory of the Human Faculty of Representation* (*Versuch einer Theorie des menschlichen Vorstellungsvermögens*) of 1789, his publication of the *Letters on Kantian Philosophy* (*Briefe über die Kantische Philosophie*) in book form in 1790, and the *Contributions toward the Correction of Past Philosophers' Misunderstandings* (*Beyträge zur Berichtigung bisheriger Missverständnisse der Philosophen*) of 1790, popularized and extended Kant's philosophy. In fact, it became customary during this time to speak of the Kant–Reinholdian philosophy. For Reinhold was no longer content just to present Kant's thought. He wanted to develop it further. In particular, he claimed that he had undercut Hume's position. Accordingly, his stance toward Hume is quite different from that of Kant. Whereas Kant did not seem to mind very much when he was called "skeptical" in some sense, his followers bristled at the charge. For them, skepticism in general and Hume's skepticism in particular was something dreadful. Thus while Reinhold, very early on, recognized and accepted the skeptical dimension in Kant, he later vehemently argued against it.

In a paper that appeared in the 1789 issue of the *Berlinische Monatsschrift*, entitled "From Which Skepticism Can We Expect a Reformation in Philosophy?," Reinhold differentiated among three different kinds of skepticism, namely "unphilosophical skepticism," "dogmatic skepticism," and "critical skepticism," rejecting the first two and opting for the third. By "unphilosophical skepticism," he had in mind the mitigated skepticism of Kant's contemporaries, such as Feder, Meiners, Platner, and other so-called popular philosophers. He did not argue against them, but simply dismissed them because he was writing for a "genuinely philosophical public" (*aechtphilosophisches Publikum*).[85] Dogmatic skepticism, on the other hand, is a "worthy opponent." It has to be disproved so that we can reach "that important doubt of critical skepticism," which, for him, marks the beginning of something new.[86] Critical skepticism is not part of traditional philosophy. Indeed, as he argues in another paper that appeared in the very same year in *Der Teutsche Merkur,* only "critical skepticism" can free a critical thinker from the necessity of adhering to any of the traditional parties in philosophy, and enable him to fight all of them.[87]

Dogmatic skepticism obviously has a special significance for critical philosophy. It seems to be, for Reinhold, the most important enemy, and his paper is designed to put as much distance between it and critical skepticism as possible. This is relatively easy, given his definition of "dogmatic skepticism."

It bears the name "dogmatic skepticism" because it attempts to demonstrate that we must forever doubt objective truth, that is, the real agreement of our representations with their object. The indemonstrability of objective truth constitutes the dogma of this sect. It can co-exist only through an obvious, though therefore no less common, inconsistency with philosophical convictions which presuppose necessity and universality. . . . Critical Skepticism doubts what dogmatic skepticism considers as settled. It seeks the foundations of the demonstrability of objective truths, while the latter believes to be in possession of reasons for the indemonstrability of objective truth. The one executes and prescribes an investigation, which the other declares to be futile and superfluous, and thus, as much as is possible for him, makes impossible.[88]

As any member of Reinhold's "*aechtphilosophisches Publikum*" could see right away, dogmatic skepticism is really inconsistent, and only critical skepticism can be considered to be true skepticism. One would hope that they also saw right away, that the inconsistency was one introduced by Reinhold's definition.[89]

It is significant, however, that in 1789 the critical point of view, for Reinhold, was a skeptical point of view, and not one that gave rise to any positive claims. Indeed, it was, so far as doctrinal content is concerned, more negative than traditional skepticism, at least as characterized by Reinhold. The most important characteristic of the critical skeptic was his more open attitude. But this constitutes only the beginning of Reinhold's objection to skepticism. Holding onto his definition of "dogmatic skepticism," and still claiming that "dogmatic skepticism" needs to be refuted, he not only abandoned "critical skepticism" as a position, but also banished the name from his vocabulary. Indeed, in some of his later writings he went so far as to argue that skepticism, in order to be philosophical at all, must be dogmatic, that is, based on principles. His "philosophy of elements," which was meant to supply Kant's critical philosophy with its foundation, was also meant to answer all skepticism.

Reinhold was by no means the only follower of Kant who found it necessary to downplay the critical element in Kant in favor of a somewhat more dogmatic view, or who built up the straw man of a dogmatic skeptic in order to destroy it. Ludwig Heinrich Jakob, the first philosopher to give university lectures on Kant in Halle, was also interested in skepticism. Between 1790 and 1792 he published what seemed to be the first German translation of Hume's *Treatise*. Its first volume contained a long Appendix of 314 pages, entitled *Kritische Versuche über die menschliche Natur* (Critical Essays Concerning the First Book of David Hume's Treatise of Human Nature).[90] The expressed goal of the long Appendix was to provide the "point of view from which Hume's *Treatise* must be seen." This point of view was characterized by the following claims: (1) that skepticism is one of the most important philosophical views (indeed, that it is inevitable given traditional philosophical assumptions); (2) that Hume's *Treatise* is the most perfect expression of skepticism; and (3) that the *Critique of Pure Reason* has given us the means to disprove Hume, and therefore all of skepticism. In disproving Hume, Jakob claimed to be disproving skepticism *überhaupt*, for he thought there could be no other justification of skepticism than that given by Hume.

With these developments a new task for philosophy had arisen, namely, the founding of all knowledge against skepticism or a fundamental philosophy. In this foundation, Kant was of extreme importance in this project, but since he had not finished the enterprise, there was need for other thinkers to complete his work.

At the same time, many of the older philosophers continued to resist and attack the critical philosophy. Some of these attacks were vicious. But J. A. Eberhard's *Philosophisches Magazin*, which appeared in four volumes between 1789 and 1792, drew Kant's special attention.[91] Eberhard maintained that Leibniz's system was superior to Kant's: whatever was contained in Kant's critical philosophy was already better expressed in Leibniz's, and where Kant disagreed with the Leibnizian view, he was mistaken. Kant was very upset, as his letters to Reinhold and Schulze during 1789 and 1790 show.[92] He decided to answer Eberhard's attacks. Thus, at the Leipzig Easter Book Fair of 1790 appeared a short treatise by Kant entitled *On a Discovery According to which Any New Critique of Pure Reason Has Been Made Superfluous by an Earlier One.*

Kant's answer came in two parts. First, he addressed Eberhard's claim that he had established the objective reality of concepts going beyond sense perception, and second, he argued against Eberhard's proposed solution to the problem of synthetic a priori judgments. Appealing to mathematical concepts, Eberhard had tried to show that we do have concepts that are independent of sense perception but yet are objectively real. Kant denies this, insisting that without corresponding intuitions, mathematical concepts cannot be shown to have objects. He also rejects Eberhard's defense of the concept of sufficient reason as an objectively real concept. His attempt to prove the principle of sufficient reason from the principle of contradiction fails, because (1) the proposition to be proved is ambiguous, (2) the proof lacks unity and really consists of two proofs, (3) Eberhard contradicts himself in some of his conclusions, and (4) the principle he purports to prove is simply false, if it is applied to things. "The teaching of the *Critique* therefore stands firm."[93] Similarly, Eberhard commits many errors in trying to prove the concept of a simple being as a legitimate concept independent of experience, and his attempts at ascending to the nonsensible from the sensible prove only that he misunderstood major portions of the *Critique of Pure Reason*.

In the second section, Kant shows that Eberhard misunderstood what the *Critique* means not only by "dogmatic," but also by "synthetic judgments a priori." Because of this, Eberhard makes a number of claims that are simply false. Thus he maintains that Kant wanted "to deny to metaphysics all synthetic judgments."[94] But the *Critique* did not do that. It only denied that they were possible apart from experience. Since Eberhard does not even understand the problem Kant wanted to solve in the *Critique,* his remarks about the dispensability of the enterprise can safely be ignored.

Kant concludes by discussing Leibnizian philosophy, and by trying to show that Eberhard misunderstood that as well. Kant sees Leibniz's system as characterized by three doctrines, namely, the principle of sufficient reason, the monadology, and the doctrine of preestablished harmony. Eberhard wants to construe the principle of sufficient reason as objective, but Leibniz thought it was subjective, and he seems to "expose Leibniz to ridicule just when he thinks he is providing him with an apology."[95] Eberhard also misunderstands the monadology when he tries to show that bodies consist of simples. It is the intelligible substrate of bodies, not the bodies themselves, that consist of simples for Leibniz. Similar things can be said about Eberhard's understanding of preestablished harmony. The three *Critiques* are quite compatible with this aspect of Leibniz. The agreement between the kingdom of nature and the kingdom of grace, or the concepts of nature and the concepts of morals, constitutes a harmony, and this harmony can be conceived as possible only because of a first intelligent cause. "The *Critique of Pure Reason* may therefore be seen as the genuine apology for Leibniz, even against his partisans, whose eulogies hardly do him honor."[96]

Kant's attack on Eberhard was effective. It convinced the younger generation, if they needed any convincing, that the Leibnizians had nothing to offer them. Philosophy continued now on a more or less Kantian path. While the attacks continued, Kant paid less and less attention to them. In any case, the criticisms no longer concerned just the master, but also his pupils; and increasingly, his pupils were criticizing the critics. The *Aetas Kantiana* had dawned. Hundreds of books and articles for and against Kant were written, and Kant was the only important philosopher as far as most Germans were concerned. He had become the king of the Philosophers. Yet he himself took less and less interest in these squabbles, concentrating on the completion of the work he had started so long ago.

The Famous Host: "King in Königsberg"

Kant was now one of the greatest names in Königsberg. Everyone who visited Königsberg wanted to see him. Some just wanted to visit him; others went to his lectures as well. One visitor who saw Kant in 1792 wrote:

I was every day with Kant [three days in all], and once I was invited to dinner. He is the most cheerful and most entertaining old man, the best *compagnon*, a true *bon-vivant* in the most honorable sense. He digests the heaviest foods as well, while his readers get indigestion over his philosophy. But you can recognize the man of the world and taste by the fact that I did not hear a word about his philosophy even during the most intimate hours.[97]

The most famous visitor in Königsberg of the period was Johann Gottlieb Fichte (1762–1814). He stayed in Königsberg from July to October 1791. His background was similar to Kant's. Having studied theology and jurisprudence in Jena, Leipzig, and Wittenberg between 1780 and 1784, he first became a private tutor. In 1790, he returned to Leipzig and agreed to tutor a student in Kantian philosophy. Soon after beginning his tutoring, he wrote that he "had thrown himself entirely into the Kantian philosophy; first from need – I had to tutor for an hour on the *Critique of Pure Reason* – but, after I became acquainted with the *Critique of Practical Reason*, with true relish."[98] He probably then decided to visit Kant in Königsberg by way of Warsaw (where he took up another position as a private tutor that did not last very long).[99] In Königsberg, he first looked at "the immense (*ungeheure*) city" and then visited Kant early the next day. He was not received "enthusiastically" (*sonderlich*), but, like many learned visitors, he stayed to attend Kant's lectures. Kant did not excite him, seeming "sleepy" to him. But he wanted a more serious interchange with Kant. Not knowing how to arrange another visit, he "finally had the idea to write a *Critique of All Revelation*." In six weeks, he finished the book and delivered it to Kant.[100]

Borowski gave the following account:

> One morning he [Fichte] brings the manuscript to Kant, asks for his judgment, and whether Kant, in case he finds it worthy of publication, might not help him to find a publisher. . . . Kant likes him because of his modesty, and he promises to do what he could. That very evening I met Kant on his walk. His first words were: "You must help me – help me very quickly – to find name and also money for a young destitute man. Your brother in law (Hartung, the book dealer) must be involved. Persuade him to publish . . . the manuscript.[101]

Though Kant thought the manuscript was good enough for publication (after reading up to paragraph three), Fichte revised it and had Borowski and Schulz read it as well. But he did not expect too much from Schulz, because he had "more orthodox (*rechtgläubige*) concepts than a critical philosopher and mathematician should have."[102] The book was soon finished, but because of difficulties with the censorship process, it appeared only at the Easter Book Fair of 1792.[103] Fichte benefited greatly from Kant's help. He did not expect much from the lectures. Indeed, he found: "His lectures are not as useful as his writings. His weak body is tired to house such a great mind. Kant is already very frail, and his memory begins to leave him."[104] Still, Fichte may perhaps be called Kant's most famous "student" of that time.

Friedrich Lupin (1771–1845) reported that Kant was especially interested in talking about mineralogy and about a mineralogist named Werner, whom he knew.[105] Lupin thought that this was because Kant himself was at that time busy with his edition of the physical geography, but it was probably motivated more by genuine interest in mineralogy. After his initial "audience," as Lupin described the encounter, he was invited to come back for lunch the next day. He gave the following account:

> When I came the next day at the agreed hour at the promised meal of honor, I found the philosopher meticulously dressed; and he received me with the voice of the host

and a proud demeanor which revealed an inner pride that looked good on him. He seemed to be another person from the one I met yesterday in his frock (*Schlafrock*); he seemed less dry in body and soul. But his high brow and his clear eyes were clearly the same, and they enlivened the little man. . . . As I was leaving, Kant said I should come tomorrow at noon for dinner.

What a triumph, to be asked to table by the king in Königsberg! . . .

We hardly had sat down, and I had prepared myself to play the role of an inferior mind, when I noticed that great minds do not just live on air. He ate not only with an appetite but with sensuality. The lower part of his face, the entire periphery of his cheeks expressed the sensual delight of satisfaction in an unmistakable way. Some of his intellectual looks were fixated so much on this or that dish that he was at that time nothing but a man of the table. He enjoyed his good old wine in the same way. Great men and scholars are never as similar to one another as they are with regard to their guests at table. After Kant had paid his tribute to nature . . . he became talkative. I have seen only few men at his age who were so lively and agile as he was. And yet he had a dry humor in everything he said, no matter how elegant and witty his remarks about even the most ordinary things were. He added some anecdotes, just as if they were made for the occasion, and one could not prevent one's laughter, even while expecting the most serious thoughts. He constantly told me to please have another helping especially of the large sea fish, alluding to the rich Jew who told his guests: "Eat, eat, this is a rare fish, bought and not stolen." I told him, however, the story of the *Magister* Vulpius, who was invited to Leibniz's house and who swallowed a piece of goose liver without chewing so that he would miss no word, and who died the next day of indigestion. . . . It was one of the characteristics of this great man that his deep thinking did not stand in the way of his cheerful socializing. He was all pure reason and deep understanding, but he did not burden either himself or others with it. In order to have a good time in his society one only had to look at him and to listen to him. In order to be virtuous, one did not merely have to believe his words, one only had to follow him and to think with him, for there is hardly a human being who lived more morally and more happy.[106]

Another visitor during April of 1795 described Kant as follows:

He lectures logic *publice* daily at 7:00 A.M. and twice a week a private course on physical geography. It's understood that I miss none of the classes. His presentation is entirely in the tone of ordinary speech, and if you will not very beautiful. Imagine an old little man (*Männchen*), who sits there, bent, in a brown coat with yellow buttons, a wig, and – not to forget – the hair bag. Imagine further that, at times, he takes his hands from the buttoned-up coat, in which they are placed folded over, and makes a small motion to his face, as he wanted to make something quite comprehensible to someone. If you imagine this, you will see him before you exactly. Even though this does not look exactly beautiful, even though his voice does not sound clear (*hell*), all that his presentation is lacking in form, if I may say so, is richly replaced by the excellence of its matter.[107]

He went on to contrast Kant's direct approach with that of his followers, who were constantly talking about difficulties, preparing their hearers for

them, and encouraging the students not to give up on Kant's difficult philosophy. Kant did not even seem to imagine in his dreams that his doctrine
might be difficult. But "once one has come so far that one understands his
voice, then it is not difficult to understand his *thought.* Last time he spoke
of space and time and I felt that I had never understood anyone as much
as him." Indeed, the visitor went on to say that he was very satisfied with
Kant's lectures, that "his was the very ideal of a learned presentation," and
that a science meant to be for the mind should be presented in just that
way. Every philosopher should lecture as Kant did. If they did, they could
lecture every day, and the students would also be able to come and listen
every day. We also hear about Kant's lecture notes. Kant used "the old logic
of Meyer" as a basis for his lectures.

He always brings the book into class. It looks so old and dirty that I believe he has
already brought it with him for forty years. All the pages are covered with small hand-
writing, some of the printed pages have paper glued on them, and many lines have been
scratched out. There is, as you might imagine, almost nothing left of Meyer's logic.
None of his students brings this book. They all just take notes from him. But he does
not even seem to notice, following the author with great fidelity from chapter to
chapter. And he corrects the author, or rather: he puts it differently. But he does so
with such innocence that one can see in his face that he does not make much of his
inventions.[108]

All in all, Kant reminds him of the "damned Wieland." He is just as "long-
winded," engages in "long asides," and even his language is reminiscent
of Wieland's.[109]

All these accounts make it clear that Kant had become very old, and that
his weakness had begun seriously to interfere with his effectiveness as a
lecturer. Visitors who attended just a lecture or two, and who saw in Kant
one of the most famous authors in Germany, tended to overlook some of
the problems. Students in Königsberg were less kind. Reusch, who began
his studies at the University of Königsberg in 1793, claims that "his voice
was weak, and he got tangled up in his presentation, and he became un-
clear." When one student could not overcome his boredom "and signified
it by a long yawn, Kant was disturbed and became angry, saying that if one
could not stop yawning one should at least have enough of good manners
to hold one's hand before one's mouth."[110] Kant's amanuensis saw to it
that this student sat further back in the classroom after that. Boredom was
especially a problem in metaphysics and logic. His lectures on physical geography and anthropology appear to have been more lively. "They were
clear and comprehensible, even highly witty and entertaining."[111] One of

Kant's students reported that he often introduced his lectures by saying that he lectured neither for the very bright (*Genies*), because they would find their own way, nor for the stupid, because they were not worth the effort, but only for those in the middle, who were seeking to be educated for a future profession.[112]

In 1788, Kant taught for thirteen hours: logic (with eighty students enrolled), natural law (twelve students), physical geography, and an "*examinatorium*" on logic (with ten students).[113] In that same year Pörschke, who lectured on aesthetics in accordance with Eberhard and on metaphysics based on Ulrich, also announced a course on Kant's *Critique of Pure Reason*.[114] In the summer semester of 1789, Kant lectured for the first time for only nine hours, and he never increased his hours again. Part of the reason for curtailing his teaching was his health and his advancing age. At sixty-five Kant found that he could only write in the morning, being too tired for it in the evening. He now could only work "for two or three hours in the morning," and every hour of teaching took an hour away from writing. Indeed, Kant had noticed around the end of 1789 a "sudden revolution" in his health. He still felt well enough, but his "inclination to intellectual work, even to giving lectures had suffered a great change."[115] In 1789–90 he lectured on metaphysics to only forty students, but for most of the following years he still seems to have lectured to between fifty and eighty students in his public lecture courses in logic and metaphysics.

Given Kant's decline, it is perhaps not surprising that his influence on the students at the university and in Königsberg began to diminish at this time.[116] Before, there had been a certain balance in the teaching of philosophy. Kraus's more "practical" and empiricist approach and Kant's theoretical and abstract style complemented each other quite well. But now "Kraus's doctrine undeniably acquired a greater weight in teaching and in reputation."[117] By this time, Kraus had made a virtue of his inability to write, and he openly declared that his goal was "to survive, not in dead books, but through men who owe their education to me."[118] While many people came from outside Königsberg to see Kant, at home his name did not shine so brightly any longer. Indeed, some who resented his success now dared to speak more openly about Kant's shortcomings.

Kant was still the most famous philosopher of the Albertina, and some came to study with him. One of his most important students during this period was Johann Gottfried Karl Kiesewetter (1766–1819), who was in the fall of 1788 sent to Königsberg by Frederick William II himself so that "he could benefit from Kant's oral instructions."[119] The king supported him with 300 Thalers. At that time Kant gave not only his regular lectures but also a private recitation, in which a select few of his students could talk to him about philosophical matters. Kiesewetter stayed until 1789, and in 1790 he came back for another three months. Kiesewetter adored Kant, frequently referring to him as his "second father in later times."[120] Beginning with his *Grundriss der reinen allgemeinen Logik nach Kantischen Grundsätzen* (1791), he became an ardent popularizer of Kant's philosophy.

Kant was not just visited; he also received the manuscripts of promising young philosophers who had written on his work. Thus he wrote on May 26, 1789, to Herz, who had sent him a manuscript by Salomon Maimon: "What were you thinking when you send me such a great package of the most subtle inquiries not just for reading but also for thinking through. I am burdened in my sixty-sixth year with the extensive task of completing my plan, that is, I must deliver the final part of the Critique, namely the Faculty of Judgment, which should appear soon, and work out the metaphysics of nature as well as the metaphysics of morals. Furthermore, I am constantly kept out of breath by many letters, which demand special explanations about particular points, and this while I am always of uncertain health."[121] The manuscript was Maimon's *Essay on Transcendental Philosophy with an Appendix on Symbolic Cognition and Notes*, which appeared in 1790. Maimon, who on his visit to Königsberg could not visit Kant's lectures, had read the first *Critique* and tried his best to consider Kant's problem in an even wider extent than Kant himself had been willing to do. Maimon found that "there was much scope left for the full force of Hume's scepticism" and that "the complete solution of this problems leads either to Spinozistic or Leibnizian dogmatism."[122] Maimon was just as much influenced by the pantheism dispute as he was by the *Critique*. But Kant liked the work, telling Herz that he was about to send the manuscript back with an excuse, but that a glance at it persuaded him otherwise. None of his opponents had understood him as well. Maimon's enquiries were profound, acute, and important. The book should be published.

Even specialists found the book difficult. The *Allgemeine Literaturzeitung* wrote to Maimon, "three of the best speculative thinkers have declined the review of your book, because they are unable to penetrate into the depth of your researches. An application has been made to a fourth, from whom a favorable reply was expected; but a review from him has not yet been received."[123] Maimon, who tried to steer Kant's critical philosophy into a more skeptical direction, became one of the most important Kantian philosophers, but he was a philosopher's philosopher. He did not help the further spread of Kantian philosophy. Instead, he took it into a new direction.

Kant had the deserved reputation of being a difficult writer, and there were many disputes about who got Kant right. Fichte, for instance, got into a dispute with an army captain in a guest house where he was staying. The captain, who professed not to believe in immortality, appealed to Kant as someone who supported his position, because he had only given a probabilistic proof of God's existence. Fichte burst out: "You did not read Kant!" He argued that, if the captain had read Kant, he would have seen that Kant had given a necessary proof.[124]

At times, the occasions for a dispute were more mundane. On December 9, 1791, some time before 7:00 A.M., there was a commotion in Kant's lecture hall about who could use one of the few tables, which were set aside for students who took notes during Kant's lectures. Kant's amanuensis at that time, one Johann Heinrich Lehmann, student of theology, tried to mediate the dispute between the two students, but one of them attacked and insulted Lehmann instead. Lehmann immediately went upstairs to inform Kant, who instructed him to file a complaint with the rector. Before beginning his lectures on metaphysics at 7:00, he warned his students, saying that "nothing like this had ever happened in his *auditorium*, and that if his students had such a dispute [again], they should take care of this on the street; otherwise he would no longer give any lectures."[125] But, whether mundane or otherwise, Kant's philosophy was apt to cause disputes, and Kantians soon acquired the reputation of being especially quarrelsome. Thus Maimon was very happy to have received Kant's own blessing, because, he said, "there are some arrogant Kantians, who believe themselves to be the sole proprietors of the Critical Philosophy, and therefore dispose of every objection, even though not intended as a refutation, but as a fuller elaboration of this philosophy, by the mere assertion . . . that the author has failed to understand Kant."[126]

The Beginning of a Conflict: "Daring Opinions"

In September 1791, Kant published an essay "On the Miscarriage of All Philosophical Trials in Theodicy." It appears to have been written immediately after he finished with the third *Critique*, and it continued the treatment of the subject matter of religion that he had begun in the final sections of that work. Kant tried to show that "every previous theodicy has failed to perform what it promised, namely the vindication of the moral wisdom of the world-government against doubts raised against it on the basis of what the experience of the world teaches."[127] While the doubts are not decisive either, traditional theodicy is a failure. Using Job as an example, Kant argues that faith can never be the result of insight into God's plans or the nature of the world. We should admit our ignorance and thus also our doubts. What is needed in religious matters is only "sincerity of heart," "openly admitting one's doubts," and "repugnance to pretending conviction where one feels none." Job's faith came from his moral disposition not to lose his integrity even under the greatest pressure. "He did not found his morality on faith, but his faith on morality." Even though every "higher consistory in our times (one alone excepted)" would likely have condemned Job, he was more pleasing to God than were his judges.[128] The reference was obvious to any reader of the essay in 1791. The king, just like the Pietists in Kant's youth, was declaring that people should pretend conviction even if there was none – and this was something Kant was unwilling to do. "Sincerity of heart" was more important than what any higher consistory might demand.

Kant believed he had shown that theodicy has little to do with the interests of science. It was "a matter of faith."[129] But more importantly, it was a matter of honesty. While one cannot always vouch for the truth of what one says, one "can and must stand by the *truthfulness* of one's declaration or confession, because one has immediate consciousness of this." But one of the basic presuppositions of truthfulness is our paying attention to whether we really consider something to be true when we declare it true, so that we never *pretend* that we believe something to be true when we are not consciously holding it true. Self-deception is the root of hypocrisy. Someone who declared that he believed "without perhaps casting even a single glimpse into himself" would be committing the "most sinful" lie, for such a lie "undermines the ground of every virtuous intention."[130] Sincerity is the property "farthest removed from human nature," yet it is the minimal condition of character.[131]

Kant's claims in the theological sections of the third *Critique* seemed at the very least questionable to Frederick William II and his censors. But his remarks about sincerity, hypocrisy, and character were openly critical of the activities of the "higher consistories" and their policies. Insofar as their mandate came directly from the king in Berlin, Kant was criticizing him. This would not have been lost on those in power in Berlin.

The Rosicrucian cronies of the king were continuing to move against the advocates of the Enlightenment. The French Revolution made them redouble their efforts. The Enlightenment ideas were dangerous not just for morality, but also for the existing order. The actions of the king had begun to affect the pastors of the Prussian church long before, and he increased the pressure. Thus he formed in 1791 a committee to examine the preachers' orthodox credentials (or their lack thereof). As might have been expected, the majority of the committee were Rosicrucians. Given the zealous persecution of rationalist preachers by Wöllner and his subordinates, the situation became more and more tense. Few preachers were dismissed, but the fear of reprisals from Berlin was significant, and it was not just the preachers and pastors who came to feel the wrath of the king. Gedike and Biester, the editors of the *Berlinische Monatsschrift*, the most important publication propagating the Enlightenment in Germany and therefore much hated by Wöllner and his cronies, had to move the journal outside Prussia to Jena early in 1792.[132]

In February of 1792, Kant sent to Biester an essay entitled "On Radical Evil in Human Nature." He also asked Biester to send it to the Berlin office of censorship. Even though this was not required, because the *Monatsschrift* was now published in Saxony, Kant wrote that he did not want to create even the appearance of trying to "express so-called daring (*kühn*) opinions only by consciously avoiding the Berlin censorship." The censors let the essay pass. It appeared in the April issue. In June, Biester received another essay from Kant, entitled "Of the Struggle of the Good Principle with the Evil Principle for Sovereignty over Man." It was rejected. Hillmer, who was responsible for moral matters in the bureau of censorship, had allowed the first essay to be published because he thought it was written for philosophers and not suitable for the public. But the second essay was theological, or so it seemed to him. He therefore sent it to Hermes, who rejected it.[133] Biester filed a complaint, but it was rejected. The article seemed doomed – at least as long as Kant persisted in playing by the rules.

At the Easter Book Fair in Leipzig appeared a book with the title *Critique of All Revelation*, published by Hartung in Königsberg. Since the book appeared anonymously, the *Allgemeine Literaturzeitung* published a note in which it found that anyone "who read even the most minor writings by means of which the Königsberg philosopher has obtained the eternal gratitude of mankind will immediately recognize the distinguished author of this work." Kant reacted quickly and pointed out in a note of "correction," dated July 31, 1793, that he had not "the slightest part (*schlichtesten Antheil*) in the work of this talented man," and that the author was "the candidate of theology Mr. Fichte." He claimed that it was his "duty to leave the undiminished honor to the one, who really deserved it."[134] This declaration made Fichte – who had not really wanted to publish the book anonymously in the first place – immediately famous as the foremost Kantian.

It could be argued that Fichte would have had much less impact if the book had been published in his own name. Kant also had other reasons to make sure that the book was not considered his own work. Though Fichte's *Critique of All Revelation* begins from the Kantian point of view, arguing that morality is prior to religion and that morality is what makes us receptive to revelation, he also assigned a greater importance to religion and revelation than Kant was willing to grant it. For Fichte, religion had to answer the problem of how "the propositions, which are accepted through the law of reason, can practically motivate us."[135] This was not really an open question for Kant, and, though he would have agreed that the "idea of God, as the lawgiver through moral laws in us, is founded on a projection from us, [that is,] on transferring something subjective to a being external to us," and that "this projection (*Entäußerung*) is the real *principle of religion*," he would not have put it in those terms. In a sense, Kant was putting distance between his own view and that of Fichte. It was Kantian, but it was not Kant.

In July, Kant also asked that the article he had sent to the *Berlinische Monatsschrift* be sent back to him, because he "did not want to hold back from the public the three essays, which belonged to . . . the article on radical evil."[136] He promised Biester that he would "soon" send another "exclusively moral" essay, which was to deal with Garve's critique of the Kantian principle of morals.[137] This was what later became Part I of his essay "On the Old Saw 'That May Be Right in Theory, but It Won't Work in Practice'." Before finishing this essay, he created the *Religion within the Limits of Mere Reason* by putting together four essays that he felt belonged together. This time, rather than submitting the entire volume to the Berlin censorship office, he decided to give it to a faculty of theology, who would determine whether it was a contribution to biblical theology or philosophy. This was not a merely theoretical matter. Prussian professors had a right to exempt themselves from the Berlin censorship and to have their books censored by a dean of their faculty. If the *Religion* was indeed a philosophical book, then the dean of the philosophical faculty could give permission to have it printed. Reluctant to involve the theological faculty in Königsberg, Kant first planned to send it to the University of Göttingen, and then considered the University of Halle. Since Halle had just rejected Fichte's *Critique of All Revelation*, however, and since the Königsberg theologians did not think they would get any trouble from the Berlin officials if they censored it themselves, he finally submitted it there. The faculty of theology declared the book to be philosophical in nature, and therefore the faculty of philosophy could decide whether it should be published. Kant did not ask the philosophical faculty at the University of Königsberg. Kraus was the dean during 1792–93, and it may have been that Kant did not want to implicate Kraus. In any case, he sent the manuscript to Jena, where it was approved for publication. The book appeared in time for the beginning of the 1793 Easter Book Fair in Leipzig.

Part of the book, namely the chapter on the struggle between the good and evil principles, had already been banned by the Berlin censors. Accordingly, its publication could only be construed as a slap in the face of Wöllner and his censors. They could not possibly let this pass. Kant had to be reprimanded. This must also have been clear to Kant. It almost appears as if he was trying to force their hand, that he was picking a fight with the censors.

This was dangerous, as the example of *Zopf-Schulz,* the preacher of atheism, had showed to everyone. Schulz had already experienced difficulties. Because of his *Moral Doctrine of All Mankind* and his open endorsement of determinism, he had been accused as an infidel, unfit to be a preacher. Minister von Zedlitz had successfully defended him by drawing a distinction between Schulz, the preacher (and thus official of the state) and Schulz, the public author. The two functions were quite distinct – one being private, the other public. Accordingly, his public writings could not be used to impeach his qualifications as a preacher. Yet in 1791 he was accused again. The court asked the *Oberkonsistorium* whether Schulz deviated from the basic principles of the Christian religion or from those of the Lutheran Church. The answer came back in two parts: (1) Schulz did deviate from Lutheran principle, but (2) he did not necessarily deviate from those of religion in general. The tribunal concluded that he should be allowed to preach because he was religious. The king was furious, and he had Schulz removed from office in 1793 on the basis of his deviance from the Lutheran principles. He also punished the members of the *Oberkonsistorium* as well as the *Probst* Teller, whom he thought had misled the members of the committee: no salary for three months. The price for perceived heresy was not as great as it had been under Frederick William I, but, given the lack of principles of Frederick William II, no one could be sure how high it might be. Those who had tried to back Schulz lost three months' salary. Schulz himself was left without any support –

and the next person to defy the king's orders might have to pay an even higher price.

Religion within the Limits of Mere Reason: "An Example of . . . Obedience"?

The *Religion within the Limits of Mere Reason* consists of the published essay "Of the Radical Evil in Human Nature" and the rejected "Concerning the Battle of the Good against the Evil Principle for Dominion over the Human Being," as well as "The Victory of the Good Principle over the Evil Principle, and the Founding of a Kingdom of God on Earth" and "Of Religion and Priestcraft." The four essays are preceded by a relatively short Preface, dated January 6, 1794.

The first sentence sounds a tone of defiance. "Morality, insofar as it is based on the concept of the human being as one who is free but who also, just because of this freedom, binds himself through his reason to unconditional laws, is in need neither of the idea of another being above him in order that he recognize his duty nor of an incentive other than the law itself in order that he observe it."[138] If we find such a need in us, it is our own fault. One of the implications is that decrees are neither necessary nor useful. Kant is still more explicit. "Obey authority!" is, he points out, also a moral command that can legitimately be extended to religion. Therefore, it is only proper that a book on religion should itself be "an example of this obedience." Still, this obedience cannot consist in blindly observing "the law in a single decree," but only in coherent respect for the totality of all laws. Kant admits that the censorship decree is indeed a law, but he suggests that insofar as it is incompatible with the large majority of the laws (passed under Frederick, one might add), it is obedience that makes defiance necessary.

In the first essay, or Book I, Kant takes up the question of whether human beings are by nature "either morally good or morally evil."[139] For Kant, this disjunction can mean only that there must be in the human being "a first ground (to us inscrutable) for the adoption of good or evil (unlawful) maxims."[140] His answer is that there is in us a first ground for moral evil. It consists in what he calls "the ultimate ground for the acceptance or the observance of our maxims according to the laws of freedom."[141] This means, in Kant's language, that the ultimate ground is rational. Indeed, the claim that each human being is evil means that "he is conscious of the moral law and yet has incorporated into his maxim the (occasional) deviation from it."[142] Every human being is necessarily evil in this sense, and yet every human being is responsible for this evil because he or she has freely adopted a deviant maxim.

This evil is *radical*, since it corrupts the ground of all maxims; as natural propensity, it is also not to be *extirpated* through human forces, for this could only happen through good maxims – something that cannot take place if the subjective supreme ground of all maxims is supposed to be corrupted. Yet it must equally be possible to *overcome* this evil, for it is found in the human being as acting freely.[143]

Furthermore, this evil has a beginning in time. This means that if we want to explain the origin of evil, we must look for the causes of every particular transgression in an earlier period of our lives "all the way back to the time when the use of reason had not yet developed."[144]

Where this evil, which is inherent in our rationality, came from, cannot be explained. It is inscrutable. Yet Kant has more to say about it. The first inscrutable ground for the adoption of good or evil maxims is disposition or *Gesinnung*. It is a single characteristic of any human being, but it is also something that we have freely adopted.[145] Nevertheless, it cannot be known. There "cannot be any further cognition of the subjective ground of or the cause of this adoption, for otherwise we would have to adduce still another maxim into which the disposition would have to be incorporated, and this maxim must in turn have its ground."[146]

If this is true, the question must be how we can ever get out of this state. Kant himself asks that question explicitly and tries to answer it.

If a human being is corrupt in the very ground of his maxims, how can he possibly bring about this revolution by his own forces and become a good human being on his own? Yet duty commands that he be good, and duty commands nothing but what we can do. The only way to reconcile this is by realizing that the revolution is necessary for the way of thinking (*Denkungsart*), but that the gradual reform is necessary for the sensible disposition (*Sinnesart*) (which places obstacles in the way of the former) and therefore must be possible as well. That is, when a human being reverses the supreme ground of his maxims by a single irreversible decision (and thereby puts on a new man), he is to this extent, by principle and way of thinking (*Denkungsart*), a subject receptive to the good; but he is a good human being only in the incessant laboring and becoming, i.e. he can hope . . . to find himself on the good (though narrow) path of constant progress from good to better.[147]

The biblical story of the Fall is suggestive. Our evil is the result of seduction, and this means that we are not ineluctably corrupt but capable of improvement.[148] We must first bring about a revolution in our thinking, that is, found a character, and then we must work on it. Nevertheless, the moral

character "for which we are responsible" does not have an origin in time.[149]
It must therefore have a beginning in reason and must be rationally explicable. Character is identical to *Denkungsart*.[150]

Character is not identical to *Gesinnung*.[151] The notion of *Gesinnung* adds
nothing new to Kant's discussion of particular moral agents. When he uses
the term in this context, he refers to the motivation, or the motivations,
expressed in our maxims. Thus Kant often speaks of "good *Gesinnungen*
and maxims" or of "principles and *Gesinnungen*," or he refers to "the maxims," adding in brackets, "*Gesinnungen*."[152] In those passages he seems
to identify *Gesinnungen* as the motivational aspect of maxims. *Gesinnungen*
refer to what is "subjective" in the "subjective principles of volition." The
singular "*Gesinnung*" is then nothing more than a way of talking about the
motivation expressed in the collectivity of our maxims. It is in this way that
Gesinnung is "the internal principle of maxims" that one has adopted.[153]

When Kant speaks of *Gesinnung* in the *Religion* as the "first subjective
ground of the adoption of maxims," he seems to be talking about something else.[154] He is talking about something that is "to us inscrutable,"
namely, the "intelligible ground of the heart (the ground of all powers of
all the maxims of the power of choice)."[155] Kant's assertion that having
a good or evil *Gesinnung* is the "first subjective ground of the adoption of
maxims," and that it is both an "innate characteristic we have by nature"
and also "adopted by free will," seems troubling, however.[156] Does this
mean that we are "choosing ourselves" in some fundamentally Sartrean
sense, that we ourselves freely adopt our own fundamental maxim?

This would certainly create problems. Since *Gesinnung* is "not acquired
in time," this raises the specter of "noumenal choice."[157] Still, Kant had in
mind neither the notion of "choosing ourselves" nor the notion of a "fundamental maxim."[158] *Gesinnung*, for Kant, is inscrutable. It is "supersensible" (*übersinnlich*).[159] It is a characteristic that a human being has, not qua
individual, but qua being a member of the human species. It is a universal
characteristic of all human beings, which shows that "by his maxims he
expresses at the same time the character of his species."[160] So it is precisely not a "choosing of ourselves." It is an expression of our "fallenness."
This is what Kant was concerned with in his essay on a "Conjectural Beginning of the Human Race." Reason, when it begins to function, comes
"into conflict with animality in all its strength," and therefore evils necessarily ensue. This is the necessary first step for rational beings like us –
or so Kant seems to believe. "From the moral point of view, therefore, the
first step . . . was a fall, and from the physical point of view, this fall was a

punishment that led to hitherto unknown evils. Thus, the history of *nature* begins with goodness, for it is the *work of God;* but the history of *freedom* begins with evil, for it is the *work of man.*"[161] We always find ourselves as already fallen.

The second essay or book of the *Religion*, which deals with the struggle of good against evil, does not postulate a Manichean ontology, as the title might suggest. Kant does not view the universe as the battlefield of two forces. Indeed, he claims that ultimately it is irrelevant whether we place that which tempts us "simply in us or also outside us."[162] If we give in, we are guilty just the same, no matter whether the temptation comes from within or without. The same also holds, of course, for the power of the good. The Son of God, who represents the idea of the perfect human being, may be thought of as having existed outside of us, but it is more important to view him as an ideal to be emulated. The Son of God, just like the tempter, is more important as a concept that might help us understand our moral situation than as anything that has a reality apart from morality. Just as Lessing had claimed in his "Education of the Human Race," Kant argues that the Bible has only a moral import. While some of Kant's analogies between religion and morality seem fanciful, they do show how much he was concerned to show that there was no necessary conflict between Lutheran doctrine and moral faith. It might almost appear that he is giving advice to preachers on how to translate the language of critical morality into the language of traditional faith.

Moral faith makes the miraculous stories of the Bible dispensable, and "the person of the teacher of the one and only religion, valid for all worlds, is a mystery . . . his appearance on earth, as well as his taking leave from it, his eventful life and his passion, are all miracles." Indeed, the story of the life of the great teacher is itself a miracle, since it is thought to be revelation. We can "leave the merit of these miracles undisturbed" and "even venerate the external cover" of the doctrine that is written into our hearts,

> provided, however, that . . . we do not make it a tenet of religion that knowing, believing, and professing them are themselves something by which we can make ourselves well-pleasing to God.[163]

What counts is a moral disposition, not the external cover. In the third book or third essay, Kant addresses again the question of hope. However, the hope he has in mind is not for eternal life and salvation for the individual, but for the "kingdom of God on earth," or the establishment of an "ethic-civil state" in which human beings are "united under laws without being coerced, that is, under *laws of virtue* alone."[164] Kant goes on to argue that such a community needs to be understood as a community "under God," and that therefore the moral state must be understood as a church. While all historical churches depend on historical, revealed, or "ecclesiastic" faith, Kant hopes there will eventually arise the "pure faith" of moral religion. Indeed, he claims that the gradual transition of ecclesiastic faith toward pure religious faith represents the coming of the Kingdom of God. These views of Kant seem a bit strained, especially his argument that the ethical community must be a community under God. We must assume that there is a God as a supreme law-giver because moral laws are essentially internal laws and a community needs juridical laws, which are external. These external laws must conform with the ethical laws, that is, they must be at the same time true duties, and someone who truly knows our hearts is the only one who can accomplish the establishment of such laws.

In the second division of the essay Kant then goes on to outline the historical course of the gradual establishment of the Kingdom of God or the dominion of the good on Earth. In the course of that outline he answers the question "Which period of the entire church history in our ken up to now is the best?" He replies "without hesitation, *the present.*" His reason is that he sees the seeds of true religion being sown at this time. "In matters which ought to be moral and soul improving by nature, reason has wrest itself free from the burden of faith constantly exposed to the arbitrariness of its interpreters."[165]

In the final section, on religion and priestcraft, he launches an all-out attack on external religious practices, arguing that we must differentiate between true service of the church and counterfeit service. Religion, "subjectively considered," is for Kant nothing but "the recognition of all our duties as divine commands." He can thus differentiate between revealed and natural religion based on whether duty or the divine command is prior. In revealed religion, I must first understand that something is a divine command in order to see it as my duty; in natural religion, duty comes first.[166]

Kant argues that Christianity can be viewed as both a natural and a learned religion. He also argues that as a natural religion it is one that "can be proposed to all human beings comprehensibly and convincingly through their own reason." It is a religion whose possibility and even necessity has been made visible in an example, "without either the truth of those teachings or the authority and the worth of the teacher requiring any other authentication."[167] This is what the first three essays have shown.

Insofar as Christianity is based not only on reason but also on facts, it is not merely a religion but also a kind of faith. If these facts assume primary importance, and the rational and moral content of religion merely secondary importance, then religious service becomes "counterfeit" or "pseudo" service. Indeed, Kant accepts as "a principle requiring no proof" that any service to God over and above *"good life-conduct"* is *"mere religious delusion and counterfeit service to God."*[168] Only moral service will make us pleasing to a moral God. Prayer, liturgy, pilgrimages, and confessions are worthless. There is no difference between the Tibetan using a prayer wheel, a Catholic saying a rosary, or a Protestant praying without a set formula. They are all fooling themselves. Nothing good will be accomplished by such forms of worship, and they may even lead to fanaticism and thus to "the moral death of reason, without which there can be no religion, because, like all morality in general, religion must be founded on principles."[169]

This still was not sufficient for Kant. In the penultimate section of the essay, he attacked the "priestcraft" of the official Christian churches, pointing out that the ways in which a primitive Wogulite and "the sublimated *puritan* and Independent in Connecticut" pray may differ, but there is no essential difference between them. The European prelate, who rules over both church and state, is no different from a shaman among the Tunguses.[170] Praying as an "inner ritual service" and a means of obtaining grace is a particularly harmful "superstitious delusion (a fetish-making)." It is also not very intelligent, for it amounts to declaring a wish to a being who, being all-knowing, does not need such declaration.[171] Such clericalism leads to fetish worship wherever it is allowed to rule. If it becomes dominant in a state, it will lead to hypocrisy, undermining the integrity and loyalty of the subjects, and thus producing the very "opposite of what was intended."[172]

This self-defeating religious policy was just what Kant observed in Prussia between 1788 and 1790. He was speaking not just to a general audience but also to Frederick William II. His *Religion* was not just a theoretical treatise, meant as a contribution to the philosophy of religion; it was also a political act. In fact, it was primarily a political act. Kant hoped (perhaps naïvely) to alter the conduct of his readers, including that of the king. The *Religion* was also Kant's declaration of loyalty to Lessing and Mendelssohn. Kant's *Religion*, Lessing's *Education of the Human Race*, and Mendelssohn's *Jerusalem*, as well as many other less well-known contributions to the *Berlinische Monatsschrift*, were all valiant attempts to introduce into Prussia the kind of religious freedom that had by then already been achieved in the United States. Lessing and Mendelssohn were dead. Kant carried on the fight. That he was concerned not only with religious freedom, but ultimately with full-fledged civil freedom, is clear from a footnote, in which he observed:

I admit that I am not comfortable with th[e] way of speaking, which even clever men are wont to use: "A certain people (intent on civil freedom) is not ripe for freedom"; "The bondsmen of a landed proprietor are not yet ripe for freedom"; and so too, "People are not yet ripe for freedom of belief." For on this assumption freedom will never come, since we cannot *ripen* to it if we are not already established in it.

In an obvious allusion to the French Revolution, he went on to say:

To be sure, the first attempts will be crude, and in general also bound to greater hard-ships and dangers . . . yet we do not ripen to freedom otherwise than through our *own* attempts. I raise no objections if those in power, being constrained by the circum-stances of the time, put off relinquishing these three bonds far, very far into the fu-ture. But to make it a principle that those who are once subjected to them are essentially unsuited to freedom . . . this is an intrusion into the prerogatives of divinity itself, which created human beings for freedom.[173]

This meant not only religious freedom, but also civil freedom and freedom from any kind of bondage. One might have expected a swift and decisive response from the powers that be.

"On the Old Saw": Addressing
One of the "Earthly Demi-Gods"

Yet nothing happened, at least at first. Kant remained somewhat cautious, but not overly so. In March of 1793 he was asked by the Berlin publisher Johann Carl Philip Spener to republish his 1784 essay on an "Idea for a Universal History from a Cosmopolitan Point of View." He declined, say-ing that a pygmy who placed great value on his hide should not get involved when "the strong ones of the world are in a state of intoxication, regard-less of whether it results from the breath of the Gods or from that of a Mufette."[174] In September 1793, the essay Kant had promised Biester a year earlier appeared in the *Monatsschrift*. It was entitled "On the Old Saw 'That May Be Right in Theory, but It Won't Work in Practice.'"[175] This was hardly an exclusively moral essay, however. Kant addressed such issues as the freedom of the press, the right to revolution, the authority to wage war, the preservation of peace, and the nature and authority of government in general. It was another contribution to a political discussion that the king would rather not have seen developing.

The essay has three parts. In the first Kant deals with the relation of moral theory to moral practice. It was written to answer "some exceptions" taken by Garve, who was more conservative than Kant. The second part discusses the relation of theory and practice in constitutional law and was ostensibly directed against Hobbes. The final part discusses theory and practice in international law. Kant develops what he calls a "cosmopolitan" view, directed against Mendelssohn. This division expresses three perspectives that a person can take on the world: the perspective of (1) a private citizen and man of business, (2) a man in a state, and (3) a man in the world.

Garve had argued that Kant's distinction between acting from duty and acting in accordance with duty, simply could not be maintained. Garve's first objection was that for us to act morally, according to Kant, we must give up our desire to be happy; but this is contrary to nature. Kant's answer: I never demanded any such thing, and if I had, I would have asked for the impossible. Garve's second objection was that we can never really know whether we acted merely from duty or from selfish reasons. Since the distinction is of fundamental importance for Kantian morality, this was a serious criticism. Kant answered:

> I gladly admit that no man can ever be conscious with certainty of *having performed* his duty quite unselfishly, for this is a matter of internal experience, and this consciousness of his state of mind would require one to have a consistently clear view of all the subsidiary notions and considerations which imagination, habit, and inclination attach to the concept of duty. We can never demand such a view . . .

This was never demanded, according to Kant. He argued that his distinction made sense if it was understood as an injunction to act in a certain way, saying

> that man *ought to perform* his duty quite unselfishly, and that his desire for happiness *must* be completely divorced from the concept of duty in order to preserve its purity – this he knows with utmost clarity . . . to make a maxim of favoring . . . motives [at odds with duty], on the pretext that human nature does not allow this kind of purity . . . is the death of all moral philosophy.[176]

The distinction has to do with a person's *Gesinnung*, with his honesty of soul, not with empirical psychology. Though our striving to do the right thing for the right reason is not independent of psychological questions, it is also not simply reducible to them.

Garve's third objection was related to the second. He claimed that in practice we never know which of the many motives we usually have made us do what we did. Duty is no better guide to action than any other motive.

Kant argues that this is false. The concept of duty is "simpler, clearer, more comprehensible, and more natural" than any motive drawn from happiness. Maxims based on happiness are notoriously difficult to formulate and act on. Yet moral education had been based on such maxims until now. Kant went on to argue that this is what impeded moral progress, and that this did not prove the old saw that moral theory could not work in practice. It would work, if only it were tried.

Garve had objected to Kant that it was incomprehensible how anyone "can be conscious of having achieved complete detachment from his desire for happiness." Kant admitted that no one could ever be conscious of having acted purely from duty. Now, if it is impossible to know in principle whether one has ever accomplished a certain thing, then one might be excused for thinking that there is a real problem in "trying" to do it. And even if it did make sense to keep trying to achieve what we can never know to have actually achieved, it still would not be true that the concept pure duty is simpler, clearer, and more comprehensible and natural. It was not an argument against Garve that provides independent evidence for Kant's view. Indeed, his admission that we can never know whether we have acted from duty alone shows that there is a problem with his derivation of duty from pure reason alone – a problem Garve did not have. Garve's view may make morality more external, but it does give a more sensible account of it. Kant's idealism was perhaps more inspiring, but it was not necessarily a clearer formulation and better defense of ordinary moral convictions.

The second part of the essay is an attempt to answer two questions: (1) why must we obey existing governments? and (2) are there circumstances in which we are justified in (a) disobeying or (b) overthrowing existing governments? The French and American Revolutions, as well as the actions of Frederick William II and his censors, had made this a highly relevant question for Kant for both political and personal reasons. Kant's answer to (2b) is simply that there are no circumstances in which we have a right to revolution. Though revolutions might improve things in some cases, they are never justified. There can be neither a legal nor a moral right to revolution. His answer to (2a) is almost equally negative. Citizens have no right to disobey, even when they perceive a law to be unjust. Indeed, they are not the ones who decide whether a law is just – only the lawmakers can do that. Yet they have the right to question the justness of laws. The lawmaker must recognize the citizen's right "to inform the public of his views on whatever in the sovereign's decrees appears to him as a wrong against the community."[177] Freedom of the pen is essential. To speak up about perceived wrongs does not necessarily constitute disobedience.

This freedom of speech follows from Kant's view of what legitimizes the power of government. This is the social contract. Disagreeing with both Hobbes and Locke, Kant argues that the social contract should not be understood as an explanation of the origin of government but as a normative idea that clarifies the relationship between a government and its citizens. It shows, according to Kant, that government can ultimately be justified only by the consent of those who are governed and that governmental power is morally justified only in cases where all rational beings can agree to it. "For right consists merely in limiting everybody else's freedom to the point where it can coexist with my freedom according to a universal law, and the public law in a community is no more than a state of actual legislation in accordance with this principle and combined with power."[178] The people have "inalienable rights" against the government, even if these rights can never justify disobedience or rebellion.

There is no contradiction between Kant's rejection of a *right* to rebellion and his enthusiasm for the French Revolution, or better: Kant himself saw no contradiction between the two. Louis XVI had in effect abdicated when he called the Estates-General. So, legally speaking, the French Revolution was not rebellion. "In France the States-General could change the national constitution, even though it was charged only with getting the finances into order. For they were representatives of the entire nation (*Volk*) after the king allowed them to pass decrees in accordance with indeterminate powers. Before that, the king represented the nation . . ."[179]

In the third part of the essay, Kant asked whether the human race as a whole should be loved or disdained. His answer was that this depended on the answer to another question, namely whether the human race had tendencies that would allow constant progress or whether it was condemned to evil forever. Mendelssohn had written that the view "that the whole of mankind down here should be moving ever forward, perfecting itself in the sequence of times," was chimerical.[180] His position was motivated, at least in part, by Jewish ideas of human corruption. Christian doctrine, of course, emphasized to an even greater extent the ineradicable evil of humanity and the impossibility of salvation by human devices. If Kant took "a different view" from that of Mendelssohn, he also took a view that was quite different from that of convinced Christians, whether they were influenced by Rosicrucianism or not.

Kant argued that if progress were impossible, the trials and tribulations of every person striving for virtue would be nothing but a farce. It would also be repugnant to a wise Creator of the world.[181]

I may be allowed to assume, therefore, that our species, progressing steadily in civilization as its natural end, is also making strides for the better in regard to the moral end of its existence . . . I rest my case on this: I have the innate duty . . . so to affect posterity through each member in the sequence of generations in which I live, simply as a human being, that future generations will become continually better. . . . I may always be and remain unsure whether an improvement in the human race can be hoped for; but this can invalidate neither the maxim nor its necessary presupposition that in a practical respect it is feasible.[182]

The perpetual progress to the better would, Kant assured his readers, ultimately "bring the states under a cosmopolitan constitution even against their will."[183] Though some might reject this theory as impractical, he declared that he put his "trust in the theory that proceeds from the principles of justice, concerning how relations between individuals and states *ought to be*." This theory has greater authority than any of the "earthly demi-gods" who actually rule. Ultimately they would have to submit. Kant had taken another stand. While he rejected the right of rebellion, which some of his followers had defended on the basis of his own theories, he also argued against conservatism in politics. The essay was thus relevant to Edmund Burke's discussion of the French Revolution and its merits. The *Reflections on the French Revolution* of 1790, which had been translated into German in 1791 and 1793, loomed large in the background. But first and foremost Kant felt the need to clarify his own position, as Kantians of various persuasions had their own views on what his theory implied about revolution.[184]

The essay was also relevant to Kant's dispute with the censors in Berlin. It was his way of addressing Frederick William II, as one of "the earthly demi-gods." He may not have been expecting a reply from the king, but he did receive one in short order. While the more conservative thinkers in Germany, especially August Wilhelm Rehberg and Friedrich Gentz, found it necessary to answer Kant publically, the king answered by a special order.[185]

During this period Kant also found time to work on another project, namely on an essay in answer to a question of the Berlin Academy, "What is the real progress that metaphysics has made since the times of Leibniz and Wolff in Germany?"[186] Kant appears to have begun working on it some time in November of 1793.[187] Whether Kant intended to submit the essay to the Academy is not clear. What is clear is that he drafted a fairly extensive answer to the question, in which he tried to show that there was indeed progress, namely, his own critical philosophy. Taking up a distinction familiar from the first *Critique*, he argued that metaphysics proceeded in three steps or stages, namely dogmatism, skepticism, and the criticism of pure reason.[188] In the historical part of the (projected) essay, he first gave a summary of Leibniz's principles, which differed from the outline given in his response to Eberhard. He now identified the four basic principles of Leibnizian metaphysics as the principle of the identity of indiscernibles, the principle of sufficient reason, the principle of preestablished harmony, and the monadology.[189] Kant called the system of preestablished harmony "the most peculiar figment ever conceived by philosophy."[190] He squarely relegates Leibniz (and Wolff) to the first stage of metaphysics. The second stage of metaphysics, that is, skepticism, he identified with the antinomy of pure reason as it was discussed in the first *Critique*. The third stage was what he called here the "Practical-Dogmatic Transition to the Supersensible."[191] It consisted in the discussion of the three ideas of Freedom (autonomy), God, and Immortality, as he had put them forward in the first, second, and third *Critiques*. In a section entitled "Solution of the Academic Question" he summarized his own views of rational faith, transcendental and moral theology, comparing them to the views of the "Leibniz–Wolffian epoch."[192] Kant points out that Leibniz–Wolffian philosophy had tried to demonstrate things that he had tried to prove unknowable but believable on sufficient moral grounds. The draft ends with an interesting summary of Kant's entire philosophy.

Metaphysics has two pivots on which it turns. The *first* is the doctrine of the ideality of space and time. It only points to what is supersensible in regard to the theoretical principles, but which remains unknowable for us. But at the same time it is theoretical-dogmatic insofar as it has to do with the a priori cognition of objects of experience. The *second* is the doctrine of the reality of the concept of freedom as the concept of something cognizable and supersensible, in regard to which metaphysics is however only practical-dogmatic. But both pivots are, as it were, fastened to the post of the concept of reason concerning the unconditional in the totality of all subordinated conditions. With it the illusion ought to be removed, which causes an antinomy of pure reason by confusing appearances with things in themselves. And in this Dialectic itself is contained the instruction for moving from the sensible to the supersensible.[193]

While one might wish that Kant had taken better care in formulating these sentences, it should be remembered that what we have are a number of drafts of an essay that Kant never finished.[194]

In some ways, the draft of this essay is alarming. It can be considered as a sign of megalomania. The only thing Kant could accept as important in the development of metaphysics from the time of Leibniz and Wolff was his own work. Everything is contained in his own philosophy. Neither Hume nor Lambert nor Mendelssohn seem to have made any contribution to the progress of metaphysics. Neither Leibniz nor Wolff are given a fair hearing. Kant, at seventy, found it difficult to free himself from his own philosophical views and to think "from the point of view of everyone else." It almost seems as if he lost his *sensus communis.*

At the same time, the philosophical discussion in Germany was moving away from his ideas. Reinhold had put forward his own *Elementarphilosophie* as an improvement of the critical position. Gottlob Ernst Schulze's *Aenesidemus*, an attack on the "Kant-Reinholdian" position, was seen as a serious challenge.[195] Fichte's review of the book in the *Allgemeine Literatur-Zeitung* early in 1794 made clear he was about to abandon Reinhold's principles, and his *On the Concept of a Doctrine of Science*, the so-called *Wissenschaftslehre*, made good on the promise. Schelling published as a response an essay *On the Possibility of a Form of Philosophy in General*, still in the same year, and Maimon's *Essay toward a New Logic or Theory of Thought* (also of 1794) took a new direction as well. It may not yet have been apparent to Kant or to most of his contemporaries, but his own brand of critical philosophy was falling out of fashion. A few years later (in 1798), in a summary of the three most important "trend-setting events of the age," Friedrich Schlegel did not even mention Kant at all, but spoke instead of the French Revolution, Fichte's *Wissenschaftslehre*, and Goethe's *Meister*.[196] *Sic gloria mundi!*

Why did Kant not submit his answer to the Academy before the deadline of June 1, 1795, and why did he choose not to finish it? The answer is not to be found in a sudden realization that such a submission might be in bad taste. Rather, it is explained by the events that took place in the second half of 1794.

Consequences: The Threat of "Unpleasant Measures for . . . Continued Obstinacy"

On October 1, 1794, Wöllner, at the special order of the king, wrote to Kant:

Our most high person has long observed with great displeasure how you misuse your philosophy to distort and negatively evaluate (*Herabwürdigung*) many of the cardinal and basic teachings of the Holy Scripture and of Christianity; how you have done this particularly in your book *Religion within the Boundaries of Mere Reason,* as well as in shorter treatises. We expected better things of you as you yourself must realize, how irresponsibly you have acted against your duty as a teacher of the youth against our paternal purpose, which you know very well. We demand that you give at once a most conscientious account of yourself, and expect that in the future, to avoid our highest disfavor, you will be guilty of no such fault. . . . Failing this, you must expect unpleasant measures for your continued obstinacy.

This was serious business. The "unpleasant measures" would certainly have meant dismissal or forced retirement without pension, and they could have included banishment. Like Wolff in 1723, Kant in 1794 was holding his post at the pleasure of His Highness. At seventy years old, the prospects of moving would have looked even less inviting to him than they had earlier. Furthermore, resistance would not have made any difference to the developments in Prussia.

Kant was not the only one affected by the king's order. It was directed against all the "renegade preachers, school teachers and professors," singling out Niemeyer and Rösselt at Halle, Reinbeck at Frankfurt (Oder), and Kant in Königsberg. The infamous Schulz, who had advocated a thorough-going determinism in a book reviewed by Kant himself, had already been dismissed. Borowski, who talked to Kant during this period, said that Kant was fully prepared to lose not only the bonus that Frederick William II had granted him earlier, "but also his entire salary." Kant was not frightened by this possibility because he had invested his money wisely and had become independently wealthy. While he had not amassed a fortune, as Hippel had done, he was well off. Thus he "spoke . . . with great calm and explained expansively (*breitete sich aus*), how advantageous it was, if one was a good economist and therefore did not have to crawl even in such situations."[197] Yet nothing happened to him. Kant's reputation was probably one of the things that saved him from more serious consequences. Thus his reprimand came in the same year in which he became a member of the Academy of Sciences of St. Petersburg.[198]

Kant decided to give in. Indeed, according to the views he had articulated in the essay on "Theory and Practice," he had to give in. On October 12 he answered, outlining two concerns of the king as he saw them: (1) that he had been misusing his philosophy to disparage religion, and was "opposing" the king's "paternal purpose," and (2) that he should no longer publish anything "of the sort" in the future. Kant argued he had not been guilty of disparaging religion in his lectures. He was not negligent in his duty as a teacher of youth. Nor was he negligent in his duty as a teacher of the people. He could not have negatively evaluated Christianity because he had not evaluated *Christianity* at all. He greatly respected religion, and he had always been tolerant, that is, he had not intruded on the beliefs of others. Finally, he wrote: "I believe the surest way, which will obviate the least suspicion, is for me to declare solemnly, as *Your Majesty's loyal subject,* that I will hereafter refrain altogether from discoursing publicly, in lectures or writings, on religion, whether natural or revealed."[199] Kant later made clear that the phrase "as *Your Majesty's loyal subject*" signaled a mental reservation. His promise applied only to himself as the subject of "His Majesty." As soon as "His Majesty" was dead, it no longer applied.

Some have argued that this was dishonest of Kant, that either he should not have made such a promise at all or he should have kept it. Some have claimed that when Kant promised to abstain from writing on religious matter, he was making a *reservatio mentis.* But is that fair? Frederick William II had made it a personal issue. Kant had opposed *his* paternal will, and he was to promise not to do it again. He did precisely that, and he kept his word. Furthermore, Kant did not know that he would survive the king. He had every reason to believe that he would not.[200] Some have argued that the whole affair showed cowardice on Kant's part, that he should have stood up for his rights. Yet apart from being difficult, this would have been ineffective. The situation was rather the following: Kant had knowingly provoked the censors in Berlin, they had been afraid to act, and the king himself had finally been goaded into action. He had shown his true colors, and that was some sort of success.

Characteristically, Kant withdrew. A more opportune moment might present itself. Following his Stoic motto, *sustine et abstine,* he was prepared to endure and abstain from making comments – at least for a time. The largely theological essay "On the Progress of Metaphysics" was one of the things that had to wait.[201]

Kant had inflicted damage on Wöllner, for the latter was reprimanded for his leniency and for not making enough progress against the forces of rationalism. On April 12, 1794, the king had stripped Wöllner of one of his offices so that he could pay more attention to religious matters. The king's special order against Kant was a further expression of his dissatisfaction with Wöllner. He was to be more zealous in the fight against rationalism and for orthodox Christianity (and Rosicrucian ideals). Wöllner still advised caution, but his more zealous subordinates pushed harder, with undesirable effects. When a commission came to examine the professors at Halle for orthodoxy, the students rioted. This riot was probably instigated by the faculty, and it was successful; after the rioting, students smashed the windows of the hotel where the members of the commission were staying; and after having received death threats, the commission quietly left town.[202] The religious politics of Frederick William II was hardly a roaring success.

Kant, on the other hand, still had some writings on religious matters ready in his desk. He had written a manuscript entitled "The Dispute of the Faculties," but he could not publish it – at least not at this time. He had written this essay probably between June and November of 1794 at the invitation of Carl Friedrich Stäudlin, who had asked him whether he would be willing to contribute to a new journal on religious studies.[203] In December 1794, he wrote to Stäudlin that he had "already for some time" finished a treatise entitled "The Dispute of the Faculties."[204] He also claimed in this letter that he had written the "Dispute" for publication in Stäudlin's journal, but that he now felt he could not publish it because of his problems with the Prussian censors. Kant had at this time written the essay on "The Dispute between the Philosophical and Theological Faculties," which became the first part of *The Dispute of the Faculties*.[205]

The subject matter of this essay is highly relevant to Kant's response to the rejection of the essay "Of the Struggle of the Good Principle with the Evil Principle for Sovereignty over Man." It not only provided justification for his actions, but also went further in arguing that a philosopher should not be required to submit his work to a theological faculty in the first place. Kant was willing to play by the rules, but the rules were wrong. Granted, theologians

have the duty incumbent on them and consequently the title, to uphold biblical faith; but this does not impair the freedom of the philosophers to subject it always to the critique of reason. And should a dictatorship be granted to the higher faculty for a short time (by religious edict), this freedom can best be secured by the solemn formula: *Provident consules, ne quid republica detrimenti capiat* (Let the counsels see to it that no harm befalls the public).[206]

The philosophical faculty should be free of "the government's commands with regard to its teachings."[207] Kant was ready to grant that the higher faculties were, in fact, subject to the government's commands, because it had a legitimate interest in them. But if the higher faculties were given authority over philosophy, then philosophy would no longer be free. Therefore, it was wrong to set up theology, one of the higher faculties, over philosophy.[208] Therefore the religious edict was wrong.

This was not the only criticism of the policies of "His Majesty." Kant also asked whether any government could "confer on a mystical sect the sanction of a church, or could it, consistently with its own aim, tolerate and protect such a sect, without giving it the honor of that prerogative?"[209] The answer, for Kant, was of course: "No." Kant's arguments for this conclusion are subtle, and some of them derive their strength from his conception of religion as universal and necessary because based on pure practical reason. His idea of a "sect" may be idiosyncratic, but his conclusion is clear and unmistakable. It is wrong for a ruler to favor any one sect. Most of all, it is wrong to elevate mystical hocus-pocus to the level of a state-sanctioned view. Pietism, which provides a "completely mystical" solution to the problem of religion and morality, should therefore not be favored.[210] Orthodoxy, which declares "belief in dogma to be sufficient for religion" and therefore places only secondary importance on morality, is also inappropriate. "But it is superstition to hold that historical belief is a duty and essential to salvation."[211] Mysticism, because it is a private affair, which "has nothing public about it," should be of the least concern to the government. Therefore it should be entirely outside the government's sphere of influence.

Kant did not go as far as the founders of the United States in minimizing the role of religion in the state. He believed – or at least he claimed to believe – that Christianity is necessary. Still, Christianity for Kant was nothing but the clearest expression of the Idea of Religion in general, and therefore it was commendable as a moral religion. He was opposed to anything having to do with the particular customs and historical origins of this faith, and he felt those matters should be left to the individual. This was a view that was radically opposed to that of Frederick William II and his ministers, as Kant well knew.[212] Kant's destiny was tied closely to Berlin – for better or worse. He was not just a passive observer of what happened in Prussia, but an active political player – and he knew how to play his cards.

Perpetual Peace: "The Theoretical Politician as an Academic"

In December of 1795, one of Hippel's friends wrote:

I have just read the Religion and the Politics (*Politik*) of our most illustrious, and this with care and respect. He probably will not get for his newest political writing (Toward Eternal Peace) a golden box with diamond inlay – and he most likely gave it up beforehand. But I am happy (and almost amazed) that there is so much political tolerance in our native fatherland; and this especially since his basic principles (of form and non-form etc.) are so different from the faith of the castes and statutes. – I see the noble old man, just like his friend Solon (I think he was indeed), who once stood before his rulers, and was asked the question: "What is it that makes you so brave?" He answered smilingly: "*Meine Herren*, it is my age."[213]

In August of that year Kant had offered the essay "Toward Perpetual Peace: A Philosophical Project" for publication to Nicolovius in Königsberg.[214] The book appeared at Michaelmas. One of the occasions for the book was the withdrawal of Frederick William II from the War of the First Coalition in March of 1795. Another occasion was a long-standing dispute about the notion of perpetual peace, going back to 1713. Kant joined the ranks of Leibniz, Voltaire, Frederick the Great, and Rousseau in addressing this issue. He also was explicating his political and legal theory.[215]

Kant was well aware of the problems this work might cause him, and he introduced the essay with a "little saving clause" (*clausula salvatoris*). The publicly expressed opinions of a mere "theoretical politician" and "academic" could not be dangerous to the state, since the "worldly-wise statesman" or practical politician, who looks down on the mere theoretician in any case, had no temptation and was under no obligation to pay attention to him.

The essay presents an argument for the thesis that a peaceful global order presupposes cosmopolitan law (*Weltbürgerrecht*). This cosmopolitan law should replace the classical law among nations (*Völkerrecht*) with one that states the rights of human beings as citizens of the world. The essay develops this idea in two sections, two supplements, and a long Appendix. Section I contains the preliminary articles for perpetual peace among states, including articles declaring that there should be no peace treaty with a secret reservation of material for another war (article 1), that states are not the kinds of things that can be acquired by other states (article 2), and that there should be no standing armies (article 3), no national debt (article 4), no forcible interference in any other state's constitution of government (article 5), and no extreme measures in case of war (article 6).

Section II formulates the "definitive articles for perpetual peace among states." The first of these is that "The civil constitution in every state shall be republican."[216] This constitution is based on three principles, namely, the principle of the freedom of the members of a society as individuals, the principle of the dependence of all members on a single legislation as subjects, and the principle of the equality of all citizens. This is the only form of government that follows from the idea of an original contract. Though Kant does not want this republican constitution to be confused with a democratic one, as "usually happens," and though he identifies democracy as a despotic system, it is clear that his view of a republic is compatible with certain forms of democracy. For his central idea of the republic is that it is based on the separation of the executive power from the legislative power. It needs a representative form of government. The second definitive article states that "The right of nations shall be based on a federalism of free states," a view that Kant had already formulated in his earlier essays; and the third article amounts to the claim that "Cosmopolitan right shall be limited to conditions of universal hospitality."[217]

In the first supplement, Kant deals with the guarantee of perpetual peace, which for him, as for the Stoics before him, comes from providence. He had already argued for this view on many previous occasions. The second supplement offers a secret article of peace that amounts to the claim that states armed for war must consider the maxims of philosophers about the conditions that make public peace possible. While one cannot reasonably expect that kings would become philosophers, they should also not silence philosophers. Philosophers should be allowed to speak publicly. This plea had, of course, a very personal meaning for Kant. The Appendix explores further the relationship between morals and politics and how it is related to the "transcendental concept of public right." This concept is expressed by the claims that "All actions relating to the rights of others are wrong if their maxim is incompatible with publicity," and that "all maxims which *need* publicity (in order not to fail in their end) harmonize with right and politics alike."[218] Publicity is a necessary condition of moral politics. Without publicity, progress toward eternal peace would be impossible, or so Kant claims. All this is a matter of historical development.

The essay ends on a more personal note. Kant finds:

If it is a duty to realize the condition of public right, even if only in approximation by unending progress, and if there is also a well-founded hope of this, then the *perpetual peace* that follows upon what have till now been falsely called peace treaties . . . is no empty idea but a task that, gradually solved, comes steadily closer to its goal . . .[219]

Kant believed he was fulfilling his duty by speaking up.

Kant's ideas about cosmopolitanism are still hotly debated today. They are dismissed by some as a "Eurocentric illusion," and praised by others as the answer to the problem of humanity's survival. Whether they are the one or the other will be for (still) future generations to discover. Nevertheless, they make clear that Kant considered himself first and foremost not a Prussian but a citizen of the world. He was glad to be alive while momentous changes were taking place in the history of mankind, and he saw himself as rising to the challenge, addressing the important issues resulting from the changes, and trying to nurture what was good in them. However insignificant some of the occasions for these essays were, Kant succeeded in transcending them and in saying something of lasting importance.

Kant's cosmopolitan ideas were meant to form part of a civil religion similar to the kind that James Madison, Thomas Jefferson, and the other framers of the American Constitution envisaged. His transcendental idealism, at least in morality, ultimately is a political idealism, in which attaining the greatest good is not something that will be accomplished in another world but is a task to be accomplished on this earth. Kant's political writings were an attempt to show how rational (or reasonable) ideas can be substituted for religious ones, and why indeed it is necessary for the good of mankind to reinterpret religious ideas to make them fit the needs of humanity.

9

The Old Man (1796–1804)

The Early Years of Retirement (1796–1798): "Somewhat Changed"

JACHMANN, who lived outside of Königsberg and who came only a few times a year to the city, was perhaps in the best position to observe changes in Kant that would have been more difficult to see for those who saw him daily, or almost daily. He wrote in 1804:

I already found him somewhat changed eight years ago, even though there were some days when he exhibited his former mental powers. This happened when nature functioned smoothly. But after this period the decrease of his powers became more noticeable . . . the power of the greatest thinker slowly disappeared until he was completely incompetent.[1]

It is this tragedy that still needs to be told.

In the records of the university senate for the winter semester of 1796–97, the following entry could be found: "Immanuel Kant, *Log. et Metaph. Prof. Ordin. Facult. Phil. Senior:* 'I did not give any lectures because of age and indisposition.'" An entry for the summer of 1797 read: "he could not lecture because of age and weakness," and the one for the winter of 1797–98: "could not give lectures because of age and sickness."[2] These notes, written by Kant himself, show – at least indirectly – that he became incapable of teaching beginning in the summer of 1796, when he had to cut his lectures short. This was the very period during which Jachmann noticed the first signs of mental weakness. This was also a year during which Kant was supposed to serve as the rector of the university. Yet he declined.[3]

His daily life went its regular way – probably it went more regularly than ever before. Having no duty to lecture, and not going to any of the meetings of the university senate, Kant now lived a much more withdrawn life than at any prior time in his life. He still got up at 5:00 A.M., drank a little tea, smoked his pipe, "and then sat down at his working table until shortly before 1:00 P.M." If we can believe his own complaints, he could not have worked the entire time, since he found extended intellectual exertion difficult. After work, he got dressed for dinner. Dinner lasted from 1:00 to 3:00, often longer. During this period, he usually invited two guests. Immediately after dinner, he went on his daily walk for about an hour. In bad weather, his servant Lampe accompanied him. Coming back, he took care of domestic affairs and read his papers and magazines. Before going to bed at 10:00 P.M., he thought about his writings, making notes on small pieces of paper.[4]

Most of his old friends either were dead or were to die during this period. On April 23, 1796, Hippel, one of his most frequent dinner guests and the closest and most original of his surviving friends, suddenly died after a short illness.[5] He was just fifty-five years old. His death raised a number of questions. He was a highly respected public figure, but he had lived two lives, of which only one was known. Hardly anyone knew that he had published a great number of books anonymously. He had confessed to some of his friends that he was the author of some of these books. Only Scheffner knew all of them. There were suspicions, of course. Hamann at times came close in his guesses, and so did others. Scheffner often had to lie, and he felt compromised. Some of Hippel's books were very successful throughout Germany. He would have been famous, had he acknowledged his authorship, but he never did. One of the reasons for this was probably his worry that his career as a high government official would have been compromised, had the king and his ministers in Berlin known that he was plagued by "demon poesy" and did not spend his entire energy serving the government.[6]

Hippel was not able to dispose of the "chaos of papers" that made up his literary estate. There were hundreds of pages with notes, observations, and quotations, compromising bits of information and unflattering character sketches of his friends.[7] His friends were upset. They felt that his papers raised questions about Hippel's character. He left the sum of 140,000 Thalers, a large amount at the time. How could this be explained, if not by avarice?[8] His secretive nature and his literary exploitation of their friendship was too much for almost all of them.

If this was not enough, he was revealed to have been a great hedonist (*Wohllüstling*), who had engaged in all kinds of sexual escapades. One of his habits had been, for instance, to have his servants flagellate his body with wet towels.[9] Scheffner, whose "obscene" poems were not yet forgotten, found it necessary to distance himself from Hippel, explaining why it was that he never suspected anything about Hippel's sexual proclivities or his other shortcomings. He, Scheffner that is, had lived far away, had known nothing of his youth, and had viewed him as his superior. Hippel, on the other hand, had done everything to remove any traces that could have allowed Scheffner to draw conclusions about Hippel's "way of thinking and acting." He was never egotistical, and hardly ever showed any of his shortcomings. "Of his proclivity to satisfy his sexual needs I never found any evidence in his household."[10] That Hippel could not have been his friend *"in the way* in which he had assured me became clear only after I saw proof after his death and others told me."[11] Hippel was a disappointment to his friends. He was materialistic, deceptive, stingy, and sex-crazed.[12] What made these shortcomings worse in the eyes of many of his friends was that he had successfully hidden them for such a long time.

While Hippel was sick, Kant inquired about his status every day, but he did not visit him. On the day the old friend died, Kant said: "It is indeed sad for those close to the deceased, but we should let the dead rest with the dead," thus cutting off any further conversation about Hippel.[13] Kant did not belong among those who reviled Hippel, and continued to refer to him as a former "intimate" and "beloved" friend. We may be sure that he had always been much more aware of the complex, even self-contradictory, nature of this man, who was as successful in the pursuit of worldly success as in his secret career of "scribbling."

Hippel had remained a Pietist all his life, had written hymns that can still be found in the *Gesangbuch* of the Protestant churches in Germany, yet he was also a Freemason, adhering to Enlightenment principles, and a skeptical writer of satires and comedies in the style of Sterne. In December 1793 he had written to Kant

Since you know how much I adore you, I may not say to you how much I miss your learned society, which – as you know yourself – gives more to me than anything that Königsberg has to give. . . . I have had the *Religion within the Limits of Mere Reason* read to me during my illness. . . . There should truly not be any reservations that the name Immanuel Kant precedes this work, which can and will do much good.[14]

Though Hippel was a religious believer in the way that Kant was not, he did not see the kind of danger in the work that so many other public officials saw in it. Jachmann asked Kant in 1794 to use his influence with Hippel, "whom you can convince of anything," to get him a position in Königsberg.

Jachmann had reason to believe that Kant had such an influence on Hippel because he had obtained a scholarship through Kant's intervention.[15]

Much of the controversy around Hippel centered on the publication of his *Lebensläufe*. Hippel had made much use of notebooks from Kant's lectures on anthropology and metaphysics in the first volume. Not long after Hippel's death, a certain G. Flemming in Göttingen promised to prove, on the basis of their similarities to Kant's published writings, that Kant was the author of the anonymous *Lebensläufe* as well as of two other books.[16] Somewhat later, a J. A. Bergk weakened that claim, arguing that Kant had only written the philosophical parts. Kant felt he had to respond. Late that year he wrote a "Declaration Concerning Hippel's Authorship," pointing out that he was neither the author nor the coauthor of the book.[17] The similarity between Hippel's text and his own work was to be explained by the fact that Hippel had used notes taken by his students. This did not mean that Hippel had committed plagiarism. His lectures were public wares, and anyone who found them useful could use them in any way he saw fit. "And so my friend, who never explicitly studied philosophy, used the materials he obtained as spice for the taste of his readers, without being allowed to tell them whether they came from his neighbor's garden or from India."[18]

Kant knew that Hippel was the author of the *Lebensläufe* almost immediately after the publication of the book, although in a draft of his declaration he claims that he never broached the subject of these books in conversation or writing, and this because he was sensitive to Hippel's needs. Since Hippel never said anything to him about the books, and since he felt that someone who wanted to remain incognito should not be forced to reveal himself in polite society, he respected Hippel. He knew how many of his own thoughts had entered into the *Lebensläufe* and the book *On Marriage* even before he himself had published them. Hippel was his "former student, later a lively (*aufgeweckter*) acquaintance and, during the last ten years, his intimate (*vertrauter*) friend," and he did not want to harm him. On the other hand, however, he also did not want to seem to be a collaborator in Hippel's literary work.[19]

Hippel had used in the *Lebenlsäufe* Kant's claim that "in reading a book it is necessary to seek out the soul of the book and to try to investigate the idea, which the author had; only then do we know the book entirely." This means that the identity of the author is not as important as what the author had to say. The idea of the author that makes up the soul of the book is someone's idea, and the two cannot be entirely separated. We may be sure that Kant had better insight into the idea of the book and the identity of the author than he let on to Hippel. We may also be sure that Hippel knew very well that Kant had a fairly good idea not only of the books he had published anonymously, but also of who the author was. That neither Kant nor Hippel found this to stand in the way of their friendship is perhaps remarkable, but what was even more remarkable was the nature of their conversations about the subjects that Hippel discussed in his works. The wit and irony involved in this was probably only heightened by the fact that some of their mutual friends were also aware to varying degrees of some of the complexities. Hippel himself argued that "oral presentation betrays the way of thinking," that writing was a pure imitation of speaking, and that "all that is as great as our art, must be said."[20] Of course, it was not always simply what was said, but who said it and how he said it.

Scheffner was aware of this, and so were Pörschke and Jensch, but it was either lost on Kant's earliest biographers, or it was one of those dimensions of Kant's life that they thought were better not talked about. Hippel was, after all, persona non grata to them, at least after his death. If they found it embarrassing that Kant continued to honor him, his close friendship with Hippel between 1786 and 1796 may have been even more embarrassing to them. Kant, on the other hand, had not just lost another friend in Hippel, his social and intellectual life had lost a most significant component.

In the summer of 1797 a notable anatomist and surgeon named Friedrich Theodor Meckel (1756–1803) visited Königsberg and also stopped at Kant's house. He found that Kant's mind had so much declined that it was unreasonable to expect Kant to contribute anything new and original to the philosophical debate from then on, and he said so publicly. Pörschke came to Kant's defense, writing to Fichte in July 1798 that Kant might be suffering from weaknesses brought on by old age, but that this did not mean "that Kant's mind is already dead. To be sure, he is no longer capable of extended and concentrated thought; he now lives largely from the rich store of his memory, but even now he makes exceptional combinations and projects."[21] This did not mean that he no longer took as active an interest in the discussion of his philosophy by others. He complained bitterly about Fichte. Indeed, it was impossible to mention Fichte and his school without making Kant angry. On the other hand, "he just dismissed Reinhold (zuckte die Achseln)." His judgment of Herder was almost as passionate as his condemnation of Fichte: Herder "wanted to be dictator and liked to have apostles."[22] Nor was he "satisfied with Beck, preferring commentators of "stricter obedience (Observanz)."[23] When someone asked him why he never said anything bad about Reinhold, he answered: "Reinhold has done me too much good for me to be angry with him."[24] The name "Fichte," on the other hand, was ominous, for "Fichte" means "pine," and bad proofs were sometimes called "proofs of pine." Furthermore, to "lead someone behind the pines" could mean to be deceptive.[25] Some of Kant's acquaintances agreed. Thus Borowski found that "the man really was extremely ungrateful" toward the old philosopher.[26] Others, like Pörschke, sided with Fichte. Kant was also hurt by Nicolai's attacks on him, saying that he and Eberhard just "did not want to understand his system."[27]

While Kant was no longer the old great conversationalist himself, he apparently still had his moments. In the summer of 1798 the theologian Johann Friedrich Abegg (1765–1840) visited Königsberg on a journey that took him to most of the important cultural centers in Germany. He took extensive notes from which we can get some idea about how diverse the opinions on Kant were in Königsberg (and elsewhere) at that time. Herz, whom Abegg had visited in Berlin, praised Kant's character, contrasting him explicitly with the "Kantians," who had not produced one decent human being.[28] All of Kant's friends, acquaintances, and students in Königsberg seemed to agree to this judgment, but some noted that he could not take criticism well. Others, like Pörschke, remarked that Kant lacked goodwill or helpfulness. Scheffner criticized Kant for having been less than generous in his declaration about Hippel. Why did he talk about the lecture notes that Hippel had used? Could he not simply have pointed out that he was his friend?[29] Bock also felt Kant had created the appearance that Hippel had stolen his ideas, and that he was an "unfeeling" (*fühlloser*) man, who "should not be allowed to speak of friendship and love."[30] Deutsch emphasized that Kant was Hippel's intimate friend, "if anyone could be said to have been Hippel's friend."[31] Hippel and Kant were "a magnificent entertainment."[32]

Borowski did not like Kant's philosophy.[33] Pörschke preferred Fichte. He also claimed that "Kant does not read his own writings any longer; does not right away understand what he has written himself before. . .[and] his weakness is that he repeats everything he is told."[34] The curious old man is a tattletale. Kraus and Kant were still quarreling. They did not see each other any longer, and when they had to sit at the same table in society, they made sure they did not sit too close to each other.[35] Kraus, who was called by Friedländer the German Bayle, did "not have the best character; he acted ignobly against Kant."[36] Kraus claimed that Hamann believed Spinoza's writings were inspired by God.[37] Kant did not really believe in

God.[38] Reinhold made a great deal of what we may hope for, but Kant really thought: "Believe nothing, hope for nothing! Do your duty here, that's what the reply should be expressed in the Kantian language. "[39]

Abegg's report also gives some insight into the subjects of conversation at Kant's dinner table. There was very little about philosophy in general, not very much about the Kantian publications then in progress (*Anthropology* and *The Dispute of the Faculties*). There was some conversation about science (e.g., mineralogy and physiognomy), and more about persons in Königsberg and elsewhere (including Hamann, Herz, Hippel, Reuss, Schmalz, Starck, and Fichte). The last was said to have fathered an illegitimate child in Königsberg. There was much talk of daily life (drinking tea, smoking the pipe, taking snuff, wine, and coal), but most of the conversation was about politics.[40] Kant found most politically current ideas and contemporary political events interesting; and he had definite ideas about all of them. France, Russia, and England were critically discussed. The civil status of the Jews and the relations between the estates interested him as much as whether a king was needed. Schulz, Kant's expositor, took a more radical position on the last question than Kant himself, but Kant was most sympathetic toward the Revolution in France. Jensch remarked, for instance, "'We see . . . the innumerable consequences of the crusades, of the reformation, etc., and what are they compared with what we see now? What kinds of consequences will these events have?' Kant answered: 'Great, infinitely great and beneficial.'"[41]

When Abegg delivered his greetings from Herz, Kant said: "Oh, this is a well-meaning man, who sends his regards at every occasion," and he was "very" glad that Herz was well. "This is why I like at times visits of someone from outside of Königsberg because he can tell me such things firsthand."[42] Brahl confided at that occasion that Kant "loved the French undertaking with his entire soul," that he did not "believe in God, even though he postulated him," and was not afraid of death.[43] "The name of the preacher who ate with me at Kant's is Sommer and he is especially well versed in chemistry. – When tea was mentioned, Kant said that he drank two cups a day. Sommer asked: 'and do you still smoke a pipe of tobacco?' Kant answered: Yes, that is one of my happiest times. Then I am not yet strained, and I try gradually to collect myself, and in the end it becomes clear what and how I will spend the day." What did he have to say about his reading of other philosophers, like Selle? "It's just as it was with Hamann when he was reading Starck's writings on freemasonry, they make my belly rumble! – Starck wanted nothing less than to become the head of all freemasons. Then freemasonry was used for all kinds of purposes. Now it seems to be only a way to spend one's time and a play."[44]

Scheffner said: "Kant was very admirable in society and in some hours he still is. What is peculiar is that as soon as he takes up his feather he can write coherently and with his old force, just not as long anymore. How good it would be if he had a better style." Borowski answered: "Words are only the clothes," but Scheffner added, "clothes make the person." Borowski does not seem to be very endeared with Kant's philosophy.[45]

Even though he never went to its meetings, Kant was still a member of the academic senate. Reccard, a theologian, was essentially in the same position. Too old to attend the meetings, he still had not resigned. Membership in the senate was not a trivial matter, if only because the members of this body received certain perquisites from foundations connected with the university.[46] In June 1798 some of the younger members of the senate felt that it was necessary to complete their numbers by allowing the next two professors to join the senate as adjuncts. Kant felt that such a course of action amounted to a violation of his rights. Accordingly, he publicly protested in July 1798. Neither he nor Reccard had given up their right to vote by not appearing at the meetings. All the privileges that pertained to the position were still rightfully theirs. The matter was brought to the attention of the king by the university official Holtzhauer. The king took the side of Kant and Reccard, "who served the academy for many years with glory and usefulness, and who we trust will continue to do so insofar as their faculties allow them." Reccard died later that year. Kant continued to be a member of the senate for another three years.

Finishing Up: "Tying the Bundle"

Goeschen wrote to his son on February 2, 1797, that Kant was not lecturing and would never lecture again. "He intends to spend the small remainder of his life ordering his papers and to give his literary estate to his publishers. Those who had asked him about his literary works three years earlier he had already answered: 'What could they be? *Sarcinas colligere.* That's all I can think of now.'"[47] Kant was planning to "tie his bundle" at least from that time on. He did not expect much from himself any longer. Between 1794 and 1796 he had not published much. There would be more during 1797 and 1798, but most of these books were the results of "ordering his papers." He had long before conceived *The Metaphysical Foundations of the Doctrine of Right* (1797) and *The Metaphysical Foundations of the Doctrine of Virtue* (1797), and he had worked on them for a long time. Still, much of the material they contain derives from his lectures, and there is little in them that is new.[48] *The Dispute of the Faculties* (1798) consisted of three essays. One of these was written in 1794, the second after October 1795, and the third in 1796–97. The *Anthropology from a Pragmatic Point of View* (1798) was entirely based on his lecture notes. Apart from this ordering of papers, he wrote a few short essays and open letters dictated by time and circumstances. His publications contained no fresh ideas, and they were highly predictable, being entirely compatible with Jachmann's observation that Kant was not quite himself any longer but had moments in which he approached his former abilities. No longer lecturing, he could spend more time on his literary pursuits, but he was not breaking new ground. His health was questionable. Never possessing the vigorous health that his "long dead friends often praised," he now defined "health" as a period in which he neither suffered from sleeplessness nor had to sleep more than two hours longer than usual, while being able to eat and to walk.[49]

In May 1796, Kant had published one of his last articles in the *Berlinische Monatsschrift*. It was entitled "Of a Recently Adopted Noble Tone in Philosophy" and seemed to be directed against J. G. Schlosser's *Plato's Letters about the State Revolution of Syracuse* of 1795. Schlosser, Goethe's brother-in-law, had been a government official in Baden, but he had retired and was now concentrating on more philosophical matters. Not well disposed toward Enlightenment theories, he was one of the most outspoken critics of Basedow's school reforms, for instance.[50] He was convinced that most children should not learn about "higher" things but instead should become accustomed to steady work. Schlosser also had developed a peculiar kind of Platonic mysticism, involving the view that true knowledge is not based on deductive reasoning but on intuition. In many ways, this view was just another expression of the *Gefühlsphilosophie* or philosophy of feeling, which was then popular in certain circles. Schlosser was close to the philosophical ideas of Jacobi and Hemsterhuis, but his mysticism was also quite compatible with the Rosicrucianism that Frederick William II and Wöllner had prescribed as the cure against the common philosophy of the Enlightenment.

Kant had attacked this view in his still unpublished essay on "The Dispute of the Faculties"; and in the letter to Stäudlin in which he declined publication, he had said that an ironic treatment of the kind of which Lichtenberg was capable was perhaps the best way to counter such obscurantism. One of the ironies of his attack on Schlosser's "noble" philosophy was that he also attacked "His Majesty" in Berlin.

Kant defined as "noble" any philosophy that does not methodically and slowly develop its insights but is visionary and based on what may be called intellectual intuition. Its motto is "Away with the hair splitting based on *concepts*, let the philosophy of *feeling* live, which leads us directly to the thing itself." This "most recent German wisdom," opposed to the "manufacture of forms," that is, critical philosophy, promises "secrets that can be felt."[51] Kant dismissed the "new proprietors" of secret philosophical truths, just as he dismissed ascetics, alchemists, and Freemasons.[52]

Though Kant never mentioned the name "Schlosser," he had quoted from the notes to his book. Schlosser quite justifiably felt attacked and wrote a response entitled "Letter to a Young Man who Intended to Study the Critical Philosophy," which appeared in 1797. In it, Schlosser argued that Kant was destroying Christianity, ruining the lives of many in the process. He even said that Kant should not be allowed to keep his office, thus encouraging the conservative forces in Berlin to do even more.

Kant responded to this attack in his "Announcement of the Soon to Be Completed Tract on Eternal Peace in Philosophy."[53] He characterized Schlosser as wanting "to relax from the administration of law, which stands under authority and is enforceable, but not wanting to engage in complete leisure," and as stepping "unexpectedly into the battle field of metaphysics, where there are many more bitter disputes than in the field he just left."[54] After recapitulating the main tenets of his own philosophy, he shows that Schlosser's critique of critical philosophy is based on mistakes and that Schlosser is out of his depth. Schlosser does not, and cannot, know what he is talking about. Either he is simply incompetent or he is pretending, which is a form of lying. He concludes by claiming that if those who deal in philosophical questions were truly honest with themselves and others, peace in philosophy would have been accomplished.

This dispute with Schlosser was, of course, also a dispute about religion and its relation to philosophy, but Kant was very careful not to transgress into the religious arena. Bound by his word, he could not openly talk about religious problems, but he did his best to show the weakness of this philosopher of intuition and mystical faith, hoping that his criticism of Schlosser and his "noble" mysticism in philosophy would be recognized in Berlin for what it was: a criticism of the Rosicrucian mysticism of Frederick William II and his ministers.

The two *Metaphysical Foundations* belong together, and they were published again as one book in 1797, namely as *The Metaphysics of Morals*. A second edition of the two parts appeared as early as 1798. Kant added to this edition an Appendix, in which he answered objections from a review in the *Göttingische gelehrte Anzeigen* of 1797. This book fulfills Kant's promise of presenting "the whole system" of human duties, plans for which go back at least to 1767. It had taken Kant much longer to unearth all of its critical presuppositions than he had anticipated. Finally, at the age of seventy-four, in the process of tying things up, he gave to the public this work, which was more comprehensive than the one planned, offering not only an account of all ethical duties but also views on the philosophy of law. Yet, compared to the *Groundwork* and the second *Critique*, the *Metaphysics of Morals* is disappointing. It exhibits none of the revolutionary vigor and novelty of the two earlier works. Indeed, it reads just like the compilation of old lecture notes that it is. Given Kant's difficulties and weakness, it is not surprising that much remains cryptic and that some of the text is corrupt.[55] Kant simply did not have the energy to satisfactorily pull together all the different strands of his arguments, let alone polish the work. Indeed, he even had difficulties with supervising the printing of the book. This, of course, does not mean that the work is without interest or even unimportant. The ideas Kant presented go back to his most productive years. It is important for understanding not only his moral philosophy but also his political thinking. It is indeed a veritable tour de force. Yet, if the work "make[s] demands upon its readers that seem excessive even by his standards," its creation made demands upon Kant that were even more excessive.[56]

The argument of the work is based on a distinction between duties of justice and duties of virtue, or between juridical and ethical duties. Kant claims that the laws freely adopted by rational agents like us are based on these two types of duties. Roughly speaking, *The Metaphysical Foundations of the Doctrine of Right* deals with the former, *The Metaphysical Foundations of the Doctrine of Virtue* deals with the latter.[57] Both have to do with legislation, but of two types: political and personal. Juridical legislation deals with what is required or permitted in an external sense, while ethical legislation is, for Kant, "inner legislation." Since both kinds of legislation give rise to laws that must be able to be freely adopted by rational beings, there are for Kant two kinds of freedom as well. They are outer freedom and inner freedom. Correspondingly, juridical laws are laws of outer freedom, and ethical laws are laws of inner freedom. The ethical laws are ultimately more important. They are prescribed by the categorical imperative, and they are the expressions of our autonomous reason. Juridical duties, which have to do with actions that we can be forced to perform by others, turn out to be only indirectly ethical. Juridical laws and duties are connected with rights that other persons have, and though we should do what others can rightfully demand of us, we do not have to perform such acts from a moral motive.

Yet, not all external laws are created the same. There are some that are merely positive laws, that is, laws adopted by a certain state or other political body, and there are others that are "prescriptive natural laws," or laws that can be derived from the categorical imperative. Only the latter are juridical.

External freedom is the absence of external constraint, or constraint by other agents. It can never be unlimited, but must necessarily be understood as limited by the legitimate concerns of others. Kant therefore formulates the following Universal Principle of Right, which states: "Any action is right if it can coexist with everyone's freedom in accordance with a universal law, or if on its maxim the freedom of choice of each can coexist with everyone's freedom in accordance with a universal law."[58] This gives rise to a universal law of right, which commands us to act externally so that our free choice "can coexist with the freedom of everyone in accordance with universal law."[59] However, this law itself does not have to be an incentive to action; it is meant to remind us of the limits upon our free actions.

Juridical duties or duties of right come in two divisions for Kant. There are private (or natural) rights, and public (or civil) rights. By far the largest part of the *Doctrine of Right* deals with private rights. Kant discusses in separate chapters "How to Have Something External as One's Own" (Chapter 1), "How to Acquire Something External" (Chapter 2), and "Acquisition That Is Dependent Subjectively Upon the Decision of a Public Court of Justice" (Chapter 3). In the first chapter Kant tries to explain and justify the legal concept of ownership. To get his point, it is necessary to understand the difference between mere physical possession and rightful ownership, a concept central to Roman law (and almost absent in common law). According to this conception, possession and ownership are radically distinct. I may physically possess something without owning it, and I may own something without being in possession of it. Thus if I lend my car to you, you possess it, but I still own it. While it is possible to possess something rightfully, it is also possible to possess it without having a right to it.

Thus, if you abscond with the car and never bring it back, you still possess it, but you no longer have any right to it. It is the owner who has the right of possession, and only the owner can transfer or give up this right.

Kant's question is, how is ownership possible in the first place? Or, what are the conditions that make ownership possible? Kant's short answer is: "a postulate of practical reason."[60] The question is, what does this mean? His arguments for this claim are difficult to understand, but the rough idea seems to be simply that the concept of ownership cannot be reduced to mere physical possession, and that it presupposes moral laws. Ownership, unlike possession, has a moral component. This component is not a direct consequence of the moral laws. Rather, it is a postulate, almost like God and immortality. This also means that ownership is not something that can be proved directly, but only something that must be presupposed for morality to be possible. We must presuppose that there is not just empirical (or physical) possession but also something like "intelligible possession," that is, rightful possession without physical possession, or ownership. "It is therefore an a priori presupposition of practical reason to regard and treat any object of my choice as something that could be objectively mine or yours."[61] This idea of intelligible possession is for Kant also the ultimate explanation of the possibility of external ownership, but this explanation shows only its possibility as a private right in the state of nature, not how it is actualizable. In order to understand the latter, we must add the necessity of a civil society. Property may precede government, but government makes it secure. For it is only in a state of right or in a body governed by public law that external ownership is really possible.

After having made clear how ownership is possible, Kant goes on to explain how we can come to own things. First he deals with property rights, then with contractual rights, and finally and perhaps most interestingly with how we can acquire rights over persons "in a thing-like fashion." Since his account of property and contractual rights is fairly straightforward, I will say something only about rights over persons "in a thing-like fashion." What Kant has in mind is obvious – at least for the most part. He is talking about marriage, parenthood, and indenture: "A man acquires a wife, a couple acquires children; and a family acquires servants." That these relationships must be seen in terms of "acquisition" is far from obvious to us, but it was obvious to Kant. However, to really understand what Kant means, it is again necessary to understand what was obvious to Kant and is no longer obvious to us, namely, the distinction between possession and ownership. When a man acquires a wife, or "a woman acquires a husband" (that phrase also occurs), he or she does not get ownership of anything, but rather possession of some things but not others. Kant thinks that a person cannot be owned at all. At best, one person may be granted physical possession of the other person. In the case of marriage, the husband and the wife get possession of each other, or more specifically, of each other's sexual organs, and this for *enjoyment* – not for procreation. Kant believes that because each partner grants the other partner an equal right over himself or herself, there is no violation of the personality of either partner. They both remain free in the most important sense, and neither treats the other merely as a thing. Kant believes, furthermore, that sexual intercourse outside of marriage makes it impossible not to treat the other merely as a thing.

The husband and wife also have the duty to treat each other as beings with moral ends. Similar considerations hold for children. Parents possess them in "a thing-like way." Children have no duties toward their parents. They have only rights to be treated in certain ways. They are always free. Servants, by contrast, are part of a household by contract only. They may be used, but they may not be used up. In other ways, they are more like children. Much of this must certainly seem strange by today's standards. Still, seen in the context of eighteenth-century Prussia, it is really quite "progressive."[62] The woman's function is not clearly subordinated to that of the man. There is mutual recognition between them. The wife's role is not exhausted by procreation. She governs the household together with the husband, and while her role is restricted to the household, it is of perhaps greater importance than any public role the husband may play.

Following the section "On Rights to Persons Akin to Rights to Things," Kant discusses acquisition that is dependent on a public court of justice, namely, contracts involving gifts, lending, recovery of something lost, guarantees by oath, and the "Transition from What is Mine or Yours [i.e. ownership] in a State of Nature to What is Mine or Yours in a Rightful Condition Generally." In this section Kant finally explicates what he has merely asserted earlier, namely, the transition from the private right of ownership in the state of nature to the public right in civil society.[63]

The second part of the Doctrine of Right, dealing with public right, and particularly with "The Right of a State" (Chapter 1), "The Right of Nations" (Chapter 2), and cosmopolitan right, seems to belong more to what today would be called political philosophy. It is firmly anchored in the tradition of Hobbes, Locke, and those who follow them. His central problem is to show that the overcoming of the state of nature is in no way arbitrary. While he does not say much about the state of nature, it is clear that it has for him the status of a rational idea. He did not want it to be dependent on anthropological elements, like the claim that human beings are naturally egotistical beings without a shred of sympathy. Whether his view is defensible or not, Kant, like many more recent political theorists, derives "legitimate government from the original contract between free persons."[64] Through government, the state of law replaces ever-present latent war with peace. The state of law is characterized by two things: (1) government determines justice, and (2) government must rule by universal law. "The legislative authority can belong only to the united will of the people" or the original contract.[65] This idea of the original contract or the *volonté general* (united will of the people) has normative force for Kant. Thus Kant rejects special privileges for the nobility on its basis.[66] Curiously enough, he does not think that this implies that everyone has a right to vote, for instance. Anyone whose "preservation in existence (his being fed and protected) depends not on his management of his own business, but on arrangements made by another (except the state)" lacks what he calls "civil personality" and therefore should not vote. Women, minors, and servants are to be excluded from the united will of the people. Lampe does not really count. Nor does anyone who hires out his labor. Independent tradesmen, like Kant's father, for instance, do possess civil personality.[67]

One of the most controversial parts of Kant's theory is his claim that citizens do not have a right to rebel against an unjust government. Though he believes that we have "inalienable rights," he does not think that active resistance is allowed. Only "negative resistance" is justified. Whether his own behavior in the censorship affair amounted to such negative resistance may be doubted. For he thinks that this negative resistance is something that belongs to parliamentary representatives rather than to private citizens. In spite of his great enthusiasm for the American and French Revolutions, Kant cannot seem to bring himself to endorse publicly the legitimacy of revolution. Perhaps he was just too afraid of the forces of irrationality that revolution could (and did) unleash.

Kant's views of the relation between states are informed by the same rational principles of public law as are his views on the internal constitution of government. He advocates a union or league of nations that would overcome the state of war in international politics. The "right of the stronger" should be replaced by the "rational idea of a peaceful . . . thoroughgoing community of all nations on the earth."[68] This is for him not a mere philanthropic ideal but "a principle having to do with rights," which for Kant means, among other things, that settlement by Europeans of newly discovered lands "may not take place by force but only by contract."[69]

The *Doctrine of Virtue* is divided into two main parts, a long part on the elements of ethics and a short part on the methods of virtue. The second part deals with the teaching of ethics and something Kant calls "ethical ascetics." He believes that ethics should be taught neither dogmatically (where only the teacher speaks) nor by dialogue (where both question and answer each other), but by catechism (where the teacher asks and the student answers, being helped by the teacher if he does not know the answer). This is to be a moral catechism, not a religious one. Indeed, Kant insists that instruction in moral duties must precede instruction in religious doctrines. Kant's idea of ethical ascetics goes back to ancient exercises in virtue. Like the Stoics and the Epicureans, Kant feels that virtues must be practiced to take hold. Punishment has no place in moral instruction for Kant. Ultimately, we must train ourselves to be moral.

Kant's "Elements of Ethics" follows the familiar division between duties to oneself and duties to others. Some of these virtues are perfect, that is, they prescribe precisely what we must do; others are imperfect, that is, it is left up to us how much we should do. An example of an imperfect duty to ourselves is the duty to better ourselves, or the duty of self-improvement. We should all work on improving ourselves, but it is far from clear how far we should go. Curiously enough, this duty of self-improvement comes for Kant in two flavors, namely, a duty to improve our "natural" perfection and a duty to improve our moral perfection. We should try to do things from the right motives, or strive for "holiness," and we should do all our duties, that is, we should strive for perfection. Kant assures us that these can be only imperfect duties:

The depths of the human heart are unfathomable. Who knows himself well enough to say when he feels the incentive to fulfill his duty, whether he proceeds entirely from the representation of the law or whether there are not many other sensible impulses contributing to it that look to one's advantage . . .and that, in other circumstance, could just as well serve vice? . . . (objectively) there is only *one* virtue (as moral strength of one's maxims); but in fact (subjectively) there is a multitude of virtues . . . our self-knowledge can never adequately tell us whether it is complete [in being virtuous] or deficient . . .[70]

Since the duty of moral self-improvement is imperfect, it is far from clear for Kant how hard we should strive to be morally perfect. This is something that those who accuse Kant of pursuing moral sainthood would do well to remember.

There is much that is interesting in the first part of the "Elements of Ethics"; but it is interesting mainly because it complements his earlier discussions of ethical principles, not because it adds anything new. Therefore it is perhaps not necessary to summarize it here. Though many of the "Casuistical Questions" Kant adds to the discussion of particular duties are interesting and show that he had a better insight into the complexities of moral life than many have given him credit for. The complete system of duties that Kant finally presents to us is a doctrine of virtue; what he ultimately aims at is a virtue-based ethics, one in which character plays a central role, and not some kind of constructivist moral system. The categorical imperative is intimately bound up with virtue:

> Virtue is the strength of a human being's maxims in fulfilling his duty. Strength of any kind can be recognized only by the obstacles it can overcome, and in this case the obstacles are natural inclinations . . . and since it is man himself who puts these obstacles in the way of his maxims, virtue is not merely a self-constraint . . . but also a self-constraint in accordance with a principle of inner freedom, and so through the mere representation of one's duty in accordance with its formal law.[71]

Indeed, the "basic principle of the doctrine of virtue" is the categorical imperative.

The Conclusion, entitled "Religion as the Doctrine of Duties to God Lies Beyond the Bounds of Pure Moral Philosophy," is of great biographical interest. For, though Kant had promised some years before that he would not treat religion in his writings, at least as long as he was His Majesty's subject, here he comes close to doing just that. In any case, not only does he take up the problem of the *Religion within the Limits of Mere Reason,* he even refers to the work. He argues that while we can explain religion as "the sum of all duties as . . . divine commands," this does not make "a duty of religion into a duty *to* God."[72] Religion has no say in morals. For in

> ethics, as pure practical moral philosophy of internal lawgiving, only the moral relations of men to men are conceivable by us. The question of what sort of moral relation holds between God and man . . . is entirely inconceivable for us . . . ethics cannot extend beyond the limits of men's duties to one another.[73]

These last few sentences of the *Doctrine of Right* go toward proving that those who accuse Kant of being a coward in his dispute with Frederick William II and the censors are wrong.

Kant's essay "On a Supposed Right to Lie Because of Love of Humanity," which also appeared in 1797, was an answer to Benjamin Constant, who had criticized Kant in an article that had appeared earlier in that year.

Constant claimed that the "moral principle stating that it is a duty to tell the truth would make any society impossible if that principle were taken singly and unconditionally." In particular, he argued that it was a duty to tell the truth, but that every duty was based on a right that someone else had, and that therefore the case might arise in which someone did not have a right to be told the truth, and that, as a matter of fact, no one has a right to a truth that harms others. Kant attacked the notion that someone might have "a right to truth." He claimed that there could be no such right, but he also claimed that a lie always harmed someone – if not a particular person, then humanity in general. "To be truthful (honest) in all declarations is . . . a sacred and unconditionally commanding law of reason that admits of no expediency whatsoever." Anyone who tells a lie is answerable for any of the consequences that might follow from the lie; but someone who tells the truth is not liable for the consequences.

This essay, often attacked because of the alleged absurdity of its conclusions, is a good example of Kant's rigorism. While some have wanted to explain it away as a product of Kant's old age, it seems clear that it represents his considered view on the subject, and that he would have presented essentially the same arguments at the time he was writing the *Groundwork*. It underlines his Stoic view of action. "Some things are up to us, and some are not are up to us. Our opinions are up to us, and our impulses, desires, aversions – in short, whatever is our own doing. Our bodies are not up to us, nor are our possessions, our reputations or our offices, or, that is, whatever is not our own doing. The things that are up to us are by nature free, unhindered, and unimpeded; the things that are not up to us are weak, enslaved, hindered, not our own."[74] Ethics is about things that are properly our own affair or are "up to us," namely our acts. Benjamin Constant, by contrast, believed it to be relevant to things that are, at least according to Kant, not properly our own affair, namely, the consequences of our acts. We cannot be responsible for all the things that follow from our actions, but only for what we do. Constant does not understand the difference between "doing harm" (*nocere*) and "doing wrong" (*laedere*). We cannot always avoid the former. In fact, it would be unreasonable to demand this; but we can and must at all costs avoid the latter.

Kant would probably also have liked to publish the essay "An Old Question Raised Again: Is the Human Race Constantly Progressing?," for this was in all likelihood the essay that Kant sent to the *Berlinische Monatsschrift*, but the censors refused it on October 23, 1797.[75] Kant later included it in *The Dispute of the Faculties*.

Unfinished Religious Business: "The Nonsense
Has Now Been Brought under Control"

On November 10, 1797, Frederick William II died, and Frederick William III assumed the throne. Frederick William II had stood all his life in the shadow of his predecessor, Frederick the Great. Yet he had fought what he thought was the good fight for Rosicrucianism. In his moral outlook, Frederick William III resembled less his father than his great-grandfather Frederick William I, but he lacked both the vision and the resolution of his ancestor. The forty-three-year reign of Frederick William III was undistinguished. One of his ministers (von Stein) complained that Prussia was governed by "a mediocre, inactive, and cold man."[76] From Kant's point of view, however, the change was good. One of the king's first actions was the closing of Wöllner's creation, the *Religionsexaminations-Kommission*. Wöllner himself was severely reprimanded early in 1798, and on March 11 was dismissed without a pension. The Edict Concerning Religion, the capstone and symbol of Wöllner's policy, "was never formally repealed, but it was allowed to fall quietly into desuetude."[77]

Kant lost no time. In the fall of 1798 he published *The Conflict of the Faculties*. This book brought together three essays Kant had written at different times, namely, the essay on the relation between the philosophical and the theological faculties, the essay on the "old" question of whether the human race was progressing, and a short essay, "On the Power of the Mind to Master Its Morbid Feelings by Sheer Resolution." The collection was preceded by an Introduction. In it, Kant gave the full text of the 1794 letter of reprimand by Frederick William II and his own answer. Not content just to relate the letter, he also commented on the entire affair, saying that "the further history of this incessant drive toward faith ever more estranged from reason" was well known. Theologians were no longer examined but made to profess their faith and to beg for repentance. This "nonsense has now been brought under control."[78] There was again an enlightened government, which was releasing the human spirit "from its chains."[79]

What follows the Introduction is a mixed bag (or, if you will, "bundle"). Even though Kant tried to unify these three disparate themes into a book by assigning the second essay to "The Conflict of the Faculty of Philosophy with the Faculty of Law," and the third to "The Conflict of the Faculty of Philosophy with the Faculty of Medicine," there is no real conflict discussed in these essays. It is only the first essay that deals with such a conflict. As we have seen, it grew out of his conflict with the censors in Berlin. Kant just added an Appendix, "On a Pure Mysticism in Religion." It consists of the cover letter that Karl Arnold Wilmans had sent to Kant with his dissertation on *The Similarity of Pure Mysticism with the Religious Doctrine of Kant* of 1797.[80]

The second essay raises an "old" question insofar as it raises the same question as does the third part of the essay "On the Old Saw 'That May Be Right in Theory but It Won't Work in Practice'" of 1793. In the earlier essay he had tried to address Mendelssohn's rejection of historical progress. In the new essay he argues against "our politicians" and also "ecclesiastics," or the forces in Berlin opposing the Enlightenment. The politicians and ecclesiastics are "just as lucky in their prophecies" as the old Jewish prophets because they make self-fulfilling prophecies. Creating the very events that they have predicted, they cannot but be right. So if people are found "stubborn and inclined to revolt," or irreligious and immoral, they are so because the government and the church have made them such, and not for any other reason. Retrogression is not necessary, and moral progress is not made impossible by the Jewish prophets, the politicians, or the ecclesiastics.

While admitting that the idea of moral progress cannot be established experientially, Kant argues nevertheless that "there must be some experience in the human race which, as an event points to the disposition and capacity of the human race to be the cause of its own advance toward the better."[81] There is such an experience:

The revolution of a gifted people which we have seen unfolding in our day may succeed or miscarry; it may be filled with misery and atrocities to the point that a right-thinking human being, were he boldly to hope to execute it successfully the second time, would never resolve to make the experiment at such a cost – this revolution, I say, nonetheless finds in the hearts of all spectators (who are not engaged in this game themselves) a wishful participation that borders closely on enthusiasm the very expression of which is fraught with danger; this sympathy, therefore, can have no other cause than a moral predisposition in the human race.[82]

The French Revolution will never be forgotten. It is the sign that we can progress or improve. Politicians (and ecclesiastics) should realize this. They should advance, not resist, the Enlightenment. For "*Enlightenment of the people* is the public instruction of the people in its duties and rights *vis-à-vis* the state to which they belong." Progress cannot be expected from the "movement of things *from bottom to top*, but *from top to bottom*." This is why education ultimately holds out more hope than revolution. In other words, philosophers, not politicians and ecclesiastics, should be in charge of education.[83]

This is indeed an interesting essay, but whether it amounts to a discussion of the relation between the faculty of philosophy and the faculty of law may be doubted. The third essay, which is conceived as a letter to Hufeland about his book *On the Art of Prolonging Human Life*, a topic always dear to Kant's heart, is even more tenuously connected to the presumed topic of the book. Still, it is highly interesting for understanding Kant's own view of life and death.[84] Kant agreed with Hufeland that the physical element in a human being needs to be treated morally, that we must adopt a regimen, that is, "the art of *preventing* illness, as distinguished from the art of *therapeutics* or *curing* it."[85] Kant argues that this is identical to Hufeland's "art of prolonging life." For Kant, such a regimen cannot prescribe a life of ease. In indulging ourselves, we would spoil ourselves – or so he believes. Stoicism's "endure and abstain (*sustine et abstine*)" is better guidance. It is important not just as "*the doctrine of virtue*, but also as the *science of medicine*." The two really complement each other. Kant thinks that "warmth, sleep, and pampering ourselves when we are not ill are some of these bad habits of a life of ease" that are incompatible with the general Stoic principle.[86] Hypochondria or pathological feelings of despondency can also be mastered in this way.[87] In fact, Kant claims that he himself has accomplished this very task.[88] Indeed, he had mastered the "art of prolonging life" early on, and he was successful – perhaps far too successful, for his life went on long after he himself wanted to live.

In the *Anthropology*, which also appeared in 1798, Kant tied up one of the most important and popular lecture courses of his years as a professor. He had regularly lectured on this subject beginning in the fall semester of 1772–73. He probably worked on putting it together during most of 1797.

Kant thought moral philosophy proper should be concerned exclusively with pure principles of morals. His famous rhetorical question whether "it is not of the utmost necessity to construct a pure moral philosophy which is completely freed from everything which may be only empirical and thus belong to anthropology" has galled many a reader. One might wish that he had not simply gone on to claim, without further argument, that it "is evident from the common idea of duty and moral laws *that* there *must be* such a philosophy."[89] Many a philosopher had disagreed even before Kant wrote this. It is difficult to believe he did not know this, but however that may be, it is clear that he believed that in "ethics . . . the empirical part may be called more specifically practical anthropology; the rational part, morals proper." It is also clear that, according to Kant himself, the metaphysics of morals, just like the metaphysics of nature, had to be "carefully purified of everything empirical so that we can know what reason can accomplish in each case and from what sources it creates its a priori teaching."[90] Kant was perhaps too successful in purifying his moral concepts. He made it difficult even for dedicated scholars of his work to make out which, as a matter of fact, were the anthropological concepts that he so carefully purified to give rise to the purely moral ones. If only for this reason, the *Anthropology* is a most important work.

What the *Anthropology* offers is, of course, different from what a present-day discussion of this subject would give to us. It is an attempt to answer the philosophical question, "What is man?" To that end, Kant presents a great deal of the empirical psychology that informs his critical philosophy. The first part, which makes up about 75 percent of the book, deals with just that. In it, Kant presents his views on the cognitive faculty (Book I), the faculty of feeling pleasure and displeasure (Book II), and the faculty of desire (Book III). It is interesting that, while these three books correspond in a fairly straightforward way to his three *Critiques*, the order in which he presents them in the *Anthropology* is different from the order in which they were written. The material critically discussed in *Critique of Judgment*, which was in fact written last, occupies the middle place. This was no accident. This is where it should belong in his philosophical system. It is his moral and political philosophy that comes last and was most important to him.

The second part of the work, which deals with "1) the character of the person, 2) the character of the sex, 3) the character of the nation, 4) the character of the race, and 5) the character of the species," is in some sense nothing but an extension of the last book of Part I. It is also a reaffirmation of the thesis Kant had pushed so hard to advance in his historical and political essays of the late eighties and the nineties. Kant says that he intends to

present the human species not as evil, but as a species of rational beings, striving among obstacles to advance constantly from the evil to the good. In this respect our intention in general is good, but achievement is difficult because we cannot expect to reach our goal by free consent of individuals, but only through progressive organizations of the citizens of the earth within and toward the species as a system which is united by cosmopolitan bonds.[91]

This also explains the title of the book. The *Anthropology* is an *Anthropology from a Pragmatic Point of View* because it is meant not just to investigate what "nature makes man," but more importantly to establish the kind of knowledge needed to understand "what man makes of himself, or should make of himself as a freely acting being."[92] Indeed, "it is properly pragmatic only when it incorporates knowledge of man as a citizen of the world."[93]

While there is much in Kant's discussion of the human race that is quaint or outright weird, while much of it is dated or just plain false, while much is of merely historical or perhaps even antiquarian interest, what he says is interesting because it does provide the empirical background of his aesthetic, moral, and political views. Even as a summary of Kant's lectures, it is an imperfect book. All of Kant's major critical works are based on his lectures, but their arguments go far beyond anything that his students would have encountered in his lectures. While this is to some extent still true of the *Metaphysics of Morals*, it is no longer true of the *Anthropology*. Though his historical essays can give us some idea of where he might have taken his anthropological reflections, we can only imagine what precisely Kant would have made of this work, had he published it earlier. Romantics such as Schleiermacher found nothing of any value in it, but this does not mean that we too should dismiss the work.[94] Kant remained an Enlightenment thinker to the end, as becomes clear from the anecdote about Frederick the Great and Sulzer, which he related at the end of the *Anthropology*. Frederick asked Sulzer, whom he regarded highly, what he thought of the character of man in general. Sulzer replied: "Since we have built on the principle (of Rousseau) that man is good by nature, things are going to get better." The king said: "my dear Sulzer, you do not sufficiently know this evil race to which we belong." Kant believed that Frederick was wrong, and that the human race was at the very least not evil through and through, and much of his work during his last years of writing was meant to show just that.

The books that appeared after the *Anthropology* during Kant's lifetime, namely the Jäsche *Logic* (1800), the *Physical Geography* (1802) by Rink, and the *Pedagogy* (1803) by Rink, shared the same fate. They were not considered to be important. Furthermore, though nominally by Kant, they cannot really be considered his works. They are compilations from his notes for his lectures taken from various periods. Kant did not really have a hand in any of them. He had given his papers to others because he knew that he could no longer accomplish the task of editing them himself. By the time they appeared, the German philosophical discussion had moved far "beyond" Kant. They remain marginal and deeply flawed texts that either already are or soon will be superseded by modern editions of Kant's lecture notes and the lecture notes taken by his students.

The *Opus postumum*: "Exceptional Combinations and Projects"

Kant's last work "and the only [surviving] manuscript" remained unfinished.[95] It is now known as the *Opus postumum*.[96] Plans for the work seem to date back to the period immediately following the completion of the *Critique of Judgment*, but he probably did not begin to work on it until after he stopped teaching in 1796.[97] On the other hand, he could not have added much of any significance after 1798, when he was "almost paralyzed" as far as thinking went.[98] Kant believed that this work was necessary for the completion of his critical system, but when he stopped working on it, he had not yet decided on a final title. He called it by many names, such as "Transition from Metaphysics to Physics," "Transition from the Metaphysical Foundations of the Metaphysics of Nature to Physics," "Transition from the Metaphysics of Nature to Physics," or as "Transition from the Metaphysics of Bodily Nature to Physics." At other times he even appears to have thought that a title like "The Highest Point of View of Transcendental Philosophy in the System of Ideas" would be appropriate. These different titles betray different purposes, and they show at the very least that Kant himself had not yet decided what his projected work ultimately was to include, and what its ultimate function in his system was to be. Wasianski's remarks about Kant's attitude toward the work make clear that Kant himself was not clear on what the manuscript amounted to:

As freely as I could speak about his death and everything he wanted me to do after his death, so reluctant he was to talk about what should be done with the manuscript. At times, he believed that he could no longer judge what he had written, that it was completed and only needed to be polished. At other times, it was his will that the manuscript should be burned after his death. After his death, I showed it to H. P. S. [Herrn Pastor Schulz], a scholar, whom Kant considered to be the best interpreter of his work, second only to himself. His judgment was that it represented only the beginning of a work, whose Introduction was not yet finished, and which was impossible to edit (*der Redaktion nicht fähig*). The effort, which Kant expended in working it out, consumed the rest of his strength more quickly. He declared it to be his most important work, but it was probably his weakness that was largely responsible for this judgment.[99]

Some scholars have argued that these fragments are interesting mainly as evidence of the deterioration of Kant's mind. This view goes back at the very least to Kant's colleague Hasse, who claimed that Kant himself at times

declared the manuscript as "his chief work . . . which represents his system as a completed whole," but then pointed out that future editors needed
to be cautious, because "Kant often deleted during his last years things
that were better than the ones he replaced them with." He also found that
he included in the book much that was nonsensical "(like the meals planned
for a given day)."[100] Rink wrote in 1801: "Kant now works on his *Transition from Metaphysics to the Physics of Nature;* but it moves slowly, I do not
believe that he will live to see the end. It cannot be published as is under
any circumstances."[101] Kraus thought similarly. In any case, he later wrote
to Scheffner: "My poor head seems to be finished; it is like . . . the last
scribblings over which Kant died: no sense or understanding wants to enter into them."[102] Other scholars have given more credence to the old Kant's
judgment, and have argued that they bear witness to Kant's ultimate intentions.[103] What these intentions were is not clear to everyone. Thus it
has also been argued that the different titles indicate different books, and
that Kant was working on at least two different projects during his last
years. What we do possess is a great number of notes, outlines, sketches,
and perhaps even some final drafts of this projected work. Still, the work
has a fragmentary character. It is not clear what it is evidence for. Would
it have become a narrow project, meant to fill a certain gap in his system,
or would it have amounted to something much more ambitious, that is, the
very capstone of his system? We will never know, simply because Kant was
not able to finish it.[104]

The manuscript, as reprinted in the Akademy edition, takes up almost
1,300 pages, but much of this material is repetitious. Kant treats "the same
matters ten and twenty times . . . and almost always with such rich additions
and wide-ranging vistas that it is impossible to establish direct connections
between ideas by just omitting such perspectives."[105] It would be difficult
to edit the work with a pair of scissors, as it were. One of the earliest proponents of publication pointed out that only about one-fifth of the actual material "taken up individually and brought into proper order" would suffice to give a good insight into Kant's proposed work.[106] Such an edition
would take up about 260 pages. The English translation and edition of this
work by Eckart Förster and Stanley Rosen comes remarkably close to this
ideal. It is as good an edition of Kant's unfinished manuscript as there is.

Central parts of the *Opus postumum* suggest that what Kant wanted to
accomplish in his last work was the specification of the a priori principles
that a physicist must employ to achieve a systematic science of nature.
Such principles would have to be more specific than those he had discussed

in the Analytic of Principles of the first *Critique*. Presumably, they would also have to be more specific than those that he had identified in the *Metaphysical Foundations of Natural Science*. Some of his remarks suggest this, but some of the titles suggest a more ambitious enterprise, namely, the formulation of the a priori principles of physics itself. Perhaps not surprisingly, Kant did not succeed.

Roughly put, Kant approached the filling of this still-remaining gap in his system, that is, the lack of a metaphysics of nature or natural science, in the following way. He postulated a kind of ether or caloric matter, which filled up the entire universe and penetrated all bodies equally. This ether, or original matter, was accordingly not subject to any change of place. Kant also wanted to show that ether, as original matter, is not a merely hypothetical principle. It is indeed the original moving force. Without it, there would be neither objects of sense nor any experience. He used this ether to explain all other moving forces, and, in what was to be the first part of the book, he tried to give an account of them in accordance with the table of the categories. In the second book, he intended to formulate the system of the world. What has come to us concerns mostly the first part.[107]

Kant worked hard on filling a perceived gap between the foundations of the metaphysics of nature and physics beginning in 1796, but a solution evaded him. The solution of postulating ether as an a priori principle suggested itself only after "several years," namely "in 1799." This solution is, according to Förster "reflected in the unique status Kant now assigned to the concept of ether, which had initially been introduced in the *Opus postumum* to explain a number of physical phenomena."[108] Ether, as hypostatized space, which is all-penetrating, all-moving, and permanent, became now the a priori principle that provides systematicity to physics. This "solution" would never have occurred to the critical Kant. Ether was a kind of matter, and no matter of any kind could be for him a priori. Indeed, a priori matter would have been a contradiction in terms for the critical Kant. Matter always was and had to be a matter of experience. Yet, now ether "as material for a world system, [was] given not hypothetical but a priori" status.[109] This is a *contradictio in adjecto,* at least from the point of view of critical philosophy.[110] Kant himself noted that a proof that establishes this kind of matter "appears strange; for such a mode of inference does not seem at all consistent or possible."[111] Yet he goes on to outline such a proof.

It is perhaps not surprising that Kant himself almost immediately realizes that this does not amount to a solution.[112] (What is surprising is that he would ever have found it worthy of writing down.) What he substitutes for the first solution is no better. Starting from the idea that we can know nature only on the basis of certain subjective conditions, Kant argues that we know the moving forces in bodies only because we are "conscious of our own activity." For this reason, he finds that the "concept of originally moving forces . . . must lie a priori in the activity of the mind of which we are conscious when moving."[113] I am conscious of moving only as an embodied being, and as an embodied being I am an object of experience among other objects of experience. The activity of the mind of which we are conscious when moving does not therefore necessarily disclose an a priori concept of originally moving forces either. This argument is just as much a non-starter as the earlier one.

In his discussion of ether and caloric forces, Kant was influenced by contemporary discussions of physics and chemistry. Pörschke claimed that "the last books he read" were physics texts, and that new discoveries in physics "disturbed him internally."[114] What he read during the last years had probably a great deal to do with the new developments in physics that resulted from Lavoisier's discoveries. Physico-chemical conceptions of physics had replaced his more mechanical views in the *Opus postumum*. Friedman is certainly correct in suggesting that "his growing awareness of the new physical chemistry, . . . more than any other factor, fuels the new optimism about the empirical or experiential sciences manifest in Kant's *Transition* project."[115] From the point of view of his critical enterprise, such confidence is misplaced. The experiential sciences cannot themselves solve the problem of his a priori foundations of physics, just because they are experiential.

Still later, Kant tried to fix the argument by introducing language first used by Fichte. The subject constitutes itself as a subject. Kant now argues that we can be aware of being moved only insofar as we move ourselves, and, more importantly, that we are aware of other things only insofar as we are aware of ourselves. In a most remarkable passage, Kant claims that "I am an object of myself and of my representations. That there is also something external to me is my own product. I make myself. We make everything ourselves." More specifically, the

understanding begins with the consciousness of itself (*apperceptio*) and performs thereby a logical act. To this the manifold of outer and inner intuition are joined, and the subject makes itself into an object by a limitless sequence. But this intuition is not empirical . . . it determines the object a priori by the act of the subject that it is the owner and originator of its own representations . . .[116]

Again, this stands in stark contrast to Kant's own critical doctrine and especially to his refutation of idealism. From the point of view of the first *Critique*, this is just nonsense, but it makes perfect sense according to one conception of his project in the *Opus postumum*. If we understand it as "Philosophy as *Wissenschaftslehre* in a Complete System," which is after all one title Kant considered for it, then it makes sense. This would also mean that Kant had made the move to Fichtean idealism. Though he never mentions Fichte in the *Opus postumum*, and though there is evidence that he disliked Fichte personally, his talk of "self-positing" in the *Opus postumum* is clearly Fichtean.[117] Yet it is of little consequence whether Kant was more influenced by Beck, Fichte, or Schelling. Nor is it clear whether Kant would have endorsed the arguments in a published version of the book. He might just have been trying to understand Fichte's position by writing it out in his own way. What is important is that he is no longer elaborating his own theories, but adapting the views of others. They are some of the "exceptional combinations and projects" that Pörschke claimed Kant was still capable of as late as 1798, but they are not representative of Kant's best thinking. While this does not mean that they are without philosophical interest, they are of lesser importance to Kant's philosophical legacy.

Decline and Death (1799–1804): "Consider Me as a Child"

"From the winter semester of 1798–99 Kant's name no longer appeared in the registers of the courses given at the university."[118] Though he had not lectured from 1796 on, by 1799 it became all too clear that Kant could never teach again. That year also saw the last independent publication by Kant himself, namely the "Open Declaration" against Fichte, which was Kant's last word on current philosophical developments. He took leave of the school and from the public, saying:

I hereby declare that I regard Fichte's *Theory of Science* [*Wissenschaftslehre*] as a totally indefensible system. For the pure theory of science is nothing more or less than mere logic, and the principles of logic cannot lead to any material knowledge . . . Since some reviewers maintain that the *Critique* is not to be taken literally in what it says about sensibility and that anyone who wants to understand the *Critique* must first master the requisite "standpoint" (of Beck or of Fichte), because Kant's precise words, like Aristotle's, will kill the mind, I therefore declare again that the *Critique* is to be understood by considering exactly what it says . . .[119]

Wasianski reported: "already in 1799, when it [his weakness] was still hardly noticeable, he said . . . in my presence: 'My Gentlemen, I am old and weak, and you must consider me as a child.'"[120] Jachmann, of course, had already noticed the "weakness" three years earlier. At another occasion, Kant explained:

My gentlemen, I am not afraid of death; I will know how to die. I assure you before God that, should I feel in the coming night that I would fold my hands and say "God be praised." But if an evil demon was on my back and was to whisper in my ear: 'You have made human beings unhappy,' then it would be different.[121]

Kant felt he had done no such thing. He was content – ready to die. In fact, he looked forward to dying. Given the choice between life or death, he would have chosen death. Yet he felt the choice was one that had not been given to him.[122] He repeatedly said to friends during his final years that he went to bed every night hoping it was his last.[123] Since his brother, who was more than eleven years younger than he was, had died in 1799, he might have felt that this hope was justified.

Yet his wish was not to be fulfilled for a long time. He had to wait another five years – slowly declining month by month. All his biographers talk about his increasing weakness. Already in 1798, he hardly ever went out for a dinner invitation in the evening, and his walks became shorter.[124] Yet what his biographers describe as "weakness" (*Schwäche*) was not so much the frailty of his body, but his diminishing mental abilities. There is indeed something tragic about the way in which one of the greatest minds who ever lived was reduced to complete helplessness. Nothing, except great physical pain, was spared him during the final years.

During the period of almost five years that it took Kant to die, his steady mental deterioration may have made this waiting easier, but the decline of his body made it more and more difficult. There is nothing extraordinary about Kant's long-drawn-out decline. Many others have had to suffer through it, and there are no new lessons to be learned from Kant's dying. Given the gradual process of decline, Kant did not prove that he knew how to die any better than anybody else. Death was something that happened to him. It was a gradual process that first robbed him of his mind and then of his body.

Gradually, all the regularities that had given order to Kant's life changed. Though he still got up at 5:00 A.M., he began to go to bed earlier. His walks now no longer took him far away from his house. He was frail. Theoretician that he still was, he developed a peculiar way of walking, trying to make his feet hit the ground by a perpendicular motion; he began to stomp. His reason was the belief that walking in a flat-footed way would maximize resistance and thus prevent him from falling. But he fell anyway. To an unknown women who once helped him up, he gave a rose he was carrying in his hand. Soon after, he gave up his walks altogether.[125] He could no longer take care of even minor monetary transactions, since he was no longer able to recognize the coins properly. Accordingly, he was taken advantage of more than once. Wasianski had to see to it that the smallest details of his life were taken care of.

Kant's short-term memory went first. He began to forget many of the ordinary things that needed to be done, and told the same stories several times a day. His long-term memory was still good. Like many old people, he began to live in the past, but he was still alert enough to notice that he was repeating himself and incessantly forgetting things. So he began to write things down. Jachmann, who visited him, wrote

Four years ago he began to use note papers (*Gedankenzettel*), on which he marked the travelers who would visit him. In the end he wrote down every little detail that others told him or that came to him.[126]

So, in 1800 Kant's memory was so bad that he no longer remembered what he had done a few hours before and what he had to do within a few hours. He no longer answered letters. Rink wrote: "I almost want to say that he is incapable of answering them."[127]

By 1801, his memory had deteriorated even further. It appears that now even his working memory, that is, the kind of memory that allows us to concentrate on a given task, was affected. Still, it was not entirely gone. Jachmann found:

Three years ago [1801] I had to inform him about the impending changes in my office and place of residence, but he found it already so difficult to remember . . . that I had slowly to dictate everything to him. He noticed during this time, that he could not think at times, and he excused himself, saying that thinking and comprehending were difficult for him, and that [at times] he had to give up on pursuing an intended line of thought. This gave him then perhaps more discomfort than it did during his greater weakness later on.[128]

The content of the notes Kant made was varied, but it manifests nothing of Kant's former acuity. Wasianski gives the following sample:

Leaving out what has to do with his kitchen or what does not belong in a text for the public, I provide the following short, abrupt sentences: . . . clerics and lay persons. The former are regulars, the latter seculars. About my former instruction to students that they should avoid blowing their noses and coughing (respiration through the nose). The word "*Fußstapfen*" (foot print) is false. It should be "*Fustappen* (also just foot print)" The nitrogen azote is the basis of nitrate and it has acidic powers. The winter fluff (*flomos*), which the sheep of Angora get, and which even the pigs grow that are combed in the heights of the mountains of Cashmere, where they are combed, is sold for much money under the name "shawls." Similarity of women to a rose bud, a rose in bloom, and a haw (fruit of a hawthorn) . . .[129]

This is the stuff that Hasse's *Notable Remarks by Kant* is made of. Other works are also full of trite, droll, or sad sayings that reveal Kant's weakness. Even Wasianski, who genuinely seems to like Kant, trades in these stories. There is much about the spelling of words, their etymology, and their meaning. This is evidence that Kant felt his language skills going and was struggling against this loss. In any case, a few months later he even had to circumscribe words like "bedroom" and was reduced to using (not-so) definite descriptions to make himself understood. Wasianski claimed that only those who knew him well could understand him any longer. His cognitive skills slowly diminished, perhaps eradicated by a series of small strokes.

After a while Wasianski began to make little notebooks for Kant to replace the many small notepapers he was carrying around.[130] This helped him to remember. His decline was not stopped, of course. He began to develop a number of strange theories, based on observations that were either completely false or distorted. For instance, when many cats inexplicably died in the city of Basel, Kant developed the theory that this was due to electricity, because cats are very "electrical" animals. Indeed, the pressure that he constantly felt in his head was also due to electricity.[131] When someone died relatively young, he declared: "He probably drank beer." Was someone sick, he asked: "Does he drink beer in the evening?" Beer was, he thought, a slow-acting poison.[132] Wasianski summed up: "Kant the great thinker now stopped thinking."[133] Many of the anecdotes about Kant's scurrilous views and habits derive, of course, from this period. They indicate nothing about his philosophy or about his true personality.[134] They are, if you will, post-philosophical.

Motherby was the only one whom Kant still visited during these years, but he became seriously ill and died in 1801.[135] Motherby's dying affected Kant deeply. Jachmann had to report to him twice daily how Motherby was doing and what the prognosis of the doctors was. When he heard Motherby had died, Kant asked: "Must I see every one of my friends go to the grave before me?"[136] After Motherby's death, Kant "rarely, if ever" left his house.

He continued to read, but he took in little. Writing was almost impossible. By August 1801, a friend wrote that Kant was able "only at singular moments to write down his thoughts on philosophical matters."[137] Often he fell asleep in his chair, slipped out of it, and fell to the ground. Having fallen, he could not get up. He calmly lay where he fell and waited until someone helped him up. It is not clear how often this happened, until Wasianski provided him with an armchair that prevented him from falling. He still read in bed. Three times, his nightcap caught fire. Kant stamped out the fire with his feet. Wasianski provided him with a bottle of water by his bed, and changed the design of his nightcap. He also instructed him to read at a greater distance from the candle. Wasianski now had to attend to Kant several times a day. Their friends began to feel sorry for Kant and Wasianski.

As early as November 1801 Kant turned all matters concerning his estate over to Wasianski. He made Wasianski a present of a commemorative coin with his likeness on it, giving him a certificate that proved he had received it as a gift. Wasianski did not know who had given him the coin, but the rumors to the effect that it had been given to him by the Jews for explaining a difficult passage in the Talmud seemed "incomprehensible" to him. To him, as to many of Kant's friends in Königsberg, "Kant and the Talmud seemed too heterogeneous."[138] Wasianski was now also responsible for Kant's estate, which amounted to about 20,000 Thalers – not nearly as much as Hippel's 140,000, but much more than one would have expected from a professor at the University of Königsberg. Money had been important to Kant, and he had invested it wisely. On November 14, 1801, Kant finally resigned his seat on the senate. He did not write the letter himself but only signed it.[139]

Meanwhile, things did not go well at home. Lampe had begun too take advantage of the "weakness" of his master. He became more quarrelsome, obtained unreasonable favors, did not do his job, was frequently drunk, and exhibited a certain kind of "brutality."[140] Wasianski talked to Lampe, who promised to improve but got worse. In January 1802 Kant reported to Wasianski: "Lampe has done such wrong to me that I am ashamed to say what it was."[141] Wasianski saw to it that Lampe, the servant who had been with Kant for forty years, was dismissed in the very same month. He received a yearly pension, under the condition that neither he nor any of the relatives were ever to bother Kant again.

Kant continued to call his new servant "Lampe." To remind himself, he wrote in one of his little notebooks: "the name Lampe must now be completely forgotten."[142] This kind of performative contradiction is perhaps more indicative of his condition than any of the other anecdotes that are told about the old Kant. There are many, most of them spurious, and all of them irrelevant for understanding who Kant was.[143] Scheffner reported on January 4, 1802: "It is quite good that the old Kant takes no part in any decision about himself any longer. The Aenesidemus Schulze may stamp on him all he wants. Kant has entrusted himself, if not to the hands of god, then at least in those of time, and time eats all human children, no matter what their abilities."[144]

Kant had always been lean, but during the last years of his life, he lost even more weight. His muscle tissue diminished constantly. He was aware of this, declaring at every meal that he believed himself to have "reached the minimum of muscular substance."[145] His miniscule buttocks created special difficulties for sitting – and sitting was pretty much all he could do at that time. In 1801 he could still joke about "the lack of eminence" in his backside, but in 1802 the lack of muscle mass made it difficult for him to walk.[146]

During the winter of 1802, Kant's health declined further. After every meal, there would appear an elevation of several inches in his abdomen, which was hard to the touch. He had to open his clothes to relieve the pressure it caused. Though apparently not accompanied by pain, it bothered him. This got better after half a year or so. In the spring of 1803 Wasianski felt it advisable to provide exercise for Kant. Though he no longer could walk by himself, he was brought into his garden, but he felt uncomfortable outside, as though "on a deserted island."[147] Over time he got more used to the outdoors again, and even undertook a short trip, but he was so frail that he could hardly enjoy anything. Other problems, such as a complete lack of teeth, constipation, difficulty in urinating, and loss of the sense of smell and taste, made life more and more burdensome. During the winter he frequently complained how tiresome life had become and expressed his wish to die. "He was of no use to the world and he did not know what to do with himself."[148]

In fact, one of the only joys remaining to him was observing a bird, a titmouse, that came every spring and sang in his garden. When this bird came late one year, he said: "It must still be very cold in the Apennines," wishing the bird good weather for its homecoming.[149] In 1803 the bird did not come back. Kant was sad and complained, "My little birdie is not coming."[150] On April 24, 1803, Kant wrote in his notebook: "According to the Bible: Our life lasts seventy years, and if it is long eighty, and when it is good, then it was effort and labor."[151] The summer of 1803 went well enough.

Among other things, he enjoyed the marches that were played at the changing of the guards. Since they were passing his house, he had all the doors opened to be better able to listen to their marches.[152]

Foreign travelers were discouraged from visiting him. He no longer took any pleasure in such encounters. His life was not altogether without other kinds of excitement, though. Twice there were attempts to rob him. His doors to the streets were always open. Once a woman – well dressed, according to Kant – came in to steal from Kant, but, surprised by his apparent agility, she asked for the time of day. Kant looked at his watch and told her the time. She left, only to return moments later, asking him to hand the watch over to her so that she could *show* him precisely what time it was. Kant got so angry that she fled in fear. Wasianski reported that Kant bragged to him about this episode and claimed that he would have physically defended himself. Wasianski was skeptical, saying that "victory would have been on her side, and Kant would have been in old age defeated by a lady for the very first time."[153] We may doubt that Kant engaged in many fights with ladies at any time in his life. Another woman, who must have been well aware of Kant's "weakness," tried to defraud him of money by telling Wasianski that her husband had lent Kant a dozen silver spoons as well as some golden rings. She was willing to take cash instead. When Wasianski offered in turn to call the police, she begged for money instead.[154]

Toward the beginning of the fall, Kant's "weakness" increased at an accelerated rate. Wasianski enlisted Kant's sister, "after getting permission" from Kant. This sister, for whom Kant had provided for a long time, "had a similar facial expression and benevolent disposition as Kant." Six years younger than Kant, she was much more healthy, "lively and fresh." Because Kant found change unnerving, and had always been more or less alone, she sat "behind" him. After a while, Kant got used to her. She took care of him with "sisterly tenderness," trying never to upset him, while always being there for him. She had the necessary "patience, good disposition, and indulgence" for taking care of an old man with many peculiarities.[155] Altogether, she spent about six months in Kant's house. When she moved in, Kant's mind had deteriorated so much that he hardly knew who he was. Jachmann saw him in August of 1803, but Kant no longer recognized him. Nor could he remember anything that had connected the two just a few years back. When Jachmann asked him about his well-being, Kant willingly talked about his condition. Still, he could not finish many a short sentence, "so that his very old sister, who sat behind his chair and who had perhaps heard the same conversation many a time, prompted him with the missing word, which he then added."[156] When Jachmann left, Kant asked him to tell his sister who he was so that she could later explain. Hasse, who told the story that Kant "apologized" to his friends for his sister's lack of culture, was therefore more than just disingenuous; and Metzger's insinuation that Kant was morally defective because he did not let his sister eat at his table was even more so. Either Hasse was not able to see how far gone Kant was, or he had other motives than he stated.[157]

On October 8, 1803, Kant's condition became life-threatening. According to Wasianski, this was a result of Kant's diet. He had eaten badly during the last few years, not liking any of the traditional dishes. On the other hand, he had developed a craving for a sandwich with grated dry English cheese (cheddar), which Wasianski considered bad for him. On October 7, he ate, against Wasianski's advice, a large quantity of it:

> He for the first time made an exception in his customary approval and acceptance of my suggestion. He insisted excitedly on the satisfaction of his craving. I do not think I err when I say that this was the first time I noticed a certain kind of animosity against me, which was meant to suggest that I had stepped over the line he had drawn for me. He appealed to the fact that this food had never harmed him and could not harm him. He ate the cheese – and more had to be grated. I had to be silent and give in, after having tried everything to change his mind.[158]

At 9:00 A.M. the next morning, being led by his sister on a walk through the house, Kant lost consciousness and fell to the ground. He was put to bed in his study, which was heated. The doctor came. Kant made noises, but he could not articulate words. Later that day he managed to speak, but he slurred the words. Though he had probably suffered a stroke rather than an attack of indigestion, he got no more cheese at Wasianski's order.[159] Still, it might have been the cheese that caused Kant's "sickness" – at least indirectly. The excitement over the forbidden food might have raised his blood pressure and brought on the stroke. Whether or not this was the case we will never know, but what we can know is that Wasianski felt responsible. Scheffner wrote on October 27 to a friend: "Kant is now almost without soul, yet he still lives; often he does not know his daily acquaintances."[160] In March he had already written that Kant could "no longer utter three connected words . . . he seems to have lost the rational soul entirely."[161]

"After this sickness Kant never was happy to the degree he was before." His dinner parties were resumed, but he no longer enjoyed them. He hurried his guests along, and while Kant's friends still showed up to his dinner parties, it was more a chore done from duty than it was a pleasure – at least for most of them. Some, like Hasse, seem to have enjoyed it as a kind of spectator sport. Many visitors from outside Königsberg engaged in this pastime as well, most of them quite willingly. Christian Friedrich Reusch, who was invited in 1803 to attend Kant's dinner parties on a regular basis, observed that

during the last period of my presence Kant began to speak, as usual, but very quietly and incoherently, often falling into daydreams when his stomach or his sleeplessness bothered him. He wanted there to be conversation, but he did not like it when his two guests spoke with each other. He was long used to be the center and the leader of the conversation. Now, weak and hard of hearing, he spoke usually alone – usually about the quality of the food, obscure memories and opinions about his sickness. His old friends could bring him to remember old times . . . he still knew some verse of his favorite poem . . . "The rule remains one must not marry . . . but, *excipe*, what honorable pair . . . placing special emphasis on "honorable." . . . After half an hour Kant was usually completely exhausted and was brought to his room. His dinner guests left with bad feelings . . .[162]

Metzger, not one to mince words, found that Kant, who had been his own doctor for the longest time, was perhaps "too anxious in observing the slow diminution of his powers," and that during his last years he "entertained his friends with this *ad nauseam*. . . ." For him, this was the swansong of his egoism or of his peculiarities.[163] For the others, it was just dreadful.

Kant went to bed early, only to spend the night awake, bothered by nightmares.[164] "Calm walking in his room was followed by anxiety, and it was most strong soon after he woke up."[165] He had to be watched every night. His relatives were called in to help. In December, Kant could not write his name any longer. Nor could he find his spoon. He had difficulties expressing himself verbally. During the last few weeks of his life, he recognized no one. Sitting in a chair, as if asleep, he passed the days. Kant was "vegetating" rather than living, Wasianski thought. A visitor from Berlin, who was allowed to see Kant, later wrote that he had found Kant's husk, but not Kant.

Jachmann, who visited him one evening late in 1803 or early 1804 found him "roaming through his room restlessly and without a goal, led by his servant. He was only vaguely aware of me, asking incessantly about the obscure grounds (*Gründe*) before him. What he could have meant by grounds has remained unknown to me, but when he touched my somewhat cool hands, he cried out about the cool grounds, which he could not grasp."[166]

At the beginning of 1804 Kant could eat hardly anything at all. "He found everything too tough and without taste." At table, he just stammered, and during the night he could not sleep.[167] Though there were still short periods during which he was coherent, they were rare. At one occasion, he surprised his doctor by waking up from his half-conscious state, assuring him: "the feeling of humanity has not yet left me."[168] On February 11, he uttered his last words. Thanking Wasianski for giving him a mixture of wine and water, he said: "*Es ist gut*," or "it is good."[169] Much has been made of these words – but "*Es ist gut*" need not have been the affirmation that this is the best of all possible worlds, it can also mean "it's enough," and it probably meant just that in the context. He had drunk enough – but he had also had enough of life.

Kant finally died on February 12, 1804, at 11:00 A.M., less than two months before his eightieth birthday. Jachmann wrote that he died toward noon, "as calmly as is possible, without any distortions and without any sign of a violent separation, but seemingly gladly . . ."[170] Wasianski said: "the mechanism halted and the machine stopped moving. His death was the cessation of life, not a violent act of nature."[171]

At his funeral, he was honored with a poem – a weak performance, by all accounts. A poem by his favorite author might have been more appropriate; for Kant, who only wanted to be human, was a most remarkable example of this species celebrated by Pope in *An Essay on Man* with these words:

> Plac'd on this isthmus of a middle state,
> A being darkly wise and rudely great:
> With too much knowledge for the sceptic side,
> With too much weakness for the Stoic's pride,
> He hangs between; in doubt to act, or rest;
> In doubt to deem himself a God or beast;
> In doubt, his mind or body to prefer;
> Born but to die, and reas'ning but to err;
> Alike in ignorance, his reason such
> Whether he thinks too little, or too much:
> Chaos of thought and passion, all confus'd,
> Still by himself abus'd, or disabus'd;
> Created half to rise, and half to fall;
> Great lord of things, yet prey to all;
> Sole judge of truth, in endless error hurl'd:
> The glory, jest, and riddle of the world.

Notes

Prologue

1. The Declaration was published on August 28 of 1799. See Immanuel Kant, *Gesammelte Schriften*, published by preuáische Akademie der Wissenschaften (Berlin: Walter de Gruyter, 1900–), pp. 370–371 [herinafter "Ak," followed by volume and page number]. See also Immanuel Kant, *Philosophical Correspondence, 1759–1799*, edited and translated by Arnulf Zweig (Chicago: University of Chicago Press, 1967), p. 253.

2. This formulation is from Johann Georg Scheffner, Kant's oldest and in some ways closest friend, in 1804. See Arthur Warda and Carl Driesch, eds., *Briefe von und an Scheffner*, 5 vols. (Munich and Leipzig, 1916), II, p. 400.

3. *Wer war Kant? Drei zeitgenössische Biographien von Ludwig Ernst Borowski, Reinhold Bernhard Jachmann und E. A. Ch. Wasianski*, ed. Siegfried Drescher (Pfullingen: Neske 1974), p. 232 [subsequently referred to as "Borowski, *Leben*" "Jachmann, *Kant*," and "Wasianski, *Kant*" respectively].

4. Scheffner, in *Briefe von und an Johann Georg Scheffner*, II, p. 451.

5. Königsberg was still the place at which the coronation took place and many governmental offices still were housed in Königsberg. But the center of power was in Berlin.

6. Scheffner to Lüdecke, March 5, 1804, *Briefe von und an Scheffner*, II, p. 443.

7. Johann F. Abegg, *Reisetagebuch von 1798*, Erstausgabe herausgegeben von Walter und Johanna Abegg in Zusammenarbeit mit Zwi Batscha (Frankfurt [Main]: Insel Verlag, 1976), p. 147. See also Rudolf Malter and Ernst Sraffa, "Königsberg und Kant im 'Reisetagebuch' des Theologen Johann Friedrich Abegg (1798)," *Jahrbuch der Albertus-Universität Königsberg/Pr.* 26/27 (1986), pp. 5–25, and *Briefe an und von Johann Georg Scheffner* II, p. 184.

8. Scheffner, *Briefe von und an Scheffner*, II, p. 444.

9. Karl Vorländer, *Immanuel Kants Leben* (Leipzig: Felix Meiner, 1911), p. 207.

10. Werner Euler and Gideon Stiening, "'... und nie der Pluralität widersprach?' Zur Bedeutung von Immanuel Kants Amtsgeschäften," *Kant-Studien* 86 (1995), pp. 54–70, 59f. See also Heinrich Kolbow, "Johann Heinrich Metzger, Arzt und Lehrer an der Albertus Universität zur Zeit Kants," *Jahrbuch der Albertus Universität zu Königsberg* 10 (1960), pp. 91–96.

11. *Äußerungen über Kant, seinen Charakter und seine Meinungen, von einem billigen Verehrer seiner Verdienste* (Königsberg, 1804), p. 7.

12. *Äußerungen über Kant*, p. 9.

13. "Misogynist" did not mean the same thing that it means today. For Metzger it seems to have meant simply an "aversion to marriage."

14. *Äußerungen über Kant*, p. 17.

15. *Äußerungen über Kant*, p. 19.

16. There was *Kant's Leben. Eine Skizze. In einem Briefe eines Freundes an einen Freund* (Altenburg: C. H. Richter, 1799). It is represented as a translation "from the English." There is also an English title published in the same year by the same publisher, called "A Sketch of Kant's Life in a Letter from One Friend to Another from the German by the Author of the Translation of the Metaphysic of Morals . . ." The author of this appears to have been John Richardson, who had studied Kantian philosophy with Beck. This "sketch" cannot be identical with "Richardson's Sketch" as published by Stephen Palmquist (ed.) in *Four Neglected Essays by Immanuel Kant* (Hong Kong: Philopsychy Press, 1994). This was written later. The earlier version was a translation of "Etwas über Kant," *Jahrbücher der preußischen Monarchie unter der Regierung Friedrich Wilhelms des Dritten* 1 (1799), pp. 94–99 (author indicated by "L. F."). Second, there was an anonymous volume called *Fragmente aus Kants Leben. Ein biographischer Versuch* (Königsberg: Hering and Haberland, 1802), probably by Johann Christoph Mortzfeld, a medical doctor who lived in Königsberg, and another anonymous biography that had appeared early in 1804, entitled *Immanuel Kants Biographie*, vol. 1 (Leipzig: C. G. Weigel, 1804). Apart from these longer treatments there had already been at least sixteen short publications, a number of public speeches on Kant in Königsberg, and many other incidental materials. For a discussion of the value of all these (and some later sources) see Karl Vorländer, *Die ältesten Kant-Biographien. Eine kritische Studie* (Berlin: Reuther & Reichard, 1918).

17. Johann Gottfried Hasse, *Äusserungen Kant's von einem seiner Tischgenossen* (Königsberg: Gottlieb Lebrecht Herlage, 1804).

18. Ak 12, p. 371.

19. Hasse, *Äusserungen Kant's*, p. 20n. According to Rüdiger Safranski, in *E. T. A. Hoffmann. Das Leben eines skeptischen Phantasten* (München/Wien: Karl Hanser Verlag, 1984), p. 42. Hasse also tried to prove in one of his publications that the Garden of Eden had been somewhere close to Königsberg (Samland).

20. Since Metzger and Hasse were close, both being "foreigners," i.e., not natives of Königsberg, one may speculate whether the two were not playing the same game, that is, taking the natives down a notch.

21. Hasse, *Äusserungen Kant's*, p. 37n.

22. Scheffner, *Briefe von und an Scheffner*, II, p. 451.

23. He himself claimed that he sat in Kant's lectures for *nine* years. Since he received his *Magister* degree in 1787, he must have attended Kant's classes even as a young *Magister*. See Jachmann, *Kant*, p. 142.

24. Wasianski kept a copy of his biography bound with empty pages between the printed ones, in which he made "remarks not appropriate for the public." They were later published by P. Czygan as "'Anmerkungen, die nicht fürs Publikum

gehören' aus Wasianskis Handexemplar," *Sitzungsbericht der Altertumsgesellschaft Prussia* 17 (1891/2), pp. 109–140, but they are not particularly interesting. See also Vorländer, *Die ältesten Kant-Biographien,* pp. 28–29.

25. Scheffner, *Briefe von und an Scheffner,* p. 448.

26. Borowski referred to Scheffner, and what he might say, several times in the latter half of his biography.

27. Rudolf Malter, *Kant in Rede und Gespräch* (Hamburg: Felix Meiner, 1990), p. 442. This book is an indispensable source for anyone interested in Kant's life.

28. Friedrich Theodor Rink, *Ansichten aus Immanuel Kant's Leben* (Königsberg: Göbbels and Unzer, 1805). See also Christian Friedrich Reusch, *Kant und seine Tischgenossen. Aus dem Nachlasse des jüngsten derselben* (Königsberg: Tag and Koch, 1848, published without date).

29. Rink, *Ansichten,* pp. 15–17, 75, 128–131.

30. Rudolph Reicke, *Kantiana. Beiträge zu Immanuel Kants Leben und Schriften* (Königsberg: Th. Theile's Buchhandlung, 1860).

31. Though Frederick William III had been relatively tolerant, Kant had the greatest difficulties under his predecessor. Furthermore, Borowski knew that circumstances could change quickly.

32. Borowski, *Leben,* p. 29.

33. Sommer had studied with Kant (beginning in the fall semester of 1771). He was a good friend of Kant's later in life. Both shared an interest in chemistry. Beginning in 1784 he was the subinspector of the *Collegium Fridericianum.*

34. The biography is the first volume of Kant's life, which had appeared in Leipzig in 1804, and which was probably written by Mellin.

35. Borowski, *Leben,* p. 127.

36. See Vorländer, *Die ältesten Kant-Biographien,* pp. 16f., 23f., 27.

37. Borowski, *Leben,* p. 105f.

38. See Ak 12, p. 323f.

39. Ak 12, p. 322.

40. The German title is: *Prüfung der Kantischen Religionsphilosophie in Hinsicht auf die ihr beygelegte Ähnlichkeit mit dem reinen Mysticismus.*

41. Jachmann, *Kant,* p. 144.

42. Borowski, *Leben,* p. 63. He claims that Kant saw this.

43. Jachmann, *Kant,* pp. 178–180.

44. I will call attention to such influences in the appropriate context. Just one example: Borowski says that Martin Knutzen, one of Kant's Pietistic professors at the university, died in 1756 (when Kant was already teaching at the university) and that Kant (naturally) applied for that position. But Knutzen had died in 1751. May we really assume that Borowski did *not* know that Knutzen had died five years before he himself entered the university? Borowski was interested in suggesting a continuity between Knutzen and Kant that simply did not exist.

45. The word "caricature" is from F. A. Schmid, "Kant im Spiegel seiner Briefe," *Kant-Studien* 9 (1914), pp. 307f.

46. Heinrich Heine, *Religion und Philosophie in Deutschland,* vol. 3. Heinrich Heine, *Lyrik und Prosa,* 2 vols., ed. Martin Greiner (Frankfurt [Main]: Büchergilde Gutenberg, 1962), II, p. 461.

47. We must remember that "ordinary" and "common" in the eighteenth century did not have the pejorative connotation they acquired mainly as a result of Romanticism.

48. See Gerhard Lehmann, "Kants Lebenskrise," in Gerhard Lehmann, *Beiträge zur Geschichte und Interpretation der Philosophie Kants* (Berlin: de Gruyter, 1969), pp. 411–421, p. 413.

49. Arsenij Gulyga, *Immanuel Kant*, tr. Sigrun Bielfeldt (Frankfurt [Main]: Suhrkamp Verlag 1981), pp. 7, 9. I quote from the German translation. All translations are my own.

50. See Friedrich Nietzsche, *Jenseits von Gut und Böse (Beyond Good and Evil)*, in Friedrich Nietzsche, *Werke. Historisch-kritische Ausgabe* (Berlin: Walter de Gruyter & Co., 1994), VI–2, aphorism 14.

51. Stephen Gaukroger, *Descartes: An Intellectual Biography* (Oxford: Clarendon Press, 1995), p. 1.

52. Hartmut Böhme and Gernot Böhme, *Das Andere der Vernunft. Zur Entwicklung von Rationalitätsstrukturen am Beispiel Kant* (Frankfurt [Main]: Suhrkamp Verlag, 1983), p. 428f.

53. The Böhmes's uncritical acceptance of a psychoanalytic and hermeneutic approach stands in stark contrast to their hypercritical view of anything rational. The other strand of their approach, namely the "critical theory" of Frankfurt provenance, is quite incompatible with their post-Freudian musings.

54. Rudolf Malter, "Einleitung," in Karl Vorländer, *Immanuel Kants Leben*. 4th ed. (Hamburg: Felix Meiner, 1986), p. xix.

55. Rudolf Malter, "Einleitung," in *Immanuel Kant. Sein Leben in Darstellungen von Zeitgenossen. Die Biographien von L. E. Borowski, R. B. Jachmann und E. Ch. Wasianski*, ed. Felix Gross (Darmstadt: Wissenschaftliche Buchgesellschaft, 1993), p. xviii.

56. Rudolf Malter, "Bibliographie zur Biographie Immanuel Kants," in Karl Vorländer, *Immanuel Kant. Der Mann und das Werk*. 2 vols., 3rd ed. (Hamburg: Meiner Verlag, 1992), pp. 405–429. See also Rudolf Malter, "Immanuel Kant (1724–1804). Ein biographischer Abriss," *Jahrbuch der Albertus Universität zu Königsberg* 29 (1994), pp. 109–123.

57. Rolf George, "The Lives of Kant" [discussion of the biographies of Vorländer, Stuckenberg, Gulyga, Cassirer, and Ritzel], *Philosophy and Phenomenological Research* 57 (1987), pp. 385–400.

58. Karl Vorländer, *Immanuel Kant. Der Mann und das Werk*. 2 vols. (Leipzig: Felix Meiner, 1924). I shall quote in accordance with the third edition, referred to above.

59. Karl Vorländer, *Immanuel Kants Leben* (Leipzig: Felix Meiner 1911; 4th ed. Hamburg: Felix Meiner, 1986).

60. Vorländer, *Kants Leben*, p. vi.

61. Other major biographies are Friedrich Wilhelm Schubert, *Immanuel Kants Biographie. Zum grossen Theil nach handschriftlichen Nachrichten* (Leipzig: Leopold Voss, 1842), Friedrich Paulsen, *Immanuel Kant, Sein Leben und seine Lehre* (Stuttgart: Friedrich Frommanns Verlag, 1904, 7th ed. 1924), and Ernst Cassirer, *Kants Leben und Lehre* (Darmstadt: Wissenschaftliche Buchgesellschaft, 1977; originally Berlin, 1918). An important corrective to Vorländer is Kurt Stavenhagen, *Kant und Königsberg* (Göttingen: Deuerlichsche Verlagsbuchhandlung, 1949). A good short summary of Kant's life is Norbert Hinske, "Immanuel Kant," in the *Neue deutsche*

Biographie, ed. Historische Kommission bei der Bayerischen Akademie der Wissenschaften (Berlin: Duncker & Humblot, 1952–1982), II, pp. 110–125.

62. J. H. W. Stuckenberg. *The Life of Immanuel Kant* (London: MacMillan, 1882; reprinted with a Preface by Rolf George, Lanham: The University Press of America, 1987). Ernst Cassirer, *Kant's Life and Thought*, tr. James Haden, Introduction by Stefan Körner (New Haven and London: Yale University Press, 1981), a translation of Ernst Cassirer. *Kants Leben und Lehre* (Berlin: Bruno Cassirer, 1918; 2nd ed. 1921; reprinted Darmstadt: Wissenschaftliche Buchgesellschaft, 1977). Arsenij Gulyga. *Immanuel Kant and His Life and Thought*, tr. M. Despalatovic (Boston: Birkhauser, 1987).

63. George, "The Lives of Kant," p. 493.

64. There are signs of change. See, for instance, Ray Monk's *Ludwig Wittgenstein: The Duty of Genius* (Harmondsworth: Penguin Books, 1990).

65. This is a biographical detail that is not understood by most Kant scholars.

66. In this I follow Stavenhagen's lead as well as Otto Schöndörffer, "Der elegante Magister," *Reichls Philosophischer Almanach* (1924), pp. 65–86, as well as other more recent discussions of Kant.

Chapter 1: Childhood and Early Youth (1724–1740)

1. The most important occasion for the ire of the zealots in Halle was Wolff's formal address to the university, "Über die praktische Philosophie der Chineser" (On the Practical Philosophy of the Chinese) of 1721, in which he argued that ethics was not dependent on revelation, that Chinese ethics and Christian ethics were not fundamentally different, that happiness need not have a religious basis, and that reason was a sufficient principle in ethics.

2. The result was an order by the king issued on November 15, 1725, which commanded Fischer to leave Königsberg within twenty-four hours and Prussia within forty-eight hours because "he had dared in his classes to dishonorably defame some of the professors newly appointed by the king, and because he already had earlier followed and defended the evil principle of Professor Wolff who has been removed from Halle." Erich Riedesel, *Pietismus und Orthodoxie in Ostpreußen. Auf Grund des Briefwechsels von G. F. Rogall und F. A Schultz mit den Halleschen Pietisten* (Königsberg: Ost-Europa Verlag, 1937), p. 39. See also Paul Konschel, "Christian Gabriel Fischer, ein Gesinnungs- und Leidensgenosse Christian Wolffs in Königsberg," *Altpreussische Monatsschrift* 53 (1916), pp. 416–444.

3. See Hasse, *Merkwürdige Äußerungen*, pp. 15f. He reported that Kant, in his last years, claimed he had learned this from Hasse himself. Hasse was right, of course, when he pointed out that Kant had thus explained his name long before. The episode provides evidence for how confused Kant was during his final years. But the fact remains that Kant was named "Emanuel," but had called himself "Immanuel" since at least 1746. In the summer of 1746, when his book was submitted to the censor, he is listed as "Immanuel Kandt." See Ak 1, p. 524. His father had died in March, and it is not improbable that he changed his name only after that.

4. I shall not say much about Kant's ancestry. It is well known that he himself believed that his father's ancestors had come from Scotland, but there is extensive

literature on the topic that disputes the correctness of Kant's belief. For a recent article, see Hans and Gertrud Mortensen, "Kants väterliche Ahnen und ihre Umwelt," *Jahrbuch der Albertus-Universität Königsberg* 3 (1953), pp. 25–57. See also Malter, "Immanuel Kant (1724–1804). Ein biographischer Abriß," pp. 109–124.

5. She was the daughter of Anna Felgenhauer, née Mülke or Wülke. Her father died early, and the mother remarried one Jakob Gause. See Gustav Springer (alias G. Karl), *Kant und Alt-Königsberg* (Königsberg, 1924).

6. Vorländer does not give the name of Kant's great-grandmother. For this see Gustav Springer (alias G. Karl), *Kant und Alt-Königsberg*, pp. 8f.

7. Vorländer, *Immanuel Kant*, I, p. 21, for comparison.

8. Vorländer, *Immanuel Kant*, I, p. 11.

9. This institution has a history that reaches back far into the Middle Ages and even to antiquity. It was essentially a feudal institution. See, for instance, Rudolf Stadelmann and Wolfram Fischer, *Die Bildungswelt des deutschen Handwerks* (Berlin: Duncker & Humblodt, 1955), pp. 66–93.

10. Haden (Cassirer, *Kant's Life*, p. 12) translates Cassirer's "*Handwerkerhaus*" as "workingman's house." Yet "*Handwerker*" does not mean "working man." Indeed, there was a world of difference between an independent member of a guild and a working man who hired out his labor to others.

11. Quoted from Ulrich Im Hof, *The Enlightenment: An Historical Introduction* (Oxford: Blackwell, 1997), pp. 59f. Im Hof's discussion of "The Craftsmen" (pp. 58–62) is most interesting in this context, though it concentrates more on the latter third of the eighteenth century. Also of interest is Klaus Epstein, *The Genesis of German Conservatism* (Princeton: Princeton University Press, 1966), pp. 213–219. Though Epstein concentrates on "The Guild Controversy" of 1774–1776, caused by the abolishment and restoration of the guilds in France, his discussion sheds light on the status of the guilds. On p. 219 he quotes Christian Wilhelm Dohm, who romanticized the guilds in 1781 as follows: "The life of a skilled artisan craftsman is perhaps the most happy one possible in our civil society. His soul is troubled by neither nagging fear nor delusive hopes concerning the future. . . . His strenuous labor keeps him healthy, while its uniformity brings his spirit the satisfaction of quiet tranquillity. . . . He is honest and just in his charges because this is dictated by the honor of his craft," etc., etc.

12. The address was Vordere Vorstadt 22, which later became Vordere Vorstadt 21/22. Vorländer got this wrong. He thought Kant was born in the house at Vordere Vorstadt 195, at the corner of the Sattlergasse, which was really the residence of the grandparents. See Springer, *Kant und Alt-Königsberg*, pp. 8f.

13. According to Springer, who still had access to relevant records, he paid 38 Thalers and 34 Thalers in taxes during the earlier years; Springer, *Kant und Alt-Königsberg*, p. 11. This was not an insignificant sum. Kant later charged students 4 Thalers per lecture.

14. This, by itself, does not prove that his business was not going well, as Vorländer suggested. The number of apprentices and journeymen a master tradesman could employ was strictly limited in the eighteenth century.

15. See Jachmann, *Kant*, p. 134.

16. Robert Forster and Elborg Forster, eds., *European Society in the Eighteenth Century* (New York: Harper & Row, 1969), p. 232.

17. Rink, *Ansichten*, p. 14. See also Herbert Sinz, *Lexikon der Sitten und Gebräuche im Handwerk* (Freiburg: Herder Verlag, 1986), p. 153: "There were drawn out confrontations between the saddle makers and the harness makers about the similarity of their tools and their trade." See also Otto Kettemann, "Sattler und Riemer," in Reinhold Reith, ed., *Lexikon des alten Handwerks. Vom Spätmittelalter bis ins 20. Jahrhundert* (München: C. H. Beck, 1990), pp. 188–191. The dispute Kant describes was obviously part of that larger conflict. Fritz Gause, *Die Geschichte der Stadt Königsberg in Preußen*, I, *Von der Gründung der Stadt bis zum letzten Kurfürsten* (Köln/Graz: Böhlau Verlag, 1965), p. 533, points out that the saddle and harness makers had a twenty-five-year-long dispute about which parts of the harness and other equipment for carriages were the work of which trade. The saddle makers also disputed the right of the harness makers to use certain (more fancy) kinds of leather (*weißgegerbtes*).

18. Wolfram Fischer, *Quellen zur Geschichte des deutschen Handwerks. Selbstzeugnisse seit der Reformationszeit* (Göttingen: Musterschmidt Verlag, 1957), pp. 79–91.

19. Kraus in Reicke, *Kantiana*, p. 5n.

20. Borowski, *Leben*, p. 12; see also Jachmann, *Kant*, p. 135, who claimed that Kant often called his education a shield (*Schutzwehr*) of the heart and morals against wicked impressions (*lasterhafte Eindrücke*). Jachmann also called Kant's education both at home and at school "entirely Pietistic."

21. Draft of a letter to Lindblom, Oct. 13, 1797 (Ak 13, p. 461; the letter itself: Ak 12, pp. 205–207). This is the only pronouncement on his parents written by Kant himself. It lends credibility to what others report. How important the moral standing of his family was to Kant can also be seen from a letter to the fiancé of his brother's daughter of December 17, 1796 (Ak 12, p. 140), where he said: "Since the blood of my two esteemed parents in its different streams has never been sullied by anything morally indecent, I hope that you will find this in your loved one . . ."

22. Emil Arnoldt, "Kant's Jugend," in Emil Arnoldt, *Gesammelte Schriften*, 6 vols., ed. Otto Schöndörffer (Berlin, 1907–1909), I, pp. 608–609. See also Stuckenberg, *Kant*, p. 6.

23. Jachmann, *Kant*, p. 169. He also says that Kant's eyes were always filled with tears when he spoke of his mother, and that he called her "a loving, sensitive, devout, and righteous woman and a tender (*zärtlich*) mother who led her children to fear God through her devout teachings and virtuous example. She often took me out of the town and called attention to the works of God." See also Wasianski, *Kant*, pp. 250f.

24. Wasianski, *Kant*, p. 246.

25. Ak 7, p. 310. The words "enthusiastic" or "*schwärmerisch*" refer to highly emotionalized religiosity, which was common in many Pietist groups, especially the Herrnhuter. It had a long history. John Locke had already argued against it in his *Essay*. See John Locke, *An Essay Concerning Human Understanding*, edited with an introduction by P. H. Nidditch (Oxford: Oxford University Press, 1975), pp. 697–706.

26. Ak 9, pp. 477f.
27. Wasianski, *Kant*, p. 246.
28. Wasianski, *Kant*, p. 247.
29. These questions might appear strange, but they are raised by the Böhmes in *Das Andere der Vernunft*, pp. 483f.
30. Böhme and Böhme, *Das Andere der Vernunft*, p. 484, argue that Kant was fixated on his mother all of his life. Part of their "reasoning" is based on false information. They claim that Kant was the first surviving child of his parents, which is false. Kant had an older sister. They also claim that Kant's father had "no influence on the son," that he was "extensively disregarded (*ausgeblendet*)." Yet it is Kant's biographers, not necessarily Kant himself, who disregard the father. One should not read too much into the words of the early biographers. There were reasons for the early biographers' emphasis on the mother, but they were quite different from the reasons the Böhmes suspect – as we shall see. Furthermore, Rink, *Ansichten*, p. 13, noted: "He [Kant] thankfully carried in his heart the image of his father even in his later years. But, if possible, he remembered his mother with greater tenderness." Rink constantly spoke of his "parents," and not just of the mother.
31. Vorländer, *Immanuel Kant*, I, p. 19, drew certain conclusions about the income of Kant's father from this fact. I doubt that this is possible. Given their religious convictions, ostentation of any kind was foreign to them. The simple burials that his mother and his father received were probably just what they considered appropriate. Furthermore, as a decree from 1748 shows, the practice of burying one's relatives "silently" appears to have become rather common during the forties. It was found necessary to tighten the rules regarding who could be buried in this fashion. See Ludwig Ernst Borowski, *Neue Preußische Kirchenregistratur . . .* (Königsberg, 1789), pp. 18f., 269f. Indeed, many of the poorest citizens of Königsberg, who could not afford the fees, buried their relatives illegally out of town. At the same time, merchants were insisting on the most luxurious funerals (reserved for nobility), although rules were made that prohibited them from driving to a funeral by carriage, for instance. See Gause, *Königsberg*, II, p. 59. As a Pietist, Kant's father might have thought that "silence" was more appropriate than pomp, even if he could have afforded it. Accordingly, one must be careful not to draw too definite a conclusion about a family's financial status from how they buried their dead. See also Paul Graff, *Geschichte der Auflösung der alten gottesdienstlichen Formen in der evangelischen Kirche Deutschlands*, II, *Die Zeit der Aufklärung und des Rationalismus* (Göttingen: Vandenhoek & Rupprecht, 1939), p. 278.
32. It is not clear what the tax rate was, but 36 Thalers was significant. The rent for a small apartment was 40 Thalers a year, and a student was expected to live on 200 Thalers a year.
33. This is the same uncle who took in Kant's younger brother after their mother died. Perhaps not surprisingly, the younger brother felt closer to this family than did Emanuel.
34. See Wasianski, *Kant*, pp. 245f.
35. His oldest sister probably died in 1792 without ever having married. His second sister (Maria Elisabeth, born on January 2, 1727) married and then divorced around 1768. She received from her brother Immanuel support after her divorce until she

died in 1796. After her death, Kant continued regular payments to her four children, and he provided for them in his will. They also received a substantial dowry from Kant when they married, and his physician treated them at Kant's expense. His third sister (Anna Luisa, born in February 1730) died in 1774. He also gave a pension to his youngest sister (Katharina Barbara, born September 15, 1731), whose husband died within a year of their marriage, and who was otherwise well taken care of ("*sonst gut versorgt*") by Kant in a position at St. George's Hospital. His younger brother Johann Heinrich (born November 28, 1735) was brought up in the household of the well-to-do brother of Kant's mother. They went to the same schools, and Johann Heinrich later also attended Kant's lectures. Though they corresponded later in life, Kant remained rather cool and reserved toward the more emotional advances of his brother, once writing on a page of a letter from Johann Heinrich: "All morality consists in the derivation of an action from the idea of the subject, *not* from *feeling (Empfindung)*." When his brother died in 1800, Kant supported the family, though not on a regular basis and, it seems, somewhat reluctantly. See Vorländer, *Immanuel Kant*, II, pp. 17–26. Again, the Böhmes, *Das Andere der Vernunft*, p. 485, like others before them, claim that Kant's relation to his closest relatives was significant, explaining his distance from them as the result of Kant's fixation on the mother. The brothers and sisters did not count. He had no relationship with them, and he simply "paid them off." This is unfair, though Kant may have had in his adult life less social intercourse with his sisters and his brother than some of his colleagues had with their relations – but not much less. Even late in Kant's life, Königsberg society was divided by social rank. Indeed, rank alone presented barriers that neither his sisters nor Kant would have wanted to transgress. That he took care of them is more significant than the absence of close relations with them. (What would they have talked about?) There may have been deeper reasons for his lack of a relationship with his brother, but he was more than ten years younger and Kant probably did not know him very well. Furthermore, the younger brother did nothing to support any of his relatives, and even failed to provide sufficiently for his wife and children.

36. Pietism also had significant effects outside of Germany. See F. E. Stoeffler, *The Rise of Evangelical Pietism*, 2nd ed. (Leiden, 1971).

37. Richard L. Gawthrop, *Pietism and the Making of Eighteenth-Century Prussia* (Cambridge: Cambridge University Press, 1993), p. 141.

38. For a useful introduction, see Albrecht Ritschl, *Geschichte des Pietismus*, 3 vols. (Bonn: 1880–1896), and Emanuel Hirsch, *Geschichte der neuen evangelischen Theologie*, 2nd ed. (Gütersloh, 1960), vol. II, pp. 91–143. See also Max Weber, *The Protestant Ethic and the Spirit of Capitalism*, tr. Talcott Parsons, foreword by R. H. Tawney (New York: Charles Scribner's Sons, 1958), pp. 128–139. For a short collection of writings by Pietists, see Peter C. Erb, ed., *Pietists: Selected Writings*, with a Preface by Ernest Stoeffler (New York: Paulist Press, 1983). For Francke and the Halle School, see especially pp. 97–215.

39. See Carl Friedrichs, *Preußentum und Pietismus. Der Pietismus in Brandenburg-Preußen als Religiös-Soziale Reformbewegung* (Göttingen: Vandenhoek & Ruprecht, 1971). He deals with Königsberg specifically on pp. 231–300. See also Mary Fulbrook, *Piety and Politics: Religion and the Rise of Absolutism in England, Württemberg*

and Prussia (Cambridge: Cambridge University Press, 1983), and Gawthrop, *Pietism and the Making of Eighteenth-Century*. For Pietism's role in education, see especially James Van Horn Melton, *Absolutism and the Eighteenth-Century Origins of Compulsory Schooling in Prussia and Austria* (Cambridge: Cambridge University Press, 1988). For the Prussian situation, see especially pp. 23–59 and pp. 109–168.

40. Friedrichs, *Preußentum und Pietismus*, p. 125.

41. A. H. Francke, "Delineation of the Entire Work," in A. H. Francke, *Pädagogische Schriften*, 2nd ed., Hermann Lorenzen (Paderborn: Ferdinand Schöningh, 1957), p. 123.

42. Fulbrook, *Pietism and Politics*, p. 163.

43. He replaced the Pietist Wolff, who had died in 1731. Schulz was not any better liked by the orthodox clergy than his predecessors had been. Like Rogall, he was a controversial figure. After his graduation he had served as a *Feldprediger*, or field chaplain, in the service of the king. In some of the older discussions, this is taken as a sign of his humility: he did not take some of the more illustrious positions available to him, but chose the position of a "mere" field chaplain. Nothing could be more misleading. In the Prussia of his day, this was the surest way to begin a promising career. The "soldier king" thought most highly of those who ministered to those who interested him most, namely his soldiers. Field chaplains became his most trusted church officials later on. Thus Schulz became first the pastor of the Old City Church by royal decree, and then in rapid succession became *Konsistorialrat*, professor of theology at the university, director of the *Collegium Fridericianum*, and member of the "Special-Church-and-School-Commission."

44. Nevertheless, this is often claimed. Benno Erdmann, *Martin Knutzen und seine Zeit. Ein Beitrag zur Geschichte der Wolffischen Schule und insbesondere zur Entwicklungsgeschichte Kants* (Leipzig, 1876; reprinted Hildesheim: Gerstenberg, 1973) gives some insight into the complexity of the situation. Paul Kalweit, *Kants Stellung zur Kirche* (Königsberg, 1904), p. 1, notes correctly that Pietism was just beginning to become dominant in Königsberg when Kant was born. Though it became more influential after 1724, other aspects of Königsberg culture remained important.

45. In fact, he had tried to mediate between Wolff and the Pietists during the famous dispute that led to Wolff's banishment from Prussia.

46. Some of the older Pietists found this approach to things difficult to take.

47. Norman Balk, *Die Friedrich-Wilhelms Universität* (Berlin, 1926), p. 30; see also F. A. von Winterfeld, "Christian Wolff in seinem Verhältnis zu Friedrich Wilhelm I und Friedrich dem Großen," *Nord und Süd* 64 (1893), pp. 224–236; Hans Droysen, "Friedrich Wilhelm I, Friedrich der Grosse und der Philosoph Christian Wolff," *Forschungen zur brandenburgischen und preussischen Geschichte* 23 (1910), pp. 1–34.

48. Borowski found that Schulz "was a declared enemy of all connection with unknown forces and all enthusiasm (*Schwärmerei*). He prevented the Count of Zinzendorf from establishing a congregation. When Zinzendorf traveled through Königsberg, Schulz, as the dean of the Faculty, invited him to a meeting. After that he pestered him for many years with pamphlets, arguing for the usefulness of a law against those who claimed to be the only true preachers of the gospel." See Erdmann, *Martin Knutzen*, pp. 47f.

49. The almost mystical and very emotional character displayed by some of the Württemberg Pietists was foreign to him. Though some of his language would have sounded very familiar to someone who had read Spener's *Pia Desideria*, his teaching was in many ways different and not always compatible with it.

50. Carl Hinrichs, *Preußentum und Pietismus*, p. 281. See also "Der Hallesche Pietismus als Politisch-Soziale Reformbewegung des 18. Jahrhunderts," *Jahrbuch für die Geschichte Mittel-und Ostdeutschlands* 2 (1953), pp. 177–189.

51. Luise Adelgunde Viktorie Gottsched's comedy *Die Pietisterey im Fischbein-Rocke, oder die doktormäßige Frau* (Pietism in Petticoats, or the Doctorlike Woman) of 1737 throws interesting light on this period. It was meant to make fun of the conditions in Königsberg. See L. A. Gottsched, *Pietism in Petticoats and Other Comedies*, tr. Thomas Kerth and John R. Russell (Columbia, S. C.: Camden House, 1994).

52. Most commentators who make this claim are rather vague about what this Pietism actually amounted to. See Ward, *The Development of Kant's View of Ethics*, p. 3, as one example of many.

53. Borowski, *Leben*, p. 37.

54. Rink, *Ansichten*, p. 13f.

55. It should be remembered that Kant himself believed that "children cannot understand all religious concepts" even though one must teach some to them, namely what "God" cannot mean. In particular, he felt it was of the utmost importance to teach that "true estimation of God consists in doing his will," and that the concepts of "God" and "duty" needed to be brought together (Kant, *Pedagogy*, p. 56).

56. Ward, *The Development of Kant's View of Ethics*, p. 3. There is no such fact, since there was no such church.

57. Kant, *Pedagogy*, pp. 38–39. Wolfgang Ritzel, "Wie ist Pädagogik als Wissenschaft möglich," in *Kant und die Pädagogik. Pädagogik und praktische Philosophie* (Würzburg: Könighausen & Neumann, 1985), pp. 37–45, p. 36, points out quite correctly that Rink's text must be used with care, since he mixed notes from different periods, and since it is not always clear which are Kant's own pronouncements.

58. Kant, *Pedagogy*, pp. 50–51.

59. Kant, *Pedagogy*, p. 52.

60. Kant, *Metaphysics of Morals*, ed. Gregor, p. 268. Kant is here talking about teachers, but it is relevant for parents too.

61. Kant, *Pedagogy*, p. 56.

62. Kant, *Metaphysics of Morals*, ed. Gregor, p. 272.

63. Kant's account of how children should be educated is not primarily a description of his own education. We should therefore be careful in drawing conclusions from it concerning Kant's early life. Given Kant's characterization of his earliest education as morally *ideal*, it is reasonable to use his mature view of education in elucidating the way he was educated. It is certainly more appropriate to use Kant's comments than those of Borowski and others. If we take Kant's own account of a good moral education seriously, then there is no room for "the demand for holiness" that Borowski identifies. Children should be taught to do their duty, not to "please" God (or anyone else, for that matter). "Holy" for Borowski and the Pietists basically meant "belonging to, derived from, or associated with God." Kant felt it was better to leave such notions for later.

64. See Justus Möser, *Patriotische Phantasien* (1774–1786), for instance, especially the
    chapters "Rich People's Children Should Learn a Trade," "Of the Deterioration
    of the Trade in Smaller Cities," and "Accordingly Every Scholar Should Learn
    a Trade." Rink, *Ansichten,* pp. 6f. and 10f., argued that the Prussian government
    had a fundamental influence on Kant's moral outlook, and asked (rhetorically):
    "Could this strict demand for law in his system not be at least indirectly the result
    of the strict care of law in his Fatherland, and could it not form the basis of its
    character?" It is also interesting how Rink connected Pietism with the Prussian
    government. Though he regretted that "the king dared to rein in the religious faith
    of his subjects and forced them to believe what he considered in their best inter-
    est," he still thought that the apparent "oppression of opinion" (*Meinungszwang*)
    was not really harmful (p. 8).
65. Wasianski, *Kant,* p. 245.
66. Ak 6, pp. 236, 464.
67. Ak 9, p. 480.
68. Such speculations about what might or might not have influenced Kant in his early
    childhood so that it affected his mature work must remain just that, speculations.
    As Mary Fulbrook has shown, Pietism was "evidently a quite flexible ideology,
    capable of representing many different social groups." While it is not reducible to
    the particular views of any one of the social groups, in eighteenth-century Königs-
    berg it was identified with townspeople, artisans, soldiers, and working men. See
    Fulbrook, *Piety and Politics,* p. 43. Fulbrook also argues that "the particular cir-
    cumstances of individuals" have a great influence on "the content and power of
    religious orientation" (p. 189). I can only agree. Puritanism in England, Pietism in
    Württemberg, and Pietism in Prussia played entirely different political roles. Thus,
    "Puritanism cannot be ignored in the genesis of the English resistance to abso-
    lutist rule; nor Pietism in the successful establishment of absolutism in Prussia.
    What is required is an analysis of the patterns of combination of elements: of the
    ways in which different projects, with different resources, and different goals and
    interests, interrelate in specific historical situations." Similar considerations are
    relevant for explaining the role of religion in the lives of individuals. The social
    strata of individuals are at least as important as their religious orientations. And
    the lives of shopkeepers and artisans did not radically differ in different countries
    during the eighteenth century.
69. One might say that the ethos of the guilds provided some of the material princi-
    ples of Kant's morality, while the Pietist insistence on the necessity of a certain
    kind of motivation was influential as a formal principle.
70. Hippel, according to Malter, *Kant in Rede und Gespräch,* p. 95. Mortzfeld, Kant's
    first biographer, spoke of the "leaden destiny of punishment" in this school (see
    Malter, *Kant in Rede und Gespräch,* p. 75).
71. Ak 10, p. 117.
72. Ak 7, p. 486.
73. Ak 25.2 (Anthropology Busolt), p. 1496.
74. See Heiner F. Klemme, *Die Schule Immanuel Kants. Mit dem Text von Christian
    Schiffert über das Königsberger Collegium Fridericianum* (Hamburg: Meiner Verlag,

1994), p. 34. The school was connected to the same hospital at which Kant later secured a place for his sister.

75. Klemme finds that it is no longer possible to determine whether or not it was Schulz because Borowski (and all those who followed him) were wrong in supposing that Schulz was already director of the *Collegium* in 1731–32, when he actually became director in the summer of 1733. Perhaps Klemme is overly skeptical. Schulz was well connected, and he could have arranged for Kant's acceptance in the *Collegium* even before he became its director. Indeed, it is likely that Schulz would have noticed the young Kant. Vorländer claimed that Schulz often visited the Kant household and became aware of Kant there (Vorländer, *Immanuel Kant*, I, p. 20). Even if Schulz never visited the Kants, he was the minister of the Church of the Old City, and the school was under the supervision of this church. In other words, Schulz was Boehm's superior. Given his hands-on attitude, he would have supervised Boehm's teaching, and thus he would have come to know the young Kant in the classroom.

76. Schiffert in Klemme, *Die Schule Immanuel Kants*, p. 63.

77. Kant probably was among the many students whose parents did not have to pay – or who paid very little – for the education of their children.

78. Schiffert in Klemme, *Die Schule Immanuel Kants*, p. 109: "Because it can hardly be imagined what kind of damage is done to the children, and how difficult they will find it to direct their energies to their studies again after they have holidays lasting entire days or weeks . . . the holidays common in other schools are not observed by us." Every once in a while, a day might be skipped, however.

79. Schiffert in Klemme, *Die Schule Immanuel Kants*, p. 69.

80. Ak 8, p. 323, reveals some of the effects of this teaching: "is this not the same as it is with the catechism, which we knew by heart in all detail when we were children, and which we believed we understood, but which we understood less and less the older and more reflective we became. We would deserve to be placed in school, if we could find anyone (apart from ourselves) who understood it better."

81. The full title of the second edition in English: Christoph Starcke, *Order of Salvation in Tabular Form for Students; in Part to Provide Them with the First Foundations of Theology, in Part to Repeat the Most Important and Most Necessary Parts of It in Order to Improve Their Recall; but Also for the Simple-Minded in Order to Give Them a Solid Conception of the Most Important Christian Doctrines which Will Enable Anyone to Impress Any Doctrine through the Added Duty and Comfort into the Heart, to Prove to Them Everything Sufficiently with Verses and to Lead Them to Scripture. Also Containing a Short Appendix of the Order of Duties in Life. Which Are Brought into This Form with Exceptional Industry for the Furthering of the Living Knowledge of God and Jesus Christ* (Erfurt, 1756). See Schiffert in Klemme, *Die Schule Immanuel Kants*, p. 71n.

82. The book used was Daniel Salthenius, *Introductio in omnes libros sacros tam veteris quam novi Testamenti, ad usum studiosae iuventius; cum praesentatione de necessariis quibusdam studii exegetico-biblici subsidiis* (Königsberg, 1736). Schiffert in Klemme, *Die Schule Immanuel Kants*, p. 72n. On the importance of the "tabular method" in Pietist pedagogy, see Melton, *Absolutism and Compulsory Schooling*, pp. 53f.

83. Schiffert in Klemme, *Die Schule Immanuel Kants*, p. 71.

84. Vorländer, *Kants Leben*, p. 25. He was only in his first year of Hebrew, but it was not taught at the lowest levels. Arithmetic also had only three classes.

85. The phrase is Vorländer's (see *Kants Leben*, p. 27).

86. Vorländer, *Kants Leben*, p. 32; Rink, *Ansichten*, p. 20; see also Borowski, for essentially the same report.

87. See also F. A. Gotthold, "Andenken an Johann Cunde, einen Freund Kant's und Ruhnken's," *Neue preussische Provincial-Blätter*, second series, 3 (1853), pp. 241–258. Cunde was born in 1724 or 1725, and he went to the same primary school as Ruhnken. So Ruhnken and Cunde knew each other before coming to Königsberg. Cunde came to the *Collegium Fridericianum* in 1735 with a stipend. He lived at the school and graduated in 1741. Like Kant, he then studied at the University of Königsberg.

88. Borowski, *Leben*, p. 39.

89. Borowski, *Leben*, p. 38.

90. Ibid.; Reicke, *Kantiana*, pp. 39, 43.

91. See also Jachmann, *Kant*, p. 148: "Of the modern languages he understood French, but did not speak it."

92. Schiffert in Klemme, *Die Schule Immanuel Kants*, p. 105.

93. Schiffert in Klemme, *Die Schule Immanuel Kants*, p. 88 (the book first appeared in 1717).

94. Ibid.

95. Borowski, *Leben*, p. 91.

96. Schiffert in Klemme, *Die Schule Immanuel Kants*, p. 91.

97. Ak 9 (*Anthropology*), p. 473.

98. Melton, *Absolutism and Compulsory Schooling*, p. 42.

99. Schiffert in Klemme, *Die Schule Immanuel Kants*, p. 97.

100. Ak 7, pp. 132f. Introspection of this sort should not be confused with the "*Höllenfahrt der Selbsterkenntnis*" which for Kant is a necessary condition for becoming moral (see Ak 6, p. 441 and related passages). Kant was careful to distinguish it from the "enthusiastic" condemnation of ourselves practiced by the Pietists. See Klemme, *Die Schule Immanuel Kants*, p. 44n.

101. Mortzfeld in Malter, *Kant in Rede und Gespräch*, p. 75; see also G. Zippel, *Geschichte des Königlichen Friedrichs-Kollegiums zu Königsberg Preussen, 1698–1898* (Königsberg, 1898), p. 114f., who said that the whip was used for corporeal punishment.

102. Jachmann, *Kant*, p. 135. The teacher who was not so strict was probably Heydenreich. Kant described him as teacher with a "fragile and droll body, who commanded always a great deal of attention, obedience, and respect in him and some other students because they could learn in his classes a great deal." This raises the question of how much "attention, obedience, and respect" other teachers commanded.

103. Borowski, *Leben*, p. 39.

104. Jachmann, *Kant*, p. 135.

105. Hasse, *Merkwürdige Äußerungen*, p. 34.

106. Francke, *Kurzer und einfältiger Unterricht*, p. 15; see also Melton, *Absolutism and Compulsory Schooling*, p. 43.

107. Ak 7 (*Dispute of the Faculties*), p. 55.

108. Ak 6, p. 184; see also Ak 6, p. 24.

109. Ak 7, p. 57.

110. See, however, Ak 8, p. 23. When Kant finds that man is the kind of animal that "needs a master that breaks his will," that this master must be a human being, and that therefore perfection on Earth is impossible, we find an echo of this view.

111. Gerhard Ritter, *Frederick the Great*, tr. Peter Paret (Berkeley: University of California Press, 1974), p. 23.

112. Ak 8, p. 40.

113. Kant, *Practical Philosophy*, p. 17 (Ak 8, p. 36).

114. Johann George Scheffner, *Mein Leben, wie ich es selbst beschrieben* (Leipzig: J. G. Neubert, 1816; 2nd ed. 1823).

115. This is not meant to give an account of the constitutional history of Prussia and Königsberg's role in it. I just mark some of the important milestones in the history of the city. The king was not "king of Prussia," for instance, but merely "king in Prussia."

116. Fritz Gause, "Königsberg als Hafen- und Handelsstadt," in *Studien zur Geschichte des Preussenlandes*, ed. Ernst Bahr (Marburg: N. G. Elwert Verlag, 1963), pp. 342–352, p. 343.

117. These numbers exclude the military (another 7,000 or 8,000 people).

118. Stavenhagen, *Kant und Königsberg*, p. 9.

119. Gause, *Königsberg*, II, p. 53; see also Robert Ergang, *The Potsdam Führer: Frederick William I, Father of Prussian Militarism* (New York: Octagon Books, 1972, reprint of Columbia University Press, 1941), pp. 118f.

120. See Ergang, *The Potsdam Führer*, p. 73.

121. Ergang, *The Potsdam Führer*, p. 74.

122. Ergang, *The Potsdam Führer*, p. 69.

123. See Ak 10, pp. 149, 190; pp. 11, 78.

124. Ak 7 (*Anthropology*), p. 120n.

125. See Vorländer, *Immanuel Kant*, I, 6, and especially Hamilton Beck, "Moravians in Königsberg," in Joseph Kohnen (ed.), *Königsberg. Beiträge zu einem besonderen Kapitel der deutschen Geistesgeschichte* (Frankfurt [Main]: Peter Lang, 1994), pp. 335–344, 347–370.

126. Springer (alias G. Karl), *Kant und Alt-Königsberg*, p. 9. Strictly speaking, it was not the house that Kant was born in, but the house that had replaced it. In 1740 the house had been torn down.

127. Beck, "Moravians in Königsberg," p. 348.

128. Since all the land masses in the city are connected by seven bridges, the question arises whether is it possible for a person to take a walk around town, starting and ending at the same location, and crossing each of the seven bridges exactly once. Euler proved this to be impossible.

129. Hinrichs, *Preußentum und Pietismus*, p. 293; Riedesel, *Pietismus und Orthodoxie in Ostpreußen*, p. 138. See also Walther Hubatsch, *Geschichte der evangelischen Kirche in Ostpreussen*, 3 vols. (Göttingen: Vandenhoek and Rupprecht, 1968), I, pp. 218f.

130. Ritter, *Frederick the Great*, p. 76.

Chapter 2: Student and Private Teacher (1740–1755)

1. These were highly regimented. Not only were no women allowed to enter them, but their doors were locked at 10:00 P.M. in the summer and at 9:00 P.M. in the winter.

2. Georg Erler, *Die Matrikel und die Promotionsverzeichnisse der Albertus-Universität zu Königsberg in Preussen*, 3 vols. (Leipzig, 1910–17), pp. lxxxiv f., pp. cxxx f. Two years of absence from the university meant the loss of this protection. Under the reign of Frederick Wilhelm I, students had to endure forcible conscription – especially if they were tall. They were relentlessly pursued by the army recruiters (see Erler, *Die Matrikel*, pp. lxxxviii f.). Academic citizenship was not restricted to students and employees of the university. Teachers of French, Italian, and English, riding, fencing, and dancing, arithmetic and writing also belonged among the academic citizens, as did many public officials, pastors, lawyers, medical doctors, apothecaries, and book dealers and printers.

3. Kant was well aware of the nature of the academic guild and placed great value on it. See Ak 7, pp. 18f., for instance. See also Richard von Dülmen, *The Society of the Enlightenment: The Rise of the Middle Class and Enlightenment Culture in Germany*, tr. Anthony Williams (New York: St. Martin's Press, 1992), p. 7.

4. We do not know when precisely Kant changed his name from "Emanuel" to "Immanuel." I will from now on refer to him as "Kant."

5. In fact, since Frederick William I was himself of the Reformed faith, he tried, with varying degrees of success, to get the two churches to cooperate. See Hubatsch, *Geschichte der evangelischen Kirche Ostpreussens*, I, pp. 173f.

6. For the fate of Jewish students, see Monika Richarz, *Der Eintritt der Juden in die akademischen Berufe. Jüdische Studenten und Akademiker in Deutschland 1678–1848* (Tübingen: J. B. Mohr, 1974), pp. 55f. The first Jewish student entered the university in 1731; the first doctorate was given only in 1781. But Königsberg had more Jews among its students than did any other university in Prussia.

7. According to the decree of October 25, 1725. See Vorländer, *Kants Leben*, pp. 15f.

8. But it is not clear that he even had to take it. See Werner Euler and Stefan Dietzsch, "Prüfungspraxis und Universitätsreform in Königsberg. Ein neu aufgefundener Prüfungsbericht Kants aus dem Jahre 1779," in Reinhard Brandt and Werner Stark (eds.), *Autographen, Dokumente und Berichte. Zu Editionen, Amtsgeschäften und Werk Immanuel Kants* (Hamburg: Meiner, 1994), pp. 91–101, p. 97n. The final report from the *Collegium Fridericianum* would have been sufficient. The professor who tested him was Langhansen.

9. But see Klemme, *Die Schule Immanuel Kants*, p. 35f. Hahn, the rector at the time, noted only whether a student wanted to study pharmacy or medicine. So we know that Kant did not declare to study either of these two subjects.

10. Apparently, every student had to choose one of the three higher faculties, i.e., theology, law, or medicine. There is some dispute about whether Kant first belonged to the school of theology. Borowski claimed that Kant first intended to study theology. Kant himself scratched out this claim when he revised Borowski's sketch for a biography. Characteristically, Borowski retained it. There is no indication that Kant seriously considered theology as a career when he was in university. See also

Malter, "Immanuel Kant (1724–1804). Ein biographischer Abriß," pp. 109–124. In fact, in none of the documents of the university is Kant ever listed in one of the three higher schools (theology, law, and medicine). See Hagen, *Altpreussische Monatsschrift* 48, pp. 533f. All of this is perhaps a red herring. Until 1771 the students did not always have to declare what they intended to study (though beginning in the 1730s they were sometimes asked). But this is irrelevant; since philosophy was a preparatory course of study that everyone had to take before going on to the higher faculties, it was rarely noted as a subject. Even if Kant had declared theology as his subject, he would have taken philosophy courses. See Erler, *Die Matrikel*, pp. xc f.

11. Reicke, *Kantiana*, pp. 48–51; Malter, *Kant in Rede und Gespräch*, p. 18.
12. He matriculated February 5, 1746.
13. For a brief account of student life in eighteenth-century German universities, see Henri Brunschwig, *Enlightenment and Romanticism in Eighteenth-Century Prussia*, tr. Frank Jellinek (Chicago: University of Chicago Press, 1975), pp. 77–81. Later in the century the authorities found it necessary to curb "brawls, debauch, slovenly dress, bathing and swimming at places not authorized by the police, unlawful entry, invasions of private gatherings, especially weddings, organized rowdyism at examinations, carrying weapons, speeding on horseback or by carriage, excesses in musketry, tobacco, fireworks, the entertainments and dinners demanded of newcomers, games of chance, etc." (p. 80).
14. Reicke, *Kantiana*, p. 49; Malter, *Kant in Rede und Gespräch*, p. 19. He spoke highly of Montaigne in his lectures as well. See Ak 25.1 (Anthropology Collins), p. 87: "One may take extracts from foreign books, but they must be short. There are not many such passages. In Montaigne we find many naïve thoughts; he wrote with great leisure, for as a *Seigneur* he did not exert himself, and no one should blame him. He wrote to please himself (*um sich wohl zu befinden*)." Erasmus, by contrast, was not often mentioned in his lectures.
15. Schulz had been accused in 1740 of taking away playing cards from poor people. See Hinrichs, *Preußentum und Pietismus*, p. 293.
16. Ak 30 (Mrongovius), p. 98. Kant was also aware that playing can become a passion that eradicates all other inclinations. For him, its main interest lay in the constant alternation between the pleasure of winning and the pain of losing.
17. See Charles E. McClelland, *State, Society, and University in Germany, 1700–1914* (Cambridge: Cambridge University Press, 1980), pp. 27f.
18. Vorländer, *Immanuel Kant*, I, p. 49. Vorländer claimed that in 1744 there were 591 theologians, 428 law students, and 13 medical students. His source seems to be either Pisanski or the document on which Pisanski bases his claim, for the numbers are identical. See Georg Christoph Pisanski, *Entwurf einer preussischen Literärgeschichte in vier Büchern*, ed. Rudolf Philippi (Königsberg, 1886), p. 472n. Stuckenberg, *Kant*, p. 453, disputes this, claiming that these numbers include the students of both the summer and winter semesters, counting many of them twice. I am not sure Stuckenberg is correct. In any case, Erler, *Die Matrikel*, makes clear in his introduction how difficult it is to count those whom we would today call "students." Many of those inscribed were not attending lectures or recitations, but were connected to the university by trade or profession; and many who were

inscribed were not present in Königsberg. When he lists 1,032 students in 1744, he probably includes all the citizens of the university.

19. Compare Stavenhagen, *Kant und Königsberg*, p. 13. See Pisanski, *Entwurf einer preussischen Literärgeschichte*, p. 472n. According to Pisanski, there were in August 1744 the following students at the university: 143 Königsbergers, 184 Germans, 119 Poles, 62 Lithuanians, 13 from Danzig, 21 from Elbing, 17 from Thorn, 31 "from the other Polish parts of Prussia," 58 from Curland, 62 from Liefland, 13 from Ingermannland, 4 Russians, 2 Cosacks, 17 Poles, 3 Hungarians, and 5 from Siebenbürgen.

20. Hinrichs, *Preußentum und Pietismus*, p. 189.

21. Erdmann, *Knutzen*, p. 6.

22. Baczko, after Stuckenberg, *Kant*, p. 38. These shortcomings may have been more a perceptual than a real problem. Though the very latest books were not available immediately, most seem to have been in Königsberg after a few months. Göttingen, being closer to Leipzig, was in a better position, but not in a much better one.

23. Vorländer, *Immanuel Kant*, I, 48.

24. Hippel, according to Vorländer, *Immanuel Kant*, I, p. 49.

25. I shall call them from now on "full professors," "associate professors," and "lecturers" (*Magisters*) respectively. Though it is somewhat misleading to equate these positions with "professor," "associate professor," and "lecturer," it is less misleading than using "ordinary" and "extraordinary" professor, which would be the literal translations.

26. This was the normal division in Protestant universities beginning with Melanchthon.

27. Kant himself wrote a treatise on some of the problems this presented. See pp. 404–407 of this volume.

28. Erdmann, *Knutzen*, p. 13.

29. The titles of some of the books published by philosophy professors during that period make this abundantly clear. See Pisanski, *Entwurf einer preussischen Literärgeschichte*, pp. 519f.

30. Erdmann, *Knutzen*, p. 13 (compare Pisanski, *Entwurf einer preussischen Literärgeschichte*, pp. 523f.).

31. Erdmann, *Knutzen*, p. 18.

32. Pisanski, *Entwurf einer preussischen Literärgeschichte*, pp. 553f.

33. Erdmann, *Knutzen*, p. 18, based on the Preface to the first edition of the *Gründe der Weltweisheit*.

34. During this year Lysius began to receive stronger official support, and the relative isolation of the Pietists at the university ended. The theological faculty was radically transformed by a number of appointments. The king first appointed Georg Friedrich Rogall as full professor of philosophy and associate professor of theology, and then Abraham Wolff (1638–1731) as a teacher and preacher at the *Collegium Fridericianum*. These two appointments were soon followed by the appointments of Langhansen, Kypke, and Salthenius. Where there had been only one Pietist, there were now four. Though they by no means constituted a majority, they had become a significant minority.

35. Hinrichs, *Preußentum und Pietismus*, p. 247.

36. These were not empty threats, as the case of Fischer shows.

37. Though the order was signed by the king in September 1727, Abraham Wolff could take up his post only after a delay of six months. But then the Pietists consistently and ruthlessly used their power to eliminate any candidate who did not conform to their standards. They advanced only those whom they judged to have a reliable Pietistic background. Rogall, Wolff, and others also took over other institutions of higher learning, like the Lithuanian seminary, of which Abraham Wolff became the new director (by royal decree). This created a great deal of resentment. There were protests by students, who threw stones into the windows of Wolff's house, for example.

38. Riedesel, *Pietismus und Orthodoxie*, p. 38. In Königsberg the primary target of the Pietists was, of course, Fischer. While the other Wolffians were careful not to mention Wolff's name or to call attention to their views, Fischer characterized the Pietists as mere simpletons, ridiculed their positions in his lectures, and confessed "the irrefutable, eternal truths" of Wolffian thought. Rogall informed on Fischer through Francke in Halle. This incident harmed the Pietists more than it helped them. Many who were not in agreement with Fischer found the tactics of the Pietists distasteful, and Fischer's followers disrupted Rogall's classes. Rogall asked the king (again through Francke) to soften the punishment (from banishment to a prohibition of lecturing), but to no avail. This was not the only incident. In fact, two years later, the Pietists had someone else removed, namely the "notorious atheist Lau," who appeared to be influenced by Spinozism.

39. Paul Konschel, *Der junge Hamann nach seinen Briefen im Rahmen der lokalen Kirchengeschichte* (Königsberg, 1915), p. 5.

40. Stuckenberg, *Kant*, p. 41.

41. Konschel, *Der junge Hamann*, p. 5.

42. Frederick the Great is reported to have said: "Quandt is the only German orator." See Walther Hubatsch, *Geschichte der evangelischen Kirche in Ostpreussen*, I, p. 200.

43. His most important student and friend was Gottsched. See Riedesel, *Pietismus und Orthodoxie*, pp. 26f.

44. Erdmann, *Knutzen*, p. 21.

45. This was Hippel, who himself had been brought up in accordance with Pietistic principles; see Hippel, *Sämtliche Werke*, XII, p. 96.

46. Erdmann, *Knutzen*, p. 27. For a discussion of the relation between Pietism and literature, see Wolfgang Martens, *Literatur und Frömmigkeit in der Zeit der frühen Aufklärung* (Tübingen: Niemeyer, 1989). Martens concentrates on Halle, but most of what he says holds for Königsberg as well.

47. Konschel, *Der junge Hamann*, p. 7.

48. Konschel, *Der junge Hamann*, pp. 20f.

49. Erdmann, *Knutzen*, p. 37; Riedesel, *Pietismus und Orthodoxie*, p. 99: "Schultz, Kypke, Salthenius and Arnoldt formed a brotherhood which remained of one opinion."

50. Malter, *Kant in Rede und Gespräch*, p. 21.

51. Vorländer, *Immanuel Kant*, I, p. 50; Arnoldt, "Kant's Jugend," pp. 322f. I quote the relevant edict in accordance with Riccardo Pozzo, *Kant und das Problem einer Einleitung in die Logik. Ein Beitrag zur Rekonstruktion der historischen Hintergruende von Kants Logik-Kolleg* (Frankfurt, 1989), p. 2: "Each Professor publicus ordinarius

... must in his Lectionibus publicis ... finish each semester one Science publique, for example logica in one and Metaphysica in the other, and so year after year, just like jus naturalae in one, moral philosophy in the other year so that the Studiosi, especially those who are poor, can hear all the parts of philosophy free at the university and have the chance to hear in at least three semesters all the fundamental subjects of philosophy."

52. Vorländer, *Immanuel Kant*, I, p. 50.

53. Pisanski, *Entwurf einer preussischen Literärgeschichte*, p. 522. According to Pisanski, Gregorovius was "one of the last" who taught and defended Aristotle. He was interested mainly in ethics; one of his books was *Observationes Aristotelicae* (Königsberg, 1730).

54. Vorländer found that Gregorovius, as an "old" Aristotelian, was irrelevant to Kant, and thus dismissed him all too quickly. See Vorländer, *Immanuel Kant*, I, p. 50.

55. Kant, *Practical Philosophy*, p. 574 (Ak 6, p. 455).

56. Schulz had arranged for him an associate professorship in 1735.

57. See Manfred Kuehn, "Christian Thomasius and Christian Wolff," in *The Columbia History of Western Philosophy*, ed. Richard H. Popkin (New York: Columbia University Press, 1999), pp. 472–475.

58. Vorländer, *Kants Leben*, p. 21.

59. *Cursus philosophicus, sive Compendium praecipuarum scientiarum philosophicarum, Dialecticae nempe, Analyticae, Politicae, sub qua comprehenditur Ethica, Physicae et Metaphysicae. Ex evidentioribus rectae rationis principium deductum, methoda scientifica adornatum* (Königsberg/Leipzig, 1703).

60. Erdmann, *Knutzen*, p. 21.

61. But he was by no means the only one. The notorious Fischer, who also had started out as an Aristotelian, had published in 1716 *Problematica dialectica, quibus extantiora dialecticae capita sub expresso problematis schemate ex locis topicis ventilanda exhibentur* (Königsberg, 1716).

62. See Borowski, *Leben*, p. 100. See also Vorländer, *Immanuel Kant*, I, pp. 50, 82. Kant went to the *Collegium Fridericianum* with Kypke's nephew, who became his friend and colleague. See also Klemme, *Die Schule Immanuel Kants*, pp. 40, 46. Werner Stark thinks it may have been the house of the younger Kypke (Werner Stark, "Wo lehrte Kant? Recherchen zu Kants Königsberger Wohnungen," in *Königsberg. Beiträge zu einem besonderen Kapitel der deutschen Geistesgeschichte*, ed. Joseph Kohnen (Frankfurt [Main]: Peter Lang, 1994), pp. 81–109, p. 88f.

63. Erdmann, *Knutzen*, p. 68.

64. Konschel, *Der junge Hamann*, pp. 26–27n.

65. Konschel, "Christian Gabriel Fischer," p. 433.

66. In 1731 he published an English grammar (in Königsberg), *Johannis Wallisis tractatus de loquela seu sonorum formatione grammatic-physicus et grammatica linguae Anglicanae per compendium edita nexis dictionis Anglicanae exemplis selectis*.

67. In 1741 he gave a lecture on Pope, and in 1742 he announced two courses on him. See Erdmann, *Knutzen*, pp. 140, 149n.

68. All this is, of course, somewhat speculative. Kant may have learned of British authors elsewhere. Their books were everywhere. British thought and culture were represented prominently at the University of Königsberg when Kant was a student.

69. Borowski mentioned only Teske and Knutzen, not Ammon (Borowski, *Leben*, p. 40).
70. Erdmann, *Knutzen*, p. 14n.
71. Reicke, *Kantiana*, p. 7. It is not clear, however, whether he thought so as a student. Teske lived until 1772, and Kraus might have had in mind what Kant thought later about him.
72. Riedesel, *Pietismus und Orthodoxie*, pp. 43f.
73. Borowski, *Leben*, pp. 39f.; Vorländer, *Immanuel Kant*, I, p. 50.
74. Borowski, *Leben*, pp. 87f. Actually it was the memory of both Teske and Knutzen that was said to be "holy" to him.
75. Pisanski, *Entwurf einer preussischen Literärgeschichte*, p. 548.
76. Pisanski, *Entwurf einer preussischen Literärgeschichte*, p. 546.
77. Johann Friedrich Lauson, *Erster Versuch in Gedichten, nebst einer Vorrede von der sogenannten extemporal Poesie, und einem Anhange von Gedichten aus dem Stegreif* (Königsberg: Driest, 1753) and *Zweyter Versuch in Gedichten, nebst einer Vorrede von den Schicksalen der heutigen Poesie, und einem Anhange von Gedichten aus dem Stegreif* (Königsberg: Driest, 1754). Herder, who studied in the early sixties in Königsberg, also took courses with Teske. His notes show that Teske's lectures in physics were crucial to him. See W. Dobbek, *J. Herders Jugendzeit in Mohrungen und Königsberg, 1744–1764* (Würzburg: Holzener Verlag, 1961), p. 94.
78. Hamann, *Brevier*, p. 19; see also Hamann, *Gedanken über meinen Lebenslauf*, p. 168; Hans-Joachim Waschkies, *Physik und Physikotheologie des jungen Kant. Die Vorgeschichte seiner allgemeinen Weltgeschichte und Theorie des Himmels* (Amsterdam: Gruner, 1987), pp. 13, 57; Konschel, *Der junge Hamann*, p. 25; Vorländer, *Immanuel Kant*, I, pp. 54, 90. This society nevertheless seems to have lasted from July 1748 until the summer of 1749, perhaps even until 1751. (Werner Stark has suggested to me that "*zu Stande kam*" means that the society was not accredited or privileged by the government, as "the German society" was.) Hamann and J. G. Lindner were members of it. Waschkies tries to show that the sources of Kant's later work on cosmogony can be found here. There is no proof that Kant actually belonged to this society, nor is such an assumption necessary for accepting Waschkies's claim.

   Several other students talked about Knutzen in similar terms. See also Borowski, *Leben*, p. 38, and Erdmann, *Knutzen*, p. 6. It should be pointed out that Hamann was sarcastic. He goes on to lament that he did not take advantage of the opportunity, and then finds: "My memory of another academic teacher, who was not as famous, is more pleasant. God permitted it that he lived under depressed, miserable, and obscure circumstances. He was worthy of a better fate. He possessed qualities, which the world does not esteem and therefore does not reward. His end was as his life: unnoticed. I do not doubt that he is saved. His name was Rappolt; a man who possessed a peculiarly keen judgment concerning natural things and at the same time the consideration, devotion, and humility of a Christian philosopher. He had an exceptional ability to emulate the spirit and the language of the ancients."
79. Borowski, *Leben*, p. 40.
80. Reicke, *Kantiana*, p. 7.
81. It is said that as a student he did not go to the Aristotelians but "to men who had sufficient strength to teach him in more recent philosophy, mathematics . . ." He

attended the lectures of "Magister Ammon (Philosophy and mathematics) and to J. G. Teske (experimental physics)." He also learned French, English, Greek, and Hebrew, and he studied theology with A. Wolff and Schulz. In 1732, he became the respondent when the newly arrived Schulz defended his Inaugural Dissertation as a requirement for becoming a professor at Königsberg. Characteristically, it was entitled "Of the Agreement of Reason with Faith . . ." Knutzen taught himself calculus, and he is said to have learned all of algebra from Wolff's Latin work on the discipline. See Johann Friedrich Buck, *Lebensbeschreibungen derer verstorbenen preußischen Mathematiker* (1764). See also J. Chr. Strodtman, *Martin Knutzen*, pp. 75–76.

82. Erdmann, *Knutzen*, p. 51.
83. He defended this thesis in 1733.
84. See Erdmann, *Knutzen*, p. 52; see also Pisanski, *Entwurf einer preussischen Literärgeschichte*, p. 539. Knutzen's writings were successful beyond Königsberg. In 1745, he republished his Inaugural Dissertation under the title *System of Efficient Causality*, and in 1747 he published *Elements of Rational Psychology, or Logic Demonstrated in the Method of General and Special Mathematics.*
85. Riedesel, *Pietismus und Orthodoxie*, p. 97. Riedesel said this of Schulz, but the same holds for Knutzen.
86. Erdmann, *Knutzen*, p. 110.
87. Gottsched, *Neuer Büchersaal*, IV, 3, p. 241; Erdmann, *Knutzen*, p. 112.
88. Locke, *Essay*, Book I, Chapter 4, p. 85, insists that even our knowledge of the principle of (non)contradiction, *"impossibile est idem esse, et nonesse,"* is derived from experience.
89. See Klemme, *Die Schule Immanuel Kants*, p. 40n. See also Alois Winter, "Selbstdenken, Antinomien, Schranken. Zum Einfluss des späten Locke auf die Philosophie Kants," in *Eklektik, Selbstdenken, Mündigkeit*, ed. N. Hinske (Hamburg: Meiner, 1986), pp. 27–66.
90. It had first appeared as a series of articles in the *Königsberger Intelligenzblätter*. It was reissued several times. The fourth edition (Königsberg: Hartung) appeared in 1747. Its title reads *Philosophischer Beweiß von der Wahrheit der christlichen Religion, darinnen die Nothwendigkeit einer geoffenbarten Religion insgemein, und die Wahrheit oder Gewißheit der Christlichen insbesondere, aus ungezweifelten Gründen der Vernunft nach mathematischer Lehrart dargethan und behauptet wird.*
91. The works of these British authors were readily available in the extensive libraries of Königsberg theologians such as the orthodox Quandt and the Pietist Salthenius. Salthenius possessed an especially outstanding collection in that area. Pisanski, *Entwurf einer preussischen Literärgeschichte*, pp. 513f.; Klemme, *Die Schule Immanuel Kants*, pp. 4, 24.
92. See also Martin Knutzen, *Vertheidigte Wahrheit der christlichen Religion gegen den Einwurf: Daß die christliche Offenbahrung nicht allgemein sey. Wobey besonders die Scheingründe des bekannten Englischen Deisten Matthäi Tindal, welche in deßen Beweise, Daß das Christentum so alt wie die Welt sey, enthalten, erwogen und widerlegt werden* (Königsberg: Hartung, 1747).
93. Borowski, *Leben*, pp. 37, 39, 50, 85.
94. From Vorländer, *Kants Leben*, p. 23.

95. Borowski, *Leben*, pp. 39f.
96. Klemme, *Die Schule Immanuel Kants*, p. 35n.
97. Borowski, *Leben*, p. 40, "*unausgesetzt.*"
98. Riedesel, *Pietismus und Orthodoxie*, p. 142; Erdmann, *Knutzen*, pp. 44f. Fischer was, by the way, neither the first nor the only "materialist" and "Spinozist" who had come out of Königsberg. Theodor Ludwig Lau was another materialist, atheist, and native of Königsberg; he had studied with Thomasius in Halle. See G. Stiehler (ed.), *Materialisten der Leibniz Zeit* (*Friedrich Wilhelm Stosch, Theodor Ludwig Lau, Gabriel Wagner, Urban Gottfried Bucher*) (Berlin: VEB Verlag der deutschen Wissenschaften, 1966). His *De Deo, Mundo, Homine* or *Philosophical Considerations of God, the World and Man* of 1717 had created something of a sensation in all of Germany. Lau had tried – unsuccessfully, of course – to obtain a position at the University of Königsberg in 1727. He was denied the position because of "paradoxical doctrines." In 1729 he had to openly recant his materialism. He died in Altona in 1740. Fischer was often compared to the "notorious Lau." Rogall complained in 1724 of "the atheism and Epicureanism that is dominant here and cannot be eradicated" (see Hinrichs, *Preußentum und Pietismus*, p. 425).
99. Konschel, "Christian Gabriel Fischer," pp. 437f.
100. Ritter, *Frederick the Great*, p. 50. The entire chapter, "The King's View of the World," is a good introduction to Frederick's thought. Frederick's view of the world is important for understanding the climate in which Kant's thought matured.
101. Konschel, "Christian Gabriel Fischer," p. 439; Kant would later offer very similar arguments defending his own view. See pp. 404–405 of this volume.
102. Waschkies, *Physik und Physikotheologie*, pp. 296–347. This prediction was apparently based on Newton's theory of the course of periodic comets, according to which they orbit the sun in ellipses.
103. This book, which Kant essentially completed in 1746, appeared in 1749.
104. See Waschkies, *Physik und Physikotheologie*, p. 310; see also Ferdinand Josef Schneider, "Kometenwunder und Seelenschlaf (Johann Heyn als Wegbereiter Lessings)," *Deutsche Vierteljahrsschrift für Literaturwissenschaft und Geistesgeschichte* 18 (1940), pp. 201–232. Schneider does not mention Knutzen, but he shows that Heyn was important at the time (and that he was close to many of the younger adherents of Enlightenment philosophy, such as Lessing and Abraham Kästner).
105. Waschkies, *Physik und Physikotheologie*, p. 310.
106. It appeared in Berlin and Leipzig in 1742 with a Preface by Gottsched. Heyn also published a translation of Maupertuis's "Lettre sur la cométe " together with a letter by himself.
107. Waschkies, *Physik und Physikotheologie*, p. 335.
108. Waschkies, *Physik und Physikotheologie*, pp. 345f.
109. See pp. 98–99 of this volume.
110. Giorgio Tonelli, "Das Wiederaufleben der deutsch-aristotelischen Terminologie bei Kant während der Entstehung der 'Kritik der reinen Vernunft,'" *Archiv für Begriffsgeschichte* 9 (1964), pp. 233–242, argues that Aristotelian terminology was

reintroduced during the 1760s and 1770s. Aristotelian terminology did not need to be revived, as it had never been abandoned.

111. Göttingen was constituted in 1736–37.

112. Cassirer's claim that among Kant's teachers "Knutzen alone represented the European ideal of universal science" is historical nonsense (Cassirer, *Life*, 25). Teske and others represented that ideal just as much, or just as little. It is perhaps more significant that they discussed all the different ideas that contributed to this European ideal. However, the Pietists in Königsberg, including Knutzen, did not represent the ideal of universal science.

113. Borowski, *Leben*, p. 92.

114. Ibid. (Borowski probably knew what he was talking about, since he must have attended Teske's lectures.)

115. Ak 1, pp. 5f., 7.

116. Ak 1, pp. 30f.

117. Knutzen's name appears only in Kant's correspondence – in a letter of application for Knutzen's position.

118. Ak 1, p. 10.

119. Ak 1, p. 13.

120. Ak 1, p. 10.

121. The degree of *Magister* is roughly equivalent to today's Ph.D.

122. Vorländer, *Immanuel Kant*, I, p. 63, asks a similar question, but to my mind takes the easy way out, saying that it was because his friend had left, and that it was rather typical for young academics to take this route.

123. Borowski, *Leben*, p. 92.

124. It is indeed interesting to compare the passages on Schulz and Knutzen in Borowski's biography that Kant could have read (Borowski, *Leben*, pp. 37, 39f.) and the passages that Kant did not read (Borowski, *Leben*, pp. 83, 92). In the passages Kant did not read, the relationship between Knutzen and Kant is characterized as being much warmer and closer.

125. Ak 1, p. 309n. He belongs to the "*Metaphysikkundigeren,*" but not to the "*Metaphysikkundigen.*" Compare Waschkies, *Physik und Physikotheologie,* pp. 461n., 462f.

126. Waschkies, *Physik und Physikotheologie,* p. 20n.

127. The claim that Kant did not study theology "because he was opposed to Pietism" is from Reicke, *Kantiana,* p. 7.

128. It is often claimed that D'Alembert tried to show in his *Essai de dynamique* of 1743 that the different parties were just fighting about words, but Carolyn Iltis, in "D'Alembert and the *Vis Viva* Controversy," *Studies in History and Philosophy of Science* 1 (1970), pp. 135–44, claims that he did this only in the 1758 edition. Precedents for the distinction between change in momentum and force acting in a given time can, however, be found in Boscovich and in Clarke's fifth reply to Leibniz. (I am thankful to Martin Curd for pointing this out.)

129. See also Larry Laudan, "The *Vis Viva* Controversy, a Post-Mortem," *Isis* 59 (1968), pp. 131–143. Laudan refers to Euler's "De la force de percussion et sa veritable mesure," in *Memoires de l'Academie Royale des Sciences et des Belles Lettres de Berlin,* Année 1745 (Berlin: Haude, 1746), pp. 27–33, as Euler's contribution to this dispute.

130. Jachmann, *Kant*, p. 157.
131. Gottfried Wilhelm Leibniz, *Philosophical Essays*, tr. Roger Ariew and Daniel Garber (Indianapolis: Hackett Publishing Company, 1989), p. 123.
132. Ernan McMullin, *Newton on Matter and Activity* (Notre Dame: University of Notre Dame Press, 1978), p. 32. I rely heavily on his account of the differences and similarities between Descartes, Leibniz, and Newton.
133. McMullin, *Newton on Matter and Activity*, p. 33. It should, however, be remembered that force was for Newton not essential to matter.
134. Ak 1, p. 17.
135. Ak 1, p. 139.
136. Ibid. (the phrase represents the subtitle of Part III). This contrast between mathematical body and body of nature can be found in Christian August Crusius, who had argued that the space that substances fill is not the same as mathematical space, that mathematical space is arbitrary, and that it can therefore not be applied to nature without problems. See *Entwurf der nothwendigen Vernunftwahrheiten, wiefern sie den zufälligen entgegengesetzt werden* (1745), now in Christian August Crusius, *Die philosophischen Hauptwerke*, ed. G. Tonelli (Hildesheim: Olms, 1964); see especially p. 175. Compare Reinhard Finster, "Zur Kritik von Christian August Crusius an den einfachen Substanzen bei Leibniz und Wolff," *Studia Leibnitiana* 18 (1986), pp. 72–82. However, it is more likely that Kant relies on Alexander Gottlieb Baumgarten's *Metaphysica*, which first appeared in 1739, and which inspired both Crusius and Kant. Baumgarten made a distinction between fictional or mathematical points and monads, which are real and determinate physical points. But whether or not Baumgarten influenced Crusius, his conception of physical monads certainly represents almost exactly Kant's own early view. See especially paragraphs 392–435 (Ak 17, pp. 109–117).
137. Ak 1, p. 140.
138. Ak 1, pp. 151f. Kant's theory must also be viewed in relation to the question that the Berlin Academy had formulated for the year 1747 (published in 1746): "We demand an examination, starting from an exact and clear presentation of the doctrine of monads, whether monads can be thoroughly disproved and destroyed by incontestable arguments, or whether it is possible to prove the monads and derive from them an intelligible explanation of the main phenomena of the universe *and especially of the origin and the motion of bodies*" (emphasis supplied). For an account of the discussion connected to this question, see Karl Vogel, *Kant und die Paradoxien der Vielheit. Die Monadenlehre in Kants philosophischer Entwicklung bis zum Antinomienkapitel der Kritik der reinen Vernunft* (Meisenheim am Glan: Anton Hain, 1975), pp. 87f.
139. At Ak 1, p. 152. Kant refers to this work.
140. McMullin, *Newton on Matter and Activity*, p. 46.
141. Baumgarten, *Metaphysica*, paragraphs 294 (Ak 17, p. 91) and 210–223 (Ak 17, pp. 70–76), especially 220 (p. 74). But compare also Erdmann, *Knutzen*, pp. 95–96. Erdmann claims that Baumgarten's preestablished harmony was different from Leibniz's because Baumgarten held that monads can act on each other. This is certainly true, but this does not mean that his theory was one of physical influx. Just like Kant, Baumgarten believes that external influences (what he calls

"real influx") awaken an inner principle of the monad that ultimately explains the action ("ideal influx"). Real influx is ultimately based on ideal influx. Even Erdmann must admit that Baumgarten's "ideal influx" is identical to the theory of preestablished harmony. Erdmann's claim that Baumgarten had "completely abandoned" Leibniz's theory seems to me to rest on his failure to take seriously the "phenomenal" character of real influx in Baumgarten (and Kant). Ideal influx provides the foundation for real influx. For an important argument against this claim, see Eric Watkins, "The Development of Physical Influx in Early Eighteenth Century Germany: Gottsched, Knutzen, and Crusius," *Review of Metaphysics* 49 (1995), pp. 295–339, "Kant's Theory of Physical Influx," *Archiv für Geschichte der Philosophie* 77 (1995), pp. 285–324, and "From Pre-established Harmony to Physical Influx: Leibniz's Reception in 18th Century Germany," *Perspectives on Science* 6 (1998), pp. 136–201. Watkins views Kant more as a follower of Knutzen's. I see him as a follower of Baumgarten. There is at least the following difference between Knutzen and Kant: Knutzen was arguing for real physical influx. Kant said, "Physical influx in the true sense of the term, however, is excluded. There exists a universal harmony (*influxus physicus proprie sic dictus excluditur, et est rerum harmonia universalis*)." See Kant, *Theoretical Philosophy, 1755–1770*, p. 44 (Ak 1, p. 415). Though Kant took pains to differentiate universal harmony from preestablished harmony, the two were close enough from the Pietistic point of view. Indeed, Kant's claim that substances do not just agree with one another (as Leibniz said), but actually "mutually depend" on one another, might have seemed worse to the Pietists.

142. Ak 1, p. 171.

143. It is likely that he would have rejected even at that time the idea that the universal harmony was preestablished. See Chapter 2 of this volume. Michael Friedman, *Kant and the Exact Sciences* (Cambridge: Harvard University Press, 1992), claims that "Kant attempts to revise the Leibniz-Wolffian monadology in light of Newtonian physics," that his "primary notion of active force is not that of an internal principle" but "that of an action exerted by one substance on another substance," and that Kant in this way has "imported Newton's second law of motion into the very heart of the monadology" (p. 5). I agree with Friedman on this. Susan Meld Shell, *The Embodiment of Reason* (Chicago: University of Chicago Press, 1996), pp. 10–30, has a nice summary of Kant's position. Still, her claim that in *The True Estimation of Living Forces* Kant "is flatly at odds with the claims of the Leibniz Wolffian school" (p. 28) seems to me not quite correct. In his most significant claims about what she describes as "cognitive dualism," Kant was close to Gottsched, his philosophical predecessor in Königsberg. The most extensive account of the problem of physical influx and its relation to Leibniz-Wolffian philosophy is found in Gerd Fabian, *Beitrag zur Geschichte des Leib-Seele Problems* (*Lehre von der prästabilierten Harmonie-und vom psychophysischen Parallelismus in der Leibniz-Wolffschen Schule*) (Langensalza: Hermann Beyer & Söhne, 1925).

144. Friedman claims that substances are connected by their mutual relations, and not by preestablished harmony. This seems to be true. But there is a difference between what connects them and the principle that governs this connection.

145. Ak 1, p. 21. See Watkins, "Kant's Theory of Physical Influx," p. 289.

146. Ak 1, p. 20. Knutzen did talk about this in terms of motion.

147. Emil Arnoldt, "Kant's Jugend," pp. 608–609. The same phrase was used when Kant himself died.

148. Ak 6, p. 382.

149. Even if no Kant biographer has ever paid attention to this fact.

150. See p. 427, note 3, this volume.

151. Although most of biographers claim that Kant left much earlier, their reasoning is suspect. I follow Waschkies here (see Waschkies, *Physik und Physikotheologie,* p. 14). Waschkies, like everyone before him, fails to take into account the family situation, which provides further support for this dating. Kant's youngest brother was already twelve when his uncle took him in. This suggests that the household was dissolved in 1748. Before then, Kant and his sisters must have cared for their little brother.

152. See Harald Paul Fischer, "Eine Antwort auf Kants Briefe vom 23. August, 1749," *Kant-Studien* 76 (1985), pp. 79–89, and "Kant an Euler," *Kant-Studien* 85 (1985), pp. 214–218.

153. The German reads: "Auf des Herrn K* Gedanken von der wahren Schätzung der lebendigen Kräfte / K* unternimmt ein schwer Geschäfte, / Der Welt zum Unterricht. / Er schätzet die lebendgen Kräfte, / Nur seine schätzt er nicht." Gotthold Ephraim Lessing, *Werke,* 8 vols., ed. Herbert G. Göpfert, Karl Eibl, Helmut Göbel, Karl S. Guthke, Gerd Hillen, Albert von Schirmding, and Jörg Schönert (München: Carl Hanser, 1970–), I, p. 47.

154. Ak 7, p. 201.

155. Reicke, *Kantiana,* p. 7. Kraus notes that he does not know anything of a stay with the Keyserlingk family. See also Fritz Schütz, "Immanuel Kant, Studiosus Philosophiae, in Judtschen," *Kant-Studien* 11 (1916), pp. 226–229. Schütz argues that Kant was not a Hofmeister with Andersch, but an adjunct or auxiliary teacher. The schoolmaster he was to have helped was Jacob Challet. Kant did become on October 23, 1748, the godfather of Challet's son Samuel. It is thus possible that Kant was primarily an adjunct of Challet, and secondarily a private teacher of Andersch's younger sons.

156. Arnoldt, "Kant's Jugend," pp. 156f. See also Waschkies, *Physik und Physikotheologie,* p. 25.

157. J. M. R. Lenz, a student of Kant, later wrote a drama called *Der Hofmeister,* which depicts the miserable lot of a member of this profession. See also Franz Werner, *Soziale Unfreiheit und 'bürgerliche Intelligenz' im 18. Jahrhundert. Der organisatorische Gesichtspunkt in J. M. R. Lenz's Drama 'Der Hofmeister oder die Vorteile der Privaterziehung'* (Frankfurt: Rita G. Fischer Verlag, 1981), pp. 93–204; and Heinrich Bosse, "Berufsprobleme der Akademiker im Werk von J. M. R. Lenz," in *'Unaufhörlich Lenz gelesen . . .' Studien zu Leben und Werk von J. M. R. Lenz,* ed. Inge Stephan and Hans-Gerd Winter (Stuttgart and Weimar: Metzler, 1994), pp. 38–51.

158. See Werner, *Soziale Unfreiheit,* and Bosse, "Berufsprobleme der Akademiker," for vivid descriptions of the usual plight of the *Hofmeister.* Also interesting is

Frank Aschoff, "Zwischen äußerem Zwang und innerer Freiheit. Fichte's Hauslehrer-Erfahrungen und die Grundlegung seiner Philosophie," *Fichte-Studien* 9 (1997), pp. 27–45.

159. See Waschkies, *Physik und Physikotheologie*, p. 28; but see also Michaelis, "Kant – Hauslehrer in Judtschen?," *Kant-Studien* 38 (1933), pp. 492–493.
160. Compare Vorländer, *Immanuel Kant*, I, pp. 65–68.
161. Though it is likely he never learned to speak it well.
162. This is about as far as Kant ever traveled from Königsberg. Though he often went on excursions around Königsberg, the only trips that are comparable are those to Goldapp (about seventy-five miles). Otherwise, Kant seems to have stayed within a thirty-mile radius. (Pillau was that far away.)
163. Rink, *Ansichten*, p. 29.
164. Ak 10, p. 2.
165. Feder, *Leben*, pp. 173.
166. Borowski, *Leben*, pp. 40f.
167. It is often assumed that Kraus's remark that he did not know anything of a "*Kondition*" with the Keyserlingks means that Kant could not have been a teacher in their household at that time. However, since the Keyserlingk family lived in Königsberg at least during part of the relevant period, Kant could well have been a teacher there, without living in their household (for that is what "*in Kondition*" means).
168. See Ak 1, p. 185.
169. Ak 1, p. 191.
170. Ak 1, p. 213.
171. Ibid.
172. Ak 1, p. 226. Another way of putting this might be that he is following up the Cartesian side of his earlier enterprise, leaving the Leibnizian aspect to one side.
173. Ak 1, p. 221; compare Ak 23, pp. 11f. These claims suggest that it is necessary to compare his work with those of Lau and Fischer. Kant knew that these would be fighting words – at least as far as the Pietists were concerned.
174. Ak 1, p. 221.

Chapter 3: The Elegant *Magister* (1755–1764)

1. See Immanuel Kant, *Kant's Latin Writings: Translations, Commentaries, and Notes*, 2nd revised edition by Lewis White Beck, Mary J. Gregor, Ralf Meerbote, and John A Reuscher (New York: Peter Lang, 1992), pp. 11–35. The dissertation is, according to Beck, interesting mainly as "a succinct, reasonably accurate and well-informed presentation of a venerable but incorrect theory in the later stage of its life" (p. 12). It also is important for revealing the corpuscularian background of Kant's mechanics.
2. See Reicke, *Kantiana*, p. 48 (Malter, *Kant in Rede und Gespräch*, p. 19).
3. In Latin, of course. This text does not appear to have survived. Its title is similar to that of Kypke's speech. (Werner Stark, "Kants akademische Kollegen," unpublished manuscript).
4. Borowski, *Leben*, p. 41.

5. Johann Georg Hamann, *Briefwechsel*, vols. 1–7, ed. Walther Ziesemer and Arthur Henkel (Frankfurt [Main]: Insel Verlag, 1955–1979), I, p. 190 (April 28, 1756).
6. Kant, *Latin Writings*, ed. Beck, p. 58.
7. Kant, *Latin Writings*, ed. Beck, p. 83.
8. Kant, *Latin Writings*, ed. Beck, pp. 82f.
9. Kant handed it in on March 23, 1756 (see Ak 1, p. 578).
10. Kant, *Latin Writings*, ed. Beck, p. 95.
11. Kant, *Latin Writings*, ed. Beck, p. 97.
12. Kant, *Latin Writings*, ed. Beck, p. 99.
13. On Boscovich and his possible influence, see Beck in Kant, *Latin Writings*, ed. Beck, pp. 88, 90n. On Euler, see H. E. Timerding, "Kant und Euler," *Kant-Studien* 23 (1919), pp. 18–64, and Wolfgang Breidert, "Leonhard Euler und die Philosophie," in *Leonhard Euler, 1707–1783: Beiträge zu Leben und Werk* (Gedenkband des Kantons Basel-Stadt Basel: Birkhauser Verlag, 1983), pp. 447–457. It is certainly significant that Kant sent his first work to Euler. See also Fischer, "Kant an Euler," pp. 214–218. Timerding argues that Euler was to some extent influenced by Baumgarten.
14. G. Krause, *Gottsched und Flottwell, die Begründer der deutschen Gesellschaft* (Leipzig, 1893), p. 47. Compare Stark, "Kants Kollegen" (unpublished manuscript).
15. Hamann, *Briefwechsel*, I, p. 98.
16. Ak 1, p. 231. See Ley, *Kant's Cosmogony*. He reprints the review.
17. References to Weitenkampf's publication show that he was still writing on it in 1754. See Waschkies, *Physik und Physikotheologie*, and Riccardo Pozzo, "Kant e Weitenkampff," *Rivista di storia della filosofia* 48 (1993), pp. 283–322.
18. Accordingly, he first offers a brief account of Newton's principles.
19. Arthur Lovejoy, *The Great Chain of Being: A Study in the History of Ideas* (New York: Harper & Brothers, 1960), pp. 265f., views Kant's theory as "a temporalized version of the principle of plenitude" (p. 265).
20. For general information about Kant's teaching see Werner Stark, "Kant als akademischer Lehrer," in *Königsberg und Riga*, ed. Heinz Ischreyt (Tübingen: Max Niemeyer Verlag, 1995), pp. 51–70.
21. Borowski, *Leben*, p. 100. This probably took place on Monday, October 13, 1755. See "Translator's Introduction" to Immanuel Kant, *Lectures on Metaphysics*, tr. Karl Ameriks and Steve Naragon (Cambridge: Cambridge University Press, 1997), p. xix.
22. Borowski, *Leben*, 100f. See also Wannowski in Malter, *Kant in Rede und Gespräch*, p. 48: "he used the textbooks his lectures were based on as a canon but only *pro forma*, following his own thoughts." Kant himself taught physical geography and anthropology without a textbook, however. But both were "new" disciplines.
23. Johannes Voigt, *Das Leben des Professor Christian Jacob Kraus . . ., aus den Mitteilungen seiner Freunde und Briefen* (Königsberg, 1819), p. 130.
24. Borowski, *Leben*, p. 103, see also p. 62.
25. Borowski, *Leben*, p. 91.
26. Scheffner, *Mein Leben*, II, p. 362.
27. Johann Georg Hamann, *Hamanns Schriften*, 7 vols., ed. Friedrich Roth (Berlin, 1821–25), III, p. 11. Watson was three years younger than Hamann. He became *Magister* in 1753 and associate professor of rhetoric in 1756.

28. Scheffner, *Mein Leben*, p. 59.

29. Scheffner, *Mein Leben*, p. 60.

30. Borowski, *Leben*, pp. 94f. Borowski may be exaggerating here. In any case, he admits that in later years Kant became very interested in church history.

31. Emil Arnoldt, "Möglichst vollständiges Verzeichnis aller von Kant gehaltenen oder auch nur angekündigten Vorlesungen nebst darauf bezüglichen Notizen," in Emil Arnoldt, *Gesammelte Schriften*, 6 vols., ed. Otto Schöndörffer (Berlin, 1907–09), IV, pp. 335f. But see also Werner Stark's more specific account in "Einleitung," to Ak 25.1 (Anthropologie Vorlesungen), pp. xcvii f. The semesters began on Easter and Michaelmas respectively, i.e., the summer semester could start at any time between March 22 and April 25, while the winter semester always started on September 29. The election of the rector was an important event at the beginning of every semester. It took place the Sunday after the beginning of the semester. But lectures usually started only eight days after the election of the rector.

32. Stark, "Introduction," Ak 25, p. xcix.

33. Arnoldt, "Möglichst vollständiges Verzeichis," p. 188.

34. 1756/57: logic, metaphysics (according to Baumeister), ethical theory, mathematics, physics; 1757: physical geography, natural science, logic, metaphysics (Baumeister or Baumgarten), mathematics; 1757/58: metaphysics, physics, mathematics, moral philosophy, and a *Disputatorium* (exercises in disputation); perhaps also logic; 1758: logic, metaphysics, disputation (on Wednesdays and Sundays), mathematics, natural science, physical geography, etc., etc. See Arnoldt, "Möglichst vollständiges Verzeichnis," pp. 173–343.

35. This was a summary of a more extensive work. He read once in accordance with the more extensive textbook also known as the "Large Meier."

36. Malter, *Kant in Rede und Gespräch*, p. 42.

37. Borowski, *Leben*, p. 101. These notebooks have not survived.

38. Kant owned the 1750 edition of the former and the 1749 edition of the latter. He seems to have lectured on this subject for sixteen semesters from the winter of 1755–56 to the summer of 1763. See Gottfried Martin, "Die mathematischen Vorlesungen Immanuel Kants," *Kant-Studien* 58 (1967), pp. 58–62. See also the translators note in Gottfried Martin, *Arithmetic and Combinatorics: Kant and His Contemporaries*, tr. and ed. Judy Wubnig (Carbondale and Edwardsville: Southern Illinois University Press, 1985), pp. 143f. This conflicts with Arnoldt's view, according to which he did not read mathematics in the winter semesters of 1757–58 and 1758–59 and the summer of 1762. Arnoldt is probably correct. This means that it is likely that Kant used the shorter *Auszug* during the preceding semester.

39. According to Arnoldt, Kant lectured on physics in the winter semesters of 1755–56, 1756–57, 1760–61, 1762–63, and in the summer semesters of 1759. He also lectured on natural science in the summer semesters of 1756, 1757, and 1758, lectured on theoretical physics in the summer of 1761, and gave a *collegium physico-mathematicum* in the winter of 1761–62.

40. Jachmann, *Kant*, p. 137.

41. Borowski, *Leben*, p. 83. Vorländer, *Leben*, p. 57, thinks that this was later and that

Kant's income fluctuated greatly during his years as a lecturer. There is no reason to assume this. The accounts of Jachmann, Borowski, and Kant are compatible.

42. At least since 1761. But the letter says that he "always" had a servant (Ak 11, p. 149). See also Borowski, *Leben*, p. 83.

43. Ak 11, p. 256.

44. See also Malter, *Kant in Rede und Gespräch*, p. 44.

45. Ak 10, p. 3.

46. Ak 12, p. 3.

47. Reicke, *Kantiana*, p. 7; see also the anonymous Leipzig biography, pp. 12, 126; Rink, *Ansichten*, p. 30; and Borowski, *Leben*, p. 31.

48. See Arthur Warda, "Zur Frage nach Kant's Bewerbung um eine Lehrerstelle," *Altpreussische Monatsschrift* 35 (1898), pp. 578–614. Warda's research makes this time very likely, though one might expect that this event took place earlier.

49. Warda, "Lehrerstelle," pp. 606f.

50. For more information on Kypke, see Werner Stark, "Hinweise zu Kants Kollegen vor 1770," unpublished manuscript. See also Ak 10, pp. 17, 19, 25, 33.

51. In 1743 he defended *"De incomprehensibilitate dei, respectu intellectu infiniti"* under Teske. He then went to Halle and returned to Königsberg, having obtained the *Magister* degree. His career is in many ways typical of that of a well-connected Königsberg Pietist, and is quite different from Kant's.

52. Stark, "Kants Kollegen" (unpublished manuscript).

53. See Winter, "Selbstdenken, Antinomien, Schranken."

54. Stark, "Kants Kollegen," points out that the title of a published book by Kypke was *Treatise on Brevity and Extensiveness in Written Presentation*. Kant spoke on "The Easier and More Thorough Presentation of Philosophy" on the occasion of receiving his doctorate.

55. Hamann, *Briefwechsel*, I, p. 226.

56. From Stark, "Kants Kollegen."

57. Compare Alexander Altmann, *Moses Mendelssohn: A Biographical Study* (Alabama: University of Alabama Press, 1973), pp. 307–309. For later developments see also pp. 216–217 of this volume.

58. Borowski also said that "among his academic colleagues, Funk was very dear to him" (see Reicke, *Kantiana*, p. 31).

59. Wannowski in Reicke, *Kantiana*, p. 39; he mentioned Kypke as his second friend, and also mentioned Lilienthal as someone he respected, "however much he disagreed with his views."

60. Borowski, *Leben*, pp. 59f.

61. I am thankful to Werner Stark for this information.

62. Th. G. v. Hippel, *Sämmtliche Werke*, 14 vols., ed. Theodor Gottlieb von Hippel (Berlin: Reimer, 1828–39; reprint de Gruyter, 1978), XII, pp. 30f.

63. Flottwell writes on January 29, 1751, that Knutzen inherited first 10,000 Thalers and then another 15,000 Thalers, "and yet this philosopher lives in bad humor (*misvergnügt*), without social intercourse, and as a complete pedant." Three days after Flottwell wrote this, Knutzen was dead.

64. Jachmann, *Kant*, p. 191; he speaks vaguely of Kant's "younger years," and adds

that "Kant, as a keen observer of himself, changed his way of life in accordance with years and circumstances."

65. The Prussian von Wallenrodt took over the administration in Königsberg on August 6, 1762.

66. Pisanski, *Entwurf einer preussischen Literärgeschichte*, p. xi.

67. Compare all this to Stavenhagen, *Kant und Königsberg*, pp. 14–18.

68. Scheffner, *Mein Leben*, p. 67.

69. Ibid.

70. Stavenhagen, *Kant und Königsberg*, p. 26.

71. Wannowski in Malter Kant in Rede und Gespräch, p. 48; he adds that Kant paid attention to fortification, military architecture, and pyrotechnics.

72. For further details see especially Wilhelm Salewski, "Kant's Idealbild einer Frau. Versuch einer Biographie der Gräfin Caroline Charlotte Amalie von Keyserlingk, geb. Gräfin Truchsess von Waldburg (1727–1791)," *Jahrbuch der Albertus Universität zu Königsberg* 26/27 (1986), pp. 27–62.

73. Ak 11, p. 56. The events he is referring to must have taken place in 1762. Compare Malter, *Kant in Rede und Gespräch*, pp. 56–7.

74. Unless etiquette required that a guest of higher social standing had to occupy it.

75. Borowski, *Leben*, p. 75; he also said that Kant had tried to convince his students that one should never be entirely out of fashion in one's dress.

76. K. A. Varnhagen van Ense, *Denkwürdigkeiten des Philosophen Arztes Johann Benjamin Erhard* in *Ausgewählte Schriften*, 15.2 (Leipzig, 1874), p. 322.

77. See Borowski, *Leben*, p. 75; see also Jachmann, *Kant*, p. 172. The sword was not unusual then. Kant stopped carrying it when merchants did so as well.

78. There is a nice description of the clothing worn by the clerics in Friedrich Nicolai, *Sebaldus Nothanker* (Berlin, 1773), Book 4, section 8. See the recent edition by Bernd Witte (Stuttgart: Reclam, 1991), pp. 213–221. See also Book 4, section 1, for a description of the dress of a typical Pietist (p. 161). See also *Fragmente aus Kants Leben*, pp. 91f.: "During the first years of his teaching when theological disputes were still on the daily agenda, there lived a certain D. and P. S. . . . according to whom a class of theologians called themselves S...ner. Apart from their quiet Pietistic lives they were also characterized by common clothing and thus wanted to be considered for children of the right faith."

79. Jachmann, *Kant*, p. 189; compare Borowski, *Leben*, p. 72.

80. His attire certainly was fashioned in accordance with this ideal: "Typical attire for men included knee breeches, jackets with embroidered vests, and shirts decorated with a throat cloth, or cravat, the ancestor of the modern necktie. The hat for men throughout the century was the tricorn, a low crowned hat with the brim turned up on three sides. By 1790 two other hats were common: a bicorn and a top hat similar to the 17th-century Puritan hat." Kant's biographers take pains to point out that Kant never changed his hat from a tricorn. When his early philosophical theories were dismissed by more orthodox thinkers as "*Tändeley*," Kant was in fact already characterized as belonging to this tradition.

81. K. W. Böttiger (ed.), *Literarische Zustände und Zeitgenossen* in *Schilderungen aus Karl Aug. Böttiger's handschriftlichen Nachlasse* (Leipzig, 1838), I, p. 133. This is later than the period under discussion (1764) but still relevant.

82. Borowski, *Leben*, p. 79 (Malter, *Kant in Rede und Gespräch*, p. 46).

83. Mortzfeld in Malter, *Kant in Rede und Gespräch*, p. 75.

84. The poem was published in 1754. See C. M. Wieland, *Sämtliche Werke*, 14 vols. (Hamburg: Hamburger Stiftung zur Förderung von Wissenschaft und Kultur, 1984; reprint of Leipzig: Göschen, 1794–1811), XIV, pp. 4–18. Wieland lived from 1753 to 1813.

85. Heilsberg, in Malter, *Kant in Rede und Gespräch*, p. 22.

86. Ibid.

87. Robin Schott, *Cognition and Eros: A Critique of the Kantian Paradigm* (Boston: Beacon Press, 1988), criticizes Kant for views he did not hold. Ursula Pia Jauch, *Immanuel Kant zur Geschlechterdifferenz. Aufklärerische und bürgerliche Geschlechtervormundschaft* (Vienna: Passagen Verlag, 1988) appreciates some aspects of Kant's views while criticizing him rather harshly for his views on marriage.

88. See Ak 10, pp. 4–6, and Ak 13, pp. 4f.

89. Borowski, *Leben*, p. 42.

90. Hamann, *Briefwechsel*, I, p.362. Compare Johann Georg Hamann, *Hamann's Socratic Memorabilia*, translated with commentary by James C. O'Flanerty (Baltimore: Johns Hopkins University Press, 1967), p. 56, and Kant, *Correspondence*, tr. Zweig, p. 35.

91. Hamann, *Briefwechsel*, I, p. 373.

92. Kant, *Correspondence*, tr. Zweig, pp. 41f.

93. The full title reads: *Socratic Memorabilia, Compiled for the Boredom of the Public by a lover of Boredom. With a Double Dedication to Nobody and to Two* (Amsterdam, 1759).

94. Hamann, *Socratic Memorabilia*, p. 167.

95. The concluding paragraph of section 10 of Hume's first *Enquiry* might indeed suggest such a reading.

96. David Hume, *Enquiries Concerning Human Understanding and Concerning the Principles of Morals*, 3rd ed., ed. L. A. Selby-Bigge, rev. P. H. Nidditch (Oxford: Clarendon Press, 1975), p. 131. There is a historical case to be made that Hume actually had a great influence on this Kierkegaardian conception, at least indirectly. His discussions of belief in the *Treatise* and the *Enquiry* influenced Hamann and Jacobi in their conception of faith. Especially Jacobi liked to talk of a *"salto mortale"* into faith. Kierkegaard knew Hamann and Jacobi. For more on this, see Philip Merlan, "From Hume to Hamann," *The Personalist* 32 (1951), pp. 11–18, "Hamann et les Dialogues de Hume," *Revue de Metaphysique* 59 (1954), pp. 285–289; "Kant, Hamann-Jacobi and Schelling on Hume," *Rivista critica di storia filosofia* 22 (1967), pp. 343–351.

97. Hume, *Enquiry*, pp. 129f. Later exploited by Jacobi in the *Pantheismusstreit* (see pp. 305–309 of this volume).

98. Vorländer and others claim that Kant had asked Hamann to help him in writing this book some time after the encounter of Berens and Kant with Hamann at the latter's house. This seems highly unlikely. Kant may have proposed such collaboration at that meeting in the same context in which he suggested that Hamann translate parts of the *Encyclopédie*, and as an attempt to reconvert Hamann. It is unlikely that he approached Hamann later. In any case, Lindner knows through Berens of Kant's plan, as the letter of December 26 shows (Ak 10, p. 25).

99. Hamann, *Briefwechsel*, I, p.445.

100. Ibid.

101. Most, indeed all, Hamann and Kant scholars I know, take the letter at face value. See, for instance, Hans Graubner, "Physikotheologie und Kinderphysik. Kants und Hamanns gemeinsamer Plan einer Physik für Kinder in der physikotheologischen Tradition des 18. Jahrhunderts," in *Johann Georg Hamann und die Krise der Aufklärung: Acta des fünften Internationalen Hamann-Kolloquiums in Münster i. W.* (Frankfurt and Bern: Peter Lang, 1990), pp. 117–145. Graubner, like most other scholars, finds it necessary to adduce arguments that make such a cooperation of Hamann and Kant "plausible" (p. 125). No such arguments are needed because there was no cooperation. It was one of Hamann's spoofs. Blumenberg is thus correct in calling this episode *"ein Paradestück der Komik."* But Blumenberg did not get the joke either. See Hans Blumenberg, *Die Lesbarkeit der Welt* (Frankfurt: Suhrkamp, 1981), p. 191.

102. Ak 17, pp. 229–239.

103. Ak 2, p. 33; Immanuel Kant, *Theoretical Philosophy, 1755–1770*, tr. David Walford and Ralf Meerbote (Cambridge: Cambridge University Press, 1992), p. 75.

104. Ak 2, pp. 461f. Most scholars think Weymann misconstrues Kant's intent. See the Introduction to Kant, *Theoretical Philosophy*, pp. liv–lvii. Stark, "Kants Kollegen," shows that Weymann understood Kant's intentions quite well.

105. Ak 10, p. 19 (compare to Kant, *Theoretical Philosophy, 1755–1770*, p. lvi).

106. See Helmuth Weiss, "Das Königsberg Kants in den Augen eines jungen russischen Teilnehmers am Siebenjährigen Krieg," *Jahrbuch der Albertus-Universität zu Königsberg* 17 (1967), pp. 49–62.

107. Andrej Bolotov, *Leben und Abenteuer des Andrej Bolotov von ihm selbst für seine Nachkommen aufgeschrieben. 1. 1738–1762*, tr. Marianne Schilow, ed. Wolfgang Gruba (München, Beck, 1990), I, pp. 357f. See also Adelheid Rexheuser, "Andrej Bolotov. Königsberg als Bildungserlebnis eines russischen Aufklärers," in *Königsberg und Riga*, ed. Heinz Ischreyt (Tübingen: Max Niemeyer Verlag, 1995), pp. 87–122, p. 114n.

108. I am thankful to Professor Thomas Newlin for a personal communication concerning this.

109. Gulyga, *Kant*, p. 57 (see also Rexheuser, "Bolotov," p. 113). Weymann refused to take payment from Bolotov, even though he lived in bitter poverty.

110. Hamann, *Briefwechsel*, I, pp. 425f.

111. Hamann, *Briefwechsel*, I, p.448.

112. Hamann, *Briefwechsel*, I, p.450.

113. Hamann, *Briefwechsel*, I, p.440 (November 17, 1759).

114. Ak 10, p. 19.

115. See Paul Tschackert, "Theodor Gottlieb Hippel, der christliche Humorist, als Student der Theologie in Königsberg 1756 bis 1759," *Altpreussische Monatsschrift* 28 (1892), pp. 355–356.

116. Ferdinand Josef Schneider, *Theodor Gottlieb von Hippel in den Jahren von 1741 bis 1781 und die erste Epoche seiner literarischen Tätigkeit* (Prague: Taussig & Taussig, 1911), pp. 47–49.

117. After Hippel experienced the freeing of his soul in Petersburg, he appreciated Kant more – or so it appears. But for what it is worth, he never appears to have viewed himself as a "student" of Kant, and he found it strange when he was later characterized in this way.

118. Schulz began his studies on September 25, 1756. Borowski is not the only one to mention him as one of Kant's important students. Wald does so too. See Reicke, *Kantiana*, pp. 31, 37. Since Schulz said in his reponse to Wald that he did not "dare" to decide who were Kant's most important students and thus left the space blank, it may have been modesty that kept him from pointing out that he was Kant's student.

119. Ak 2, p. 41.

120. Ak 2, p. 42.

121. I am grateful to Werner Stark for this information.

122. Hamann, *Briefwechsel*, I, 234.

123. Hagen in Malter, *Kant in Rede und Gespräch*, p. 76. While the anecdote is probably spurious, it does illustrate the social climate of the time. A professor seemed to count for less than an officer. See also Mortzfeld according to Malter, *Kant in Rede und Gespräch*, p. 75

124. Ak 10, p. 34 (April 5, 1761). Borowski was at the house of the Knoblochs at Kant's recommendation.

125. Molyneux had proposed in 1690 in a letter to Locke that the question of how much in perception was native and how much was learned could be solved by depriving people from birth of all visual sensory experience and therefore also of the opportunity for visual perceptual learning. When normal sensory function was restored, they could be tested to see whether any perceptual functions were still intact. This problem was hotly debated during the eighteenth century. Such operations as the one Kant attended yielded only ambiguous evidence, insufficient to answer the question.

126. Schneider, *Hippel*, p. 124.

127. Johann Gottfried Herder, *Briefe, Gesamtausgabe 1763–1803*, ed. Karl-Heinz Hahn (Weimar: Herman Böhlaus Nachfolger, 1977–88), I, p. 95. Kant also recommended Herder to Schiffert as a teacher at the *Collegium Fridericianum*. But Herder apparently did not find teaching at this institution a pleasant experience.

128. Dobbek, *Herders Jugendjahre*, p. 94.

129. Dobbek, *Herders Jugendjahre*, p. 93. He apparently moved into his own house in 1761 (see also Hamann, *Briefwechsel*, II, p. 119).

130. It is not known when Kant moved from his quarters in Kypke's house to the *Magistergasse*. But it probably was sometime during the early sixties.

131. Stark, "Wo lehrte Kant," p. 90.

132. Borowski, *Leben*, pp. 73f., 69.

133. Borowski, *Leben*, p. 72.

134. I quote from Lewis White Beck's translation in "Kant's Life and Work," in Immanuel Kant, *Foundations of the Metaphysics of Morals* (New York: Macmillan, 1990), p. xxvi. At another place Herder said: "I have heard in Königsberg Kant's judgments on Leibniz, Newton, Wolff, Crusius, Baumgarten, Helvétius, Hume,

Rousseau . . ." See Johann Gottfried Herder, *Sämmtliche Werke,* 33 vols., ed. Bernhard Suphan (Berlin: Weidmannsche Buchhandlung, 1877–1913), XVIII, p. 325; VIII, p. 211.

135. Herder, *Werke,* ed. Suphan, XXI, pp. 12f.

136. Herder, *Werke,* ed. Suphan, XX, pp. 324f.

137. Herder, *Werke,* ed. Suphan, XX, p. 325.

138. Herder, *Werke,* ed. Suphan, XVII, p. 404.

139. Abegg, *Reisetagebuch,* p. 251.

140. Herder, Preface to *Kalligone,* in Herder, *Werke,* ed. Suphan, XXII, p. 12.

141. Some have been translated. See Kant, *Lectures on Metaphysics,* pp. 3–16; and Immanuel Kant, *Lectures on Ethics,* tr. Peter Heath, ed. Peter Heath and Jerry Schneewind (Cambridge: Cambridge University Press, 1997), pp. 1–36. There are also notes taken in Kant's lectures on physical geography, which will be published in vol. 26 of the Academy edition.

142. Ak 24.1 (Logik Herder), pp. 3–6, pp. 4f.

143. Ak 29.1,1 (Mathematik Herder and Physik Herder), pp. 49–66, 69–71.

144. See Ak 27.1 (Praktische Philosophie Herder), pp. 3–89; and Ak 28.1 (Metaphysik Herder), pp. 1–166.

145. Kant, *Lectures on Ethics,* p. 5 (Ak 27.1, p. 6). I will not follow the translation exactly.

146. Kant, *Lectures on Ethics,* p. 5 (Ak 27.1, p. 6).

147. Kant, *Lectures on Ethics,* p. 7 (Ak 27.1, p. 11).

148. Ak 27.1, p. 23 (not translated in Kant, *Lectures on Ethics*).

149. Ak 27.1, p. 8 (not translated in Kant, *Lectures on Ethics*).

150. Kant, *Lectures on Ethic,* p. 23 (Ak 27.1, p. 49).

151. Ak 27.1, p. 85 (not translated in Kant, *Lectures on Ethics*).

152. Ak 20, p. 44. To get some idea of the background of his former view one should consult Wieland's "Platonische Betrachtungen über den Menschen" (Platonic Meditations on Man) of 1755 (Wieland, *Sämmtliche Werke,* XIV, pp. 65–100). Wieland divides human beings into four classes, and only the class of speculative minds and those of genius have any real value. The other two classes are unfortunate because they are driven by their sensible nature alone. Curiously enough, Kant's mature view is in some ways a return to such "Platonic Meditations on Man."

153. Ak 20, p. 30. There is a popular anecdote to the effect that Kant forgot his regular walk because he was so engrossed in Rousseau. Since he did not live the highly regulated life of his later years in 1764, this anecdote is probably false.

154. Ak 20, p. 43.

155. See also Klaus Reich, "Rousseau und Kant," *Neue Hefte für Philosophie* 29 (1989), pp. 80–96. Also of interest in this connection are Ernst Cassirer, *Rousseau, Kant, Goethe,* tr. James Gutmann, Paul-Oskar Kristeller, and John Hermann Randall (Princeton: Princeton University Press, 1970), and Richard L. Velkley, *Freedom and the End of Reason: On the Moral Foundation of Kant's Critical Philosophy* (Chicago: University of Chicago Press, 1989).

156. Ak 20, pp. 58f. Rousseau also influenced Kant in other ways. See Reinhard Brandt, "Rousseau und Kants 'Ich denke,'" in *Autographen, Dokumente und Berichte,* ed. Brandt and Stark, pp. 1–18.

157. Ak 28.1, p. 5 (not translated in Kant, *Lectures on Metaphysics*).
158. Ak 28.1, p. 6 (not translated in Kant, *Lectures on Metaphysics*).
159. Ak 28.1, p. 14 (not translated in Kant, *Lectures on Metaphysics*).
160. Ak 28.1, p. 102.
161. Ak 28.1, pp. 103f.
162. Ak 28.1, p. 108.
163. This description of Kant's effects on a young mind is taken from R. G. Colling-wood, *An Autobiography* (Oxford: Oxford University Press, 1939), who tried to read the *Foundations of the Metaphysics of Morals* at the age of nine. It also describes, better than I ever could, my own first exposure to Kant – and, I am sure, that of many others.
164. Malter, *Kant in Rede und Gespräch*, p. 66; see also Dobbek, *Herders Jugendjahre*, p. 111. Hippel was similarly affected by Rousseau. See Emil Brenning, "Hippel and Rousseau," *Altpreussische Monatsschrift* 16 (1873), pp. 286–300.
165. Herder, "Versuch über das Sein," in Gottfried Martin, "Herder als Schüler Kants, Aufsätze und Kolleghefte aus Herders Studienzeit," *Kant-Studien* 41 (1936), pp. 294–306.
166. Martin, "Herder als Schüler Kants," p. 304.
167. See Herder, *Werke*, ed. Suphan, XXIX, p. 255.
168. Herder, *Werke*, ed. Suphan, IV, p. 175.
169. Schneider, *Hippel*, p. 124. See also Hamann, *Briefwechsel*, IV, p. 65, where Herder wrote: "I am not conscious of having done anything against Hippel either in word or deed. My course never limited his, even though he amply ridiculed all my first steps in Königsberg."
170. Böttiger, *Literarische Zustände und Zeitgenossen* (1838), p. 133 (Malter, *Kant in Rede und Gespräch*, p. 27).
171. Hamann, *Briefwechsel*, I, 234.
172. Rink, *Ansichten*, p. 81.
173. Hamann, *Briefwechsel*, II, p. 188.
174. This is Werner Stark's suggestion.
175. The first is an attempt to describe illness of the faculty of cognition. Kant talks about idiocy, foolishness, insanity, craziness, melancholy (depression), enthusiasm, hypochondria, etc., in a lighthearted fashion. His description of hypochondria is interesting from a biographical point of view (see Ak 2, pp. 259–271). The review (Ak 2, pp. 272f.) is simply a short announcement of a book on a meteor. But Kant could not refrain from poking fun at Weymann; having spoken of Weymann's meteoric rise before, he characterized the meteor as "bright and terrible, just like colossal human beings at times, but just as quickly absorbed in the wide chasm of nothingness" (p. 272).
176. Ak 2, p. 57. Actually he says "in the logical presentation" or "*in dem logischen Vortrage.*"
177. Ak 2, pp. 466f.
178. Compare Kant, *Theoretical Philosophy, 1755–1770*, pp. lvii f. However, the book was reviewed by Resewitz, not by Mendelssohn, as is claimed by Vorländer and in Kant, *Theoretical Philosophy, 1755–1770*, p. lx. In fact, Resewitz reviewed most of the writings from this period.

179. Kant, *Theoretical Philosophy, 1755–1770*, p. lxii.
180. Ak 2, p. 301.
181. His friend Funk had published in Danzig a book that had not passed censorship in Königsberg during the occupation, and this was not taken well. See Hamann, *Briefwechsel*, II, p. 52.
182. Kant, *Theoretical Philosophy, 1755–1770*, p. 274 (Ak 2, p. 300).
183. Kant, *Theoretical Philosophy, 1755–1770*, p. 273 (Ak 2, p. 299).
184. Kant, *Theoretical Philosophy, 1755–1770*, p. 272 (Ak 2, p. 299): Kant argues that "just as nothing follows from the primary formal principles of our judgments of truth except when primary material grounds are given, so also no particular definite obligations follow from these two rules except when indemonstrable material principles of practical knowledge are connected with them." He believes the converse to be true as well.
185. Paul Arthur Schilpp, in *Kant's Pre-critical Ethics*, 2nd ed. (Evanston: Northwestern University Press, 1960), pp. 22–40, is perhaps too eager to disprove all that Menzer had to say about the British influence on Kant. In any case, he does not pay enough attention to the skeptical note on which Kant closes.
186. Kant, *Theoretical Philosophy, 1755–1770*, p. 201 (Ak 2, p. 163).
187. Abegg, *Reisetagebuch*, p. 184.
188. See Ak 2, pp. 200–202.
189. Ak 2, p. 199.
190. Ak 2, p. 204.
191. Ak 2, p. 202.
192. Ak 2, p. 204.
193. Ak 2, p. 199.
194. See Manfred Kuehn, "Mendelssohn's Critique of Hume," *Hume Studies* 21 (1995), pp. 197–220.
195. Ak 2, p. 66.
196. Kant, *Theoretical Philosophy, 1755–1770*, p. lix. The editors think only of the former. That the preparation of his lectures interfered more than usual is still less likely.
197. Arnoldt according to Malter, *Kant in Rede und Gespräch*, p. 43.
198. Kant, *Theoretical Philosophy, 1755–1770*, p. 196 (Ak 2, p. 156).
199. Kant, *Theoretical Philosophy, 1755–1770*, p. 196 (Ak 2, p. 157).
200. Kant, *Theoretical Philosophy, 1755–1770*, p. 123 (Ak 2, p. 78).
201. Kant, *Theoretical Philosophy, 1755–1770*, p. 191 (Ak 2, p. 151).
202. Daniel Weymann, *Bedenklichkeiten über den einzig möglichen Beweisgrund des M. Kant vom Daseyn Gottes* (Königsberg, 1763), p. 30. Compare Stark, "Kants Kollegen."
203. Weymann, *Bedenklichkeiten*, pp. 12f. He later says: "It is not appropriate to doubt principles which God has implanted in us. Because of this the Idealists have become a laughing stock."
204. *Briefe die neueste Literatur betreffend* 18 (1764), pp. 69–102.
205. Scheffner, *Briefe an und von Johann Georg Scheffner*, I, p.447.
206. Immanuel Kant, *Observations on the Feeling of the Beautiful and Sublime*, tr. John T. Goldthwait (Berkeley: University of California Press, 1960), p. 13.
207. Kant, *Of the Beautiful and Sublime*, tr. Goldthwait, p. 74.

Chapter 4: A Palingenesis and Its Consequences (1764–1769)

1. Ak 7 (*Anthropologie*), p. 201.
2. Ak 7, p. 294.
3. Ak 7, 294f.; compare Ak 25.1 (Antropologie Collins), p. 150.
4. Ak 25.1 (Anthropologie Friedländer), p. 629; see also p. 353.
5. Ak 25.1 (Anthropologie Friedländer), p. 523.
6. Ak 25.1 (Anthropologie Friedländer), p. 617.
7. Henry Allison, *Kant's Theory of Freedom* (Cambridge: Cambridge University Press, 1990), p. 136. Allison does not endorse this view
8. See also Ak 9, p. 475.
9. Ak 25.2 (Anthropologie Pillau), p. 822.
10. Ak 25.2 (Anthropologie Mrongovius), p. 1385.
11. Borowski, *Leben*, p. 71.
12. See Lehmann, "Kants Lebenskrise," pp. 411–421. Lehmann argues that Kant underwent such a "life crisis" in 1764. He takes the "Observations on the Feeling of the Beautiful and Sublime" as an indication of it, but he sees it entirely in theoretical terms, wanting to understand his *"Denkkrisen als Lebenskrisen"* (p. 412). This is too one-sided.
13. Hamann, *Briefwechsel*, II, pp. 82, 119. This fallow period lasted until the end of his life. Hamann, who was very interested in Kypke's library and manuscripts during 1779–80, found nothing of significance in his literary remains.
14. Immanuel Kant, *Religion and Rational Theology*, tr. and ed. Allan W. Wood and George DiGiovanni (Cambridge: Cambridge University Press, 1996), pp. 277f. (Ak 7, pp. 55f.).
15. Kant, *Religion and Rational Theology*, p. 280 (Ak 7, p. 59). Compare p. 367, this volume.
16. Kant, *Religion and Rational Theology*, p. 280 (Ak 7, p. 58).
17. Ak 25.2 (Menschenkunde), p. 1174.
18. It is all-too-often forgotten that for the ancient philosophers, philosophy was more a "way of life," akin to "religion," than a theoretical pursuit in our sense of the term. See Pierre Hadot, *Philosophy as a Way of Life*, tr. A. I. Davidson (London: Blackwell, 1995); see also Martha C. Nussbaum, *The Therapy of Desire: Theory and Practice in Hellenistic Ethics* (Princeton: Princeton University Press, 1994), especially pp. 383f.
19. Plato, *Republic*, 604E.
20. Ak 7, p. 104, emphasis supplied.
21. In his draft for the *Dispute of the Faculties*, he said: "I formulated rules for myself early on," attributing his long life to these rules (Ak 23, p. 463).
22. See "Insanity," in John W. Yolton et al. (eds.), *The Blackwell Companion to the Enlightenment* (Cambridge, Mass: Blackwell Publishers, 1991). See also Böhme and Böhme, *Das Andere der Vernunft*, pp. 389f. True to form, the Böhmes claim that hypochondria "is a product of the Enlightenment." In particular, "the denial of affects, the discipline of the body, and the thorough intellectualization of the entire world (*Dasein*) led to a deep malfunctioning of the immediate bodily existence" (p. 419). Kant's hypochondria is the result of his rationalism. This is false.

To say that the concept of "hypochondria" was a creation of the Enlightenment is historical nonsense. Nor did Kant have to wait for the publication of J. U. Bilguer's *Nachrichten an das Publikum in Absicht der Hypochondrie* of 1767. Hypochondria was all around him, in literature (in the novels of Laurence Sterne and Tobias Smollett, and in Samuel Butler's *Hudibras*, for instance) and in daily life. The claim that attempts to keep one's emotion in check lead to hypochondria is psychological nonsense. Indeed, it seems to be well understood – at least in some psychological circles – that keeping distressing emotions in check is a key to emotional well-being, and that expressing emotions (such as anger) too freely is what leads to distress – not that the Stoics would have disagreed. Finally, it is a mistake to treat Kant's hypochondria as a uniform phenomenon. His early complaints, having to do with his chest and palpitations, were different from the complaints of his later years, which were more "hepatick," as we shall see.

23. Susan Baur, *Hypochondria: Woeful Imaginings* (Berkeley: University of California Press, 1988), p. 22. See also Shell, *The Embodiment of Reason*, pp. 266–305 (Chapter 10, "Kant's Hypochondria: A Phenomenology of Spirit," which contains a short history of hypochondria). Shell's conclusions go too far, however.

24. Robert Burton, *The Anatomy of Melancholy*, ed. Floyd Dell and Paul Jordan-Smith (New York: Tudor Publishing Company, 1927), p. 154.

25. Baur, *Hypochondria*, p. 27.

26. Ak 2, p. 266.

27. Ibid.

28. Ak 10, p. 231, see also p. 344; and Ak 23, p. 463; also of interest are Borowski, *Leben*, p. 73; Ernst König, "Arzt und ärztliches in Kant," *Jahrbuch der Albertus Universität zu Königsberg* 5 (1954), pp. 113–154.

29. Lehmann, "Kant's Lebenskrise," p. 418.

30. Josef Heller, *Kants Persönlichkeit und Leben. Versuch einer Charakteristik* (Berlin: Pan Verlag, 1924), p. 65.

31. Lehmann, "Kant's Lebenskrise," p. 420.

32. It had already been reviewed in the March 22 issue of the *Königsbergische Gelehrten und Politischen Zeitungen*. For more information, see Pia Reimen, "Struktur und Figurenkonstellation in Theodor Gottlieb von Hippels Komödie der Mann nach der Uhr," in Joseph Kohnen (ed.), *Königsberg. Beiträge zu einem besonderen Kapitel der deutschen Geistesgeschichte* (Frankfurt [Main]: Peter Lang 1994), pp. 199–263. Reimen believes that the model is Kant, but she fails to see that Jachmann's description of Kant, on which she relies, is the Kant of the 1780s and 1790s, not the young Kant (see pp. 224f.). Jachmann claimed that Green was the model. Green was also the model for a merchant in Johann Timotheus Hermes's novel *Sophien's Reise von Memel nach Sachsen*. Hermes and Hippel studied together in Königsberg in 1757.

33. Jachmann, *Kant*, p. 154.

34. See Gause, *Die Geschichte der Stadt Königsberg*, II, p. 192; see also Bogislav von Archenholz, *Bürger und Patrizier. Ein Buch von Städten des Deutschen Ostens* (Darmstadt: Ullstein Verlag, 1970), pp. 311f.

35. Archenholz, *Bürger und Patrizier*, p. 311.

36. Karl Hagen, ""Gedächtnisrede auf William Motherby," *Neue Preußische Provincial-Blätter* 3 (1847), pp. 131f.

37. Karl Hagen, "Kantiana," *Neue Preußische Provincial-Blätter* 6 (1848), pp. 8–12, p. 9. He also pointed out that his love of order and punctuality had deteriorated into *"Sonderbarkeit,"* and that the massive English watch that he wore still served its present owner, that is, it still worked forty years later. See also F. Reusch, "Historische Erinnerungen," *Neue preußische Provincial-Blätter* 5 (1848), p. 45.

38. Scheffner, *Briefe von und an Scheffner,* I, p.255 (August 16). The German is somewhat ambiguous. Green need not have written the letters. Perhaps he just transmitted some "letters" (perhaps even a published book of letters) to Kant. Werner Stark suggested as much to me (and this would explain why they cannot be found in Kant's correspondence).

39. Vorländer, *Immanuel Kant,* I, p. 122 (Jachmann, *Kant,* p. 161).

40. This was a significant event, which surprised the British, and may be seen as the first sign of the coming revolution. The delegates to the so-called Stamp Act Congress expressed the colonists' opposition to the Stamp Act in a Declaration of Rights and Grievances, an address to the king, and in petitions to both houses of the British Parliament. The petitions were rejected. These developments inspired Samuel Adams to found a section of the Sons of Liberty.

41. Theodor Gottlieb von Hippel, *Der Mann nach der Uhr oder der ordentliche Mann. Lustspiel in einem Aufzuge,* ed. Erich Jenisch (Halle, 1928), pp. 36f. (scene 2).

42. Hippel, *Der Mann nach der Uhr,* pp. 59f. (scene 11).

43. Kraus in Reicke, *Kantiana,* p. 60 (Malter, *Kant in Rede und Gespräch,* p. 73). Compare Jachmann, *Kant,* p. 161.

44. Jachmann, *Kant,* p. 185.

45. Reicke, *Kantiana,* p. 35: "But he most likely never played an instrument." Furthermore, though Kant was probably never much of a dancer, he was at many a ball. But later, he did not like any of these diversions.

46. Compare Vorländer, *Immanuel Kant,* II, p. 27.

47. Two of her other sisters also played a role in Kant's life, namely Albertine, who married Hartknoch, Kant's later publisher, and Sophie, who became one of the best friends of Hamann.

48. Hamann, *Briefwechsel,* II, p. 416. This also throws interesting light on his relation to Knutzen.

49. Ak 25.2 (Menschenkunde), p. 966.

50. Ak 25.2 (Menschenkunde), p. 967.

51. Borowski, *Leben,* p. 83 (Kant did not see this).

52. Heilsberg said that "in his final years" he put all his money into this firm (Reicke, *Kantiana,* p. 49).

53. Ingrid Mittenzwei, *Preussen nach dem Siebenjährigen Krieg: Auseinandersetzungen zwischen Bürgertum und Staat um die Wirtschaftspolitik* (Berlin: Akademie Verlag, 1979), p. 11.

54. Beck, "Moravians in Königsberg," pp. 347f.

55. Hamann, *Briefwechsel,* II, p. 285. See also Ak 10, p. 48, pp. 13, 25.

56. Ak 13, p. 24. Compare Borowski, *Leben,* p. 43.

57. Indeed, in a postscript to the letter confirming Lindner's appointment, the Berlin authorities basically instructed the university officials to see to it that Kant was soon given a position (a later letter reconfirms this; see Ak 13, p. 25).

58. The salary also included "*Emolumente*" or material goods, such as firewood. This was a usual part of the salary in eighteenth-century Prussia (and elsewhere). Given the inflationary tendencies of the period, this was significant. But whether or not Kant received these goods is not known.

59. Kant's own phrase (Ak 10, p. 49). During the latter part of the sixties he also administrated a collection of stones and fossils, which had been collected by Saturgus. See Vorländer, *Immanuel Kant,* I, p. 180.

60. See also Werner Stark, "Wo lehrte Kant?," p. 91. Hamann reported to Scheffner, who was looking for a place to live, that one of his friends had an apartment that cost him 40 Thalers a year, but was fairly small. The 62 Thalers would have allowed Kant to rent a fairly decent apartment. Yet the sum did not amount to much. A student was expected at that time to live on 200 Thalers.

61. All the works of the sixties, and some of the later ones.

62. Hamann, *Briefwechsel,* II, p. 245: "Kant insisted very much to work immediately on your return." What he could have done is not clear. But it seemed to involve petitioning the minister von Braxein. Kant also seems to have had a hand in the appointment of Lindner's successor, Kreutzfeld. See Euler, "Kant's Amtstätigkeit," p. 83.

63. In a letter to Kant of April 7, 1774, Hamann referred to "my friend Dr. Lindner." This would have been odd had he considered him at this point Kant's friend as well.

64. Compare Kant, Ak 24.1 (Logik Blomberg), p. 36: "Pyrrho was a man of great insights. He had the motto: *non liquet,* which he constantly held up to the prudent sophists to dampen their pride. He was the founder of the skeptics, who also called themselves Zetetici. But this sect soon exaggerated skepticism so much that they finally doubted everything – even mathematical propositions." Hamann compared Kant to Socrates as early as 1759, and he used Hume and (what he took to be) Humean arguments in order to persuade Kant that it was "reasonable" to reject Enlightenment ideals in favor of a fundamentalist religious faith. See pp. 118–122, this volume.

65. Ak 2, p. 307. See also Ak 20, p. 175: "The doubt which I adopt is not dogmatic but a doubt of waiting (*Aufschub*). *Zetetici* (zeten) seeker. I will strengthen the reasons on both sides. It is peculiar that one is afraid of this. Speculation is not a matter of necessity. The cognitions of the latter in regard to ultimate reasons are certain. The method of doubting is useful because it makes the soul act not from speculation but from healthy understanding (common sense). I seek the honor of Fabius Cunctator."

66. See, for instance, Sextus Empiricus, *Selections from the Major Writings on Scepticism, Man and God,* ed. Philip P. Hallie, tr. Sanford G. Etheridge (Indianapolis: Hackett, 1985), p. 32: "Now the sceptic discipline is called the 'zetetic' (searching) . . ."

67. Ak 2, p. 308.

68. Ak 2, pp. 309f.

69. See Martin L. Davies, *Identity or History? Marcus Herz and the End of the Enlightenment* (Detroit: Wayne State University Press, 1995), p. 7. See also Steffen Dietzsch, "Kant, die Juden und das akademische Bürgerrecht in Königsberg," in *Königs-*

berg. Beiträge zu einem besonderen Kapitel der deutschen Geistesgeschichte, ed. Kohnen, pp. 111–126.

70. Dietzsch, "Kant, die Juden und das akademische Bügerrecht," pp. 123f.

71. But see Stark, "Wo lehrte Kant?", p. 94. Stark points out that Herz attended Kant's lectures *"nachweislich"* only in the summer of 1768. But nothing speaks against him having attended the lectures in the winter semester of 1766–7.

72. See Stark, "Wo lehrte Kant?", p. 94. Johann Friedrich Reichardt made this claim.

73. See Davies, *Marcus Herz,* p. 228. Davies believes that these pains were of a somewhat psychosomatic nature, having to do with the lack of social acceptance and the strains of acculturation (p. 29). But Kant and Kraus had similar problems without such strains.

74. Ak 10, p. 99. I follow the translation of Davies, *Marcus Herz,* p. 19.

75. Davies, *Marcus Herz,* p. 227.

76. More about that in the next chapter. Another student of Kant's during this period was Karl Gottlieb Fischer (1745–1801), who studied with Kant around 1763. He attended Kant's lectures in physical geography and theoretical physics. Later, in 1774, he went to Kant's lectures again with his charge Karl Ludwig Alexander zu Dohna. See Stark, "Kant als akademischer Lehrer," pp. 51–70.

77. Ak 10, p. 83.

78. Mortzfeld according to Malter, *Kant in Rede und Gespräch,* p. 75.

79. Hippel, *Sämtliche Werke* XIII, pp. 66f.

80. von Dülmen, *The Society of the Enlightenment,* pp. 87f.

81. Henriette Herz, in Rolf Strube (ed.), *Sie saßen und tranken am Teetisch. Anfänge und Blütezeit der Berliner Salons, 1789–1871* (München: Pieper Verlag, 1991), p. 46.

82. Herz, in *Berliner Salons, 1789–1871,* p. 47.

83. von Dülmen, *The Society of the Enlightenment,* p. 93. His entire discussion of "literary friendship circles" (pp. 93–104) is relevant here.

84. Malter, *Kant in Rede und Gespräch,* p. 92.

85. See Hamann, *Briefwechsel,* II, p. 405. To Herder on December 27, 1767: "Yesterday I was visited by the master of the mint Goeschen and Magister Kant." In June of the same year, Hippel named Goeschen as "the only person" with whom he has social relations (see Schneider, *Hippel,* p. 162).

86. The offices of Jacobi's business were located at *Magistergasse* 29, the very street Kant lived on during the sixties. See Archenholz, *Bürger und Patrizier,* p. 302, and Stark, "Wo lehrte Kant?", p. 90.

87. Hamann, *Briefwechsel,* V, p. 315 (Malter, *Kant in Rede und Gespräch,* p. 53). Hamann did not know Jacobi himself when the arrangement was made.

88. Jachmann, *Kant,* p. 157.

89. Ak 10, p. 39.

90. Archenholz, *Bürger und Patrizier,* pp. 299–302.

91. Ak 10, p. 58.

92. Schneider, *Hippel,* p. 173. For the reviews of sixteen French, two Italian, two Danish, and fifteen German performances, see Schneider, *Hippel,* pp. 173f. and Appendix 9–27, which reprints them.

93. See Hippel, *Werke,* XIII, pp. 59, 60, 64–67.

94. Hippel *Werke,* XIII, p. 103.

95. Hippel *Werke*, XIII, p. 120.

96. Hippel, *Werke*, XIII, p. 121; see also Vorländer, *Kants Leben*, pp. 136f.

97. Later they had contact again. Hamann, who knew Goeschen well and who was invited often during the early seventies did not keep up the relation either. In November 1786 he reported that "his former connection with this house had ceased for some years," but that he had received some books (Hamann, *Briefwechsel*, VII, p. 56). In December of the same year he spoke of a dinner "at which were present Hippel, Kant, Kriminalräte Lilienthal and Jenisch, and Goeschen, whom I have not seen for years and where I used to eat every Thursday" (Hamann, *Briefwechsel*, VII, p. 75; see also p. 216, where he mentions that after "many years" he was again invited by the Goeschens). The fact that Kant did not go to the house of the Goeschens did not keep him from socializing with his former friend at other occasions – at least after Jacobi was dead.

98. Ak 20, p. 99.

99. Jachmann, *Kant*, p. 166.

100. Schneider, *Hippel*, p. 169.

101. Hippel, *Sämtliche Werke*, XIII, p. 85 (Schneider, *Hippel*, p. 169).

102. Hippel, *Sämtliche Werke*, XIII, p. 84 (Schneider, *Hippel*, p. 167).

103. Hippel, *Sämtliche Werke*, XIII, p. 129.

104. Hippel, *Sämtliche Werke*, XIII, p. 33.

105. Ak 7, p. 308.

106. The poem is very long. It gives various reasons for not marrying: the Pope is not married, the most famous philosophers did not marry, the world is old, women are not as they used to be, marriage is expensive, etc., etc. The entire poem is somewhat tedious, at least by today's standards. The last two stanzas read: "Komm ich nach schon geschloßnem Bunde / zu spät mit meinen Gründen an; / so führ ich einen Spruch im Munde, / Der euch die Zeit vergülden kann / Da habt ihr ihn so kurz als möglich: Gefallet Gott und seyd vergnügt, / lebt glücklich, fröhlich, redlich, klüglich / liebt, küsset, hoffet, kriegt und wiegt.

Wird nichts von allem diesen wanken, / und hält ein jedes sein Gewicht; / so schraub ich meinen Satz in Schranken, / denn widerrufen schickt sich nicht. / Wenn Regeln noch so gut gedeyen, / kommt doch was auszunehmen dar; / Die Regel bleibt: Man muß nicht freyen, / doch excipe, solch ein würdig Paar!!" See Hagen, "Kantiana," pp. 8–12. Hagen claims that a friend of Kant kept the poem in his library because he respected Kant so much.

107. Scheffner, *Mein Leben*, pp. 123, 125.

108. Scheffner, *Mein Leben*, p. 205; in April of 1771 Scheffner was permanently transferred to Königsberg (Scheffner, *Mein Leben*, p. 144).

109. Scheffner, *Briefe*, I, p. 272; compare also Malter, *Kant in Rede und Gespräch*, p. 92.

110. See Ak 13, pp. 20f. One may add to the arguments adduced there, the fact that the Russian occupation ended only in the summer of 1762 (and that Prussia and Russia had been making plans to wage war against Denmark earlier that year).

111. The Swedish scientist and theologian, known for his visions of spirits or souls of the dead, had become rather famous at this time. His writings inspired his followers to establish the Church of the New Jerusalem after his death.

112. Ak 10, p. 71 (compare Kant, *Theoretical Philosophy, 1755–1770*, p. lxvii).

113. Herder, *Werke,* ed. Suphan XXIV, pp. 24f. (Malter, *Kant in Rede und Gespräch,* p. 67).

114. Ak 10, p. 69.

115. Immanuel Kant, *Dreams of a Spirit-Seer Illustrated by Dreams of Metaphysics,* tr. E. F. Goerwitz (New York: MacMillan, 1900; reprint Glasgow: Thoemmes, 1992), pp. 83f. I quote from this edition, but I also give the page numbers in Kant, *Theoretical Philosophy, 1755–1770* (pp. 335f.; Ak 2, p. 348).

116. Kant, *Theoretical Philosophy, 1755–1770,* p. 336 (Ak 2, p. 348).

117. Ak 2, p. 271. Kant wrote this essay because the private tutor of the young man asked him to; the tutor thought it would help calm the mother. Borowski, *Leben,* p. 52 (Kant saw this and made no comment).

118. Kant, *Theoretical Philosophy, 1755–1770,* p. 306 (Ak 2, p. 319); *Dreams,* p. 39.

119. Kant, *Theoretical Philosophy, 1755–1770,* p. 355 (Ak 2, p. 369); *Dreams,* p. 115.

120. Kant, *Theoretical Philosophy, 1755–1770,* p. 359 (Ak 2, p. 373); *Dreams,* p. 121.

121. Kant, *Theoretical Philosophy, 1755–1770,* p. 358 (Ak 2, p. 372); *Dreams,* p. 120.

122. Kant, *Theoretical Philosophy, 1755–1770,* p. 355 (Ak 2, p. 369); *Dreams,* p. 115.

123. Kant, *Theoretical Philosophy, 1755–1770,* p. 339 (Ak 2, p. 352); *Dreams,* p. 90.

124. Kant, *Theoretical Philosophy, 1755–1770,* p. 315 (Ak 2, p. 328); *Dreams,* p. 53.

125. Kant, *Of the Beautiful and Sublime,* tr. Goldthwait, p. 8.

126. Ak 2, p. 311.

127. Erich Adickes, *Kant-Studien* (Kiel and Leipzig, 1895), p. 52. Compare also his long paper on "Die bewegenden Kräfte in Kant's philosophischer Entwicklung und die beiden Pole seines Systems," *Kant-Studien* 1 (1897), pp. 9–59, 161–196, 352–415, especially pp. 11f.

128. Adickes, *Kant-Studien,* p. 67.

129. Adickes, *Kant-Studien,* p. 70. However, in the early sixties, Kant's view of analysis is still "entirely rationalistic" (p. 81), and the basic starting point of his philosophy has not changed: "The rationalist background of Kant's epistemology is thus in 1763 precisely the same as that in 1755. What is given, the starting point, are concepts that are potentially contained in the mind. They only require the influxus physicus . . . and propensity becomes reality" (p. 82).

130. Adickes, *Kant-Studien,* p. 99.

131. Adickes, "Die bewegenden Kräfte," p. 18.

132. While "*Umkippungen*" is Kant's own term (Ak 10, p 55), it does not necessarily indicate radical change. Kant also said that in each of these changes, he tried to show how his errors and insights depended on the method he followed.

133. See, for instance, Herman-J. de Vleeschauwer's *The Development of Kantian Thought: The History of a Doctrine,* tr. A. R. C. Duncan (London: Thomas Nelson & Sons, 1962), p. 37. Vleeschauwer places more emphasis on Kant's Newtonianism, but he also argues that Kant never really became an empiricist. See also Lewis White Beck, "The Development of Kant's Philosophy before 1769," in *Early German Philosophy: Kant and His Predecessors* (Cambridge, Mass.: The Belknap Press of Harvard University Press, 1969), pp. 438–456. Beck argues that Kant "was never an orthodox Wolffian" (p. 439), that he was "a Newtonian not only in his cosmology but also in the *theory* of science" (p. 441), and places more emphasis on Crusius than does Adickes (pp. 451f.). See also his "A Prussian Hume

and a Scottish Kant," in Lewis White Beck, *Essays on Kant and Hume* (New Haven/London: Yale University Press, 1978), pp. 113f., where he discusses Kant's development with special emphasis on the problem of causality and distinguishes between a "pre-Humean" phase around 1755/6 and a "quasi-Humean" phase from 1762/3 to 1770. On the other hand, Karl Ameriks, relying mainly on Kant's theory of mind, argues, for instance, that there was a move from a more empiricist position to a more rationalist one in Kant. Thus he observes that "in his first publications Kant can be described as (relatively speaking) an empiricist," and that in the second period (around 1762) his philosophy is "much more oriented towards non-empirical and rationalistic concerns." He then goes on to differentiate a "third or sceptical period," which, he thinks, is only natural "in view of some obvious difficulties with the preceding rationalistic developments," and "a fourth or critical period in Kant's philosophy after approximately 1768." Karl Ameriks, *Kant's Theory of Mind: An Analysis of the Paralogisms of Pure Reason* (Oxford/New York: Clarendon Press, 1982), pp. 14f. In a certain sense, Ameriks and other Kant scholars are right, of course. There were rationalist, empiricist, and even skeptical concerns in Kant. In different works, different concerns were predominant.

134. Vleeschauwer, *Development*, p. 1.
135. Louis E. Loeb (among others) has argued convincingly that these labels are seriously distorting even our picture of the broad outlines of early modern philosophy. See his *From Descartes to Hume: Continental Metaphysics and the Development of Modern Philosophy* (Ithaca: Cornell University Press, 1981). See also John Cottingham, *The Rationalist*, vol. 4 of *A History of Western Philosophy* (Oxford: Oxford University Press, 1988), pp. 1–10. Cottingham quite correctly points out that rationalism is not a seamless web, but rather a cluster of overlapping views.
136. Beck, *Early German Philosophy*, p. 267.
137. This is not to say, of course, that his "critical philosophy" contains no "precritical elements" or that Kant's early life and thought are irrelevant to a discussion of the mature position. It only means that we must be careful not to conceive the "precritical Kant" in accordance with our idea of the "critical Kant."
138. Ak 10, p. 74 (not in Kant, *Correspondence*, tr. Zweig).
139. George S. Pappas, "Some Forms of Epistemological Scepticism," in George S. Pappas and Marshall Swain (eds.), *Essays in Knowledge and Justification* (Ithaca: Cornell University Press 1978), pp. 309f.
140. We know that Kant believed he could trace back the failure of his predecessors, his contemporaries, and even of himself to the method they had followed so far, and that he hoped to achieve more by a better method.
141. Ak 10, p. 97.
142. Immanuel Kant, *Critique of Pure Reason*, tr. Norman Kemp Smith (New York: St Martin's Press, 1965), pp. Aix f. (Subsequent references to this work will be given in the body of the text and consist of an "A" and/or "B" followed by page number.)
143. Kant adds in a footnote that "indifference, doubt and, in the final issue, severe criticism, are themselves proofs of a profound habit of thought," at least until critical philosophy has done its work.

144. Kant, Ak 16, p. 457 [Refl. 2660]; see also *Logik Blomberg* (1771), Ak 24.1, pp. 36, 83, 212f., 105, 159. Kant claims that the "tendency to decide is the most certain way to error" and ascribes "dogmatic pride" to many philosophers. Compare also Giorgio Tonelli, "Kant und die antiken Skeptiker," in *Studien zu Kants philosophischer Entwicklung,* ed. Dieter Henrich and Giorgio Tonelli (Hildesheim: Olms, 1967). This is a useful *Materialübersicht.* See also Enno Rudolph, *Skepsis bei Kant. Ein Beitrag zur Interpretation der Kritik der reinen Vernunft* (München: Eugen Fink Verlag, 1978) and Ludwig Weber, *Das Distinktionsverfahren im mittelalterlichen Denken und Kants skeptische Methode* (Meisenheim am Glan: Verlag Anton Hain, 1976).

145. Ak 24.1 (Logik Herder), p. 4.

146. Ak 27.1 (Praktische Philosophie Herder), p 23.

147. Ak 27.1 (Praktische Philosophie Herder), p. 79.

148. Kant, *Theoretical Philosophy, 1755–1770,* p. 316 (Ak 2, p. 329).

149. Kant, *Correspondence,* tr. Zweig, p. 55.

150. Beck, "A Prussian Hume and a Scottish Kant," pp. 65f. Ameriks also emphasizes the skeptical dimension in Kant's writings of this period.

151. Dieter Henrich, "The Concept of Moral Insight," tr. Manfred Kuehn, in D. Henrich, *The Unity of Reason: Essays on Kant's Philosophy,* ed. R. Velkley (Cambridge: Harvard University Press, 1994), pp. 55–88.

152. *Bibliothek der schönen Wissenschaften und der freyen Künste,* II, 2 (1759). I quote from the 2nd. ed. of 1762, pp. 290f.

153. *Allgemeine Theorie des Denkens und Empfindens* was the title of a book by Johann August Eberhard (Berlin, 1776). The book was a response to a question by the Prussian Academy, asking for a more precise theory of thinking and sensation. Eberhard reported that the question specifically demanded that "(i) one precisely develop the original conditions of this twofold power of the soul as well as its general laws; (ii) thoroughly investigate how these two powers of the soul are dependent on each other, and how they influence each other; and (iii) indicate the principles according to which we can judge how far the intellectual ability (genius) and the moral character of man depends upon the degree of the force and liveliness as well as on the increase of those two mental faculties . . ." (pp. 14f.).

154. Moses Mendelssohn, *Gesammelte Schriften,* ed. F. Bamberger et al. (Stuttgart/ Bad Canstatt, 1931–), II, p. 183.

155. Mendelssohn, *Schriften,* II, p. 184.

156. I borrow this term from Lewis White Beck, *Kant Selections* (New York/London: Scribner Macmillan Publishing Co., 1988), p. 28. But whereas he uses it to refer to the continuity of science and metaphysics, I use it to designate his related view on the relation of sensibility and reason.

157. Immanuel Kant, *Enquiry into the Distinctness of the Fundamental Principles of Natural Theology and Morals,* in *Critique of Practical Reason and Other Writings on Moral Philosophy,* tr. Lewis White Beck (Chicago: University of Chicago Press, 1949), p. 285 (Ak 2, p. 300).

158. Kant, *Of the Beautiful and Sublime,* tr. Goldthwait, p. 60 (Ak 2, p. 217).

159. Kant, *Of the Beautiful and Sublime,* tr. Goldthwait, p. 59. See also p. 74, where he finds that "good-hearted impulses" cannot be estimated as "a particular merit of

the person." Though general rules may be more dangerous, they are also more meritorious when they are correct.

160. Kant, *Theoretical Philosophy 1755–1770*, p. 273 (Ak 2, p. 299).
161. Kant, *Theoretical Philosophy 1755–1770*, p. 372 (Ak 2, p. 383).

Chapter 5: Silent Years (1770–1780)

1. Ak 10, p. 91.
2. See Paul Schwartz, *Die Gelehrtenschule Preußens unter dem Oberschulkollegium (1787–1806) und das Abiturientenexamen. Monumenta Germaniae Paedagogica,* Nr. 50 (1912), pp. 586f. See also Euler and Stiening, "'. . . und nie der Pluralität widersprach'?," p. 64.
3. However, the salary of sublibrarian, amounting to 60 Thalers, must be added to this.
4. Davies, *Identity or History*, p. 20. Davies refers to Jolowicz, *Geschichte der Juden in Königsberg*, p. 92, and Hans Jürgen Krüger, *Die Judenschaft in Königsberg in Preußen 1700–1802* (Marburg, 1966).
5. Ak 12, p. 208. See also Kant, *Correspondence,* tr. Zweig, p. 239.
6. Kant, *Theoretical Philosophy, 1755–1770*, p. 384 (Ak 2, p. 392). I give the reference in this edition, but for the most part I follow Beck's translation in Kant, *Latin Writings.*
7. Kant, *Theoretical Philosophy, 1755–1770*, p. 384 (Ak 2, p. 393).
8. Kant, *Theoretical Philosophy, 1755–1770*, p. 384 (Ak 2, p. 392)
9. Kant, *Theoretical Philosophy, 1755–1770*, p. 387 (Ak 2, p. 395).
10. Kant, *Theoretical Philosophy, 1755–1770*, p. 386 (Ak 2, p. 394).
11. This bit of dogmatism was abandoned by Kant later, but that's a different part of the story.
12. Kant, *Theoretical Philosophy, 1755–1770*, p. 385 (Ak 2, p. 393).
13. Kant, *Theoretical Philosophy, 1755–1770*, p. 408 (Ak 2, p. 412).
14. Kant, *Theoretical Philosophy, 1755–1770*, pp. 415f. (Ak 2, p. 419).
15. Ibid.
16. Kant, *Theoretical Philosophy, 1755–1770*, p. 388 (Ak 2, p. 396).
17. I use A 576/B604 to flesh out this notion.
18. Kant, *Theoretical Philosophy, 1755–1770*, p. 388 (Ak 2, p. 396).
19. Kant seems to have read Plato himself. But, as Michael Gill has pointed out to me, much of this can also be found in the works of the so-called Cambridge Platonists. Cudworth is a good example of this. Kant probably knew them as well. See Ralph Cudworth, *A Treatise Concerning Eternal and Immutable Morality, with A Treatise of Freewill*, ed. Sarah Hutton (Cambridge: Cambridge University Press, 1996)
20. Kant, *Theoretical Philosophy, 1755–1770*, p. 388 (Ak 2, p. 396).
21. Kant, *Theoretical Philosophy, 1755–1770*, p. 415 (Ak 2, p. 419).
22. Kant, *Theoretical Philosophy, 1755–1770*, p. 406 (Ak 2, p. 411).
23. Reinhard Brandt, "Materialien zur Entstehung der *Kritik der reinen Vernunft* (John Locke und Johann Schultz)," in *Beiträge zur Kritik der reinen Vernunft, 1781–1981,* ed. Ingeborg Heidemann and Wolfgang Ritzel (Berlin: de Gruyter, 1981), pp. 37–

68, p. 66. There is an English translation of this review in Johann Schultz, *Exposition of Kant's Critique of Pure Reason*, tr. James C. Morrison (Ottawa: University of Ottawa Press, 1995).

24. Ak 10, p. 133.
25. Ak 10, p. 134; Lambert made essentially the same objection, Kant thought. He also dismissed another objection as a misunderstanding.
26. Kant, *Correspondence*, tr. Zweig, p. 74 (Ak 10, p. 133).
27. Kant, *Correspondence*, tr. Zweig, pp. 67f. (Ak 10, pp. 113f.).
28. Kant, *Latin Writings*, ed. Beck, p. 134 (Ak 2, p. 399).
29. Kant, *Correspondence*, tr. Zweig, p. 69 (Ak 10, p. 115).
30. Kant, *Correspondence*, tr. Zweig, pp. 69f. (Ak 10, pp. 115f.).
31. Kant, *Correspondence*, tr. Zweig, p. 66 (Ak 10, pp. 110).
32. Lambert did not just claim this but tried to prove it in the remainder of the letter. An analysis of the arguments would lead too far afield, but they impressed Kant and made him think harder on the problems he had tackled in the dissertation.
33. Ak 10, p. 132.
34. Lambert reviewed it in the *Allgemeine deutsche Bibliothek* 20 (1773), p. 227, and characterized it as a further elaboration of comments made at the thesis defense that did not go much beyond Kant.
35. Markus Herz, *Betrachtungen aus der spekulativen Weltweisheit*, ed. Elfried Conrad, Heinrich P. Delfosse, and Birgit Nehren (Hamburg: Meiner Verlag, 1990), p. 64.
36. Herz, *Betrachtungen*, p. 64.
37. Herz, *Betrachtungen*, pp. 64f. He continues: "No doubt, you will object to the view I maintain here by citing a case in which the cause precedes the effect in the order of nature, but in which, in accordance with existence, both are simultaneous, such as fire and light. Here the former contains the cause of the latter, but can still never exist without the latter. Yet, however undeniably this can be proved by pure reason, you will find by a more exact observation of the way in which we represent it to us that whenever we think of fire and light, we do not think of them as cause and effect but as determinations which constantly co-exist in a common subject. As soon as we call one of these the cause of the other, we implicitly presuppose that there was some moment at which the one existed without the other. It is entirely impossible for us to think an efficient cause without representing it to ourselves as being concerned – as it were – with the production of the effect. This is what forces us to assign to the cause a moment at which it still seemed to be at work."
38. The editor of Hamann's *Complete Works* believed that it was Hamann's work and included it as one of his original works. See Johann Georg Hamann, *Sämtliche Werke*, ed. Josef Nadler (Wien, 1949–1953), IV, pp. 364–370.
39. See Rudolf Unger, *Hamann und die Aufklärung. Studien zur Vorgeschichte des romantischen Geistes im 18. Jahrhundert*, 2nd ed. (Halle, 1925), II, p. 932. See also Charles W. Swain, "Hume and the Philosophy of David Hume," *Journal of the History of Philosophy* 5 (1967), pp. 343–351.
40. David Hume, *A Treatise of Human Nature*, 2nd ed., ed. L. A. Selby Bigge (Oxford: The Clarendon Press, 1985).
41. Hume, *Treatise*, p. 272. See also O. Bayer, "Hamann's Metakritik im ersten Entwurf," *Kant-Studien* 81 (1990), pp. 435–453. Bayer notes the change to "in our

land," but not the missing last paragraph. So anyone who did not know Hume's *Treatise* very well – and there were not many in eighteenth-century Germany who did – would certainly have been justified in assuming that Hamann was the author. It is perhaps not quite so easily to be excused that several of the editors of Hamann's work have made this mistake. The most egregious mistake is probably the one by Stefan Majetschak, whose *Vom Magus im Norden und der Verwegenheit des Geistes. Ein Hamann Brevier* (Munich: Deutscher Taschenbuch Verlag, 1988) contains the first part of the translation as Hamann's original text long after it should have been known to anyone that it was not Hamann's own work.

42. Hume, *Treatise*, p. 266. If we define an "antinomy" as a contradiction between the basic principles of the human mind, then this passage does contain an antinomy. For more on this, see Manfred Kuehn, "Kant's Conception of Hume's Problem," *Journal of the History of Philosophy* 21 (1983), pp. 175–193, and "Hume's Antinomies," *Hume Studies* 9 (April 9, 1983), pp. 25–45, as well as "Kant's Transcendental Deduction: A Limited Defense of Hume," in *New Essays on Kant,* ed. Bernard den Ouden (New York/Bern: Peter Lang Publishing, 1988), pp. 47–72, and "Reid's Contribution to Hume's Problem," in *The Science of Man in the Scottish Enlightenment: Hume, Reid, and their Contemporaries,* ed. Peter Jones (Edinburgh: University of Edinburgh Press, 1989), pp. 124–148. The paper on "Kant's Conception Hume's Problem" has created some controversy – especially in Germany. Much of this controversy is due to the fact that Lothar Kreimendahl and Günter Gawlick took over much of my story in their *Hume in der deutschen Aufklärung: Umrisse einer Rezeptionsgeschichte* (Stuttgart: frommann-holzboog, 1987). Agreeing that the translated passage offers an antinomy, and that it was this passage that awakened Kant, Gawlick and Kreimendahl criticized my dating of Kant's awakening to 1771 and offered a somewhat different interpretation of *why* Hume's Antinomies were important to Kant. In particular, they claimed that Kant read the Humean "Night Thoughts" two years earlier, i. e., in 1769, and that Hume's Antinomies led Kant to formulate the final version of his own doctrine of the Antinomies. Kreimendahl elaborated this view further in *Kant – Der Durchbruch von 1769* (Köln: Dinter, 1991) Several of the critics of Gawlick and Kreimendahl's work also found it necessary to criticize my position (and most of these have criticized it as if it were essentially the same as theirs). See Rudolf Lüthe, review of G. Gawlick and L. Kreimendahl, *Hume in der deutschen Aufklärung* in *Philosophischer Literaturanzeiger* 40 (1987), pp. 209–212; Lewis White Beck, review of G. Gawlick and L. Kreimendahl, *Hume in der deutschen Aufklärung* in *Eighteenth-Century Studies* 21 (1988), pp. 405–408; Wolfgang Carl, review of G. Gawlick and L. Kreimendahl, *Hume in der deutschen Aufklärung* in *Philosophische Rundschau* 35 (1988), pp. 207–214, p. 211; Wolfgang Carl, *Der schweigende Kant. Die Entwürfe zu einer Deduktion der Kategorien vor 1781*, Abhandlungen Akademie Göttingen 182 (Göttingen/Zürich: Vandenhoek & Ruprecht, 1989), pp. 50, 150, 156; and Reinhard Brandt, review of L. Kreimendahl, *Der Durchbruch von 1769* in *Kant-Studien* 83 (1992), pp. 100–111. The only one who properly differentiates my position from that of Gawlick and Kreimendahl is Lorne Falkenstein, "The Great Light of 1769 – A Humeian Awakening? Comments on Lothar Kreimendahl's Account of Hume's Influence on Kant," *Archiv für Geschichte der Philosophie* 77 (1995), pp. 63–79. As

Lorne Falkenstein points out quite correctly, Kreimendahl and Gawlick argue that Kant, as a result of Hamann's Hume translation, discovered *the* Antinomy of Pure Reason as it is found in the first *Critique*. I have never made such a claim. In fact, I believe that Kant could not have discovered the Antinomy of Pure Reason in 1770 simply because he did not have a clear conception of reason as opposed to the understanding. All I tried to show was that, borrowing a concept from biology, phylogenetically the Antinomy as a specific part of Kant's system evolved from a problem that was at first quite undifferentiated, consisting both of what later became the problem of the Transcendental Deduction and the Transcendental Analytic. It presents some of the origins of the critical problem Kant tries to answer in the first *Critique*.

43. Ak 19, pp. 116, 118f.; see also p. 133.

44. Ak 19, pp. 116f.

45. Ak 19, p. 103.

46. Ak 19, p. 117.

47. Though this also recalls Hutcheson's distinction between justifying and exciting reasons.

48. Ak 19, p. 119.

49. Ibid. See also p. 120: "The highest principles of moral judgment are rational, yet they are merely formal principles. They do not determine any goal, but only the moral form of any goal . . ."

50. Ak 19, p. 122.

51. Ak 19, p. 120.

52. Ak 19, p. 108.

53. Ak 19, p. 110.

54. Ak 5, p. 152. See also pp. 144–151 of this volume.

55. In several letters he complained about his health. See, for instance, Ak 10, pp. 83, 95, 99.

56. Ak 10, p. 95.

57. Stark, "Kant als akademischer Lehrer," p. 57n.

58. Stark, "Introduction," Immanuel Kant, *Kant's Gesammelte Schriften,* published by the Königlich Preussische Akademie der Wissenschaften. Part IV: *Kants Vorlesungen,* vol. 25, ed. Reinhard Brandt and Werner Stark (Berlin: Walter de Gruyter & Co., 1997), 25.1, pp. ci f. Vorländer's supposition that Kant did so to get time for writing is wrong; Vorländer, *Immanuel Kant,* I, p. 199.

59. Arnoldt, "Möglichst vollständiges Verzeichnis," p. 337. He taught this subject also in 1775, 1777–78, 1779–80, and 1781–82. He usually taught it from 8:00 to 9:00 A.M., but a few times also between 10:00 and 11:00 A.M. and 3:00 and 4:00 P.M.

60. Arnoldt, "Möglichst vollständiges Verzeichnis," pp. 236, 239. See also Vorländer, *Immanuel Kant,* I, p. 199; Stark, *Nachforschungen,* p. 321.

61. Stark, "Einleitung," Ak 25.1, p. c.

62. Ak 10, p. 145.

63. Ak 10, p. 242. Given the popularity of Kant's lectures on anthropology, it is perhaps somewhat surprising that he only published a version of these lectures in 1798 at the very end of his academic career, and that the multitude of transcripts made by students was made available only sparingly. Apart from Fr. Chr. Starke's

publication in 1831 of a transcript of Kant's lectures and a book giving advice on how to know man and world, based on lecture transcripts, not much happened. Volume 15 (1913) of the Academy edition, which contains Kant's very own reflections on anthropological subjects, represented a further step toward a better knowledge of Kant's anthropological views, but the different transcripts of Kant's lectures on anthropology had to wait until 1997. They are now available in vol. 25 of the Academy edition.

64. Werner Stark, *Nachforschungen zu Briefen und Handschriften Immanuel Kants* (Berlin: Akademie Verlag, 1993), p. 326. See also Jachmann, *Kant*, p. 126, and Rink, *Ansichten*, p. 33.

65. Arnoldt, "Möglichst vollständiges Verzeichnis," pp. 220f.

66. The group of academic citizens was much larger than the group made up of student and faculty. See pp. 438–439 of this volume. The dean was a temporary member of the senate. As one of the four most senior professors, Kant became a permanent member of the senate in 1780.

67. Vorländer, *Immanuel Kant*, I, p. 44 and Euler, "Kants Amtsgeschäfte," p. 75. Kant was dean in the summer semester of 1776, the winter semesters of 1779–80, 1782–83, 1785–86, 1787–88, the summer semester of 1791, and the winter semester of 1794–95.

68. Reicke, *Kantiana*, p. 19 (Malter, *Kant in Rede und Gespräch*, pp. 132f.). See also Euler and Dietzsch, "Prüfungspraxis und Universitätsreform in Königsberg," pp. 99–101. Euler and Dietzsch show that Kant did not, in fact, allow everyone to pass.

69. Jachmann, *Kant*, p. 146 (Malter, *Kant in Rede und Gespräch*, pp. 221f.). This was in 1783. Jachmann contradicted, however, what the others said. He said that he had the reputation of being strict. Kant may have been stricter the second time around.

70. He was first teaching at the Löbenichts school, but later became vice principal at the *Altstädtische Gymnasium*. Since he was no longer allowed to teach at the university (at least in part because of Kant; his invectives against Kant must have been pervasive). It is also interesting that the director was not alone in his fear. The "Inspector of the school shared it," and he took on the task. This episode by itself explains why Jachmann thought Kant was "strict."

71. On Basedow, see pp. 227–229 of this volume. See Stark, *Nachforschungen*, pp. 327f.

72. It appeared in Königsberg in 1780.

73. Vorländer, *Immanuel Kant*, I, p. 227.

74. In an unpublished anthropology manuscript (Dohna) Kant points out that "it was Basedow's failure that he drank too much Malaga [wine]."

75. Jakob Michael Reinhold Lenz, *Werke und Briefe in drei Bänden*, ed. Sigrid Damm (München/Wien: Hanser Verlag, 1987), III, pp. 83f. The entire poem consists of twelve verses.

76. Lenz, *Werke und Briefe*, II, p. 499. He also claimed that faith is a "*complementum moralitatis*," just as did Kant (p. 513).

77. Not all of Lenz's theory is Kant, of course. Lenz thought that perfection and happiness (in accordance with perfection) were the two pillars of moral philosophy. The essay was written in Straßburg, not long after Lenz had left Königsberg.

78. Voigt, *Kraus*, p. 21.
79. See Kurt Röttgers, "Christian Jakob Kraus (1753–1807)," *Jahrbuch der Albertus Universität zu Königsberg* 29 (1994), pp. 125–135, p. 128.
80. Voigt, *Kraus*, pp. 26f.
81. Hamann, *Briefwechsel*, III, p. 205.
82. Hamann, *Briefwechsel*, III, p. 242.
83. Hamann, *Briefwechsel*, III, p. 260.
84. Hamann, *Briefwechsel*, III, p. 261.
85. Kant, *Correspondence*, p. 93 (Ak 10, p. 248).
86. Voigt, *Kraus*, p. 87.
87. Ludwig von Baczko, *Geschichte meines Lebens*, vol. I (Königsberg: Unzer, 1824), pp. 187f. (Malter, *Kant in Rede und Gespräch*, pp. 118f.).
88. Kant, *Correspondence*, tr. Zweig, pp. 90f., p. 91. Kraus later said that he "read only for the best heads in his lecture hall" (Voigt, *Kraus*, p. 401). This is not precisely the same approach Kant followed. See pp. 358–359 of this volume.
89. Kant, *Correspondence*, tr. Zweig, p. 91.
90. Ak 10, p. 242.
91. Baczko, *Geschichte meines Lebens*, I, pp. 220f. See also Thomas Studer, "Ludwig von Baczko. Schriftsteller in Königsberg um 1800," in *Königsberg. Beiträge zu einem besonderen Kapitel der deutschen Geistesgeschichte*, ed. Kohnen, pp. 399–424, see especially p. 413. Studer quotes another passage in which Baczko explains that Kant's advice was the result, at least in part, of a more private encounter. Kant, who lived at Kanter's house, noticed that Baczko took out travel books and read them, and therefore encouraged him to study geography and anthropology. The two accounts are not necessarily incompatible.
92. Baczko, *Geschichte meines Lebens*, II, pp. 222–223 (Malter, *Kant in Rede und Gespräch*, pp. 120f.).
93. Hamann, *Briefwechsel*, IV, p. 210.
94. Baczko, *Geschichte meines Lebens*, II, pp. 13f. (not in Malter, *Kant in Rede und Gespräch*).
95. Adolf Porschmann, "Die ersten Kantianer in England," in *Studien zur Geschichte des Preussenlandes*, ed. Ernst Bahr (Marburg: N. G. Elwert Verlag, 1963), pp. 470–482.
96. See A. F. M. Willich, *The Elements of the Critical Philosophy* (1798; reprint New York: Garland, 1977).
97. Salomon Maimon, *The Autobiography of Salomon Maimon*, tr. Hugo Bergmann (London: The East and West Library, 1954), p. 94
98. See pp. 360–361 of this volume.
99. Stark, "Hinweise zu Kants Kollegen vor 1770."
100. Stark, "Kant als akademischer Lehrer," p. 67.
101. Rink, *Ansichten*, pp. 43f.
102. Ak 10, p. 231.
103. Ak 10, p. 236.
104. Ibid.
105. Ak 10, p. 244 (Nov. 24, 1778).
106. Ak 10, p. 254.

107. Vorländer, following the lead of many before him, claimed that Kant was close only to Johann Ernst Schulz and Kraus (Vorländer, *Immanuel Kant*, II, p. 318). This is demonstrably false, as I hope to have shown (I have relied to some extent on Stark, "Kants Kollegen").

108. Altmann, *Mendelssohn*, p. 309.

109. Hamann, *Briefwechsel*, IV, p. 260.

110. See Kant, *Latin Writings*, ed. Beck, pp. 161–183. There is some evidence that Kant, who was dean during this semester, had some influence on this appointment. See Euler, "Kant's Amtstätigkeit," p. 83.

111. Hamann, *Briefwechsel*, IV, p. 199.

112. Hamann, *Briefwechsel*, IV, p. 206.

113. Hamann, *Briefwechsel*, IV, p. 261.

114. In Kant, *Latin Writings*, ed. Beck, p. 179, Kant directly addresses Kraus in a public defense, saying: "I turn finally to you, honored respondent, whom I have long counted among my best students. Endowed by nature with excellent gifts of intellect, you possess rich knowledge," etc.

115. Kraus in Reicke, *Kantiana*, p. 60 (Malter, *Kant in Rede und Gespräch*, p. 121).

116. Malter, *Kant in Rede und Gespräch*, pp. 146f. Bernoulli goes on to describe how Kant first took him to the Court Library and then to a museum.

117. See K. Hagen, "Gedächtnisrede auf B. William Motherby," *Neue preußische Provincial-Blätter* 3 (1847), pp. 131f.

118. Hamann, *Briefwechsel*, VI, p. 364 (in 1786).

119. Reusch, "Historische Erinnerungen," p. 365.

120. Reusch, "Historische Erinnerungen," p. 297.

121. Ak 10, p. 231.

122. Borowski, *Leben*, p. 76f. See also Stark, "Wo lehrte Kant?", p. 98. Hamann speaks in a letter of November 24, 1777, of his own cock, "which has never been heard crowing, and which accordingly does not belong to the race of those loud-mouths (*Schreihälse*) which our Professor Kant does not like." Hamann, *Briefwechsel*, III, p. 387.

123. Voigt, *Kraus*, p. 146. For the move see Hamann, *Briefwechsel*, V, p. 222, and Stark, "Wo lehrte Kant?", p. 99. But see Gulyga, *Kant*, p. 112, and Vorländer, who think the move took place as early as 1775.

124. Voigt, *Kraus*, p. 121.

125. Borowski, *Leben*, p. 74.

126. Ibid.

127. Karl Rosenkranz, *Politische Briefe und Aufsätze, 1848–1856*, ed. Paul Herre (Leipzig, 1919), p. 140. I quote in accordance with Stark, "Wo lehrte Kant?", p. 107. See Czygan, "Wasianskis Handexemplar," p. 118.

128. Stark, "Wo lehrte Kant?", p. 107. Stark points out that Hippel had his meals sent to his house from this establishment.

129. Borowski, *Leben*, p. 74.

130. Borowski, *Leben*, p. 71.

131. Christian Wilhelm Dohm, *Über die bürgerliche Verbesserung der Juden* (Berlin, 1781). I quote in accordance with Epstein's translation, *The Genesis of German Conservatism*, p. 219.

132. Mittenzwei, *Preussen nach dem Siebenjahrigen Krieg*, pp. 135–147. The "partition of Poland" refers to three territorial divisions of Poland (1772, 1793, 1795). It was initiated by Prussia, Russia, and Austria. Poland's territory was progressively reduced until, after 1795, the state of Poland ceased to exist.

133. See Stark, "Wo lehrte Kant?", p. 100. But it would be a mistake to think that he held a grudge. Late in his life, Lampe's wife and her daughter helped Lampe in his duties. They cleaned Kant's house and took care of other matters.

134. See Manfred Kuehn, *Scottish Common Sense in Germany, 1768–1800: A Contribution to the History of Critical Philosophy*, with a Preface by Lewis White Beck (Kingston/Montreal: McGill-Queen's University Press, 1987), pp. 154–6. For a good discussion of Herder's views in English, see Robert E. Norton, *Herder's Aesthetics and the European Enlightenment* (Ithaca and London: Cornell University Press, 1991).

135. Hamann, *Briefwechsel*, III, p. 82.

136. Malter, *Kant in Rede und Gespräch*, p. 132.

137. Ak 10, pp. 177f.

138. Paul Konschel, *Hamanns Gegner, der Kryptokatholik D. Johann August Starck, Oberhofprediger und Generalsuperintendent von Ostpreußen* (Königsberg, 1912), pp. 14f. Vorländer, by the way, failed even to mention Starck's name. How important this man was for all of Germany can be seen from Epstein, *The Genesis of German Conservatism*, especially pp. 506–517.

139. Starck, "Heathen Importations into Christendom," p. 70, translated from Konschel, *Der Kryptokatholik Starck*, p. 24. If this sounds vaguely Kantian, this is no accident. Starck's doctrine belongs just as much to the Enlightenment as Kant's does.

140. Hamann, *Konxompax* (1779), *Hierophantische Briefe*. Relevant in this context also is Hippel's *Des Ritters von Rosencreuz letzte Willensmeinung der Sprache . . .* See Joseph Kohnen, "Konxompax und die Kreuz und Querzüge des Ritters A bis Z," in *Königsberg. Beiträge zu einem besonderen Kapitel der deutschen Geistesgeschichte*, ed. Kohnen, pp. 308–320. Though Hamann's writings against Starck appeared only much later, their origins date back to this time.

141. Hamann, *Briefwechsel*, III, p. 84.

142. Hamann, *Briefwechsel*, III, pp. 86f.

143. Hamann, *Konxompax*, p. 225.

144. See pp. 339–340 of this volume.

145. See Hamann, *Briefwechsel*, III, p. 193, 218, 220; see also Archenholz, *Bürger und Patrizier*, pp. 316f.

146. Hamann, *Briefwechsel*, III, p. 260.

147. This was also Kant's view. See pp. 42–45, this volume.

148. Johann Georg Schlosser, "Zweites Schreiben über die Philanthropinen," *Ephemeriden der Menschheit* 1 (1776), pp. 38–39. I use the translation of Epstein, *The Genesis of German Conservatism*, p. 79.

149. "Neues Schulreglement für die Universität Breslau, July 26, 1800," as quoted in Epstein, *The Genesis of German Conservatism*, p. 560.

150. Kant, *Correspondence*, tr. Zweig, pp. 83–85 (Ak 10, pp. 179–180).

151. Ak 2, pp. 445–452.

152. Ak 2, p. 452.
153. Ak 10, pp. 217f. (not in Kant, *Correspondence*, tr. Zweig).
154. Ak 2, p. 449.
155. For Mendelssohn's biography see especially Altmann, *Mendelssohn*. See also his *Moses Mendelssohns Frühschriften zur Metaphysik* (Tübingen, 1969). Mendelssohn lived from 1729 to 1786. Though not born in Berlin, he lived most of his life there. Starting from relatively humble beginnings, he became the most prominent member of the Jewish community in that city. He was one of the closest friends of Gotthold Ephraim Lessing, who portrayed him in one of his plays as "Nathan the Wise." Advocating the cultural assimilation of the Jewish community into German society, he became famous as "the Jewish Socrates" for his philosophical thought. He was also the target of attack by fundamentalist Christians, who challenged him to explain why – given the enlightened beliefs he held – he had not yet converted to Christianity. He defended his cause admirably. Georg Christoph Lichtenberg, who came to his defense in a satirical attack on the fundamentalists, summed up their fears, saying: "A Jew who was a natural honest man would be regarded as a fellow human being and might even be preferred to a Christian? The very idea makes one shudder." Many enlightened Germans took Mendelssohn to be the very model of an enlightened person. He not only was important for his thought, but also became an icon for their most deeply held beliefs.
156. Kant, *Correspondence*, tr. Zweig, p. 87.
157. Immanuel Kant, *Prolegomena to Any Future Metaphysics*, ed. Lewis White Beck (Indianapolis: Bobbs-Merrill, 1950), pp. 8f. (Ak 4, pp. 260f.).
158. Kant, *Correspondence*, tr. Zweig, pp. 58f. (Ak 10, pp. 96f.).
159. Ak 10, p. 122 (not in Zweig).
160. Ak 10, p. 123 (not in Zweig).
161. Kant, *Correspondence*, tr. Zweig, pp. 73 (Ak 10, p. 132). See also p. 74 (Ak 10, p. 133): "The Göttingen reviewer [of the dissertation] dwells on some applications of system that in themselves are not essential and with respect to which I myself have since changed my view – with the result, however, that my main aim has only been furthered."
162. Kant, *Correspondence*, tr. Zweig, pp. 77f. (Ak 10, p. 144).
163. Kant, *Correspondence*, tr. Zweig, p. 86 (Ak 10, p. 199).
164. Kant, *Correspondence*, tr. Zweig, p. 89 (Ak 10, p. 213). I have changed the translation.
165. Ak 10, pp. 231f. (not in Zweig).
166. Kant, *Correspondence*, tr. Zweig, p. 90 (Ak 10, p. 241).
167. Ak 10, p. 241.
168. Kant, *Correspondence*, tr. Zweig, pp. 93f. (Ak 10, p. 266).
169. Kant, *Correspondence*, tr. Zweig, pp. 100f. (Ak 10, p. 338). I have slightly changed the translation.
170. For a more systematic discussion of the issues connected with this claim, see Heiner F. Klemme, *Kants Philosophie des Subjekts. Systematische und entwicklungsgeschichtliche Untersuchungen zum Verhältnis von Selbstbewußtsein und Selbsterkenntnis* (Hamburg: Meiner Verlag, 1996).

171. The story is not quite as simple as these remarks suggest. Whereas Kant simply speaks of an opposition between "rational" and "sensitive" in the dissertation, he distinguishes two "rational" faculties in 1781, namely the "understanding" and "reason." The separation of these two faculties is a significant part of the story.

172. Ak 18, p. 69 (emphasis supplied).

173. *Die philosophischen Hauptvorlesungen Immanuel Kants*, ed. Arnold Kowalewski (Hildesheim: Olms, 1965), p. 505 (Ak 24.2 [Logic Dohna-Wundlacken], pp. 783f.; Kant, *Lectures on Logic*, pp. 515f.). The student was impressed by this confession, for he noted "NB. This happened in the repetitorium on Saturday, for the collegium had already finished on Friday."

174. The most decisive change appears to have happened before February 1772. What Kant calls "decisive" in the letter to Herz is just what most radically differentiates the Inaugural Dissertation from the first *Critique*, namely the emphasis on the necessary interdependence of rational cognition and sensible intuition. The "all-important rule" that we must "*carefully prevent the principles proper to sensitive cognition from passing their boundaries and affecting the intellectual*" for which he argued in 1770 had to be radically reformulated as a result of his meditations during the seventies. He ultimately transformed this rule into two principles. He called the first one "Hume's principle," that is, the prescription to consider knowledge as restricted to experience, and the second one the boundary principle, or the claim that experience does not exhaust reality. His "essential point" involves both these principles. It is what defines the essential outlook of the first *Critique*. See pp. 000–000, this volume.

175. Kant, Ak 12, p. 361 (emphasis supplied).

176. For all this see Hamilton Beck, *The Elusive 'I' in the Novel: Hippel, Sterne, Diderot, and Kant* (Bern and New York: Peter Lang, 1987), pp. 99–126, and his "Kant and the Novel: A Study of the Examination Scene in Hippel's 'Lebensläufe nach aufsteigender Linie,'" *Kant-Studien* 74 (1983), pp. 271f. See also Anke Lindemann-Stark, "Kants Vorlesungen zur Anthropologie in Hippels *Lebensläufen*" (Magisterarbeit Marburg, 1990), and her "Leben und Lebensläufe des Theodor Gottlieb von Hippel" (Dissertation, Phillips Universität Marburg, 1998).

177. See Hippel, *Sämtliche Werke*, II, pp. 148–167. Compare Beck, "Kant and the Novel," p. 287. The scene is also of interest for Kant's philosophy.

Chapter 6: "All-Crushing" Critic of Metaphysics (1780–1784)

1. William James, *The Varieties of Religious Experience*, in his *Writings, 1902–1910* (New York: Library of America, 1987), pp. 183f. See also Erik H. Erikson, *Young Man Luther: A Study in Psychoanalysis and History* (New York: Norton, 1962), pp. 41f.

2. Hamann, *Briefwechsel*, V, p. 36.

3. Ak 10, pp. 212f.

4. The former is claimed by the Böhme brothers in *Das Andere der Vernunft;* the latter is claimed by Shell in *The Embodiment of Reason*.

5. Kant, *Religion and Rational Theology*, pp. 326 (Ak 7, p. 115).

6. Hamann, *Briefwechsel*, IV, p. 196.

7. Hamann, *Briefwechsel*, IV, p. 210. On October 6, he asked Hartknoch to give him a copy of Kant's *Critique*, should he become its publisher. By the end of the month it was certain that Hartknoch would be the publisher (Hamann, *Briefwechsel*, IV, pp. 226, 230, 232).

8. Borowski, *Leben*, p. 103.

9. Jachmann, *Kant*, p. 162.

10. Ibid.

11. Compare Vorländer, *Kant*, II, p. 108.

12. Benno Erdmann, *Reflexionen Kants zur kritischen Philosophie. Aus Kants hand-schriftlichen Aufzeichnungen herausgegeben* (Stuttgart and Bad Canstatt: frommann-holzboog, 1992, originally Leipzig 1882/1884), pp. 315f. (Ak 18, p. 64).

13. Hamann, *Briefwechsel*, IV, p. 292f.

14. Hamann, *Briefwechsel*, IV, p. 312; see also Vorländer, *Immanuel Kant*, I, pp. 261f.

15. The short account I offer of the contents of the *Critique of Pure Reason* will not, of course, do justice to Kant's work. It is meant only as a first introduction, and the reader, who is interested in understanding it better should consult one of the many good works that are available in English. No one seriously interested in Kant's *Critique* can ignore Henry Allison, *Kant's Transcendental Idealism: An Interpretation and Defense* (New Haven and London: Yale University Press, 1986), and Paul Guyer, *Kant and the Claims of Knowledge* (Cambridge: Cambridge University Press, 1987).

16. More precisely: the physico-theological argument presupposes the cosmological argument, and the cosmological argument in turn presupposes the ontological argument. Thus both arguments presuppose the ontological argument and fail for that reason.

17. Ak 10, p. 270; Kant, *Correspondence*, tr. Zweig, p. 96.

18. Ak 10, p. 341; Kant, *Correspondence*, tr. Zweig, pp. 102f.

19. Ak 10, p. 345; Kant, *Correspondence*, tr. Zweig, p. 106.

20. Ak 10, p. 346; Kant, *Correspondence*, tr. Zweig, p. 107.

21. Mendelssohn, *Morgenstunden* (in 1785).

22. Reinhard Brandt, "Feder und Kant," *Kant-Studien* 80 (1989), pp. 249–264; see also Kurt Röttgers, "J. G. H. Feder – Beitrag zu einer Verhinderungsgeschichte eines deutschen Empirismus," *Kant-Studien* 75 (1984), pp. 420–41. See also Walther Ch. Zimmerli, "'Schwere Rüstung' des Dogmatismus und 'anwendbare Eklektik'. J. G. H. Feder und die Göttinger Philosophie im ausgehenden 18. Jahrhundert," *Studia Leibnitiana* 15 (1983), pp. 58–71.

23. Hamann, *Metakritik* (*Werke*, ed. Nadler, III, p. 283).

24. For an extended discussion of Hamann's relationship to Kant, see Heinrich Weber, *Hamann und Kant* (München, 1904). For the significance of Hamann's library, see Immendorfer, *Johann Georg Hamann und seine Bücherei*.

25. Hamann, *Briefwechsel*, III, p. 418.

26. See Immanuel Kant, *Prolegomena zu einer jeden künftigen Metaphysik die als Wissenschaft wird auftreten können*, ed. Rudolf Malter (Stuttgart: Philip Reclam Jun., 1989), pp. 200–205 (Beilage 3: "Die Gotha Rezension").

27. Ak 8, pp. 3f. (see also Ak 10, p. 280).

28. See pp. 351–355, this volume. Later that year (April 18) the Newspaper published another article by Kant, namely his "Announcement to Doctors," which intro-

duced Kraus's translation of an essay on influenza by a certain Fothergill that had appeared in the *Gentleman's Magazine* of February 1776 (see Ak 8, pp. 6–8). This Introduction and the circumstances surrounding its writing is interesting in the context of Kant's lifelong fascination with medicine as well as his relationship with a member of the faculty of medicine at the University of Königsberg.

29. Ak 10, p. 271.
30. Ak 10, p. 273.
31. Hamann, *Briefwechsel*, IV, p. 319, see also pp. 323, 331.
32. Hamann, *Briefwechsel*, IV, p. 336.
33. Hamann, *Briefwechsel*, IV, p. 341; see also pp. 344, 350. For further details see Ak 4, pp. 598f.
34. Hamann, *Briefwechsel*, IV, pp. 376, 400, 418.
35. Kant, *Prolegomena*, p. 123 (Ak 4, p. 374). Thus the second edition of his first *Critique*, like many of the textbooks and popular treatises of the time, contains a "Refutation of Idealism," but quite unlike most of these, it lacked a "Refutation of Skepticism."
36. Kant, *Prolegomena*, ed. Beck, p. 123 (Ak 4, p. 374). This position comes close to his own view in the Inaugural Dissertation. Though sensitive knowledge is not "sheer illusion" in the Inaugural Dissertation, the ideas of the pure understand-ing and reason (which are not clearly differentiated in the Inaugural Dissertation) are the only genuine parts of metaphysics.
37. Kant, *Prolegomena*, ed. Beck, pp. 10f. (Ak 4, pp. 260f.).
38. Kant, *Prolegomena*, ed. Beck, pp. 6f. (Ak 4, pp. 258f.).
39. Kant, *Prolegomena*, ed. Beck, pp. 5 (Ak 4, p. 257).
40. Kant, *Prolegomena*, ed. Beck, p. 67 (Ak 4, p. 320).
41. Kant, *Prolegomena*, ed. Beck, p. 80 (Ak 4, p. 332).
42. Kant, *Prolegomena*, ed. Beck, pp. 108f. (Ak 4, pp. 359f.).
43. Hume, *Enquiries*, pp. 11f.
44. Hume, *Enquiries*, pp. 26f., 44n.
45. Hume, *Enquiries*, p. 16.
46. Kant, *Prolegomena*, ed. Beck, p. 110 (Ak 4, p. 361). See also Bxxiv: "on a cursory view of the present work it may seem that its results are merely negative, warning us that we must never venture beyond the limits of experience. Such is in fact its primary use . . . So far as our Critique limits speculative reason, it is indeed negative."
47. Hume's principle is today perhaps better known by P. F. Strawson's name: "Kant's principle of significance." It is, as he says, a principle "with which empiricist philosophers have no difficulty sympathizing." Kant's "espousal of the principle of significance and in his consequential repudiation of transcendent metaphysics, Kant is close to the tradition of classical empiricism, the tradition of Berkeley and Hume." "Kant's principle of significance" is a principle of meaning for Strawson. Kant was not necessarily concerned with meaning per se. See P. F. Strawson, *The Bounds of Sense: An Essay on Kant's Theory of Knowledge* (London: Methuen, 1966), p. 16.
48. Kant, *Prolegomena*, ed. Beck, p. 104 (Ak 4, p. 356).
49. Kant, *Prolegomena*, ed. Beck, pp. 104f. (Ak 4, pp. 356f.).

50. Kant, "What Is Orientation in Thinking?" in *Critique of Practical Reason and Other Writings*, tr. Beck, p. 298. He makes the same point, though not as clearly, in the *Prolegomena*, p. 110.

51. Kant, *Prolegomena*, ed. Beck, p. 114 (Ak 4, p. 365).

52. Ralph C. S. Walker, *Kant* (London: Routledge & Kegan Paul, 1978), p. vii.

53. Barry Stroud, "Kant and Skepticism," in *The Skeptical Tradition* (Berkeley: University of California Press, 1983), pp. 413–434, p. 415. See also Stroud's *The Significance of Philosophical Scepticism* (Oxford: The Clarendon Press, 1984), especially pp. 128–169.

54. Stroud, "Kant and Skepticism," p. 419. Stroud has a narrow view of skepticism as a form of "skeptical idealism." Accordingly, Kant's antiskepticism is really a form of anti-idealism (which creates further problems for Stroud's view).

55. Richard Rorty, *Philosophy and the Mirror of Nature* (Princeton: Princeton University Press, 1979), p. 6.

56. Rorty, *Philosophy and the Mirror of Nature*, p. 114. For him, "[s]kepticism and the principal genre of modern philosophy have a symbiotic relationship. They live one another's life."

57. P. F. Strawson, in his *Skepticism and Naturalism: Some Varieties* (London: Methuen, 1985) seems to want to make a more fundamental distinction between the Humean and the Kantian projects than does Rorty.

58. Kant, *Prolegomena*, ed. Beck, p. 22 (Ak 4, p. 275).

59. Kant, *Prolegomena*, ed. Beck, pp. 6, 9 (Ak 4, pp. 259, 261).

60. Kant, *Prolegomena*, ed. Beck, p. 8 (Ak 4, p. 260).

61. Kant, *Prolegomena*, ed. Beck, p. 10 (Ak 4, p. 262).

62. Kant, *Prolegomena*, ed. Beck, pp. 108f. (Ak 4, p. 360).

63. W. H. Walsh, *Kant's Criticism of Metaphysics* (Chicago: University of Chicago Press, 1975), pp. 1f.

64. The copy was "defective" because there is so much he does not seem to know. But that could also be explained by the fact that he got his information about it second-hand, i.e., from Hamann, Green, or Kraus (or perhaps from all three of them).

65. Kant, *Prolegomena*, ed. Beck, p. 122n (Ak 4, p. 373).

66. See Kant, *Prolegomena*, ed. Beck, p. 11 (Ak 4, p. 263). Beck's Introduction to the *Prolegomena* still is among the best that has been written on this work (see p. xix).

67. The German title of Part I of the anonymous work reads *Versuch einer Anleitung zur Sittenlehre für alle Menschen ohne Unterschied der Religionen nebst einem Anhange von der Todesstrafe* (Berlin, 1783). Part II appeared in the same year, Part III in 1790. Kant's review appeared in the *Räsonierendes Bücherverzeichnis*, issue 7 (Königsberg, 1783). See Ak 8, pp. 10–14. See also Immanuel Kant, *Practical Philosophy*, tr. and ed. Mary J. Gregor, general introduction by Allen Wood (New York: Cambridge University Press, 1996), pp. 7–10.

68. He wrote a great number of books on religious matters between 1783 and 1788. He was called "ponytail Schulz" because he argued for the abolition of the wigs of pastors and preachers (for health reasons). He preached wearing a ponytail.

69. Kant, *Practical Philosophy*, p. 8 (Ak 8, p. 11).

70. I quote after Ritter, *Frederick the Great*, p. 54.

71. Kant, *Practical Philosophy*, p. 9 (Ak 8, p. 13).

72. Kant, *Practical Philosophy*, p. 10 (Ak 8, p. 14).
73. Hamann, *Briefwechsel*, V, p. 107.
74. Hamann, *Briefwechsel*, V, p. 87.
75. The letters are translated in Schulz, *Exposition*, pp. 145–162.
76. For a more extensive discussion of this, see James C. Morrison, "Introduction," in Johann Schultz, *Exposition of Kant's Critique*, p. xi–xxxi. See Ak 10, pp. 351f.
77. Ak 10, p. 367. Hamann followed these developments with great interest and reported them to his friends. See Hamann, *Briefwechsel*, V, pp. 36, 71, 87, 108, 123, 131, 217, 227.
78. Ak 10, pp. 368f.
79. Hamann, *Briefwechsel*, V, p. 134.
80. Ak 10, p. 362.
81. Ak 10, pp. 389f. Immanuel Kant, *Briefwechsel*, selection and notes by O. Schöndorffer, revised by R. Malter, introduction by R. Malter and J. Kopper, 3rd. ed. (Hamburg: Meiner, 1986), pp. 932f., 935f. See also Walter Kuhrke, *Kant's Wohnhaus. Zeichnerische Wiederherstellung mit näherer Beschreibung*, 2nd ed. (Königsberg: Gräfe und Unzer, 1924).
82. Ak 10, p. 391.
83. Borowski, *Leben*, p. 76 (Malter, *Kant in Rede und Gespräch*, p. 255).
84. Borowski, *Leben*, p. 76 (Malter, *Kant in Rede und Gespräch*, p. 254).
85. Euler, "Kants Amtsgeschäfte," p. 63.
86. Euler, "Kant im akademischen Senat," unpublished manuscript; see also Euler and Stiening, "'. . . und nie der Pluralität widersprach'?", pp. 57f., 59f.
87. Hasse, *Kant's Tischgenossen*, pp. 5f.
88. Voigt, *Kraus*, p. 199; compare also Borowski, *Leben*, p. 83 (Malter, *Kant in Rede und Gespräch*, p. 406).
89. Puttlich, in Malter, *Kant in Rede und Gespräch*, p. 263.
90. Voigt, *Kraus*, p. 199. This problem was, of course, not just Kant's. The walls in eighteenth-century houses had to be given a new cover of paint (usually just white chalk) at least once a year. Kant was apparently not very regular in having this done.
91. Scheffner, in Malter, *Kant in Rede und Gespräch*, p. 320.
92. Hamann wrote on June 1, 1785, that Kant spent "all his afternoons until 7:00 P.M. at Green's house" (Hamann, *Briefwechsel*, V, p. 448); this is supported by Kraus in Reicke, *Kantiana*, p. 60: Kant "during Green's last years he [Kant] spent several hours every afternoon at Green's house, since he could no longer leave the house on foot." Jachmann, *Kant*, p. 162, said: "Kant went there [to Green's] every afternoon."
93. Hamann, *Briefwechsel*, IV, p. 396; see also Malter, *Kant in Rede und Gespräch*, p. 188.
94. Hamann, *Briefwechsel*, IV, pp. 78, 232, 355, 359, 439; V, pp. 316, 448.
95. Hamann, *Briefwechsel*, IV, p. 205. Hamann's plan to translate the book goes back to these conversations.
96. Hamann, *Briefwechsel*, IV, p. 393.
97. Jachmann, *Kant*, p. 162.
98. Rink, *Ansichten*, p. 45.

99. Rink, *Ansichten*, p. 82. Rink's account describes the situation after Kant had his own cook. But his routine differed little from the way it was two years earlier.
100. Rink, *Ansichten*, p. 148.
101. Rink, *Ansichten*, p. 47.
102. Puttlich, in Malter, *Kant in Rede und Gespräch*, p. 263.
103. Hamann, *Briefwechsel*, IV, pp. 386f; VI, 6, p. 199; and VII, p. 204.
104. Hamann, *Briefwechsel*, IV, pp. 386f. See also Ak 10, pp. 475.
105. Hamann, *Briefwechsel*, VI, p. 199.
106. See Ak 10, p. 463. See also Hamann, *Briefwechsel*, VI, p. 349 and VII, p. 44.
107. See Kuehn, *Scottish Common Sense in Germany*, p. 211.
108. See Voigt, *Kraus*, pp. 315, 392; Beck is called Kraus's "charge" and "Kraus's protegée" (*Zögling*).
109. Ak 11, p. 442.
110. See D. E. Walford, "Introduction," in *Selected Pre-Critical Writings and Correspondence with Beck*, ed. G. B. Kerferd and D. E. Walford, with a contribution by P. G. Lucas (Manchester: Manchester University Press, 1968), p. xxxv.

Chapter 7: Founder of a Metaphysics of Morals (1784–1787)

1. Hamann, *Briefwechsel* (September 19–20, 1784): "Kant has sent off the manuscript of the *Foundations*." See also Ak 10, p. 308, where Kant claims that the work was at the printer's twenty days before Michaelmass.
2. Thus he wrote on December 31, 1765, to Lambert that he had finished a minor work on the "Metaphysical Foundations (*Anfangsgründe*, not *Grundlegung*) of Practical Philosophy," which, together with the "Metaphysical Foundations (*Anfangsgründe*) of Theoretical Philosophy" was soon to be published. If it had appeared, it would no doubt have looked rather different from what he published twenty years later. See Ak 10, p. 56. In the winter semester of 1770–71 he expressed again hopes to complete a "pure moral philosophy in which *no empirical principles can be met.*" The matters he would have dealt with in this work would undoubtedly have been much closer to the *Foundations*, but they would have still been treated differently from the way they are treated in the final product. See Ak 10, p. 97. See also pp. 136–138 and pp. 201–204, this volume.
3. Ak 10, pp. 279.
4. Ak 10, pp. 346f. "This winter I will finish the first part of my morals, if not completely then at least in part. This work allows of greater popularity . . ." (August 16, 1783, to Mendelssohn).
5. Ak 10, p. 346.
6. *Philosophische Anmerkungen und Abhandlungen zu Ciceros Büchern von den Pflichten.* This was a translation or adaptation of Cicero's *On Duties.*
7. See Klemme, *Die Schule Immanuel Kants*, pp. 76–78; see also pp. 48–49 of this volume.
8. Ak 9, p. 47. See also Johan van der Zande, "In the Image of Cicero: German Philosophy between Wolff and Kant," *Journal of the History of Ideas* 56 (1995), pp. 419–442.

9. Hamann, *Briefwechsel*, V, pp. 129f. He also reported: "but the title has not yet been formulated" and then that Kant wanted to send something "on Beauty" to the Berlin *Monatsschrift*. See also his letter to Hartknoch, March 14, 1784 (p. 131).

10. Hamann, *Briefwechsel*, V, pp. 134, 141.

11. Several scholars have argued that Garve's Cicero was actually important to Kant in dealing with fundamental issues. The most extensive argument to this effect is to be found in Carlos Melches Gibert, *Der Einfluss Christian Garve's Übersetzung Ciceros "De Officiis" auf Kants "Grundlegung zur Metaphysik der Sitten"* (Regensburg: S. Röderer Verlag, 1994).

12. See Gregory DesJardins, "The Terms of *De Officiis* in Hume and Kant," *Journal of the History of Ideas* 28 (1967), pp. 237–242. DesJardins is following the lead of Klaus Reich, *Kant und die Ethik der Griechen* (Tübingen: J. C. B. Mohr [Paul Siebeck], 1935); translated by W. H. Walsh as "Kant and Greek Ethics," *Mind* 48 (1939). Reich is criticized by Pierre Laberge in his "Du passage de la Philosophie Moral Populaire a la Métaphysique des Moers," *Kant-Studien* 71 (1980), pp. 416–444.

13. Cicero, *On Duties*, ed. M. T. Griffin and E. M. Atkins (Cambridge: Cambridge University Press 1991), p. 6.

14. Cicero, *On Duties*, p. 6.

15. Cicero, *On Duties*, p. 7.

16. Cicero, *On Duties*, p. 59.

17. Cicero, *On Duties*, p. 9.

18. Cicero, *On Duties*, p. 21.

19. Cicero, *On Duties*, p. 62.

20. Cicero, *On Duties*, p. 43.

21. Christian Garve, *Eigene Betrachtungen über die allgemeinen Grundsätze der Sittenlehre. Ein Anhang zu der Übersicht der verschiedenen Moralsysteme* (Breslau, 1798), p. 265. Garve's *Übersicht der vornehmsten Principien der Sittenlehre von dem Zeitalter des Aristotles an bis auf unsere Zeit . . .* (Breslau, 1798) contained also an extensive (and interesting) discussion of Kant's "system" (pp. 183–318). It was dedicated to Kant. Kraus called it "the best presentation of the Kantian system from the point of view of bon sens" (Kraus in Reicke, *Kantiana*, p. 53).

22. See Chapter 1 of this volume, pp. 26–31.

23. Wasianski, *Kant*, p. 245.

24. Ak 6, pp. 236, 464.

25. Kant, *Practical Philosophy*, p. 45 (Ak 4, p. 389).

26. He seemed more positive in his lectures on anthropology, claiming that "a more subtle, or well-understood concept of honor or a correct concept of honor can amount to the best *analogon* of a good character, even if, by itself, it isn't." But this really is no more than a change in emphasis. He still holds that any behavior that is merely based on honor, being concerned with appearances, not with reality, falls short of true moral worth. Though it may be behavior in accordance with duty, it has no moral worth.

27. Frederick, *Anti-Machiavel*. I use the translation of Epstein, *The Genesis of German Conservatism*, p. 342.

28. Kant, *Practical Philosophy*, p. 51.
29. Kant, "Old Saw," p. 53. That the concept of duty must be understood in this way by everyone is a central claim of the *Foundations* as well.
30. Hamann, *Briefwechsel*, V, p. 147.
31. Hamann, *Briefwechsel*, V, pp. 176, 182; see also p. 189, where Hamann predicts that it will soon be sent off.
32. Kant, *Practical Philosophy*, pp. 43–108 (Ak 4, pp. 387–463). In the following summary I shall concentrate on the metaphysical aspects of the work, and not on the practical implications or applications of the categorical imperative. For a perceptive account of the latter, see especially Barbara Herman, *The Practice of Moral Judgment* (Cambridge, Mass.: Harvard University Press, 1993). For a collection of some of the most important recent essays on this work, see Paul Guyer (ed.), *Kant's Groundwork of the Metaphysics of Morals: Critical Essays* (Lanham, Md: Rowman & Littlefield, 1998).
33. Kant, *Practical Philosophy*, p. 44 (Ak 4, p. 389).
34. Kant, *Practical Philosophy*, p. 47 (Ak 4, p. 392).
35. See pp. 144–151, this volume.
36. Kant, *Practical Philosophy*, p. 52 (Ak 4, p. 397).
37. Kant, *Practical Philosophy*, p. 57 (Ak 4, p. 402).
38. Kant, *Practical Philosophy*, p. 61 (Ak 4, p. 406).
39. Kant, *Practical Philosophy*, p. 65 (Ak 4, p. 412).
40. Kant, *Practical Philosophy*, p. 46 (Ak 4, p. 390).
41. Ibid.
42. This cannot be overemphasized, given the contemporary tendency (one that is almost universal) to treat Kant's *Foundations* as being about the everyday situations of ordinary moral agents.
43. Kant, *Practical Philosophy*, p. 72 (Ak 4, p. 420).
44. Kant, *Practical Philosophy*, p. 108 (Ak 4, p. 463).
45. Kant, *Practical Philosophy*, p. 73 (Ak 4, p. 421). He also formulates it as follows: "act as if the maxim of your action were to become a universal law of nature." Kant, *Practical Philosophy*, p. 73 (Ak 4, p. 421).
46. Kant, *Practical Philosophy*, pp. 80, 83 (Ak 4, pp. 429, 433). Since Kant does not clearly identify the third version, there may be some dispute about this.
47. Kant, *Practical Philosophy*, p. 87 (Ak 4, p. 438).
48. Kant, *Practical Philosophy*, p. 89 (Ak 4, p. 440).
49. Kant, *Practical Philosophy*, p. 94 (Ak 4, p. 446).
50. Kant, *Practical Philosophy*, p. 96 (Ak 4, p. 448).
51. Kant, *Practical Philosophy*, p. 96 (Ak 4, p. 449).
52. Kant, *Practical Philosophy*, pp. 96f. (Ak 4, p. 449). This description of the circle is somewhat different from Kant's own, but I do not think it is incompatible with what he says. The entire problem is difficult, and this short summary should not be taken as an attempt to solve it. For a good discussion of the problem see Henry E. Allison, "The Reciprocity Thesis," in *Kant's Theory of Freedom*, pp. 201–230.
53. Kant, *Practical Philosophy*, p. 98 (Ak 4, p. 451).
54. Kant, *Practical Philosophy*, p. 77 (Ak 3, p. 425).

55. Hamann, *Briefwechsel*, V, p. 222; see also p. 238 (October 18, 1784), where he says that "Kant has until now worked hard for the *Berlinische Monatsschriften.*"

56. Ak 8, pp. 15–31. I shall quote from Kant, *Political Writings*, ed. Reiss, pp. 41–53.

57. Kant, *Political Writings*, ed. Reiss, pp. 52f.

58. Kant, *Political Writings*, ed. Reiss, p. 41.

59. Kant, *Political Writings*, ed. Reiss, p. 43.

60. Kant, *Political Writings*, ed. Reiss, p. 45.

61. Kant, *Political Writings*, ed. Reiss, p. 46 (but I use the translation from Kant, *Political Writings*, pp. 17f.).

62. Kant, *Political Writings*, ed. Reiss, p. 47.

63. Kant, *Political Writings*, ed. Reiss, p. 53.

64. Norbert Hinske (ed.), *Was ist Aufklärung: Beiträge Aus Der Berlinischen Monatsschrift*, 4th ed. (Darmstadt: Wissenschaftliche Buchgesellschaft, 1981), p. 115. Hinske's Introduction and postscripts are indispensable for anyone who wants to better understand Kant and the context in which he answers the question. See also *What Is Enlightenment? Eighteenth-Century Answers and Twentieth-Century Questions*, ed. James Schmidt (Berkeley: University of California Press, 1996).

65. Kant, *Practical Philosophy*, p. 22 (Ak 8, pp. 41f.).

66. Kant, *Practical Philosophy*, p. 21 (Ak 8, p. 41).

67. Ibid.

68. The motto comes from Horace, one of Kant's favorite Latin poets.

69. Kant, *Practical Philosophy*, p. 18 (Ak 8, p. 36).

70. There was no separation of state and church in Prussia. Much has been written about the distinction between private and public use of reason, and Kant has often been accused of being a reactionary in this regard. But this is a mistake; see, for instance, Hinske, "Introduction," in *Was Ist Aufklärung*, and John Christian Laursen, "'The Subversive Kant: The Vocabulary of 'Public' and 'Publicity,'" *Political Theory* 14 (1986), pp. 584–603.

71. Kant, *Practical Philosophy*, p. 20 (Ak 8, p. 39).

72. Ak 10, pp. 393f.

73. Hamann, *Briefwechsel*, V, p. 175. In this letter, dated August 6, 1784, Hamann tells Herder that he has begun reading the *Ideas* for the second time, but that he had been interrupted because he had to show it (*mitgetheilt*) to all his friends – "Kant and Fischer first, and then . . . Scheffner." He also tells him that their judgment, like his own, was not entirely positive. Herder has not written with "the maturity, calmness, and humanity, which such a subject requires," but he also tells him that only he, Herder, could be expected ultimately to succeed in dealing with this topic.

74. Ak 10, p. 396.

75. Beck, *Historical Writings*, p. 27.

76. Beck, *Historical Writings*, p. 36.

77. Beck, *Historical Writings*, p. 35.

78. Beck, *Historical Writings*, p. 39.

79. Herder, *Sämtliche Werke* (Cotta, 1830), III, p. 123; see also Vorländer, *Immanuel Kant*, I, p. 316.

80. Hamann, *Briefwechsel*, V, p. 347 (February 3, 1785).

81. Ak 8, p. 74.
82. Ak 10, p. 397.
83. Hamann, *Briefwechsel*, V, pp. 362f.
84. Hamann, *Briefwechsel*, V, p. 418.
85. Hamann, *Briefwechsel*, V, p. 432.
86. Beck, *Historical Writings*, p. 40.
87. Beck, *Historical Writings*, p. 41.
88. Beck, *Historical Writings*, p. 42.
89. Ak 10, p. 421; see also pp. 406f., 408.
90. Beck, *Historical Writings*, p. 43.
91. Beck, *Historical Writings*, p. 45.
92. Beck, *Historical Writings*, p. 47.
93. Beck, *Historical Writings*, p. 51. The second principle Kant defended was also one that he had adopted and that had figured centrally in his "What Is Enlightenment?" It consisted in the claim that the human species needs education just as much as the human individual. This principle is, of course, not just Kant's. Lessing's "Education of the Human Race," and indeed much of Enlightenment pedagogy, depended on it as well.
94. Hamann, *Briefwechsel*, VI, pp. 212f.
95. See also Hamann, *Briefwechsel*, VI, p. 140.
96. Ak 8, p. 100.
97. Herder, *Ideas* in *Sämmtliche Werke*, ed. Suphan, XIII, p. 258.
98. Clearly, such a difference cannot justify an institution like slavery for Kant.
99. For a discussion of the views of Herder and Kant as well as their historical background, see Eric Voegelin, *The History of the Race Idea: From Ray to Carus*, tr. Ruth Hein, ed. Klaus Vondung (Baton Rouge: Louisiana State University Press, 1998).
100. Ak 8, pp. 107–127.
101. Kant, *Political Writings*, ed. Reiss, p. 221.
102. Kant, *Political Writings*, ed. Reiss, p. 222.
103. Kant, *Political Writings*, ed. Reiss, pp. 223f.
104. Kant, *Political Writings*, ed. Reiss, pp. 225f.
105. Kant, *Political Writings*, ed. Reiss, p. 227.
106. Kant, *Political Writings*, ed. Reiss, p. 231.
107. Kant, *Political Writings*, ed. Reiss, p. 231.
108. Kant, *Political Writings*, ed. Reiss, p. 233.
109. Herder, *Werke*, ed. Suphan, XIII, p. 339.
110. Kant, *Political Writings*, ed. Reiss, p. 234.
111. Hamann, *Briefwechsel*, V, p. 290.
112. Lessing to Nicolai on August 25, 1769; I quote after Epstein, *The Genesis of German Conservatism*, p. 350.
113. Hamann, *Briefwechsel*, V, p. 402.
114. Ak 10, p. 406.
115. Ibid.
116. Kant, *Metaphysical Foundations of Natural Science*, tr. James Ellington (Indianapolis: Bobbs-Merrill, 1970), p. 8 (Ak 4, p. 471).

117. Kant, *Metaphysical Foundations*, pp. 4f. (Ak 4, pp. 468f.).
118. Kant, *Metaphysical Foundations*, p. 12 (Ak 4, p. 476).
119. Kant, *Metaphysical Foundations*, p. 16 (Ak 4, p. 478).
120. Kant, *Metaphysical Foundations*, p. 28 (Ak 4, p. 487).
121. Kant, *Metaphysical Foundations*, p. 18 (Ak 4, p. 480). The distinction between relative and absolute space is interesting, if only because it seems to be central to what Kant is trying to do in this book, namely trying to find a middle ground between Leibniz, who held a relationalist view of space, and Newton, who viewed space as absolute. See Friedman, *Kant and the Exact Sciences*, pp. 136f.
122. Kant, *Metaphysical Foundations*, p. 40 (Ak 4, p. 496).
123. Kant, *Metaphysical Foundations*, p. 41 (Ak 4, p. 497).
124. See especially Observation 2 (Kant, *Metaphysical Foundations*, p. 48; Ak 4, pp. 501f.).
125. Kant, *Metaphysical Foundations*, p. 77 (Ak 4, p. 523).
126. This is tricky. The two opposed camps within seventeenth- and eighteenth-century mechanical philosophy were the corpuscularians (Descartes, etc.) and the atomists (Gassendi, Newton). The corpuscularians insisted that matter was infinitely divisible; the atomists denied this. Yet, both parties maintained that matter is impentrable. They disagreed about whether matter (atoms) is absolutely hard. So the concepts of "hardness" and "impenetrability" are not necessarily identical.
127. See Friedman, *Kant and the Exact Sciences*, pp. 138f., but it may not be Leibniz whom Kant has in mind here.
128. Kant, *Metaphysical Foundations*, p. 95 (Ak 4, p. 536).
129. See Immanuel Kant, *Metaphysische Anfangsgründe der Naturwissenschaft*, ed. Konstantin Pollok (Hamburg: Meiner, 1997), pp. 145f. I am deeply indebted to Martin Curd and Konstantin Pollok for their help with this account of the *Metaphysical Foundations*.
130. Kant, *Metaphysical Foundations*, p. 118 (Ak 4, p. 554).
131. Kant, *Metaphysical Foundations*, p. 126 (Ak 4, p. 559).
132. In the *Allgemeine Literatur-Zeitung* of August 29, 1789. See Konstantin Pollok's very helpful "Introduction" to Kant, *Metaphysische Anfangsgründe der Naturwissenschaft*, ed. Pollok, p. xxiii.
133. Ak 12, p. 23.
134. He must have written at least parts of the Preface during the winter of 1785. For the dating, see Pollok, "Introduction," p. xxi. Kant eventually returned to work on the problems of natural philosophy in his so-called *Opus postumum*. See pp. 409–413 of this volume.
135. The ensuing dispute was the so-called Pantheism Controversy. For more extensive English accounts, see Frederick Beiser, *The Fate of Reason: German Philosophy from Kant to Fichte* (Cambridge: Harvard University Press, 1987), pp. 92–126; Beck, *Early German Philosophy*, pp. 352–360; Altmann, *Mendelssohn*, pp. 553–712.
136. Friedrich Heinrich Jacobi, *Werke*, ed. Friedrich Roth and Friedrich Köppen (Darmstadt: Wissenschaftliche Buchgesellschaft, 1976; reprint of the edition Leipzig, 1812–1820), IV, pp. 121f.
137. See Ak 10, pp. 417f., 433, 453–458.

138. Ak 10, p. 442.
139. Kant, *Political Writings*, ed. Reiss, pp. 237f.
140. Kant, *Political Writings*, ed. Reiss, p. 240.
141. Kant, *Political Writings*, ed. Reiss, p. 242.
142. Ibid.
143. Kant, *Political Writings*, ed. Reiss, p. 244.
144. Kant, *Political Writings*, ed. Reiss, p. 248f.
145. For a more extensive discussion of this aspect, see Charles Taylor, "Aims of a New Epoch," Chapter 1 of his *Hegel* (Cambridge: Cambridge University Press, 1975), pp. 3–50.
146. See Ak 10, pp. 435–438, 450f., 458–462, 467f.
147. See Ak 10, pp. 467f. The Preface is dated August 4. Hamann reported on August 11 that Kant had received the proofs of part of Jakob's book, and that he had written the Preface. He was well informed about the contents. See Hamann, *Briefwechsel*, VII, pp. 44f.
148. Ak 8, p. 153.
149. Ak 8, p. 154.
150. Kant, *Practical Philosophy*, pp. 109–118 (Ak 8, pp. 125–130).
151. Ak 10, pp. 412f., 422.
152. Kant, *Practical Philosophy*, p. 115 (Ak 8, p. 128).
153. Kant, *Practical Philosophy*, p. 117 (Ak 8, p. 129). Kant, *Practical Philosophy*, has mistakenly "appropriate" for "*unschicklich.*"
154. Ak 10, p. 441.
155. Hamann, *Briefwechsel*, VII, pp. 104f.
156. Hamann, *Briefwechsel*, VII, p. 149.
157. Jachmann, *Kant*, p. 171. Jachmann said the two men were friends.
158. Ak 10, p. 490.
159. Ak 10, p. 514; for a discussion of all who were meant, see Karl Vorländer, in "Introduction," in Immanuel Kant, *Kritik der reinen Vernunft* (Leipzig: Meiner, 1951), pp. xvi–xx. He mentions Flatt, Tittel, Pistorius, Selle, and Meiners in addition to Feder, Abel, and Wizenmann (who is the only critic whom Kant mentions by name).
160. For more on this, see Kuehn, *Scottish Common Sense in German*, pp. 214f., and Beiser, *The Fate of Reason*, pp. 181f.
161. Ak 10, p. 490.
162. Ibid.
163. Compare with Mary Gregor, "Introduction," in Immanuel Kant, *The Metaphysics of Morals*, introduction, translation, and notes by Mary Gregor (Cambridge: Cambridge University Press, 1991), p. 1
164. Kant, *Practical Philosophy*, p. 178 (Ak 5, p. 47).
165. Kant, *Practical Philosophy*, p. 269 (Ak 5, p. 162).
166. Kant, *Practical Philosophy*, p. 255 (Ak 5, p. 143).
167. Ak 12, pp. 451; see also Dietzsch, "Kant, die Juden und das akademische Bürgerrecht," pp. 124f., and Richarz, *Der Eintritt der Juden in die akademische Berufe*, pp. 56f. Richarz claims that at least eight Jewish students of medicine can be called "Kant's students in the narrow sense of the term." Euchel was probably,

besides Herz, the most important. He also had a great effect on the Jewish community in Königsberg, founding a Society of Hebraic friends of Literature in 1782, which published beginning in 1784 the journal *Ha Measef* (The Collector).

168. Hamann, *Briefwechsel*, VII, pp. 47, 59f.

169. Euler and Stiening, "'. . . und nie der Pluralität widersprach'?", pp. 59f. This was by no means the only trouble that the deanship carried with it. Kant also had to examine whether those who wanted to enter the university were ready for it. In 1786 he failed two students. See Ak 10, pp. 439–440.

170. Rink, *Ansichten*, pp. 48f. Rink claims that this was the only time he was rector. This is false, for in 1788 he held that office again. (Even though the normal turnus took five years, there were often exception because someone among the seniors died.)

171. Vorländer, *Kant*, II, pp. 40f. Vorländer's description of this matter is not entirely correct. See Euler, "Kant's Amtstätigkeit," pp. 61, 64f.

172. Euler, "Kant's Amtstätigkeit," pp. 65f., does a good job of sorting this out. Since it is not necessary to know all the details, I will not report them here.

173. Ak 10, pp. 434, 435; Ak 13, pp. 166–168.

174. Hamann, *Briefwechsel*, VI, p. 330.

175. Rink, *Ansichten*, pp. 49f.

176. Euler, "Kant's Amtstätigkeit," pp. 67f. See also Ak 13, p. 589, and Borowski, *Leben*, p. 44; and see Hamann, *Briefwechsel*, VII, p. 15: "Our deserving (*verdienter*) critic was received with special honors by the Minister Herzberg as well as by the king, who, it is said, has decided to give him a place in the academy."

177. Euler and Stiening, "'. . . und nie der Pluralität widersprach'?", p. 61.

178. Hamann, *Briefwechsel*, VI, pp. 38f.

179. Malter, *Kant in Rede und Gespräch*, p. 299.

180. Rink, *Ansichten*, pp. 47f. See also Baczko, *Geschichte meines Lebens*, II, pp. 137f. He claims, obviously relying at least to some extent on Rink, that he found these administrative duties "bothersome (*lästig*)" and that he never "contradicted the plurality."

181. See Malter, *Rede und Gespräch*, p. 395; he actually said this of both Kant and Kraus.

182. The extent and importance of Kant's administrative work has not been thoroughly investigated yet. There are beginnings of such investigations, however. See Euler and Stiening "'. . . und nie der Pluralität widersprach'?"; see also Werner Euler, "Immanuel Kants Amtstätigkeit. Aufgaben und Probleme einer Gesamtdokumentation," in *Autographen, Dokumente und Berichte*, ed. Brandt and Stark, pp. 58–90, and Werner Stark, "Kants Amtstätigkeit," *Kant-Studien* 85 (1994), pp. 470–472.

183. See pp. 314–315, this volume, for instance.

184. Rink, *Ansichten*, p. 60. Rink also reports that Kant sent all of this yearly bonus to the family of his brother after he died in 1799 and left his family without support.

185. Rink, *Ansichten*, p. 60.

186. Rink, *Ansichten*, pp. 40–43 (Malter, *Kant in Rede und Gespräch*, pp. 289f.). Malter thinks that the person Rink has in mind was Metzger. This is doubtful. It must

have been a former student of Kant's, and that makes it likely that it was either Kraus or Borowski.

187. Rink, *Ansichten*, p. 148.

188. Hamann, *Briefwechsel*, VI, p. 380.

189. Jachmann, *Kant*, p. 143.

190. Jachmann, *Kant*, p. 144.

191. Rink, *Ansichten*, p. 50 (Malter, *Kant in Rede und Gespräch*, p. 290).

192. Hamann, *Briefwechsel*, VI, p. 376, p. 472: "Kant complained yesterday in bitter desperation that he could not get his *sphincter* to open."

193. Reusch, *Kant und seine Tischgenossen*, p. 290.

194. Malter, *Kant in Rede und Gespräch*, p. 341.

195. Ak 10, p. 430; Hamann *Briefwechsel*, VI, p. 302 (Malter, *Kant in Rede und Gespräch*, p. 291).

196. Malter, *Kant in Rede und Gespräch*, p. 307.

197. A second edition of the former appeared as early as 1788.

198. Vorländer, *Kant*, pp. 150f. This order was rescinded at the end of 1787.

199. Christoph Meiners, *Grundriss der Seelenlehre*, Preface. In his *Outline of the History of Philosophy* of the same year, he continued to criticize Kant in a book called *Grundriss der Geschichte der Weltweisheit*.

200. Ak 10, pp. 430f.

201. Hamann, *Briefwechsel*, VI, p. 349.

202. Hamann, *Briefwechsel*, VI, p. 349; see also p. 401.

203. Anthony Quinton, "The Trouble with Kant," *Philosophy* 72 (1997), pp. 5–18.

204. Quinton "The Trouble with Kant," p. 18.

205. Hamann, *Briefwechsel*, VI, p. 350.

206. Hamann, *Briefwechsel*, VII, p. 46.

207. Hamann, *Briefwechsel*, VI, p. 353. Hamann wrote: "he could not read it because it was too psychological," and then goes on to say that Herz was "his best student and respondent," but that Kant had complained "pretty loudly" about misunderstandings of his philosophy that he had perpetrated in the *Betrachtungen* of 1771.

208. Borowski, *Leben*, p. 88 (Malter, *Kant in Rede und Gespräch*, p. 292).

209. See Davies, *Identity and History*, pp. 32f., for a discussion of Kant's and Herz's relationship.

210. Jachmann, *Kant*, p. 165 (Malter, *Kant in Rede und Gespräch*, p. 329).

211. Voigt, *Kraus*, pp. 175f. Stark, "Kant und Kraus," should be consulted in reading this part of Voigt because he has identified and published one of Voigt's sources (see especially pp. 182–191).

212. Kant had been asked by the *Allgemeine Literatur-Zeitung* to write a review (Ak 10, p. 470). He obviously got Kraus to do it instead. See Stark, "Kant und Kraus," pp. 170f.

213. Voigt, *Kraus*, p. 177.

214. Voigt, *Kraus*, p. 178. As Kraus was finishing the review, Kant was writing the Preface to the second edition of the *Critique of Pure Reason*. See Hamann, *Briefwechsel*, VII, p. 123 (see also p. 122).

215. Hamann, *Briefwechsel*, VII, p. 184.

216. See Stark, "Kant and Kraus," p. 179.

217. Kant, *Metaphysical Foundations of Natural Science*, p. 11n (Ak 4, p. 474n). The footnote must have been added either in December of 1785 or early in 1786.
218. Hamann, *Briefwechsel*, VI, p. 349; see also p. 338.
219. Rink, *Ansichten*, p. 82.
220. The literature is vague on the date of Green's death (1786 or 1787). I am grateful to Dr. Lindemann-Stark for information about the exact date (based on *Altpreussische Biographie*, I, p. 229).
221. Hamann to Jacobi on May 26, 1786; see Hamann, *Briefwechsel*, VI, p. 401.
222. Jachmann, *Kant*, p. 163. Jachmann should have known, because both he and his brother had also been friends of Green.
223. Hamann, *Briefwechsel*, VII, pp. 104f., wrote on January 30, 1787: "I ate at Jacobi's together with Kant, who intends to prepare his own household, and his head is full with this. *Crispus* [Kraus] is to be his companion . . ."
224. Hamann, *Briefwechsel*, VII, p. 148.
225. Hamann, *Briefwechsel*, VII, p. 198.
226. See Voigt, *Kraus*, pp. 264f.
227. Jachmann, *Kant*, p. 186, said that these were the people who came to Kant's dinners "until 1794." I have left out Kraus, whom he also mentioned, since he did not come after 1790, and because he was not really a guest before then.
228. Reusch, *Tischfreunde*, p. 11.
229. Voigt, *Kraus*, p. 198.
230. Abegg, *Reisegeschichte*, pp. 255f. (Malter, *Kant in Rede und Gespräch*, p. 318); see also Jachmann, *Kant*, p. 163 (Malter, *Kant in Rede und Gespräch*, p. 319).
231. Jachmann, *Kant*, pp. 163f. (Malter, *Kant in Rede und Gespräch*, p. 319).
232. Brahl in Malter, *Kant in Rede und Gespräch*, p. 319. For more on this, see pp. 331–334 of this volume.
233. Hasse, *Kant's Tischgenossen*, pp. 6f.
234. Abegg, *Reisetagebuch*, pp. 255f. (see Malter, *Kant in Rede und Gespräch*, p. 318).
235. For a discussion of Reid's influence on Jacobi, see Kuehn, *Scottish Common Sense*, pp. 141–162.
236. Jacobi, *Werke*, II, pp. 299–304.
237. Jacobi, *Werke*, II, pp. 303f.
238. Jacobi, *Werke*, II, p. 308: "The very word 'sensibility' does not make sense, if we do not mean a distinct and real medium between two realities, and if the conceptions of externality and connection, of active and passive, of causality and dependency are not already contained as real and objective determinations in it; and contained in it in such a way that the absolute universality and necessity of these conceptions as prior presuppositions is given at the very same time."
239. Jacobi, *Werke*, II, p. 309.
240. Jacobi, *Werke*, II, p. 304. Herder later followed Hamann and Jacobi's lead, saying that Kant created too many artificial distinctions. In his *Vernunft und Sprache. Eine Metakritik zur Kritik der reinen Vernunft* of 1799, he characterized Kant's philosophy as a "splitting" (*zerspaltende*) one, as a "*philosophia schismatica*." Wherever Kant looks, antinomies and splits arise; dichotomies are the work of critical philosophy.
241. For a short summary, see Beiser, *The Fate of Reason*, pp. 159–164. Beiser does,

however, unfairly criticize Herder for not responding to Kant's essay "On the Use of Teleological Principles in Philosophy." Since the essay was written after the appearance of his *God* and published only at the beginning of 1788, he did not know it.

Chapter 8: Problems with Religion and Politics (1788–1795)

1. Jachmann, *Leben*, p. 130.
2. Stark, "Kant und Kraus," pp. 179f. See also pp. 267–269, this volume.
3. Kant, *Practical Philosophy*, p. 128.
4. Ibid.
5. Kant, *Practical Philosophy*, p. 130.
6. Kant, *Practical Philosophy*, p. 131. For some notes by Kant, see Ak 23, pp. 79–81.
7. Quoted after Stark, "Kant und Kraus," p. 174.
8. Quoted after Stark, "Kant und Kraus," p. 175.
9. Quoted after Stark, "Kant und Kraus," p. 177.
10. Stark, "Kant und Kraus," p. 190.
11. It is the author of the notes who speaks of a "union into which they had entered with this ring, namely to live only for each other." Whether or not something like this existed in the heads of Kraus and Kant is far from clear. Similarly, there seems no reason to doubt that Kant gave Kraus a ring, but what this meant apart from being a sign of Kant's gratefulness to Kraus is open to speculation. I am inclined to think that it meant no more than that.
12. Voigt, *Kraus*, p. 202.
13. Brahl in Malter, *Kant in Rede und Gespräch*, p. 319.
14. Brahl in Malter, *Kant in Rede und Gespräch*, p. 318.
15. The witness is Brahl. Kant had a standing invitation with the Keyserlingks on Tuesday. Kraus had to eat alone on Tuesdays anyway (see Hamann, *Briefwechsel*, VII, p. 164). So what Brahl observed must have taken place when Kant no longer attended the Keyserlingks' dinners. The countess died on August 15, 1791. Her husband had died in 1787. But, as the following section shows, Kant still attended her dinner parties after her husband died. It is not unlikely, though, that Kant no longer came or that she stopped giving the dinners in early 1789.
16. Voigt, *Kraus*, p. 132.
17. Voigt, *Kraus*, p. 271.
18. This is false. The agreement was to share the expenses.
19. Hamann, *Briefwechsel*, IV, p. 78. On the other hand, Hamann said about Kant in 1780 that "he cannot appreciate any hero from this race (*Volk*)." This was about Lessing's "Nathan the Wise," which was among other things a tribute to Mendelssohn. These remarks are contradicted by an account about what took place shortly after Mendelssohn's death; see pp. 319–320, this volume.
20. Borowski, *Leben*, p. 69 (Malter, *Kant in Rede und Gespräch*, p. 318).
21. Ak 6, p. 428 (*Practical Philosophy*, pp. 552f.).
22. Hamann, *Briefwechsel*, VII, p. 164 (Malter, *Kant in Rede und Gespräch*, p. 321). At least at this time. Before he had his own household, i. e., before the middle April 1787, he attended these dinner parties even more often.

23. A certain J. L. Schwarz reports that there were daily about twelve scholars or "other interesting people," who had a perpetual invitation, "and I was lucky enough to sit four times right across from Kant during my five day stay there" (Malter, *Kant in Rede und Gespräch*, p. 314). This was in February or March 1787.
24. Schwarz in Malter, *Kant in Rede und Gespräch*, p. 314, and Elise von der Recke in Malter, *Kant in Rede und Gespräch*, p. 248. She also claims that she saw Kant almost daily at the Keyserlingks (around 1784).
25. Malter, *Kant in Rede und Gespräch*, p. 248.
26. For a discussion of Kant's conception of wit and his wit, see Wolfgang Ritzel, "Kant über den Witz und Kants Witz," *Kant-Studien* (1991), pp. 102–109. Though Ritzel is inclined to overstate the difference between "wit" in the eighteenth century and today, it is a good introduction to the topic.
27. Schwarz in Malter, *Kant in Rede und Gespräch*, p. 314.
28. This is a translation of the entire scene. Though Kant plays a relatively minor role in it and exhibits none of his wit or command of conversation, it does throw an interesting light on this part of his environment.
29. Hippel, *Werke*, I, pp. 294–297 (Malter, *Kant in Rede und Gespräch*, p. 340).
30. Epstein, *The Origin of German Conservatism*, p. 352.
31. See P. Bailleu, "Woellner, Johann Christof," in *Allgemeine deutsche Biographie*, pp. 148–159, pp. 151f. See also Christopher McIntosh, *The Rose Cross and the Age of Reason: Eighteenth-Century Rosicrucianism in Central Europe and Its Relationship to the Enlightenment* (Leiden: E. J. Brill, 1992), and Hans Möller, "Die Bruderschaft der Gold- und Rosenkreuzer," in *Freimaurer und Geheimbünde im 18. Jahrhundert in Mitteleuropa*, ed. Helmut Reinalter (Frankfurt: Suhrkamp, 1983), pp. 199–239, especially pp. 218–222; and Michael W. Fischer, *Die Aufklärung und ihr Gegenteil. Die Rolle der Geheimbünde in Wissenschaft und Politik* (Berlin: Duncker & Humblot, 1982), pp. 144–169, 242–255. Manfred Agethen, *Geheimbund und Utopie. Illuminaten, Freimaurer und deutsche Spätaufklärung* (München: R. Oldenbourg Verlag, 1987), deals with a group of Freemasons, on the whole opposed to the Rosicrucians. But when it was disbanded, many of its members ended up as Rosicrucians.
32. Quoted after Epstein, *The Genesis of German Conservatism*, p. 143
33. The sister of Stark's wife was Kraus's aunt. For this reason Kraus would not take a public position against him. But he did not think highly of him, saying in confidence: "der Mann taugt nichts" (Voigt, *Kraus*, p. 245).
34. See pp. 224–226 of this volume. Lady von Recke did publish a book against him in 1788.
35. François Furet, *The French Revolution, 1770–1814*, tr. Antonia Nevill (Oxford: Blackwell, 1988), p. 68.
36. Furet, *The French Revolution*, p. 74.
37. Malter, *Kant in Rede und Gespräch*, p. 348.
38. Quoted after Epstein, *The Genesis of German Conservatism*, p. 436.
39. Michael Hughes, *Early Modern Germany, 1477–1806* (Philadelphia: University of Philadelphia Press, 1992), p. 173. But see especially Epstein, *The Genesis of German Conservatism*, pp. 434–538, "The Challenge of the French Revolution" and "The Conspiracy Theory of the Revolution." These two chapters are a must

for anyone wishing to understand the background of Kant's views on the French Revolution.

40. Metzger, *Äußerungen über Kant*, pp. 14f. (Malter, *Kant in Rede und Gespräch*, p. 351); compare Borowski, *Leben*, p. 77; he also noted that Kant spoke his mind without concern about the rank or status of those to whom he was speaking.

41. Borowski, *Leben*, p. 81 (Malter, *Kant in Rede und Gespräch*, p. 349).

42. Borowski, *Leben*, p. 77.

43. Anonymous; see Malter, *Kant in Rede und Gespräch*, pp. 351f.

44. Jachmann, *Kant*, p. 179 (Malter, *Kant in Rede und Gespräch*, pp. 349f.). Jachmann was interested in downplaying Kant's enthusiasm for the French Revolution, which is otherwise very well documented.

45. Abegg, *Reisetagebuch*, p. 148; see also Vorländer, *Immanuel Kant*, II, p. 222.

46. Vorländer, *Immanuel Kant*, II, p. 222.

47. Voigt, *Kraus*, p. 311; see also p. 408; Kraus could not have thought very highly of Schulz as a mathematician (see Voigt, *Kraus*, p. 398).

48. Ak 10, p. 490 (June 25, 1787). The book was already listed in the catalogue of the Leipzig book fair of 1787 under the same title (see Ak 10, p. 488).

49. Ak 10, pp. 497–500.

50. Ak 8, p. 183.

51. Ak 8, p. 174 and 174n.

52. Ak 8, p. 184.

53. John H. Zammito, *The Genesis of Kant's Critique of Judgment* (Chicago: University of Chicago Press, 1992), pp. 7f.

54. Zammito, *The Genesis of Kant's Critique of Judgment*, p. 7.

55. Zammito, *The Genesis of Kant's Critique of Judgment*, pp. 9f.

56. Ak 1, p. 222.

57. Zammito, *The Genesis of Kant's Critique of Judgment*, p. 47 (Ak 10, p. 514).

58. For some of the background, see Kant's notes to *Eberhard's Vorbereitung zur natürlichen Theologie*, dated by Adickes to the period 1783–86, Ak 18, pp. 489–606, especially pp. 566f. Zammito's identification of the different layers of Kant's third *Critique* remains nothing but conjecture. Of course, Kant had had the three concerns Zammito identifies, but they were concerns that he had at least since the inception of the critical problem. Though Zammito is right in identifying three different and apparently quite unrelated concerns within the text of the third *Critique*, it is a mistake to think that these three concerns can be relegated to different stages in Kant's development.

59. For a systematic discussion of the issues, see Paul Guyer, *Kant and the Claims of Taste* (Harvard: Harvard University Press, 1979).

60. Ak 5, p. 236. All translations should be considered as my own. Even though I have heavily leaned on Meredith's translation, there are many significant departures from it. See Immanuel Kant, *Critique of Judgment*, tr. J. C. Meredith (Oxford: Clarendon Press, 1952). Since this edition gives the page numbers of the Academy edition in the margin, the references can easily be verified.

61. Ak 5, p. 240.

62. Ak 5, p. 238.

63. Ak 5, p. 248.

64. Ak 5, p. 247.
65. Ak 5, p. 267.
66. Ak 5, p. 268.
67. Ak 5, p. 274.
68. Ak 5, p. 280.
69. Ak 5, p. 285.
70. Ak 5, p. 290.
71. Ak 5, pp. 338f.
72. Ak 5, p. 340.
73. Ak 5, p. 354.
74. Ak 5, p. 279.
75. Ak 5, p. 387.
76. Ak 5, p. 394.
77. Ak 5, p. 395.
78. Ak 5, p. 417.
79. Ak 5, p. 433.
80. Ak 5, p. 436.
81. Ak 5, p. 442.
82. Ak 5, p. 450.
83. Ak 11, pp. 95, 106; see also pp. 121, 122f.
84. Ak 11, pp. 121, 129f., 136, 140f., 141, 142f., 193, 383.
85. See *Between Kant and Hegel: Texts in the Development of Post-Kantian Idealism*, tr. and ed. George di Giovanni and H. S. Harris (Albany: State University of New York Press, 1985), pp. 104–135. The volume also has a helpful Introduction.
86. di Giovanni and Harris, *Between Kant and Hegel*, p. 61.
87. Reinhold, "Allgemeiner Gesichtspunkt einer bevorstehenden Reformation der Philosophie," *Der Teutsche Merkur* (June 1789), pp. 243–274, pp. 251–252n.
88. di Giovanni and Harris, *Between Kant and Hegel*, p. 61–2.
89. di Giovanni and Harris, *Between Kant and Hegel*, p. 26.
90. *Über die menschliche Natur, aus dem Englischen, nebst kritischen Versuchen zur Beurtheilung dieses Werks* (On Human Nature, from the English, with Critical Essays for Judging This Work) (Halle: Hemmerde and Schwetschke, 1790–92). This is most significant, as this first translation is rather peculiar. It was never meant primarily as an accurate source for Humean philosophy, but was designed to present an object for criticism. Nor was it a translation of the *Treatise*, because Jakob left out the passages rewritten for the *Enquiry* and included instead the version found in the *Enquiry*.
91. It was published with J. J. Gebauer in Halle.
92. See Ak 11, pp. 17f., 59–73, 88f., 111f. See Henry Allison, *The Kant-Eberhard Controversy* (Baltimore: Johns Hopkins University Press, 1973), pp. 1–21, for a discussion of the details of this affair.
93. Ak 8, p. 198.
94. Ak 8, p. 235.
95. Ak 8, p. 249.
96. Ak 8, p. 250.
97. Malter, *Kant in Rede und Gespräch*, p. 387.

98. J. G. Fichte, *Gesamtausgabe*, III.1, ed. R. Lauth, H. Jacob, and M. Zahn (Stuttgart/ Bad Canstatt: F. Frommann, 1962), p. 168.

99. See Aschoff, "Zwischen äußerem Zwang und innerer Freiheit," p. 43.

100. This is Fichte's own account. I quote from Malter, *Kant in Rede und Gespräch*, pp. 372f.

101. Malter, *Kant in Rede und Gespräch*, p. 371.

102. Malter, *Kant in Rede und Gespräch*, p. 376.

103. Malter, *Kant in Rede und Gespräch*, p. 377. The dean of the theological faculty at Halle, who had to censor the book, did not give permission for printing.

104. Malter, *Kant in Rede und Gespräch*, p. 375.

105. He visited Kant in the summer of 1794 with letters of introduction from Blumenbach, Kästner, Heyne, and Werner.

106. Malter, *Kant in Rede und Gespräch*, p. 414.

107. Karl Hügelmann, "Ein Brief über Kant. Mitgeteilt von Karl Hügelmann," *Altpreussische Monatsschrift* 16 (1879), pp. 607–612, pp. 608f.

108. Hügelmann, "Ein Brief über Kant," p. 610. Another, more famous, visitor to Kant was Karamsin, the Russian writer, who visited Kant in June 1789. He found, among other things: "He lives in a small shabby (*unansehnlich*) house; and, all in all, everything about him is ordinary, except his metaphysics" (Malter, *Kant in Rede und Gespräch*, p. 348).

109. Hügelmann, "Ein Brief über Kant," p. 611.

110. Reusch, *Kant und seine Tischgenossen*, p. 6 (Malter, *Kant in Rede und Gespräch*, p. 401).

111. Ibid.

112. Malter, *Kant in Rede und Gespräch*, p. 398.

113. Arnoldt, "Möglichst vollständiges Verzeichnis," pp. 301f.

114. Arnoldt, "Möglichst vollständiges Verzeichnis," p. 303. Pörschke also lectured on the *Critique* during the following semester, and in the summer of 1795.

115. Ak 11, p. 288; Arnoldt, "Möglichst vollständiges Verzeichnis," pp. 305–312.

116. But this does not mean that the influence of Kantian philosophy per se diminished. Pörschke lectured several times on the first *Critique*, and Schulz gave a course on natural theology on the basis of the *Religion within the Limits of Mere Reason* in the summer semester of 1795, and in the winter semester 1795–96.

117. Voigt, *Kraus*, p. 376; see also Pörschke in Malter, *Kant in Rede und Gespräch*, p. 442 (letter to Fichte, 1798). Freiherr von Stein's close collaborator, Schroetter decreed in 1800 that "no one would henceforth be permitted to enter East Prussian administrative service without a certificate of having attended Kraus's lectures." See Epstein, *The Origins of German Conservatism*, p. 181.

118. Voigt, *Kraus*, p. 154. Kraus also assumed that Kant wrote so much in his later years because he "no longer attended social events in the evening, yet wanted to rid himself of his thoughts" (Voigt, *Kraus*, p. 154). Kraus was at this time no longer close to Kant and did not know of his "weakness."

119. Jachmann, *Leben*, p. 156 (Malter, *Kant in Rede und Gepräch*, p. 330).

120. Ak 11, pp. 107, 254, for instance. See also Malter, *Kant in Rede und Gepräch*, p. 342.

121. Ak 11, pp. 48f.

122. Maimon, *Autobiography*, p. 144.

123. Maimon, *Autobiography*, pp. 145f.
124. Malter, *Kant in Rede und Gespräch*, p. 372.
125. Malter, *Kant in Rede und Gespräch*, p. 380. The incident led to official proceedings against the student, which went all the way to the king in Berlin. He was to be incarcerated for fourteen days. But after Kant and other professors attested to his otherwise good character, the punishment was reduced to a fine, which ultimately he did not have to pay.
126. Maimon, *Autobiography*, p. 145.
127. Kant, *Religion and Rational Theology*, p. 30 (Ak 8, p. 263).
128. Kant, *Religion and Rational Theology*, p. 33 (Ak 8, p. 267).
129. Kant, *Religion and Rational Theology*, p. 34 (Ak 8, p. 267).
130. Kant, *Religion and Rational Theology*, p. 35 (Ak 8, p. 269).
131. Kant, *Religion and Rational Theology*, p. 36 (Ak 8, p. 270).
132. Nicolai had to move his *Allgemeine deutsche Bibliothek* to Danish Altona after an order issued on April 17, 1794. See Epstein, *The Origin of German Conservatism*, p. 365; see also P. Bailleu, "Woellner."
133. For all this, see Hermann Noack, "Einleitung," in Immanuel Kant, *Die Religion innerhalb der Grenzen der bloßen Vernunft*, ed. Karl Vorländer, introduction by Hermann Noack, bibliography by Heiner Klemme (Hamburg: Meiner, 1990), pp. xxxi f.
134. Ak 12, pp. 359f.
135. Johann Gottlieb Fichte, *Fichtes Werke*, ed. Immanuel Hermann Fichte, 8 vols. *Nachgelassene Werke*, 3 vols. (Berlin: Walter De Gruyter, 1971), V, p. 59.
136. Ak 11, p. 349.
137. Ak 11, p. 350. In December of 1792 he had not yet sent the essay. See Ak 11, p. 397.
138. Kant, *Religion and Rational Theology*, p. 57. I have had to change the translation to restore the emphasis of the original (compare Ak 6, p. 3).
139. Kant, *Religion and Rational Theology*, p. 71 (Ak 6, p. 22).
140. Kant, *Religion and Rational Theology*, p. 71 (Ak 6, p. 21).
141. Kant, *Religion and Rational Theology*, p. 79 (Ak 6, p. 32).
142. Ibid.
143. Kant, *Religion and Rational Theology*, p. 83 (Ak 6, p. 37).
144. Kant, *Religion and Rational Theology*, p. 88 (Ak 6, pp. 42f.).
145. Kant, *Religion and Rational Theology*, p. 74 (Ak 6, p. 25). Kant also calls *Gesinnung* "the first subjective ground of the adoption of maxims."
146. Kant, *Religion and Rational Theology*, p. 74 (Ak 6, p. 25).
147. Kant, *Religion and Rational Theology*, p. 92 (Ak 6, pp. 47f.).
148. Kant, *Religion and Rational Theology*, p. 89 (Ak 6, p. 44).
149. Kant, *Religion and Rational Theology*, p. 88 (Ak 6, p. 43).
150. This is important, and it is often not understood. Thus Allison claims that "character or nature in the full Aristotelian sense . . . for Kant, is to a large extent a function of factors such as temperament or 'way of sensing' (*Sinnesart*), over which a person has relatively little control" (*Kant's Theory of Freedom*, p. 141). To support this view, he refers to the *Anthropology from a Pragmatic Point of View*. But the passage he refers to does not support the claim. Kant always opposes character as *Denkungsart* to mere temperament as *Sinnesart*, emphasizing that the

former is acquired and the latter innate. Character is a moral achievement and thus something over which we do have control.

151. Again, there are misconceptions in the current literature. In *Kant's Theory of Freedom,* Allison, conflating character and *Gesinnung,* claims that "in the *Critique of Practical Reason* and other later writings Kant seems to go even further by referring to a timeless noumenal choice of one's entire character (*Gesinnung*)" (p. 48). Allison recognizes that "the notion of intelligible character operative in the second critique cannot be equated with that of the first," and therefore argues that "the introduction of the conception of *Gesinnung* marks a significant deepening of the first *Critique* theory of freedom." *Gesinnung* is to "consist of a choice of intelligible character . . . in the adoption of 'unchangeable principles'" (p. 140). It "refers to the enduring character or disposition of an agent which underlies and is reflected in particular choices" (p. 136). While in the *Foundations* and other earlier works "Kant creates the impression that Kant conceives of [particular] actions as free-floating, isolated decisions (for the law or inclinations) that stand in no connection with an enduring moral agent with a determinate nature and interests" (p. 136), his discussion of *Gesinnung* in the *Religion* fixes that problem. It shows that "the choices of rational agents, or in his terms the maxims they adopt must be conceived in relation to an underlying set of intentions, beliefs, interests, and so on which collectively constitute that agent's disposition or character" (p. 136). Yet, this is not a problem that needs fixing, as long as we understand maxims as character-constituting devices, i.e., as the rules that "constitute that agent's disposition or character."

152. Ak 5, pp. 56, 327, for instance.

153. Ak 5, p. 116.

154. Kant, *Religion and Rational Theology,* p. 71n (Ak 6, p. 21n).

155. Kant, *Religion and Rational Theology,* pp. 71, 92 (Ak 6, pp. 21, 48).

156. Kant, *Religion and Rational Theology,* p. 74 (Ak 6, p. 25).

157. Allison tries to save Kant from the accusation that he thereby has committed himself to a notion of "noumenal choice" or the "choice of a noumenal character." He claims that Kant can be saved by construing *Gesinnung* as "an agent's fundamental maxim with respect to the moral law" (*Kant's Theory of Freedom,* p. 140). Though we are "choosing ourselves" in a sense (p. 142), this is not a metaphysical but a conceptual claim. As soon as we exercise our freedom, we already have chosen or adopted a certain kind of fundamental maxim. Allison finds that Kant's claim is perfectly appropriate, if we understand that the pretemporal or nontemporal acquisition amounts to nothing more than the claim that our *Gesinnung* is coextensive with our moral personality. Since it is nothing more than "the internal principle" of the maxims themselves, there is no problem with nontemporal choice.

158. This is a good thing, for how can one "choose" oneself before one is a self? More importantly perhaps, one may ask how changing "*Gesinnung*" (or "the ultimate subjective ground of the adoption of maxims") into a maxim solves any problem. If *Gesinnung* is itself a maxim, then it presupposes another *Gesinnung,* and so on ad infinitum. Kant himself points out that this is no solution (Ak 6, pp. 22–23n).

159. Kant, *Religion and Rational Theology,* p. 109 (Ak 6, p. 67).

160. Kant, *Religion and Rational Theology*, p. 71 (Ak 6, p. 21).
161. Kant, *Political Writings*, ed. Reiss, p. 227; see also p. 000, this volume.
162. Kant, *Religion and Rational Theology*, p. 103 (Ak 6, p. 60).
163. Kant, *Religion and Rational Theology*, p. 123 (Ak 6, p. 85).
164. Kant, *Religion and Rational Theology*, p. 130 (Ak 6, p. 95).
165. Kant, *Religion and Rational Theology*, p. 159 (Ak 6, p. 131).
166. Kant, *Religion and Rational Theology*, p. 177 (Ak 6, pp. 153f.).
167. Kant, *Religion and Rational Theology*, p. 184 (Ak 6, p. 162).
168. Kant, *Religion and Rational Theology*, p. 190 (Ak 6, pp. 170f.).
169. Kant, *Religion and Rational Theology*, p. 194 (Ak 6, p. 175).
170. Kant, *Religion and Rational Theology*, p. 195 (Ak 6, p. 176).
171. Kant, *Religion and Rational Theology*, p. 194 (Ak 6, p. 194).
172. Kant, *Religion and Rational Theology*, p. 210 (Ak 6, p. 180).
173. Kant, *Religion and Rational Theology*, pp. 204f. (Ak 6, p. 188).
174. Ak 11, p. 417.
175. See Ak 8, pp. 274–339. See also Immanuel Kant, *Über den Gemeinspruch "Das mag in der Theorie richtig sein, taugt aber nicht für die Praxis,"* ed. Heiner Klemme (Hamburg: Meiner Verlag 1992), and Immanuel Kant, *On the Old Saw That May Be Right in Theory But It Won't Work in Practice*, ed. George Miller (Philadelphia: University of Pennsylvania Press, 1974).
176. Ak 8, pp. 284f (Kant, *On the Old Saw*, ed. Miller, pp. 51f.).
177. Kant, *On the Old Saw*, ed. Miller, p. 72.
178. Kant, *On the Old Saw*, ed. Miller, p. 60.
179. Ak 19, p. 595.
180. Kant, *On the Old Saw*, ed. Miller, p. 76.
181. Which, according to orthodox belief, it of course was not.
182. Kant, *On the Old Saw*, ed. Miller, p. 77.
183. Kant, *On the Old Saw*, ed. Miller, p. 79.
184. Karl von Klauer, for instance, had argued in the *Berlinische Monatsschrift* of 1790 that the right of revolution followed from Kant's theory. See Klemme, "Einleitung," in Kant, *Über den Gemeinspruch*, pp. ix f. See also Dieter Henrich, "Einleitung," in *Kant, Gentz, Rehberg. Über Theorie und Praxis*, introduction by Dieter Henrich (Frankfurt [Main]: Suhrkamp Verlag, 1967). Henrich thinks that a satire of Kästner was the occasion of the essay, and he wants to exclude Burke. It seems to me a mistake to view the essay as occasioned by just one of the many issues to which it was relevant. Kant was concerned about *all* of them.
185. Epstein, *The Origin of German Conservatism*, pp. 547–594, calls Rehberg a "reform conservative." The same holds true of Gentz. Neither of them was satisfied with the status quo, but both opposed the French Revolution. Furthermore, both believed that Kant's optimism was a mistake. In their view, theory could never be sufficient for practice.
186. The question was asked in French: "Quels sont les progrès réels de la Metaphysique en Allemagne depuis le temps de Leibnitz et de Wolf?" It was originally announced in 1788 with a deadline of 1791, but the deadline was changed to January 1, 1792. Johann Christian Schwab (1743–1821), a Wolffian, who had contributed to Eberhard's *Philosophical Archive*, sent in the only submission.

Though the work was found to be worthy of a prize, the deadline was extended to June 1, 1795. The second prize was ultimately awarded to two Kantians, namely, Reinhold and Johann Heinrich Abicht (1762–1816), and the three contributions were published in 1796. See Ak 20, p. 480. Compare Vleeschauwer, *Development*, pp. 151f. See also Karl Rosenkranz, *Geschichte der Kant'schen Philosophie*, ed. Steffen Dietzsch (Berlin: Akademie-Verlag, 1987), pp. 350–354. (The book was originally published in 1840.)

187. There is an outline of an answer on the back of a letter to Kant, dated November 5, 1793 (see Ak 11, pp. 466f.). The text was first published by Theodor Friedrich Rink in 1804. It can be found in Ak 20, pp. 255–332.

188. Ak 20, p. 264, pp. 281f.

189. In the earlier essay it was the principle of sufficient reason, the monadology, and the doctrine of preestablished harmony.

190. Ak 20, p. 284.

191. Ak 20, p. 293.

192. See Ak 20, pp. 306–310.

193. Ak 20, p. 231. I will say nothing about the first draft of the first section, as it rehearses well-known Kantian themes (which is not to say that they are not of great interest to the specialist).

194. They are just two sentences in German.

195. The full title reads in English: *Aenesidemus, or Concerning the Foundations of the Elements Issued by Prof. Reinhold in Jena. Together with a Defence of Skepticism against the Pretensions of the Critique of Pure Reason.* It appeared anonymously in 1792. For the entire discussion see di Giovanni and Harris, *Between Kant and Hegel*.

196. See George J. Seidel, "Introduction," in *Fichte's Wissenschaftslehre of 1794: A Commentary on Part I*, ed. George J. Seidel (West Lafayette, Ind.: Purdue University Press, 1993), p. 1. See also Martin Oesch (ed.), *Aus der Frühzeit des deutschen Idealismus. Texte zur Wissenschaftslehre Fichtes, 1794–1804* (Würzburg: Königshausen & Neumann, 1987).

197. Borowski, *Leben*, pp. 82f.

198. Rink, *Ansichten*, p. 60.

199. Kant published both the letter and his response in *The Conflict of the Faculties* of 1798. See *Religion and Rational Theology*, pp. 240–2. All translations are taken from this volume. I have substituted "evaluated negatively" for "disparaging" because it makes Kant's point clearer.

200. Rink, *Ansichten*, p. 60.

201. It was published by Rink only after his death in 1804.

202. Epstein, *The Origin of German Conservatism*, p. 367.

203. Ak 11, pp. 507f. The letter is dated June 14, 1794. Since he received the special order only in October, he may have been working on this treatise right after Stäudlin's invitation to contribute.

204. Ak 11, p. 533.

205. However, the Appendix on mysticism (Ak 7, pp. 69–75) of the first part could have been written only after 1797, i.e., after the appearance of Wilmans's book on the relationship between the Kantian philosophy and mysticism. The second part of *The Dispute* on the progress of humanity, or the dispute between the fac-

ulties of philosophy and law (Ak 7, pp. 79–94), must also have been written after 1797. For this dating see Reinhard Brandt, "Zum 'Streit der Fakultäten,'" in *Neue Autographen und Dokumente zu Kants Leben, Schriften und Vorlesungen*, ed. Reinhard Brandt and Werner Stark (Hamburg: Meiner, 1987), pp. 31–78, especially pp. 31, 45, 59, 65f.

206. Kant, *Religion and Rational Theology*, p. 287.

207. Kant, *Religion and Rational Theology*, p. 249.

208. On the organization of the university and its faculties, see pp. 66–68, this volume.

209. Kant, *Religion and Rational Theology*, p. 280.

210. Kant, *Religion and Rational Theology*, p. 277. On this, see also pp. 52–54 of this volume.

211. Kant, *Religion and Rational Theology*, p. 285.

212. Brandt, "Zum 'Streit der Fakultäten,'" shows that Kant makes use of Thomasius and Walch in his conception of the faculties. R. Selbach, "Eine bisher unbeachtete Quelle des 'Streits der Fakultäten,'" *Kant-Studien* 82 (1991), pp. 96–110, shows that he also was aware of Wolff's critique of this position and was in many ways close to Wolff.

213. Malter, *Kant in Rede und Gespräch*, p. 425.

214. Ak 12, p. 35.

215. For a collection of contemporary papers on this subject, see James Bohmann and Matthias Lutz-Bachmann (eds.), *Perpetual Peace: Essays on Kant's Cosmopolitan Ideal* (Cambridge, Mass.: MIT Press, 1997).

216. Kant, *Practical Philosophy*, p. 322 (Ak 8, p. 349).

217. Kant, *Practical Philosophy*, p. 328 (Ak 8, p. 357).

218. Kant, *Practical Philosophy*, pp. 347, 351 (Ak 8, pp. 381, 386).

219. Kant, *Practical Philosophy*, p. 351 (Ak 8, p. 386).

Chapter 9: The Old Man (1796–1804)

1. Jachmann, *Kant*, p. 203.

2. Arthur Warda, "Ergänzungen zu E. Fromm's zweitem und drittem Beitrage zur Lebensgeschichte Kants," *Altpreußische Monatsschrift* 38 (1901), pp. 75–95, 398–432. See also Arthur Warda, "Zur Frage: Wann hörte Kant zu lesen auf," *Altpreussische Monatsschrift* 41 (1904), pp. 131–135; and Arnoldt, "Möglichst vollständiges Verzeichnis," pp. 328–331.

3. Arthur Warda, "Die Kant-Manuscripte im Prussia Museum," *Altpreußische Monatsschrift* 36 (1899), pp. 337–367, p. 355.

4. Hasse, *Merkwürdige Äußerungen*, p. 4, claimed that Kant was still at times invited for a meal in the evening, but not as often as he used to be. This contradicts what others said, namely that after Green's death he no longer went out in the evening.

5. "*Brustwassersucht*" or "dropsy of the chest" was the diagnosis. His health had been damaged before. Baron of Schrötter, who supervised the incorporation of Danzig into Prussia after the second partition of Poland, had called on Hippel to supervise the process. The stress and the change in his daily routine were too much for him. There were already signs of declining health before he returned to Königsberg in March of 1794. He also had lost an eye due to an infection.

6. See Timothy F. Sellner, "Introduction" to Theodor Gottlieb von Hippel, *On Improving the Status of Women,* tr. Timothy F. Sellner (Detroit: Wayne State University Press, 1979), pp. 28f.

7. Sellner, "Introduction" to Hippel, *On Improving the Status of Women,* p. 29.

8. See Timothy F. Sellner, "The Eheeiferer in Goethe's Wahlverwandtschaften: Could Mittler be Hippel?," in *Königsberg. Beiträge,* ed. Kohnen, pp. 321–334, p. 328.

9. Abegg, *Reisetagebuch von 1798,* p. 254.

10. Scheffner, *Mein Leben,* pp. 126–8.

11. Scheffner, *Mein Leben,* p. 129.

12. Scheffner, *Mein Leben,* p. 130: "He tried to hide his materialism almost more than his proclivity to enjoy bodily pleasure."

13. Borowski, *Leben,* p. 79 (Malter, *Kant in Rede und Gespräch,* p. 432). Borowski claims that was the way he always acted, i.e., that he was very concerned when someone among his friends was sick, but never visited the sick. When someone died, he no longer spoke of his illness and death. Yet, he remembered and continued to speak of his interactions with the dead friend.

14. Ak 11, pp. 472f.

15. Ak 11, p. 505; see also pp. 371, 434.

16. See Beck, *The Elusive 'I' in the Novel: Hippel, Sterne, Diderot, and Kant,* and "Kant and the Novel," pp. 271f. Actually, there had been rumors about the book before. See Arthur Warda, "Kants Erklärung wegen der v. Hippelschen Autorschaft," *Altpreussische Monatsschrift* 41 (1904), pp. 61–93.

17. Ak 12, pp. 360–1. The declaration is dated December 6, 1796.

18. Ak 12, p. 361.

19. Ak 13, pp. 537, 540.

20. Compare all this to Beck, *The Elusive 'I',* p. 111.

21. Malter, *Kant in Rede und Gespräch,* p. 442 (see also Ak 13, p. 473).

22. Hasse, *Ansichten,* p. 29.

23. Abegg, *Reisetagebuch,* p. 184.

24. Malter, *Kant in Rede und Gespräch,* p. 353.

25. Ibid.

26. Reicke, *Kantiana,* p. 32.

27. Reicke, *Kantiana,* p. 40. Friedrich Nicolai had published several essays critical of Kant at that time. See Friedrich Nicolai, *Philosophische Abhandlungen* in *Gesammelte Werke,* vol. 11, ed. Bernhard Fabian and Marie-Luise Spieckermann (Hildesheim: Olms, 1991).

28. Abegg, *Reisetagebuch,* p. 104.

29. See also Warda, "Kants Erklärung," pp. 91f.

30. Abegg, *Reisetagebuch,* p. 245.

31. Abegg, *Reisetagebuch,* p. 252.

32. Abegg, *Reisetagebuch,* p. 255.

33. Abegg, *Reisetagebuch,* p. 202.

34. Abegg, *Reisetagebuch,* p. 247.

35. Abegg, *Reisetagebuch,* p. 255.

36. Abegg, *Reisetagebuch,* p. 192.

37. Abegg, *Reisetagebuch,* p. 238.

38. Abegg, *Reisetagebuch,* pp. 147f., 184, 229. Compare Malter, "Königsberg und Kant im 'Reisetagebuch,'" p. 14.
39. Abegg, *Reisetagebuch,* p. 184.
40. I follow Malter, "Königsberg und Kant im 'Reisetagebuch,'" p. 19, in this list.
41. Abegg, *Reisetagebuch,* p. 249.
42. Abegg, *Reisetagebuch,* p. 147.
43. Abegg, *Reisetagebuch,* p. 148.
44. Abegg, *Reisetagebuch,* pp. 186–191.
45. Abegg, *Reisetagebuch,* p. 202.
46. See Schubert, *Kants Biographie,* pp. 165–8, and Warda, "Die Kant-Manuscripte," pp. 351f. There were just ten senators, the ten most senior full professors. Though Kant did not go to the meetings, he probably voted in absentia.
47. Translated from Vorländer, *Kants Leben,* II, p. 270.
48. This does not mean that he did not extensively rewrite the material. See Ak 23, pp. 209–419, for some of Kant's early drafts of these books.
49. Ak 23, p. 403. "Vigorous health" is a translation of the state of being *"blühend gesund"* or *"vegetus."* Kant claims in this context that he has no memory of how he felt in his childhood.
50. See pp. 227–228 of this volume.
51. Ak 8, p. 395.
52. Ak 8, p. 389.
53. Ak 8, pp. 411–422. Though the article appeared nominally in December 1796, it was published only in July 1797. Apart from these essays, Kant published only two short pieces in his name in 1796, namely the Appendix to Sömmering's book *On the Organ of the Soul,* which he had written in 1795 (see p. xxi, this volume), and a short note on how to solve a mathematical dispute.
54. Ak 8, p. 419.
55. See Mary Gregor, "Introduction," in Kant, *Metaphysics of Morals,* p. 7, and Bernd Ludwig, "Einleitung," Immanuel Kant, *Metaphysische Anfangsgründe der Rechtslehre,* ed. Bernd Ludwig (Hamburg: Meiner, 1986), for instance.
56. Gregor, "Introduction," in Kant, *Metaphysics of Morals,* p. 8.
57. I keep the translations "metaphysical foundations of right" and "metaphysical foundation of virtue." Gregor translates, more literally, "metaphysical first principles of the doctrine of right" and "metaphysical first principles of the doctrine of virtue."
58. Kant, *Practical Philosophy,* p. 387 (Ak 6, p. 230).
59. Kant, *Practical Philosophy,* p. 388 (Ak 6, p. 231).
60. Kant, *Practical Philosophy,* p. 409 (Ak 6, p. 255).
61. Kant, *Practical Philosophy,* p. 406 (Ak 6, p. 246).
62. I am indebted in this account to John Ladd's paper on "Kant on Marriage" read at the Midwest Study Group of the North American Kant Society at Purdue University in the fall of 1997.
63. Kant, *Practical Philosophy,* pp. 450f. (Ak 6, pp. 306f.).
64. Otfried Höffe, *Immanuel Kant,* tr. Marshal Farrier (Albany: State University of New York Press, 1994), p. 181.
65. Kant, *Practical Philosophy,* p. 457 (Ak 6, p. 314).

66. Kant, *Practical Philosophy*, p. 471 (Ak 6, p. 329).
67. Kant, *Practical Philosophy*, p. 458 (Ak 6, pp. 314f.).
68. Kant, *Practical Philosophy*, p. 489 (Ak 6, p. 352).
69. Kant, *Practical Philosophy*, p. 490 (Ak 6, p. 353).
70. Kant, *Practical Philosophy*, p. 567 (Ak 6, p. 447).
71. Kant, *Practical Philosophy*, pp. 524f. (Ak 6, p. 394).
72. Kant, *Practical Philosophy*, p. 599 (Ak 6, p. 487).
73. Kant, *Practical Philosophy*, p. 602 (Ak 6, p. 491).
74. Epictetus, *The Handbook*, ed. Nicholas P. White (Indianapolis: Hackett Publishing Company, 1983), p. 11.
75. Kant, *Religion and Rational Theology*, pp. 297–309 (Ak 7, pp. 78–94). For Part II of *The Dispute of the Faculties*, see Brandt, "Zum 'Streit der Fakultäten,'" p. 65.
76. Epstein, *The Origin of German Conservatism*, p. 388.
77. Epstein, *The Origin of German Conservatism*, p. 391.
78. Kant, *Religion and Rational Theology*, p. 243 (Ak 7, p. 10).
79. Kant, *Religion and Rational Theology*, p. 239 (Ak 7, p. 5).
80. For the contents of the essay, see Chapter 7 of this volume.
81. Kant, *Religion and Rational Theology*, p. 301 (Ak 7, p. 84).
82. Kant, *Religion and Rational Theology*, p. 302 (Ak 7, p. 85).
83. Compare Brandt, "Zum 'Streit der Fakultäten,'" pp. 45f. Brandt argues on the basis of an early draft by Kant that the targets of the essay are pseudo-Kantians, but it is more likely that the parties named in the essay, namely "our politicians" and the "ecclesiastics," really are the targets. The censors in Berlin must have seen it that way, as well. This does not mean that he might not also have had some of his followers in mind (secondarily).
84. See pp. 153–154 of this volume.
85. Kant, *Religion and Rational Theology*, p. 314 (Ak 7, p. 99).
86. Kant, *Religion and Rational Theology*, p. 316 (Ak 7, p. 101).
87. Kant, *Religion and Rational Theology*, p. 318 (Ak 7, pp. 103f.).
88. See pp. 150–152, this volume.
89. Kant, *Practical Philosophy*, p. 44 (Ak 4, p. 389).
90. Kant, *Practical Philosophy*, p. 44 (Ak 4, p. 388).
91. Ak 7, p. 333.
92. Ak 7, p. 119.
93. Ak 7, p. 120.
94. Schleiermacher found that an "extract of the particulars could almost be nothing else than a collection of trivialities." See Friedrich Schleiermacher, *Kritische Gesamtausgabe*, I/2 (Berlin: de Gruyter, 1984), pp. 365–369, 365
95. Wasianski, *Kant*, p. 283.
96. The manuscript is published in volumes 21 and 22 of the Academy edition of Kant's works, edited by Arthur Buchenau and Gerhard Lehmann. These volumes contain most of these notes. But the editors failed to include all of the relevant fragments. On the other hand, they included some material that is irrelevant to Kant's last work. There is an English translation of this work in the Cambridge edition of Kant's works, which in some ways is a better one than that to be found in the Academy edition. See Immanuel Kant, *Opus postumum*, edited, with an in-

troduction and notes, by Eckart Förster, translated by Eckart Förster and Stanley Rosen (New York: Cambridge University Press, 1993). See also *Übergang, Untersuchungen zum Spätwerk Immanuel Kants*, edited by the Forum für Philosophie Bad Homburg (Siegfried Blasche, Wolfgang R. Köhler, Wolfgang Kuhlmann, Peter Rohs) (Frankfurt [Main]: Vittorio Klostermann, 1991). This volume provides the necessary background to the recent discussion of the *Opus postumum*.

97. See Eckart Förster, "Introduction, " Kant, *Opus postumum*, pp. xvi f.

98. König, "Arzt und ärztliches in Kant, " pp. 113–154.

99. Wasianski, *Kant*, p. 283.

100. Hasse, *Äusserungen Kant's*, p. 20n.

101. Hans Vaihinger, "Briefe aus dem Kantkreis," *Altpreussische Monatsschrift* 17 (1880), pp. 286–299, p. 290.

102. *Briefe von und an Scheffner*, ed. Warda, II, p. 424

103. Most of the authors in *Übergang, Untersuchungen zum Spätwerk Immanuel Kants*, seem to believe this.

104. I disagree with Eckart Förster on this. He claims in his "Fichte, Beck and Schelling in Kant's Opus Postumum," in *Kant and His Influence*, ed. G. M. Ross and T. McWalter (Bristol: Thoemmes, 1990), pp. 146–169, p. 146, that "the manuscript is virtually complete, Kant did not live to edit it."

105. See Ak 22, p. 758 (K. Christian Schoen).

106. See Ak 22, p. 758.

107. See Ak 22, 757f. I closely follow the summary given there.

108. Förster, "Fichte, Beck and Schelling in Kant's *Opus Postumum*," p. 151. In his "Kant's Selbstsetzungslehre," in *Kant's Transcendental Deductions*, ed. E. Förster (Stanford: Stanford University Press, 1989), pp. 217–238, Förster dates this "solution" to April 1799 (p. 224). If it is true that Kant found this "solution" at that time, then it falls just into the period where his weakness began to become more noticeable.

109. Kant, *Opus postumum*, ed. Förster, p. 71 (Ak 21, p. 222).

110. See Ak 4, p. 515; pp. 4, 534, 564, 467; pp. 9, 67, for instance. In his *Metaphysical Foundations of Natural Science*, Kant had indeed treated the "empirical concept" of matter a priori, but only insofar as "the intuition corresponding to the concept" was given a priori (Ak 4, p. 470), that is, insofar as it is spatial and temporal. "Ether," being a much richer (and thus more questionable) concept, could not be treated in this way without collapsing into the concept of "matter."

111. Kant, *Opus postumum*, ed. Förster, p. 74 (Ak 21, p. 226).

112. Compare Förster, "Fichte, Beck and Schelling in Kant's *Opus Postumum*," p. 153.

113. Ak 21, p. 490; I follow Förster, "Fichte, Beck and Schelling in Kant's *Opus Postumum*," p. 154f. Even though I am much more critical of Kant's supposed achievements than is Förster, I have benefited tremendously from his discussion.

114. Malter, *Rede und Gespräch*, p. 595.

115. Friedman, *Kant and the Exact Sciences*, p. 240. Friedman's judicious discussion of the development of chemistry during the eighties and nineties in relation to Kant's thought should be consulted by anyone wanting to understand Kant's motivations in the *Transitions* project. Some of Kant's personal acquaintances are important sources for understanding his interest in chemistry. Pastor Sommer

had an avid interest in this subject, and Karl Gottfried Hagen wrote one of the first textbooks on pharmacy in 1786. It was called *Grundriss der Experimental-chemie zum Gebrauch bey dem Vortrage derselben* (Basic Outline of Experimental Chemistry for Use in Lectures); beginning with the third edition it was called *Grundsätze der Experimentalchemie* (Basic Principles of Experimental Chemistry). Kant called this textbook a "logical masterpiece." Hagen was a regular dinner guest at Kant's house. See Wolfgang Caesar, "Karl Gottfried Hagen (1749–1829)," *Jahrbuch Der Albertus Universität Zu Königsberg* 29 (1994), pp. 389–395.

116. Ak 22, pp. 82f.

117. Förster argues in his "Kant's Selbstsetzungslehre" that this is not a Fichtean in-fluence, appealing to other instances of "positing" in Kant. This approach has precedents in Kant, but this does not make a Fichtean influence impossible. Fichte was indebted to Kant on just these points, but the idea that "we make *every-thing*" is closer to Fichte's than it is to Kant's critical view. See also Förster, "Fichte, Beck and Schelling in Kant's *Opus Postumum*," pp. 158f. Förster emphasizes the differences between Fichte and Kant as well as he can, but I do not think his ar-guments are successful in showing that Fichte did not influence Kant.

118. Warda, "Ergänzungen zu E. Fromm's Lebensgeschichte Kants," p. 86.

119. Kant, *Briefwechsel*, ed. Zweig, pp. 253f.

120. Wasianski, *Kant*, p. 232.

121. Ibid.

122. Rink, *Ansichten*, p. 70.

123. See Malter, *Kant in Rede und Gespräch*, p. 475 (from *Der Freimütige*, 1804), and Rink, *Ansichten*, p. 71.

124. Hasse, *Merkwürdige Äußerungen*, p. 4 . See also Pörschke's comments to Fichte in Malter, *Kant in Rede und Gespräch*, p. 442: "Kant, who no longer lectures, and who has withdrawn from all society, the house of his friend Motherby excepted, is slowly becoming less known even here; even his reputation is decreasing" (July 7, 1788).

125. According to Hasse, *Merkwürdige Äußerungen*, p. 4, this was at the end of 1800.

126. Jachmann, *Kant*, p. 203.

127. Rink to Villers, a popularizer of Kant in France: "Please do not blame Kant for not having answered your letter. He is old and weak. He answers almost no letter any longer, though he receives so many . . . I almost want to say he is incapable of answering them." See Vaihinger, "Briefe aus dem Kantkreis," pp. 287f. This is supported by his published correspondence. See Kant, *Briefwechsel*, ed. Schön-dorfer and Malter. Kant was never a great correspondent. But after 1799, there are very few letters, and many of them were short.

128. Jachmann, *Kant*, p. 203; Rink to Villers in June 1801: "Kant's weakness is in-creasing dramatically (*ungemein*)," in Vaihinger, "Briefe aus dem Kantkreis," p. 292; Hasse, *Merkwürdige Äußerungen*, p. 8: "From 1801 he had become noticeably weaker. His thoughts were no longer as well ordered as before; but he still expe-rienced clear insights at frequent occasions, which went like lightning strikes through his head. They proved his uncommon acuity, and deserved to be recorded." What Hasse recorded shows nothing of the sort.

129. Wasianski, *Kant*, p. 23.
130. Some of these have survived. See Hermann Degering (ed.), *Immanuel Kants Mittagsbüchlein vom 17. August bis 25. September 1802* (Berlin, 1926).
131. Wasianski, *Kant*, p. 231; compare Jachmann, *Kant*, p. 207, as well as Rink, *Ansichten*, pp. 105–119 (Malter, *Kant in Rede und Gespräch*, pp. 479–484).
132. Wasianski, *Kant*, p. 264; see also Rink, *Ansichten*, pp. 111f. Kant hardly ever drank beer.
133. Wasianski, *Kant*, pp. 231f.
134. I will not mention most of them, since they add nothing to our understanding of Kant. A few samples should be sufficient to show that they were signs of senility.
135. Rink, *Ansichten*, p. 77; Vorländer, *Kant*, II, p. 28, claims Motherby died in 1799.
136. Jachmann, *Kant*, p. 163; Ruffmann had died in 1794, Count Keyserlingk in 1788, and the Countess in 1791 (see Vorländer, *Kant*, II, p. 28).
137. Rink to Villers, in Vaihinger, "Briefe aus dem Kantkreis," p. 294. He also said that he had given up any hope that Kant would get better. Yet, Kant was still spending three hours at his dinner parties.
138. Wasianski, *Kant*, p. 242.
139. Ak 12, p. 443. The letter was occasioned by an earlier letter from the rector (November 12, 1801), asking for his resignation (Ak 12, p. 442).
140. Wasianski, *Kant*, p. 251.
141. Wasianski, *Kant*, p. 253. See also *Briefe von und an Scheffner*, ed. Warda, II, 401: "Kant has divorced Lampe by the power of the police."
142. Wasianski, *Kant*, p. 257.
143. Andrew Cutrofello, *Discipline and Critique: Kant, Poststructuralism, and the Problem of Resistance* (Albany: State University of New York Press, 1994), pp. 103–115, used this note and Lampe's relationship to Kant in construing a certain picture of Kant's sexuality. He asks "Did Lampe make some sort of explicit sexual advance on Kant?" (pp. 112f.). He claims that the "imperative to forget the name of Lampe can be read in the light of Kant's moral condemnation of homosexuality. A man who approaches another man sexually no longer deserves to be a person. If Lampe did approach Kant sexually, Kant would have had a moral obligation to stop thinking of Lampe as a person" (p. 113). This is pure fantasy or wish fulfillment. Neither the drunk servant nor the feeble and feeble-minded Kant had anything of the sort in mind.
144. Scheffner, *Briefe von und an Scheffner*, II, p. 379.
145. Jachmann, *Kant*, p. 210.
146. Ibid.
147. Wasianski, *Kant*, p. 258.
148. Wasianski, *Kant*, p. 261.
149. Wasianski, *Kant*, p. 259.
150. Hasse, *Merkwürdige Äußerungen*, p. 46.
151. Wasianski, *Kant*, p. 265.
152. Wasianski, *Kant*, p. 268. Compare p. 156, this volume.
153. Wasianski, *Kant*, p. 279.
154. Wasianski, *Kant*, p. 280.

155. Wasianski, *Kant*, p. 269: the German words are *"Geduld, Sanftmut und Nachsicht."* Especially the word *"Nachsicht"* seems revealing to me. It suggests that caring for the brother was difficult at times.

156. Jachmann, *Kant*, pp. 201f.

157. Compare pp. 5–6 of this volume.

158. Wasianski, *Kant*, p. 276.

159. Jachmann, *Kant*, p. 211, speaks of "a nervous stroke" (*Schlagfluß*). This stroke probably had little to do with Kant's constipation, a permanent feature of his old age.

160. Scheffner, *Briefe von und an Scheffner*, II, p. 426.

161. Scheffner, *Briefe von und an Scheffner*, II, p. 423.

162. Reusch, *Kants Tischgenossen*, p. 10.

163. *Äußerungen über Kant*, pp. 28f. (Malter, *Kant in Rede und Gespräch*, p. 475).

164. Wasianski, *Kant*, p. 263.

165. Wasianski, *Kant*, p. 277.

166. Jachmann, *Kant*, p. 209.

167. Hasse, *Merkwürdige Äusserungen*, p. 48 (Malter, *Kant in Rede und Gespräch*, p. 584).

168. Wasianski, *Kant*, p. 287.

169. Wasianski, *Kant*, p. 290 (Malter, *Kant in Rede und Gespräch*, p. 592). Malter gives February 11, 1804, as a date for the incident.

170. Jachmann, *Kant*, p. 212.

171. Wasianski, *Kant*, p. 291.

Works Cited

This is not a complete account of everything ever written on Kant's life. Such a bibliography can be found in Rudolf Malter's "Bibliographie zur Biographie Immanuel Kants," listed here. Because some of the materials listed in Malter's complete bibliography are only of marginal interest to most readers, they are not included. On the other hand, this bibliography is more extensive than Malter's in other respects, because it includes many sources on the more general eighteenth-century background, on Kant's friends and acquaintances, as well as on Kant's philosophy.

Abegg, Johann Friedrich. *Reisetagebuch von 1798.* 1st. ed. Hrsg. v. Walter und Jolanda Abegg in Zusammenarbeit mit Zwi Batscha. Frankfurt: Insel Verlag, 1976 (second edition 1977).

Adickes, Erich. *Kant-Studien.* Kiel and Leipzig, 1895.

"Die bewegenden Kräfte in Kant's philosophischer Entwicklung und die beiden Pole seines Systems." *Kant-Studien* 1 (1897), pp. 9–59, 161–196, 352–415.

Agethen, Manfred. *Geheimbund und Utopie. Illuminaten, Freimaurer und deutsche Spätaufklärung.* München: R. Oldenbourg Verlag, 1987.

Allison, Henry E. *The Kant-Eberhard Controversy.* Baltimore: Johns Hopkins University Press, 1973.

Kant's Transcendental Idealism: An Interpretation and Defense. New Haven and London: Yale University Press, 1986.

Kant's Theory of Freedom. Cambridge: Cambridge University Press, 1990.

Altmann, Alexander. *Moses Mendelssohns Frühschriften zur Metaphysik.* Tübingen: J. C. B. Mohr, 1969.

Moses Mendelssohn: A Biographical Study. Alabama: University of Alabama Press, 1973.

Ameriks, Karl. *Kant's Theory of Mind: An Analysis of the Paralogisms of Pure Reason.* Oxford and New York: Clarendon Press, 1982.

Archenholz, Bogislav von. *Bürger und Patrizier. Ein Buch von Städten des deutschen Ostens.* Darmstadt: Ullstein Verlag, 1970.

Arnoldt, Emil. *Kant's Jugend.* In Emil Arnoldt, *Gesammelte Schriften,* 6 vols., ed. Otto Schöndörffer. Berlin, 1907–1909 (vol. 3, pp. 103–210).

Möglichst vollständiges Verzeichnis aller von Kant gehaltenen oder auch nur angekündigten

Vorlesungen nebst darauf bezüglichen Notizen. In Emil Arnoldt, *Gesammelte Schriften,* 6 vols., ed. Otto Schöndörffer. Berlin, 1907–1909 (vol. 4, pp. 173–344).

Aschoff, Frank. "Zwischen äußerem Zwang und innerer Freiheit. Fichtes Hauslehrer-Erfahrungen und die Grundlegung seiner Philosophie." *Fichte-Studien* 9 (1997), pp. 27–45.

Bailleu, P. "Woellner, Johann Christof." *Allgemeine deutsche Biographie,* pp. 148–159.

Balk, Norman. *Die Friedrich-Wilhelms Universität.* Berlin, 1926.

Baur, Susan. *Hypochondria: Woeful Imaginings.* Berkeley: University of California Press, 1988.

Bayer, O. "Hamanns Metakritik im ersten Entwurf." *Kant-Studien* 81 (1990), pp. 435–453.

Beck, Hamilton. "Kant and the Novel: A Study of the Examination Scene in Hippel's 'Lebensläufe nach aufsteigender Linie.'" *Kant-Studien* 74 (1983), pp. 271ff.

The Elusive 'I' in the Novel: Hippel, Sterne, Diderot, and Kant. Bern and New York: Peter Lang, 1987.

"Framing the Debate: Hippel's Response to Zimmermannn's Attack on the Enlightenment." *Eighteenth-Century Life* 14 (1990), pp. 29–38.

"Moravians in Königsberg." In *Königsberg. Beiträge zu einem besonderen Kapitel der deutschen Geistesgeschichte,* ed. Joseph Kohnen. Frankfurt (Main): Peter Lang, 1994 (pp. 335–374).

"Neither Goschen nor Botany Bay: Hippel and the Debate on Improving the Civic Status of the Jews." *Lessing Yearbook* 27 (1995), pp. 63–102.

Beck, Lewis White. *A Commentary on Kant's Critique of Practical Reason.* Chicago: University of Chicago Press, 1960.

Early German Philosophy: Kant and His Predecessors. Cambridge: Belknap Press of Harvard University Press, 1969.

Essays on Kant and Hume. New Haven and London: Yale University Press, 1978.

Review of G. Gawlick and L. Kreimendahl, *Hume in der deutschen Aufklärung. Eighteenth-Century Studies* 21 (1988), pp. 405–408.

Kant Selections. New York and London: Scribner Macmillan Publishing Co., 1998.

Beiser, Frederick. *The Fate of Reason: German Philosophy from Kant to Fichte.* Cambridge, Mass.: Harvard University Press, 1987.

Bilguer, J. U. *Nachrichten an das Publikum in Absicht der Hypochondrie.* 1767.

Blasche, Siegfried, Köhler, Wolfgang R., Kuhlmann, Wolfgang, and Rohs, Peter, Editors. *Übergang, Untersuchungen zum Spätwerk Immanuel Kants.* Herausgegeben vom Forum für Philosophie Bad Homburg. Frankfurt (Main): Vittorio Klostermann, 1991.

Blumenberg, Hans. *Die Lesbarkeit der Welt.* Frankfurt (Main): Suhrkamp Verlag, 1981.

Böhme, Hartmut, and Böhme, Gernot. *Das Andere der Vernunft. Zur Entwicklung von Rationalitätsstrukturen am Beispiel Kant.* Frankfurt (Main): Suhrkamp Verlag, 1983.

Böttiger, K. W., Editor. *Literarische Zustände und Zeitgenossen.* In *Schilderungen aus Karl Aug. Böttiger's handschriftlichem Nachlasse,* Vol. 1. Leipzig, 1838.

Bohmann, James, and Lutz-Bachmann, Matthias, Editors. *Perpetual Peace: Essays on Kant's Cosmopolitan Ideal.* Cambridge, Mass.: MIT Press, 1997.

Bolotow, Andrej. *Leben und Abenteuer des Andrej Bolotov von ihm selbst für seine Nach-*

kommen aufgeschrieben. 1. 1738–1762, tr. Marianne Schilow, ed. Wolfgang Gruba. München: Beck, 1990.

Borowski, Ludwig Ernst. *Darstellung des Leben und Charakters Immanuel Kants*. Königsberg, 1804.

Neue Preußische Kirchenregistratur. Königsberg, 1789.

Bosse, Heinrich. "Berufsprobleme der Akademiker im Werk von J. M. R. Lenz. '*Unaufhörlich Lenz gelesen.*'" In *Studien zu Leben und Werk von J. M. R. Lenz*, ed. Inge Stephan and Hans-Gerd Winter. Stuttgart and Weimar: Metzler, 1994 (pp. 38–51).

Brandt, Reinhard. "Materialien zur Entstehung der *Kritik der reinen Vernunft* (John Locke und Johann Schultz)." In *Beiträge zur Kritik der reinen Vernunft, 1781– 1981*, ed. Ingeborg Heidemann and Wolfgang Ritzel. Berlin: de Gruyter, 1981.

"Rousseau und Kants 'Ich denke.'" In *Neue Autographen und Dokumente zu Kants Leben, Schriften und Vorlesungen*, ed. Reinhard Brandt und Werner Stark. Hamburg: Meiner, 1987 (pp. 1–18).

"Zum 'Streit der Fakultäten.'" In *Neue Autographen und Dokumente zu Kants Leben, Schriften und Vorlesungen*, ed. Reinhard Brandt und Werner Stark. Hamburg: Meiner, 1987 (pp. 31–78).

"Feder und Kant," *Kant-Studien* 80 (1989), pp. 249–264.

Review of L. Kreimendahl, *Der Durchbruch von 1769*. *Kant-Studien* 83 (1992), pp. 100–111.

Brandt, Reinhard and Stark, Werner, Editors. *Autographen, Dokumente und Berichte. Zu Editionen, Amtsgeschäften und Werk Immanuel Kants*. Hamburg: Meiner, 1994.

Breidert, Wolfgang. "Leonhard Euler und die Philosophie." In *Leonhard Euler, 1707– 1783: Beiträge zu Leben und Werk: Gedenkband des Kantons Basel-Stadt Basel*. Basel: Birkhauser Verlag, 1983 (pp. 447–457).

Brenning, Emil. "Hippel and Rousseau." *Altpreussische Monatsschrift* 16 (1873), pp. 286–300.

Brunschwig, Henri. *Enlightenment and Romanticism in Eighteenth-Century Prussia*, tr. Frank Jellinek. Chicago: University of Chicago Press, 1975.

Buck, Johann Friedrich. *Lebensbeschreibungen derer verstorbenen preußischen Mathematiker*. 1764.

Burton, Robert. *The Anatomy of Melancholy*, ed. Floyd Dell and Paul Jordan-Smith. New York: Tudor Publishing Company, 1927.

Caesar, Wolfgang. "Karl Gottfried Hagen (1749–1829)." *Jahrbuch der Albertus Universität zu Königsberg* 29 (1994), pp. 389–395.

Campbell, Georg. *Die Philosophie der Rhetorik*. Berlin, 1791 (translation of *The Philosophy of Rhetoric*).

Carl, Wolfgang. Review of G. Gawlick and L. Kreimendahl, *Hume in der deutschen Aufklärung*. *Philosophische Rundschau* 35 (1988), pp. 207–214.

Der schweigende Kant. Die Entwürfe zu einer Deduktion der Kategorien vor 1781. Abhandlungen Akademie Göttingen 182. Göttingen and Zürich: Vandenhoek & Ruprecht, 1989.

Cassirer, Ernst. *Kant's Life and Thought*, tr. James Haden, introduction by Stefan Körner. New Haven and London: Yale University Press, 1981.

Kants Leben und Lehre. Darmstadt: Wissenschaftliche Buchgesellschaft, 1977 (originally Berlin, 1918).

Rousseau, Kant, Goethe, tr. James Gutmann, Paul-Oskar Kristeller, and John Hermann Randall. Princeton: Princeton University Press, 1970.

Cicero. *On Duties,* ed. M. T. Griffin and E. M. Atkins. Cambridge: Cambridge University Press, 1991.

Collingwood, R. G. *An Autobiography.* Oxford: Oxford University Press, 1939.

Cottingham, John. *The Rationalists. A History of Western Philosophy,* Vol. 4. Oxford: Oxford University Press, 1988.

Crusius, Christian August. *Die philosophischen Hauptwerke,* ed. G. Tonelli. Hildesheim: Olms, 1964.

Cudworth, Ralph. *A Treatise Concerning Eternal and Immutable Morality, with A Treatise of Freewill,* ed. Sarah Hutton. Cambridge: Cambridge University Press, 1996.

Cutrofello, Andrew. *Discipline and Critique: Kant, Poststructuralism, and the Problem of Resistance.* Albany: State University of New York Press, 1994.

Czygan, P. "'Anmerkungen, die nicht fürs Publikum gehören' aus Wasianskis Handexemplar." *Sitzungsbericht der Altertumsgesellschaft Prussia* 17 (1891/2), pp. 109–140.

Davies, Martin L. *Identity or History? Marcus Herz and the End of the Enlightenment.* Detroit: Wayne State University Press, 1995.

Degering, Hermann, Editor. *Immanuel Kants Mittagsbüchlein vom 17. August bis 25. September 1802.* Berlin, 1926.

DeJardins, Gregory. "The Terms of *De Officiis* in Hume and Kant." *Journal of the History of Ideas* 28 (1967), pp. 237–242.

di Giovanni, George, and Harris, H. S., Editors. *Between Kant and Hegel: Texts in the Development of Post-Kantian Idealism.* Albany: State University of New York Press, 1985.

Dietzsch, Steffen. "Kant, die Juden und das akademische Bürgerrecht in Königsberg." In *Königsberg. Beiträge zu einem besonderen Kapitel der deutschen Geistesgeschichte,* ed. Joseph Kohnen. Frankfurt (Main): Peter Lang, 1994 (pp. 111–126).

Dobbek, W. J. *Herders Jugendzeit in Mohrungen und Königsberg, 1744–1764.* Würzburg: Holzener Verlag, 1961.

Dohm, Christian Wilhelm. *Über die bürgerliche Verbesserung der Juden.* Berlin, 1781.

Drescher, Siegfried, Editor. *Wer war Kant? Drei zeitgenössische Biographien von Ludwig Ernst Borowski, Reinhold Bernhard Jachmann und E. A. Ch. Wasianski.* Pfullingen: Neske, 1974.

Droysen, Hans. "Friedrich Wilhelm I, Friedrich der Grosse und der Philosoph Christian Wolff." *Forschungen zur brandenburgischen und preussischen Geschichte* 23 (1910), pp. 1–34.

Dülmen, Richard von. *The Society of the Enlightenment: The Rise of the Middle Class and Enlightenment Culture in Germany,* tr. Anthony Williams. New York: St. Martin's Press, 1992.

Eberhard, Johann Georg Heinrich. *Philosophisches Magazin.* Halle: J. J. Gebauer, 1788–1792.

Epictetus. *The Handbook,* ed. Nicholas P. White. Indianapolis: Hackett Publishing Company, 1983.

Epstein, Klaus. *The Genesis of German Conservatism.* Princeton: Princeton University Press, 1966.

Erb, Peter C., Editor. *Pietists: Selected Writings.* Preface by Ernest Stoeffler. New York: Paulist Press, 1983.

Erdmann, Benno. *Martin Knutzen und seine Zeit. Ein Beitrag zur Geschichte der Wolff-ischen Schule und insbesondere zur Entwicklungsgeschichte Kants.* Leipzig, 1876 (reprinted Hildesheim: Gerstenberg, 1973).

Reflexionen Kants zur kritischen Philosophie. Aus Kants handschriftlichen Aufzeichnungen herausgegeben. Neudruck der Ausgabe Leipzig 1882/1884. Reprint with a new preface by Norbert Hinske. Stuttgart and Bad Canstatt: frommann-holzboog, 1992.

Ergang, Robert. *The Potsdam Führer: Frederick William I, Father of Prussian Militarism.* New York: Octagon Books, 1972 (reprint of New York: Columbia University Press, 1941).

Erikson, Erik H. *Young Man Luther: A Study in Psychoanalysis and History.* New York: Norton, 1962.

Erler, Georg. *Die Matrikel und die Promotionsverzeichnisse der Albertus-Universität zu Königsberg in Preussen.* 3 vols. Leipzig, 1910–1917.

Euler, Werner. "Immanuel Kants Amtstätigkeit. Aufgaben und Probleme einer Gesamtdokumentation." In *Autographen, Dokumente und Berichte. Zu Editionen, Amtsgeschäften und Werk Immanuel Kants,* ed. Reinhard Brandt and Werner Stark. Hamburg: Meiner, 1994 (pp. 58–90).

"Kant im akademischen Senat." Unpublished manuscript.

Euler, Werner, and Dietzsch, Steffen. "Prüfungspraxis und Universitätsreform in Königsberg. Ein neu aufgefundener Prüfungsbericht Kants aus dem Jahre 1779." In *Autographen, Dokumente und Berichte. Zu Editionen, Amtsgeschäften und Werk Immanuel Kants,* ed. Reinhard Brandt and Werner Stark. Hamburg: Meiner, 1994 (pp. 91–101).

Euler, Werner, and Stiening, Gideon. "'. . . und nie der Pluralität widersprach?' Zur Bedeutung von Immanuel Kants Amtsgeschäften." *Kant-Studien* 86 (1995), pp. 54–70.

F., L. "Etwas über Kant." *Jahrbücher der preußischen Monarchie unter der Regierung Friedrich Wilhelms des Dritten* 1 (1799), pp. 94–99.

Fabian, Gerd. *Beitrag zur Geschichte des Leib-Seele Problems (Lehre von der prästabilierten Harmonie-und vom psychophysischem Parallelismus in der Leibniz-Wolffschen Schule).* Langensalza: Hermann Beyer & Söhne, 1925.

Falkenstein, Lorne. "The Great Light of 1769 – A Humeian Awakening? Comments on Lothar Kreimendahl's Account of Hume's Influence on Kant." *Archiv für Geschichte der Philosophie* 77 (1995), pp. 63–79.

Fichte, Johann Gottlieb. *Gesamtausgabe,* ed. R. Lauth, H. Jacob, et al. Stuttgart and Bad Canstatt: F. Frommann, 1962–.

Fichtes Werke, ed. Immanuel Hermann Fichte, 8 vols., and *Nachgelassene Werke,* 3 vols. Berlin: Walter De Gruyter, 1971.

Fichte's Wissenschaftslehre of 1794. A Commentary on Part I, ed. George J. Seidel. West Lafayette, Ind: Purdue University Press, 1993.

Finster, Reinhard. "Zur Kritik von Christian August Crusius an den einfachen Substanzen bei Leibniz und Wolff." *Studia Leibnitiana* 18 (1986), pp. 72–82.

Fischer, Michael W. *Die Aufklärung und ihr Gegenteil. Die Rolle der Geheimbünde in Wissenschaft und Politik.* Berlin: Duncker & Humblot, 1982.

Fischer, Paul. "Eine Antwort auf Kants Brief vom 23. August, 1749." *Kant-Studien* 76 (1985), pp. 79–89. "Kant an Euler." *Kant-Studien* 76 (1985), pp. 214–218.

Fischer, Wolfram. *Quellen zur Geschichte des deutschen Handwerks. Selbstzeugnisse seit der Reformationszeit.* Göttingen: Musterschmidt Verlag, 1957.

Förster, Eckart. "Kant's Selbstsetzungslehre." In *Kant's Transcendental Deductions,* ed. E. Förster. Stanford: Stanford University Press, 1989 (pp. 217–238). "Fichte, Beck and Schelling in Kant's Opus Postumum." In *Kant and His Influence,* ed. G. M. Ross and T. McWalter. Bristol: Thoemmes, 1990 (pp. 146–169).

Forster, R. and Forster, E. *European Society in the Eighteenth Century.* New York: Harper & Row, 1969.

Francke, A. H. *Pädagogische Schriften,* ed. Hermann Lorenzen. 2nd ed. Paderborn: Ferdinand Schöningh, 1957.

Friedman, Michael. *Kant and the Exact Sciences.* Cambridge: Harvard University Press, 1992.

Friedrichs, Carl. *Preußentum und Pietismus.* Göttingen: Vandenhoek & Ruprecht, 1971.

Fulbrook, Mary. *Piety and Politics: Religion and the Rise of Absolutism in England, Württemberg and Prussia.* Cambridge: Cambridge University Press, 1983.

Furet, François. *The French Revolution, 1770–1814,* tr. Antonia Nevill. Oxford: Blackwell, 1988.

Garve, Christian. *Philosophische Anmerkungen und Abhandlungen zu Ciceros Büchern von den Pflichten.* 3 vols. Breslau, 1783.
Übersicht der vornehmsten Principien der Sittenlehre von dem Zeitalter des Aristoteles an bis auf unsere Zeit . . . Breslau, 1798.
Eigene Betrachtungen über die allgemeinen Grundsätze der Sittenlehre. Ein Anhang zu der Übersicht der verschiedenen Moralsysteme. Breslau, 1798.

Gaukroger, Stephen. *Descartes: An Intellectual Biography.* Oxford: Clarendon Press, 1995.

Gause, Fritz. "Königsberg als Hafen- und Handelsstadt." In *Studien zur Geschichte des Preussenlandes,* ed. Ernst Bahr. Marburg: N. G. Elwert Verlag, 1963.
die Geschichte der Stadt Königsberg in Preußen. Vol. 1. *Von der Gründung der Stadt bis zum letzten Kurfürsten.* Köln and Graz: Böhlau Verlag, 1965.

Gawthrop, Richard L. *Pietism and the Making of Eighteenth-Century Prussia.* Cambridge: Cambridge University Press, 1993.

George, Rolf. "The Lives of Kant" [discussion of the biographies of Vorländer, Stuckenberg, Gulyga, Cassirer, and Ritzel]. *Philosophy and Phenomenological Research* 57 (1987), pp. 385–400.

Gibert, Carlos Melches. *Der Einfluss Christian Garves Übersetzung Ciceros "De Officiis" auf Kants "Grundlegung zur Metaphysik der Sitten."* Regensburg: S. Röderer Verlag, 1994.

Gotthold, F. A. "Andenken an Johann Cunde, einen Freund Kant's und Ruhnken's." *Neue preussische Provincial-Blätter,* second series, 3 (1853), pp. 241–258.

Gottsched, L. A. *Pietism in Petticoats and Other Comedies,* tr. Thomas Kerth and John R. Russell. Columbia, S. C.: Camden House, 1994.

Graff, Paul. *Geschichte der Auflösung der alten gottesdienstlichen Formen in der evangelischen Kirche Deutschlands.* Vol. II. *Die Zeit der Aufklärung und des Rationalismus.* Göttingen: Vandenhoek & Rupprecht, 1939.

Graubner, Hans. "Physikotheologie und Kinderphysik. Kants und Hamanns gemeinsamer Plan einer Physik für Kinder in der physikotheologischen Tradition des 18. Jahrhunderts." In *Johann Georg Hamann und die Krise der Aufklärung: Acta des fünften Internationalen Hamann-Kolloquiums in Münster i. W.* Bern and New York: Lang, 1990 (pp. 117–145).

Gregor, Mary. "Introduction." In Kant, *Metaphysics of Morals,* introduction, translation, and notes by Mary Gregor. Cambridge: Cambridge University Press, 1991.

Gulyga, Arsenij. *Immanuel Kant,* tr. Sigrun Bielfeldt. Frankfurt (Main), 1981.

Immanuel Kant and His Life and Thought. Translated by M. Despalatovic. Boston: Birkhauser, 1987.

Guyer, Paul. *Kant and the Claims of Taste.* Harvard: Harvard University Press, 1979.

Kant and the Claims of Knowledge. Cambridge: Cambridge University Press, 1987.

Editor. *Kant's Groundwork of the Metaphysics of Morals: Critical Essays.* Lanham, Md: Rowman & Littlefield, 1998.

Hagen, Karl. "Gedächtnisrede auf B. William Motherby." *Neue preußische Provincial-Blätter* 3 (1847), pp. 131ff.

"Kantiana." *Neue preußische Provinzial-Blätter* 6 (1848), pp. 8–12.

Hagen, Karl Gottfried. *Grundriss der Experimentalchemie zum Gebrauch bey dem Vortrage derselben.* Königsberg, 1786.

Hamann, Johann Georg. *Sämtliche Werke,* ed. Josef Nadler. Wien: Herder Verlag, 1949–1953.

Socratic Memorabilia, translation and commentary by James O'Flaherty. Baltimore: Johns Hopkins University Press, 1967.

Briefwechsel, ed. Walther Ziesemer and Arthur Henkel. 7 vols. Frankfurt (Main): Insel Verlag, 1955–1979.

Vom Magus im Norden und der Verwegenheit des Geistes. Ein Hamann Brevier, ed. Stefan Majetschak. Munich: Deutscher Taschenbuch Verlag, 1988.

Hasse, Johann Gottfried. *Äusserungen Kant's von einem seiner Tischgenossen.* Königsberg: Gottlieb Lebrecht Herlage, 1804.

Heine, Heinrich. *Religion und Philosophie in Deutschland.* In Heinrich Heine, *Lyrik und Prosa,* 2 vols., ed. Martin Greiner. Frankfurt (Main): Büchergilde Gutenberg, 1962.

Heller, Josef. *Kants Persönlichkeit und Leben. Versuch einer Charakteristik.* Berlin: Pan Verlag, 1924.

Henrich, Dieter, Editor. *Kant, Gentz, Rehberg. Über Theorie und Praxis.* Frankfurt (Main): Suhrkamp Verlag, 1967.

"The Concept of Moral Insight and Kant's Doctrine of the Fact of Reason:" tr. Manfred Kuehn. In D. Henrich, *The Unity of Reason. Essays on Kant's Philosophy,* ed. R. Velkley. Cambridge, Mass.: Harvard University Press, 1994.

Herder, Johann Gottfried. *Sämmtliche Werke,* ed. Bernhard Suphan. 33 vols. Berlin: Weidmannsche Buchhandlung, 1877–1913.

Briefe, Gesamtausgabe 1763–1803, ed. Karl-Heinz Hahn. Weimar: Herman Böhlaus Nachfolger, 1977–1988.

Herman, Barbara. *The Practice of Moral Judgment*. Cambridge, Mass.: Harvard University Press, 1993.

Herz, Markus. *Betrachtungen aus der spekulativen Weltweisheit*, ed. Elfried Conrad, Heinrich P. Delfosse, and Birgit Nehren. Hamburg: Meiner Verlag, 1990.

Hinrichs, Carl. "Der Hallesche Pietismus als Politisch-Soziale Reformbewegung des 18. Jahrhunderts." *Jahrbuch für die Geschichte Mittel- und Ostdeutschlands* 2 (1953), pp. 177–189.

Preußentum und Pietismus. Der Pietismus in Brandenburg-Preußen als Religiös-Soziale Reformbewegung. Göttingen: Vandenhoeck & Ruprecht, 1971.

Hinske, Norbert. "Immanuel Kant." In *Neue deutsche Biographie*, ed. Historische Kommission bei der Bayerischen Akademie der Wissenschaften. Berlin, Duncker & Humblot, 1952–1982 (vol. 2, pp. 110–125).

Editor. *Was Ist Aufklärung: Beiträge aus der Berlinischen Monatsschrift*. 3rd ed. Darmstadt: Wissenschaftliche Buchgesellschaft, 1981.

Hippel, Theodor Gottlieb von. *Sämmtliche Werke*, ed. Theodor Gottlieb von Hippel, 14 vols. Berlin: Reimer, 1828–1839 (reprint Berlin: de Gruyter, 1988).

On Improving the Status of Women, tr. Timothy F. Sellner. Detroit: Wayne State University Press, 1979.

Der Mann nach der Uhr oder der ordentliche Mann. Lustspiel in einem Aufzug, ed. Erich Jenisch. Halle, 1928.

Hirsch, Emanuel. *Geschichte der neuen evangelischen Theologie*. 2nd ed. Gütersloh, 1960.

Höffe, Otfried. *Immanuel Kant*, tr. Marshal Farrier. Albany: State University of New York Press, 1994.

Hubatsch, Walther. *Geschichte der evangelischen Kirche in Ostpreussen*. 3 vols. Göttingen: Vandenhoek and Rupprecht, 1968.

Hügelmann, Karl. "Ein Brief über Kant. Mitgeteilt von Karl Hügelmann." *Alpreussische Monatsschrift* 16 (1879), pp. 607–612.

Hughes, Michael. *Early Modern Germany, 1477–1806*. Philadelphia: University of Philadelphia Press, 1992.

Hume, David. *A Treatise of Human Nature*, L. A. Selby Bigge. 2nd. ed. Oxford: The Clarendon Press, 1985.

Enquiries Concerning Human Understanding and Concerning the Principles of Morals, ed. L. A. Selby-Bigge, rev. P. H. Nidditch. 3rd ed. Oxford: The Clarendon Press, 1975.

Über die menschliche Natur, aus dem Englischen, nebst kritischen Versuchen zur Beurtheilung dieses Werks, tr. Ludwig Heinrich Jakob. Halle: Hemmerde and Schwetschke, 1790–92.

Iltis, Carolyn. "D'Alembert and the *Vis Viva* Contoversy." *Studies in History and Philosophy of Science* 1 (1970), pp. 135–44.

Im Hof, Ulrich. *The Enlightenment: An Historical Introduction*. Oxford: Blackwell, 1997.

Jachmann, Reinhold Bernhard. *Immanuel Kant geschildert in Briefen an einen Freund*. Königsberg, 1804.

Jacobi, Friedrich Heinrich. *Werke*, ed. Friedrich Roth and Friedrich Köppen. Darmstadt: Wissenschaftliche Buchgesellschaft, 1976 (reprint of Leipzig, 1812–1820).

James, William. *The Varieties of Religious Experience*. In *Writings, 1902–1910*. New York: The Library of America, 1987.

Jauch, Ursula Pia. *Immanuel Kant zur Geschlechterdifferenz. Aufklärerische und bürgerliche Geschlechtervormundschaft.* Vienna: Passagen Verlag, 1988.

Kalweit, Paul. *Kants Stellung zur Kirche.* Königsberg, 1904.

Kant, Immanuel. *Gesammelte Schriften.* Edited by the Prussian Academy. Berlin: Walter de Gruyter, 1902–.

Critique of Practical Reason and Other Writings on Moral Philosophy, tr. Lewis White Beck. Chicago: University of Chicago Press, 1949.

Critique of Judgment, tr. J. C. Meredith. Oxford: The Clarendon Press, 1952.

Observations on the Feeling of the Beautiful and Sublime, tr John T. Goldthwait. Berkeley: University of California Press, 1960.

Critique of Pure Reason, tr. Norman Kemp Smith. New York: St. Martin's Press, 1965.

Philosophical Correspondence, 1759–1799, edited and translated by Arnulf Zweig. Chicago: University of Chicago Press, 1967.

Selected Pre-Critical Writings and Correspondence with Beck, translated and introduced by G. B. Kerferd and D. E. Walford, with a contribution by P. G. Lucas. Manchester and New York: Manchester University Press, 1968.

Metaphysical Foundations of Natural Science, tr. James Ellington. Indianapolis: Bobbs-Merrill, 1970.

Briefwechsel, selection and notes by O. Schöndörffer, revised by R. Malter, introduction by R. Malter and J. Kopper. 3rd ed. Hamburg: Meiner, 1986.

Die Religion innerhalb der Grenzen der bloßen Vernunft, ed. Karl Vorländer, introduction by Hermann Noack, bibliography by Heiner Klemme. Hamburg: Felix Meiner Verlag, 1990.

Foundations of the Metaphysics of Morals, tr. Lewis White Beck. New York: Macmillan, 1990.

The Metaphysics of Morals, introduction, translation, and notes by Mary Gregor. Cambridge: Cambridge University Press, 1991.

Dreams of a Spirit-Seer Illustrated by Dreams of Metaphysics, tr. E. F. Goerwitz. New York: Macmillan, 1900 (reprint Glasgow: Thoemmes, 1992).

Kant's Latin Writings: Translations, Commentaries, and Notes, 2nd revised edition by Lewis White Beck, Mary J. Gregor, Ralf Meerbote, and John A Reuscher. New York: Peter Lang 1992.

Lectures on Logic, translated and edited by J. Michael Young (The Cambridge Edition of the Works of Immanuel Kant). New York: Cambridge University Press, 1992.

Theoretical Philosophy, 1755–1770, tr. David Walford and Ralf Meerbote (The Cambridge Edition of the Works of Immanuel Kant). Cambridge: Cambridge University Press, 1992.

Opus postumum, edited, with an introduction and notes, by Eckart Förster, translated by Eckart Förster and Stanley Rosen (The Cambridge Edition of the Works of Immanuel Kant). New York: Cambridge University Press, 1993.

Practical Philosophy, translated and edited by Mary J. Gregor, general introduction by Allen Wood (The Cambridge Edition of the Works of Immanuel Kant). New York: Cambridge University Press, 1996.

Religion and Rational Theology, translated and edited by Allen W. Wood and George

Di Giovanni (The Cambridge Edition of the Works of Immanuel Kant). Cambridge: Cambridge University Press, 1996.

Lectures on Ethics, tr. Peter Heath, ed. Peter Heath and J. B. Schneewind (The Cambridge Edition of the Works of Immanuel Kant). Cambridge: Cambridge University Press, 1997.

Lectures on Metaphysics, tr. Karl Ameriks and Steve Naragon (The Cambridge Edition of the Works of Immanuel Kant). Cambridge: Cambridge University Press, 1997.

Critique of Pure Reason, tr. Paul Guyer and Allen Wood (The Cambridge Edition of the Works of Immanuel Kant). Cambridge: Cambridge University Press, 1998.

Kettemann, Otto. "Sattler und Riemer." In Reinhold Reith, *Lexikon des alten Handwerks. Vom Spätmittelalter bis ins 20. Jahrhundert*. München: C. H. Beck, 1990.

Klemme, Heiner F. *Die Schule Immanuel Kants. Mit dem Text von Christian Schiffert über das Königsberger Collegium Fridericianum*. Hamburg: Meiner Verlag, 1994 (Kant-Forschungen, Bd. VI).

Kants Philosophie des Subjekts. Systematische und entwicklungsgeschichtliche Untersuchungen zum Verhältnis von Selbstbewußtsein und Selbsterkenntnis. Hamburg: Meiner Verlag, 1996.

Knutzen, Martin. *Philosophischer Beweiß von der Wahrheit der christlichen Religion, darinnen die Nothwendigkeit einer geoffenbarten Religion insgemein, und die Wahrheit oder Gewißheit der Christlichen insbesondere, aus ungezweifelten Gründen der Vernunft nach mathematischer Lehrart dargethan und behauptet wird*. 4th ed. Königsberg, 1745.

Vertheidigte Wahrheit der christlichen Religion gegen den Einwurf: Daß die christliche Offenbahrung nicht allgemein sey. Wobey besonders die Scheingründe des bekannten Englischen Deisten Matthäi Tindal, welche in deßen Beweise, Daß das Christentum so alt wie die Welt sey, enthalten, erwogen und widerlegt werden. Königsberg: Hartung, 1747.

König, Ernst. "Arzt und Ärztliches in Kant." *Jahrbuch der Albertus Universität zu Königsberg* 5 (1954), pp. 113–154.

Kohnen, Joseph, Editor. *Königsberg. Beiträge zu einem besonderen Kapitel der deutschen Geistesgeschichte*. Frankfurt (Main): Peter Lang, 1994.

"Konxompax und die Kreuz- und Querzüge des Ritters A bis Z." In *Königsberg. Beiträge zu einem besonderen Kapitel der deutschen Geistesgeschichte*, ed. Joseph Kohnen. Frankfurt (Main): Peter Lang, 1994 (pp. 309–320).

Kolbow, Heinrich. "Johann Heinrich Metzger, Arzt und Lehrer an der Albertus Universität zur Zeit Kants." *Jahrbuch der Albertus Universität zu Königsberg* 10 (1960), pp. 91–96.

Konschel, Paul. "Christian Gabriel Fischer, ein Gesinnungs- und Leidensgenosse Christian Wolffs in Königsberg." *Altpreussische Monatsschrift* 53 (1916), pp. 416–444.

Der junge Hamann nach seinen Briefen im Rahmen der lokalen Kirchengeschichte. Königsberg, 1915.

Hamanns Gegner, der Kryptokatholik D. Johann August Starck, Oberhofprediger und Generalsuperintendent von Ostpreußen. Königsberg, 1912.

Kowalewski, Arnold, Editor. *Die philosophischen Hauptvorlesungen Immanuel Kants*. Hildesheim: Olms, 1965.

Krause, G. *Gottsched und Flottwell, die Begründer der deutschen Gesellschaft.* Leipzig, 1893.

Kreimendahl, Lothar. *Hume in der deutschen Aufklärung: Umrisse einer Rezeptionsgeschichte.* Stuttgart: Frommann-Holzboog, 1987.

Kant – Der Durchbruch Von 1769. Köln: Dinter, 1991.

Kroner, Richard. *Kant's Weltanschauung,* tr. John E. Smith. Chicago: University of Chicago Press, 1956.

Kuehn, Manfred. "Kant's Conception of Hume's Problem." *Journal of the History of Philosophy* 21 (1983), pp. 175–193.

Hume's Antinomies," *Hume Studies* 9 (1983), pp. 25–45.

Scottish Common Sense in Germany, 1768–1800: A Contribution to the History of Critical Philosophy. Preface by Lewis White Beck. Kingston and Montreal: McGill-Queen's University Press, 1987.

"Kant's Transcendental Deduction: A Limited Defense of Hume." In *New Essays on Kant,* ed. Bernard den Ouden. New York and Bern: Peter Lang Publishing, 1988 (pp. 47–72).

"Reid's Contribution to Hume's Problem." In *The Science of Man in the Scottish Enlightenment: Hume, Reid, and Their Contemporaries,* ed. Peter Jones. Edinburgh: University of Edinburgh Press, 1989 (pp. 124–148).

"Mendelssohn's Critique of Hume," *Hume Studies* 21 (1995), pp. 197–220.

"The 'Moral Dimension' of Kant's Great Light of 1769." In *Proceedings of the Eighth International Kant Congress,* vol. I, 2, ed. H. Robinson. Milwaukee: Marquette University Press, 1995 (pp. 373–392).

"Christian Thomasius and Christian Wolff." In *The Columbia History of Western Philosophy,* ed. Richard H. Popkin. New York: Columbia University Press, 1999 (pp. 472–475).

Kuhrke, Walter. *Kant's Wohnhaus. Zeichnerische Wiederherstellung mit näherer Beschreibung.* 2nd ed. Königsberg: Gräfe und Unzer, 1924.

Krüger, Hans Jürgen. *Die Judenschaft in Königsberg in Preußen 1700–1802. Wissenschaftliche Beiträge zur Geschichte und Landeskunde Ost-Mitteleuropas* 76. Marburg, 1966.

Laberge, Pierre. "Du passage de la Philosophie Moral Populaire a la Métaphysique des Moers." *Kant-Studien* 71 (1980), pp. 416–444.

Ladd, John. "Kant on Marriage." Unpublished manuscript.

Lambert, Johann Heinrich. *Philosophische Schriften,* ed. Hans-Werner Arndt. Hildesheim: Olms, 1965.

Laursen, John Christian. "The Subversive Kant: The Vocabulary of 'Public' and 'Publicity.'" *Political Theory* 14 (1986), pp. 584–603.

Lauson, Johann Friedrich. *Erster Versuch in Gedichten, nebst einer Vorrede von der sogenannten extemporal Poesie, und einem Anhange von Gedichten aus dem Stegreif.* Königsberg: Driest, 1753.

Zweyter Versuch in Gedichten, nebst einer Vorrede von den Schicksalen der heutigen Poesie, und einem Anhange von Gedichten aus dem Stegreif. Königsberg: Driest, 1754.

Lehmann, Gerhard. "Kants Lebenskrise." In Gerhard Lehmann, *Beiträge zur Geschichte und Interpretation der Philosophie Kants.* Berlin: de Gruyter, 1969 (pp. 411–421).

Leibniz, Gottfried Wilhelm. *Philosophical Essays*, tr. Roger Ariew and Daniel Garber. Indianapolis: Hackett Publishing Company, 1989.

Lessing, Gotthold Ephraim. *Werke*, ed. Herbert G. Göpfert, Karl Eibl, Helmut Göbel, Karl S. Guthke, Gerd Hillen, Albert von Schirmding, and Jörg Schönert. 8 vols. München: Carl Hanser, 1970–.

Lindemann-Stark, Anke. "Kants Vorlesungen zur Anthropologie in Hippels *Lebensläufen*." Magisterarbeit: Phillips Universität Marburg, 1990.

———. "Leben und Lebensläufe des Theodor Gottlieb von Hippel." Dissertation, Phillips Universität Marburg, 1998.

Locke, John. *An Essay Concerning Human Understanding*, edited with an introduction by P. H. Nidditch. Oxford: Oxford University Press, 1975.

Loeb, Louis E. *From Descartes to Hume: Continental Metaphysics and the Development of Modern Philosophy*. Ithaca: Cornell University Press, 1981.

Lovejoy, Arthur. *The Great Chain of Being: A Study of the History of Ideas*. New York: Harper & Brothers, 1960.

Ludwig, Bernd. "Einleitung." In Immanuel Kant, *Metaphysische Anfangsgründe der Rechtslehre*, ed. Bernd Ludwig. Hamburg: Meiner, 1986.

Lüthe, Rudolf. Review of G. Gawlick and L. Kreimendahl, *Hume in der deutschen Aufklärung*. *Philosophischer Literaturanzeiger* 40 (1987), pp. 209–212.

Maimon, Salomon. *The Autobiography of Salomon Maimon*, tr. Hugo Bergmann. London: The East and West Library, 1954.

Malter, Rudolf. "Königsberg und Kant im 'Reisetagebuch' des Theologen Johann Friedrich Abegg (1798)." *Jahrbuch der Albertus-Universität Königsberg/Pr.* 26–7 (1986), pp. 5–25.

———. "Einleitung." In Karl Vorländer, *Immanuel Kants Leben*. 4th ed. Hamburg: Felix Meiner, 1986. *Immanuel Kant in Rede und Gespräch*. Hamburg: Felix Meiner Verlag, 1990.

———. "Bibliographie zur Biographie Immanuel Kants." In Karl Vorländer, *Immanuel Kant. Der Mann und das Werk*, 2 vols. 3rd ed. Mit einer Bibliographie zur Biographie von Rudolf Malter und einem Verzeichnis der Bibliographien zum Werke Immanuel Kants von Heiner Klemme. Hamburg: Meiner Verlag, 1992.

———. "Einleitung." In *Immanuel Kant. Sein Leben in Darstellungen von Zeitgenossen. Die Biographien von L. E. Borowski, R. B. Jachmann und E. Ch. Wasianski*, ed. Felix Gross. Darmstadt: Wissenschaftliche Buchgesellschaft, 1993.

———. "Immanuel Kant (1724–1804). Ein biographischer Abriss." *Jahrbuch der Albertus Universität zu Königsberg* 29 (1994), pp. 109–123.

Martens, Wolfgang. *Literatur und Frömmigkeit in der Zeit der frühen Aufklärung*. Tübingen: Niemeyer, 1989.

Martin, Gottfried. "Herder als Schüler Kants. Aufsätze und Kolleghefte aus Herders Studienzeit." *Kant-Studien* 41 (1936), pp. 294–306.

———. "Die mathematischen Vorlesungen Kants." *Kant-Studien* 58 (1967), pp. 58–63.

———. *Arithmetic and Combinatorics: Kant and His Contemporaries*, tr. Judy Wubnig. Carbondale and Edwardsville: Southern Illinois University Press, 1985.

McClelland, Charles E. *State, Society, and University in Germany, 1700–1914*. Cambridge: Cambridge University Press, 1980.

McIntosh, Christopher. *The Rose Cross and the Age of Reason: Eighteenth-Century Rosi-*

crucianism in Central Europe and Its Relationship to the Enlightenment. Leiden: E. J. Brill, 1992.

McMullin, Ernan. *Newton on Matter and Activity*. Notre Dame: University of Notre Dame Press, 1978.

Meiners, Christoph. *Grundriss der Geschichte der Weltweisheit*. Lemgo, 1786.

Grundriss der Seelenlehre. Lemgo, 1786.

[Mellin, G. S. A.] *Immanuel Kants Biographie*, Vol. 1. Leipzig: C. G. Weigel, 1804.

Melton, James Van Horn. *Absolutism and the Eighteenth-Century Origins of Compulsory Schooling in Prussia and Austria*. Cambridge: Cambridge University Press, 1988.

Mendelssohn, Moses. *Gesammelte Schriften*, ed. F. Bamberger et al. Stuttgart and Bad Canstatt, 1931–.

Merlan, Philip. "From Hume to Hamann." *The Personalist* 32 (1951), pp. 11–18.

"Hamann et les Dialogues de Hume." *Revue de Metaphysique* 59 (1954), pp. 285–89.

"Kant, Hamann-Jacobi and Schelling on Hume." *Rivista critica di storia filosofia* 22 (1967), pp. 343–51.

[Metzger, Johann Heinrich.] *Äußerungen über Kant, seinen Charakter und seine Meinungen, von einem billigen Verehrer seiner Verdienste*, 1804.

Michaelis, K. "Kant – Hauslehrer in Judtschen?" *Kant-Studien* 38 (1933), pp. 492–493.

Mittenzwei, Ingrid. *Preussen nach dem Siebenjährigen Krieg: Auseinandersetzungen zwischen Bürgertum und Staat um die Wirtschaftspolitik*. Berlin: Akademie Verlag, 1979.

Möller, Hans. "Die Bruderschaft der Gold- und Rosenkreuzer." In *Freimaurer und Geheimbünde im 18. Jahrhundert in Mitteleuropa*, ed. Helmut Reinalter. Frankfurt: Suhrkamp, 1983.

Möser, Justus. *Sämtliche Werke*, Historisch-kritische Ausgabe in 14 Bänden, ed. Akademie der Wissenschaften zu Göttingen. Hamburg, 1943–.

Monk, Ray. *Ludwig Wittgenstein: The Duty of Genius*. Harmondsworth: Penguin, 1990.

Mortensen, Hans and Gertrud. "Kants väterliche Ahnen und ihre Umwelt." *Jahrbuch der Albertus-Universität Königsberg* 3 (1953), pp. 25–57.

[Mortzfeld, Johann Christoph.] *Fragmente aus Kants Leben. Ein biographischer Versuch*. Königsberg: Hering und Haberland, 1802.

Nicolai, Friedrich. *Philosophische Abhandlungen* in *Gesammelte Werke*, Vol. 11, ed. Bernhard Fabian and Marie-Luise Spieckermann. Hildesheim: Olms, 1991.

Sebaldus Nothanker, ed. Bernd Witte. Stuttgart: Reclam, 1991 (first published Berlin, 1773).

Nietzsche, Friedrich. *Jenseits von Gut und Böse*. In *Werke. Historisch-kritische Ausgabe*. Berlin: Walter de Gruyter & Co., 1994.

Noack, Hermann. "Einleitung." In Immanuel Kant, *Die Religion innerhalb der Grenzen der bloßen Vernunft*, edited by Karl Vorländer, introduction by Hermann Noack, bibliography by Heiner Klemme. Hamburg: Meiner, 1990 (pp. li–lxix).

Norton, Robert E. *Herder's Aesthetics and the European Enlightenment*. Ithaca and London: Cornell University Press, 1991.

Oesch, Martin, Editor. *Aus der Frühzeit des deutschen Idealismus. Texte zur Wissenschaftslehre Fichtes, 1794–1804*. Würzburg: Königshausen & Neumann, 1987.

Palmquist, Stephen, Editor. *Four Neglected Essays by Immanuel Kant*. Hong Kong: Philopsychy Press, 1994.

Pappas, George S. "Some Forms of Epistemological Scepticism." In *Essays in Knowledge and Justification*, ed. George S. Pappas, and Marshall Swain. Ithaca: Cornell University Press, 1978.

Paulsen, Friedrich. *Immanuel Kant, Sein Leben und seine Lehre.* 7th ed. Stuttgart: Fri. Frommanns Verlag, 1924.

Pisanski, Georg Christoph. *Entwurf einer preussischen Literärgeschichte in vier Büchern*, ed. Rudolf Philippi. Königsberg, 1886.

Pollok, Konstantin. "Einleitung." In *Immanuel Kant, Metaphysische Anfangsgründe der Naturwissenschaft*, ed. Konstantin Pollok. Hamburg: Meiner, 1997.

Porschmann, Adolf. "Die ersten Kantianer in England." In *Studien zur Geschichte des Preussenlandes*, ed. Ernst Bahr. Marburg: N. G. Elwert Verlag, 1963 (pp. 470–482).

Pozzo, Riccardo. *Kant und das Problem einer Einleitung in die Logik. Ein Beitrag zur Rekonstruktion der historischen Hintergründe von Kants Logik-Kolleg.* Frankfurt, 1989.

"Kant e Weitenkampff." *Rivista di storia della filosofia* 48 (1993), pp. 283–322.

Quinton, Anthony. "The Trouble with Kant." *Philosophy* 72 (1997), pp. 5–18.

Reich, Klaus. *Kant und die Ethik der Griechen.* Tübingen: J. C. B. Mohr (Paul Siebeck), 1935.

"Kant and Greek Ethics." *Mind* 48 (1939) [translation of *Kant und die Ethik der Griechen* by W. H. Walsh].

"Rousseau und Kant." *Neue Hefte für Philosophie* 29 (1989), pp. 80–96.

Reicke, Rudolph. *Kantiana. Beiträge zu Immanuel Kants Leben und Schriften.* Königsberg: Th. Theile's Buchhandlung, 1860.

Reimen, Pia. "Struktur und Figurenkonstellation in Theodor Gottlieb von Hippels Komödie der Mann nach der Uhr." In *Königsberg. Beiträge zu einem besonderen Kapitel der deutschen Geistesgeschichte*, ed. Joseph Kohnen. Frankfurt (Main): Peter Lang, 1994 (pp. 199–263).

Reusch, Christian Friedrich. "Historische Erinnerungen." *Neue preußische Provincialblätter* 5 (1848).

Kant und seine Tischgenossen. Aus dem Nachlasse des jüngsten derselben. Königsberg: Tag and Koch, 1848 [published without date].Rexheuser, Adelheid. "Andrej Bolotov. Königsberg als Bildungserlebnis eines russischen Aufklärers." In *Königsberg und Riga*, ed. Heinz Ischreyt. Tübingen: Max Niemeyer Verlag, 1995 (pp. 87–122).

[Richardson, John.] *Kant's Leben. Eine Skizze. In einem Briefe eines Freundes an einen Freund.* Altenburg: C. H. Richter, 1799.

"A Sketch of the Author's Life by the Translator" [1819]. In *Four Neglected Essays by Immanuel Kant*, ed. Stephen Palmquist. Hong Kong: Philopsychy Press, 1994 (pp. 88–103).

Richarz, Monika. *Der Eintritt der Juden in die akademischen Berufe. Jüdische Studenten und Akademiker in Deutschland 1678–1848.* Tübingen: J. C. B. Mohr, 1974.

Riedesel, Erich. *Pietismus und Orthodoxie in Ostpreußen. Auf Grund des Briefwechsels von G. F. Rogall und F. A Schultz's mit den Halleschen Pietisten.* Königsberg: Ost-Europa Verlag, 1937.

Rink, Friedrich Theodor. *Ansichten aus Immanuel Kant's Leben.* Königsberg: Göbbels and Unzer, 1805.

Ritschl, Albrecht. *Geschichte des Pietismus.* 3 vols. Bonn: 1880–1896.

Ritter, Gerhard. *Frederick the Great,* tr. Peter Paret. Berkeley: University of California Press, 1974.

Ritzel, Wolfgang. *Immanuel Kant. Zur Person.* Bonn: Bouvier, 1975.

Kant, eine Biographie. Berlin and New York: Walter de Gruyter, 1985.

"Wie ist Pädagogik als Wissenschaft möglich." IN *Kant und die Pädagogik. Pädagogik und praktische Philosophie,* ed. Jürgen Eckardt Pleines. Würzburg: Könighausen & Neumann, 1985 (pp. 37–45).

"Kant über Den Witz und Kants Witz." *Kant-Studien* (1991), pp. 102–109.

Rorty, Richard. *Philosophy and the Mirror of Nature.* Princeton: Princeton University Press, 1979.

Rosenkranz, Karl. *Politische Briefe und Aufsätze, 1848–1856,* ed. Paul Herre. Leipzig, 1919.

Geschichte der Kant'schen Philosophie, ed. Steffen Dietzsch. Berlin: Akademie-Verlag, 1987 (originally Leipzig: Leopold Voss, 1840).

Röttgers, Kurt. "J. G. H. Feder – Beitrag zu einer Verhinderungsgeschichte eines deutschen Empirismus." *Kant-Studien* 75 (1984), pp. 420–441.

Kants Kollege und seine ungeschriebene Schrift über die Zigeuner. Heidelberg, 1993.

"Christian Jakob Kraus (1753–1807)." *Jahrbuch der Albertus Universität zu Königsberg* 29 (1994), pp. 125–135.

"Kants Zigeuner." *Kant-Studien* 88 (1997), pp. 60–86.

Rudolph, Enno. *Skepsis bei Kant. Ein Beitrag zur Interpretation der Kritik der reinen Vernunft.* München: Eugen Fink Verlag, 1978.

Safranski, Rüdiger. *E. T. A. Hoffmann. Das Leben eines skeptischen Phantasten.* München and Wien: Karl Hanser Verlag, 1984.

Salewski, Wilhelm. "Kants Idealbild einer Frau. Versuch einer Biographie der Gräfin Caroline Charlotte Amalie von Keyserling, geb. Gräfin Truchsess von Waldburg (1727–1791)."

Jahrbuch der Albertus Universität zu Königsberg 26–27 (1986), pp. 27–62.

Salthenius, Daniel. *Introductio in omnes libros sacros tam veteris quam novi Testamenti, ad usum studiosae iuventius; cum praesentatione de necessariis quibusdam studii exegetico-biblici subsidiis.* Königsberg, 1736.

Scheffner, Johann George. *Mein Leben, wie ich es selbst beschrieben.* Leipzig: J. G. Neubert, 1816.

Schilpp, P. A. *Kant's Pre-Critical Ethics.* Evanston, Ill: Northwestern University Press, 1960.

Schleiermacher, Friedrich. *Kritische Gesamtausgabe,* Vol. I/2. Berlin: de Gruyter, 1984.

Schmid, F. A. "Kant im Spiegel seiner Briefe." *Kant-Studien* 9 (1914), pp. 307f.

Schmidt, James, Editor. *What is Enlightenment? Eighteenth-Century Answers and Twentieth-Century Questions.* Berkeley: University of California Press, 1996.

Schneider, Ferdinand Josef. *Theodor Gottlieb von Hippel in den Jahren von 1741 bis 1781 und die erste Epoche seiner literarischen Tätigkeit.* Prague: Taussig & Taussig, 1911.

"Kometenwunder und Seelenschlaf (Johann Heyn als Wegbereiter Lessings)." *Deutsche Vierteljahrsschrift für Literatur-wissenschaft und Geistes-geschichte* 18 (1940), pp. 201–232.

Schöndörffer, Otto. "Der elegante Magister." *Reichls Philosophischer Almanach* 1924, pp. 65–86.

Schott, Robin. *Cognition and Eros: A Critique of the Kantian Paradigm.* Boston: Beacon Press, 1988.

Schubert, Friedrich Wilhelm. *Immanuel Kants Biographie. Zum großen Teil nach handschriftlichen Nachrichten dargestellt.* Leipzig, 1842.

Schultz, Johann. *Exposition of Kant's Critique,* translation and introduction by James C. Morrison. Ottawa: University of Ottawa Press, 1995.

Schulz, Johann Heinrich. *Versuch einer Anleitung zur Sittenlehre für alle Menschen ohne Unterschied der Religionen nebst einem Anhange von der Todesstrafe.* 3 vols. Berlin, 1783–1790.

Schütz, Fritz. "Immanuel Kant, Studiosus Philosophiae, in Judtschen." *Kant-Studien* 11 (1916), pp. 226–229.

Schwartz, Paul. "Die Gelehrtenschule Preußens unter dem Oberschulkollegium (1787–1806) und das Abiturientenexamen." *Monumenta Germaniae Paedagogica* 50 (1912), pp. 586f.

Selbach, R. "Eine bisher unbeachtete Quelle des 'Streits der Fakultäten'." *Kant-Studien* 82 (1991), pp. 96–101.

Sellner, Timothy F. "The *Eheeiferer* in Goethe's *Wahlverwandtschaften:* Could Mittler be Hippel?" In *Königsberg. Beiträge zu einem besonderen Kapitel der deutschen Geistesgeschichte,* ed. Joseph Kohnen. Frankfurt (Main): Peter Lang, 1994 (pp. 321–334).

Sextus Empiricus. *Selections from the Major Writings on Scepticism, Man and God,* ed. Philip P. Hallie, tr. Sanford G. Etheridge. Indianapolis: Hackett, 1985.

Shell, Susan Meld. *The Embodiment of Reason.* Chicago: University of Chicago Press, 1996.

Sinz, Herbert. *Lexikon der Sitten und Gebräuche im Handwerk.* Freiburg: Herder Verlag, 1986.

Springer, Gustav [alias G. Karl]. *Kant und Alt-Königsberg.* Königsberg, 1924.

Stadelmann, Rudolf, and Fischer, Wolfram. *Die Bildungswelt des deutschen Handwerks.* Berlin: Duncker & Humblodt, 1955.

Stark, Werner. *Nachforschungen zu Briefen und Handschriften Immanuel Kants.* Berlin: Akademie Verlag, 1993.

"Wo lehrte Kant? Recherchen zu Kants Wohnungen." In *Königsberg. Beiträge zu einem besonderen Kapitel der deutschen Geistesgeschichte des 18. Jahrhunderts,* ed. Joseph Kohnen. Frankfurt (Main): Peter Lang, 1994 (pp. 81–110).

"Kants Amtstätigkeit." *Kant-Studien* 85 (1994), pp. 470–472.

"Kant als akademischer Lehrer." Tübingen: Max Niemeyer Verlag, 1995 (pp. 51–70).

"Kants akademische Kollegen." Unpublished manuscript.

Stavenhagen, Kurt. *Kant und Königsberg.* Göttingen: Deuerlichsche Verlagsbuchhandlung, 1949.

Stiehler G., Editor. *Materialisten der Leibniz Zeit (Friedrich Wilhelm Stosch, Theodor Ludwig Lau, Gabriel Wagner, Urban Gottfried Bucher).* Berlin: VEB Verlag der deutschen Wissenschaften, 1966.

Stoeffler, E. *The Rise of Evangelical Pietism.* Leiden, 1965.

Strawson, P. F. *The Bounds of Sense: An Essay on Kant's Theory of Knowledge.* London: Methuen, 1966.

Skepticism and Naturalism: Some Varieties. London: Methuen, 1985.

Stroud, Barry. "Kant and Skepticism." In *The Skeptical Tradition,* ed. Myles Burnyeat. Berkeley: University of California Press, 1983.

The Significance of Philosophical Scepticism. Oxford: The Clarendon Press, 1984.

Strube, Rolf, Editor. *Sie saßen und tranken am Teetisch. Anfänge und Blütezeit der Berliner Salons, 1789–1871.* München: Pieper Verlag, 1991.

Stuckenberg, J. W. H. *The Life of Immanuel Kant.* Preface by Rolf George. Lanham and London: University Press of America, 1986 (reprint of London: MacMillan, 1882).

Studer, Thomas. "Ludwig von Baczko. Schriftsteller in Königsberg um 1800." In *Königsberg. Beiträge zu einem besonderen Kapitel der deutschen Geistesgeschichte,* ed. Joseph Kohnen. Frankfurt (Main), 1994 (pp. 399–424).

Swain, Charles W. "Hamann and the Philosophy of David Hume." *Journal of the History of Philosophy* 5 (1967), pp. 343–351.

Taylor, Charles. *Hegel.* Cambridge: Cambridge University Press, 1975.

Timerding, H. E. "Kant und Euler." *Kant-Studien* 23 (1919), pp. 18–64.

Tonelli, Giorgio. "Das Wiederaufleben der deutsch-aristotelischen Terminologie bei Kant während der Entstehung der 'Kritik der reinen Vernunft'." *Archiv für Begriffsgeschichte* 9 (1964), pp. 233–242.

Tschackert, Paul. "Theodor Gottlieb Hippel, der christliche Humorist, als Student der Theologie in Königsberg 1756 bis 1759." *Altpreussische Monatsschrift* 28 (1892), pp. 355–356.

Unger, Rudolf. *Hamann und die Aufklärung. Studien zur Vorgeschichte des romantischen Geistes im 18. Jahrhundert.* 2 vols. 2nd ed. Halle, 1925.

Vaihinger, Hans. "Briefe aus dem Kantkreis." *Altpreussische Monatsschrift* 17 (1880), pp. 286–299.

Varnhagen van Ense, K. A. *Denkwürdigkeiten des Philosophen Arztes Johann Benjamin Erhard* in *Ausgewählte Schriften,* 15.2. Leipzig, 1874.

Velkley, Richard L. *Freedom and the End of Reason: On the Moral Foundation of Kant's Critical Philosophy.* Chicago: University of Chicago Press, 1989.

Vleeschauwer, Herman-J. de. *The Development of Kantian Thought: The History of a Doctrine,* tr. A. R. C. Duncan. London: Thomas Nelson and Sons, 1962.

Voegelin, Eric. *The History of the Race Idea: From Ray to Carus,* tr. Ruth Hein, ed. Klaus Vondung. Baton Rouge: Louisiana State University Press, 1998.

Vogel, Karl. *Kant und die Paradoxien der Vielheit. Die Monadenlehre in Kants philosophischer Entwicklung bis zum Antinomienkapitel der Kritik der reinen Vernunft.* Meisenheim am Glan: Anton Hain, 1975.

Voigt, Johannes. *Das Leben des Professor Christian Jacob Kraus . . . , aus den Mitteilungen seiner Freunde und Briefen.* Königsberg, 1819.

Vorländer, Karl. *Die ältesten Kant-Biographien. Eine kritische Studie.* Berlin, 1918. *Kants Leben.* 4th ed. Hamburg: Meiner, 1986.

Immanuel Kant: Der Mann und das Werk. 2nd enlarged edition, ed. Konrad Kopper and Rudolf Malter, with a contribution on "Kant's Opus postumum" by Wolfgang Ritzel. Hamburg: Meiner, 1977.

Walker, Ralph C. S. *Kant*. London: Routledge & Kegan Paul, 1978.

Walsh, W. H. *Kant's Criticism of Metaphysics*. Chicago: University of Chicago Press, 1975.

Ward, Keith. *The Development of Kant's View of Ethics*. Oxford: Basil Blackwell, 1972.

Warda, Arthur. "Zur Frage nach Kant's Bewerbung um eine Lehrerstelle." *Altpreussische Monatsschrift* 35 (1898), pp. 578–614.

"Kants Bewerbung um die Stelle des Sub-bibliothekars an der Schloßbibliothek." *Altpreussische Monatsschrift* 36 (1899), pp. 473–524.

"Ergänzungen zu E. Fromms zweiten und drittem Beitrage zur Lebensgeschichte Kants." *Altpreussische Monatsschrift* 38 (1901), pp. 75–95, 398–432.

"Kants Erklärung wegen der v. Hippelschen Autorschaft." *Altpreussische Monatsschrift* 41 (1904), pp. 61–93.

"Zur Frage: Wann hörte Kant zu lesen auf." *Altpreussische Monatsschrift* 41 (1904), pp. 131–135.

"Blätter der Erinnerung an Christian Jacob Kraus." *Altpreussische Monatsschrift* 48 (1911), pp. 24–36.

Immanuel Kants Bücher. Berlin: Martin Breslauer, 1922.

Warda, Arthur, and Driesch, Carl, Editors. *Briefe von und an Johann Georg Scheffner*. München and Leipzig, 1916.

Waschkies, Hans-Joachim. *Physik und Physikotheologie des jungen Kant. Die Vorgeschichte seiner allgemeinen Weltgeschichte und Theorie des Himmels*. Amsterdam: Gruner, 1987.

Wasianski, E. A. Chr. *Immanuel Kant in seinen letzten Lebensjahren*. Königsberg, 1804.

Watkins, Eric. "Kant's Theory of Physical Influx." *Archiv für Geschichte der Philosophie* 77 (1995), pp. 285–324.

"The Development of Physical Influx in Early Eighteenth Century Germany: Gottsched, Knutzen, and Crusius" *Review of Metaphysics* 49 (1995), pp. 295–339.

"From Pre-established Harmony to Physical Influx: Leibniz's Reception in 18th Century Germany." *Perspectives on Science* 6 (1998), pp. 136–201.

Weber, Ludwig. *Das Distinktionsverfahren im mittelalterlichen Denken und Kants skeptische Methode*. Meisenheim (Glan): Verlag Anton Hain, 1976.

Weber, Max. *The Protestant Ethic and the Spirit of Capitalism*, tr. Talcott Parsons, foreword by R. H. Tawney. New York: Charles Scribner's Sons, 1958.

Weiss, Helmuth. "Das Königsberg Kants in den Augen eines jungen russischen Teilnehmers am Siebenjährigen Krieg." *Jahrbuch der Albertus-Universität zu Königsberg* 17 (1967), pp. 49–62.

Werner, Franz. *Soziale Unfreiheit und 'bürgerliche Intelligenz' im 18. Jahrhundert. Der organisatorische Gesichtspunkt in J. M. R. Lenz's Drama 'Der Hofmeister oder die Vorteile der Privaterziehung.'* Frankfurt: Rita G. Fischer Verlag, 1981.

Weymann, Daniel. *Bedenklichkeiten über den einzig möglichen Beweisgrund des M. Kant vom Daseyn Gottes*. Königsberg, 1763.

Wieland, C. M. *Sämtliche Werke*. Vols. 1–14. Hamburg: Hamburger Stiftung Zur Förderung Von Wissenschaft und Kultur, 1984 (reprint of the edition Leipzig: Göschen, 1794–1811).

Willich, A. F. M. *The Elements of the Critical Philosophy*. Leipzig, 1798 (reprint New York: Garland, 1977).

Winter, Alois. "Selbstdenken, Antinomien, Schranken. Zum Einfluss des späten Locke auf die Philosophie Kants." In *Eklektik, Selbstdenken, Mündigkeit,* ed. N. Hinske. Hamburg: Meiner, 1986 (pp. 27–66).

Winterfeld, F. A. von. "Christian Wolff in seinem Verhältnis zu Friedrich Wilhelm I und Friedrich dem Großen." *Nord und Süd* 64 (1893), pp. 224–236.

Zammito, John H. *The Genesis of Kant's Critique of Judgment.* Chicago: University of Chicago Press, 1992.

Zimmerli, Walther Ch. "'Schwere Rüstung' des Dogmatismus und 'anwendbare Eklektik'. J. G. H. Feder und die Göttinger Philosophie im ausgehenden 18. Jahrhundert." *Studia Leibnitiana* 15 (1983), pp. 58–71.

Zippel, G. *Geschichte des Königlichen Friedrichs-Kollegiums zu Königsberg Preussen, 1698–1898.* Königsberg, 1898.

Index

Lichtenberg, Georg Christoph, 394, 478n155
Lilienthal, Auditeur, 466
Lindner, Gottlieb Immanuel, 77, 103, 107,
110–11, 119, 123, 125, 127, 160, 164,
170, 217, 443n78, 455n98, 463n57,
464n62
literary societies, 163, 167, 173
Locke, John, 67, 75, 79–80, 83, 111, 178, 181,
183, 197, 348, 375, 399, 429n25, 444n88,
457n125, 470n23
Loeb, Louis E., 468n135
Lossow, Daniel Friedrich von, 128, 163
Louis XVI, xx, 341, 375
Lovejoy, Arthur, 451n19
Lucian, 48
Lucretius, 49, 99
Lupin, Friedrich, 356
Lüthe, Rudolf, 472n42
Luther, Martin, 47, 336, 479n1
Lysius, Johann Heinrich, 36, 37, 68, 70, 77,
440n34

Maimon, Salomon, xix, xx, 214, 360, 361,
378, 475n97, 499n123
Majetschak, Stefan, 472n41
Malebranche, Nicolas, 75, 132, 252
Malter, Rudolf, 16–17, 423n7, 426n55,
428n4, 480n26, 483n81
Marquardt, Conrad Theophil, 68, 70, 75–6,
81, 85, 93
Martens, Wolfgang, 441n46
Martin, Gottfried, 452n38, 459n165
Maupertuis, Pierre-Louis Moreau de, 141,
445n106
McClelland, Charles E., 439n17
McIntosh, Christopher, 495n31
McMullin, Ernan, 447n132–33
Meckel, Friedrich Theodor, 390
Meier, Georg Friedrich, 108–9, 136, 212,
358, 452n35
Meiners, Christoph, 318, 320–21, 351,
490n159, 492n199
Melton, James Van Horn, 51, 432n39,
435n82, 436n98
Mendelssohn, Moses, xiii, xvii–xviii, xix,
108, 122, 135–37, 140, 160, 171–73,
183–85, 195–96, 201, 214, 216, 230–32,
251, 253, 268, 277, 302, 305–9, 315,
318–19, 333, 371, 373, 375, 378, 405,
453n57, 459n178, 460n194, 469n154,
478n155, 484n4, 489n135, 494n19
Merlan, Philip, 455n96
metaphysics, xvii, 1, 71, 73, 75, 79, 84–6, 88,
90, 100, 104, 108, 110, 118, 125, 131–34,
137–38, 141, 159, 161–62, 172–75, 178,

180–81, 183, 188, 190, 191–94, 198,
203–5, 209–12, 231–32, 236, 242,
245–46, 248, 254–62, 264, 273–74, 277,
285, 293, 306, 310, 312, 317, 321, 331,
354, 358, 359–61, 377–78, 389, 395, 407,
411, 452, 469, 481, 498; of morals, xviii,
23, 42, 74, 94, 266, 277, 283, 285, 312,
396, 408, 457, 486, 490, 505; possibility
of, 199
Metzger, Johann Daniel, 4–6, 8, 11, 16, 271,
314–16, 342, 420–21, 423n10, 424n13,
491n186
Meyer, General von, 128
Michaelis, Johann David, 450n159
Mittenzwei, Ingrid, 463n53, 477n132
Molière, 166
Möller, Hans, 495n31
Möser, Justus, 342, 434n64
Molyneux problem, 457n125
monads, 68, 91, 93, 102–3, 191, 447n136,
447n138
Monk, Ray, 427n64
Montaigne, Michel de, 22, 64, 85, 121, 130,
439n14
moral sense, 131, 144, 178, 184, 185, 186,
189, 192, 201–3, 207
mortality, 293
Mortensen, Hans and Gertrud, 428n4
Mortzfeld, Johann Christoph, 51, 424n16,
434n70, 436n101, 455n83, 457n123,
465n78
Motherby, Johann Benjamin, xii, xiii, 219,
223, 228–29, 273, 322–23, 334, 462n36,
476n117, 508n121
Motherby, Robert, xiii, 156–57
Muretus, 48
mysticism, 11, 35, 253, 272, 394, 395,
502n205

Naragon, Steve, 451n21
naturalism, 175–76
Necker, Jacques, 340, 341
needs, 3, 93, 120, 153, 200, 219, 222, 258–60,
287, 289, 298, 344, 370, 385–86, 388–89,
406
Negroes, 344
Nepos, 48, 271n108
Newlin, Thomas, 456
Newton, Isaac, 83–8, 90–1, 98, 102, 104, 129,
137, 176, 304, 445n102, 447n132–33,
448n143, 451n18, 457n134, 489n126
Nicolai, Friedrich, xxi, 301, 391, 454n78,
488n112, 499n132, 504n27
Nicolovius, Friedrich, 6, 383
Niemeyer, August Hermann, 379